INFORMATION TECHNOLOGY CONTROL AND AUDIT

Second Edition

OTHER INFORMATION SECURITY BOOKS FROM AUERBACH

INFORMATION TECHNOLOGY CONTROL AND AUDIT

Second Edition

Frederick Gallegos, CGFM, CISA, CDE
Sandra Senft, CISA, CIA
Daniel P. Manson, Ph.D.
Carol Gonzales, CISA

AUERBACH PUBLICATIONS

A CRC Press Company
Boca Raton   London   New York   Washington, D.C.

Library of Congress Cataloging-in-Publication Data

Information technology control and audit / Frederick Gallegos ... [et al.].--2nd ed.
  p. cm.
  ISBN 0-8493-2032-1 (alk. paper)
  1. Information technology--Auditing--Handbooks, manuals, etc. I. Gallegos, Frederick.

T58.5I5372 2004
004--dc22

2003065985

Visit the Auerbach Web site at www.auerbach-publications.com

© 2004 by CRC Press LLC
Auerbach is an imprint of CRC Press LLC

No claim to original U.S. Government works
International Standard Book Number 0-8493-2032-1
Library of Congress Card Number 2003065985
Printed in the United States of America 2 3 4 5 6 7 8 9 0
Printed on acid-free paper

Contents

Contents

Contents

Contents

Contents

Contents

Contents

Contents

Contents

Contents

About the Authors

Carol Gonzales, CISA, MSBA, has 20 years of combined IT operational and IT auditing experience. She is currently a project manager with the Information Technology Division at California State Polytechnic University, Pomona. She is also a part-time faculty member with the Computer Information Systems Department, College of Business Administration at California State Polytechnic University, teaching IT audit and general IT courses.

Ms. Gonzales graduated from California State Polytechnic University, Pomona, with a master of science degree in business administration option information systems auditing and a bachelor's degree in computer science. She is currently pursuing her doctoral degree in information science at Claremont Graduate University. Ms. Gonzales is a Certified Information Systems Auditor and member of the Information Systems Audit & Control Association (ISACA) and teaches local CISA review courses. She is also a member of the Association for Information Systems. Ms. Gonzales was co-author of the *Instructor's Guide to Information Technology Control and Audit, First Edition.*

Sandra Senft, CISA, MSBA, is currently Assistant Vice President of IT Support Services with an insurance company in Los Angeles, responsible for IT governance, finance, project management, asset management, strategic sourcing, vendor management, service management, process improvement, employee development, and administration.

A faculty member of California State Polytechnic University, Pomona from 1997 to 2000, she taught undergraduate and graduate courses in information technology and information systems auditing. She also has presented information systems auditing at seminars and conferences specializing in project management and systems development auditing. She has co-authored several articles for Auerbach Publications.

Ms. Senft graduated from California State Polytechnic University, Pomona, with a master of science degree in business administration option in information systems auditing and a bachelor of science degree in accounting. She has six years' experience as an information systems auditor and ten years as an accounting manager and controller. She is a Certified Information Systems Auditor and past-president of the Los Angeles Chapter of Information Systems Audit & Control Association, past-president of Farmers Toastmasters, and founder and charter president of the Inland Empire Accounting Managers and Controllers Network.

Daniel P. Manson, Ph.D., is currently professor of Computer Information Systems, College of Business Administration at California Polytechnic University, Pomona. Daniel received a doctorate in the Management of Information Systems at Claremont Graduate University. He is also an MSBA–Information Systems Audit graduate of California State Polytechnic University, Pomona. He has co-authored more than 15 articles that have been published in the Auerbach *EDP Audit* series, *Data Management* series, and *Data Security* series. He was a lead researcher for the Information Systems Audit and Control Association Control Objectives in Information Technology (COBIT).

He is currently co-principal investigator on a three-year National Science Foundation grant project, with Mt. San Antonio College, to develop a regional information systems security center. Prior to teaching full time at Cal Poly, Daniel worked as a specialist systems analyst with McDonnell–Douglas Space Systems Company, a senior EDP auditor with McDonnell–Douglas Corporation, an EDP auditor with Avery International, and an internal auditor with Coldwell Banker.

Frederick Gallegos, CISA, CDE, CGFM, MBA, focuses on IT audit education, IT auditing, security and control of information systems, legal environment of information systems, local area and wide area network security and controls, computer ethics, management information systems, executive support systems, and the Internet as an audit resource. He has over 30 years of teaching and practical experience in the field, published three textbooks, and authored or co-authored over 150 articles in the subjects listed. In 2000, he received the Best Research Paper of the Year Award from the International Association For Computer Information Systems. He received his bachelor's and master's degrees from California State Polytechnic University, Pomona. He has received the following professional certifications: Certified Information Systems Auditor (CISA), Certified Government Financial Manager (CGFM), and Certified Data Educator (CDE).

Prior to teaching full-time at Cal Poly, he was with the U.S. General Accounting Office–Los Angeles Regional Office (1972–1996) and served as a GAO evaluator progressing to manager, management and evaluator support group. Aside from participating in GAO audits, he managed staff involved in office automation and support, computer audit, training, human resource planning and staffing, technical information retrieval, and security/facilities management. He is the recipient of several awards from GAO, EDPACs, and ISACA, recognizing his contributions to the field. While with the GAO, he helped a number of universities establish coursework in IS auditing, control, and security at the undergraduate level. In 1980, he assisted Cal Poly to establish the now AACSB-accredited and NSA/CNSS courseware certified (2003) Master of Science in Business Administration

Degree program in Information Systems Auditing. He has spoken widely on topics in the information systems audit, control, and security fields. Professionally, he has served in a number of assignments and positions with the Information Systems Audit and Control Association, as follows:

- ISACA Foundation — Member of the Standards Board and Committee (1984–1996), involved in the Issuance of General Standards for the EDP Audit Profession and named as a contributor on the General Standards and 9 Information Systems Audit Standards
- ISACA — Member of the History Committee (1986 to present)
  - Involved in writing the history of the EDP Auditors Association for their 25th Anniversary.
- Editorial Board Member for ISACA Journal (1995 to present)
- Member — Academic Liaison Committee (1984–1990, 1995–1997)
- Chair, President's Task Force–ISACA for the Development of Curricula for Undergraduate and Graduate Education In Information Systems Auditing (May 1995 — issued March 1998), member of current ISACA Model Curriculum Task Force (2001 to present)
- Member of the Institute of Internal Auditors Website Policy and Oversight Subcommittee (2000 to present).

He is also a member of the International Association for Computer Information Systems — Member (1978 to present), IFIPS Workgroup 11.8 Information Security Training, and the Association of Government Accountants.

Foreword and Acknowledgment

The authors have many to thank for their support of our efforts to provide this textbook. Our combined 75 years of information systems audit, control, and security experience, includes four textbooks and more than 200 professional articles, and 280 presentations in this field. This textbook is designed for those who wish to learn and possibly select this career field as their profession and those who wish to retool and enhance their audit tool kit with new experiences and techniques. In essence, we have collected our past experiences, successes, and lessons learned. We hope you will profit from this and share with your colleagues.

We thank our past editor, Christian Kirkpatrick, for having supported the first edition effort. We also thank Richard O'Hanley for his interest and support of a second edition of this publication. We would also like to thank Andrea Demby, our project editor at CRC Press, for her fine support. And, Ms. Claire Miller, Managing Editor and Art Director, for her support and fine work. Their support was critical in the evolution of the second edition.

We wish to thank the IT audit faculty worldwide who have been in the trenches teaching this profession to the many who want to learn. Specifically, we credit the research and writings of Professors A. Faye Borthick, Ron Weber, Peter Best, Roger Jamieson, John Wyber, Alan Friedberg, Dan Kneer, Nils Kandelin, Tommie Singleton, Sokratis Katsikas, Gary McCombs, Damaso Lopez, Howard Kanter, Karen Forcht, Alan T. Lord, Joe Gelinas, Kil C. Kim, Hiroshi Yoshida, Jae Up Kim, Josef Vyskoc, Gordon B. Davis, Elsie Jancura, Allen Bragan, Efrim Boritz, Wim Van Grembergen, Margareth van Biene-Hershey, Michael and Virginia Cerullo, and many more. And, we thank the professionals past who paved the way: Joseph Wasserman, Harold J. Highland, Wayne Snipes, Stan Halper, Keagle Davis, Francis Langlinais, and Donald C. Scantlebury. We honor those professionals who continue the search for excellence in this field, specifically John Lainhart IV, Robert B. Parker, Michael Cangemi, Steven Ross, Steven Jue, Art Foreman, David Irvin, William Perry, Bill Mair, Donald Wood, Carl Pabst, John Kuyers,

Dana "Rick" Richardson, Belden Menkus, Robert Roussey, Akira Matsuo, Paul Williams, Fred Lilly, Michael Parkinson, John Beveridge, Michael Villegas, Hugh H. Peri-Williams, Hugh Parkes, John Tongren, and many others.

We also thank our past and current employers for allowing us the opportunity to experience this challenging environment and excel in our IT audit careers: the U.S. General Accounting Office, Coldwell Banker, Avery International, McDonnell–Douglas, Transamerica Corporation, Air Quality Management District, Farmers Insurance, and California State Polytechnic University, Pomona. Finally, we acknowledge the involvement and experience with the professional associations worldwide that support this field and mentioned in this text for their many contributions, especially those members of the ISACA Model Curriculum Task Force and Academic Relations Committee, and their subsequent product which was issued in March 1998, and the ongoing efforts of the current ISACA committee currently revising this model.

Also, we thank our colleagues, alumni, and students for their participation and contributions to the writings and editing of this work. At Cal Poly we are a large extended family as all authors of this book are alumni and have or are currently teaching in this field. We thank Professors Steven Powell, Robert Stumpf, Leonard Friebott, Louise Soe, Larisa Preiser-Houy, Steven Curl, Ida Masouris, Ruth Guthrie, Ward Testerman, and Anna Carlin for their written contributions, and for their technical review, our thanks to IT professionals Roger Lux and Paul Senft of Farmers Insurance. We thank alumnus Carin Ruiz, Anita Montgomery, Rodney Kocot, Anu Tandon, Maribel Tomenis, Jennifer Campbell, Amanda Xu, John Barger, Aleksandra Looho, Michael Miller, Bill Liao, Mark Wickham, Cathy Chen, Cathy Wang, Janet Zhu, Cynthia Huang, Rita Leung, Edson Gin, Girard Sadowski, Joseph Yin, Julie Ni, Mohammad Al-Abdullah, Naz Nageer, Sally Xu, Linda Su, Novel Anwar, Stephanie Doda, Irina Orlova Kessinger, Rory Robison, Brandon Brown, Boulton Fernando, Martin Rojas, Jeff Cowherd, Mattie Woods, Scott Kandel, Roin Nance, Matt Touquet, Karen Seketa, Kevin Powell, Dan Dow, Amin Leiman, Larry Lam, Richard Leonard, Ron Proulx, Anna Carlin, Harry Soo, Charles Bent, Tessa Rogge, David Wright, Lana Nino, Karen Nelson, Gerald Morris, Henry Townsend, John Carvala, Steven Barnes, Debbie Newman, Isabelle Prieve-Theisen, Christine Kartawidjaja, Lidya Kartawidjaja, Heru Subroto, Nurullah Askan, Gatu Prihartoyo, Kim Phelps-Kneough, Paul Wan, Roehl Amante, Waberyn Wambugi, Rosina Liu, Loida Tison-Dualan, Seth Cox, Randy Coneby, Lorne Dear, Phoung Quach, Benny Hsu, Helen Yamashiro, Sherman Hung and more than 300 others we have placed into the IT audit, security, and control profession since 1980.

We thank our current students at the undergraduate and graduate levels with a special thanks to Carin Ruiz, Femi Olarewaju, Unity Gwanzura, Agus Haryanto, John Lee, Nadia Porter, Mohammad Al-Abdullah, Stephanie

Doda, Edson Gin, and Steven Tanner for their assistance and support. Also, sincere thanks go to our faculty support, Kathleen Von Velasco, Martha Guarnett, and Victoria Galvez. My wife Susan Gallegos has provided so much support to our sons, David and Chris, and me, and accomplished the work on the glossary. The other authors wish to thank their families as well for their support during this update.

This work is the combined efforts of the many we have worked with, the many we have shared with, and the many we have taught to go on into this profession worldwide. We hope you will use it and add to it in your professional development in this exciting field. For us, IT audit has been a dynamic, challenging, and evolutionary field. There has never been a dull moment in this field and we do not think there will ever be.

Part I
A Foundation for IT Audit and Control

A FOUNDATION FOR IT AUDIT AND CONTROL

Chapter 1 through Chapter 4

The first part of this text examines the foundation for Information Technology (IT) audit and control. This foundation has evolved through the recognition of the need for strong IT controls by professional organizations, business, and government. For the novice IT auditor, it provides a prospective as to how far the evolution of IT control guidance and techniques has come.

Chapter 1 presents the IT environment today and discusses why issues involving IT control and audit are so important. It briefly discusses what IT auditing involves and the development of guidance by a number of organizations worldwide to deal with IT control and auditability issues. Information integrity, reliability, and validity are extremely important in today's competitive business world. Also, with the increased demand for IT has come growing legal issues of concern to the CEO, the CIO, and the IT professional. The IT auditor must keep pace with legal issues that may impact business processes and profitability. Control and audit are global concerns, especially in such areas as electronic funds transfer, electronic payment systems, and wireless technology.

Chapter 2 discusses the process of audit and review and its IT role. Who are IT auditors? What are their roles? What do they do? What are their Standards of Practice? What level of knowledge or skills should an IT auditor possess and how do they obtain them? Again, this discussion provides the novice IT auditor and IT audit manager/supervisor with important baseline information to help in the training and preparation of the IT auditor.

Chapter 3 covers the IT audit process for the auditing of IT and the demands it will place on the profession in the years ahead. IT auditing is both basic and complex. This chapter discusses its basics and beginnings and its evolution. With the evolution, professional associations and government have taken an active role in generating guidance for the practitioner. Worldwide, all of these efforts have contributed to the IT audit process and the array of tools and techniques being used by practitioners today.

Chapter 4 discusses the use of computer-assisted audit tools and techniques in auditing. This chapter discusses the planning steps necessary for use and application of computer assisted tools and techniques. The various types of tools and techniques available for the auditor to use will be described as well as their advantages and disadvantages. Recognition and selection of the tools and techniques available to the auditor is an important step in the audit process.

Chapter 1

Information Technology Environment: Why Are Controls and Audit Important?

Much has changed in the world since the first edition. With these changes, the role of information technology (IT) control and audit has become a critical mechanism for ensuring the integrity of information systems and the reporting of corporation finances to avoid and hopefully to prevent future financial fiascos such as Enron, WorldCom, and Global Crossing. Also, the events of September 11, 2001, have changed the way Americans think and operate. Homeland Security has become a high priority within the United States and other countries, and that extends to the electronic infrastructure of commerce worldwide. The need to control and audit IT has never been greater.

Initially, IT auditing (formerly called electronic data processing [EDP] auditing, computer information systems [CIS] auditing, and information systems [IS] auditing) evolved as an extension of traditional auditing. At that time, the need for an IT audit function came from several directions:

- Auditors realized that computers had impacted their ability to perform the attestation function.
- Corporate and information processing management recognized that computers were key resources for competing in the business environment and similar to other valuable business resource within the organization, and therefore the need for control and auditability is critical.
- Professional associations and organizations, and government entities recognized the need for IT control and auditability.

The early components of IT auditing were drawn from several areas. First, traditional auditing contributes knowledge of internal control practices and the overall control philosophy. Another contributor was information systems management, which provides methodologies necessary to achieve successful design and implementation of systems. The field of behavioral science provided such questions and analysis to when and why information systems are likely to fail because of people problems. Finally, the field of computer science contributes knowledge about control concepts, discipline, theory, and the formal models that underlie hardware and software design as a basis for maintaining data validity, reliability, and integrity.

IT auditing is an integral part of the audit function because it supports the auditor's judgment on the quality of the information processed by computer systems. Initially, auditors with IT audit skills are viewed as the technological resource for the audit staff. The audit staff often looks to them for technical assistance. As you will see with this textbook, within IT auditing there are many types of audit needs, such as organizational IT audits (management control over IT), technical IT audits (infrastructure, data centers, data communication), application IT audit (business/financial/operational), development/implementation IT audits (specification/requirements, design, development, and post-implementation phases), and compliance IT audits involving national or international standards. The IT auditor's role has evolved to provide assurance that adequate and appropriate controls are in place. Of course, the responsibility for ensuring that adequate internal controls are in place rests with the management. The audit's primary role, except in areas of management advisory services, is to provide a statement of assurance as to whether adequate and reliable internal controls are in place and are operating in an efficient and effective manner. So, whereas management is to ensure, auditors are to assure.

Today, IT auditing is a profession with conduct, aims, and qualities that are characterized by worldwide technical standards, an ethical set of rules (ISACA Code of Ethics), and a professional certification program (Certified Information Systems Auditor, CISA). It requires specialized knowledge and practicable ability, and often long and intensive academic preparation. Often, where academic programs were unavailable, significant in-house training and professional development had to be expended by employers. Most accounting, auditing, and IT professional societies believe that improvements in research and education will definitely provide an IT auditor with better theoretical and empirical knowledge base to the IT audit function. They feel that emphasis should be placed upon education obtained at the university level.

The breadth and depth of knowledge required to audit IT and systems are extensive. For example, IT auditing involves the:

- Application of risk-oriented audit approaches
- Use of computer-assisted audit tools and techniques
- Application of standards (national or international) such as ISO 9000/3 and ISO 17799 to improve and implement quality systems in software development and meet security standards
- Understanding of business roles and expectations in the auditing of systems under development as well as the purchase of software packaging and project management
- Assessment of information security and privacy issues which can put the organization at risk
- Examination and verification of the organization's compliance with any IT-related legal issues which may jeopardize or place the organization at risk
- Evaluation of complex systems development life cycles (SDLC) or new development techniques (e.g., prototyping, end-user computing, rapid systems, or application development)
- Reporting to management and performing follow-up review to ensure actions taken at work

The auditing of complex technologies and communications protocols involves the Internet, intranet, extranet, electronic data interchange, client servers, local and wide area networks, data communications, telecommunications, wireless technology, and integrated voice/data/video systems.

IT Today and Tomorrow

High-speed information processing has become indispensable to organizations' activities. For example, CoBiT (Control Objectives for Information and Related Technology) emphasizes this point and substantiates the need to research, develop, publicize, and promote up-to-date, internationally accepted IT control objectives. The primary emphasis of CoBiT (issued by Information Systems Audit and Control Foundation, 1996) is to ensure that information needed by businesses is provided by technology and the required assurance qualities of information are both met. CoBiT, Third Edition, has evolved and improved in its guidance to incorporate the essential elements of IT governance and risk management.

From a worldwide perspective, IT processes need to be controlled. From a historical standpoint, much has been published about the need to develop skills in this field. In its 1992 discussion paper, "Minimum Skill Levels in Information Technology for Professional Accountants," and its 1993 final report, "The Impact of Information Technology on the Accountancy Profession," the International Federation of Accountants (IFAC) acknowledged the need for better university-level education to address growing IT control concerns and issues. From this, it has published more recent guidance and information as cited in Appendix III. The Institute of Internal Auditors 1992 document

"Model Curriculum for Information Systems Auditing" was developed to define the knowledge and skills required by internal auditors to be proficient in the information age of the 1990s and beyond. The IIA has developed and produced guidance for its membership as cited in Appendix III. Around the world, reports of white-collar crime, information theft, computer fraud, information abuse, and other information/technology control concerns are being heard more frequently thanks to surveys and reports by SANS Institute, U.S. General Accounting Office (GAO), Federal Bureau of Investigation (FBI), Federal Trade Commission (FTC) and Computer Security Institute (CSI), Computer Emergency Response Teams (CERT), and others. Organizations are more information conscious and conscious of the pervasive nature of technology across the business enterprise. The increased connectivity and availability of systems and open environments have proven to be the lifelines of most business entities. IT is used more extensively in all areas of commerce around the world.

Due to the rapid diffusion of computer technologies and the ease of information accessibility, knowledgeable and well-educated IT auditors are needed to ensure that effective IT controls are in place to maintain data integrity and manage access to information. Globally, private industry, professional associations, and organizations such as International Federation of Information Processing (IFIPS), Association for Computing Machinery (ACM), Association of Information Technology Professionals (AITP), Information Systems Security Association (ISSA), and others have recognized the need for more research and guidance as identified in Appendix III. Control-oriented organizations such as the American Institute of Certified Public Accountants (AICPA), the Canadian Institute of Chartered Accountants (CICA), Institute of Internal Auditors (IIA), Association of Fraud Examiners, and others have issued guidance and instructions and supported studies/research in this area. The need for improved control over IT has been advanced over the years in earlier and continuing studies by the AICPA's Committee of Sponsoring Organizations of the Treadway Commission (COSO), International Organization for Standardization (ISO) issuance of ISO 9000 and ISO 17799, OECD's "Guidelines for the Security of IS by the Organization for Economic Cooperation and Development (OECD)," IIA's "Systems Auditability and Control Report," and the U.S. President's Council on Integrity and Efficiency in Computer Audit Training Curriculum. The most recent addition to these major studies is the aforementioned CoBIT research. Essentially, technology has impacted three significant areas of the business environment:

- It has impacted what can be done in business in terms of information and as a business enabler. It has increased the ability to capture, store, analyze, and process tremendous amounts of data and information, which has increased the empowerment of the business decision maker. Technology has also become a primary enabler to various production and service processes. It has become a critical component to business processes. There is a residual effect in that the increased use of technology has resulted in increased budgets, increased successes and failures, and increased awareness of the need for control.

- Technology has significantly impacted the control process. While control objectives have generally remained constant, except for some that are technology specific, technology has altered the way in which systems should be controlled. Safeguarding assets, as a control objective, remains the same whether it is done manually or is automated. However, the manner by which the control objective is met is certainly impacted.

- Technology has impacted the auditing profession in terms of how audits are performed (information capture and analysis, control concerns) and the knowledge required to draw conclusions regarding operational or system effectiveness, efficiency and integrity, and reporting integrity. Initially, the impact was focused on dealing with a changed processing environment. As the need for auditors with specialized technology skills grew, so did the IT auditing profession.

Information Integrity, Reliability, and Validity: Their Importance in Today's Global Business Environment

The virtual corporation's dynamic global multi-enterprise organization and team-oriented collaborative approach to work will place very stringent requirements on the venture's telecommunications network. The design of such systems is complex and management will be very difficult. As the name implies, the virtual corporation is critically dependent on the timely flow of accurate information throughout the organization. A good way to view how stringent the network requirements are is to analyze them in terms of the quality of the telecommunications service. Perhaps two examples of the world's dependency on IT come as a result of two past reported events where IT failure impacted world commerce and communications. In 1998, an AT&T major switch failed due to two software errors and a procedural error, causing communications at that switch to become overloaded and making customers using credit cards unable to access their funds for 18 hours. In another 1998 event, a communication satellite went into an uncontrollable rotation causing pager communication systems worldwide to be "useless," and those companies using this technology for E-account transaction and verification were unable to process credit card information for 24 hours, thus causing their customers to pay cash for their transactions. The disruption of the paging services caused severe impact to services provided by both private and governmental organizations that depended on this communication. Even today, these types of events are repeated over and over again where organizations dependent on technology encounter failure and disruption to services and business. In August 2003, the northeast quadrant and part of Canada were still recovering from a massive power outage to the area that shut down ATMs and all electrical services (elevators, phone service, street signals, subways, etc.).

Most telecommunication experts believe the network must be able to reach anyone anywhere in the world and be capable of supporting the sharing of a wide range of information, from simple voice, data, and text messages to cooperative transactions requiring the information updating of a variety of databases. The CEO and CIO want to meet or exceed their business objectives and attain maximum profitability through an extremely high degree of availability, fast response time, extreme reliability, and a very high level of security.

This means that the products for which IT provides consumer feedback will also be of high quality, rich in information content, and come packaged with a variety of useful services to meet the changing business conditions and competition. Flexible manufacturing and improvement programs such as Just-In-Time (JIT), Lean Manufacturing, and Total Quality Management (TQM) will enable low-cost production. Flexible manufacturing will permit products to be produced economically in arbitrary lot sizes through modularization of the production process.

The unpredictability of customer needs and the shortness of product life cycles will cause the mix of production capabilities and underlying resources required by the virtual corporation to change constantly. The virtual corporation must be capable of assembling its capabilities and resources quickly, thereby bringing a product to market swiftly. In order to achieve the high degree of organizational flexibility and value-chain coordination necessary for quick market response, excellent product quality, and low cost, the virtual corporation will employ a network, team-oriented, distributed decision-making organizational approach rather than a more traditional hierarchical, vertically integrated, command-and-control approach.

The virtual corporation will possess a dynamic network organization synthesizing the best available design, production, supply, and distribution capabilities and resources from enterprises around the world and linking them and the virtual corporation's customers together. Its multi-enterprise nature will enable the virtual corporation to respond to a competitive opportunity quickly and with the requisite scale, while, at the same time, enabling the individual network participant's cost and risk to be reduced. The network will be dynamic because participant identities and relationships will change as capabilities and resources required change. The global scope of the network will enable virtual corporations to capitalize on worldwide market opportunities. Work will be performed by multidisciplinary, multi-enterprise teams which will work concurrently and, in order to reduce production time, be granted significant decision-making authority. Team members will be able to work collaboratively regardless of location and time zone. Openness, cooperativeness, and trust will characterize the relationships among the organizations in the network and their personnel.

Aside from reach, range, and service responsiveness, the network must be highly interconnective so that people, organizations, and machines can communicate at any time, regardless of location. Also, the network must be very flexible because the organization is constantly changing. Finally, the network must be cost-effective because low cost is one of the ingredients in the mass-customization strategy. In addition, a control structure must be designed, developed, and implemented which provides assurances of integrity, reliability, and validity.

So how can this be accomplished? The ability to reach anyone anywhere in the world requires global area networks. Clearly, the Internet and global carrier services will be crucial. Also, because the intended receiver need not be in the office or even at home, wireless networks will play a major part. This will be true on-premise, such as with the use of wireless PBXs or LANs, and off-premise, with the use of cellular networks, global satellite networks such as Iridium, and Personal Communications Networks. To support the sharing of a wide range of voice, data, and video information, bandwidth-on-demand will be required all the way to the desktop as well as the mobile terminal. Also, various collaborative service platforms such as Lotus Notes will be necessary. Finally, perfect service will have to be designed into the network. Speed can be achieved through broadband networking: locally via fast Ethernet, gigabit, and ATM LANs, and over a wide area via SMDS and ATM services, and reliability through quality hardware/software and proven wired and wireless solutions where possible.

Legal Issues Impacting IT

In recent years, the events of September 11, 2001, and the financial scandals involving Enron and Arthur Andersen LLP, and the others to follow generated a demand for new legislation to prevent, detect, and correct such aberrations. Added to this, the advancements in network environments technologies have resulted in bringing to the forefront issues of security and privacy that were once only of interest to the legal and technical expert but which today are topics that affect virtually every user of the information superhighway. The Internet has grown exponentially from a simple linkage of a relative few government and educational computers, to a complex worldwide network that is utilized by almost everyone from the terrorist who has computer skills to the novice user and everyone in between. Common uses for the Internet include everything from marketing, sales, and entertainment purposes to electronic mail, research, electronic commerce, and virtually any other type of information sharing.

Unfortunately, as with any breakthrough in technology, advancements have also given rise to various new problems that must be addressed, such as security, privacy, and homeland security. President Bush recently announced the U.S. government's National Strategy for Securing Cyberspace. These problems are often being brought to the attention of IT audit and control specialists because they have public and private organization impact. Hence, in a later chapter security and privacy legislation will be discussed as they relate to the networked environment and the Internet. Current federal legislation and government plans will effect the online community and, along with the government's role in the networked society, will have a lasting impact in future business practices.

Federal Financial Integrity Legislation

The Enron–Arthur Andersen LLP financial scandal continues to plague today's financial market as the trust of the consumer, the investor, and the government to allow the industry to self regulate have all been violated. The Sarbanes–Oxley Act of 2002 will be a vivid reminder of the importance of due professional care. The Sarbanes–Oxley Act prohibits all registered public accounting firms from providing audit clients, contemporaneously with the audit, certain nonaudit services including internal audit outsourcing, financial-information-system design and implementation services, and expert services. These scope-of-service restrictions go beyond existing Security and Exchange Commission (SEC) independence regulations. All other services, including tax services, are permissible only if preapproved by the issuer's audit committee and all such preapprovals must be disclosed in the issuer's periodic reports to the SEC.

The act requires auditor (not audit firm) rotation. Therefore, the lead audit partner and/or the concurring review partner must rotate off the engagement if he or she has performed audit services for the issuer in each of the five previous fiscal years. The act provides no distinction regarding the capacity in which the audit or concurring partner provided such audit services. Any services provided as a manager or in some other capacity appear to count toward the five-year period. The provision starts as soon as the firm is registered, so, absent guidance to the contrary, the audit and concurring partner must count back five years starting with the date in which Public Company Accounting Oversight Board registration occurs. This provision has a definite impact on small accounting firms. The SEC is currently considering whether or not to accommodate small firms in this area; currently, there is no small-firm exemption from this provision.

This act is a major reform package mandating the most far-reaching changes Congress has imposed on the business world since the Foreign Corrupt Practices Act of 1977 and the SEC Act of the 1930s. It seeks to thwart future scandals and restore investor confidence by, among other things, creating a public company accounting oversight board, revising auditor independence rules, revising corporate governance standards, and significantly increasing the criminal penalties for violations of securities laws.

Federal Security Legislation

The IT auditor should recognize that the U.S. federal government has passed a number of laws to deal with issues of computer crime and security and privacy of information systems. Private industry has in the past been reluctant to implement these laws because of the fear of the negative impact it could bring to a company's current and future earnings and image to the public. The recent passage of the Homeland Security Act of 2002 and the inclusion of the Cyber Security Enhancement Act will have a substantial impact on private industry. Below is an example of a number of past laws in place.

The Computer Fraud and Abuse Act (CFAA)

The CFAA was first drafted in 1984 as a response to computer crime. The government's response to network security and network-related crimes was to revise the act in 1994 under the Computer Abuse Amendments Act to cover such crimes as trespass (unauthorized entry) into an online system, exceeding authorized access, and exchanging information on how to gain unauthorized access. Although the Act was intended to protect against attacks in a network environment, it does also have its fair share of faults. More details may be found in Chapter 18 and Chapter 19. The IT auditor must be aware of it significance.

Under this act, penalties are obviously less severe for "reckless destructive trespass" than for "intentional destructive trespass." The reasoning behind this is that reckless attackers may not necessarily intend to cause damage, but must still be punished for gaining access to places that they should not have access to. However, the impact of such terminology appears to possibly create some confusion in prosecuting the trespasser because it resides in such a "gray area." In Morris v. United States it was determined that "intent" applied to access and not to damages. The implication here would be that if the "intentional" part of the violation was applied to access and not the damage, then the culprit could possibly be prosecuted under the lesser sentence.

For example, if an individual intentionally intended to release a virus over a network, it would seem difficult for prosecutors to prove the motive for the violation. What if the individual stated that he or she was conducting some type of security test (as Morris contested) and "accidentally" set off a procedure which released a virus over the network? Intentional could refer to access to a system but it may not apply to damage. In this case, the lesser penalty of "reckless destructive trespass" may be applied. Within the courts, this is a matter that must be contemplated on a case by case basis, observing the facts of each individual case. In some instances, however, it would appear that even "intentional" trespass could be defended by claims that the violation was due to negligence and therefore fall under the less severe of the two circumstances.

This legislation has been helpful as a legal tool for prosecuting crimes involving some of the above-mentioned intruders and violators of system security, but it also seems to have a loophole in certain cases. Unfortunately, this loophole may be large enough for a serious violator of the act to slip through and be prosecuted under a lesser penalty by virtue of having to prove intent. All states have closed a portion of that loophole through statutes prohibiting harassment or stalking, including "electronic mail." This act has been amended several times since 1984 to keep it current.

The Computer Security Act of 1987

Another Act of importance is the Computer Security Act of 1987, which was drafted due to congressional concerns and public awareness on computer security-related issues and because of disputes on the control of unclassified information. The general purpose of the act was a declaration from the government that improving the security and privacy of sensitive information in federal computer systems is in the public interest. The Act established a federal government computer-security program that would protect sensitive information in federal government computer systems. It would also develop standards and guidelines for unclassified federal computer systems and facilitate such protection.

The Computer Security Act also assigned responsibility for developing governmentwide computer system security standards, guidelines, and security training programs to the National Bureau of Standards. It further established a Computer System Security and Privacy Advisory Board within the Commerce Department, and required federal agencies to identify those computer systems containing sensitive information and develop security plans for those systems. Finally, it provided periodic training in computer security for all federal employees and contractors who managed, used, or operated federal computer systems.

The Computer Security Act, as discussed later in this book, is particularly important because it is fundamental to the development of federal standards of safeguarding unclassified information and establishing a balance between national security and other nonclassified issues in implementing security and privacy policies within the federal government. It is also important in addressing issues concerning government control of cryptography, which, as can be seen later, has recently become a hotly contested topic.

The Act was also a legislative response to overlapping responsibilities for computer security among several federal agencies. Some level of federal computer security responsibility rests with the Office of Management and Budget (OMB), The General Services Administration (GSA), and the Commerce Department (particularly The National Institute of Standards and Technology [NIST] and the National Telecommunications and Information Administration [NTIA]). OMB maintains overall responsibility for computer security policy. GSA issues regulations for physical security of computer facilities and oversees technological and fiscal specifications for security hardware and software. The National Security Administration (NSA) is responsible for security of information that is classified for national security purposes. Such overlapping responsibilities were found to impede the development of one uniform federal policy regarding the security of unclassified information. This is an area that has surfaced and is being dealt with in the Homeland Security Act of 2003.

The Office of Technology Assessment found in its 1994 report on information security and privacy implementation that the Computer Security Act has not been without problems. Numerous reports issued by the GAO since 1995 have continued to identify the Government's inability to secure and protect its information systems and compliance with this law and others. For example, it was found that although the agencies follow the rules set forth by the act regarding security plans and training, they do not necessarily follow the intent of the act. Many of these reports issued by GAO have shown that although agencies do develop the required security plans, the act does not require their periodic reviewing or updating as technologies change. Because of this, existing security of systems may remain stagnant over time unless the agencies review them regularly. As a result, the required security plans, if not evaluated on a regular basis, can become outdated and ultimately less effective, and may not be able to properly address the new problems associated with computer security.

The Homeland Security Act of 2002
(Inclusion of the Cyber Security Enhancement Act)

In the wake of the events of September 11, 2001, the United States has discovered that it is no longer an island exempt from terrorism. Much as December 7, 1941, was a day of infamy for the United States and plunged it into World War II, September 11, 2001, has become quite similar, as the country declared war on terrorism. The follow-on work of the U.S. federal agencies uncovered the terrorist use of the Internet and electronic financial systems to fund their actions and activities of terrorists to an extent not realized or understood until now.

The Cyber Security Enhancement Act (HR 3482) was included in the passage of the Homeland Security Act. The Act demands life sentences for those hackers that "recklessly" endanger lives. It seeks to allow Net surveillance to gather telephone numbers, IP addresses, and URLs or e-mail information without recourse to a court, where an "immediate threat to a national security interest" is suspected. Finally, Internet Service Providers (ISPs) will also be permitted to hand users' records over to law enforcement authorities, overturning current legislation that outlaws such behavior.

The Act itself is a statement that protection of the homeland is everybody's business. It outlaws the publication anywhere of details of such tools as PGP, which encode e-mails so that they cannot be read by snoops. It allows police to conduct Internet or telephone eavesdropping randomly with no requirement to ask a court's permission first. Finally, in this act is a provision that calls for punishment of up to life in prison for electronic hackers who are found guilty of causing death to others through their actions.

Hackers, if convicted of causing injuries to others, could face prison terms up to 20 years under cyber crime provisions, which are in Section 225 of a bill known as the Cyber Security Enhancement Act of 2002.

Privacy on the Information Superhighway

Private Information Available for the Taking

Now that some issues associated with computer security have been reviewed, how the issue of privacy is impacted when computer security is breached will be examined. As is well known, there is a tremendous amount of information that companies and agencies are able to retrieve on any individual. People, corporations, and government are active in trading personal information for their own gain. In Virginia, a resident filed suit in state court against *U.S. News & World Report*, challenging the right of the magazine to sell or rent his name to another publication without his express written consent. It is astonishing to find out that criminals, competitors, and basically anybody else can buy a person's IRS form for $500. It is known that individuals share private information on a daily basis, but how has it affected the network world and the Internet? This issue will be analyzed in the following section.

The large number of users on the Internet has resulted in the availability of an enormous amount of private information on the network. This information unfortunately seems to be available for the taking by anyone who might be interested. A person's sexual orientation, bank balance, Social Security number, political leanings, medical record, and much more is there for anyone who may want it. Information identity theft has been one of the fastest growing crimes, and use of the information systems highway has been a key component of such crimes. In 2003, it was revealed that a hacker penetrated the State of California Payroll system and gained access to personal information. This information potentially could be put up for sale to anyone who might be interested in it. Someone has been collecting information and making it available for use, and a large number of these individuals seem to be refusing to follow any sort of fair information practice. In another 2003 incident, all it took was a phone call for an Internet hijackers to steal 65,000 Web addresses belonging to the County of Los Angeles. The addresses were then sold and used to send pornographic material and junk e-mail and to try to hack into other computers.

Fortunately, the Federal Trade Commission has been very active in providing the public alerts to the various ongoing scams, and by visiting its Web site at www.ftc.gov, people can be helped by the information it can provide if they become victims. This activity causes everyone alarm and the question is asked — Is it entitled to one's information? What is the government's policy regarding privacy of an individual and keeping a strong security policy? Ideally, citizens would like to limit the amount of monitoring that the government is allowed to do on them, but is the government in a position to monitor communications on the information superhighway? How will this affect one's right to privacy as guaranteed by the U.S. Constitution? The focus of the following section will then be to address these issues, paying especially close attention to the security-based measures that have affected the ideal of individual right to privacy.

Privacy Legislation and the Federal Government Privacy Act

In addition to the basic right to privacy that an individual is entitled to under the U.S. Constitution, the government also enacted the Privacy Act of 1974. The purpose of this is to provide certain safeguards to an individual against an invasion of personal privacy. This act places certain requirements on federal agencies, which include the following:

- Permits an individual to determine what records pertaining to him or her are collected and maintained by federal agencies.
- Permits an individual to prevent records pertaining to him or her that were obtained for a particular purpose from being used or made available for another purpose without consent.
- Permits an individual to gain access to information pertaining to him or her in federal agency records and to correct or amend them.
- Requires federal agencies to collect, maintain, and use any personal information in a manner that assures that such action is for a necessary and lawful purpose, that the information is current and accurate, and that safeguards are provided to prevent misuse of the information.

Even though the Privacy Act is an important part of safeguarding individual privacy rights, it is important for the IT auditor to recognize that there are many exemptions under which it may be lawful for certain information to be disclosed. This could, in some cases, for various agencies, both federal and nonfederal, allow the means by which they can obtain and disclose information on any individuals simply because they may fall under one of the many exemptions that the Privacy Act allows. For example, the subsequent Freedom of Information Act provides the federal government a way to release historical information to the public in a controlled fashion. The Privacy Act has also been updated over time through the amendment process.

Electronic Communications Privacy Act

In the area of computer networking, the Electronic Communications Privacy Act is one of the leading early pieces of legislation against violation of private information as applicable to online systems. Before analyzing some of the implications that the Act has had on the network community, let us briefly analyze some of the provisions defined by the Act, as it seems to be quite complicated in giving privacy protection in some instances and not others.

Section 2511 of the Act makes interception and disclosure of wire, oral, or electronic communications prohibited, and prohibits the manufacture and possession of intercepting devices under Section 2512. Section 2516, however, seems to transcend these two as it authorizes and makes exceptions for the interception of wire, or electronic communications under certain circumstances. In spite of the exceptions under 2516, Section 2515 prohibits the use, as evidence, of intercepted wire or oral communications. Even if evidence were allowed to be intercepted and collected, it would seem that agencies could not introduce that evidence in court! Does that make sense?

To continue with the analysis, a very important provision in the sense of government intervention in online privacy is to be considered. Under Section 2701; it is unlawful for anyone (including the government) to access stored communications without proper authority (i.e., warrant). Once again, however, an exception is made in this provision. Under Section 2701(c)(1) it is stated that the person or entity providing a wire or electronic communications service can intercept communications with prior user consent. Under Section 2702(b)(6)(B) on disclosure, such a person can then report the information to a law enforcement agency if such contents appear to pertain to the commission of a crime (again with prior consent). Upon reading this, most people may think that clearly anyone desiring privacy would not give prior consent. But what about cases where consent is given when the contract is agreed upon? Some services will include fine print on the terminal screen: at the time the user first joins the service, which indicate the role of the system operator/system administrator. It can contain statements regarding privacy rights as they apply to that specific service. If people do not scrutinize the fine print closely enough, then they may be setting themselves up, having their private information intercepted by and disclosed to others. For these reasons, the subscriber must take special care to read the policy guidelines when signing up for an online service.

The point of seizure of private information stored on computer without a warrant was made clear in the landmark case of *Steve Jackson Games Inc. v. U.S. Secret Service*. Secret service officials raided the office of Steve Jackson Games as part of a nationwide investigation of data piracy in 1990. Agents first violated privacy rights by searching and seizing messages without proper authority and without a warrant. It was then found, when the gaming company did receive a copy of the Secret Service warrant affidavit, that it was unbelievably flimsy. It seems as though the author of the game GURPS Cyberpunk was suspected to be guilty by "remote association." The author had corresponded with a variety of people, from computer security experts to computer hackers. That was enough to put him on a federal list of "dangerous hoodlums." More than three years later, a federal court awarded damages over $50,000, plus over $250,000 in attorney's fees, ruling that the raid had been careless, illegal, and completely unjustified. This was an important case on the topic because it was the first step toward establishing that online speech is entitled to Constitutional protection and that law enforcement agents cannot seize and hold a Bulletin Board Service (BBS) with impunity.

In summary, the Electronic Communications Privacy Act, although very good in its intentions to protect privacy rights, may have too many exceptions to be fully effective. This would hold true for the user and law enforcement agencies alike. Ideally, citizens would like to keep any information regarding their private affairs from being shared by others, but as mentioned previously, this is not always easy to do. In addition, even though law enforcement officials may get access to private information, it would appear to be difficult at times for authorities to base their prosecution solely on electronic communication.

Communications Decency Act of 1995

The Communication Decency Act (CDA) bans the making of "indecent" or "patently offensive" material available to minors via computer networks. The Act imposes a fine of up to $250,000 and imprisonment for up to two years. The CDA does specifically exempt from liability any person who provides access or connection to/or form a facility, system, or network that is not under the control of the person violating the Act. Also, the CDA specifically states that an employer shall not be held liable for the actions of an employee unless the employee's conduct is within the scope of his or her employment.

Health Insurance Portability and Accountability Act — 1996

On August 21, 1996, President Clinton signed the HIPAA into law. The original purpose of the law was to make it easier for Americans to maintain their health insurance when they switch jobs and restrict the ability of insurers to reject them based on preexisting health conditions. Unfortunately, the digital age added the provision of "administrative simplifications" to the law. According to the U.S. Department of Health:

> The "administrative simplifications" provisions require the adaptation of national standards for electronic health care transactions. By ensuring consistency throughout the industry, these national standards will make it easier for health plans, doctors, hospitals, and other healthcare providers to process claims and other transactions electronically. The law also required security and privacy standards in order to protect personal information.

The provisions for administrative simplification came "At the time when hospitals and insurers used more than 400 different software formats to transmit healthcare data. These covered everything from the headers on insurance forms to the codes describing diseases and medication." Many in the healthcare industry have viewed the "administrative simplification" component of the laws to be the most expensive and most difficult to implement. Part of the reason for the difficulty in implementation involves the issue of privacy. According to InfoWorld, "Medical organizations will need to invest in some of the new technologies currently available in other industries. Technologies like digital certificates, authentication, and biometric standards are needed to ensure that those authorized to view something are the only ones that have access." The cost and difficulty of implementing these new technologies to meet the requirements of HIPAA can be both time consuming and expensive, most especially for smaller hospitals and clinics with little or no IT support. This is a challenge for internal and external auditors of the U.S. healthcare industry. Noncompliance by organizations can face stiff fines and penalties.

Current Legislative Activities: Security, Privacy, and Audit

In summary, it appears that traditional as well as new security methods and techniques are simply not working. Although many products are quite efficient in securing the majority of attacks on a network, no single product seems to be able to protect a system from every possible intruder. Current security legislation, although addressing the issues of unwanted entry into a network, may also allow for ways by which some criminals can escape the most severe penalties for violating authorized access to a computer system. Moreover, some legislation, in effect, does not require periodic review, thus allowing for various policies and procedures to get outdated. The computer networking industry is continually changing. Because of this, laws, policies, procedures, and guidelines must constantly change with it; otherwise they will have a tendency to become outdated, ineffective, and obsolete.

On the subject of privacy, it has been seen that in the online world, private information has begun to leak out of systems as though it were water from a running faucet. Even then, some of the legislation passed in recent years does protect the user against invasion of privacy. Some of the laws observed contain far too many exceptions and exclusions to the point that their efficacy suffers. In addition, the government continues to utilize state of the art techniques for the purpose of accessing information for the sake of "national security" now justified under the Homeland Security Act. New bills and legislation continue to attempt to find a resolution to these problems, but new guidelines, policies, and procedures need to be established, and laws need to be enforced to their full extent if citizens are to enjoy their right to privacy as guaranteed under the Constitution. Several recent pending bills are currently being evaluated by the government, which would affect the issues of personal privacy protection such as the State of California's SB 1386 and the Privacy Act of 2003. These will be covered in Chapter 18 and Chapter 19.

Thus, if security products are not safe from every attack, and if current laws may not always be efficient in addressing the problem correctly, is there anything a user might be able to do? Even though there is nothing at this time that will guarantee a system's security, a good starting point might be the establishment and implementation of a good computer security policy. A good policy can include:

- Specifying required security features
- Defining "reasonable expectations" of privacy regarding such issues as monitoring people's activities
- Defining access rights and privileges and protecting assets from losses, disclosures, or damages by specifying acceptable use guidelines for users. Also, providing guidelines for external communications (networks)
- Defining responsibilities of all users
- Establishing trust through an effective password policy
- Specifying recovery procedures
- Requiring violations to be recorded
- Providing users with support information

A good computer security policy will differ for each organization, corporation, or individual depending on security needs, although such a policy will not guarantee a system's security or make the network completely safe from possible attacks from cyberspace. With the implementation of such a policy, helped by good security products and a plan for recovery, perhaps the losses can be targeted for a level that is considered "acceptable" and the leaking of private information can be minimized.

Control and Audit: A Global Concern

The events of September 11, 2001, and the collapse of Americans' trust in the financial reports of private industry (Enron, WorldCom, etc.) have caused much reflection and self-assessment within the business world. The evolution of the economic society parallels the evolution of exchange mechanisms because advancement in the latter allows the facilitation of the former. Society started with the primitive use of the barter system. In this way, individuals were both consumers and producers because they brought to market that commodity which they had in excess and exchanged it directly for a commodity for which they were in need. Simply, society exercised an exchange of goods for goods. Due to its numerous inefficiencies and societies' demands to accommodate for the increased population, production, communication, and trading areas, this system was soon replaced by a modified barter exchange mechanism. In the modified barter exchange system, a common medium of exchange was agreed upon so that the time and effort expended in trying to find a trading partner with the need for one's product would be reduced. In the early stages of economic development, precious metals such as gold and silver gained widespread acceptance as exchange media. Precious metals characterized acceptability, durability, portability, and divisibility, but it gradually played the role of money. Thus, when emerging central governments began minting or coinage of these metals to begin the money-based exchange system, its monetary role was even more strengthened.

As economies became more commercial in nature, the influential mercantile class shaped the new society. The needs of the mercantilists, which included the promotion of exchange and accumulation of capital, led to the development of money warehouses that served as depositories for the safekeeping of funds. A receipt would be issued for those who opened a deposit account, and upon presentation of the receipt, the warehouse would return the specified amount to the depositor. These warehouses represented an elementary banking system because, like banks of today, they collected fees to cover their costs as well as earned profits for their owners. Soon the warehouses began issuing bills of exchange or their own drafts because of the idea that not all depositors would withdraw their funds at the same time. This created the fractional reserve banking system in which banks used the deposits not only to back up the receipts that they issued but also to extend credit.

The coin, currency, and demand deposit payment mechanism flourished for many decades because of its convenience, safety, efficiency, and widespread acceptance by the public. However, another major change is now at hand for payment mechanisms: electronic funds transfers.

E-Commerce and Electronic Funds Transfer

E-commerce and electronic funds transfer (EFT) open the next chapter for payment systems. They have been around since the 1960s. The banking industry is considered to be one of the forerunners in the use of computers. The industry started with mechanizing bookkeeping and accounting tasks, automating transaction flows, implementing magnetic ink character recognition (MICR) technology, and finally, utilizing online terminals to update depositor's account and to record receipt or disbursement of cash. The advancement of both computer and communication technologies has spurred the phenomenal growth of EFT systems in the last 20 years. As more consumers become familiar and trusting of electronic financial transactions, EFTs will continue to be more widely used. Today, EFTs have already gone beyond the banking industry and can be seen in almost all retail establishments such as supermarkets, clothing stores, gas stations, and even amusement parks. EFTs allow the convenience of paying for goods and services without having to use checks or currency. In today's society of ever more computer literate individuals, a transition is being witnessed from the traditional cash and check system to electronic payment systems.

Future of Electronic Payment Systems

The increased used of the Internet has brought with it a new form of exchange: virtual commerce. The cashless society that futurists have long forecast is finally at hand and it will replace today's paper money, checks, and even credit cards. Virtual commerce involves a new world of electronic cash (E-cash). Virtual transactions work very much like physical cash but without the physical symbols.

Although the use of E-cash has its positive aspects such as more convenience, flexibility, speed, cost savings, and greater privacy than using credit cards or checks on the Internet, it also has negative ramifications. Uncontrolled growth of electronic cash systems could threaten bank and government-controlled payment systems, which would fuel the growth of confusing and inefficient systems. Also, current technology has not yet deemed E-cash to be more secure than bank money because money stored in a PC could be lost forever if the system crashes. In addition, E-cash could permit criminal activity such as money laundering and tax evasion to hide behind cyber dollars. Counterfeiters could also design their own mints of E-cash that would be difficult to differentiate from real money. Lastly, criminals such as computer hackers could instantaneously pilfer the wealth of thousands of electronic consumers.

Therefore, many companies have been compelled to develop electronic payment systems that will solve these consumer concerns. According to studies, it is expected that 63 percent of the online population will be making retail purchases online by the year 2006. In 2000, it was about 40 percent of the online population. There is a definite need for the security and privacy of payments made over the Internet as millions of transactions occur daily and will be increasing at a rapid pace in the future. With this increase of E-commerce, the likelihood of fraud increases as well. Electronic commerce depends on security and privacy because, without them, neither consumers nor businesses would have an adequate level of comfort in digital transmission of transaction and personal data. In the newly revolutionized economy, it is a necessity for companies to conduct business online and/or reach out to customers through the Internet. The primary areas of concern with E-commerce are confidentiality, integrity, nonrepudiation, and authentication. These areas are addressed through several ways, such as encryption, cryptography, and the use of third parties.

In addition, the credit card industry has been motivated to find secure technology for electronic commerce. The NIST has done some extensive work in this area under its Information Technology Laboratory, devoting an emphasis to Smart Card Standards and Research at http://smartcard. nist.gov/. Organizations like these are only a fraction of the massive experiments that will transform the way people think about money. This is a worldwide commerce movement, not just a U.S. movement. Electronic cash is the next inevitable payment system for an increasingly wired world. Economic history has once again reached another crossroads. Just as the mercantile class transformed the money exchange system to one of money warehouses, electronic commerce (trade on the Internet) will be a revolutionary opportunity for global society to transform today's traditional system of exchange into a system of electronic payments. Thus, the need for auditability, security, and control of IT has become a worldwide issue.

Conclusion

The computer is changing the world. Business operations are also changing, sometimes very rapidly, because of the fast continuing improvement of technology. World events such as September 11, 2001, and financial upheavals from corporate scandals such as Enron and Global Crossing have resulted in increased awareness. Yes, IT controls are very important. Today, people are shopping around at home via networks. People use "numbers" or accounts to buy what they want via shopping computers. These "numbers" are "digital money," the modern currency in the world. Digital money will bring us benefits as well as problems. One major benefit of digital money is its increased efficiency. However, it will also create another problem for us. "Security" is perhaps the biggest factor for individuals interested in making online purchases by using digital money. Also, it must be remembered that vigilance needs to be maintained over those who use the Internet for illegal activities, including those who are now using it for scams, crime, and covert activities that could potentially cause loss of life and harm to others. IT control and security is everyone's business.

Most people fear giving their credit card numbers, phone numbers, or other personal information to strangers. They are afraid that people will be able to use these to retrieve their private or other valuable information without their consent. With identity theft and fraud on the rise, much care is needed in the protection, security, and control of such information. Security, indeed, is the biggest risk in using digital money on the Internet. Besides the problem of security, privacy is a significant factor in some electronic payment systems. In order to encourage people to use digital money, those electronic payment systems should ensure that personal and unrelated information is not unnecessarily disclosed.

For the IT auditor, the need for audit, security, and control will be critical in the areas of IT and will be the challenge of this millennium. Perhaps George Washington University said it best in its Forecast of Emerging Technologies and their impact on society and industry (see Exhibit 1). There are many challenges ahead; everyone must work together to design, implement, and safeguard the integration of these technologies in the workplace.

Review Questions

1. What is IT auditing? What does it involve?
2. Briefly, what are the skills needed to audit information systems? Are they technical or nontechnical?
3. List five professional associations or organizations that support the needs of IT auditors today.
4. List at least three studies or documents issued that discuss the need for improved IT control.
5. Technology has impacted the business environment in three areas. What are those areas?
6. Why is IT control and auditability so important in today's virtual environment?
7. List and explain three U.S. federal laws which impact IT auditors.
8. What are some of the major concerns regarding control and auditability of IT in today's global environment?
9. What is EFT and what are its areas of vulnerability?
10. What is E-cash? What are the IT control concerns associated with E-cash?

Multiple Choice

1. One reason why IT auditing evolved from traditional auditing was that:
   a. Auditors realized that computers had impacted their ability to perform the attestation function.
   b. Computers and information processing were not a key resource.

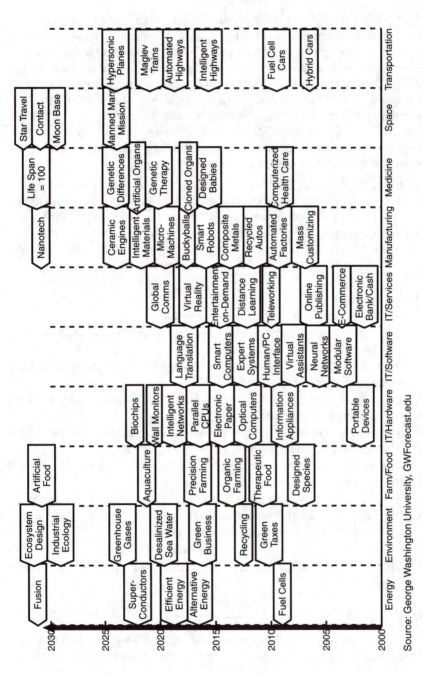

Source: George Washington University, GWForecast.edu

Exhibit 1. George Washington University Forecast of Emerging Technology

      c. Professional associations such as AICPA and ISACA did not recognize the need.

      d. Government did not recognize the need.

2. IT auditing may involve:

      a. Organizational IT audits

      b. Application IT audits

      c. Development/implementation IT audits

      d. All of the above

3. The breadth and depth of knowledge required to audit IT and systems are extensive and may include:

      a. Application of risk-oriented audit approaches

      b. Reporting to management and performing follow-up review to insure action taken

      c. Assessment of security and privacy issues that can put the organization at risk

      d. All of the above

4. CoBiT stands for:

      a. A computer language

      b. A federal agency

      c. Control Objective for Information and Related Technology

      d. None of the above

5. ISACA stands for:

      a. Information Systems Security Association

      b. Institute of Internal Auditors

      c. Information Systems Audit and Control Association

      d. International Association for Computer Educators

6. ISO is:

      a. A government organization

      b. A private company

      c. The International Organization for Standardization

      d. None of the above

7. The federal government plan for improving security on the Internet is called:

      a. FIP 102 Computer Security and Accreditation

      b. National Strategy for Securing Cyberspace

      c. Computer Abuse Act of 1984

      d. Privacy Act of 1974

8. The Sarbanes–Oxley Act of 2002:

      a. Does not affect the attestation function

      b. Applies only to the Big Four accounting firms

      c. Requires auditor rotation

      d. Does not apply to small accounting/audit firms

9. Which is the most recent federal law that addresses computer security or privacy:

      a. Computer Fraud and Abuse Act

    b. Computer Security Act
    c. Homeland Security Act
    d. Electronic Communications Privacy Act

10. Which act has a provision where punishment can be up to life in prison if electronic hackers are found guilty of causing death to others through their actions?
    a. Computer Fraud and Abuse Act
    b. Freedom of information Act
    c. Communications Decency Act
    d. Homeland Security Act

Exercises

1. List and explain five Web sites you can go to for information about IT auditing.
2. List and explain five Web sites you can go to for information about IT security and privacy issues.
3. List and explain five Web sites you can go to for information about recent U.S. or World Court laws or court cases involving IT issues.
4. You are asked by your IT audit manager to do a background search on auditing IT disaster recovery planning. List and summarize five Web sites where information can be obtained to help you in your background research.
5. You are asked by your IT audit manager to obtain studies and articles on conducting performing control self-assessment reviews. List five articles or Web sites that can provide such information.

Answers to Multiple Choice Questions

1 — a; 2 — d; 3 — d; 4 — c; 5 — c; 6 — c; 7 — b; 8 — c; 9 — c; 10 — d.

References

1. Basel Committee on Banking Supervision, Sound Practices for the Management and Supervision of Operational Risk, Bank for International Settlements, published online, December 2001. http://www.bis.org/publ/bcbs86.htm
2. COBIT Steering Committee and The IT Governance Institute, COBIT 3rd edition, Rolling Meadows, IL, Information Systems Audit and Control Foundation, 2002.
3. Federal Financial Institutions Examination Council, FFIEC IS Examination Handbook. Published online, 1996. http://www.ncua.gov/ref/ffiec/ffiec_handbook.html
4. Gallegos, F., Federal Laws affecting IS Auditors, EDP Auditing Series, #72-10-23, Auerbach Publishers, Boca Raton, FL, January 2001, pp. 1–24.
5. Gallegos, F. et al., Information Technology Control and Audit, Auerbach Publishers, Boca Raton, FL, 1999.
6. Gallegos, F. et al., Audit and Control of Information Systems, Thomson Corporation–South-Western Publishers, Cincinnati, OH, 1987.
7. Gallegos, F., Due professional care, Inf. Syst. Control J., Vol. 2, 2002, pp. 25–28.
8. Gallegos, F., Electronic funds transfer: Control issues in a cashless, checkless society, Inf. Strategy Executive's J., Vol. 17, No. 2, winter 2001, pp. 36–39.

9.   George Washington University, Forecast of Emerging Technology, 2002.
10. The IT Governance Institute and the IT Control Practices Committee of ISACA, IT Control Practice Statement for the CobiT High-Level Control Objective PO-9 Assess Risks, Rolling Meadows, IL: IT Governance Institute, 2001.
11. Lam, J., Enterprise-wide risk management and the role of the chief risk officer, *ERisk*, March 25, 2000. http://www.erisk.com/portal/resources/archive/011_lamriskoff.pdf
12. Miccolis, J., Enterprise Risk Management in the Financial Services Industry, From Concept to Management Process, IRMI, published online, November 2000. http://www.irmi.com/expert/articles/miccolis003.asp
13. Miccolis, J. and C. Lee, Implementing Enterprise Risk Management: The Emerging Role of the Chief Risk Officer, IRMI, published online, January 2001. http://test.www.irmi.com/expert/articles/miccolis006.asp
14. Office of the Comptroller of the Currency, OCC Bulletin 98-3 Technology Risk Management, February 4, 1998.
15. Office of the Comptroller of the Currency, OCC Bulletin 98-38 Technology Risk Management: PC Banking, August 24, 1998.
16. OTA, Information Security and Privacy in Network Environments, Office of Technology Assessment — Congress of the United States. Government Printing Office, Washington, D.C., 1995. http://www.ota.gov
17. Rester, M., Hacker steals Web addresses, Inland Valley Daily Bulletin, June 28, 2003, A6.
18. Smiechewicz, W., Case Study: Implementing Enterprise Risk Management, Institutional Investor Bank Accounting & Finance, 2001, 14.4: 21.
19. Walton, S.V. and A.S. Marucheck, The relationship between EDI and supplier reliability, *Int. J. Purchasing Mater. Manage.*, Vol. 33, No. 3, 1997.
20. Upton, D. and A. McAfee, The real virtual factory, *Harvard Business Review*, July-August 1996, 123–133.
21. United States General Accounting Office, Information Security Risk Assessment Practices of Leading Organizations, Washington, D.C., November 1999. http://www.gao.gov/special.pubs/ai00033.pdf
22. United States General Accounting Office, Protecting Information Systems Supporting the Federal Government's and the Nation's Critical Information, GAO High Risk Series, GAO-03-121. Washington, D.C., January 2003.
23. United States General Accounting Office. Executive Guide: Information Security Management, Learning from Leading Organizations, GAO Report AIMD-98-68. Washington, D.C., May 1998.
24. United States General Accounting Office, Executive Guide: Maximizing the Success of Chief Information Officers, GAO Report AIMD-00-83. Washington, D.C., March 2000.
25. United States General Accounting Office, Executive Guide: Measuring Performance and Demonstrating Results of Information Technology Investments, GAO Report AIMD-99-89. Washington, D.C., March 1998.

Chapter 2
Audit and Review: Its Role in Information Technology

For the information technology (IT) manager, or any manager, the words "audit" and "auditor" send chills up and down the spine. Yes, the auditor or the audit has been considered an evil that has to be dealt with by all managers. In the IT field, auditors in the past had to be trained or provided orientation in IS Concepts and Operations in order to evaluate IT practices and applications. IT managers cringed at the auditor's ability to effectively and efficiently evaluate the complexities and grasp the issues. Exhibit 1 lists the top 10 reasons for the start of IT auditing.[1]

In today's environment, organizations must integrate their IT with business strategies to attain their overall enterprise objectives, get the most value out of their information, and capitalize on the technologies available to them. Where IT was formerly viewed as an enabler of an enterprise's strategy, it now is regarded as an integral part of that strategy to attain profitability and service.

As computerized applications are penetrating nearly all business functions and processes, organizations are mixing hardware platforms from different vendors with a combination of commercially available software and in-house developed software. Issues such as IT governance, international information infrastructure, E-commerce, security, and privacy and control of public and enterprise information have driven the need for self-review and self-assurance.

As a result, business risk increases. IT auditing is needed to evaluate the adequacy of information systems to meet processing needs, to evaluate the adequacy of internal controls, and to ensure that assets controlled by those systems are adequately safeguarded. Recent situations such as those at Enron, WorldCom, and others give weight to the need for audit and independence. The passage in the United States of the Sarbanes–Oxley Act of 2002 provides the needed support for organizations to clean up their act and rely on their internal audit capability.

Exhibit 1. The Top Ten Reasons for the Start-Up of IT Auditing

1. Auditing around the computer was becoming unsatisfactory for the purpose of data reliance.
2. Reliance on controls was becoming highly questionable.
3. Financial institutions were losing money due to creative programming.
4. Payroll databases could not be relied on for accuracy due to sophisticated programmers.
5. The security of data could no longer be enforced effectively.
6. Advancements occured in technology.
7. Internal networks were being accessed by employees' desktop computers.
8. Personal computers became accessible for office and home use.
9. Large amounts of data required advanced software programs to audit them, known as CAATs (Computer Assisted Audit Technique).
10. The tremendous growth of corporate hackers, either internal or external, warranted the need for IT auditors.

Today, even in these economic times the demand for qualified IT auditors exceeds the supply. IT governance has created opportunities for the IT auditor.

The Need for the IT Audit Function

Organizations continue to rely heavily on computer technology. With the increased reliance on computers to perform daily transactions and with the higher risks associated with new technology, management needs assurance that the controls governing its computer operations are adequate. Management looks toward the audit function to provide this assurance. However, because of the rapidly changing technology and the new risks associated with that technology, specialists are needed to perform these control assessments. The EDP auditors of the past have evolved into the IT auditors of today and the future.

There have been many changes in the way enterprises address IT issues, resulting in a new framework called IT governance. CEOs, CFOs, COOs, CTOs, and CIOs agree on the founding principles of IT governance, which focus on strategic alignment between IT and enterprise objectives. This, in turn, creates changes to tactical and day-to-day operational management of IT in the organization.

In simple terms, IT governance is the process by which an enterprise's IT is directed and controlled. Effective IT governance helps ensure that IT supports business goals, maximizes business investment in IT, and appropriately manages IT-related risks. IT governance also helps ensure achievement of critical success factors by efficiently and effectively deploying secure, reliable information and applied technology.

Auditing Concerns

Auditors involved in reviewing information systems should focus their concerns on the system's control aspects. They must look at the total systems environment — not just the computerized segment. This requires their involvement from the time a transaction is initiated until it is posted to the organization's general ledger. Specifically, auditors must ensure that provisions are made for:

- An adequate audit trail so that transactions can be traced forward and backward through the system
- The documentation and existence of controls over the accounting for all data (e.g., transactions) entered into the system and controls to ensure the integrity of those transactions throughout the computerized segment of the system
- Handling exceptions to, and rejections from, the computer system
- Unit and integrated testing, with controls in place to determine whether the systems perform as stated
- Controls over changes to the computer system to determine whether the proper authorization has been given and documented
- Authorization procedures for system overrides and documentation of those processes
- Determining whether organization and government policies and procedures are adhered to in system implementation
- Training user personnel in the operation of the system
- Developing detailed evaluation criteria so that it is possible to determine whether the implemented system has met predetermined specifications
- Adequate controls between interconnected computer systems
- Adequate security procedures to protect the user's data
- Backup and recovery procedures for the operation of the system and assurance of business continuity
- Ensuring technology provided by different vendors (i.e., operational platforms) is compatible and controlled
- Adequately designed and controlled databases to ensure that common definitions of data are used throughout the organization, that redundancy is eliminated or controlled, and that data existing in multiple databases is updated concurrently

This list affirms that the auditor is primarily concerned with adequate controls to safeguard the organization's assets and that the Sarbanes–Oxley Act of 2002 will ensure that quality and independence are maintained in this review process.

The Reviewers of Information System Policies, Procedures, Standards, and Their Applications

Today, the auditor, especially the new breed of IT auditors, has the level of knowledge, skills, and abilities to do a quality job and provide a quality assessment. But how can the IT manager better utilize the IT auditor to assist in providing objective, value-added contributions to their work? Such techniques as risk assessment, participation in corporate audit planning, developing IT audit skill and capability, and holding auditors to their standards of practice are ways of accomplishing this goal.

The techniques mentioned above could work if supported by top management and IT management. The support of top management is essential. It is precisely the managerial initiatives that provide the opportunity for reducing threats of carelessness, corruption, and incompetence. It is equally essential to gain the support of all members of the organization and design security systems so that they are as unintrusive in the work place as possible. These managerial initiatives to reduce risk can be combined with the more traditional defensive strategies and tactics of information systems security to provide the best (most cost effective) approach to protecting corporate information assets.

What Are the Policies and Procedures of Management?

When conducting an audit of an external client or in-house management, one must take into consideration the policies and procedures of management. Management dictates how the organization will be divided into subgroups that control small portions of a company. In order to accurately assess the scope of the audit environment, the IT auditor should first verify the existence of a policies and procedures manual. This step becomes very important in most audits because, if a finding is made, it helps the auditor establish where to place the cause and how to rectify the problem.

> Policies and procedures are only as good as the management structure which formed them and enforces the action taken. The IT auditor should examine the corporate structure of the policies and procedures set by management. The auditor should then verify that the policies and procedures follow audit standards set by ISACA. ISACA has some very good examples of proper IT environment procedures that are easy to adopt for almost any organization.[2]

A good rule of thumb to keep in mind is that the client's management developed the policies and procedures with the hopes of meeting their company's desired goals more efficiently with the maximum amount of control and profit.

> Each function in the organization, including internal audit and IT, needs complete, well documented polices and procedures to describe the scope of the function of its activities and the interrelationships with other

departments. As policies and procedures are developed and organized into a standards manual, they should be tied directly to the goals and objectives of the organization.[3]

Even today, many companies are lacking in written polices and procedures so it is hard for the auditor to compare them to compliance standards. This is where the auditor can aid them in developing a new set of procedures that would be written and given to each employee who worked in that IT area. Thus, the auditor can provide value added recommendations and help the organization to establish new policies and procedures for the upcoming year. By doing so, this helps the auditor gauge compliance with known standards that are acceptable in the IT audit profession. IT auditors will use this gauge the following year to test personnel compliance to the administration's new directives.

Learning new ways of auditing is always a priority of internal and external IT auditors. Most auditors want tools or audit methodologies that will aid them in accomplishing their task faster and easier. Almost every large organization and/or company has some sort of IT audit function or shop that involves an internal audit department. Today, the "Big Four" CPA firms have designated special groups that specialize in the IT audit field. PriceWaterhouseCoopers LLP, Ernst & Young LLP, Deloitte & Touché LLP, and KPMG LLP have staff that perform IT audits.

Most of these groups assist the financial auditors in establishing the correctness of financial statements for the companies in which they audit. Others focus on special projects such as Internet security dealing with penetration studies, firewall evaluations, bridges, routers, and gateway configurations. Some other areas in which IT audit skills are needed are listed in Exhibit 2.

Auditors Have Standards of Practice

As a manager at any level, you must remember that auditors, whether internal or external, have standards of practice that they are suppose to follow. Like IT professionals, auditors may belong to one or more professional associations and have code of ethics and professional standards of practices and guidance that help them in performing their evaluations/audits. Some of the organizations that produced such standards of practice are the American Institute of Certified Public Accountants (AICPA), Institute of Internal Auditors (IIA), International Federation of Accountants (IFAC), Canadian Institute of Chartered Accountants (CICA), and the Information Systems Audit and Control Association (ISACA). Even government auditors have standards of practice. The U.S. General Accounting Office, the watchdog of Congressional spending, has for many years influenced government auditing standards worldwide. Appendix III provides an overview of these standards.

Exhibit 2. Skills Related to IT Auditing

Number	Subject	Description
1.	Performance of general controls	Internal and external shop operations
2.	Preparation of application assessments	Featured on mainframe, UNIX, Windows NT, and other operating systems
3.	Transfer control protocol/Internet protocol (TCP/IP)	Internet-related data security practice
4.	Asynchronous transfer method (ATM)	Telecommunications
5.	Electronic funds transfer (EFT)	Telecommunications
6.	Database management systems (DBMS)	Knowledge of Oracle, Access, and other DBMS
7.	Business continuity planning (disaster recovery planning)	The planning and recommended implementation of a corporate disaster recovery plan
8.	Systems under change	The use of system development methodology, security and control design, and post-implementation reviews
9.	Audit integration services	Working with financial auditors in order to make assertions on a company's financial statements
10.	Information security services	Internet penetration studies using ISS, SATAN, COPS, and other Internet security tools of trade

Anyone who wants to impress the audit committee or the auditors they are working with should ask for their credentials. If they are seen not performing their work to "standards of practice" for their profession, they know they could be open to a potential lawsuit or even "de-certified." Understand that auditors as the IT professionals take their work seriously and try to do their best to provide a quality effort.

Auditors Must Have Independence

Audit independence is a very critical component if a business wishes to have an audit function that can add value to the organization. The audit report and opinion must be free of any bias or influence if the integrity of the audit process is to be valued and recognized for its contribution to the organization's goals and objectives. A number of professional organizations (such as AICPA, IIA, ISACA, AGA, and others) have addressed this point in very clear context and language. Governmental organizations such as the U.S. General Accounting Office and the International Organization of Supreme Audit Organizations have also addressed this area in-depth.

The Sarbanes–Oxley Act of 2002 will be a vivid reminder of the importance of due professional care. The Sarbanes–Oxley prohibits all registered public accounting firms from providing audit clients contemporaneously with the audit; certain nonaudit services including internal audit outsourcing, financial-information-system design and implementation services, and expert services. These scope-of-service restrictions go beyond existing Security and Exchange Commission (SEC) independence regulations. All other services, including tax services, are permissible only if preapproved by the issuer's audit committee and all such preapprovals must be disclosed in the issuer's periodic reports to the SEC.

The act requires auditor (not audit firm) rotation. Therefore, the lead audit partner and/or the concurring review partner must rotate off the engagement if he or she has performed audit services for the issuer in each of the five previous fiscal years. The act provides no distinction regarding the capacity in which the audit or concurring partner provided such audit services. Any services provided as a manager or in some other capacity appear to count toward the five-year period. The provision starts as soon as the firm is registered so, absent guidance to the contrary, the audit and concurring partner must count back five years starting with the date in which Public Company Accounting Oversight Board registration occurred. This provision has a definite impact on small accounting firms. The Security and Exchange Commission is currently considering whether or not to accommodate small firms in this area; currently, there is no small-firm exemption from this provision.

This act is a major reform package mandating the most far-reaching changes Congress has imposed on the business world since the Foreign Corrupt Practices Act of 1977 and the Security & Exchange Commission Act of 1934. It seeks to thwart future scandals and restore investor confidence by, among other things, creating a public company accounting oversight board, revising auditor independence rules, revising corporate governance standards, and significantly increasing the criminal penalties for violations of securities laws.

The Practice of Continuous Reassessment

The authors believe that this is a very critical component. Continuous reassessment of audit goals is necessary to stay on track with audits lasting more than two to four weeks. Auditors should verify that they have not lost sight of their original intentions and that the scope of the audit still remains the same. Auditors can easily lose themselves in other areas or go off on tangents because of the seemingly unending audits. The client, whoever it may be, is not paying for a jumbled mess of information or any information on areas not previously agreed upon.

For this reason and this reason alone, the auditor needs to step back and reassess the situation. The auditor should make sure the goal of the audit has not changed. If the goal has changed and auditors find themselves encompassing more information in audits to support conclusions then reevaluation of the audit scope is necessary. It is possible that the scope of the audit may need to be expanded. In a later chapter, we have provided guidance on how to accomplish this.

High Ethical Standards

In order for one to act as an auditor, one must have a high standard of moral ethics. The term *auditor* is Latin for one that hears complaints and makes decisions or acts like a judge. To act as a judge one definitely must be morally ethical or it defeats the purpose. Ethics are a very important basis for our culture as a whole. If the auditor loses favor in this area it is almost impossible to regain the trust the auditor once had with audit management and auditees.

Trust is the mainstay thrust upon all auditors as they enter into the position. Whether an auditor is ethical in the beginning or not, they should all start off with the same amount of trust and good favor from the client or auditee. If the bond is not broken, the auditor establishes a good name as someone who can be trusted with sensitive material.

In today's world economy, trust is an unheard of word. No one can trust anyone these days and for this reason it is imperative that high ethics are at the top of the manager's list of topics to cover with new staff. Times are changing and so are the clients requesting our services. Most managers will tell you that they cherish this aspect called ethics because it distinguishes them from others without it.

For example, say a budget calls for numerous hours. It is unethical to put down hours not worked. It is also unethical to overlook something during the audit because the client says it is not important.

> One has to be objective, one has to be fair, and one has to be ethical. If I have to stress one thing above all with respect to Due Professional Care, it's ethics. Sometimes, our wants and desires to succeed and produce the best profit margin for our company get in the way of our ethical standing. I think at times we use gray areas with ethics. It's black, it's white, it's right or it's wrong. So, if there is one message I can give, it's to have a high standard of ethics.[4]

A fine line exists between what is ethical and what is legal. Something can be ethically wrong but still legal. However, with that being said, some things initially thought to be unethical become illegal over time. If there is a large enough population opposed to something ethically incorrect, you will see legislation introduced to make it illegal.

When IT auditors attain their CISA certification, they also subscribe to a Code of Professional Ethics. This code applies to not only the professional conduct but also the personal conduct of IT auditors. It requires that: the ISACA standards are adhered to, confidentiality is maintained, any illegal or improper activities are reported, the auditor's competency is maintained, due care is used in the course of the audit, the results of audit work is communicated, and high standards of conduct and character are maintained.[5]

The Auditor: Knowledge, Skills, and Abilities

Traditionally, there have been three commonly accepted sources of obtaining an IT auditing education:

- The first source is to participate in a mixture of on-the-job training and in-house programs. These are most appropriate where the technology presented has been adopted and implemented by the organization.
- The second source is to participate in seminars presented by professional organizations or vendors. These are valuable in presenting information that is new or for exploring various approaches to information systems auditing problems. In the seminar environment, a peer group can share perspectives not available from a single instructor. However, seminars involve costs, not only for the program, but also for travel, accommodations, and loss of time at work. Also, some seminars do not provide the in-depth technical hands-on competence required in information systems auditing.
- The third source is found in the traditional university academic environment. Past studies have shown that as much as 70 percent of audit training is on-the-job, compared to only 8 percent learned in school. Thus, one of the purposes of proposing a model curriculum for undergraduate and graduate education in IT auditing is to increase the level of education received in this field. Further, a model curriculum provides a framework for universities in structuring or restructuring their courses as well as developing new courses that meet the needs of employers of their graduates.

In the information-based business environment, business professionals who are technically competent in IT or IT specialists who understand the accounting, commerce, and financial operations are in high demand for IT auditing careers. The IT specialist and the IT auditor must continuously receive education to upgrade their knowledge, skills, and abilities. Universities, with the appropriate curriculum, can generate employable candidates for the IT audit, security, and control profession. A university-sponsored proactive IT auditing curricula at the undergraduate and graduate levels is very desirable to those professionals wishing to change their career path or upgrade their skills for job enhancement. The ISACA "Model Curricula for IS Auditing Education at the Undergraduate and Graduate Levels" was developed and issued in March 1998 and should be viewed as a guideline, not absolute criteria. The undergraduate and graduate model curricula provide a goal for universities worldwide to strive towards in meeting the demand for IT auditing, security, and control education. As of this writing, a new update of this model may be in place by 2004.

In the Information Assurances Community, INFOSEC has made significant strides in gaining support from U.S. universities. The National INFOSEC Education and Training Program (NIETP) operates under national authority and its initiatives provide the foundation for a dramatic increase in the population of trained, professionally competent security experts. Activities in this area directly support government efforts to develop professionally competent and certified system administrators and associated network positions in security practices and procedures. There is no single vehicle to accomplish this task. NIETP initiatives are multi-faceted and strive to address all aspects of its role in education, training, and awareness by creating partnerships among government, academia, and industry. Through these partnerships, the NIETP can assess current offerings in INFOSEC courses from a variety of sources to identify gaps and determine how to fill those gaps. To date, 55 U.S. universities have been identified as Centers of Excellence in Information Assurances Education and 66 have had their courses certified to meet federal standards. The U.S. National Security Agency is continuing in its leadership role with national level programs via the NSTISSC for assuring the very finest preparation of professionals entrusted with securing the national security systems.

These models can also serve those who are interested in obtaining an IT auditing education or in educational institutions worldwide that are developing curricula in IT auditing. The sample syllabi of courses identified are offered as examples of what content and requirements courses may include or contain. Universities that have been successful in starting and maintaining such programs at the undergraduate and graduate levels have shared or provided their syllabi to other educational units. Non-U.S. educational institutions may substitute sequence, courses, and content due to government or educational requirements/restrictions imposed within their environment.

Broadest Experiences

Experience in IT management is a definite must, and this is equally true with regard to IT audit management. Nothing in this world can compare to actual on the job, real-world experiences. Theory is also valuable, and for the most part an IT auditor should rely on theory to progress through an audit. For example, if IT auditors wish to demonstrate their commitment and knowledge level of the field, they can select an area to be tested. A number of professional certifications exist that can benefit the auditor. In the IT audit area, to pass the CISA (Certified Information Systems Auditor) exam, one must know, understand, and be able to apply the theory of modern IT auditing to all exam questions posed. In other situations, certifications such as the Certified Public Accountant (CPA), Certified Chartered Accountant (CA), Certified Internal Auditor (CIA), Certified Computer Professional (CCA), Certified Government Financial Manager (CGFM), Certified Information Systems Security Professional (CISSP), Certified Information Security Manager (CISM), and Certified Fraud Examiner (CFE) are examples of certifications that may be very useful to one's career and future plans.

The understanding of theory is definitely essential to the successful IT auditor. However, theory can only take one so far. This textbook and others available should be viewed as a guide. In this field, due to the technology complexity and situation, there comes a time when an IT auditor has to rely on experience to confront a new never-before-encountered situation. Experience in the field is a definite plus, but having experience in a variety of other fields can sometimes be more beneficial. For example, if you are working for a Big Four public accounting firm as an IT audit manager, you are going to be exposed to a wide variety of IT audit situations and scenarios. The experience you receive will help broaden your horizons and further your knowledge in the IT audit field.

This textbook is designed for the professional and those who wish to learn about the Information Systems Audit and Control community as well as those aspiring to enter the profession. It can be used as a resource for training and learning about this field.

Certainly, support for education and the need to share experiences in this area has been recognized and training materials provided for many years by accounting, auditing, and information security professional societies such as the American Institute of Certified Public Accountants, the Institute of Internal Auditors, ISACA, Information Systems Security Association, and the Institute for Management Accountants. The Association of Information Technology Professionals (AITP, formerly Data Processing Management Association — DPMA), in the issuance of its Model Curriculum for Undergraduate Computer Information Systems Education in 1981, included the need for an elective course on IT auditing. This course is still in their most recent model curriculum. From an international perspective, organizations such as the International Federation of Accountants and IFIP/WG11.8 (Information Security Education and Training) have published documents advocating the need for university-developed training in IT auditing, security, and control.

Direct entry into the profession, as is the situation today, may change with entry-level requirements, including experience in business processes, systems, and technology, as well as sound knowledge of general auditing theory supplemented by practical experience. In addition, IT auditors may require specific industry expertise, such as telecommunications, transportation, or finance and insurance to adequately address the industry specific business/technology issues. This book provides current information and approaches to this complex field, which can help the practitioners and those wanting to learn more.

Individuals seeking entry into this profession must understand that experiences in auditing IT applications and operations will provide exposure to languages such as JAVA, C++, a 4GL or Cobol, or others that are relevant. Also, exposure to computer-based communications networks, for example, can include additional technical or programming work such as object-oriented programming or general knowledge of operating systems/programming issues. IT-related experiences provide both exposure to and awareness of the complexities of IT operations and the management of IT. For example, the experience may include discussion on IT project management, IT risk management, and recognizing success and failure factors in IT related projects. Universities worldwide can provide such exposure, experiences, and training in their coursework.

A measure of success is the fact that employers for this career field continuously seek candidates from these universities. Such employers are active in providing speakers and funding for joint research/education. The following courses were suggested and cover 11 areas in the IFAC study "The Impact of Information Technology on the Accountancy Profession" and the follow-up discussion paper, "Minimum Skill Levels in Information Technology for Professional Accountants." Thus, the blend of accounting, business, and IT education at the graduate level can enrich a person with the basic skills to perform in the area of IT auditing. The eleven areas are:

1. IT and its application
2. Systems analysis, design, development, and implementation
3. Internal controls and documentation of information systems
4. Data structures and data base concepts and management
5. Information systems applications and processing cycles
6. Management of information systems and technology
7. Computer programming languages and procedures
8. Computer communications and networks
9. Model-based systems (decision support and expert systems)
10. Systems security and disaster recovery planning
11. Auditing of IT and its role in business

A program beyond the bachelor's degree should be designed to satisfy the following eight technical proficiency requirements:[6]

1. Proficiency as an auditor
2. Ability to review and evaluate IT internal controls and recommend the extent of audit procedures required
3. Understanding of IT system design and operations
4. Knowledge of programming languages and techniques and the ability to apply computer-assisted audit techniques and assess their results
5. General familiarity with computer operating systems and software
6. Ability to identify and reconcile problems with client data file format and structure
7. Ability to bridge the communications gap between the auditor and the IT professional, providing support and advice to management
8. Knowledge of when to seek the assistance of an IT professional

Supplemental Skills

In addition to the experience and technical skills, effective information systems auditors possess a variety of skills that enable them to add value to their organizations and clients. The finest technical training does not fully prepare auditors for the communication and negotiation skills, among others, that are required for success.

Many of the nontechnical or supplemental skills are concerned with gathering information from and, of comparable importance, presenting information to, people. As such, these supplemental skills are readily transferable to other disciplines, e.g., finance, management, and marketing. The final product auditors create is the information presented in their audit report. If this information is not effectively and efficiently delivered via solid oral and written communication skills all value accruing from the audit process could potentially be lost.

Experience comes with time and perseverance, as is well known, but auditors should not limit themselves to just one industry, software, or operating system. They should challenge themselves and broaden their horizons with a multitude of exposure in different environments, if possible. The broader and more well-rounded the IT auditor is, the better the chance for a successful audit career. The auditor can pull on experiences in other fields, software packages, or even operating systems to act as a mental guide during the audit. A side note: Having a well-rounded diverse background never hurts when one is working with an auditee. For example, a junior auditor was recently conducting an audit in which she was faced with a client/auditee that was not very cooperative.

During the questioning process, the junior auditor established a rapport with the client by using people skills or "soft skills." The role of an auditor is not an easy one when we are asked to review and question the work of others. Many times, the auditee must have a clear understanding of our role and that the auditor's focus is not to be critical of the individual but of the organizational policies, procedures, and process. The audit objectives focus on the organization's goals and objectives.

Trial and Error

Some of the best learning comes from the mistakes of others and one's own errors. Errors committed by a simple oversight teach the auditor to become thorough and exacting before releasing the work papers to upper management. No one is perfect in this world. Everyone makes mistakes. It is for this reason that most audit managers realize the importance of error and the valuable lessons that can be learned from such errors. Nobody wants to be a failure. However, it is inevitable, and, for that matter, inconceivable, to believe that employees are not going to make mistakes. The key to success in any business environment is the individual employee. An efficient auditor will learn from errors and improve productivity so that the same error is never committed again.[7]

Most IT audit managers will admit that they all have done things on audits as an inexperienced staff member that they would like to forget. The thing to remember here is that all IT audit professionals who are successful have learned from their mistakes and have built a solid foundation on which to grow.

Committing errors will always happen in day-to-day life. That is just a fact, and anyone who believes otherwise is just fooling himself. Learn to accept that perfection is not possible and that faults must be worked on to enhance productivity and quality of work.

Objective and Context

The objective and context of the work one is to perform is a key element in any audit environment and should not be overlooked. It is the basis by which all audits should be approached.

> *The Objective is what we are trying to accomplish. The Context is the environment in which we perform our work. Thus, everything ultimately depends on both our objective and the context of the work we are to perform. That is to say, the decisions we make about the scope, nature and timing of our work depends on what we're trying to do (i.e., gain assurance of an A/R balance, gain assurance that a Web site is secure, gain assurance that a new application will work correctly when implementation is complete, gain assurance that a business is prepared to continue functioning after a riot) and that the environment we are working in (i.e., a big company vs. a small company, a domestic organization with a centralized common systems vs. a multinational organization with multiple divisions using a variety of disparate applications on a multitude of computer platforms, an organization based in Los Angeles or New York vs. an organization based in Fargo, North Dakota or Portland, Oregon). Keep in*

> *mind what works well for one organization, may not work as well in another, based on many combinations of objective and context.*[8]

For example, if the auditor has a General Controls Assessment, the audit objectives may be to verify that all controls related to (the data center, the building in which the data center is located, A/R, A/P) are adequate. Therefore, the IT auditor needs to verify the controls because the financial auditors were relying on the computer system to provide them with the correct financial information. The Context is where the auditor's true analytical skills come into play. Here the environment is for the most part always different from shop to shop. The auditor must assess the context for which he/she has entered and make a decision as to how the environment should be addressed (i.e., big company, small company, large staff, small staff, etc.).

The Role of the IT Auditor

The auditor evaluating today's complex systems must have highly developed technical skills to understand the evolving methods of information processing. Contemporary systems carry risks such as noncompatible platforms, new methods to penetrate security through communication networks (e.g., the Internet), and the rapid decentralization of information processing with the resulting loss of centralized controls.

Auditing the processing environment is divided into two parts. The first and most technical part of the audit is the evaluation of the operating environment, with major software packages (e.g., the operating and security systems) representing the general or environmental controls in the automated processing environment. This part is usually audited by the IT audit specialist. The second part of the processing environment is the automated application, which is audited by the general auditor who possesses some computer skills.

As the use of IT in organizations continues to grow, auditing computerized systems must be accomplished without many of the guidelines established for the traditional auditing effort. In addition, new uses of IT introduce new risks, which in turn require new controls. IT auditors are also in a unique position to evaluate the relevance of a particular system to the enterprise as a whole. Because of this, the IT auditor often plays a role in senior management decision making.

The role of IT auditor can be examined through the process of IT governance and the existing standards of professional practice for this profession. As mentioned earlier, IT governance is an organizational involvement in the management and review of the use of IT in attaining the goals and objectives set by the organization.

Because IT impacts the operation of an entire organization, everyone should have an interest and role in governing its use and application. This growing awareness has led organizations to recognize that, if they are to make the most of their IT investment and protect that investment, they need a formal process to govern it.

Reasons for implementing an IT governance program include:

- Increasing dependence on information and the systems that deliver the information
- Increasing vulnerabilities and a wide spectrum of threats
- Scale and cost of current and future investments in information and information systems
- Potential for technologies to dramatically change organizations and business practices to create new opportunities and reduce costs.

As long as these factors remain a part of business, there will be a need for effective, interdependent systems of enterprise and IT governance.

An open-standard IT governance tool that helps nontechnical and technical managers and auditors understand and manage risks associated with information and related IT was developed by the IT Governance Institute and the Information Systems Audit and Control Foundation. Control Objectives for Information and Related Technology (CoBiT) is a comprehensive framework of control objectives that helps IT auditors, managers, and executives discharge fiduciary responsibilities, understand their IT systems, and decide what level of security and control is adequate. CoBiT provides an authoritative, international set of generally accepted IT practices for business managers and auditors.

CoBiT can be downloaded on a complimentary basis from www.isaca. org. It includes a publication containing detailed management guidelines to bridge the gaps among business risks, control needs, and technical issues. These new tools help businesses monitor processes by using critical success factors (CSFs), key goal indicators (KGIs), key performance indicators (KPIs), and Maturity Models (MMs). Additional resources and information are available at www.ITgovernance.org.

The IT Auditor as Counselor

In the past, users have abdicated responsibility for controlling computer systems, mostly because of the psychological barriers that surround the computer. As a result, there are few checks and balances, except for the IT auditor. Therefore, auditors must take an active role in developing policies on auditability, control, testing, and standards. Auditors also must convince users and IT personnel of the need for a controlled IT environment.

An IT audit staff in a large corporation can make a major contribution to computer system control by persuading user groups to insist on a policy of comprehensive testing for all new systems and all changes to existing systems. By reviewing base-case results, user groups can control the accuracy of new or changed systems by actually performing a complete control function.

Insisting that all new systems be reviewed at predefined checkpoints throughout the system's development life cycle also can enhance control of IT. The prospect of audit review should prompt both user and systems groups to define their objectives and assumptions more carefully. Here, too, IT auditors can subtly extend their influence.

The IT Auditor as Partner of Senior Management

Although the IT auditor's roles of counselor and skilled technician are vital to successful company operation, they may be irrelevant if the auditor fails to view auditing in relation to the organization as a whole. A system that appears well controlled may be inconsistent with the operation of a business.

Decisions concerning the need for a system traditionally belonged to senior management, but because of a combination of factors (mostly the complex technology of the computer), computer system audits were not successfully performed. When allocating funds for new systems, management has had to rely on the judgment of computer personnel. Although their choices of new and more effective computer systems cannot be faulted, computer personnel have often failed to meet the true business needs of the organization.

Management needs the support of a skilled computer staff that understands the organization's requirements, and IT auditors are in such a position to provide that information. They can provide management with an independent assessment of the effect of IT decisions on the business. In addition, the IT auditor can verify that all alternatives for a given project have been considered, all risks have been accurately assessed, the technical hardware and software solutions are correct, business needs will be satisfied, and costs are reasonable.

Types of Auditors and Their Duties, Functions, and Responsibilities

There are two types of audit functions that exist today. They have very important roles in assuring the validity and integrity of financial accounting and reporting systems. They are the internal audit and external audit function.

A FOUNDATION FOR IT AUDIT AND CONTROL

The Internal Audit Function

The internal audit function is a control function with a company or organization. The primary purpose of the internal audit function is to assure that management authorized controls are being applied effectively. The internal audit function, although not mandatory, exists in most private enterprise or corporate entities, and in government (such as federal, state, county, and city governments). The mission, character, and strength of an internal audit function vary widely within the style of top executives and traditions of companies and organizations. IT audits is one of the newer, emerging areas of support for internal audit.

The internal audit group, if appropriately staffed with the resources, performs the monitoring and testing of IT activities within control of the organization. Of particular concern to private corporations is the processing of data and the generation of information of financial relevance or materiality.

As mentioned in the next section, management has a very large part to play in the effectiveness of an internal audit function. Their concern with the reliability and integrity of computer-generated information from which decisions are made from is critical. In organizations where management shows and demonstrates concern about internal controls, the role of the internal audit grows in stature. As the internal audit function matures through experience, training, and career development, the external audit function and the public can rely on the quality of the internal auditor's work. With a good, continuously improving internal audit management and staff, corporate management is not hesitant to assign reviews, consultation, and testing responsibilities to the internal auditor. These responsibilities are often broader in scope than those of the external auditor.

Within the United States, internal auditors from government agencies often come together to meet and exchange experiences through conferences or forums. For example, the Intergovernmental Audit Forum is an example of an event where auditors come together from city, county, state, and federal environments to exchange experiences and provide new information regarding audit techniques and methods. The Institute of Internal Auditors holds a national conference that draws an auditor population from around the world, both private and government, to share experiences and discuss new audit methods and techniques.

The External Auditor

The external auditor evaluates the reliability and the validity of systems controls in all forms. The principal objective in their evaluation is to minimize the amount of substantial auditing or testing of transactions required to render an opinion on a financial statement.

External auditors are provided by public accounting firms and also exist in government as well. For example, the U.S. General Accounting Office is considered an external reviewer because they can examine the work of both federal and private organizations where federal funds are provided. The Watchdogs of Congressional Spending provide a service to the taxpayer in reporting directly to Congress on issues of mismanagement and poor controls. Interestingly, in foreign countries, an Office of the Inspector General or Auditor General's Office within that country prepares similar functions. Also, the GAO has been a strong supporter of the International Audit Organization, which provides government audit training and guidance to its international audit members representing governments worldwide.

From a public accounting firm standpoint, firms like Deloitte & Touché, Ernst & Young, Price Waterhouse Coopers (formerly Price Waterhouse and Coopers and Lybrand), and KPMG have provided these types of external audit services worldwide. The external auditor is responsible for testing the reliability of client IT systems and should have a special combination of skills and experience. Such an auditor must be thoroughly familiar with the audit attest function. The attest function encompasses all activities and responsibilities associated with the rending of an audit opinion on the fairness of the financial statements. Besides the accounting and auditing skills involved in performing the attest function, these external auditors also must have substantial IT audit experience. The Sarbanes–Oxley Act of 2003 now governs their role and limits of services that can be offered beyond audit.

Legal Implications

In the pre-Sarbanes–Oxley years, the establishment of "limited liability partnerships" came as a result of a "Big Five" organization that was taken to court by a client. The client, who selected a support system based on the firm's recommendation, failed to perform in the manner recommended and caused the company financial loss. The courts held the Big Five firm liable for not exercising "due professional care" in the conduct of their work performed. The company sought the protection of a limited liability partnership with its auditee.

Today, we now have a Big Four due to the Enron scandal and the demise of Arthur Andersen LLP. The guidance the courts used to evaluate the issues of this case was issued by the American Institute of Certified Public Accountants. Since the firm held itself and its professionals compliant with AICPA's governing standards and guidance, the courts used this guidance as a basis for evaluating the evidence of the case and their professional conduct. Arthur Andersen LLP was the first major international accounting firm taken to court and successful convicted for a lack of due professional care in the destruction of client documents and obstructing justice. A jury on June 16, 2002, found Arthur Andersen LLP guilty of obstructing justice, all but sealing the fate of this accounting firm.

After a month-and-a-half trial and ten days of deliberations, jurors convicted Andersen for obstructing justice when it destroyed Enron Corp. documents while on notice of a federal investigation. Andersen and their lawyers had claimed that the documents were destroyed as part of its housekeeping duties and not as a ruse to keep Enron documents away from the regulators.

Management Responsibilities Today

Sarbanes–Oxley provides today's senior management vivid reminders of the need to support the internal and external audit function. Senior management participation offers more than the availability of adequate resources to accomplish the assigned tasks; it offers the possibility of radically altering the situation and thereby reducing the risks that must be managed. Specifically, there are managerial actions at all levels, which can be taken to decrease the probability of carelessness and of fraud and corruption within the organization while reducing outside threat and the probability of hostile penetration of the information systems by others. Even the best preventive system can never completely remove the threats to the system, however, and it must be supplemented by adequate defensive safeguards to protect the physical assets of the corporate group and block unauthorized access to information resources. Ultimately, getting top management involved means creating a radical change in corporate culture and structure. Thinking must become more global, with competitors at home converted into partners and friendly rivals and the overseas international competitors defined as possibly the opposition or the trading partner in today's global environment.

Risk Assessment

Contemporary risk assessment and security methodologies recognize the need for a multidimensional approach to determining and administering access control and physical security for computer information systems. At least three different approaches to providing this security emerge from the current literature, which are distinguished by the emphasis that they place on different dimensional attributes of the security system. We might designate these three perspectives as the Castellans, the Guardians, and the Gatekeepers based on the nature of their primary emphasis in establishing and maintaining a secure system.

The Castellans see the creation of a "fortress" (Smith) to provide a physically secure system as the best approach. The Guardians tend to see the imposition and enforcement of laws and administrative regulations as the best defense against the depredations of disgruntled and incompetent employees, devious competitors, and marauding hackers. The Gatekeepers place their faith in the implementation of hardware and software controls to provide adequate protection of programs and data by limiting access and by verification and validation of interactions with the system. Clearly, each of these kinds of defensive tactics has its place in establishing and maintaining reasonable assurance of the protection of corporate information assets. Each of these three perspectives recognizes the need for top and IS management support if the security efforts are to succeed.

Three Perspectives on Risk

The Castellan approach has received the least contemporary attention in the literature of the three traditional approaches to assessing risk and providing security for information systems. The civil unrest within the United States during the 1960s combined with a rapid increase in the importance of computer information systems for major corporations, universities, and governmental agencies, led to recognition of an inherent vulnerability to physical attack by dissident forces. Strategies were developed to respond to this threat, which typically focused on the creation of a "fortress" for the information system. This fortress concept included the use of inner and outer fences to isolate the building that housed the system.

Within the inner fence a berm or earthwork was often constructed to further isolate the building. The building, itself, was generally constructed of masonry without windows and with steel fire and blast-proof doors. These same precautions are built into some new facilities but the 1970s and 1980s have not provided the empirical validation to the presumed threat to lead many corporations to install full physical security.

Current literature and recent studies frequently mention the need for physical security but there is a greater concern with other aspects of the problem. One leading authority on data security goes so far as to suggest the view that security is a technical problem. Other experts have stated the current orthodoxy that information systems security is a people problem and the primary threats are incompetence and "unintentional human error." Malicious and malignant acts are a measurable possibility but they are seen as calling for much less draconian responses than building an impregnable fortress to house the information system. This concept has been further eroded by the extensive use of microcomputers, distributed data processing systems, and Client/Server Architecture, which simply cannot be effectively confined within the secure walls of the windowless redoubt.

The Guardians. The Guardians have offered a view of risk assessment and security access control that portrays it as another form of crime and corruption within organizations and within the larger society. These specialists tend to talk about "computer crimes" and failures of management controls and procedures as a serious risk to the integrity, accuracy, and reliability of the information system. Experts such as Dr. Jerry Fitzgerald, Robert Parker, Belden Menkus, J.J. Bloombecker, and the late Dr. Harold J. Highland have catalogued specific types of computer criminals including the data diddler, the Trojan horse, the salami slicer, the logic bomber, the asynchronous attacker, the scavenger, the leak catcher, the piggybackers, and the simulation and modeling criminals. Recent articles in national magazines and (IT) professional journals have emphasized the importance of federal legislative initiatives for managers and information systems professionals. They stress responsibilities that these laws create for the practice of management as a profession and the responsibilities for enforcement that reside with both the company's own auditors and with the public and governmental auditors. This point of view became all too real for many of us on September 11, 2001. It serves to remind us that the Guardian point of view is real and must be respected in management decisions.

It is difficult, indeed futile, to argue that the introduction of state and federal laws does not represent the presence of risk for integrity, reliability, and accuracy. These laws do more than reflect a level of risk within the environment that society believes to be of a sufficient magnitude to represent a threat to the welfare of the community. The Homeland Security Act of 2002 has made IT security everyone's business. Such laws recognize a real and quantifiable risk for managers and systems professionals by imposing specific responsibilities for taking those actions necessary to protect the security and privacy of information resources entrusted to their administration. Until the recent release of the U.S. government's "National Strategy for Securing Cyberspace," most would point out that the principle problem with the guardians approach is that laws, regulations, and administrative procedures do not protect assets. These laws, regulations, and procedures only establish a kind of uniform pattern of expected behavior and provide retribution for transgressors. The report identifies such assets.

The Gatekeepers. The Gatekeepers view risk as endemic to all organizational information systems. Like the Castellans, the Gatekeepers believe the best way to protect the information resources is by limiting the access individuals have to those resources. The approach to limiting that access is quite different. The Gatekeepers recognize the ubiquitousness of the means of accessing information systems in this era of distributed and networked information systems. Three primary generic types of gate-keeping activities have been suggested in the literature. These techniques include the use of passwords and access tables, the use of encryption schemes, and the use of natural and artificial "hardware" identification devices to limit access.

Application of Risk Assessment

From this point of view, we would expect that internal corruption in the form of computer fraud, unauthorized use of corporate assets, and disclosure of private or proprietary information would be intentional hostile acts directed at the corporation-as-enemy. Errors of both commission and omission that arise from the carelessness of some actor would seem to reflect a definition of the situation in which that actor defines the particular type of action as trivial, unimportant, or worse, as in some way detrimental to the organization or its members. Also, these errors of both commission and of omission often arise from the incompetence of members within the organization. Experts believe that others outside the organization are likely to contribute to the resulting situation, causing top management to impose the unneeded pressure upon the organization. An example would be the issuance of a policy or strategic mission statement that classifies the peoples who make up the working ranks of the corporate group as "cost factors" rather than as organizational assets.

The greatest threats to the integrity and privacy of the information system come from inside the organization. These threats include (1) degradation of the validity, accuracy, and reliability of data resulting from errors produced by incompetence or carelessness, (2) loss or destruction of assets by malicious acts, and (3) deliberate disclosure of private or privileged information. The best defense against these threats is a combination of actions to reduce the threats supplemented by actions, which will install and maintain basic routine safeguards like password protection of computer access and the use of access tables to authorize the kinds and extent of access that each individual is given to the information assets of the corporation. The symbolic interactionist perspective suggests that the probability of these untoward acts occurring could be significantly reduced by redefining the situation within the organization.

Thus, the outcome of risk assessment could identify prioritized areas that IT and management need to concentrate on. These can also be areas that an IS audit needs to concentrate on as well. This will assist corporate and IS Management in monitoring the most critical, sensitive, and high-risk areas.

Participation in Corporate IT Audit Planning

If IT management wants more effective and cost-efficient audits, they should get involved either through formal or informal channels and assist their audit planning committee by providing their ranking of high-risk areas identified from their risk assessment process as areas for audit consideration. In essence, IT management can openly contribute to corporate audit objectives by identifying areas of high risk through their self-evaluation or risk assessment process. Thus, this action or report will allow corporate management to provide support to critical areas and use the audit reports to gauge the effectiveness and efficiency of added resources.

If areas that are not identified by risk assessment are of concern to IT management, again these areas should be brought to the attention of the audit committee or corporate management for their action and attention. Again, these could potentially be referred to internal audit for their review or action.

The Organization's Responsibility in Developing IT Audit Skills

"If you build it, they will come" has been a familiar phrase used in reference to the coming of the auditor. An IT manager, has a right to receive a quality audit. However, managers can do much to ensure that they receive such a review by asking such questions and making such preparations as given below.

Preaudit checklist:

1. Who are members of the audit team, and what are their roles and assignments?
2. What are the credentials and experience of the assigned audit team?
3. What orientation or training can you provide them to be comfortable within the environment?
4. Communicate with your managers and staff in the areas to be audited.
5. If an area was audited before, review the prior report to see the issues raised and recommended made. Get an update of corrections or changes made as a result of prior audit work and give your staff and the audit department credit.

Audit checklist:

1. Purpose of the audit?
2. Scope and objectives?
3. Who are the audit staff assigned? (Ask to be notified if any staff are changed.)
4. Timeframe for work to be performed?
5. Use of computer time/access to system/logs/training needed.
6. Access to IT management and staff?
7. Communicate (1) and (2) to all IT staff affected.
8. Set weekly or biweekly meetings with audit manager/audit team to discuss audit progress and issues.
9. Before the audit is finished, request close-out conference from audit group.
10. Request a copy of audit report.

Post-audit checklist:

1. When the audit report is issued, pull your team together and discuss the report; if you follow the steps above there should be no surprises. If there are, there was a communication breakdown somewhere.
2. If you disagree with the report or portions of the report, do so in writing with supporting evidence. Remember, the auditor has supporting evidence for their reports, and this exists in their working papers. For those areas you agree, indicate what corrective actions your team plans to take.
3. Have your team provide a status report to you on a 3- to 6-month cycle with a copy to go to Internal Audit. This shows you value their work.

Conclusion

The audit function, whether internal or external, is part of the corporate environment. It is a process to objectively validate, verify, and substantiate a process, activity, function, system, subsystem, or project within a company. Auditors have a unique set of skills and abilities that allows them to evaluate varied issues and environments. They also have standards of professional practice that they follow, depending on their level of qualifications and any certifications they may have attained.

Assessment of strategic and operational events is not beyond their scope as well as their ability to assess issues involving efficiency, effectiveness, and economic resources. As an auditor, the use of this scarce, highly valued resource can be helpful and cost effective. Corporate management can successfully use this resource to help them manage a very complex environment and work toward achieving the organizational goals and objectives. In addition, several career path studies have shown that IT auditors at some point in time in their career path move into other parts of the organization. So, as managers, the IT auditor with their corporate overview, communication skills, analytical skills, and technology skills may be candidates for operational or support positions within IT.

This chapter has discussed the audit process and its role. Also, we have covered some approaches on how IT management can cost effectively use an IT audit, but IT managers must remember that they can do many things to ensure the quality of the IT audit. Certainly, the establishment of an in-house IT risk assessment process was one such example provided. Others mentioned and discussed were the development of IT audit skills and the awareness of Standards of Audit Practice, all of which contribute to more cost-effective IS audit work being performed and value added to all involved.

Chapter Review Test

1. List and explain three reasons for the startup of an IT audit.
2. What are management policies and procedures and why are they so important to the audit process?
3. What are the skills related to IT auditing? List and describe three areas.
4. What are examples of the auditor's Standards of Practice? Which organizations have issued standards or guidance to the auditor?
5. What and where are the resources available to train auditors, especially IS auditors?
6. What are the basic skills needed to perform in the area of IT auditing?
7. For education in IT auditing beyond the bachelor's degree, what technical proficiency areas are suggested?
8. What are some supplemental skill development areas for auditors?
9. What are external auditors? What are their roles and responsibilities? Provide and discuss two examples of external auditors.
10. What are internal auditors? What are their roles and responsibilities?
11. What are management's responsibilities with regard to the audit process?
12. How can risk assessment help management and the auditor?
13. How can the organization develop IT audit skills?
14. What can management do to ensure audit quality?

Multiple Choice

1. Which of the following is not one of the ten top reasons for the startup of IT audit:
   a. Auditing around the computer was becoming unsatisfactory for the purposes of data base reliance
   b. Accessibility of personal computers for office and home use
   c. Very little advancement in technology
   d. The growth of corporate hackers
2. IT governance is:
   a. The process by which an enterprise's IT is directed and controlled
   b. The evaluation of computers and information processing not as key resources
   c. Management only involved in making decisions
   d. User dominance in IT decision making
3. Professional associations that have Standards of Practice:
   a. IIA
   b. ISACA
   c. AICPA
   d. All the above

4. A federal agency that develops and issues government auditing standards is:
   a. GSA
   b. GAO
   c. FBI
   d. FTC

5. A special condition where an auditor must be free of any bias or influence, and have:
   a. IT skills
   b. Good writing skills
   c. Professional development
   d. Independence

6. Which recent federal law was developed and passed by U.S. lawmakers in reaction to the recent financial frauds such as Enron, WorldCom, and others:
   a. Foreign Corrupt Practices Act
   b. Security and Exchange Commission Act
   c. Sarbanes–Oxley Act
   d. Computer Fraud and Abuse Act

7. In the authors' opinion, an auditor must have:
   a. High ethical standards
   b. Limited training
   c. Poor communication skills
   d. Poor time management skills

8. The approximate number of universities that have been identified as Centers of Excellence in Information Assurances:
   a. Greater than 49
   b. Between 26–49
   c. Between 11–25
   d. Less than 10

9. Certifications that may be helpful to an IT auditor:
   a. CIA
   b. CFE
   c. CISSP
   d. All of the above

10. An auditor who works for IBM directly and is on its audit staff is considered to be:
    a. An external auditor
    b. An internal auditor
    c. A consultant
    d. None of the above

Exercises

1. Visit the Web sites of four external audit organizations: two private and two government sites. Provide a summary of who they are and their roles, function, and responsibilities.

2. Visit the Web sites of two internal audit organizations: two private and two government sites (federal, state, county, or city). Provide a summary of who they are and their roles, functions, and responsibilities.

3. You are asked by your audit supervisor to identify national colleges or universities that provide training or education in the internal audit or IT auditing area. List five colleges or universities that can provide that type of training worldwide.

4. You are asked by your audit supervisor to obtain a list of professional certifications and organizations that would be helpful for the audit staff to take or join and become involved in. Provide a list of five professional certifications and state why you think membership would be helpful. Provide a list of five professional organizations and tell why it would be beneficial to join or become involved with them.

5. Your audit supervisor has asked you to study the area of control self-assessment and business continuity planning. Provide five articles and/or Web sites that can provide your supervisor useful information on these current topics

Answers to Multiple Choice Questions

1 — c; 2 — a; 3 — d; 4 — b; 5 — d; 6 — c; 7 — a; 8 — a; 9 — d; 10 — b

Notes

1. Singleton, T. and L.F. Dale, The Developments of EDP Auditing, Education, Research and Literature in North America: 1977 to 1994, *IS Audit & Control J.*, Vol. IV, 1994, p. 38.

2. Anonymous, Price Waterhouse LLP, National, ISRM, 1996.

3. The Institute of Internal Auditors Research Foundation, Systems Auditability and Control (SAC), module 2, Audit and Control Environment, 1991, p. 2–4.

4. Truglio, T., Best Practices of IS Audit Management, ISACA International Conference, Universal Sheraton Hotel, 1995.

5. ISACA, The Code of Professional Ethics, Information Systems Audit Control Association Web site.

6. Kneer, et al., *op. cit.*, pp. 13–20.

7. Myers, J., Chair of the Accounting Department, Woodbury University, Burbank, CA, 1994.

8. Hudoba, S.J., Best Practices of IS Audit Management, ISACA International Conference, Universal Sheraton Hotel, 1995.

References

1. American Institute of Certified Public Accountants (AICPA) 1987, Statement on Auditing Standard 48 and Statement on Auditing Standard 55, "Consideration of the Internal Control Structure in a Financial Statement," April 1988. Statement on Auditing Standard 78, "Amendment to SAS 55," and Statement on Auditing Standard 82, "Consideration of Fraud in Financial Statements," 1996 and Statement on Auditing Standard 94, "The Effect of Information Technology on the Auditor's Consideration of Internal Control in a Financial Statement Audit," 2001 and Statement on Auditing Standard 99, "Consideration of Fraud in a Financial Statement Audit," 2002.
2. Cangemi, M.P. and Gallegos, F., CIS Auditing: A Career Plan, *New Accountant*, R.E.N. Publishing, Chicago, February 1991, pp. 27–30.
3. CEO Task Force for Securing Cyberspace, www.technet.org
4. Flesher, D.L. and Singleton, T., The Future of Information Systems Audit Education, *EDPACS*, 22 (4).
5. Gallegos, F., IT Auditor Careers: IT Governance Provides New Roles and Opportunities, *IS Control J.*, 3: 40–43, 2003.
6. Gallegos, F., IT audit career development plan, *IS Control J.*, 2: 16, 17, 2003.
7. Gallegos, F., Maintaining IT audit proficiency: the role of professional development planning, *IS Control J.*, 6: 20–23, 2002.
8. Gallegos, F., Due professional care, *IS Control J.*, 2: 25–28, 2002.
9. Gallegos, F., A Decade of excellence in EDP audit education, *EDP Auditor J.*, 1: 37–42, 1991.
10. Gallegos, F., Educating Auditors for The Twenty First Century, Accepted for presentation and publication at the EDPAC96 Conference, Perth, Australia, May 1996.
11. Gallegos, F., Richardson, R., and Borthick, F., *Audit and Control of Information Systems*, Thomson Corporation–South-Western, 1987.
12. Information Systems Audit and Control Association, 2003 CISA Examination Domain, ISACA Certification Board, Rolling Meadows, IL, 2002.
13. INFOSEC Professionalization: A Road to Be Traveled, *Forum for Advancing Software Engineering Education*, 9(1), January 15, 1999.
14. Institute of Internal Auditors, *Model Curriculum for Information Systems Auditing*, Altamonte Springs, Florida, ISBN 0-89413-274-1, August 1992.
15. International Federation of Accountants Education Committee. Minimum Skill Levels in Information Technology for Professional Accountants, Discussion paper issued by the *IFAC*, November 1993.
16. International Federation of Accountants, The Impact of Information Technology on the Accountancy Profession, *IFAC*, December 1995.
17. Katsikas, S.K. and Gritzalis, D.A., Eds., *A Proposal for A Postgraduate Curriculum in Information Security, Dependability and Safety*, New Technology Publications, Athens, Greece, September 1995.
18. Kneer, D., Vyskoc, J., Manson, D., and Gallegos, F., Information Systems Audit Education, *IS Audit Control J.*, 4: 1–20, 1994.
19. Looho, A. and Gallegos, F., IS audit training needs for the 21st century: a selected assessment, *J. Comput. Inf. Syst.*, International Association of Computer Information Systems, 41 (2): 9–15, 2000–2001.
20. McCombs, G. and Sharifi, M., Meeting the market needs: an undergraduate model curriculum for information systems auditing, *IS Audit Control J.*, 1: 50–54, 1997.
21. Menkus, B. and Gallegos, F., *An Introduction to IT Auditing*, Auerbach EDP Auditing Series, 71-10-10.1, CRC Press LLC, 2001, pp. 1–14.
22. Model Curricula for Information Systems Auditing at the Undergraduate and Graduate Levels, first edition, Information Systems Audit and Control Association, March 1998.
23. President's Council on Integrity and Efficiency, Computer Audit Training Curriculum, *PCIE*, Washington, D.C., September 1989.

24. Singleton, T., The Ramifications of the Sarbanes–Oxley, *IS Control J.*, 3: 11–16, 2003.
25. Singleton, T. and Flesher, D.L., The Developments of EDP Auditing Education Research and Literature in North America: 1977 to 1994, *IS Audit Control J.*, 4: 38–48, 1994.
26. National Strategy for the Physical Protection of Critical Infrastructures and Key Assets, 2002, http://www.whitehouse.gov/pcipb/physical.html
27. The National Strategy for Securing Cyberspace, 2002, http://www.whitehouse.gov/pcipb/
28. U.S. General Accounting Office, Executive Guide: Measuring Performance and Demonstrating Results of Information Technology Investments (GAO/AIMD-98-89), 1998.
29. U.S. General Accounting Office, Federal Management: Major Management Issues (GAO/OCR-98-1R), 1998.
30. U.S. General Accounting Office, Government Audit Standards, Exposure Draft, 2002.
31. Weber, R., Information Systems Control and Audit, Prentice Hall, New York, 1998.

Chapter 3
The Audit Process in an Information Technology Environment

Whether the information technology (IT) audit reviews the IT facility operations or it examines applications or systems development, the controls applied in these areas need to be verified. The IT auditor's function complements that of the internal auditor by providing reasonable assurance that assets are safeguarded, information is timely and reliable, and all errors and deficiencies are discovered and corrected promptly. Equally important objectives of this function are better control, complete audit trails, and strict compliance with organizational policies.

Today's IT auditor is faced with many concerns about the exposure of computer information systems (IS) to a multitude of risks. From these concerns arise the objectives for the audit process and function. Achieving these objectives requires the support and involvement of all the participants described in this chapter.

This chapter looks at the IT audit process for computer auditing and the demands that will be placed on the profession in the future. Computer auditors must prepare for and move into a world that literally depends on large, heavily integrated computer IS. These systems may be characterized by the use of emerging technologies, such as distributed processing, local area networking, client/server (C/S), Internet/intranet, microtechnology, firmware, satellite transmissions, and others.

IT Auditing: What Is it?

The evaluation of IS and IT by auditors has generated the term IS auditing. IT auditing is the evaluation of IS, practices, and operations to assure the integrity of an entity's information. Such evaluation can include assessment of the efficiency, effectiveness, and economy of computer-based practices. This involves the use of the computer as an audit tool. The evaluation should also determine the adequacy of internal controls within the IT environment to assure valid, reliable, and secure information services.

The computer auditor's evaluation of systems, practices, and operations may include one or both of the following:

- Assessment of internal controls within the IT environment to assure the validity, reliability, and security of information.
- Assessment of the efficiency and effectiveness of the IT environment in economic terms.

An example to illustrate that the roles of auditor, accountant, and internal auditor will converge on the computer auditor of tomorrow are the changes being made by senior managers. The senior vice president and director of internal audit for a major international bank stated that 80 percent of his audit staff are integrated computer audit specialists (financial, operational, and IT), and by 2005, all of the 500 staff within the department are expected to have computer audit competency.

As for the computer auditors of today, their advanced knowledge and skills will progress in two ways. One direction is continued growth and skill in this profession, leading the way in computer audit research and development and progressing up the external and internal audit career paths. The other direction involves capitalizing on a thorough knowledge of organizational systems and moving into more responsible career areas in general management.

The Audit Process

The time-honored method of using the general ledger as the starting point for audits does not always work in examinations of modern computer systems. However, the experienced auditor or financial manager recognizes the value of having a consistent, logical, audit or management approach that accommodates both manual and computerized methods. Although auditing computer systems requires changes from the traditional general-ledger approach, any new audit approach should be applicable universally.

Universal approaches that apply equally to manual and computerized systems were formalized for the accounting profession in the Statement on Auditing Standards (SAS 1). This standard has the effect of mandating a uniform, process-oriented approach to audit engagements. The approach depicted is a true process technique. That is, audit engagements follow a series of logical, orderly steps, each designed to accomplish specified end results. In implementation, initial efforts in the audit examination center are on gaining a basic understanding of the accounting systems. The process continues to increase in depth in the study and examination of the applications that develop financially significant data for inclusion in financial statements.

Although schematic diagrams tend to indicate distinct steps, actual audit processes are less rigid. The phases of auditing activities typically overlap and involve some reassessment and retracing of procedures performed earlier.

The Situation and the Problem — from EFCA to Enron

Computers have been in use commercially since 1952. Computer-related crimes were reported as early as 1966. However, it was not until 1973, when the significant problems at Equity Funding Corporation of America (EFCA) surfaced, that the auditing profession looked seriously at the lack of controls in computer IS. In 2002, almost 30 years later, another major fraud was uncovered, which brought skepticism and downfall to the financial markets. This time, neither the major accounting firms nor the security and exchange regulated businesses in major exchanges were able to avoid the public outrage, lack of investor confidence, and increased government regulation that befell the U.S. economy.

When EFCA declared bankruptcy in 1973, the minimum direct impact and losses from illegal activity were reported to be as much as $200 million. Further estimates from this major financial fraud escalated to as much as $2 billion, with indirect costs such as legal fees and depreciation included. These losses were the result of a "computer assisted fraud" in which a corporation falsified the records of its life insurance subsidiary to indicate the issuance of new policies. In addition to the insurance policies, other assets, such as receivables and marketable securities, were recorded falsely. These fictitious assets should have been revealed as nonexistent during the corporation's regular year-end audits but were never discovered. As the computer was used to manipulate files as a means of covering the fraud, the accounting profession realized that conventional, manual techniques might not be adequate for audit engagements involving computer application.

In 1973, the American Institute of Certified Public Accountants (AICPA), in response to the events at EFCA, appointed a special committee to study whether the auditing standards of the day were adequate in such situations. The committee was requested to evaluate specific procedures to be used and the general standards to be approved. In 1975, the committee issued its findings. Another critical review of the existing auditing standards was begun in 1974, when the AICPA created its first standards covering this area. Then, 29 years later, the Enron–Arthur Andersen fiasco of 2002 took us back to 1973.

The issue of "due professional care" has come to the forefront of the audit community at the beginning of this decade as a result of the financial scandals of Enron, Global Crossing, and others. The EFCA scandal of 1973 led to the development of strong state and federal regulation of the insurance industries and corporate creative accounting in the aerospace industry which provided support for the Foreign Corrupt Practices Act (FCPA) of 1977. Now, perhaps the Sarbanes–Oxley Act of 2002 will be a vivid reminder of the importance of due professional care. This act is a major reform package, mandating the most far-reaching changes Congress has imposed on the business world since the FCPA of 1977 and the Securities and Exchange Commission (SEC) Act of 1934. It seeks to thwart future scandals and restore investor confidence by creating a public-company-accounting-oversight board, revising auditor independence rules, revising corporate governance standards, and significantly increasing the criminal penalties for violations of securities laws.

Prior to the end of 2002, there were several public frauds that focused public attention on all aspects of financial reporting. The frauds and financial misreporting at companies such as Global Crossing, Adelphia, and Tyco were just the beginning. The Enron and the WorldCom collapse shook the financial community with reports of fraud up to billions of dollars. As a result of these frauds and the events that followed, and the pressures brought on Congress by the public, including investors, pensioners, and taxpayers, the Sarbanes–Oxley Act was passed on July 30, 2002. This law supports efforts to increase public confidence in capital markets by seeking to improve corporate governance, accountability, and audit quality. The Act will result in more attention being given to financial versus operational controls. Thus, internal audit will be a more critical resource for management and cause IT auditors to extend their work. There will be rework needed on corporate governance (especially the role and independence of audit committees).

Audit Standards

The IACPA committee, charged with the responsibility of reviewing auditing standards as a result of EFCA's collapse, stated that "generally accepted auditing standards are adequate and no changes are called for in the procedures commonly used by auditors."

However, the Sarbanes–Oxley Act will have a dramatic effect on public accounting. Section 404 — Management Assessment of Internal Controls of the Act states that the companies that are affected will be required to:

- State the responsibility of the management for establishing and maintaining an adequate internal control structure and procedures for financial reporting.

- Prepare an assessment at the end of the issuer's fiscal year of the effectiveness of the internal control structure and procedures of the issuer for financial reporting.

These requirements will have a major impact on the internal and IT auditors, as they are most likely having to complete this work as well as to evaluate, assess, and report on internal controls for management's report required by Sarbanes–Oxley.

The AICPA has responded to these audit failures and financial frauds in Enron, WorldCom, Adelphia, etc., by changing the previously issued SAS 82. SAS 99 — "Consideration of Fraud in a Financial Statement Audit" deals with brainstorming the risk of fraud and increasing professional views that it could happen here; use of unpredictable audit tests; and responding to management override controls by requiring on every audit certain procedures to detect management override.

Similarities

It appears that whenever the audit process has a breakdown, new auditing standards are required for examination of financial statements based on computer-generated records. In general, the standards of fieldwork are the same as those applied to manually generated records. Also, the basic elements of adequate internal control remain the same. The main purposes of the study and evaluation of internal control still are to provide evidence for an opinion and to determine the basis for the scope, timing, and extent of future audit tests.

Differences

With computer-based financial reporting systems, new auditing procedures must be continually developed and improved. The computations performed, addition or deletion of records or fields within records, and assurances that the transactions were authorized must be done through the computer in concert with the transaction flow. As one can experience, there are significant differences in the techniques of maintaining adequate internal control in computer-based processes. Also, there is some variation in the manner in which the study and evaluation of internal control is made. A major difference is that people have been removed from some phases of internal accounting control and reliance given to computer generated validation processes and procedures. The other factor is that irregularities identified could go beyond fraud and into the domain of the Homeland Security Act of 2002 and the provisions of the Cyber Security Enhancement Act discussed earlier in the book.

The Importance of Audit Independence

Audit independence is a very critical component if a business wishes to have an audit function; it can add value to the organization. The audit report and opinion must be free of any bias or influence if the integrity of the audit process is to be valued and recognized for its contribution to the organization's goals and objectives. A number of professional organizations (such as AICPA, the Institute of Internal Auditors [IIA], the Information Systems Audit and Control Association [ISACA, formerly EDP Auditors Association], Association of Government Accounts [AGA], and others) have addressed this point in very clear context and language. Governmental organizations such as the U.S. General Accounting Office (GAO) and the International Organization of Supreme Audit Organizations have also reviewed this area in depth.

The Sarbanes–Oxley Act of 2002 will be a vivid reminder of the importance of due professional care. The Sarbanes–Oxley prohibits all registered public accounting firms from providing audit clients, contemporaneously with the audit, certain nonaudit services such as internal audit outsourcing, financial IS design and implementation services, and expert services. These scope-of-service restrictions go beyond existing SEC independence regulations. In addition, all other services, including tax services, are permissible only if preapproved by the issuer's audit committee and all such preapprovals must be disclosed in the issuer's periodic reports to the SEC.

The act also requires auditor (not audit firm) rotation. The lead audit partner and/or the concurring review partner must rotate off the engagement if he or she has performed audit services for the issuer in each of the five previous fiscal years. There is no distinction regarding the capacity in which the audit or concurring partner provided such audit services. Accordingly, services provided as a manager or in any other capacity appear to count toward the five-year period. In addition, the provision applies as soon as the firm is registered. So, without guidance to the contrary, the audit and concurring partner must count back five years, starting from the date on which Public Company Accounting Oversight Board registration occurs. This provision is particularly important because of its potential impact on small accounting firms. The SEC is considering whether or not to accommodate small firms in this area; currently there is no small-firm exemption from this provision.

As mentioned earlier, this act is a major reform package mandating the most far-reaching changes Congress has imposed on the business world since the FCPA of 1977 and the SEC of 1934. It seeks to thwart future scandals and restore investor confidence by creating a public-company-accounting-oversight board, revising auditor independence rules, revising corporate governance standards, and significantly increasing the criminal penalties for violations of securities laws.

Past and Current Accounting and Auditing Pronouncements

The AICPA SAS are the professional standards for Certified Public Accountants (CPAs). These standards are interpretations of generally accepted auditing standards (GAAS), and the AICPA requires its members to adhere to the statements or to be prepared to justify any departure from them. Appendix III identifies several major AICPA SAS.

AICPA Pronouncements — from the Beginning to Now

The accounting profession began addressing the topic of internal control of IT systems officially in 1974 when the AICPA issued SAS 3, "The Effects of EDP on the Auditor's Study and Evaluation of Internal Control." SAS 3 was concerned with the evaluation of internal control of clients who processed significant records using a computer system. Growing use of computer-based financial systems created a need for auditors to go beyond matters of internal control in audits of financial statements. Consequently, in 1984, the AICPA superseded SAS 3 with SAS 48, "The Effects of Computer Processing on the Examination of Financial Statements." SAS 48 requires auditors to consider the effects of computer processing throughout the whole audit process, not just during the evaluation of internal control. SAS 48 amended other SASs to synchronize audit practice with the increased use of computer-based processing in client financial systems.

SAS 48 provides the basic framework for the auditing procedures necessary in examining the financial statements of entities that use computer accounting applications. The pronouncement describes the basic procedures and areas of concern with which the auditor should be familiar. The pronouncement specifically covers the following topics:

- How the audit is affected by the following:
  - Extent of computer use in each significant accounting application
  - Complexity of the organization's computer operations
  - Organizational structure of IT activities
  - Availability of data for audit use
  - Use of computer-assisted audit techniques to increase the efficiency of audit procedures (AU Sec. 311.09)
- Need for auditors with specialized expertise in IT (AU Sec. 311.10)
- Influence of internal control procedures on the methods an organization uses to process significant data
- Characteristics distinguishing computer processing from manual processing are:
  - Abbreviated life of transaction trails
  - Greater uniformity of processing, which decreases processing errors but increases vulnerability to programming errors
  - Potential for concentration of incompatible functions

- – Increased chance for errors and irregularities due to ease of gaining unauthorized access to systems and files
- – Potential for increased management supervision
- – Automatic initiation of processing functions
- – Interdependence of manual and automated controls (AU Sec. 320.33)
- Interdependence of control procedures (AU Sec. 320.57)
- Adequacy of general and application controls. General controls relate to several computer-based activities, such as control over system development. Application controls are application-specific controls (AU Sec. 320.58)
- Need to obtain reasonable assurance for the reliability of the operation of programmed controls (AU Sec. 320.65-66)
- Unchanging nature of audit objectives, even though evidence collection methods may vary (AU Sec. 326.12)

SAS 48 represents the current position of the AICPA on audit of computer-based financial systems. In addition, the following supportive SASs were issued:

- SAS 55, "Consideration of the Internal Control Structure in a Financial Statement," 1988
- SAS 78, "Amendment to SAS 55," 1990 and SAS 82, "Consideration of Fraud in Financial Statements," 1996
- SAS 94, "The Effect of Information Technology on the Auditor's Consideration of Internal Control in a Financial Statement Audit," 2001 (note this SAS amends SAS 55)
- SAS 99, "Consideration of Fraud in a Financial Statement," 2002

Several SASs apply in general to IT auditing and are mentioned in detail in Appendix III. For example, SAS 16, "The Independent Auditor's Responsibility for the Detection of Errors or Irregularities" (AU Sec. 327) is general in nature and applies to both manual and computerized systems. It defines the auditor's responsibility for detecting errors and irregularities in an accounting system. AU Sec. 327.05 states:

> ... Under GAAS the independent auditor has the responsibility, within the inherent limitations of the auditing process, to search for errors or irregularities that would have a material effect on the financial statements, and to exercise due skill and care in the conduct of that examination.

A limitation, however, is placed on the auditor's responsibility. Paragraph 13 states:

> ... The auditor is not an insurer or guarantor; if his examination was made in accordance with GAAS, he has fulfilled his professional responsibility.

From this emerged other AICPA standards to address the changes in technology that impact the audit process and the financial statements. SAS

94 was issued in and has been effective from June 2001. This supplementary audit standard was issued to provide guidance to auditors concerning the appropriate types of assessment vehicles, which can be used in the evaluation of internal controls within IT systems. The auditing standard states that computer-assisted auditing techniques (CAATs), which we will discuss more in depth in the next chapter, are needed to test certain types of IT controls in certain types of IT environments. Prior to this, the auditing standards (SAS 48, 55, and 78) were the major standards relevant and applied to computer-based audits. Unfortunately, as mentioned above, a large percentage of auditors using these standards assessed control risk at the maximum and performed only substantive tests of account balances and transactions to gather evidence of financial statement assertions. SAS 94 states that this past approach may not be viable in complex IT environments.

Other Standards

Other standards-setting organizations have also issued guidelines. For example, the IIA, ISACA, and the GAO have been quite active in providing audit-related guidelines. Another such organization is the National Institute of Standards and Technology (NIST), a division of the U.S. Department of Commerce. NIST issues the Federal Information Processing Standards (FIPS) Publication Series. FIPS that focus on computer security and related publications are listed in Appendix II and Appendix III.

Although the FIPS standards are not considered GAAS by the accounting profession, they do provide valuable guidelines on specific topics not addressed by the AICPA. Also, those companies engaged in providing services or support to the federal government through contracts or subcontracts are required to comply with FIPS if they do not have the equivalent in place.

Internal auditors are not required to follow the GAAS in the performance of their audits. However, most internal auditors are familiar with the standards and use them as general guidelines. Again, with Sarbanes–Oxley, this may change soon.

Professional associations such as IIA and the ISACA and their foundations have issued their own professional guidelines. In 1978, the IIA issued its Standards for the Professional Practice of Internal Auditing and subsequently issued the Statements on Internal Auditing Standards (SIAS), which has now evolved to Standards Related to Performance and Attributes. In 1991, with a revision in 1994, the IIA Foundation's Systems Auditability and Control (SAC) was issued and offered assistance to internal auditors on the control and audit of IS and IT.

In 1984, the ISACA issued its "EDP Control Objectives — Update 1984," a set of EDP control standards to replace the original Control Objectives issued in 1975. There have been four sets of updates to the Control Objectives. Most recently, the Information Systems Audit and Control Foundation issued Control Objectives for Information and Related Technology (CoBiT), which is a framework providing a tool for business owners to efficiently and effectively discharge their control responsibilities. Today, the 3rd edition is the most current and extensive look at internal control infrastructure in a business environment. Chapters 5 through 12 will provide an application of those techniques and methodologies.

The federal government has issued standards for internal auditors in the private sector in its announcement of the Sarbanes–Oxley Act of 2002. Prior to this, federal laws such as the Foreign Corrupt Practices Act had provided strength to the need for internal controls. Up until the Enron scandal, the SEC staff personnel had alluded to the importance of the internal auditor's role. The Sarbanes–Oxley Act provides greater support for the SEC's position of having internal auditors review internal control, as an important part of an organization's plan to devise and maintain an adequate control system, as discussed in the earlier chapter. Ten years prior to the Sarbanes–Oxley Act, the Committee of Sponsoring Organizations of the Treadway Commission (CSOTC) issued its "Internal Control–Integrated Framework" report, also known as the COSO Report. This report makes specific recommendations to management on how to evaluate, report, and improve control systems. COSO completed a study of 200 fraud cases from the 300 filed with the SEC from 1989 to 1999. These cases were studied for trends and "red flags." It was found that 83 percent of these cases of financial fraud involved either a CEO or CFO or both.

One way of evaluating an organization's internal audit function is to measure it against the audit standards issued by the GAO. The "Yellow Book" or Government Auditing Standards which GAO has issued are audit standards that must be followed in audits of federal organizations, programs, activities, and funds received by contractors, nonprofit organizations, and other external organizations (such as companies with federal contracts). In addition, it has recently released a supplement that provides auditor guidance in the use of computer-generated information in reports. GAO reports, publications, and references in this area are identified in Appendix II and Appendix III.

These standards relate to the scope and quality of the audit effort and to the characteristics of professional and meaningful audit reports. The three elements of expanded auditing covered in the standards are finance and compliance, economy and efficiency, and program results. Also, federal legislation requires that the inspectors general in federal agencies follow these standards.

Financial Auditing

Financial auditing encompasses all activities and responsibilities concerned with the rendering of an opinion on the fairness of financial statements. The basic rules governing audit opinions indicate clearly that the scope of an audit covers all equipment and procedures used in processing significant data.

Financial auditing, as carried out today by the independent auditor, was spurred by legislation in 1933 and 1934 that created the SEC. This legislation mandated that companies whose securities were sold publicly be audited annually by CPAs. CPAs, then, were charged with attesting to the fairness of financial statements issued by companies that reported to the SEC. The AICPA issued in 1993 a document called "Reporting on an Entity's Internal Control Structure over Financial Reporting (Statement on Standards for Attestation Engagements 2)" to further define the importance of internal control in the attestation engagement.

Within the CPA profession, two groups of standards have been developed that affect the preparation of financial statements by publicly held companies and the procedures for their audit examination by CPA firms: generally accepted accounting principles (GAAP) and generally accepted auditing standards (GAAS).

Generally Accepted Accounting Principles (GAAP)

GAAP establishes consistent guidelines for financial reporting by corporate managers. As part of the reporting requirement, standards are also established for the keeping of financial records upon which periodic statements are based. An auditor, rendering an opinion indicating that financial statements are stated fairly, stipulates that the financial statements conform to generally accepted accounting principles. These accounting principles have been formulated and revised periodically by private sector organizations established for this purpose. The present governing body is the Financial Accounting Standards Board (FASB). Implementation of GAAP is the responsibility of the management of the reporting entity.

Generally Accepted Auditing Standards (GAAS)

The major national professional organization of CPAs is the AICPA. In 1949, the AICPA adopted standards for audits, known as GAAS. These standards cover three categories:

General Standards

General standards relate to professional and technical competence, independence, and due professional care.

Field Work Standards

Field work standards encompass planning, evaluation of internal control, sufficiency of evidential matter, or documentary evidence upon which findings are based.

Reporting Standards

Reporting standards stipulate compliance with all accepted auditing standards, consistency with the preceding account period, adequacy of disclosure, and, in the event that an opinion cannot be reached, the requirement to state the assertion explicitly.

The standards referred to above provide broad guidelines, but not specific guidance. The profession has supplemented the standards by issuing statements of authoritative pronouncements on auditing. The most comprehensive of these is the SAS series. SAS publications provide procedural guidance relating to many aspect of auditing. In 1985, the AICPA released a codification of the SAS 1-49. Today, the number of SASs exceed 100.

Planning the Audit

A professional computer audit environment supports a professional staff by maximizing the effect of special skills and abilities and by minimizing redundant activity. A key prerequisite for professional environment is a firm management commitment to discipline and orderly planning.

Under its charter, the computer audit function should formulate both long-range and annual plans. Such plans describe what must be accomplished, include budgets of time and costs, and state priorities according to organizational goals and policies. At a minimum, a computer audit plan should:

- Define scope
- State objectives
- Structure an orderly approach
- Provide for measurement of achievement
- Assure reasonable comprehensiveness
- Provide flexibility in approach

At this level, the computer audit plan is stated in general terms. The intent is to provide an overall approach within which audit engagements can be conducted. Plans for specific audit engagements are then carried out to sufficient levels of detail to prepare budgets and actual work assignments. There is, however, another rationale for conceptualizing the computer audit plan at a general level; both the systems in development and the state of the art in computer technology are undergoing constant, dynamic change. Detailed plans at the functional level cannot hope to anticipate the pattern of such change. Thus, detailed plans would quickly become obsolete and ineffective.

A computer audit plan partitions the audit of IT into discrete segments. These segments describe a computer systems audit as a series of manageable audit engagements and steps. At the detailed planning or engagement level, these segments will have objectives that are custom-tailored to implement organizational goals and objectives within the circumstances of the audit.

Thus, computer auditing does not call for "canned" approaches. There is no single series of detailed steps that can be outlined once and then repeated in every audit. The computer audit plan, therefore, is an attempt to provide an orderly approach within which flexibility can be exercised.

Using the Plan to Identify Problems

The computer audit objectives, charter, and plan guide integral processes. The organization and its management must participate in and support this effort fully. Commitment can be gained if participants recognize that a good plan can help pinpoint problems in a highly dynamic, automated IT environment. Thus, it should be the responsibility of all participants not only to help pinpoint such problems, but also to assist in the measurement and quantification of problems.

Identifying, measuring, and quantifying problems in the IT area is difficult. The IT field is technologically complex and has a language of its own. Participants in the formulation of the computer audit plan, and particularly the computer auditors themselves, must have sufficient experience and training in technical matters to be able to grasp key concepts and abstractions about systems. For example, abstractions about IT might include significant aspects that are susceptible to naming, counting, or conceptualizing. Understanding the systems at this level can lead to the identification of major problem areas. Audit concentration, then, may be directed to the major problem areas most likely to yield significant results.

Based on this identification of problems, the auditor determines what additional data might be required to reach evaluation decisions. The audit process, therefore, must be flexible enough to combine skilled personnel, new technology, and audit techniques in new ways to suit each situation. However, this flexibility of approach requires documentation in planned, directed steps. Systems that are understood poorly (or that have been designed without adequate controls) can result in lost revenues, increased costs, and perhaps disaster or fraud.

Modern management accounting has an obligation in this new environment. Fulfilling this obligation can be addressed in two fundamental steps. First, management must encourage and support the development of professional audit teams. Second, management must assure more vigorous and effective accounting participation in the development and evaluation of systems controls.

Organizing the Audit

The typical phases of an audit engagement include:

- Preliminary review
- Application analysis
- Preliminary evaluation of internal controls
- Compliance testing
- Final evaluation of internal controls
- Substantive testing

Note that the scope of each type of testing depends on the outcome of the previous step. This relationship is discussed further below.

The final, necessary phase of each audit engagement is reporting. However, reporting is not affected by the introduction of computers into a client's financial system and, thus, is not treated separately in the discussion below. This chapter discusses the first two phases of audit engagement in depth to provide an understanding of preliminary work needed to build the audit base. Later chapters discuss the other cited phases in greater depth.

Preliminary Review

The purpose of the preliminary review phase of an audit engagement is to gather information as a basis for formulating an audit plan, which is the end product of the phase. During preliminary review, the auditor will gather general information on the company and its accounting systems, including:

- Nature of business
- Financial history
- Organization structure
- An accounting system overview at sufficient depth to establish which applications are financially significant
- Extent of automation of financial systems

The auditor conducts this preliminary review at a general level, without examining details of individual applications and the processing they involve. The three separate activities included in the preliminary review phase are:

- General data gathering
- Identifying financial application areas
- Preparing an audit plan

General Data Gathering

The auditor begins the examination process by becoming acquainted, generally, with the company, its line of business, and its financial systems. Typically, an external auditor would tour the client company's plant and observe general business operations that bear upon customer service as well as on strictly financial functions.

Given this familiarity, the next level of general data gathering would include the accumulation or preparation of organization charts, particularly those for the accounting and IT functions. These audit requirements are no different from those for manual systems.

Should adequate organization charts be unavailable, the auditor must develop them. Once drawn, the charts should be reviewed with the client to secure agreement that they represent the actual organization structure. This verification would be done through interviews and discussions with key executives in the accounting and IT areas. In addition, during these interviews, the auditor would secure copies of the company's chart of accounts and an accounting standards manual, if available.

For systems in which the client company uses computers to process financially significant data, the auditor would also gather a number of other specific items of evidential matter, including:

- An overall narrative or an overview flowchart of the major applications subsystems and their interrelationships, including inputs and outputs
- Descriptions of the make and model of equipment units in the client's computer installation
- Programming languages, data processing standards, and procedures manuals used in the computer system
- Data control procedures
- Assurance that an uninterruptible power supply is in place or that an alternate power source is available
- Procedures and provisions for backup, recovery, and restart of operations in the event of equipment failure or accidental destruction of data
- Data and source statement library procedures
- Procedures for job setup and operations within the data center
- The installation's documentation standards manual or such documentation standards as exist
- Descriptions of physical security control transactions

Methods applied in gathering these data are chiefly interviews and reviews of documentation. Physical inspection techniques are used both to gather data and to validate existing documents or representations made during the interviews. For example, a single visit to the computer center can provide both data gathering and validation opportunities for determining equipment configurations, library procedures, operating procedures, physical security controls, and data control procedures.

Many of these procedures are substantially the same regardless of whether the accounting system is computerized or not. Differences associated with the audit of computerized systems center around changes in controls, documentation, audit techniques, and technical qualifications required by audit staff members.

Identifying Financial Application Areas

Once the auditor has gained a general familiarity with the client's accounting procedures, specific areas of audit interest must be identified. The auditor must decide what applications or subsystems will have to be examined at a more detailed level. As a basis for preparation of the audit plan, the auditor also must determine, in general, how much time will be required; what types of people and skills will be needed to conduct the examination; and, roughly, what the schedule will be.

This requirement applies even if the client is not using a computer. If computers are being used for financially significant applications, the auditor must determine their sophistication and extent of use. This preliminary study goes just deep enough for the auditor to evaluate the complexity and sophistication of the systems and to determine the procedures to be followed in evaluating internal control. During the preliminary review phase, it is not necessary to go into detailed analysis, such as flowcharting of applications, be they manual or computerized.

Preparing an Audit Plan

The concluding activity in the preliminary review phase of an audit engagement will be the preparation of an audit plan. One form often used is a descriptive audit plan that includes tables and schedules as appropriate. Typical sections for an audit plan might include:

- Description of client organization
- Description of accounting systems and procedures
- Engagement staffing
- Audit scope
- Accounting and auditing problems
- Tax scope and problems
- Work schedules

Field Work and Implementing Audit Methodology

There are seven basic steps that can assist an auditor in the review of a computer-based system. These steps are valid regardless of computer environment, audit area, or system complexity. For each audit, the steps must be understood clearly, planned, and coordinated with the organizational objectives set for the audit function.

1. Define objectives: The auditor defines the general objectives to verify those processes and controls necessary to make the area being audited free from significant exposures to risk. This objective also encompasses validating adherence of the systems under examination to appropriate standards; e.g., financial accounting should conform to GAAP.
2. Build a basic understanding of the area being audited: The auditor obtains and reviews summary-level information and evaluates it in relation to the audit objectives.
3. Build a detailed understanding of the area being audited: The auditor interviews key personnel to determine policies and practices, and prepares supplemental audit information as required to complete the understanding.
4. Evaluate controls, strengths, and weaknesses: The auditor determines which controls are essential to the overall audit objectives.
5. Design the audit procedures: The auditor prepares an audit program for the area being audited, selects the verification techniques applicable to each area, and prepares the instructions for their performance.
6. Test the critical controls, processes, and apparent exposures: The auditor performs the necessary testing by using documentary evidence, corroborating interviews, and personal observation.
7. Evaluate the results: In this last step, the auditor evaluates the results of the work and prepares a report on the findings.

The seven basic steps that comprise the computer auditor's review, the functional areas, as mentioned in Chapter 1, the qualities of a good computer auditor, as mentioned in Chapter 2, the computer auditor's commitment, management's commitment, and the organization's commitment all form a solid foundation upon which the computer audit function is built.

Audit Tools and Techniques

Emphasis on developing an understanding of client accounting systems is particularly appropriate during the application analysis phase of an audit engagement. It is important for the auditor to understand the relationship of each application to the conduct of the client company's business. Even where a computer plays a critical role, the auditor should avoid having audit activities become too technical and detailed too soon.

Another practice to be avoided is the tendency to treat manual and computerized elements of accounting systems as separate, distinct entities. Companies process data manually and on computers in a planned continuum. Manual and mechanized procedures usually are interdependent. The auditor should treat them accordingly. Thus, in walking through applications or subsystems, the auditor should include the entire manual and mechanized procedures that go into the preparation and presentation of information in client financial statements.

Where individual applications are concerned, the auditor concentrates on two primary functions:

- Gathering samples of source documents, input forms, and output documents on reports. Documents should include both manually and computer-produced forms and reports.
- Flowcharting each application in continuity. The relationship between manual and automated procedures and identification of control points, where applicable, should be included.

Auditors prepare application flowcharts using standard symbols and techniques. Flowcharts developed during the application analysis phase of an audit engagement are most useful if they distinguish processing according to department, function, or company area. There are some very good application support packages for flowchart development as well as the power of the word processor to build diagrams and illustrations of the process as illustrated in Exhibit 1.

Flowcharting as an Analysis Tool

As illustrated in Exhibit 2, for a computer auditor, flowcharts represent a method for identifying and evaluating control strengths and weaknesses within a system under examination. It can be time-consuming to build an understanding of strengths and weaknesses within a system to be audited. However, identification of strengths and weaknesses often is crucial because the entire direction of the remainder of an audit is toward substantiating and determining the effect of identified control weaknesses.

As a step toward building the needed understanding of control weaknesses, the audit staff should develop a flow diagram of all information processed. The flow diagrams, or audit data flow diagrams, as depicted in Exhibits 1 and 2 should encompass all information processed, from source documents through to final outputs. Either automated or manual techniques can be used in preparing these audit data flow diagrams. With either approach, the process leads to evaluation of a number of elements of a system, including the following:

- Quality of system documentation
- Adequacy of manual or automated controls over documents
- Effectiveness of processing by computer programs (i.e., whether the processing is necessary or redundant, whether the processing sequence is proper, etc.)
- Usefulness of outputs including reports and stored files

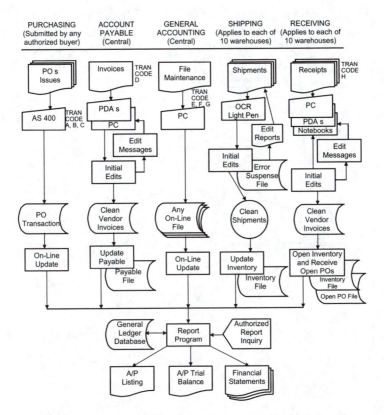

Exhibit 1. Database Computer Accounting System Implemented under Distributed Processing Concept

Steps followed in development of flowcharts and their use as audit evaluation tools include:

- Understanding how data is processed by computers
- Identifying documents and their flow through the system
- Defining critical data
- Developing audit data flow diagrams
- Evaluating the quality of system documentation
- Assessing controls over documents
- Determining the effectiveness of processing under computer programs
- Evaluating the usefulness of reports

Understanding How Computers Process Data

The auditor should build an understanding of how the system under examination generates its data. This understanding should encompass the entire scope of the system from preparation of source documents through

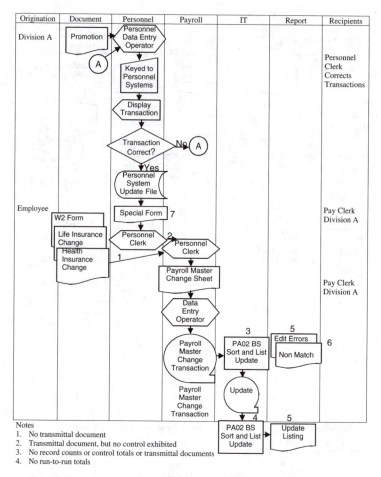

Exhibit 2. The Payroll Process from an Auditor's Control-Oriented Views

to final distribution and use of outputs. While learning how the system works, the auditor should identify potential areas for testing, using familiar audit techniques such as:

- Reviewing corporate documentation including system documentation files, input preparation instructions, and users' manuals
- Interviewing organization personnel including users, systems analysts, and programmers
- Inspecting, comparing, and analyzing corporate records

Identifying Documents and Their Flow through the System

To understand document flow, certain background information must be obtained through discussions with corporate officials, from previous audits or evaluations, or from system documentation files. Because this information may not be current or complete, it should be verified with the responsible programmer or analyst. The auditor will have to obtain:

- Name (title) of the computer product
- Purpose of the product
- System name and identification number
- Date the system was implemented
- Type of computer used (manufacturer's model) and location
- Frequency of processing and type of processing (batch, on-line)
- Person(s) responsible for the computer application and database that generates the computer product

A user or member of the computer center staff may already have a document flow diagram that shows the origin of data and how it flows to and from the computer. (This diagram should not be confused with either a system flowchart that shows detailed computer processing of data or a program flowchart that describes a computer program.)

More often than not, the auditor will have to develop document flow diagrams in a format that is workable in a given situation, whether it is a narrative description, a block diagram using simple symbols, a flowchart using standard symbols, or some combination. The document flow diagram or narrative description should include:

- Each source document, by title and identification number, with copies of the forms attached
- Point of origin for each source document
- Each operating unit or office through which data is processed
- Destination of each copy of the source document and the action applied to each copy (filed, audited, entered into a computer, etc.)
- Actions taken by each unit or office in which the data is processed (recorded in books of account, unit prices or extensions added, control numbers recorded and checked, etc.)
- Controls over the transfer of source documents between units or offices to assure that no documents are lost, added, or changed (controls include record counts, control totals, arithmetic totals of important data, etc.)
- Recipients of computer outputs

Document flow descriptions should not encompass actual computer processing that takes place within a portion of the system treated as a "black box." Processing details are beyond the scope of reliability assessment. If computer output is the product of more than one input, this condition should be noted clearly in the document flow description.

Defining Critical Data

The auditor must build a clear understanding of the data being recorded within the system under study. Therefore, the individual elements of data must be defined. Titles can be deceptive. For example, is a cost derived from the current period or is it cumulative? Is the cost accrued or incurred? What are the components of a cost? Has the composition of cost changed during the fiscal periods under review?

The organization's data element dictionary is a good source for such definitions. If a data dictionary is not available, a record layout may contain the needed definitions. In many instances, there is no one-to-one relationship between data elements and the data in a computer-processed report or file.

Developing Audit Data Flow Diagrams

Inputs from which data flow diagrams are prepared should include copies of the following:

- Narrative descriptions of all major application programs
- All manually prepared source documents that affect application processing, as well as corresponding coding sheets and instructions for data transcription
- Record layouts for all major computer input and output records, computer master files, and work files (such as update or file maintenance tapes, computation tapes, etc.)
- All major outputs produced by the automated system
- Lists of standard codes, constants, and tables used by the system

The documents listed above, along with the information developed in the previous tasks, should enable the audit staff to prepare an audit data flow diagram identifying:

- Point of origin (title or individual) for all source documents
- All transfers of source documents from one person or office to another (make sure that all control points are identified)
- Transcriptions of source documents into machine-readable format
- Computer processing of application data
- All major outputs created from the source documents
- Recipients of all essential outputs

Evaluating the Quality of System Documentation

On the basis of user and IT staff inputs, as well as on the degree of difficulty experienced in constructing an audit data flow diagram, the auditor should be able to comment upon the quality of system documentation. There are two basic questions to answer: Is the documentation accurate? Is the documentation complete?

To illustrate, if a federal auditor were examining IT internal control issues at a U.S. Navy computer facility, he or she might use the Standards for Internal Control in the Federal Government recently updated by the GAO. This publication would provide a basis for assessing internal controls compliance to federal guidelines.

Assessing Controls over Documents

Control points identified during preparation of the audit data flow diagram, along with information on controls developed in the background segment, should enable the auditor to identify system controls. With a diagram of this type, the auditor can determine whether the following controls are used:

- Turnaround documents. (Transmittal documents [manual or automated] should be returned to the originator to make sure that all documents were received and none were added during transmittal.)
- Record counts. (Record counts [manual or system-generated] should be maintained for all documents to make sure that none are added or lost.)
- Predetermined control totals. (For payroll, predetermined control totals should be developed for important data items, such as hours worked, leave taken, hourly rates, gross pay, and deductions. The purpose is to make sure that records are not altered.)
- Run-to-run totals. (These totals should be maintained to assure that no records are added or lost during steps in the computer processing sequence.)

Determining the Effectiveness of Processing under Computer Programs

The audit staff should identify any problem areas in the processing cycle including but not limited to:

- Redundant processing of data or other forms of duplication
- Bottlenecks that delay processing
- Points in the operating cycle at which clerks do not have enough time to review output reports and make corrections

Evaluating the Usefulness of Reports

The audit staff should review the key or major outputs (such as edit listings, error listings, control of hours listings, etc.) of the application system and determine if the outputs are:

- Accurate
- Useful as intended

The auditor should confirm findings by interviewing the users of the output reports. One appropriate technique might be completion of a questionnaire or survey, perhaps conducted by e-mail on user satisfaction with output reports.

Appropriateness of Flowcharting Techniques

A distinction should be noted between the use of systems flowcharts in computer auditing and in the broader field of systems analysis. In recent years, systems analysts have begun to favor other methods of modeling and documentation. Data flow diagrams, for example, are often preferred over systems flowcharts for purposes of analysis. The rationale is that data flow diagrams are process-oriented and emphasize logical flows and transformations of data. By contrast, systems flowcharts emphasize physical processing steps and controls. It is just this type of control-oriented view, however, that is the auditor's primary focus. Thus, though use of systems flowcharting may be declining for systems development purposes, this modeling tool remains important for computer auditors.

Systems flowcharting is not necessarily always the most practical approach for the auditor. Existing documentation including data flow diagrams, narratives written in structured English, or descriptions of programs in pseudo code may be used as points of departure. Based on a review of existing documentation, the auditor can decide what additional modeling is needed to gain adequate understanding of the systems under examination.

The auditor also should be aware of the increasing use of automated tools in preparing flowcharts. Software packages are available, many of which run on mainframes and microcomputers that accept program source code as input and generate finished flowcharts. Also, microcomputer-based software packages now available can aid in documentation or verification of spreadsheets or database applications.

The technique for departmental segregation of processing in the preparation of flowcharts is important. For example, separate vertical columns on the flowchart can show processing by function or department. This representation is useful because one of the important controls the auditor evaluates is the segregation of duties within the accounting system. Structuring flowcharts in this way helps both to discipline the auditor's thinking and to identify any incompatible functions that may exist within accounting applications.

During both the preliminary review and application analysis phases, the auditor should be accumulating notes to be considered for later inclusion as comments within a letter of recommendations to client management.

At the conclusion of the preliminary review and application analysis phases of the engagement, the audit team briefs audit firm partners and client managers associated with the audit. All responsible parties should have a clear understanding of the sources and procedures for development of information reflected in the financial statements on which the audit firm will render an opinion.

On completing its preliminary review and application analyses, the audit team should have built an understanding that includes:

- Establishing of sources for all financially significant accounting information
- Identifying processing steps, particularly of points within applications at which major changes in accounting information take place
- Determining and understanding processing results
- Analyzing the nature and progress of audit trails to the extent that they exist and can be followed within individual applications

Validation of Work Performed

Validation of the information obtained is prescribed by the auditor's work program. Again, this work program is the organized, written, and preplanned approach to the study of the IT department. It calls for validation in several ways:

- Asking different personnel the same question and comparing the answers
- Asking the same question in different ways at different times
- Comparing checklist answers to work papers, programs, documentation, tests, or other verifiable results
- Comparing checklist answers to observations and actual system results
- Conducting mini-studies of critical phases of the operation

Such an intensive program allows an auditor to become informed about the operation in a short time.

Auditing through the computer involves some additional steps in addition to those mentioned above. Programs are run on the computer to test and authenticate application programs that are run in normal processing. Usually, the audit team will select one of the many generalized audit software (GAS) packages such as Examine, DYL, or Easytrieve and determine what changes are necessary to run the software at the installation. The auditor will use this software to do sampling, data extraction, exception reporting, summarize and foot totals, and other tasks. Also, the auditor via microcomputer or client/server support can use packages such as Microsoft Access or Excel, IDEA, or ACL to perform in-depth analysis and reporting capability.

Computer audit teams increasingly are using such audit packages. Many large installations already have GAS installed for their internal auditors. Reasons include the fact that auditors are becoming qualified technically to alter programs and the facility's job control procedures so that packages may run successfully or similar support software may be integrated into the client server environment. Also, better and easier to use audit tools are available for use in both environments. However, the auditor must be aware that each installation is unique in its own scheduling and eccentricities. Also, the installation may have to disrupt its normal processing schedule to accommodate these testing procedures.

Using Personal Computing Technology

Today's auditors work constantly with computerized records. It is likely that many audit clients either have eliminated or will eliminate a substantial portion of their paper documents and replace them with electronic documents filed only in computerized form. An auditor who is unable to use computerized audit tools effectively will be at a tremendous disadvantage. Therefore, today's auditor must be equipped with an understanding of alternative tools and approaches to test the operations of computerized systems and to gather and analyze data contained in computerized files.

Computer technology has become an integral part of most organizational functions. Experts are forecasting continued improvement in the power and flexibility of computers and communication devices while costs are expected to decrease. Competitive factors have made it necessary for both auditors and clients to utilize new technological developments.

The following are five major reasons for an auditing firm to incorporate computers in their practices:

1. Increased productivity because auditors can complete routine tasks faster (24 percent to 75 percent), improve consistency, and focus more on significant issues
2. Audited tasks that might be impractical or impossible to be performed manually can be completed
3. Reduced cost due to diminished time required to complete audit work
4. Competitive advantage gained and client perception of the auditor, the firm, and quality of the services provided improved
5. Ability to cope with difficult tasks without corresponding staff increases

As a result of the above, IT auditors are in high demand because auditing firms have to ensure that the firm's level of knowledge is compatible with the client's. When a client requests information, computers permit a quick response that can enhance client satisfaction.

CAATTs and use of GAS are one of an auditor's most powerful assets. They empower auditors to increase their efficiency and effectiveness by harnessing the power of the computer. Limited control over the computer environment, however, means that carrying out CAATTs on mainframe or other central computer or client/server environment is a risky approach.

The Audit Report and Follow-Up

Through the various phases of the audit, the team will make positive comments as well as point out items that could be instituted or improved. At the completion of the audit program, the team manager will review a list of significant items with the IT manager. These points are not meant to be derogatory, but are suggested improvements for upgrading the operation and protecting the IT function from fraud or loss.

These suggestions will be discussed more thoroughly in the exit interview. The IT manager will be expected to prepare answers to the items listed. These answers will be in the form of an affirmative plan to correct or eliminate observed deficiencies. The report will include positive comments about things that are done particularly well or that are effective in achieving good control and protection of management interests.

In rare instances, an IT manager may be given a choice as to whether a formal report must be prepared or not. However, it is best that the report be prepared in all cases. A written report will provide excellent documentation for both the positive and negative points made and will serve as a reference for future audits and improvements. The value of the audit must be assessed to assure that the findings and recommendations — reflecting cost-conscious, workable, and timely solutions — have been achieved to some quantifiable degree and provide value to the organization. Unfortunately, this is something that does not happen as often as it should in practice. More organizations would not outsource their audit function if they gained a thorough understanding of the savings and improvement to operations and processes the audit can bring.

The bottom line is how does audit enhance an organization's value? Follow-up is the answer if an organization is to understand what value audit can have on improving operational integrity, efficiency, and effectiveness. By looking at the prior audit recommendations of earlier work, auditors are able to assess if the agency, company, or corporation had taken any action toward the report recommendations. If it had, a process should be in place to try to assess what impact those recommendations had and formally report the assessment and findings. Often, auditors will receive direct feedback from managers, supervisors, or staff in place that their actions were the results of an earlier audit report. In some instances, they may even provide direct information and cost figures on how much was being saved as the result of new controls in place or improvements to the existing processes.

Audit support systems can make this an integral process by looking at the example of the GAO's Status of Open Recommendation Support System (see Exhibit 3).

Exhibit 3. GAO's Status of Open Recommendation Support System

Director: Randolph C. Hite, (202) 512-6256
Information Technology
Business Systems Modernization: IRS Needs to Better Balance Management Capacity with System Acquisition Workload GAO-02-356 February 28, 2002

Recommendations for Executive Action
RECOMMENDATION: To address the escalating risks facing the Internal Revenue Service (IRS) on its Business Systems Modernization (BSM) program, the Commissioner of IRS should reconsider the planned scope and pace of the BSM program as defined in the fifth expenditure plan, with the goal of better balancing the number of systems acquisition projects underway and planned with IRS's capacity to manage this workload. At a minimum, the Commissioner's reconsideration should include (1) slowing ongoing projects and delaying new project starts to reduce BSM Office resource demands, (2) making correcting modernization management weaknesses a top priority and a matter of top management attention, and (3) reapplying resources — financial and human capital — available from slowed and delayed projects toward correction of control weaknesses.

TARGET: Department of the Treasury: Internal Revenue Service
STATUS: Open
STATUS COMMENTS:
RECOMMENDATION: The Commissioner of IRS should address weaknesses in software acquisition management by immediately assessing critical BSM projects (i.e., Customer Account Data Engine, Security and Technology Infrastructure Release, and e-services) against the Software Engineering Institute's Software Acquisition Capability Maturity Model (SA-CMM) level 2 requirements.

TARGET: Department of the Treasury: Internal Revenue Service
STATUS: Open
STATUS COMMENTS:
RECOMMENDATION: The Commissioner of IRS should, based on this assessment, develop a plan for correcting identified weaknesses for these projects, including having an independent SA-CMM evaluation performed on them before submission of the next BSM expenditure plan.

TARGET: Department of the Treasury: Internal Revenue Service
STATUS: Open
STATUS COMMENTS:
RECOMMENDATION: The Commissioner of IRS should submit, with the next expenditure plan, the results of this independent evaluation, along with a plan for ensuring that all BSM projects that have passed milestone 3 will meet SA-CMM level 2 requirements.

Exhibit 3. GAO's Status of Open Recommendation Support System (Continued)

TARGET: Department of the Treasury: Internal Revenue Service
STATUS: Open
STATUS COMMENTS:
RECOMMENDATION: The Commissioner of IRS should require all projects that did not pass milestone 3 as of December 31, 2001, to be assessed as SA-CMM level 2, and have a plan for correcting any project weaknesses found as a condition of milestone 3 approval.

TARGET: Department of the Treasury: Internal Revenue Service
STATUS: Open
STATUS COMMENTS:
RECOMMENDATION: The Commissioner of IRS should, for configuration management, risk management, enterprise architecture implementation, human capital strategic management, integrated program scheduling, and cost and schedule estimating, ensure that commitments discussed herein for addressing residual weaknesses are implemented as planned, and report any deviations from these planned commitments to IRS's appropriations subcommittees.

TARGET: Department of the Treasury: Internal Revenue Service
STATUS: Open
STATUS COMMENTS:
RECOMMENDATION: The Commissioner of IRS should, until contractor quality assurance weaknesses are corrected, increase the level of IRS oversight, scrutiny, and quality assurance of contractor activities.

TARGET: Department of the Treasury: Internal Revenue Service
STATUS: Open

This example shows how an organization can follow up on recommendations made by prior reports. The specific recommendations made to the organization and their status, the responsible GAO official contact, and the report and date of report are shown.

Post-Audit

Upon receipt of the formal report by the IT department staff, IT management and affected staff should review the document immediately. Those items not already completed should be handled. Within a relatively short time, the fact that all discrepancies have been corrected should be transmitted to the audit staff in a formal manner. These actions are noted in the audit files, and such cooperation reflects favorably in future audits.

Conclusion

Over decades, the computer has been used to support daily operations, especially in science and business environments. Most companies find that they must use computer technology effectively to remain competitive. The nature of technology, however, continues to change rapidly. As a result, companies continue to integrate their accounting systems and operations. Diverse operating units are becoming computerized and end-user computing is growing rapidly. The audit profession has made these adjustments as well. Worldwide, professional organizations have issued useful guidance and instruction to assist managers and the audit professional.

Auditors are entrusted with a unique public service. The profession is increasingly called on to perform expanded services for its clients and the public at large. To maintain this high public image, auditors' services must be performed at the highest level of technical competence and integrity. Computers can be helpful in many ways, but auditors are also faced with certain problems when they must audit complexities.

The nature of auditing will undoubtedly continue to undergo substantial change as the level of technology improves. A proliferation in the number of computers and workstations (desktop to handheld) also is expected in the next millennium. Today's auditor must be able to identify important auditing controls available with computers and determine the impact of those controls on the company's overall structure. Auditors must understand the design of the client's computer system in order to carry out an efficient audit.

In short, it is necessary to integrate computers into the audit process from project initiation to the final reporting stage. Full automation will enable auditors to make more efficient use of all available resources and enhance the credibility of the audit performed. Effective use of computer technology can empower auditors to conduct audits in today's highly automated environments.

Chapter Review Questions

1. What would the computer auditor's evaluation of system, practices, and operations include?
2. What is SAS 1 and why is it important to the audit process today?
3. Why is the Equity Funding event and the Enron event of 2002 so important to computer auditing?
4. What are the differences in "auditing through the computer" versus the more traditional book and records audit?
5. What are SAS Nos. 48, 55, 78, 94, and 99? Why are these important to the Big Four external and internal auditors?
6. Who are the IIA, ISACA, GAO, AICPA, and IFAC? Why are they important to internal or external auditors and IT auditors?
7. Why are GAAP and GAAS important to the IT auditor?
8. What are the steps in planning the audit?
9. How can the audit plan help identify problems?

10. What is the preliminary review portion of an audit and why is it important?
11. What are the seven basic steps in reviewing computer-based systems?
12. What are IT audit tools and techniques? How can they help auditors at their work?
13. What are data flow diagrams and why are they important tools for the IT auditor?
14. What is GAS? What are CAATTs?
15. The audit report and post-audit follow-up are important steps in the audit process. What are some of the major tasks that should be accomplished by the audit in these steps?

Multiple Choice

1. In 1973, EFCA:
   a. Declared bankruptcy
   b. Was one of the first major corporation frauds where the computer was used to manipulate files
   c. Experienced direct and indirect losses, which amounted to approximately $2 billion due to fraud
   d. All of the above
2. One of the provisions of the Sarbanes–Oxley Act of 2002, Section 404 states:
   a. Companies that are affected require no procedures for financial reporting.
   b. Companies that are affected are required to only set up an internal control structure.
   c. Companies that are affected must state the responsibility of management for establishing and maintaining an adequate internal control structure and procedures for financial reporting.
   d. None of the above.
3. SAS 48 is:
   a. A computer audit standard developed by the IIA
   b. A computer audit standard developed and issued by ISACA
   c. A computer audit standard developed and issued by NIST
   d. A statement on auditing standards developed and issued by the AICPA
4. As a CPA, when examining the effect of IT on the auditor's consideration of internal control in a financial statement audit, one should consult and comply with:
   a. SAS 72
   b. SAS 73
   c. SAS 94
   d. SAS 99

5. GAS is developed and issued by:
   a. NIST
   b. GAO
   c. FTC
   d. NSA
6. COBIT was developed and issued by:
   a. AGA
   b. ISACA
   c. IIA
   d. NIST
7. At the minimum, a computer audit plan should include all but:
   a. Definition of scope
   b. Objectives stated
   c. An orderly, structured approach
   d. A lack of flexibility in approach
8. The activities of a preliminary review may include:
   a. General data gathering
   b. Identifying financial application areas
   c. Preparing the audit plan
   d. All of the above
9. The first step in conducting field work and implementing audit methodology is:
   a. Design audit procedures
   b. Define audit objectives
   c. Evaluate results
   d. Build a detailed understanding of area being audited
10. The purpose of follow-up is to:
    a. Determine if the audit recommendations have been implemented
    b. Determine the progress made in implementing the audit recommendations
    c. Assess any potential savings/value added as a result of the recommendations.
    d. All of the above

Exercises

1. Examine the Web sites of the following organizations and summarize what information they provide that could be valuable to you in your role as an IT auditor.
   a. AICPA
   b. IIA
   c. International Federation of Accountants (IFA)
   d. ISACA
   e. GAO
   f. NIST

    g. International Federation of Information Processing (IFIPS)

    h. Information Systems Security Association (ISSA)

2. Comparison of Control Concepts: (obtain copies of CoBiT, SAC, and COSO; SAS Nos. 55, 78, 94, and 99, and Sarbanes–Oxley Act of 2002):

    a. Who is their primary audience?

    b. How does each study view internal control?

    c. Who is responsible for the internal control system?

    d. What are the internal control objectives from an organization's view?

    e. What is the focus of this document?

    f. Has the Sarbanes–Oxley Act of 2002 changed the role of the internal and external auditor?

3. You are an external auditor being asked to perform an application review of an end-user developed system. In this financial company, EUC development systems were causing a problem with the general ledger system due to the timing of the transfer of transactions. Data was transferred late, causing end of the month reports to be inaccurately stated. Managers who met to review reports of previous months' activity noticed a shortfall of $50,000 in some accounts. Prepare an audit plan for conducting an audit of this situation.

4. You are an internal auditor and you have been assigned an audit of the organization's software inventory. The Copyright Act of 1976 makes it illegal to copy computer programs except for backup or archival purposes. Any business or individual convicted of illegally copying software is liable for both compensatory and statutory damages of up to $100,000 for each illegal copy of software found on the premises. Software piracy is also a federal crime that carries penalties of up to five years in jail. Prepare a preliminary review for conducting this audit.

5. Briefly describe the characteristics and potential uses of the following CAATTs products:

    a. ACL

    b. IDEA

    c. CA Easytrieve

    d. SQL

    e. MS Office

    f. Surveyor

    g. CA Examine

    h. WizRule

    i. NIST's Asset

    j. NIST's Webmetrics

Multiple Choice Answers

    1 — d; 2 — c; 3 — d; 4 — c; 5 — b; 6 — b; 7 — d; 8 — d; 9 — b; 10 — d

References

1. American Institute of Certified Public Accountants (AICPA), 1988b, Consideration of the Internal Control Structure in a Financial Statement Audit (SAS 55).
2. American Institute of Certified Public Accountants (AICPA), 1990, Consideration of the Internal Control Structure in a Financial Statement Audit: An Amendment to SAS 55 (SAS 78).
3. American Institute of Certified Public Accountants (AICPA), 1993, Reporting on an Entity's Internal Control Structure over Financial Reporting (Statement on Standards for Attestation Engagements 2).
4. American Institute of Certified Public Accountants (AICPA), 2001, The Effect of Information Technology on the Auditor's Consideration of Internal Control in a Financial Statement Audit (SAS 94).
5. American Institute of Certified Public Accountants (AICPA), 2002, Consideration of Fraud in a Financial Statement Audit (SAS 99).
6. Cerullo, M.V. and Cerullo, M.J, Impact of SAS No. 94 on Computer audit techniques, *Inf. Syst. Control J.*, Vol. 1, 2003, pp. 53–57.
7. Committee of Sponsoring Organizations of the Treadway Commission (COSO), Internal Control — Integrated Framework, Jersey City, NJ: American Institute of CPAs Inc., 1994.
8. Committee of Sponsoring Organizations of the Treadway Commission (COSO), Report to SEC of 200 Actual Fraud Cases, 2001.
9. Gallegos, F., Due professional care, *Inf. Syst. Control J.*, Vol. 2, 2002, pp. 25–28.
10. Gallegos, F., The Audit Report and Followup: Methods and Techniques for Communicating Audit Findings and Recommendations, *Inf. Syst. Control J.*, Vol. 4, 2002, pp. 17–20.
11. Gallegos, F. and Preiser-Houy, L., *Reviewing Focus Database Applications*, EDP Auditing Series, 74-10-23, Auerbach Publishers, Boca Raton, FL, January 2001, pp. 1–24.
12. Institute of Internal Auditors Research Foundation (IIARF), 1991, revised 1994. Systems Auditability and Control, Altamonte Springs, FL.
13. ISACF, *CobiT: Control Objectives for Information and Related Technology*, Rolling Meadows, IL, 3rd ed., 2002.
14. Manson, D. and Gallegos, F., *Auditing DBMS Recovery Procedures*, EDP Auditing Series, 75-20-45, Auerbach Publishers, Boca Raton, FL, September 2002, pp. 1–20.
15. Singleton, T., The ramifications of the Sarbanes–Oxley Act, *Inf. Syst. Control J.*, Vol. 3, 2003, pp. 11–16.
16. U.S. General Accounting Office, Assessing the Reliability of Computer Processed Data Reliability, External Version 1, issued October 2002.
17. U.S. General Accounting Office, Federal Information Control Audit Manual, issued January 1999, Vol. 1, Financial Audits, GAO/AIMD 12.19.6.
18. U.S. General Accounting Office, Government Auditing Standards, Exposure Draft, July 1999.
19. U.S. General Accounting Office, Standards for Internal Control in the Federal Government, November 1999, GAO/AIMD 00-21.3.1.

Chapter 4

Auditing Information Technology Using Computer-Assisted Audit Tools and Techniques

The auditor's role is to assist management in identifying risks and formulating control solutions that minimize those risks. Organizations are changing at an ever-increasing pace. Auditing must change as well to keep pace with organizational environment. Auditing is a cyclical process that uses historical and current information for risk assessment, analysis of controls, reporting to management, and then incorporating audit results into risk assessment (see Exhibit 1).

The core of the audit process is analyzing controls to determine if they are adequate or need improvement. Many of the tasks associated with performing an audit, such as planning, developing, and documenting, while necessary, take time away from doing the actual analysis work.

Automation provides the following benefits:

- Reduces the time to complete audit analysis, tests, and reports
- Increases audit coverage by reducing the amount of time spent on manual processes
- Provides greater flexibility and responsiveness to the change
- Identifies and quickly addresses high-risk areas by integrating the elements of the auditing process with the risk assessment process
- Provides quality audit services by having a standard set of audit tools and procedures
- Monitors and follows up corrective action
- Centrally manages field staff by having work products online for immediate review

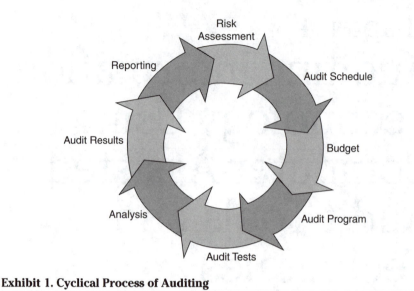

Exhibit 1. Cyclical Process of Auditing

- Leverages the knowledge gathered as a result of our audit projects to provide immediate, quality feedback to management

The computer is an important tool for many occupations. The auditing profession is particularly dependent on computers to perform most of the functions of the job. All types of audits and all types of auditors can take advantage of software tools and techniques to be more efficient and effective. This chapter describes two categories of software tools:

- *Audit productivity tools* that help auditors to reduce the amount of time spent on administrative tasks by automating the audit function and integrating information gathered as part of the audit process
- *Computer-assisted audit tools* (CAATs) that help auditors evaluate application controls, and select and analyze computerized data for substantive audit tests.

Auditor Productivity Tools

Mainframe, client/server, and all forms of personal computers are an integral part of the audit processes. Technology is used as part of the audit process for the following activities:

- *Planning and tracking the annual audit schedule* using spreadsheets, database, and project management software
- *Documentation and presentations* using word processing, flowcharting, and graphics software
- *Communication and data transfer* using electronic connectivity and a centralized server

- *Resource management* using online workpapers review and e-mail
- *Data management* using database, groupware, and intranet software

Audit Planning and Tracking

Risk assessment, audit schedule preparation and tracking, and budget preparations are necessary tasks in audit planning. Spreadsheets or database software can be used to record risk values, develop an "audit universe," and prepare a budget. Project management software can be used to schedule audits and track the current status. Each of these solutions is stand-alone. Their integration may not even be possible. Because planning tasks are interdependent, an integrated application would provide quicker update and ensure that all phases of planning are kept in sync. For example, the budget should provide sufficient costs to accomplish the audit schedule, or the audit schedule should not exceed the resources available.

Documentation and Presentations

The use of packages such as Microsoft Office Suite provides "cut and paste" and linking functionality. These features facilitate the creation of consistent, accurate documents. For example, spreadsheet data containing functional testing results can be incorporated into a report document with a few clicks of a mouse. This same data can then just as easily be copied to a presentation slide and also be "linked," so that changes to the source documents will be reflected in any of the related documents. Software suite functionality saves time and ensures consistency and accuracy.

Communication

Because the auditor operates as part of a team, the need to share data as well as communicate with other members of the group is important. Providing immediate access to current data, electronic messaging, and online review capabilities allows staff to quickly communicate and gather research information for audits and special projects. In addition, auditors may occasionally need to operate from a host computer terminal yet still have all the capability of a dedicated desktop processor. Therefore, it is necessary to have the required computer hardware, protocol handlers, desired terminal software emulators, high-speed modems, and wireless connectivity at the audit site.

Electronic connectivity not only allows auditors to communicate but also provides access for audit clients to exchange information. For example, a member of senior management can be given access to the auditing risk universe database. This allows them to browse the database and suggest additions or changes to risk areas.

Data Management

Establishing electronic connectivity provides audit personnel with the capability to access and input data into a central data repository or knowledge base. The central data repository can archive historical risk, audit schedule, and budget data that can be accessed electronically by all authorized users throughout the audit group, regardless of physical location. Database applications can be developed to automatically consolidate data input electronically from all audit functions.

Through the use of databases, audit management can centrally monitor and have immediate access to critical activity such as audit schedule status, field audit status, fraud or shortage activity, and training and development progress. Database applications can automatically consolidate functionwide data and generate local and consolidated status and trending reports. Auditors can produce more effective products by leveraging off the knowledge of other auditors by having access to functionwide data. The database can contain information such as risk areas, audit programs, findings, corrective action, industry standards, best practices, lessons learned, etc. This information could be available for research whenever needed. Online storage of information will allow auditors to do text and word searches to find specific information in voluminous documents (e.g., insurance code).

It helps auditors to research an audit area to determine prior risk areas and functional testing approaches, identify related or interrelated areas, and review local or organizationwide corrective action. In addition to historical data, a repository provides a platform for interactive activities such as electronic bulletin boards. Audit personnel (and others, if authorized) can post new information or update old information.

A central repository provides immediate access to historical data (e.g., prior audit programs) so that time will not be wasted "reinventing the wheel." Building a central knowledge base facilitates applying lessons learned and increases the level of understanding about the business environment throughout the entire organization.

Resource Management

Another challenge for audit managers is to manage a remote workforce. Whether an auditor is working on a local audit or out in the field, managers need to be able to provide guidance and review work in progress. Managers need to provide feedback while the auditor is on location in case follow-up action is necessary.

A distributed workforce requires a very informed and responsive management team that can gather and disseminate information quickly. Important information can be rapidly gathered and disseminated functionwide through e-mail and internal electronic bulletin boards. Supervisors can provide immediate feedback and direction on audit projects through online review of electronic workpapers.

Groupware

Groupware is a specialized tool or assembly of compatible tools that enables business teams to work faster, share more information, communicate more effectively, and do a better job of completing tasks. Groupware systems vary greatly. Today, we are seeing desktop conferencing, video-conferencing, co-authoring features and applications, e-mail and bulletin boards (b-boards), meeting support systems, paging and voice applications, workflow systems, and group and subgroup calendars as examples of groupware products and support systems. A popular groupware application is Lotus Notes. Notes is a client/server application development platform. It is designed to enhance group productivity by allowing users to share information, while also allowing individuals to customize private views of the information. Notes differs from traditional relational database software through its use of document-oriented databases. In Notes, a document is defined as an object containing text, graphics, video, and audio objects or any other kind of rich-text data.

Groupware is "a natural" for automating the audit function. These products use database features and workflow processing that can be used to store and integrate information gathered and used in the audit process. For example, risk assessment information feeds audit planning, and audit results feed audit reporting and update the risk assessment model. There are several products on the market that use groupware products such as Lotus Notes to automate the audit process.

Using CAATs in the Audit Process

As mentioned in Chapter 2, the AICPA issued the Statement on Audit Standard (SAS) 94, "The Effect of Information Technology on the Auditor's Consideration of Internal Control in a Financial Statement Audit." This SAS does not change the requirement to perform substantive tests on significant amounts but states that "It is not practical or possible to restrict detection risk to an acceptable level by performing only substantive tests." When assessing the effectiveness and integrity of the design and operation of controls, it is necessary for the auditor to test and evaluate these controls. The decision to test and evaluate is not related to the size of the firm but the complexity of the IT environment. Therefore, computer-assisted audit tools and techniques (CAATs) play a very important role in the performance of audit work.

CAATs can be used in a variety of ways to evaluate the integrity of an application, determine compliance with procedures, and continuously monitor processing results. Information systems auditors review application systems to gain an understanding of the controls in place to ensure the accuracy and completeness of the data. When adequate application controls are identified, the auditor performs tests to verify their effectiveness. When controls are not adequate, auditors must perform more extensive testing to verify the integrity of the data. To perform tests of applications and data, the auditor may use CAATs. Many tools and techniques have been developed that offer significantly improved management control and reduced costs if properly applied. Automated techniques have proven to be better than manual techniques when confronted with large volumes of information. The auditor, by using automated techniques, can evaluate greater volumes of data and quickly perform analysis on data to gather a broader view of a process. Four leading software packages are ACL, DYL, SAS, and IDEA. These tools can be used to select a sample, analyze the characteristics of a data file, identify trends in data, and evaluate data integrity. In addition to auditing software, other software products can be used for analyzing data. For example, Access can be used to analyze data, create reports, and query data files. Excel can also be used to analyze data, generate samples, create graphs, and perform regression or trend analysis.

Also, as mentioned earlier, there may be situations where the auditor may be required to conduct tests and evaluate IT controls and perform substantive tests to obtain sufficient information and evidence regarding financial statement assertions. Examples of some of these situations can be:

- Applications or systems involving electronic data interchange (EDI)
- Electronic payment systems that transmit electronic transactions from one company network to another
- Decision support systems that involve automatic reasoning or artificial intelligence or heuristic scenarios where they support decision making within the organization processes
- Applications that use technology like neural network to assess financial conditions using ratio application in calculation of credit worthiness
- In systems where enterprise resource architecture is used to integrate the enterprise resource planning systems, blending legacy data with newer support systems
- In systems that provide electronic services of all types to customers, especially where the IT system initiates bills for services rendered and processes the billing transaction
- Computer programs that perform complex calculations involving money or resulting in a financial decision, present or future, such as reorder points, commissions, retirement or pension funds, collection of accounts, etc.

Technical Skills and Tools

Auditing applications require specific and general knowledge about hardware and software. In addition, familiarity with system utilities helps in conducting control and substantive tests. For auditing applications and data integrity there is a variety of auditing tools that are useful. There are tools that analyze spreadsheet logic and calculations for accuracy. There are tools that analyze a database application and produce a logical flow-chart. Finally, generalized audit software can be used to analyze data produced from most applications.

Generalized Audit Software

Use of generalized audit software makes it possible to perform required functions directly on application files. Audit software can be used to:

- Analyze and compare files
- Select specific records for examination
- Conduct random samples
- Validate calculations
- Prepare confirmation letters
- Analyze aging of transaction files

IT auditors can also use the same software tools as the programming staff or additional tools used by auditors. There are a variety of query and analysis tools, as shown in Exhibit 2.

Application Testing

Once controls have been identified, the next step in an audit is to verify the control's effectiveness. This can be accomplished by:

- Submitting a set of test data that will produce known results if the application functions properly
- Developing independent programs to reperform the logic of the application
- Evaluating the results of the application

In any case, the auditor will need to understand the processing logic of the application to simulate the application or to evaluate the application's results.

Designing Tests of Controls

Reproducing an application can be very time consuming if the application being reviewed is fairly complex. The simulated application will need to be coded and tested before being able to rely on the results. Consider only partially duplicating the application logic in order to test key functions.

Exhibit 2. Query and Analysis Tools

Product	Features	Platform
Access	A database program that provides data selection, analysis, and reporting	Client/server, personal computers, notebooks, PDAs
ACL IDEA	General audit software that reads files from most formats (e.g., EBCDC, TXT) and provides data selection, analysis, and reporting	Mainframe, client/server, personal computers, notebooks
Excel	Spreadsheet software that provides analysis, calculation, graphing, and reporting	Client/server, personal computers, notebooks, PDAs
CA-Examine	A programming language that provides data selection, analysis, and reporting	Mainframe
CA-Easytrieve	A programming language that provides data selection, analysis, and reporting	Mainframe and Unix
Vbasic, C, C++, JAVA, SQL, Perl	A programming language that provides data selection, analysis, and reporting	Mainframe, client/server, personal computers, notebooks
SAS, SPSS	A programming language that provides data selection, analysis, and reporting	Mainframe

Data Analysis

Organizations develop a wealth of information from their transaction processing systems. Auditors can use this information to gain an overall understanding of an area to identify general trends and to decide where best to focus audit tests. For example, when performing an audit of accounts receivable, the auditor could quickly age payables or receivables and then look in more detail at items over a certain number of days or over a certain dollar value. CAATs can also be used to scan for invalid values or combinations of values that indicate a breakdown in controls or potential fraud. CAATs can also be used to join two files, identify sequence gaps in check or purchase order files, and check for duplicates (Lanza 36).

Compliance Testing

Information systems auditors can help determine compliance with a particular procedure for operational and financial audits. This can be accomplished by developing programs to detect data outside of expected values.

Continuous Monitoring

Rather than wait for an audit to review the results of applications, programs can be created that continuously capture and analyze processing results. These are called imbedded audit routines. Imbedded audit routines can be built at the time an application is originally developed or added later. These audit routines or modules may capture transaction data, statistics, or other information. For example, an audit routine can be added to an application that automatically triggers a purchase order when inventory drops below a certain point. The audit routine may capture quantity ordered and compare that to an expected range. An order quantity outside the expected range would create an exception report for follow-up to make sure there was no application error or fraud. If the auditor is evaluating the results of processing for errors, data files can be analyzed for the existence of incorrect data values. For example, required fields should have no null data values and amount fields should have no alpha characters.

Application Controls

Auditors need to apply the same standards to their own applications as they recommend to others. Whether the application involves downloading a file from the mainframe to a spreadsheet or the creation of a department database, controls should be in place.

Spreadsheet Controls. Spreadsheets may seem to be relatively straightforward because of their widespread use. However, the risks presented are significant if the spreadsheet results are relied on for decision making. Lack of reliability, lack of auditability, and lack of modifiability are all risks that are associated with poor spreadsheet design. Auditors use spreadsheets for analyzing data and forming opinions. The risk of relying on inaccurate information for audit opinions can be professionally embarrassing. Particularly if spreadsheets are reused, controls should be implemented to minimize the risk of bad data and incorrect logic. Some of the key controls that minimize the risks in spreadsheet development include:

- *Analysis:* understanding the requirements before building the spreadsheet
- *Source of data:* assurances that data being used is valid, reliable, and can be authenticated to originating source
- *Design review:* review by peers or system professionals
- *Documentation:* formulas, macro command, and any changes to the application should be documented externally and within the application
- *Verification of logic:* reasonableness checks and comparison with known outputs
- *Extent of training:* formal training in spreadsheet or application design, testing, and implementation
- *Extent of audit:* informal design review or formal audit procedures
- *Support commitment:* ongoing application maintenance and support from IT personnel

Database Controls. Department databases should be protected with controls that prevent unauthorized changes to the data. In addition, once the database application is implemented, the application should be kept in a separate program directory and limited to "execute only." The database can also be protected by enabling "read only" abilities to users for data that remains static. Access rights should be assigned to specific users for specific tables (access groups). The input screens should include editing controls that limit data entry to valid options. This can be accomplished by having a table of acceptable values for the data fields. Data accuracy can also be enhanced by limiting the number of free-form fields and providing key entry codes with look-up values for the full description. Database integrity controls can include:

- *Referential integrity:* prevent deleting key values from related tables
- *Transaction integrity:* restore value of unsuccessful transactions
- *Entity integrity:* create unique record identification
- *Value constraints:* limit values to a selected range
- *Concurrent update protection:* prevent data contention
- *Backup and recovery protection:* ability to back up critical information and applications and restore to continue
- *Testing protection:* perform tests at the systems, application, and unit level

Auditing professionals can play a key role in identifying standards and testing controls for end-user-computing (EUC). Where controls are already in place, auditors can review systems to verify that they are working as intended and have the necessary controls to minimize the risks of EUC. There may be situations in this environment where auditing around the computer may be adequate when automated applications are relatively simple and straightforward. Unfortunately, SAS 94 does not eliminate the use of this technique. The major weakness of the auditing-around-the-computer approach is that it does not verify or validate whether the program logic is correct. Also, this method does not evaluate how the application and their imbedded controls respond to various types of transactions (anomalies) that can contain errors.

Certainly, when audits involve the use of advanced technologies or complex applications, then the IT auditor must draw upon techniques combined with tools to successfully test and evaluate the application. Some of these tools were mentioned earlier in the latter part of Chapter 3. The techniques most commonly used are represented in Exhibit 3. Again, many of these techniques should be embedded into the application for use by auditors and security personnel. These techniques provide continuous audit and evaluation of the application or systems and provide management and the audit or security personnel assurances that controls are working as planned, designed, and implemented.

The techniques and the tools provide the auditor the mechanisms to perform their audit. Using technology to audit technology has long been a practice applied by the authors. They have used these tools and techniques to support the audit functions.

Audit Functions

A large part of the professional skills required to use computer-assisted auditing techniques lies in understanding and applying the appropriate audit functions. The computer has a broad range of capabilities. By way of illustration, four broad categories of computer auditing functions can be identified:

- Items of audit interest
- Audit mathematics
- Data analysis
- System validation

Items of Audit Interest. The auditor can use the computer to select material items, unusual items, or statistical samples of items from a computer-maintained file. The auditor has alternatives for the application of the computer to select items of audit interest. For example, the auditor can:

- Stipulate specific criteria for selection of sample items.
- State relative criteria and let the computer do the selection.

An example of selection by specific criteria might be a specification that the computer identifies all transactions of $100,000 or more and prepares a report for audit review. On the other hand, the auditor could take a relative approach and instruct the computer to select the largest transactions that make up 20 percent of the total dollar volume for a given application.

This approach abridges manual audit procedures because the auditor can rely on the computer's selection of items of interest. If the computer were not used, the auditor would have to validate the selection process. Under traditional approaches, for example, it would be common for an auditor to ask client personnel to list all transactions of $100,000 or more. With the computer, the auditor can be satisfied that the selection program has looked at the total universe of accounts payable items. The validation of the selection process is inherent in the auditor's developing and accepting the computer-auditing application program.

Audit Mathematics. Performing extensions or footing can be a cost-effective payoff area for the application of computers in auditing — particularly if the calculations can be performed as a by-product of another audit function. For example, suppose the computer is being used to select significant items from an accounts receivable file. In the process of looking at

Exhibit 3. Computer-Assisted Audit Techniques for Complex Systems

Technique	Description
Integrated test facility	Integrated test facilities are built-in test environments within a system. This approach is used primarily with large-scale, online systems serving multiple locations within the company or organization. The test facility comprises a fictitious corporation or branch, set up in the application and file structure to accept or process test transactions as though it was an actual operating entity. Throughout the financial period, auditors can submit transactions to test the system.
Test data	This technique involves methods of providing test transactions to a system for processing by existing applications. Test Data provides a full spectrum of transactions to test the processes within the application and system. Both valid and invalid transactions should be included in the Test Data as the objective is to test how the system processes both correct and erroneous transaction input. For a consumer credit card service, such transactions may be invalid account numbers, accounts that have been suspended or deleted, and others. If reliance is placed on program, application, or system testing, some form of intermittent testing is essential. Test Data generators are very good tools to support this technique but should not be relied on entirely for extreme condition testing.
Parallel simulation	Parallel simulation involves the separate maintenance of two presumably identical sets of programs. The original set of programs is the production copy used in the application under examination. The second set could be a copy secured by auditors at the same time that the original version was placed into production. As changes or modifications are made to the production programs, the auditors make the same updates to their copies. If no unauthorized alteration has taken place, using the same inputs, comparing the results from each set of programs should yield the same results. Another way is for the auditor to develop psuedo code using higher-level languages (Vbasic, SQL, JAVA, etc.) from the base documentation following the process logic and requirements. Again, both applications would utilize same inputs and results compared.
Continuous monitoring or continuous assurance	These techniques require planning, design, development, implementation, and continuous monitoring and assurance if they are to be used and applied successfully. The application of statistical sampling, regression, and advanced analytics to identify unusual events or situations. These anomalies can be extracted in real time via embedded audit modules or audit hooks designed into the application.
Sample audit review file	Sample Audit Review File (SARF) selects transactions and processes via sampling techniques and places these into log files for evaluation by auditor and security personnel.

Exhibit 3. Computer-Assisted Audit Techniques for Complex Systems (Continued)

Technique	Description
System control audit review file	Systems Control Audit Review File (SCARF) is another real-time technique that can collect specific transactions or processes that violate certain predetermined conditions or patterns. This may be enhanced by decision support software that alerts designated personnel (audit, security, etc.) of unusual activity or items out of the ordinary. Data can be collected to log files for further review and examination by computer forensic specialists.
Transaction tagging	The ability to follow a selected transaction through the entire application from input, transmission, processing, and storage to output to verify the integrity, validity, and reliability of the application under review. Some applications have a Trace or debug function, which can allow you to follow the transaction through the application. This may be a way to ensure that the process for handling unusual transactions is followed within the application modules and code.
Snapshot	The ability to look at a selected execution of application code and variables used to validate the values going into the process and the values being generated by the process to ensure that they meet requirement.

this file, the computer can be programmed to extend and foot all invoicing transactions. Because of the speed of the computer, these calculations can be performed on 100 percent of the items in a file with no significant addition of time or cost for this processing.

By contrast, extensions and footings are both tedious and costly under conventional manual examination techniques. Typically, the auditor must limit examination of any given application to extension and footing of a judgmental sample covering a few short intervals of the period under examination. Clearly, reliance can be far higher when these verification calculations are performed on complete files.

Remember, however, that the computer has limitations in this area. Although it can be programmed to make many logical comparisons and tests, the computer cannot supplant human judgement in examining items to be tested.

Data Analysis. Using the computer for analysis of data represents a major opportunity for innovation by the auditor. The computer can compare and summarize data and can represent data in graphic form. Data analysis programs use such techniques as:

- Histograms
- Modeling
- Comparative analysis

Histograms are bar charts showing graphic relationships among strata of data. In computer-assisted auditing, histograms typically are graphic representations of frequency distributions of records within data files. By picturing these relationships in graphic form, histograms give the auditor an improved perspective on the analysis of financial statements. The histogram is, in effect, a snapshot showing the substance, makeup, and distribution of data within an organization's accounting system.

With a histogram, auditors can apply their judgment in identifying and selecting appropriate testing techniques. By comparison, given a large collection of data about which such distribution data are not known, the auditor performs testing on a relatively blind basis. In such cases, the auditor cannot be sure of the significance of data until after testing is well along. With a histogram, items of significance for testing can be identified in advance because their relationship to the accounting universe is emphasized graphically.

Modeling is a technique by which the auditor can compare current data with a trend or pattern as a basis for evaluating reasonableness. For example, the auditor can develop a model based on several years of financial statements. Then the current year's total revenue can be put into the model. The computer can generate a pro forma financial statement based on past revenue or cost relationships. The pro forma statement is compared with the actual financial statements as a test of reasonableness.

Both techniques — histograms and modeling — add new content and dimensions of information to the audit process through the use of the computer. With these methods, the auditor is no longer restricted simply to validating data provided by applications personnel. With these automated techniques, the auditor generates figures or snapshots of financial data to test the reasonableness of representations under examination.

Comparative analysis is a proven, cost-effective application of computers within audit examination that involves the comparison of sets of data to determine relationships that may be of audit interest. For example, the computer may be used to compare the inventory files of the previous and current years. Wide variations in year-end balances could lead to reviews for possible obsolescence. A failure to match part numbers from the previous and current years might trigger testing procedures to determine whether old items have been dropped or new ones added.

System Validation. System validation is a method for testing the reliability of programs through simulation with either test data or actual data.

With parallel simulation techniques, the auditor may be able to satisfy both compliance and substantive testing needs in one process.

Sampling

Some audit tools assist in defining sample size and selecting the sample. For example, ACL, an audit analysis tool, will automatically calculate the sample size and select a sample from the population, and spreadsheet applications will generate random numbers for selecting a sample. There are two types of sampling techniques:

- *Judgmental sampling:* The sample is selected and the results evaluated based on the auditor's experience. The judgment may be to select a specific block of time, geographic region, or function.
- *Statistical sampling:* The sample is randomly selected and evaluated through the application of the probability theory.

Both methods allow the auditor to project to the population. However, only statistical sampling allows the auditor to quantify the risk that the sample is not representative of the population. The specific method selected for a sample will depend on the audit objectives and the characteristics of the population. Some of the techniques mentioned earlier in Exhibit 2 can be integrated with sampling techniques. For example, the sample audit review file (SARF) technique can apply a number of different sampling methodologies mentioned later in Exhibit 4. The appropriateness of the methodology selected should be reviewed for validity purposes by statistical or actuarial staff that has expertise in this area. Also, the applied technique should be revisited and reassessed over time to see if there is any change to the characteristics or attributes of the population under review.

Random Attribute Sampling. Random attribute sampling is a statistical technique that tests for specific, predefined attributes of transactions selected on a random basis from a file. Attributes for which such testing is done could include signatures, account distribution, documentation, and compliance with policies and procedures. To perform attribute sampling, the auditor must specify three parameters that determine sample size:

- Estimate the *expected error rate*, or estimated percentage of exception transactions, in the total population.
- Specify the required *precision*, or degree of accuracy desired, of the sample conclusion to be made.
- Establish an acceptable *confidence level* that the conclusion drawn from the sample will be representative of the population.

The size of the sample will be determined by the combination of the precision, confidence level, and expected error rate parameters.

Exhibit 4. Statistical Sampling Techniques

Sampling Method	Description
Random number sampling	Items are randomly selected from a population so that each item has an equal chance of being selected.
Systematic sampling (interval sampling)	A method of random sampling that begins the sample by selecting a random starting point in a population the remaining items at fixed intervals. This method should not be used for selection from a population that has a fixed pattern.
Stratified sampling	A method of random sampling that separates the population into homogeneous groups before selecting a random sample. This method should be used for selection from a population with wide variances in value.
Cluster sampling (block sampling)	A method of random sampling that separates the population into similar groups and then selects a random sample from the group.
Stop-or-go sampling (sequential sampling)	Minimizes the sample size by assuming a low error rate. It estimates the error rate of the population within a specified interval (e.g., plus or minus number).
Discovery sampling	Tests for a significant error or irregularity. It should not be used where there are known deviant conditions.
Dollar-unit sampling (probability proportional to size)	This method uses the dollar as a sampling unit, which increases the probability that larger dollar values will be selected. It primarily detects overpayments.
Mean per unit	The mean value of a sample is calculated and multiplied by the units in the population to estimate the total value of the population.
Difference estimation	The average difference between the audit value and book value for a sample unit is calculated. This difference is then multiplied by the population to estimate total value.
Ratio estimation	The sample ratio to book value is multiplied by the population book value to estimate the total value.

Variable Sampling Techniques. Variable sampling estimates the dollar value of a population or some other quantifiable characteristic. To determine sample size, the auditor must specify four parameters:

- Acceptable *confidence level* that the conclusion drawn from the sample will be representative of the population
- Absolute value of the *population* for the field being sampled
- *Materiality* or maximum amount of error allowable in the population without detection
- *Expected error rate* or estimated percentage of exception transactions in the total population

The size of the sample will be determined by the combination of confidence level, population value, materiality, and expected error rate.

Exhibit 4 lists various statistical sampling techniques.

Computer Forensics: Methods and Techniques

As a result of increased legislation and the use of computer evidence within the courts, the ability to capture and document computer-generated information related to criminal activity is critical for purposes of prosecution. The awareness and use of computer-assisted tools and techniques in performing forensic support work have provided new opportunities for the IT auditor, IT security personnel, and those within law enforcement and investigation. For the IT audit professional, computer forensics is an exciting, developing field. The IT auditor can work in the field of computer forensics or work side-by-side with a computer forensics specialist, supplying insight into a particular system or network. The specialists can ask the IT audit professionals questions pertaining to the system and get responses faster than having to do research and figure everything out on their own. Although the specialist is highly trained and can adapt to almost any system or platform, collaboration can make the jobs of the forensic specialist and the IT professional easier and more efficient.

Since its birth in the early 1970s, computer forensics has continuously evolved into what is now a very large field. New technologies and enhancements in protocols are allowing for engineers and developers to create more stable and robust hardware, software, and tools for the specialist to use in computer-related criminal investigations. As computers become more advanced and more abundant, so do criminal activities. Therefore, the computer-forensics niche is also in constant progression along with the technological advancements of computers.

With new complex advancements, there are also complicated challenges. One of these challenges facing the field of computer forensics is the advancement of encryption. As encryption standards rise and the algorithms become more complex, it will be more difficult and more time consuming for specialists to decrypt and then piece together encrypted files into meaningful information. Another major challenge is maintaining credible certifications and industry standards in the field. Currently, there are a few cardinal rules that specialists tend to follow to ensure that no forensic evidence is damaged, destroyed, or otherwise compromised by the procedures used during the investigation: (1) never work on the original evidence, (2) establish and maintain a continuing chain of custody, and (3) document everything (DOD). These rules are especially important because they help ensure that the data gathered will be done so in a structured manner even though there is not now a solid set of standards. Currently the National Institute of Standards and Technology (NIST) creates the various standards for the technology industry. More standards need to be adopted for this field in order to make the gathered evidence and the compiled information used in court more credible in the eyes of the judge, jury, and opposing attorneys. Once better standards are addressed and adopted, then information gathered by specialists will be more reliable in court and for the general public.

At times individuals might attempt to hide data that contains incriminating information which they do not want others to find. One method that is commonly used to hide data is to rename a file of a particular type to another, thus, changing the extension of a file. "One of the most challenging aspects of a forensic analysis of a computer is the possibility of data being intentionally hidden by your suspect" (Heiser and Kruse 105). For example, an individual might be keeping child pornography pictures on his computer, but he does not want others to find it; therefore, it is possible that he might change the .jpg extension to .xls for Microsoft Excel. Renaming the file makes it nearly impossible for someone to search through and determine the correct file type. In cases such as this, EnCase can be utilized to flag suspicious file types. Using tools to run a HASH analysis of the hard drive will interpret the file headers and mark them as containing incorrect header information. Thus, after the file has been flagged, the analyst can read the file header information and make a determination of the correct file type.

Computer forensic specialists gather evidence against the individual who has committed a crime in several ways. They can image a hard drive or other types of media that the illegal information might be stored on. Data can come on a variety of media, such as data tapes, zip disks, CD-ROM disks, 3.5-inch floppy disks, and 5.25-inch floppy disks (Vacca 210). For example, if the attacker has saved the database to a floppy and formatted the floppy disk, the specialist can most likely retrieve the illegal data from the drive. Specialists can decrypt and crack passwords that have been imposed on files, as criminals might encrypt their files and set passwords to inhibit others from gaining access to their illegal files.

The science of computer forensics is meticulous and requires a tremendous amount of patience and dedication. Some have been called in to work round the clock to investigate, gather, identify, and document their findings. Specialists must be extremely careful to preserve the original file or device for that is all that they have to work with. Therefore, it is extremely important to first create exact images of the information and examine that information on a different type of media. Forensic specialists work hard to find vital information, and aim towards gathering enough evidence for prosecution or disciplinary action.

Often, these specialists investigate under extreme secrecy so that other individuals do not know exactly what they are doing or what information they have gathered. Once they have thoroughly gathered all the information and evidence that they can, specialists compile a report to be used in court. At times, the specialists themselves have testified in court when an independent opinion is needed on complex technical issues as these individuals are specially trained, have an extensive background in working with computers and dealing with technical issues, and are, of course, familiar with gathered information and the methods used to acquire that information.

Conclusion

The use of IT to audit IT is not a new idea. It is one of auditor innovation, knowledge, skills, and ability. The continued evolution of IT has placed advanced features of both hardware and software in the hands of IT auditors to apply in support of conducting, documenting, and executing the audit process. With the advancements in both hardware and software, we can see that even at the applications level, software tools and techniques exist for the auditor to apply innovative approaches to validating processes. IT has created new skills and new opportunities such as computer forensics.

As discussed in Chapter 3 and later chapters, even object-oriented applications have both tools and techniques available to the auditor for use in auditing through the system. CAATs can be used efficiently, and effective tools in documenting audit work can be performed to validate application processing. We have provided an extensive look at the use of CAATs to support the audit process. The domain of CAATs extends from the workstation or notebook level to the client/server, mainframe, and network level. The IT audit professional must use due professional care in the application of CAATs to support the audit process and the possibility of computer forensics application if a crime has been committed in their organization.

Chapter Review Questions

1. What are computer-assisted audit tools and techniques?
2. What role do CAATs play in performing the audit work?
3. What are audit query and analysis tools? List and explain two such tools.
4. What is transaction tagging? What is Snapshot? How are these techniques used in application audits?
5. What is an integrated test facility? How does it differ from test files? From Snapshot? From SCARF?
6. Decision support systems and knowledge support systems are being applied in the audit process; what are the areas of their application?
7. What are some of the benefits being reported by audit organizations in their use of IT to support the audit process? Please discuss.
8. What are some of the benefits of using CAATs?
9. What are the critical areas that management needs to consider when introducing new technologies into the audit process? What are some of the typical phases an organization goes through?

10. Can software tools and techniques that IT professionals use for application design, development, testing, and maintenance, be used for audit purposes as well? Please discuss the pros and cons, providing three examples in each area.
11. What is computer forensics? Where and how would an IT auditor use this resource?

Multiple Choice

1. Audit productivity tools can be used in:
   a. Planning and tracking
   b. Documentation and presentations
   c. Communications and data transfer
   d. All of the above
2. Generalized audit software can:
   a. Validate calculations
   b. Select specific records for examination
   c. Analyze and compare files
   d. All of the above
3. The task of examining a spreadsheet for reasonableness checks and comparison with known outputs is:
   a. Documentation
   b. Extent of training
   c. Verification of logic
   d. Support commitment
4. Which is not a database integrity control?
   a. Value constraints
   b. Biometrics
   c. Backup and recovery protection
   d. Referential integrity
5. This approach is used primarily with large-scale, online systems serving multiple locations within the company or organization. It comprises a fictitious corporation or branch, set up in the application and file structure to accept or process test transactions as though it was an actual operating entity. Throughout the financial period, auditors can submit transactions to test the system. This is called:
   a. Snapshot
   b. SARF
   c. Integrated test facility
   d. Transaction tagging
6. The ability to follow a selected transaction through the entire application from input, transmission, processing, and storage to output to verify the integrity, validity, and reliability of the application under review. Some applications have a "trace" or debug function, which

can allow you to follow the transaction through the application. This may be a way to ensure that the process for handling unusual transactions is followed within the application modules and code. This technique is called:
   a. Snapshot
   b. Transaction tagging
   c. SCARF
   d. Test data
7. Which of the following are categories of computer audit functions?
   a. Items of audit interest
   b. Data analysis
   c. Systems validation
   d. All of the above
8. The histogram analysis technique allows the auditor to:
   a. Apply judgment in identifying and selecting appropriate testing techniques.
   b. Validate transmission of data
   c. Prepare the audit plan
   d. All of the above
9. Which automated technique can apply a sampling methodology to the collection of transactions or records?
   a. Test data
   b. Snapshot
   c. SARF
   d. None of the above
10. Computer forensic specialists are experts who:
   a. Investigate under extreme secrecy so other individuals do not know exactly what they are doing or what information they have gathered
   b. May testify in court where an independent opinion is needed on complex technical issues
   c. Have an extensive background working with computers and dealing with technical issues, and are, of course, familiar with gathered information and the methods used to acquire that information
   d. All of the above

Exercises

1. List three software tools that IT professionals use which can be employed to audit the application. Explain their application.
2. List three software techniques that IT professionals use which can support the audit of an application. Explain their application.
3. What specific benefits can CAATs bring to the audit? Please list and explain four benefits.

4. Read Appendix 1, Case 1, Wooback City; solve Part 1 and Part 2.
5. Read Appendix 1, Case 2, ReadyorNot Auto Insurance; complete assignment.

Answers to Multiple Choice Questions

1 — d; 2 — d; 3 — c; 4 — b; 5 — c; 6 — b; 7 — d; 8 — a; 9 — c; 10 — d

References

1. Allen-Senft, S. and F. Gallegos, *Audit concerns for end-user computing and application development,* EDP Auditing, #72-30-20, Auerbach Publishers, Boca Raton, FL, 1996, pp. 1–11.
2. Allen-Senft, S. and F. Gallegos, *Putting together an audit program for end-user computing applications,* EDP Auditing, #72-30-22, Auerbach Publishers, Boca Raton, FL, 1996, pp. 1–12.
3. Barbin, D. and J. Patzakis, Cyber crime and forensics, *IS Control J.,* Vol. 3, pp. 25–27, 2002.
4. Cerullo, V.M. and M.J. Cerullo, Impact of SAS No. 94 on computer audit techniques, *IS Control J.,* Vol. 1, pp. 53–57, 2003.
5. Gallegos, F., W. Testerman, and J.M. Klosky, The use and application of computer performance evaluation tools as an EDP audit resource, *Proceedings of the South East Decision Sciences Conference Proceedings,* Miami, FL, November 1991.
6. Gallegos, F., J.M. Klosky, and V. Klosky, Auditing Decision Support Systems: An Approach, *South East Decision Sciences Conference Proceedings,* Savannah, GA, Spring 1992, pp. 161–164.
7. Gallegos, F., *Personal computers in IT auditing,* EDP Auditing, #73-20-05, Auerbach Publishers, Boca Raton, FL, December 2002, pp. 1–7.
8. Gillevet, J., Utilizing CAATs to determine the possibility of input errors in automated systems, *IS Audit Control J.,* Vol. 4, pp. 17–24, 1995.
9. Heiser, J. and W. Kruse, *Computer Forensics — Incident Response Essentials,* Addison-Wesley, Reading, MA, 2002.
10. Ireland, D., M. Hunt, and F. Gallegos, Automating assessments of internal controls: a GAO perspective, *Gov. Acc. J.,* Vol. 40, No. 4, pp. 33–39, Winter 1992.
11. Kneer, D.C., Continuous assurance: we are way overdue, *IS Control J.,* Vol. 1, pp. 30–34, 2003.
12. Lanza, R., Take my manual audit, please, *J. Acc.,* pp. 33–36, June 1998.
13. Legner, D., F. Gallegos, J.M. Klosky, and V. Klosky, paper entitled, An Analysis of Documentation Sufficiency for PC and LAN Based Database Applications, *Proceedings of the South East Decision Sciences Conference,* Savannah, GA, Spring 1992, pp. 64–66.
14. Lou, H. and R.W. Scammel, Acceptance of groupware: the relationships among use, satisfaction and outcomes, *J. Organ. Comput. Electron. Commer.,* Vol. 6, No. 2, pp. 173–190, 1996.
15. Manson, D. and F. Gallegos, *DBMS Recovery Procedures,* Data Base Management Series, #24-03-61, Auerbach Publishers, Boca Raton, FL, October 1997, pp. 1–11.
16. McFadden, P., Seven good reasons to test the entire population versus just a sample, *IS Audit Control J.,* Vol. 2, pp. 14–16, 1998.
17. Preiser-Houy, L. and F. Gallegos, *Auditing FOCUS Data Base Applications,* EDP Auditing, #74-01-21.1, Auerbach Publishers, Boca Raton, FL, April 1995, pp. 1–28.
18. Sayana, S.A., Using CAATs to support IS audit, *IS Control J.,* Vol. 1, pp. 21–23, 2003.
19. U.S. Department of Defense, Department of Defense: Computer Forensics Laboratory, 2003, http://www.dcfl.gov/DCFL/aboutdcfl.asp
20. Vacca, J.R., *Computer Forensics — Computer Crime Scene Investigation,* Charles River Media Inc, Hingham, MA, 2002.

Part II
Auditing IT Planning and Organization

Chapter 5 through Chapter 8

The second part of this text examines IT governance and control of new and existing systems.

- *Governance* is a structure of relationships and processes to direct and control the enterprise in order to achieve the enterprise's goals by adding value while balancing risk versus return over IT and its processes.
- *Controls* are the policies, procedures, practices, and organizational structures designed to provide reasonable assurance that business objectives will be achieved and that undesired events will be prevented or detected and corrected.

COBIT

Effectively managing an IT organization requires a solid foundation of governance and control over IT resources. Governance guides the decision rights, accountability, and behaviors of an organization. This is controlled through a series of processes and procedures that identify who can make decisions, what decisions can be made, how decisions are made, how investments are managed, and how results are measured. This section covers the critical issues and best practices in governing and controlling IT resources. Key processes like project management and quality management ensure that investments made in IT deliver on their promised value. This section is organized according to the COBIT framework and covers key controls identified in the Planning and Organization Domain (Exhibit 1). COBIT groups IT processes into four major domains.

This section focuses on the following domains:

- *Planning and Organization:* This domain covers strategies and tactics, and concerns the identification of the way IT can best contribute to the achievement of the business objectives.
- *Acquisition and Implementation:* To realize the IT strategy, IT solutions need to be identified, developed, or acquired, as well as implemented and integrated into the business process. In addition to these processes, this domain makes sure that the life cycle is continued in order for the systems to cover changes in and maintenance of existing systems.

Chapter 5 covers the foundation for IT governance by aligning IT decisions with business strategy. This process is a very important step for management, auditors, and users in that it sets a framework for accomplishing control of the objectives within the organization and allows activity involvement of organization's stakeholders.

Chapter 6 discusses the processes needed to ensure that investment decisions support business objectives. This is not an easy process in economic times where justification and priorities must be reconciled. There is a price for audit, control, and security and often one must be assured that this does not exceed the level of risk or potential loss the organization may face.

Chapter 7 examines and discusses project management processes needed to ensure projects are well controlled from inception through implementation. Systems development failures and project management failures continue to appear in reports and studies. Managing technology in today's dynamic times is not an easy process or solution. Change in organization management, operations, technology, project resources, and other factors add weight to the complexity of this area.

The quality assurance processes needed to ensure that the IT systems meet the stated objectives are examined and discussed in Chapter 8. Quality is a goal that enhances product and process. It can lead to leadership in the market and ability to compete in new markets. Controls help ensure quality. They can provide measurement tools and techniques to assess and adjust the business processes. They can also assure continuity in processing and recovery if necessary to protect and preserve a company's leadership.

Exhibit 1. 11 Processes for Planning and Organization

PO 1 Define a Strategic IS Plan

Control Objectives
1. IT as part of the organization's long and short-range plans
2. IT long-range plan
3. IT long-range planning — approach and structure
4. IT long-range plan changes
5. Short-range planning for the IT function
6. Communication of IT plans
7. Monitoring and evaluating IT plans
8. Assessment of existing systems

PO 2 Define the Information Architecture

Control Objectives
1. Information architecture model
2. Corporate data dictionary and data syntax rules
3. Data classification scheme
4. Security levels

Exhibit 1. 11 Processes for Planning and Organization (Continued)

PO 3 Determine Technological Direction

Control Objectives
1. Technological infrastructure planning
2. Monitor future trends and regulations
3. Technological infrastructure contingency
4. Hardware and software acquisition plans
5. Technology standards

PO 4 Define the IT Organization and Relationships

Control Objectives
1. IT planning or steering committee
2. Organizational placement of the IT function
3. Review of organizational achievements
4. Roles and responsibilities
5. Responsibility of quality assurance
6. Responsibility for logical and physical security
7. Ownership and custodianship
8. Data and system ownership
9. Supervision
10. Segregation of duties
11. IT staffing
12. Job or position description for IT staff
13. Key IT personnel
14. Contracted staff policies and procedures
15. Relationships

PO 5 Manage the IT Investment

Control Objectives
1. Annual IT operating budget
2. Cost and benefit monitoring
3. Cost and benefit justification

PO 6 Communicate Management Aims and Direction

Control Objectives
1. Positive information control environment
2. Management's responsibility for policies
3. Communication of organization policies
4. Policy implementation resources
5. Maintenance of policies
6. Compliance with policies, procedures, and standards
7. Quality commitment
8. Security and internal control framework policy
9. Intellectual property rights

Exhibit 1. 11 Processes for Planning and Organization (Continued)

10. Issue-specific policies
11. Communication of IT security awareness

PO 7 Manage Human Resources

Control Objectives
1. Identification of training needs
2. Training organization
3. Chargeable items
4. Costing procedures
5. Chargeable items
6. Costing procedures
7. Chargeable items
8. Costing procedures

PO 8 Ensure Compliance with External Requirements

Control Objectives
1. External requirements review
2. Practices and procedures for complying with external requirements
3. Safety and ergonomic compliance
4. Privacy, intellectual property, and data flow
5. Electronic commerce
6. Compliance with insurance contracts

PO 9 Assess Risks

Control Objectives
1. Business risk assessment
2. Risk assessment approach
3. Risk identification
4. Risk measurement
5. Risk action plan
6. Risk acceptance
7. Safeguard selection
8. Risk assessment commitment

PO 10 Manage Projects

Control Objectives
1. Project management framework
2. User department participation in project initiation
3. Project team membership and responsibilities
4. Project definition
5. Project approval
6. Project phase approval
7. Project master plan

Exhibit 1. 11 Processes for Planning and Organization (Continued)

8. System quality assurance plan
9. Planning of assurance methods
10. Formal project risk management
11. Test plan
12. Training plan
13. Post-implementation review plan

PO 11 Manage Quality

Control Objectives

1. General quality plan
2. Quality assurance approach
3. Quality assurance planning
4. Quality assurance review of adherence to IT standards and procedures
5. Systems development life-cycle methodology
6. Systems development life-cycle methodology for major changes to existing technology
7. Updating of the systems development life-cycle methodology
8. Coordination and communication
9. Acquisition and maintenance framework for the technology infrastructure
10. Third-party implementer relationship
11. Program documentation standards
12. Program testing standards
13. System testing standards
14. Parallel/pilot testing
15. System testing documentation
16. Quality assurance evaluation of adherence to development standards
17. Quality assurance review of the achievement of IT objectives
18. Quality metrics
19. Reports of quality assurance reviews

Chapter 5
IT Strategy and Standards

During the past ten years, organizations have undergone significant change at a rapid pace. The pace of change is increasing in tempo and at the same time the global economy continues to diminish the autonomy and independent stability of local markets. These changes, coupled with new concepts for managing global enterprise and the dramatic advancement of IT, combine to challenge previously successful business practices as never before. Although predicting the future of global business and the technology it will use this century is certainly not something that can be done with certainty, we can proactively position ourselves to shape the future rather than be shaped by it. We must be positioned to take best advantage of emerging opportunities while also responding to the global requirements of the 21st century.

IT has become a strategic part of most businesses, enabling the redefinition of markets and industries and the strategies and designs of firms competing within them (Applegate). An IT strategic plan is a formal vision to guide in the acquisition, allocation, and management of information technology resources to fulfill the organization's objectives. It should be part of an overall corporate strategy for information technology and should align to the business strategy it supports. The business strategy needs to be in lock step with the technology strategy to ensure that resources are not wasted on projects or processes that do not contribute to achieving the organization's overall objectives (see Exhibit 1). This alignment should occur at all levels of the planning process to provide continued assurance that the operational plans continue to support the business objectives.

IT management involves combining technology, people, and process to provide solutions to organizational problems (Pearlson). The most effective strategy will be determined by the combination of the environment, culture, and technology used by an organization. IT must take the lead in

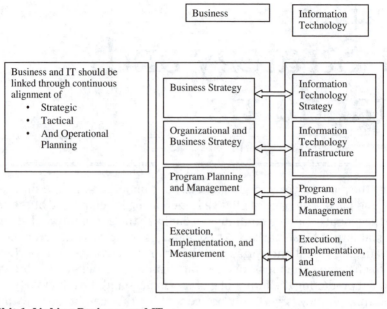

Exhibit 1. Linking Business and IT

gathering information to incorporate user departments' needs with technological feasibility to create an overall strategy.

An IT strategic plan provides a roadmap for operating plans and a framework for evaluating technology investments. The IT strategy supports the business strategy to ensure that technology resources are applied to meeting business objectives while minimizing ongoing support costs. This task sounds fairly simple, but according to a Gartner Group report "95 percent of enterprises lack a well-defined business strategy." In most cases, the business strategy has to be assumed based on conversation with business executives (Mack). The first step in defining an IT strategic plan is to understand the business objectives, whether stated or implied. These objectives guide management in evaluating investments, assessing risk, or implementing controls.

So why should IT have a strategic plan if the enterprise has none? The main risk of not having an IT strategic plan is increased cost of technology. If there is no roadmap, organizations run the risk of investing in technology that increases costs but adds no business value. IT spending as a percent of revenue declined in the early 2000s due to financial losses and an uncertain economic environment. Because of this, organizations are more careful about where they invest their technology dollars and demand a solid business case before approving new projects (Working Council).

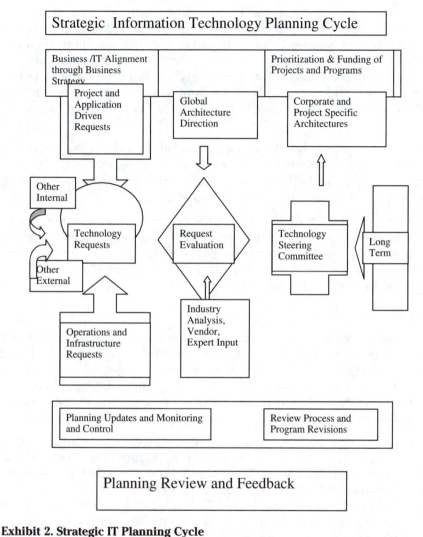

Exhibit 2. Strategic IT Planning Cycle

Architecture and Standards

The IT strategy provides a vision for the IT organization, and architecture translates vision into infrastructure (Pearlson). The architecture group establishes the standards and blueprint for the software developers (see Exhibit 2). Business applications must run on underlying technology. Whether it is mainframe or distributed, the underlying infrastructure drives the total cost of ownership (Mack). With the economic downturn in the past few years, many organizations have been attempting to drive IT costs down (Working Council). Many cost-cutting measures can be effective

123

in the short term, but long-term cost saving requires standardizing and simplifying applications and infrastructure. Simplified applications and infrastructure are easier to maintain and change because there are fewer technology products and components. Simplified applications and infrastructures are also more reliable, resulting in improved productivity and reduced cost. There are many other advantages to standardizing and simplifying systems: system reuse, faster implementation, improved flexibility, etc.

Standards guide industries and organizations in selecting hardware and software and in developing new applications. Hardware and software standards ensure compatibility between applications and ease the burden of technology integration and technical support.

Once there is an understanding of the organization's objectives and IT strategy, that strategy needs to be translated into operating plans. Operating plans will define the projects that will be initiated and the service levels expected of IT. Delivery of these plans should be controlled by a series of governance processes discussed in Chapter 6.

Policies and Procedures

Organizations establish and communicate policies and procedures for information systems to ensure that organizational goals are met. These policies and procedures should communicate the organization's stand on such issues as systems architecture, testing and validation of requirements and systems, and documentation. These areas are critical to establishing an institutional process for managing applications.

A number of professional societies have issued guidelines to assist managers in this area. Organizations such as the Association of Information Technology Professionals (AITP), Society for Information Management (SIM), International Federation of Accountants (IFAC), and Information Systems Audit and Control Association (ISACA) are examples of professional societies that recognize the need for general guidance. Examples of these can be found in Appendices 2 and 3.

Audit Involvement

As IT becomes more important to the success of organizations, it is becoming increasingly necessary to use and control this resource as effectively and efficiently as possible. To help organizations integrate IT with business objectives, the Information Systems Audit and Control Foundation (ISACF) developed a framework that links IT control objectives to business objectives. This study resulted in the Control Objectives for Information Technology (COBIT). COBIT was built on the Committee of Sponsoring Organization (COSO) model of internal controls and the Software Engineering Institute's Capability Maturity Model (CMM). COBIT provides best practices for the management of IT processes in a manageable and logical structure, meeting the multiple needs of enterprise management by bridging the gaps between business risks, technical issues, control needs, and performance-measurement requirements.

The IT Governance Institute summarized four reasons for the criticality of information and its related technology (CoBiT).

- Increasing dependence on information and the system that delivers this information
- Increasing vulnerabilities and a wide spectrum of threats such as cyber threats and information warfare
- Scale and cost of the current and future investments in information and information systems
- Potential for technologies to dramatically change organizations and business practices, create new opportunities, and reduce cost

CoBiT groups IT processes into four major domains (see Exhibit 3):

- *Planning and Organization:* This domain covers strategies and tactics and concerns the identification of the way IT can best contribute to the achievement of the business objectives.
- *Acquisition and Implementation:* To realize the IT strategy, IT solutions need to be identified, developed, or acquired, as well as implemented and integrated into the business process. In addition, changes in and maintenance of existing systems are covered by this domain to make sure that the life cycle is continued for the systems.
- *Delivery and Support:* This domain is concerned with the actual delivery of required services, which range from traditional operations over security and continuity aspects to training. In order to deliver services, the necessary support processes must be set up. This domain includes the actual processing of data by application systems, often classified under application controls.
- *Monitoring:* All IT processes need to be regularly assessed over time for their quality and compliance with control requirements. This domain thus addresses management's oversight of the organization's control process and independent assurance provided by internal and external audit or obtained from alternative sources.

In the next three chapters, the 11 processes of the CoBiT Planning and Organization domain (PO11) will be discussed in more detail and compared to other existing standards.

An Example of Standards: Technology Risk Management Regulations

Technology risk management (TRM) for financial institutions is now more than just a buzzword. An effective TRM program has been required by regulatory bodies as early as 1996. Two of the main agencies offering

---

Exhibit 3. IT Process Domain

PO 1 Define a Strategic IS Plan

Control Objectives

1   IT as part of the organization's long- and short-range plan
2   IT long-range plan
3   IT long-range planning — approach and structure
4   IT long-range plan changes
5   Short-range planning for the IT function
6   Communication of IT plans
7   Monitoring and evaluating IT plans
8   Assessment of existing systems

PO 2 Define the Information Architecture

Control Objectives

1   Information architecture model
2   Corporate data dictionary and data syntax rules
3   Data classification scheme
4   Security levels

PO 3 Determine Technological Direction

Control Objectives

1   Technological infrastructure planning
2   Monitor future trends and regulations
3   Technological infrastructure contingency
4   Hardware and software acquisition plans
5   Technology standards

---

regulatory guidance to financial institutions, which requires a risk management program, are FFIEC (Federal Financial Institutions Examination Council) and the Basel Committee on Banking Supervision.

FFIEC is a council made up of representatives from the Federal Reserve Board (FRB), Federal Deposit Insurance Corporation (FIDC), Office of the Comptroller of the Currency (OCC), Office of Thrift Supervision (OTS), and National Credit Union Administration (NCUA). This council, with representatives from each bank regulatory body in the United States, was created to address and standardize IT supervision in financial institutions, and it provides guidance on the minimum requirements for financial institutions' IT controls. The handbook also contains audit work programs used by each member agency to test compliance with FFIEC's minimum requirements. Two of the first areas addressed are risk and risk management (1). According to their Handbook, TRM programs at financial institutions should include identification, measurement, control, and monitoring of risk. TRM programs require an informed board, capable management, and appropriate staffing (2).The Basel Committee on Banking Supervision is a group of representatives from large banks and regulatory bodies from several different countries, primarily North America, Europe, and Japan. Through the Bank of International Settlements, the Basel Committee gathers to publish guidance on various aspects of banking and to further the dialogue between the financial industry and the committee on topics such as operational risk management (3). The Basel Committee's purpose is to create principles that can be widely applied to banks, with the realization that each financial institution is different. Basel recognizes that each financial institution's risk profile will be different, depending on the types of activities and lines of business it takes on. The risk management principles outlined by the Basel Committee are not to be taken as absolute requirements but should be used as a guide and a flexible framework when creating a risk management program. According to the Basel Committee, the following are the basic tenets of an operational risk management program:

- The board of directors must be involved with approval of the operational risk management plan, which includes technology risk.
- Senior management has responsibility for implementing the plan and spreading information about the plan throughout the organization.
- Processes must be in place to identify risks, measure them, monitor their occurrence, and control or mitigate their occurrence.

Where Does Technology Risk Management Belong?

Technology risk can occur at two levels. It can be enterprisewide, for example, as the choice of a new standard operating system. This type of technology risk is normally managed by the enterprise head of technology or chief technology officer (CTO). Technology risk can also occur at the business unit level. This is the more common type of technology risk at financial institutions due to the type of IT used and the structure of the bank's IT department. In most cases, the IT department, not the business owner, is the vendor of the system. It is managed by the line of business with IT support and guidance.

There are two general possible structures for a TRM program at a financial institution. Both structures have their own associated pros and cons. The first approach is to have a central risk management department, of which TRM would be a subset. This fits due to the FFIEC statement that all risk management activities should be independent of risk-taking activities (4). In this scenario, a chief risk officer (CRO) would have a staff of risk management and TRM professionals. This department would perform all the risk management functions for the entire enterprise.

This structure can add value because risk management professionals, rather than business units, are identifying, measuring, controlling, and monitoring the entire enterprise's risks. In enterprises where the business units have poor communication, this structure has the advantage of allowing a central area to evaluate risks in light of risks of other business units. There may be a specific risk at each business unit level that could be more effectively managed enterprisewide. For example, if a risk occurs for each of several different business units but each business unit is independently purchasing insurance to offset that risk, combining the policies into one coverage for the entire enterprise or affected business units may result in cost savings, premium reduction, less administration time, and uniformity of coverage.

The possible drawbacks to this type of structure are that it has the possibility to isolate TRM from business units and place it in an "ivory tower" of the executive suite. This may result in negative situations, such as too little involvement from the business units with risk identification or all the risks may not be fully understood. The business units may feel that the TRM program exists only to satisfy the auditors, while creating more work for them. Additionally, controls put in place by the central risk management area may be seen as unrealistic for the business units to execute.

If each business unit is responsible for its own TRM, the risks may be better understood. Potential controls could be evaluated based on cost and value by the business units who can best determine what controls are feasible for their unit. For example, to mitigate the risk of power outages to normal company computer processing, a central risk management department without adequate technology understanding might determine that having a dual electrical feed (feed from two different power grids) is adequate protection. They may feel that the lower cost option is acceptable and that it reduces risk of power outages to an acceptable minimum. However, the data center management might make the decision that installing a generator, although much more costly, would ensure operability in case of a natural disaster, wide-area blackout, or other occurrence. In such a case, the business unit owner (data center manager) is better able to decide how to mitigate risks. The business units often know better what is going on in their area and have the most timely information regarding potential costs of failure or the possibility of adverse events taking place.

In this second scenario, potential issues may also arise. Each business unit becomes responsible for monitoring and controlling its own technology risk and cannot rely on the IT department to do it for them. The business units may downplay their risks to intentionally avoid implementing controls that may be seen as time-consuming, unimportant, and a hindrance to normal business operations. Or the business units may not have enough technology knowledge to adequately assess the risks of their technology.

The OCC's guidance on TRM leads to the conclusion that while technology is created and maintained by the IT department, the technology itself, the use of that technology, and the risks associated with it belong to the business unit and not to the IT department (5). This attitude mirrors the thoughts of the FFIEC's statement that while financial institutions may have different structures of Risk Management programs, all risk management should be independent of risk-taking activities (4). According to Walter Smiechewicz (6), who has been a CRO at several large financial institutions, Risk Management must be an enterprisewide goal headed by the board of directors and exemplified in the CRO or other similar position. In facilitating the risk management program, the CROs will encourage the business units to identify, manage, control, and accept their own risks. This program should increase companywide communication about risk and add value through reducing risk.

Regulatory and best-practice guidance seem to point towards a blended approach for the structure of a risk management function, with a central risk management figure or department working with the business units to identify, measure, monitor, and control their risk. This blended approach achieves the advantages of a central risk management area heading the risk management effort, coordinating the process, ensuring it complies with regulatory requirements, and reviewing all risks for duplication of risks or risk transfer. This approach also has the benefit of including business management in the risk management process, making them accountable for the risks of their own area, and working with them to successfully monitor and control those risks.

The Strategy: An Effective Technology Risk Management Program

An effective TRM program will be part of an overall risk management program. Within the enterprise information technology area, there should be a designated TRM manager or coordinator, possibly several. This function would fit well with disaster recovery planning and the making of IT policy, as it is another management function of IT. The TRM coordinator should be a contact point for business management with questions, and will work with the CRO to roll out TRM as a subset of the enterprisewide risk management program.

A CRO officer should exist for the entire enterprise at a senior management level. The CRO should report to the CEO or the board of directors or both. The CRO, in collaboration with the board of directors, should determine risk limits the organization is willing to take on. These risk limits should not be static but should be subject to change — a working document. These risk limits should be published and available to the business units as each business manager will be held accountable for assessing the line of business' risks, creating a risk action plan, and determining if their risks fall within or outside of the established tolerances.

As part of the strategic planning process each year (or yearly at another time, or on a sliding schedule that runs annually by department, or on a cycle decided by the business unit and CRO if there is no annual strategic planning process), each business manager should be required to complete a risk assessment of their area. Included in that is a risk assessment of the business risks of each application, system, or program that the line of business owns. CobiT or a similar standard should be agreed upon and required to be used as a guideline. This will put all technology risk assessments on similar terms and make them somewhat standardized as to the types of risks identified. These risk assessments should be completed by the line of business with assistance from the TRM coordinator or internal audit. The TRM coordinator can give insight and information to the line of business regarding the specific technical risks faced by the application, system, or program. The business manager would be able to assess these in light of the overall risk facing the line of business. The enterprise technology department should perform the risk assessments of enterprisewide applications, systems, and programs, such as the network or the enterprisewide e-mail software. The enterprise technology department, headed by the chief technology officer, would be evaluating, managing, and accepting the risks associated with this type of enterprisewide technology.

In some ways the CRO and the officer's staff will serve as facilitators of this process. They will determine if the risk assessments are not adequate, fully considered, or lacking information. They will create tools to assist the line of business in identifying risks and possible controls, deciding which controls to implement, and monitoring and measuring those controls for effectiveness. Appendix V is a sample, partially completed risk assessment for a data center, in a format that could be used for both business and technology risks.

After the risk assessments are filled out and all the risks the particular line of business is facing fully identified, the business manager, with the assistance of the CRO's staff, should review the risks and associated controls. These should be compared to applicable regulatory requirements and board-of-director-approved limits to risk taking. If any risks fall outside of either regulatory or board limits, the CRO and the business management can work together to find solutions to lower the risks to an acceptable level. This could include implementing more controls — for example, requiring two appraisals on high-dollar loans, or requiring two management signatures before processing a master file change. It could include purchasing insurance to transfer some of the risk to a third party, such as hazard insurance for the data center if a natural disaster were to strike. Or it could mean deciding not to offer a particular service, such as opening accounts online, due to an unacceptably high risk of fraud. All of these possible solutions result in the risk being lowered, and the goal is to reduce the risk to a level acceptable to both the financial institution's regulatory agencies and its board of directors.

In a yearly cycle the risk assessments would be reviewed and reconsidered each year. This review should include adding any new risks to the business unit due to new products or services, or perhaps a new technology that has been implemented. The review should also assess whether the ratings for each risk were warranted or may need to be adjusted. The organization may decide to require review of the risk assessments more frequently in the beginning of the implementation until satisfied that all potential risks have been identified and included in the risk management process. The CRO should also implement a scorecard and metrics, such as a maturity model (7), against which line of business risk management can be measured. Lines of business with good risk management practices should be rewarded. Financial institutions must ensure that they do not monetarily reward management that does not adequately control their risks (8) as this could be perceived as discouraging risk management. This could give the wrong message to the rest of the company and make management feel that ignoring set risk limits and policies is tolerated.

Internal audit will independently evaluate the risk assessments each time they audit a function, area, or application. If audit feels the risk assessments are not adequate or that all the potential risks have not been identified or adequately controlled, that would be an issue for both the business and the CRO. Periodic audits by external auditors and regulatory bodies are also a necessary part of TRM. Many regulatory bodies have their own TRM experts or examiners who specialize in reviewing the adequacy of TRM at financial institutions. These examiners use FFIEC and other related guidance as well as best practice information to assess the adequacy and effectiveness of each financial institution's TRM program. Exhibit 4 shows the basic yearly or cyclical flow of the risk management process. The IT auditor would use this to see if the organization is following the standard in compliance with organizational or regulatory guidance.

Example: Importance of Business Strategy in Customer Relationship Management

In the planning of corporate support system, the importance of IT standards and strategy comes into play when confronted with management's interest in better control of their relationships with their customers. Despite the billions of dollars spent on customer relationship management (CRM) products and services, as much as 12 percent of all CRM implementations are complete failures, meaning the systems never even go live. One research study by AMR Research of Boston, Massachusetts found that "only 16 percent of all CRM installations have actually improved business performance in a measurable way." That means roughly 85 percent of all CRM users cannot quantify any benefits at all. In a rough economy this is bad news as CEOs want to see strong tangible benefits. The top three obstacles to success of such systems have been (1) lack of a strategic plan,

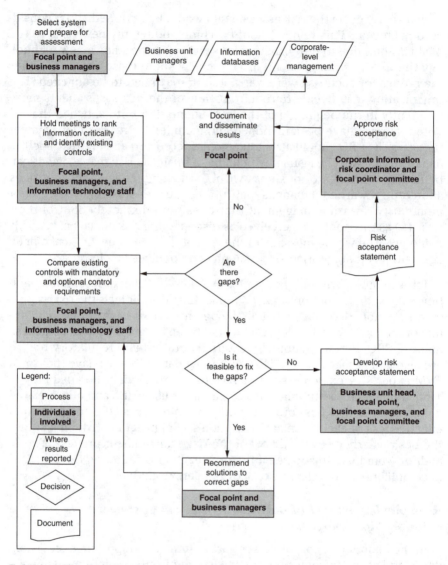

Exhibit 4. The Risk Management Process

(2) lack of executive sponsorship, and (3) poor alignment of technology and business processes.

Focus on Technology

One of the common myths is that CRM software will fix all of the company's problems, and they need the newest software to fix lagging sales. Analysts and users claim that vendors have hyped CRM's capabilities far beyond what is being delivered, and that since so many customers did not know what they wanted in the first place, many CRM implementations should never have been started. Vendors are hyping their products to all levels of the organization as a solution in all problem areas. In a troubled economy companies buy the vendors' message and bet on CRM software to turn around their sales. Companies need to understand how to change their business processes and leverage CRM software and best practices to help facilitate this change. The CRM software itself is not going to make a company customer-focused, but proper business process change will. This requires business strategy and IT strategy to coincide.

Resistance to Change

Another common mistake, made by big and small businesses alike, is underestimating the resistance to a new system such as CRM, which is created by organizational habits. New systems fail most often because of cultural barriers, not systems problems. The turf issues that exist within organizations — the invisible but thick walls that exist between parts of the organization and even between different product groups within an organization — really get in the way.

Regardless of any company's current dynamics, the sales force must support a CRM implementation if the system is to succeed. Many large sales organizations, such as Ford Motor, Kodak, Coca-Cola, and others, are justifiably wary, having suffered an ill-conceived attempt at sales-force automation in the past. To ease their fears, the strategic plan needs input from the sales team even before a system has been planned. Sales teams will always get behind a solution if it has been introduced in the right manner.

The real problem is that people do not like change, cannot deal with loss of control, like stability, and fear the unknown. If the business and IT management fail to address these issues and adequately communicate these changes to the users, the CRM project will be doomed from the start. The key to changing management is to address the concerns of all levels of employees and to gain user acceptance and buy-in.

Sales teams typically demonstrate acceptance of a solution that:

- Helps organize and streamline their day
- Saves them time
- Improves their response to their customers
- Is easy to use

As long as the sales teams can answer the question of what's in it for them, they will be much more likely to embrace the new CRM solution.

Barriers to User Adoption

The top three obstacles that we have seen that arise with CRM solutions are:

- Poor performance
- Difficult to navigate and access information
- Limited value

These key barriers have resulted in lower adoption and utilization levels than management desires to reap the anticipated benefits. In most organizations, CRM has been designed around the sales reporting needs of management and not the needs of the end user. As a result, these systems tend to be forced on the sales staff without necessarily addressing their main points or fitting easily into their daily workflow. Project managers need to focus on what functionality and data the users need to be effective.

To determine the needs of the users, they need to identify common frustrations and the best ways to fix them. If the sales representatives do not see value, they simply will not use CRM; so design the CRM solution around their everyday lives. Find out what barriers are coming between the sales rep and the customer. For example, if the sales team member in the field has not been able to access the most up-to-date marketing, product, and pricing information in the field, it is likely that he could not answer customer questions. It makes sense to empower representatives with the information they need to answer questions on the spot, thus maximizing customer interactions. Reps need the right information that is timely and relevant. It is critical to build an architecture that will flexibly aggregate corporate information.

The system needs to react quickly and not frustrate the users. Monster.com spent $1 million in 1998 on a CRM solution to increase sales force efficiency by providing "immediate" access to information on potential customers. The system was reputed to be so sluggish that field personnel could not download data on their laptops. This forced the company to abandon the solution and build a completely new system from scratch; the company had to spend a million more to get it right. One of the most popular complaints received from various users on a daily bases is the poor performance of the application. This forces the call centers to take more time on calls and to frustrate customers that have been on hold for several minutes. Users will scratch down notes on paper instead of in the system and, hopefully, will enter that data into the system later, but at a cost. Others will refuse to use the system at all because it slows them down or does not give them enough value to be worth their time.

This is where Standards such as CobiT or COSO can help an organization establish a framework. COSO among other things provides criteria against which control systems can be evaluated. COSO defines internal control as a process, influenced by an entity's board of directors, management, and other personnel, that is designed to provide reasonable assurance in the following categories:

- Effectiveness and efficiency of operations
- Reliability of financial reporting
- Compliance with applicable laws and regulations

The report emphasizes that the internal control system is a tool of, but not a substitute for, management and that controls should be built into, rather than built onto, operating activities. According to COSO, the internal control system consists of five interrelated components: (1) control environment, (2) risk assessment, (3) control activities, (4) information and communication, and (5) monitoring.

*The **control environment** provides the foundation for the other components. It encompasses such factors as management's philosophy and operating style, human resource policies and practices, the integrity and ethical values of employees, the organizational structure, and the attention and direction of the board of directors. COSO provides guidance for evaluating each of these factors.*

***Risk assessment** consists of risk identification and risk analysis. Risk identification includes examining external factors such as technological developments, competition, and economic changes, and internal factors such as personnel quality, the nature of the entity's activities, and the characteristics of information system processing. Risk analysis involves estimating the significance of the risk, assessing the likelihood of the risk occurring, and considering how to manage the risk.*

***Control activities** consist of the policies and procedures that ensure employees carry out management directives. Control activities include reviews of the control system, physical controls, segregation of duties, and information system controls. Controls over information systems include general controls and application controls. General controls are those covering access, software, and system development. Application controls are those, which prevent errors from entering the system or detect and correct errors present in the system.*

*The entity obtains pertinent **information and communicates** it throughout the organization. The information system identifies, captures, and reports financial and operating information that is useful to control the organization's activities. Within the organization, personnel must receive the message that they must understand their roles in the internal control system, take their internal control responsibilities seriously, and, if necessary, report problems to higher levels of management. Outside the entity, individuals and organizations supplying or receiving goods or services must receive the message that the entity will not tolerate improper actions.*

***Management's monitoring** of the control system by reviewing the output generated by regular control activities and by conducting special* *evaluations. Regular control activities include comparing physical assets with recorded data, training seminars, and examinations by internal and external auditors. Special evaluations can be of varying scope and frequency. Deficiencies found during regular control activities are usually reported to the supervisor in charge; deficiencies located during special evaluations are normally communicated to higher levels of the organization.*

The above are situations that the auditor has to be aware of and report to prevent the organization from making a costly mistake in the IT planning and organization process. The examples cited from the report are common in today's dynamic environment and are among the challenges organizations face.

Conclusion

Because IT and information security are integral parts of the information system's internal controls, we have discussed above and in earlier chapters the Internal Control Integrated Framework publication by COSO in 1997 that specifically includes IT controls. Also addressed are The Institute of Internal Auditors' Systems Auditability and Control (SAC) and Information Systems Audit and Control Association's (ISACA) CobiT that are both directly related to the frameworks identified by COSO in their reports. These are standards of practice we mentioned earlier to help guide business in its IT strategic planning process. This chapter has provided guidance and examples of how critical these components are in setting the direction for what will follow.

Review Questions

1. What is the purpose of developing an IT strategic plan?
2. How can an IT strategic plan be developed without a corresponding business plan?
3. How does architecture fit into the IS strategic plan?
4. What are the advantages of having architectural standards?
5. In what way does CobiT help in the alignment of business and IT objectives?
6. What are the two agencies that offer regulatory guidance to financial institutions?
7. Who is the FFIEC?
8. What is OCC's guidance on TRM?
9. What are the top three obstacles to CRM Solutions? Please explain.
10. What is COSO? Why is it important from a strategic standpoint?

Multiple Choice Questions

1. What is the purpose of developing an IS strategic plan?
   a. Define the IT goals and objectives.
   b. Guide the acquisition, allocation, and management of IT resources.

    c. Define the technology to be used by the organization for the current year.

    d. Provide a process for governing investments in information technology.

2. Architectural standards are needed to:

    a. Determine which vendor products to use.

    b. Simplify and standardize infrastructure costs.

    c. Communicate programming standards to software developers.

    d. Speed the implementation process for new technology.

3. The CoBiT model is based on the following:

    a. COSO model of internal controls

    b. Capability Maturity Model

    c. Project Management Body of Management

    d. ISO 9000–Quality Management and Quality Assurance Standards

4. The Planning and Organization domain includes all the following except:

    a. Project management standards

    b. Architecture planning process

    c. Strategic planning process

    d. Operational readiness process

5. TRM Programs have been required by U.S. regulatory bodies as early as:

    a. 1980

    b. 1990

    c. 1996

    d. 2000

6. The Federal Financial Institutions Examination Council is made up of representatives from:

    a. Federal Reserve Board and Federal Deposit Insurance Corporation

    b. Office of Comptroller of the Currency

    c. Office of Thrift Supervision and National Credit Union Administration

    d. All the above plus representatives from each bank regulatory council

7. The Basel Committee believes:

    a. The board of directors must be involved with approval of the operational risk management plan which includes technology risk.

    b. Senior management has responsibility for implementing the plan and spreading information about the plan throughout the organization.

    c. Processes must be in place to identify risks, measure them, monitor their occurrence, and control or mitigate their occurrence.

    d. All of the above.

8. One of the obstacles to the success of CRM has been:

    a. Project management standards

    b. Lack of strategic plan

    c. Strategic planning process

    d. Architecture planning process

9. A common mistake made by big and small businesses alike may involve:

    a. Project management standards

    b. Architecture planning process

    c. Resistance to change

    d. Operational readiness process

Exercises

1. Create an outline of an IT strategic plan including the key components.
2. List the key processes included in the planning and organization domain.
3. List and discuss four key reasons for the criticality of information systems.
4. List and describe the four domains in COBIT.
5. List and describe IT governance standards.

Multiple Choice

1 — b; 2 — b; 3 — a; 4 — d; 5 — d; 6 — c; 7 — d; 8 — d; 9 — b; 10 — c

References

1. Applegate, L. et al. (2003). *Corporate Information Strategy and Management: Text and Cases*. McGraw-Hill. New York.
2. Banham, R. (2002, August 1). CRM Rollouts: Mulligans Required. *CFO*, from http://www.cfo.com/article/1,5309,7514 I IC I 3,00.html
3. Basel Committee on Banking Supervision. *Sound Practices for the Management and Supervision of Operational Risk*. Bank for International Settlements, published online. Accessed July 2, 2002 http://www.bis.org/publ/bcbs86.htm
4. Blundon, W. (2003, April 11). How to make CRM work. *Computerworld*, from http://www.computerworld.com/softwaretopics/crm/story/0,10801,80251,00.html
5. Bolles, G.A. (2002, November 2). Can Your CRM Project Be Saved? *CIO Insight*, from http://www.cioinsight.com/article2/0,3959,686268,00.asp
6. Campbell, B. (2002, August). CRM How To: Close Encounters. *Oracle Magazine*, from http://www.oracle.com/oramag/profit/02-aug/index.html?p32crm_close.html
7. Close, W. (2002, October 30). CRM at Work: Eight Characteristics of CRM Winners. *CRM Project*, Vol. 3, from http://www.crmproject.com/documents.asp?d_ID=1433
8. COBIT Framework (1996). Information. Systems Audit & Control Foundation. Rolling Meadows, IL.
9. COBIT 3rd ed. (2000, July). *Audit Guidelines*: www.isaca.org/@member/ag.pdf
10. Conlon, G. (2003, July). Driving Sales. *CRM Magazine*, from http://www.destinationcrm.com/articles/default.asp?ArticleID=3227
11. Connell, J. (2001, September 7). Business goals should come before IT needs in a CRM project. *TechRepublic*, from http://techrepublic.com/article.jhtml?id=r00520010907 con02.htm
12. CRM Magazine (2003, June). A Slice of the Good Life: Introduction, from http://www.destinationcrm.com/articles/default.asp?ArticleID=3150

13. Federal Financial Institutions Examination Council. *FFIEC IS Examination Handbook.* 2 vols, published online 1996. Accessed July 2, 2002. <http://www.ncua.gov/ref/ffiec/ffiec_handbook.html>

14. Fuchs, G. (2003, June 20). Aspects of ROI. *DM Review*, from http://www.dmreview.com/editorial/dmdirect/dmdirect_article.cfm?EdID=6924

15. Gray, P. and J. Byun (2001, March). Customer Relationship Management. *Claremont Graduate School,* Claremont, CA.

16. Hass, B., M. Gorsage, and E. Barker (2002, November). Four CRM Strategies for Adapting to the Changing Economy. *CRM Magazine*, from http://www.destinationcrm.com/articles/default.asp?ArticleID=2662

17. IT Governance Institute and the IT Control Practices Committee of ISACA. (2001). *IT Control Practice Statement for the CobiT High-Level Control Objective PO-9 Assess Risks.* IT Governance Institute. Rolling Meadows, IL.

18. Lam, J. (2000, March 25). Enterprise-wide risk management and the role of the chief risk officer. *ERisk.* < http://www.erisk.com/portal/resources/archive/011_lamriskoff.PDF>

19. Mac Neela, A. and J. Disbrow. Research Note: (2003, May 19). Three Steps to Savings in Application Support. Gartner, Stamford, IL.

20. Mack, R. and N. Frey (2002, December 11). Gartner Group. *Six Building Blocks for Creating Real IT Strategies.* Gartner Group. R-17-63607.

21. Miccolis, J. *Enterprise Risk Management in the Financial Services Industry: From Concept to Management Process.* IRMI, published online (2000, November). Accessed August 28, 2002 <http://www.irmi.com/expert/articles/miccolis003.asp>

22. Miccolis, J. and C. Lee (2001, January). *Implementing Enterprise Risk Management: The Emerging Role of the Chief Risk Officer.* IRMI, published online. Accessed August 28, 2002 <http://test.www.irmi.com/expert/articles/miccolis006.asp>

23. Office of the Comptroller of the Currency (1998, February 4). OCC *Bulletin 98-3 Technology Risk Management.*

24. Office of the Comptroller of the Currency (1998, August 24). OCC *Bulletin 98-38 Technology Risk Management: PC Banking.*

25. Smiechewicz, W. (2001). Case Study: Implementing Enterprise Risk Management. *Institutional Investor Bank Accounting and Finance* 14(4): 21.

26. Stoner, J.A.F. (1982). *Management,* 2nd ed. Prentice Hall. Englewood Cliffs, NH.

27. United States General Accounting Office. *Information Security Risk Assessment Practices of Leading Organizations.* Washington, D.C.: U.S. GAO, November 1999. Accessed September 2, 2002. <http://www.gao.gov/special.pubs/ai00033.pdf>

28. Pearlson, K.E. (2001). *Management and Using Information Systems — A Strategic Approach.* John Wiley & Sons. New York.

29. Weber, R. (1999). *Information Systems Control and Audit.* Prentice Hall. Upper Saddle River, NJ.

30. Working Council for Chief Information Officers. Budget Watch: IT Spending Trends for 2003. Corporate Executive Board 2003.

Chapter 6
Planning and Controlling

Information Technology (IT) is measured both by the services it delivers and the cost of those services. IT organizations need to have defined standard services, service level agreements (SLAs), and metrics to track performance. IT is responsible for delivering services in support of the organization's objectives. The organization is responsible for determining the appropriate level of investment in technology as part of the overall business plan, and profit and loss goals. IT cannot plan or budget in a vacuum, but rather takes direction from the organization it supports to determine what and how much to budget. The drivers of cost for IT include the number of employees, customers, locations, and the type and scope of applications. An organization may decide it wants to move from a call center support desk to a Web-based application for customer self-service. This new application will drive the amount budgeted by the IT organization for the initial development costs and the on-going support costs. "After years of double-digit spending increases in IT, CFOs and their finance staff articulated the need to bring discipline to the management of technology funding, as well as the ever-present desire to improve yields on IT investments." (Working Council for Chief Financial Officers) This trend has increased the need for financial control over IT investments and operating budgets.

Governance Processes

Governance processes are needed to ensure the effective use of resources and alignment with business objectives (see Exhibit 1). This includes processes to initiate projects, design solutions, manage resources, provision services, procure products, and control financial investments. Investments in technology require significant resources in terms of people and dollars that need to be directed in support of the organization's objectives.

Demand Management

Projects need to be reviewed at the beginning of the project life cycle to make sure they have senior management support and a strong business case (see Exhibit 2). Researching technology solutions takes time and consumes

141

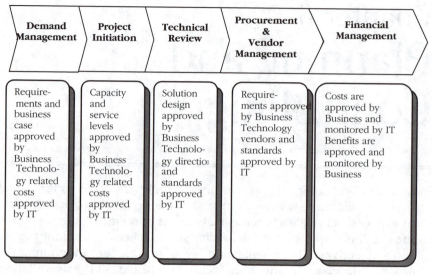

Demand Management	Project Initiation	Technical Review	Procurement & Vendor Management	Financial Management
Requirements and business case approved by Business Technology related costs approved by IT	Capacity and service levels approved by Business Technology related costs approved by IT	Solution design approved by Business Technology direction and standards approved by IT	Requirements approved by Business Technology vendors and standards approved by IT	Costs are approved by Business and monitored by IT Benefits are approved and monitored by Business

Exhibit 1. Business Objectives

Demand-Management Process

➤ Ensures that Project has a business justification

➤ Ensures that projects have a business and IT sponsor

➤ Provides a consistent approach to approving all projects

➤ Ensures that all major projects identify all costs to improve decision-making

➤ Provides a means to "weed out" non-essential projects

➤ Provides a means to control IT capacity and spending

Business or IT Initiates Project Estimates

Joint Requirement Planning and High-Level Solution Design

Business Case and Return on Investment

Cost and Savings Estimates from all Functions

Capital Appropriations Committee

Project Funding Approval and Project Initiation

Exhibit 2. Demand-Management Process

resources that could be devoted to providing business value. Managing the project evaluation process requires a governance process that manages IT demand. A demand-management process can help ensure that resources are devoted to projects that have a strong business case which has been approved by senior management. The demand-management process helps ensure that senior management has provided conceptual approval to the project to proceed through the initial requirements definition and conceptual design phases of the development life cycle. All projects should have an appropriate sponsor from senior management before evaluating the costs of implementing a solution to avoid wasted effort on a project that will not get approved.

Project Initiation

Once a project has been approved, it should undergo a project initiation process that determines the total cost and benefit of a project by defining high-level business requirements and a conceptual solution. Building a project estimate takes time and resources. It takes time from business users to develop requirements and a business case. It takes time from software developers to develop a solution and cost estimates. After a project has conceptual approval, the business users and software developers can work together to develop detailed requirements and project estimates that will be used in the final business case and form the basis for the project budget.

Technical Review

The technical solution needs to be evaluated before moving forward to ensure compliance with technology standards. A technical review process helps ensure that the right solution is selected, that it integrates with other components of technology (e.g., network), and that it can be supported with minimal investments in infrastructure. One way to control technology solutions is to implement a technical steering committee with representatives from the various technical disciplines and the enterprise architects. A technical steering committee provides a control mechanism for evaluating and approving new technology solutions. A formal product evaluation process assesses:

- Technical feasibility
- Alternative technologies
- Architecture
- In-house skill compatibility
- Existing environments/replacements
- Implementation, licensing, and cost considerations
- Research and analyst views
- Vendor company profile and financial viability

Procurement and Vendor Management

Once a technical solution has been selected, the procurement process helps ensure that the right terms and conditions are negotiated. One of the integral processes in any project is the procurement of services, hardware, and software (see Chapter 9). In most cases, organizations consider whether to make or buy systems. In either case, the procurement of external services is usually required. Depending on the extent of the service, a formal request for proposal (RFP) or other requirements document needs to be prepared to request competitive bids. The requirements should include service levels with contract penalties and tracking metrics/success criteria (see Exhibit 3).

Once a contract is signed, the vendor management process begins once a contract is signed and helps ensure that vendors live up to their commitments. This should include SLAs with measurable criteria and mechanisms to monitor actual performance to goal on a regular basis.

Strategic Sourcing and Vendor Management

Spending with third-party vendors on hardware, software, and services consumes 45 to 60 percent of an average IT budget (Working Council of Chief Information Systems Officers). This increases the risk of reliance on third parties for service delivery, but also provides an opportunity to drive costs down by negotiating purchases, contracts, and services. Using external resources provides flexibility and scalability by leveraging the expertise and staff of third-party vendors for temporary staffing needs for development projects. There is also an opportunity to drive development costs down by outsourcing programming to offshore vendors with mature development processes and inexpensive labor rates. There are a variety of sourcing models from internal delivery to full outsourcing. All models require internal processes to manage service levels, costs, and risk. Key criteria to making a decision to insource or outsource include strategy, competency, and risk (Da Rold).

Resource Management and Service Management

Resource management is the process used to effectively manage people by creating an environment for the training and development of skills and knowledge that lets individuals perform their software management and technical roles capably. The purpose is to match the right people with the right skills for the right projects.

Service management includes processes to manage third-party vendors as well as the process to deliver IT services to users. SLAs specifically state expectations between the service provider and receiver. This includes measurable criteria that can be monitored on a regular basis. "You can't manage what you don't measure" (Gartner). Measurement should include service response time, quality level, operating efficiency, pricing, escalation process, and penalties for noncompliance. Services need to be actively managed to ensure the organization receives the greatest value.

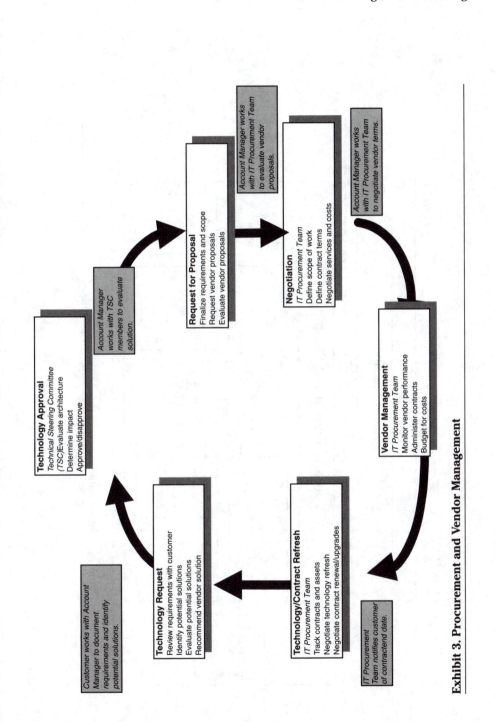

Exhibit 3. Procurement and Vendor Management

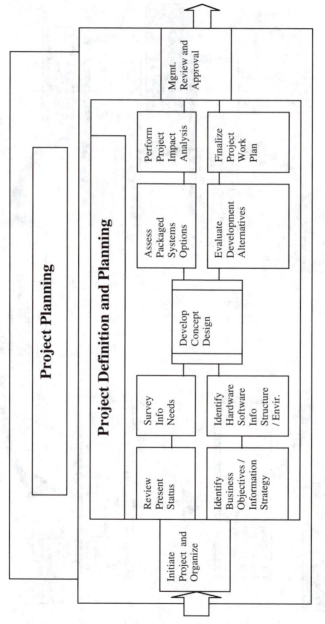

Exhibit 4. Project Planning Components

Financial Management and Budgeting

As more business processes have been converted to IT applications and the Internet infrastructure has grown, IT spending as a percentage of total spend has continued to increase. In an environment where there is an unlimited demand for technology and limited resources available, the IT spend has to be controlled and managed. IT spending is controlled by preparing an operating budget and a capital budget for new technology investments.

Operating Budget

Budgeting should begin with an understanding of the annual business plans, including business volume growth projections and new technology investments. Business demands can then be factored into staffing plans for application development that can be factored into infrastructure capacity plans. Capacity plans can then be translated into a budget for labor, hardware, software, etc. Once the budget is completed, it needs to be reviewed and approved by the organization responsible for funding. Funding of the IT budget can be achieved by gaining approval for a stand-alone cost-center budget, allocating costs to business units based on a business metric, or developing a chargeback process based on usage.

Chargeback. The method of chargeback is a controversial topic as it creates conflict between the user and IT. There is no single approach that can be identified as the best possible method and the cost of implementing various chargeback models has to be taken into consideration against the benefit. Theoretically, charging for services drives user behavior, as users have to pay for what they consume. The assumption is that if it is free, users will not be careful with the use of the resource. This would increase demand and IT costs.

Advantages

- Holds individuals accountable for the IT resources they consume
- Provides visibility into the cost of IT resources
- Encourages organizations to understand their IT costs as part of an overall profit and loss

Disadvantages. Charging for services allows the customer to see the total cost of a particular service that they may not have been aware of and do not understand. For example, the cost to deliver a desktop to a user includes the cost of the hardware itself, maintenance, software licensing, software imaging, testing, configuration and distribution, software support, help desk, desktop support, network cabling, network equipment, data circuits, server hardware, server software, backup hardware, shared file storage hardware, monitoring software, server support, facilities, management overhead, etc. This fully-loaded cost can create the misperception that IT costs are high compared to an individual buying a PC at the local technology super store and plugging it into the Internet. Users do not realize that there is a tremendous amount of infrastructure required when you consider enterprisewide applications, networking, security, etc.

Capital Budgeting

The application development budgeting process should prioritize the various business-sponsored projects as well as the technology refresh projects. Capital appropriations requests should include five major components:

- Business need
- Financial return and contingencies
- Alternatives considered
- Business issues and assumptions
- Legal, legislative, environment, and safety issues

Project cost estimates should include the total development costs and infrastructure costs to allow management to understand the impact on the operating budget and make an informed decision.

The Importance of Project Planning and Control in the Systems Development Life Cycle (SDLC)

The SDLC compartmentalizes the software development process into phases and tasks that enable the software engineer to proceed logically step-by-step through all activities of the life cycle of the software being developed. As such, the software engineers, as well as other individuals such as the IT auditor, should be involved in the development process and follow certain tasks having to do with each phase of the SDLC in an effort to deliver a complete software application. These phases range from the initial stages of project planning through rollout of the software. The SDLC identifies six generic phases. These phases are project planning, analysis, design, construction, test, and rollout. Each of these phases has certain tasks that need to be carried out.

The first of these phases is a conceptual phase in which a high-level perspective on the intended project and goals is determined. This phase is referred to as project planning. The planning stage provides a view of the proposed software product, uses this to establish the basic project structure, and evaluates feasibility and risks associated with the project. It should also describe appropriate management and technical approaches. The main purpose of this phase is to identify the software development requirements in an effort to address business objectives (see Exhibit 4).

There are several key tasks or activities that take place in project planning. The first of these tasks is project initiation. This task includes obtaining management approval for the development effort. This entails identifying the scope of the development, the outputs of the project, and the development of a project plan. Moreover, feasibility studies are performed to determine whether or not the proposed solution is cost effective. Software boundaries, goals, objectives, performance measures, and success factors are determined in the project initiation task of project planning.

Following project initiation is the review of present status. Ideally, this task can be combined with the feasibility study. In this task, existing software is evaluated in an effort to provide input for the development of new software. Such a review gives software engineers an idea of what the software will eventually function like and what environment it will operate in. Also, strengths and weakness of existing software applications are incorporated in this assessment. Data from this review can be added to the feasibility study performed in this stage. Moreover, this review also includes determining the cost effectiveness of the project. Return on investments (ROI) is taken into consideration in terms of the effort and money that will be put into the development of this new software. The cost/benefit analysis will also compare value delivered from the existing software applications to determine the added value realized from the development of the new software. The feasibility study should describe business considerations, reviews anticipated, benefits and costs, and recommend a course of action based on economic, technical, and operational factors.

Subsequent to reviewing the present status, the next task in project planning is identifying business objectives and information strategy. When encountering a new project, more often than not, the project is defined by the technology that the business plans on implementing. Instead, the opposite should happen. The business objective should define the technology to be implemented. For instance, a business may want to develop a new Web site without determining why or if one is actually needed. There could be many ways to develop a Web site. Many different tools and many different methods can be used to maintain the Web site. Just as the tools to develop vary, the impact on the organization can vary as well. Failing to define whether or not the development of a Web site is in line with business objectives can have adverse effects on the business. After investing a large amount of money into developing a Web site, a company may not realize as much ROI as anticipated. If the company had determined that having an online presence would not benefit the business, then time, effort, and money would have been saved. Many studies and authors of textbooks on systems development have repeatedly stated that defining business objectives is the key to understanding what you are trying to build and has an impact on how you are going to build it.

After it has been determined that the business objectives meet the software development directives, the conceptual design can be developed. The conceptual design is a high-level notional design of what the development environment will look like. This will include identifying the hardware and software environments needed for the development of the software. Moreover, this design will also incorporate business functions to be maintained by the new system, the software/system architecture, and interfaces with other systems. Essentially, developing a conceptual design is the estimate or vision of what it will be like to develop a piece of software with a customer. The conceptual design assists in providing the best guess toward a direction to take in development of the software. The conceptual design is used to determine an estimated level of effort before gathering formal user requirements.

When this is done, the next task under project planning is to evaluate development alternatives. In this task, other possible technical solutions are examined such as the decision to use commercial-off-the-shelf (COTS) products as opposed to developing custom software. Examples of other alternatives include contracting the project out to a third party or hiring consultants to come in and do the work. Alternatives will be considered and a cost/benefit analysis will be performed against each alternative. When every alternative has been evaluated, a decision will be made in regard to how the development will be performed.

The final and, arguably, the most significant task of project planning is development of the project work plan. Each phase of the SDLC has a deliverable that is a prerequisite for the subsequent phase. For the project planning phase, the deliverable is the project management plan, often referred to as the PMP or simply the project plan. The culmination of all the tasks in this phase results in the development of a project plan. The project plan should document the approach to be used and at a minimum include a discussion of methods, tools, tasks, resources, project schedules, and user inputs. It is a critical review point for the IT auditor.

Other important items included in the project plan are personnel assignments, cost estimates, risks, and organizational impacts associated with the project, and, of course, plans for future phases of development including the related cost estimates. It should also include the resources and the application plan and the constraints that must be adhered to during development. In an effort to gain the go-ahead from management, the project plan will incorporate everything that has been researched up to this point and will be presented to the customer and management. The project plan represents an agreement between the acquirer and developer on how the information system and its components will be produced.

Exhibit 5. Cost of Cyber-Crime in the United States (in Millions of U.S. Dollars)

	1997	1998	1999	2000	2001	2002
Theft of proprietary info.	20.05	33.55	42.50	66.71	151.23	170.83
Sabotage of data of networks	4.29	2.14	4.42	27.15	5.18	15.13
Telecom eavesdropping	1.18	0.56	0.77	0.99	0.88	6.02
System penetration by outsider	2.91	1.64	2.89	7.10	19.07	13.06
Insider abuse of Net access	1.00	3.72	7.58	27.98	35.00	50.10
Financial fraud	24.89	11.24	39.71	56.00	92.94	115.75
Denial of service	n/a	2.79	3.26	8.25	4.28	18.37
Spoofing	0.51	n/a	n/a	n/a	n/a	n/a
Virus	12.50	7.87	5.27	29.17	45.29	49.98
Unauthorized insider access	3.99	50.57	3.57	22.55	6.06	4.50
Telecom fraud	22.66	17.26	0.77	4.03	9.04	0.35
Active wiretapping	n/a	0.25	0.02	5.00	0.00	0.00
Laptop theft	6.13	5.25	13.04	10.40	8.85	11.77
Total Annual Loss	**100.11**	**136.82**	**123.78**	**265.34**	**377.82**	**455.85**

Source: 2002 CSI/FBI Computer Crime and Security Survey.

Project Planning and Control: E-Commerce Security as a Strategic and Structural Problem

An effective security management system should be made an integral part of an organization's business strategy. The development and management of security should support the core business of the organization. Security management, therefore, consists of guidelines that are based on the security practices that support the business strategy as a whole. These guidelines form the basic security policy to develop an information security management system. They are then monitored to assess their vulnerability to attack and misuse. The result is guarantee of data confidentiality, integrity, and availability both inside and outside the organization.

In E-commerce businesses, information security should be seen as a strategic asset and not as a cost. The increase in a company's E-commerce investment will automatically increase the system's vulnerability to attack; lack of security management measures and policies will result in a greater cost.

Exhibit 5 shows the results of a survey of the cost of cyber-crime in the United States, completed by the Computer Security Institute and the FBI.

The damage caused by cyber-crime has not only affected companies financially but could also damage their reputation.

151

Information Security Management Systems (ISMS)

An information security management consists of an infrastructure and a set of procedures to guarantee that confidentiality, integrity, and availability of data are met. Defining such a system is a very complicated task. Not only does the technology have to be secure but the security itself has to be maintained over time.

The complex nature of E-commerce companies' IT systems means that they are always at risk if they do not monitor internal and external security trends at all times. Financial damage caused by lack of security management can be very serious. Thus, E-commerce companies must implement an organizationally validated security management system.

The following steps need to be taken to identify and document the technical and organizational controls and their objectives:

- *Policy and procedures:* Define IT security policy and procedures.
- *Scope:* Define scope of ISMS. The environments should be defined in terms of an organization's characteristics, resources, technology, and location.
- *Risk assessment:* Identify dangers to resources, vulnerabilities, and impacts on the organization, and determine the degree of risk.
- *Risk areas:* Identify the risk areas to be managed based on the company's information security policy and the degree of protection required.
- *Controls:* Apply necessary and appropriate controls for implementation by the company and justify their selection.
- *Documentation:* Prepare documentation of the chosen technical and organizational measures/controls, their objectives, and the reason for choosing them.

The Planning and Control Approach to E-Commerce Security Management

The corporate approach to a high-level security management involves different aspects within the organization. These planning and control areas are strategic, organizational, technical, financial, and legal. Each of these aspects involves specific activities, which will be discussed in the following paragraphs.

Strategic Aspect

Once the organization has realized and accepted security as of strategic value, the approach to security begins with analyzing the strategic aspect. The strategic aspect involves the following activities:

- *Planning corporate objectives:* Define the company's E-commerce objectives clearly. This would help to form an effective security plan and give an adequate level of security for the E-commerce initiatives.

- *Defining budgets:* Define budgets according to the required security to meet agreed upon objectives.
- *Defining information security policy:* Develop a policy that includes the corporate E-commerce objectives, actions, and methods required to protect the information and make every employee in the company aware of this policy.

Organizational Aspect

The next aspect involves developing and implementing organizational measures to support the security related infrastructure. The organizational aspect involves the following activities:

- *Setting up security team of managers and technical personnel:* Assign responsibility for the development, management, and maintenance of the information security and corporate structure.
- *Defining responsibility:* Specify responsibilities for each member of the security team and everyone with operational involvement in E-commerce.
- *Drawing up training programs in technology and methods:* Train all staff in security related issues and the use of the security systems. Make sure all the staff has access to security information, policies, and technical documentation. Update staff responsible for systems and network security through classes and conferences on the latest technology in security.
- *Documenting information security procedures:* Document in detail all organizational procedures required to implement the security policy. Describe methods of doing every task such as analyzing and managing information risk, physical security of hardware/software resources, software management, anti-virus controls, backup, disaster recovery, secure use of information systems (IS), secure use of the Internet, secure use of e-mail, operating systems (OSs) security, Web server security, and incident management.
- *Application of security procedures:* Distribute security policies and procedures within the organization in the form of documentation, tools, and methods.
- *Compliance with security procedures:* Conduct periodic audits to assess the validity and adequacy of the policies. This will help the company to ensure that the systems comply with the written policies and procedures.

Technical Aspect

Once the organizational aspect has been created, an appropriate technology infrastructure can be developed that provides both physical and logical security for IS, as follows:

- IT infrastructure security
  - *Firewall:* It is a must for an E-commerce company to use firewall to protect the company's local networks against outside attacks.
  - *Access control:* The organization also needs to establish an access control system to information.
  - *Authentication:* Access authentication systems need to be established and implemented using technology according to the security classification assigned to data, systems, and networks.
  - *Cryptography:* The right cryptographic method needs to be chosen to protect transmitted information whether it is internal or external. This access must be secure both locally and remotely.
  - *Virus protection:* Anti-virus systems must be implemented to protect data and critical information.
  - *Backup:* Backup systems will be required in case of accidents that would result in data loss.
  - *Intrusion detection:* Intrusion detection tools are necessary to monitor critical networks, identify any attacks or intrusions, and take immediate corrective action.
  - *Operation systems and applications:* Guidelines on how to protect OSs and applications are necessary to prevent attacks.
  - *Database and file systems:* Appropriate security measures will be required to protect data and file systems against attacks.
  - *Vulnerability management:* Each element of the IT infrastructure will need to be systematically managed for vulnerability. Identify vulnerabilities from time to time by using software tools. Analyze and assess the risk. Lastly, and most important, take corrective action to resolve the problem found in the vulnerabilities analysis.
  - *Monitor threats:* IT staff needs to be alert at all times about current threats. New threats and attacks are reported each day in security alerts on Web sites and in newsgroups.

Financial Aspect

A financial evaluation must be carried out of the company resources requiring protection. Cost analysis should be carried out of the cost of the security solutions to be adopted. Remember that for an E-commerce company, no security would result in greater cost.

Legal Aspect

E-commerce organizations also need to consider the legal requirements in force in each country before the implementation of technical and organizational controls to ensure the security of company information. Security policies need to comply with national and international laws. For example, if you have operations in England, then the organization must comply with the Data Protection Act of 1998.

The above scenario represents the type of checkpoints IT auditors and management should typically look for in the planning and control phase. As covered later, it represents the action plan to accomplish the product and deliverable. The project plan is a controlling document with which deviations against the plan can be monitored, identified, and justified with supporting documentation.

Conclusion

IT resources represent a significant component of today's organizational cost. As such, they must be controlled and managed to deliver value. Organizations need processes in place to govern the initial investment, solution selection, sourcing decisions, service levels, costs of those services, and the business benefits from technology. Thus, it is imperative that an organization establish a formal SDLC, complete with defined phases of development and specified points for review and evaluation. The SDLC would also adequately utilize IT auditor benefits in the following ways:

- Auditor influence is significantly increased when there are formal procedures and guidelines identifying each phase in the SDLC and the extent of auditor involvement.
- Auditors will be able to review all relevant areas and phases of the SDLC and report independently to management the adherence to planned objectives and company procedures.
- Auditors can identify selected parts of the system and become involved in the technical aspects based upon their skills and abilities.

As mentioned earlier, the SDLC can be divided into categories involving the following steps showing the associated role of the auditor. Auditors can provide an evaluation of the methods and techniques applied in the SDLC. The completion of each step marks an audit control point that provides a stimulus for analyzing and sharing audit concerns with organization management and provides a timely auditing perspective on internal control decisions.

Audit Involvement in Planning and Analysis

Planning and analysis for the system is the first area of concern for the auditor. A business need exists as a reason for the development of each system. The business need is formulated into an objective, and a plan is developed to accomplish the objective.

Initial efforts consist primarily of organizing the audit and a review and evaluation of the development controls over the SDLC. The auditor function is predominately compliance. The SDLC is a control structure and the auditor assures project conformity to the control structure.

Conception of the Plan

Poor planning and lack of involvement of key people in a project plan are the main key causes of system implementation failure. A good plan will clarify the system objectives. User desires and misunderstandings can be highlighted and resolved early in the development process. Thus, conception of the plan involves the following activities:

- The auditor makes a determination of the reasonableness and merits of the project, potential for satisfying the business need, and consistent agreement with company policy and objectives. There should be periodic project evaluation points designed in the plan where the project can be altered or totally abandoned.
- The auditor identifies the existence of the communication of organizational goals from top management downward. The plan should therefore include methods for satisfying high-level organizational mandates as well as those of user management and specific users.
- Auditor requirements are introduced in a timely manner. There are no surprises from the auditor and the stigma of auditor hindrance to the project is minimized. The confidence of all parties to the SDLC is enhanced. Projects are often comprised of team members from different parts of the organization. Project coordinators must accomplish work without having direct line responsibility over team members. The auditor participating in system development will encounter this matrix organization structure and will be required to influence the project team members and users based on logic and force of evidence. The auditor must become a trusted and open contributor to influence the project plan and attain his objectives.

Project Organization

The auditor evaluates the appropriateness of the organizational structure to adequately support system development. Decisions as to the content of the project development team belong to user management. Often, this user involvement has been overlooked as management has abdicated its responsibilities to the IT specialist.

Project organization involves the following activities:

- Staff responsibilities should be clearly defined. In addition, all team members should have a general understanding of how the project will be conducted and the relationship of the project to the company business strategy as well as the desires of the particular user of the system.
- Methods of communication should be established and approved by all participants. The auditor should pay particular attention to communication with user management. It is essential that management develop an understanding of the various aspects of the project. This ensures that the project does not deviate from basic goals.

- The project team should expend considerable effort toward the analysis of the business problem and what the system is to produce without initially attempting to develop the design of the system (conventionally, the IT programmer mentality). The auditor should observe that the primary responsibility is not to develop a product but to satisfy the user. Often the user does not understand what is truly needed. Only by understanding the users' businesses, problems, goals, constraints, weaknesses, and strengths can the project team deliver the products users need.

Each of these areas is critical in the development of SDLC, security planning and control for E-commerce support, or any other IT component function. By using Control Objectives for Information and Related Technology (COBIT) or Committee of Sponsoring Organizations (COSO) as a checkpoint or guidance, the IT auditor or manager can determine if the planning and control structure is in place and working.

Review Questions

1. Why are governance processes needed in the IT area?
2. What processes can be implemented to enforce technology standards?
3. What is the process used to ensure that right terms and conditions are negotiated with vendors?
4. Why is the demand management process needed to control IT projects?
5. What is the purpose of measuring service levels?
6. In the SDLC example, what are the six phases? Why are these phases so important to planning and control?
7. What planning and control function does a feasibility study perform?
8. In project planning, why is the Project Plan an important planning and control document?
9. According to the CSI/FBI Computer Crime and Security Survey of 2002, what has been the total annual loss reported over the last six years? What is your assessment?
10. What are the planning and control areas when establishing security management?

Multiple Choice Questions

1. Governance processes are needed to:
   a. Ensure new technology is approved by the appropriate groups.
   b. Ensure projects are completed on time, on budget, and with full functionality.
   c. Ensure effective and efficient information technology operations.
   d. Ensure the effective use of resources and alignment with business objectives.

2. A technical review process helps ensure that:
   a. The project has included all the costs of the technology solution.
   b. The right solution is selected that integrates with other technology components.
   c. The current infrastructure is sufficient to support the new technology.
   d. The appropriate level of senior management approvals has been received.
3. Effective vendor management is based on:
   a. SLAs with contract penalties
   b. Clearly defined requirements in the RFP
   c. Measurable service levels and regular monitoring
   d. Strong negotiation skills of the procurement team
4. A technical steering committee provides:
   a. A control mechanism for evaluating and approving new technology solutions
   b. A framework for organizing and assessing software development and maintenance
   c. Leadership in advancing the practice of software engineering
   d. Guide in the acquisition, allocation, and management of information technology resources
5. Project capital budget requests should include:
   a. The business benefits of the proposed solution
   b. The financial impact on the operating budget
   c. The total development costs and infrastructure costs
   d. The project staffing and schedule
6. In the project initiation task of project planning, which of the following factors are determined:
   a. Software boundaries, goals, objectives, performance measures, and success factors
   b. Test criteria factors
   c. Call center factors
   d. Performance measures and success factors only
7. Identifying business objectives and information strategy is part of the:
   a. Construction phase
   b. Test and rollout phase
   c. Project planning phase
   d. None of the above
8. The project plan:
   a. Determines only the SLAs with contract penalties
   b. Clearly defines requirements in the RFP
   c. Documents the approach to be used and includes a discussion of methods, tools, tasks, resources, project schedules, and user inputs
   d. Focuses on the testing criteria only

9. Over the past six years the total annual loss due to cyber-crime has:
    a. Decreased 40 percent
    b. Quadrupled
    c. Increased 50 percent
    d. None of the above
10. The planning and control areas for security management are:
    a. Strategic and organizational
    b. Legal and technical
    c. Financial
    d. All of the above

Exercises

1. Create an outline of an IT strategic plan including the key components.
2. List the governance processes that control the use of IT resources.
3. List the areas assessed by a formal product evaluation process.
4. List and discuss the processes used to procure technology and manage vendors.
5. List and discuss the advantages and disadvantages of chargeback.

Answers to Multiple Choice Questions

1 — d; 2 — b; 3 — c; 4 — a; 5 — c; 6 — a; 7 — c; 8 — c; 9 — b; 10 — d

References

1. Cangemi, M.P. Issues and Comments, *Information Systems Control Journal*, Vol. 2, 2000.
2. Da Rold, C. and T. Berg. Sourcing Strategies: Relationship Models and Case Studies. Gartner R-18-9925. Gartner, Inc. February 7, 2003.
3. Drew, G.N. *Using SET for Secure Electronic Commerce.* Englewood Cliffs, NJ: Prentice Hall PTR, 1999.
4. Ford, W. and M.S. Baum. *Secure Electronic Commerce.* Englewood Cliffs, NJ: Prentice Hall PTR, 2001.
5. Health, J. Internet Security Risk and Solutions, accessed October 15, 2002; available: http://www.ecommercecentre.online.wa.gov.au/matrix/security.htm
6. IPNet 2001. The Basic of Business-to-Business E-Commerce Security, accessed October 15, 2002; available: http://www.ipnetsolutions.com
7. Sherif, M.H. *Protocols for Secure Electronic Commerce.* Boca Raton, FL: CRC Press, 2000.
8. Symantec Enterprise Solutions 2000. A Comprehensive Risk Management Guide, accessed October 15, 2002; available: http://enterprisesecurity.Symantec.com
9. Tivoli System, Inc. Managing e-Business Risks, accessed October 9, 2001; available: http://www_8.ibm.com/e-business
10. Unknown. A Security Management Framework for Online Services, accessed October 15, 2002; available: http://www.indtech.wa.gov.au/doit/publications.
11. Unknown. Risk Management and Security, accessed October 9, 2002; available: http://www.asisonline.org/ITSC/library/hout99lv.html
12. Working Council for Chief Financial Officers. Improving the Yield on Information Technology. Research Brief 2003.

13. Working Council for Chief Information Officers. Budget Watch: IT Spending Trends for 2003. Corporate Executive Board 2003.
14. Working Council for Chief Information Officers. Strategic Vendor Management and Outsourcing. Corporate Executive Board 2003.

Chapter 7
Project Management

IT project management refers to the processes and techniques used in the beginning-to-end development of software or other systems. Program management is one of the key controls that ensures delivery of projects on time, on budget, and with full functionality. The purpose of project management is to identify, establish, coordinate, and monitor activities, tasks, and resources for a project to produce the product or services meeting the requirements. Effectively controlling projects requires a disciplined approach to project initiation, execution, implementation, and post-implementation. This includes having the right people involved, following standard project management processes, and using a set of project management tools for effective execution. COBIT recognizes project management as a process that impacts both the effectiveness and efficiency of information systems and involves IT resources that include people, applications, technology, and operational facilities. It describes the controls over the IT process of managing projects that satisfy the organizational business requirement. It takes into consideration the following:

- Business management sponsorship of project
- Program management
- Project management capabilities
- User involvement
- Task breakdown, milestone definition, and phase approvals
- Allocation of responsibilities
- Rigorous tracking of milestones and deliverables
- Cost and manpower budgets, and balancing internal and external resources
- Quality assurance plans and methods
- Program and project risk assessments
- Transition from development to operations (COBIT)

Project Management Process

The project management process involves two basic elements:

- A project management life cycle (PMLC) that can be applied generically — but often tailored to fit the project size — to any project. This chapter focuses on project management processes.

161

- A development life cycle that addresses the specific needs of the application or other deliverable being considered. There can be many of these in use. A mainframe application may follow one type of system development life cycle (e.g., waterfall approach) and a distributed computing application another (e.g., iterative). This topic is discussed in more detail in Chapter 8.

Auditors must understand these two elements to synchronize the auditing needs to those of the project controls and schedules.

Project management has often been described as part art and part science. The part art side of it involves the human element, the experience project managers bring to the project, the support they can muster from their management, and, a critical point, how project managers relate to the client and the client's willingness to provide the right level of support to make the project succeed. As an auditor, the part art side of the equation is sometimes difficult to assess. Many times the relationship between the project manager and the client has not been built as a partnered approach. This can lead to loss of productivity by the project team and should be captured as a project risk as soon as recognized. The second part of the equation, the part science side, is somewhat easier to deal with. The auditor can quickly assess if the project manager has put in place the right project governance, a project management life cycle, and integrated these two elements with the appropriate system development life cycle. The IT industry analysts have made general and specific recommendations on why projects are successful. While not foolproof, the recommendations below are a good place to start. Other IT industry organizations have built their own Body of Knowledge to document acceptable practices. These documents should be understood prior to beginning an audit.

Gartner Group (Kapur) identifies what it calls "Project Management's 10 Best Practices":

1. All projects (other than IT infrastructure projects) must be owned by business units.
2. All projects must be launched in an orderly and rational fashion — i.e., ideas must go through appropriate due diligence before they become projects.
3. A consistent and stable system must be established to manage cross-project priorities.
4. Project success criteria is defined early and monitored throughout the project-development cycle.
5. The roles and responsibilities of sponsorship are well understood and taken seriously.
6. The rules and responsibilities for the management of projects are clearly defined and understood by all.

7. The process for assigning individuals to projects is rational, and assignments are reasonably stable.
8. Projects are expected to have comprehensive plans, realistic estimates, and viable schedules.
9. Project status is systematically, forthrightly, and consistently reported.
10. Projects are not considered complete until functionality is fully operational and benefits are realized.

Strategic and tactical initiatives are dependent upon effective, efficient, timely, and quality project initiation, planning, execution, management, and completion.

Project Management Body of Knowledge (PMBOK)™

The primary standards organization for project management is the Project Management Institute (PMI). The PMI developed project management standards published as the Project Management Body of Knowledge (PMBOK)™. This document represents the sum total of all knowledge within the project management profession.

Project Management Framework

A project management framework or a project management life cycle (PMLC) provides guidelines to project managers on the processes that must be followed to ensure successful project implementation. The PMLC is different from the software development life cycle (SDLC). The PMLC provides a structure around the SDLC being used to ensure that the project has the proper controls to succeed. It is focused on the project scope, schedule, and budget, and the SDLC is focused on the analysis, construction, and testing. As an additional clarification, the SDLC deals with developing an application, and the PMLC applies whether developing software, upgrading infrastructure, or moving an office. The SDLC is discussed in Chapter 8.

The PMLC begins where the project initiation process ends (i.e., after project approval). It provides an organized structure around every project and guidance for both new and experienced project managers as well as a reference point for auditors, executives, and business sponsors. The PMLC assists the project manager with project controls by ensuring that the proper mechanics and infrastructure are in place. It also provides a standard for the program management office or auditors to assess projects and project managers' compliance with the defined project management processes. The PMLC does reference the defined SDLC to ensure that the project team is following the company standard. One final point about the difference between the PMLC and the SDLC is that there may be multiple SDLCs in use at an organization, but there should only be one PMLC.

Exhibit 1. Tools for Preparing a Project Plan

Task	1st Quarter			2nd Quarter			3rd Quarter		
	Jan	Feb	Mar	Apr	May	Jun	Jul	Aug	Sep
Planning	■								
Analysis		■							
Design			■						
Construction				■	■	■			
Testing							■		
Implementation								■	■

Establishing and complying with the PMLC and the SDLC will provide the environment required for the project's success, but does not guarantee success. The project manager and the project team have the ultimate accountability for the success or failure of the project.

Project Management

Effective project management ensures that the project tasks are adequately defined, resources are available and used efficiently, quality is maintained, and the project is completed on time and within budget. Auditors can assist by reviewing the project plan to ensure that tasks and deliverables are defined in sufficient detail, resource requirements are defined, time estimates are reasonable, resources are available at the right time, and project progress is regularly reported.

Depending on the organization, project planning may be formal or informal. In either case, basic project management techniques should be used to ensure that the project is well planned and effectively monitored. There are many tools available to assist the project manager in preparing a project plan (see Exhibit 1).

Project management tools allow the user to define tasks, dependencies, and track progress. A project plan should include interim milestones and regular review of project deliverables. Examples of deliverables include:

Project Phase	Deliverable
Planning	Project plan
Analysis	User requirements
Design	Program specifications
Testing	Test objectives
Implementation	System documentation

Resource Management

There are many individual functions that are required to deliver a successful project. The business has to define the requirements, the application developers have to deliver the code, the quality assurance group and testers have to validate the code, and the infrastructure groups have to support the application. People with various skill sets may be assigned to a project team. Project assignments may be full-time or part-time. Team members may be transferred or matrixed to the project team. The challenge for the project manager is making sure that:

- An appropriate governance is in place.
- The right resources (money, people, facilities) are available at the right time.
- The project has a work breakdown structure that is sufficiently detailed to carry out the project.
- The project tasks are prioritized to prevent interference with other projects' due dates.
- The deliverables are produced in a timely fashion and are the right quality.
- Management (all levels) is being communicated with and sufficiently involved.
- The end user is involved and takes delivery of the agreed-to project results.

The program manager helps ensure that all groups are connected throughout the process.

Program Management versus Project Management

The business and technology environments drive the demand for multiple, complex programs and the need for enterprise-wide program coordination (see Exhibit 2). Because no development project is completed by just one function, program management is required to ensure success.

Project Planning

The objective of project planning is to be able to predict the project duration, resources required, and cost. The project manager should establish reasonable plans by estimating the work to be performed, establish commitments, and define the plan (see Exhibit 3).

Project Tracking and Oversight

An oversight and tracking process helps ensure that a project lives up to its commitments. As with anything, the best laid plans can fail due to poor execution. Controls need to be put in place to identify projects that are running astray. Oversight and tracking during all phases of the development

Exhibit 2. Program Management versus Project Management

Program Management
- Keeper of "The Vision"
- Source of "Leadership"
- Master communicator
- Deliverable and process focused
- Leadership discipline focused on delivering results
- Focused on the process to create a deliverable or subdeliverable
  (domain of methodology, process improvement)

Project Management
- Focused on a deliverable or set of deliverables
- Planning and control based on output and deliverables, milestones and schedule, resource consumption, quality attributes, and risk management
- Work management

---

process helps ensure that standard processes are followed and control is maintained. Oversight and tracking continues after the project is implemented to ensure that the business benefit promised when the project was approved is realized and the ongoing costs stay in line with the original estimates. The objective of project tracking and oversight is to provide adequate visibility into actual progress so that management can take effective actions when the project's performance deviates significantly from the plans. These requirements must be documented and controlled (see Exhibit 4).

Project Management Tools

Effective project management requires the use of a set of tools that enables plan development and tracking. There are many tools on the market for both standalone and enterprise-wide project management. There are several functions that can be automated and integrated by selecting an enterprise-level project management tool:

- Project task planning and tracking
- Resource and time tracking
- Labor hour tracking
- Time capture and billing
- Time reporting
- Project budgeting
- Project communication
- Project documentation

Enterprise-level project management tools allow for tracking multiple people working on multiple projects and aid in identifying cross-project

Exhibit 3. Project Planning

Goals

1. Estimates are documented.
2. Activities and commitments are planned and documented.
3. Impacted groups and individuals agree to their commitments.
4. Commitments.
5. Project manager is designated.
6. Project manager negotiates commitments and develops plan.
7. Policy and plan for managing planning activities are documented and followed.
8. Allocated requirements used as basis for planning.
9. Involvement of other entities is negotiated and documented.
10. Plans and estimates are reviewed by impacted groups following a documented plan.
11. Plans are reviewed by senior management.
12. Plans are managed and controlled following documented procedures and processes.
13. Changes are incorporated in a controlled and documented manner.
14. Both "version" and "change" control are utilized following a documented process.

Abilities

1. A documented and approved statement of work exists.
2. Statement of work includes scope, technical goals and objectives, standards, assigning responsibilities, goals, costs and schedule constraints, dependencies, resource constraints, and other constraints and goals.
3. Statement of work is reviewed by all involved parties.
4. Plan development responsibilities are assigned and documented.
5. Adequate resources and funding are provided.
6. Tools required for planning are provided.
7. Responsible parties are trained in estimating and planning functions.
8. Results documented.

Activities

1. Software engineering group participates in the project proposal activity.
2. Software project planning begins concurrently with overall project planning.
3. Software project planning group participates in overall project planning throughout the project life cycle.
4. All commitments, internal and external, are reviewed by senior management.
5. The project life cycle is identified and defined with predefined stages of manageable size.
6. Development and planning activities follow a documented process and procedure.
7. The project plan is documented.
8. The project plan includes purpose, scope, goals, and objectives.
9. The project plan identifies procedures, methods, and standards for developing and maintaining the plan.
10. The work products, size estimates, effort and cost estimates, use of computer resources, schedules, milestones, reviews, and risks are identified and described in the plan.
11. Facilities and support tools are identified.
12. Estimates for size, effort, cost, required computer resources, schedule, risks, and engineering facilities and support tools are developed using documented procedures.
13. Software planning data is recorded, managed, and controlled.

Exhibit 3. Project Planning (Continued)

Measurements

1. Measurements are devised and utilized to monitor management of all planning activities.

Verification

1. Management activities reviewed periodically with senior management.
2. Management activities reviewed periodically with project management.
3. Quality Assurance audits management of planning activities and reports the results.

Exhibit 4. Project Tracking and Oversight

Goals

1. Actual results and performance are tracked against the plans.
2. Corrective actions are taken and managed to closure when actual results and performance deviate significantly from the plans.
3. All changes to commitments are agreed to by affected groups or parties.

Commitments

1. Project manager is designated to be responsible for the project's activities and results.
2. Project follows a documented organizational policy for managing software projects that includes a documented software development plan.
3. Project manager is informed of project status and issues.
4. Corrective action is taken as necessary.
5. Affected groups are involved and agree with all changes to commitments.
6. Senior management reviews all changes to commitments.

Abilities

1. Software development plan is documented and approved.
2. Project manager explicitly assigns responsibilities for work products and activities.
3. Adequate resources and funding are provided for tracking and oversight activities.
4. Managers are trained.
5. First-line managers understand the technical aspects of the project.

Activities

1. A documented development plan is used for tracking project activities and communicating status.
2. Revisions to the plan are made using documented procedures.
3. Commitments and changes to commitments, either to individuals or groups, are reviewed with senior management.
4. Changes to commitments are communicated to all affected individuals and groups according to a documented procedure.
5. The size of work products or changes to work products are tracked and corrective action taken when necessary.
6. The effort and cost of the project are tracked and corrective action taken when necessary.

Exhibit 4. Project Tracking and Oversight (Continued)

7. Critical computer resources are tracked and corrective action taken when necessary.
8. Project schedule is tracked and corrective action taken when necessary.
9. Technical activities are tracked and corrective action taken when necessary.
10. Risks are tracked and corrective action taken when necessary.
11. Actual measurement and replanning data are recorded.
12. Periodic internal reviews to track technical progress, plans, performance, and issues against the plan are conducted.
13. Formal reviews are conducted at selected project milestones according to a documented procedure.

Measurements

1. Measurements are devised and utilized to monitor management of all tracking and oversight activities.

Verification

1. Management activities are reviewed periodically with senior management.
2. Management activities are reviewed periodically with project management.
3. Quality Assurance audits management of planning activities and reports the results.

---

dependencies and issues. They also integrate tasks, resources, and costs into a single repository.

If management has decided to use time and measurement tools (e.g., Project manager, CPM, PERT, GANTT charts), then the auditor must ensure that these tools are used according to management's specifications. The use of one of these tools during the system development life cycle (SDLC) can help the auditor and managers with the time management for the entire project. The auditor can use these charts to help get recommendations through and to show management how much time is needed to implement recommended controls at early and late stages of systems development.

Additional project management tools are task sheets used to allocate time (actual versus forecasted), assign personnel, and log the completion date and cost. In this way, the auditor and management can obtain a more detailed account of the time and money spent on a project and can track what is being worked on and what is finished. Future projects benefit most from these sheets because management can base future SDLC estimates on a history of times and costs (see Exhibit 5).

The auditor may often find it easier to enforce controls than standards (e.g., time sheets, CPM, PERT). Unfortunately, standard costs are more difficult to show than control costs. With a control cost, an exposure can be discovered and fixed, but the necessity for a standard is often overlooked because project phases are often completed without the standard.

Exhibit 5. Systems Design Task List

Project Name: _____ Customer: _____

Systems Manager Assigned: _____

Lead Analyst Assigned: _____

Start Date __/__/__

End Date __/__/__

Design Tasks	Corporate Priority	Worker-Days (Est)	Worker-Days (Act)	Completion Date (Est)	Completion Date (Act)	Cost (Est)	Cost (Act)	Risk H	Risk M	Risk L
Describe the business or system problem										
Describe the existing environment										
Describe the possible solutions										
Recommend a proposed solution										
Prepare a data flow diagram of the proposed solution										
Determine the educational requirements of users of the proposed system										
Estimate the staff needed to meet the educational requirements										
Define the legal considerations										
Estimate the staff needed to resolve the legal issues										
Define the security and audit requirements										
Prepare a general design and feasibility report										
Estimate the cost and time frame for the next sequential project phases										
Prepare an implementation strategy for the proposed solution										
Prepare a presentation to management on the proposed solution										
Give the presentation to management										
Obtain management approval to proceed to the next phase										
Totals:										

Footnotes:

Supervisor and review date: __/__/__

The Auditor's Role in the Project Management Process

The auditor's role in project management depends on the organization's culture, maturity of the information systems function, and philosophy of the auditing department. The objective of a project management audit is to provide an early identification of those issues that may hinder an on-time, within-budget implementation of an application that is controlled, documented, and able to be operated by an adequately trained user community. Auditing project management requires specific knowledge about the PMLC and development process. Understanding these allows the auditor to identify key areas that would benefit from independent verification. The scope of a project management audit can include an evaluation of the administrative controls over the project (e.g., feasibility results, staffing, budgeting, assignment of responsibilities, project plans, status reports, etc.) or an evaluation of specific deliverables to validate that the project is following established standards.

By becoming involved at strategic points, the auditor can ensure a project that is well controlled. The following list highlights some of the key tasks the auditor may perform during a project's development:

- Gain the support and cooperation of the users and IT professionals.
- Check project management tools for proper usage.
- Perform project reviews at the end of each phase.
- Assess readiness for implementation.
- Present findings to management.
- Maintain independence in order to remain objective.

These tasks can help provide early warning of project management issues.

To determine the level of involvement, the auditor should first complete a risk assessment of the project development process and determine the amount of time to be allocated to a particular project. Next, the auditor should develop an audit plan that includes a schedule for the specific review points tied to the project schedule. Finally, the auditor needs to communicate the scope of involvement and any findings to the project manager, users, and IT management. A summary of this entire process is shown in Exhibit 6. During the early phases, auditors do not determine how controls will be implemented, but they should establish the review points. This helps IT personnel to better understand audit objectives.

Audit Risk Assessment

Depending on the organization, auditors may not have enough time to be involved in all phases of every project. Project involvement will depend on the assessment of process risks and project risks (see Exhibit 7).

Exhibit 6. Summary of Auditor Involvement in Systems Development Phases

Planning	Development	Implementation and Operation
Conception of Plan • Project reasonableness • Adequate communications • Auditor becomes partner	**Project Coordination** • Initial control recommendations • Project budgeting • Time schedules	**System Testing** • Test logic of program • User involvement • All eventualities • Control test process
Project Organization • Project team structure • Define responsibilities • Understand the user	**General Design** • Functional specification relates to business goals • User approval of basic system • Use of structured programming techniques and best practices • Specification includes recommended controls • Insertion of embedded audit routines	**Installation** • Effects on user • Resolving user problems • Solidifying procedures • User training
Preliminary Requirements • Gathering user information • Group sessions • System concept documentation	**Detailed Design** • Design relates to functional specification • Completed documentation	**Documentation** • Allows system operation • Ease of update • Complete description of system • Hierarchical format
Feasibility Study • Formal management documentation • System justifications • Terminate or proceed	**Programming** • Structured programs • Analysis of code • Inclusion of controls	**System Conversion** • Parallel operation of old system • Retention of data • Control data integrity
Cost–Benefit Analysis • Economic feasibility • Management approvals	**Hardware and Software** • Selection process • Proper approvals • Adaptability of system	**Post-Implementation** • Solve original business problem • Perform control analysis • Ensure continued operation
		Maintenance • Control of changes • Testing system integrity

Exhibit 7. Audit Risk Assessment

Process Risks:
- Lack of strategic direction
- Lack of project management standards
- Lack of a formal project management process
- Negative organizational climate

Project Risks:
- Resource unavailability and budget
- Project complexity and magnitude
- Inexperienced staff
- Lack of end-user involvement
- Lack of management commitment

The level of risk may be a function of the size of the project, scope of organizational change, complexity of the system being developed, the number of people involved, and the importance of the project to the organization.

The scope of the audit involvement will depend on the maturity of project management in the organization. Audit involvement may be minimal if the IT group has a well-established PMLC and project office that perform regular oversight and tracking activities. In this case, the auditor may focus more on project-specific risks rather than on project management risks. For less mature organizations, the auditors may take on the role of oversight and tracking for the project.

Audit Plan

The audit plan will detail the objectives and the steps to fulfill the audit objectives. As in any audit, a project management audit will begin with a preliminary analysis of the control environment by reviewing existing standards and procedures. During the audit, these standards and procedures should be assessed for completeness and operational efficiency. The preliminary survey should identify the organization's strategy and the responsibilities for managing and controlling development.

Project Management Process Review

A project management process review would assess the adequacy of the control environment for managing projects. The review points listed represent checkpoints in the project management process. Auditors can use these checkpoints to determine both the status of the project's internal control system and the status of the development project itself. These reviews eliminate the necessity of devoting large amounts of audit

173

resources to the development effort. As long as the development process is well controlled, the need for audit involvement is minimized.

Project Management

Auditors may assist the project manager in identifying project risks and evaluating plans to mitigate and manage risks (e.g., training, devoted resources, management support, and end-user commitment). Auditing can provide management with an independent review of project deliverables (e.g., project charter, task list, schedule, budget). Auditing may also review the project task list and budget to verify that all project tasks are defined and all milestones have a deliverable.

During the planning phase the auditor can facilitate communication between functions and raise issues that may impact the quality or timeliness of the project. In a development project, resources from various departments need to come together to implement an automated process that may affect multiple user functions. Because of various audit projects, auditors develop an overall knowledge of the organization and establish relationships in multiple departments. These relationships are helpful in a development project for making sure information is flowing between the development team and other functionaries. Consider the following groups:

- Primary users
- Secondary users
- Vendors and consultants
- Programmers and analysts
- Database administrators
- Testing teams
- Computer operations
- Interfacing systems
- Implementation team
- Production support (i.e., maintenance programmers)

Verify that adequate resources are assigned responsibility for tasks and have the time to complete assignments. This includes development, computer operations, user, and support functions (e.g., help desk).

Communication

The first area to communicate is the auditor's role in the systems development project. It is very important to make sure that the management and development teams' expectations of the auditor's role are understood and communicated to all participants. In order to influence the systems development effort, the auditor must develop an open line of communication with both management and users. If a good relationship between these groups does not exist, information might be withheld from the auditor. This type of situation could prevent the auditor from doing the best job possible. In addition, the auditor must develop a good working relationship with the manager, the analysts, and the programmers. Although the auditor should cultivate good working relationships with all groups that have design responsibilities, he or she must remain independent.

Recommendations

Throughout the development project, the auditor will be making control recommendations. Depending on the organization's culture, these recommendations may need to be handled informally by reviewing designs with the project team or formally by presenting recommendations to the steering committee. In either case, the auditor must always consider the value of the control recommendation versus the cost of implementing the control. Also, recommendations should be specific, identifying the problem and not the symptom. This allows the proper controls to be implemented and tested.

Recommendations are often rejected because of a time and cost factor. Managers may sometimes feel that implementing an auditor's recommendations will put them behind schedule. The auditor must convince management that if the recommendations are not implemented, more time and money will be spent in the long run (see Exhibit 6). Informing management of the cost of implementing a control now rather than shutting down the system later to repair it or leaving possible exposures open will help convince management of the need to spend time and money now.

Example of Project Management Checkpoints and Tools in a Telecom Project

In telecommunication projects it is very hard to avoid new technology implementation. Often, the telecommunication manager has to avoid using new, cutting-edge technology for its own sake. The temptation to test new products almost always exists for telecommunications project managers. The success of a design is not measured by how many brand new products it involves; it is measured by how well it works and how well it meets a business need. A good network project manager has the ability to weigh the temptation to use cutting-edge technology against the desire for a solution that is mature, time-proven, and stable. It is extremely important that all members of a project realize that the benefits of using brand new technology may be outweighed by the risk associated with using an unproven product.

A telecommunications project manager should also consider organizational objectives when implementing a telecommunications project. A project's development should not occur in a vacuum, separated from the organizational directives and goals. It is also important for a project manager to convey to his or her team the impact the project will have on the current infrastructure and how its project supports corporate objectives.

While supporting corporate objectives, it is equally important that a project manager ensures that his or her project does not become excessively expensive. Respect for project and departmental budgets is definitely a must in telecommunications project management. Often, the greatest technical design in the world is useless if it costs too much money to implement. Managers must consider that as design progresses, for most projects the costs of hardware and software are not the only project-related costs. The costs of tangible equipment or applications are easily calculated. The tougher costs to identify are less tangible and include those associated with training, installation, configuration, and ongoing administration of the design product. Effective telecommunications project management requires identifying the fixed costs and the hidden costs up front, defining a total cost of ownership figure, and then aligning those figures with a design and a given budget.

Combating User Resistance to Telecommunications Project Implementation: Involve the User

In many telecommunication project implementations, a great deal of emphasis is placed on the technical aspects of the implementation and interfaces, and often the entity most affected by the project, the end user, is ignored. Essentially, consideration of the end users' needs should be a high priority in the project implementation process. If a telecommunications project manager neglects the consideration of user preferences and inclusion in the project design and execution processes, they run a high risk of user resistance. Often, if end users are not informed or knowledgeable about a project, they can become withdrawn and uncooperative. The diagram below graphically describes a good method to combat the user's propensity for rejecting a telecommunications project. Exhibit 8 shows that in the three major phases of a project — preparation, iterative design and development, and usage analysis — the user has been integrated. Everything from the user interface to project requirements and training requires input and involvement from the end user.

While all end-user interaction with a project team may not be perfect, certainly including users in the project implementation process can create a more seamless interaction.

Project Management Tools: Project Management Software

A significant element to a successful telecommunications project is the integration of powerful project management software tools. Project management software allows project managers to produce plans and forecasts in graphical, easy-to-read formats. They also help keep the entire project team on task. The complexity of today's projects virtually requires the use of high-powered tools such as Microsoft Project and Open Plan.

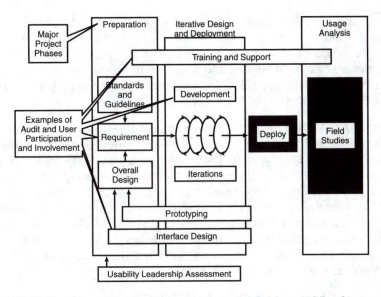

Exhibit 8. Methodology for Integrating Users in the Design and Deployment Phase of a Project

One of the project management tools is Microsoft's Project 2000. On the Project 2000 Web site Microsoft states that this product is a powerful, flexible tool designed to help a project manager manage a full range of projects. The project manager can schedule and closely track all tasks and use Microsoft Project Central, the Web-based companion to Microsoft Project 2000, to exchange project information with the project team and senior management. Some of the benefits and features of Microsoft Project 2000 include:

- *Personal Gantt chart:* Renders Gantt views like those in Microsoft Project to outline each team member's own tasks across multiple projects.
- *Task delegation:* Once assigned by the project manager, tasks may be delegated from team leaders to team members or from peer to peer. The delegation feature can also be disabled if desired.
- *View nonworking time:* Team members can report nonworking time to the project manager, such as vacation or sick leave, and also report work time that cannot be devoted to the project.
- *Database performance:* Gets improved performance and access to data with changes to the Microsoft Project database.
- *Network diagram:* Customizes network diagrams with new filtering and layout options, increased formatting features, and enhanced box styles (formerly the PERT chart).

Project 2000 is especially useful if an organization currently uses Microsoft Office because Project integrates very well with the Office 2000 suite. PowerPoint presentations and Word documents encompassing project charts can be designed and distributed throughout an organization with ease. Essentially, the telecommunications project manager's tasks are streamlined with the use of Microsoft Project 2000.

Another powerful project management tool is Open Plan, a software package designed by Welcom. Open Plan is an enterprise project management system that substantially improves an organization's ability to complete multiple projects on time and on budget. With multi-project analysis, critical path planning, and resource management, Open Plan offers the power and flexibility to serve the differing needs of businesses, resources, and project managers. Welcom also offers a product suite that is designed to be a totally integrated solution for enterprise project environments. The Welcom suite includes Cobra, a cost and earned value management tool, and WelcomHome, a Web-based project collaboration tool.

Features of Open Plan and the Welcom suite include:

- Integration with other existing enterprise applications
- Secure multi-user access to data
- Multi-project analysis
- Risk management tools
- Cost analysis applications

(*Source:* http://www.welcom.com)

The methods for project planning and implementation vary among different organizations. Each telecommunications project manager and team member develops and follows some type of schema for project management. For example, at ChevronTexaco, they implement projects based on CPDEP (pronounced "chip dip"), Chevron Process Development and Execution Planning. The details of this process are somewhat proprietary and privileged, so they cannot be disclosed. However, the methodology of CPDEP is very detailed and seeks to eliminate error and project failure by outlining, during each phase of project implementation, what is required and by whom.

A good planning and project management case example is Stanford University Information Technology Services department. The Network Transport Service project was a major component of a large infrastructure redesign that Stanford conducted, beginning in 1996. The project documentation is very thorough. The scope of the project includes history of SUNet, Stanford University's network, and the problems that were associated with it. An especially attractive element of the project plan is that it outlines what elements would make the project successful, including management commitment, organizational change, and staff training. The goals of the Network Transport Service project include:

- Ensuring that the SUNet planning and design process is accountable to the requirements of all areas of campus
- Improving the security, reliability, and functionality of the basic data transport infrastructure at Stanford
- Providing methods to evaluate whether the operational requirements established for the transport system are being met

Finally, the project documentation is complete with a Gantt chart that displays due dates for each element of the project, which spanned over two years.

Telecommunications project management requires a great deal of consideration to reach success. The design and budgeting elements must coincide well with business objectives and user needs. The costs and relevance of a project must also be thoroughly considered. Furthermore, a telecommunications project manager may look towards the future study and implementation of technology such as voice-over IP (VoIP). VoIP can significantly reduce telecommunications costs because it allows organizations to use networking equipment to route data packets as well as voice packets, eliminating the need for separate PBX phone systems. Also, Microsoft's .NET technology may also be a practical future implementation for project managers. The .NET allows organizations to not only securely communicate over long distances but interorganizational transactions to occur automatically via computer. The telecommunications project manager now has immense options when designing project implementation. In the present business environment, and with the current telecommunications technology available, the telecommunications manager most assuredly should take into account both the organizational and global implications of his or her project.

Conclusion

Developing new systems can be a costly and time-consuming endeavor. A well-controlled environment with an overall strategy, standards, policies, and procedures helps ensure the success of development efforts. There are many processes that need to be well controlled to ensure the overall success of a project and system. There are many opportunities for auditor involvement in the development process. Auditors need to develop the skills and relationships to work with the development team to ensure that controls are built into the system. Auditors can assist organizations by reviewing the project management environment — including tools, evaluating standards for project management, monitoring project progress, and evaluating phases in the project.

Review Questions

1. What are the main components of a project plan?
2. What is the intent of the planning phase?
3. When auditors do not have enough time to be involved in every phase of the development project, how do they minimize the project's risk?
4. What are the key causes of system implementation failure?
5. What skills must auditors have in order to provide a quality audit on a systems development project?

Multiple Choice Questions

1. The project management life cycle:
   a. Provides a structure for defining requirements and developing applications
   b. Is focused on project scope, schedule, and budget
   c. Is focused on the analysis, construction, and testing of applications
   d. Provides a structure for evaluating IT investments
2. Effective project management ensures that:
   a. Processes are explicitly defined, managed, measured, controlled, and effective.
   b. Applications are designed, developed, and implemented.
   c. Project tasks are defined, resources are available, and completed on time and within budget.
   d. The project has included all the costs of the technology solution.
3. During the planning phase, the auditor can:
   a. Review project deliverables to identify control weaknesses
   b. Review project management processes for appropriateness
   c. Facilitate communication between the project team and senior management
   d. Facilitate communication between functions and raise issues
4. A project management process review would assess:
   a. The adequacy of the control environment for managing projects
   b. The right solution is selected that integrates with other technology components
   c. Clearly defined requirements in the Request for Proposal
   d. Ensure projects are completed on time, on budget, and with full functionality
5. Project management tools allow the user to:
   a. Track metrics for measuring third-party vendors
   b. Help determine which vendor products to use
   c. Provide a process for governing investments in information technology
   d. Define tasks, dependencies, and track progress

6. Key tasks an IT auditor should perform:
   a. Check project management tools for proper usage.
   b. Assess readiness for implementation.
   c. Maintain independence in order to remain objective.
   d. All of the above.
7. Which of the following is not a process risk?
   a. Processes are explicitly defined, managed, measured, controlled, and effective.
   b. Lack of strategic direction.
   c. Lack of project management standards.
   d. Negative organizational climate.
8. Which of the following is not a project risk?
   a. Review project deliverables to identify control weaknesses
   b. Inexperienced staff
   c. Lack of management commitment
   d. Project complexity and magnitude
9. One of the biggest obstacles in implementation is:
   a. The adequacy of the control environment for managing projects
   b. User resistance
   c. Clearly defined requirements in the request for proposal
   d. Ensuring projects are staffed
10. Project management tools could be:
    a. Project 2000
    b. Open Plan
    c. CPM or PERT
    d. All of the above

Exercises

1. List and describe key tasks that should be included in a project plan. Consider phases in the development process as well as support tasks that are needed for implementation and maintenance.
2. List and describe the best practices in project management.
3. List and describe possible review areas that auditors may be involved in during the project life cycle.
4. List and describe controls over the project management process.
5. Develop an audit program for auditing the project management process.

Answers to Multiple Choice Questions

1 — b; 2 — c; 3 — d; 4 — a; 5 — d; 6 — d; 7 — a; 8 — a; 9 — b; 10 — d

References

1. Allen, S., F. Gallegos, and D. Manson. *Audit Concerns for End-User Computing and Application Development*. EDP Auditing. Auerbach Publishers, Boca Raton, FL, 1996.
2. Audit Guidelines: CobiT 3RD ed., p. 78. www.isaca.org/@member/ag.pdf
3. Brown, C.V. and H. Topi, Eds. *IS Management Handbook*. CRC Press, Boca Raton, FL, 2000.
4. Dow, D.P. and F. Gallegos. *Key Review Points for SDLC Audits*. EDP Auditing. Auerbach Publishers, Boca Raton, FL, 1987.
5. Dow, D.P. and F. Gallegos. *Auditing Systems Maintenance: A How-to Approach*. EDP Auditing. Auerbach Publishers, Boca Raton, FL, 1986.
6. Gallegos, F. *CIS Auditors Role in Systems Development*. EDP Auditing. Auerbach Publishers, Boca Raton, FL, 1998.
7. Gallegos, F. *Auditing DSS: Review Points for IS Managers*. EDP Auditing. Auerbach Publishers, Boca Raton, FL, 1998.
8. Gallegos, F. *Software Tools and Techniques*. EDP Auditing. Auerbach Publishers, Boca Raton, FL, 1985.
9. Gallegos F. and S. Schneider. *The Audit Process and the Information Center*. EDP Auditing. Auerbach Publishers, Boca Raton, FL, 1988.
10. Gartner Group. *Managing Distributed Computing: Stabilizing an Exploding Universe*. 1995 Western Region Briefing. Universal City, CA, April 18, 1995.
11. Gaston, S.J. *Managing and Controlling Small Computer Systems Including LANs*. The Canadian Institute of Chartered Accountants 1992.
12. Gaston, S.J. *Audit of Small Computer Systems Including LANs*. The Canadian Institute of Chartered Accountants 1993.
13. Kapur, G.K. *Project Management — 10 Key Practices*. Gartner Research Report. January 30, 1999.
14. King, D. *Current Practices in Software Development*. Yourdon Press, New York, 1984.
15. Lientz, B.P., E.B. Swanson, and G.E. Tompkins. Characteristics of application software maintenance. *Communications of the ACM* 21(6): 466–471, 1978.
16. Lientz, B.P. and E.B. Swanson. Problems in application software maintenance. *Communications of the ACM* 24(11): 763–769, 1981.
17. Swanson, E.B. and C.M. Beath. Departmentalization in software development and maintenance. *Communications of the ACM* 33(6): 658–667, 1990.
18. Williams, P. *Getting a Project Done on Time*. American Management Association 1996.

Chapter 8
Quality Management

Organizations are constantly building, replacing, and maintaining information systems. There are many different approaches to systems development, but the most successful systems follow a well-defined development methodology. The success of a system development project is dependent on the success of key processes: project management, analysis, design, testing, and implementation. Because development efforts can be costly, organizations are recognizing the need to build well-controlled, quality systems. Information systems process information that is integral to the financial stability and profitability of organizations. Therefore, these systems must be built with adequate internal controls to ensure the completeness and accuracy of transaction processing. The CobiT 11th process (PO11) in the Planning and Organization Domain emphasizes quality management and lists 19 control objectives (see Exhibit 1).

CobiT recognizes quality management as a process that impacts the effectiveness, efficiency, integrity, and availability of information systems and involves IT resources that include people, applications, technology, and facilities. It describes the controls over the IT process of managing quality that satisfies the business requirement. It takes into consideration the following:

- Establishment of a quality culture
- Quality plans
- Quality assurance responsibilities
- Quality control practices
- System development life-cycle methodology
- Program and system testing and documentation
- Quality assurance reviews and reporting
- Training and involvement of end-user and quality assurance personnel
- Development of a quality assurance knowledge base
- Benchmarking against industry norms

Software Development Standards

In support of quality management is extensive research into the processes that drive maturity. CMM is at the foundation of CobiT and other process models that identify "best practices" in controlling the delivery of

Exhibit 1. Planning and Organization Domain

PO 11 Manage Quality

Control Objectives
1. General Quality Plan
2. Quality Assurance Approach
3. Quality Assurance Planning
4. Quality Assurance Review of Adherence to IT Standards and Procedures
5. Systems Development Life-Cycle Methodology
6. Systems Development Life-Cycle Methodology for Major Changes to Existing Technology
7. Updating of the Systems Development Life-Cycle Methodology
8. Coordination and Communication
9. Acquisition and Maintenance Framework for the Technology Infrastructure
10. Third-Party Implementor Relationship
11. Program Documentation Standards
12. Program Testing Standards
13. System Testing Standards
14. Parallel/Pilot Testing
15. System Testing Documentation
16. Quality Assurance Evaluation of Adherence to Development Standards
17. Quality Assurance Review of the Achievement of IT Objectives
18. Quality Metrics
19. Reports of Quality Assurance Reviews

IT services. There are two key standards that govern the system development process (Brotbeck). These include:

- Capability Maturity Model® (CMM) for Software (Software Engineering Institute)
- 9000 Quality Management and Quality Assurance Standards (International Organization for Standardization [ISO])

Capability Maturity Model (CMM)

The Capability Maturity Model provides a framework for organizing and assessing the maturity level of information technology processes for software development and maintenance. Software process maturity is the extent to which a specific process is explicitly defined, managed, measured, controlled, and effective. Maturity implies a potential for growth in capability and indicates both the richness of an organization's software process and the consistency with which it is applied in projects throughout the organization. CMM was developed by the Software Engineering Institute (SEI), a research and development center established in December 1984 by the U.S. Department of Defense and operated as an extension of Carnegie Mellon University in Pittsburgh. CMM provides a model for

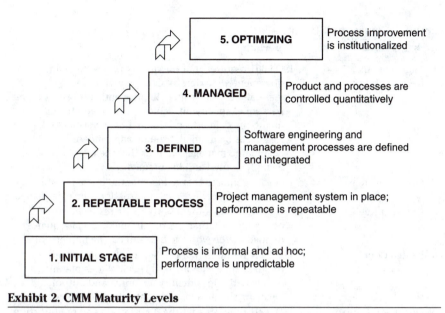

Exhibit 2. CMM Maturity Levels

assessing the level of process maturity within an organization. With CMM, maturity is defined in one of five levels (see Exhibit 2).

The specific practices to be executed in each key process area evolve as the organization achieves higher levels of process maturity. The U.S. Department of Defense established the Software Engineering Institute to advance the practice of software development with the goal of having quality systems produced on schedule and within budget — a critical need for the U.S. Defense industry. SEI's mission was to provide leadership in advancing the practice of software engineering so as to improve the overall quality of defence systems. And, although CMM was initially created for defence industry use, the model was found to be applicable to companies in the private sector that also depended on software development. The SEI combined two other source models with software maturity levels — the Electronic Industries Alliance Interim Standard and the Integrated Product Development Capability Maturity Model — into a single improvement framework, the CMMI, for use by organizations pursuing enterprisewide process improvement. The CMMI model defines two representations (staged and continuous) and four models (systems engineering, software engineering, integrated product and process development, and supplier sourcing).

The International Standards of Organizations (ISO) 9000 series of standards is a set of documents dealing with quality systems that can be used for external quality assurance purposes. They specify quality system requirements for use where a contract between two parties requires the demonstration of a supplier's capability to design and supply a product (see Exhibit 3 and Exhibit 4). The standard ISO 9001, Model for Quality

Exhibit 3. Clauses in ISO 9001

ISO 9001 Clause	Description
1. Management Responsibility	ISO 9001 requires that the quality policy be defined, documented, understood, implemented, and maintained; that responsibilities and authorities for all personnel specifying, achieving, and monitoring quality be defined; and that in-house verification resources be defined, trained, and funded. A designated manager ensures that the quality program is implemented and maintained.
2. Quality System	ISO 9001 requires that a documented quality system, including procedures and instructions, be established.
3. Contract Review	ISO 9001 requires that contracts be reviewed to determine whether the requirements are adequately defined, agree with the bid, and can be implemented.
4. Design Control	ISO 9001 requires that procedures to control and verify the design be established. This includes planning design activities, identifying inputs and outputs, verifying the design, and controlling design changes.
5. Document Control	ISO 9001 requires that the distribution and modification of documents be controlled.
6. Purchasing	ISO 9001 requires that purchased products conform to their specified requirements. This includes the assessment of potential subcontractors and verification of purchased products.
7. Purchaser-Supplied Product	ISO 9001 requires that any purchaser-supplied material be verified and maintained.
8. Product Identification and Traceability	ISO 9001 requires that the product be identified and traceable during all stages of production, delivery, and installation.
9. Process Control	ISO 9001 requires that production processes be defined and planned. This includes carrying out production under controlled conditions, according to documented instructions. Special processes that cannot be fully verified after the fact are continuously monitored and controlled.
10. Inspection and Testing	ISO 9001 requires that incoming materials be inspected or verified before use and that process inspection and testing be performed. Final inspection and testing are performed prior to release of finished product. Records of inspection and testing are kept.
11. Inspection, Measuring, and Test Equipment	ISO 9001 requires that equipment used to demonstrate conformance be controlled, calibrated, and maintained. When test hardware or software is used, it is checked before use and rechecked at prescribed intervals.
12. Inspection and Test Status	ISO 9001 requires that the status of inspections and tests be maintained for items as they progress through various processing steps.

Exhibit 3. Clauses in ISO 9001 (Continued)

ISO 9001 Clause	Description
13. Control of Nonconforming Product	ISO 9001 requires that nonconforming product be controlled to prevent inadvertent use or installation.
14. Corrective Action	ISO 9001 requires that the causes of nonconforming product be identified. Potential causes of nonconforming product are eliminated; procedures are changed resulting from corrective action.
15. Handling, Storage, Packaging, and Delivery	ISO 9001 requires that procedures for handling, storage, packaging, and delivery be established and maintained.
16. Quality Records	ISO 9001 requires that quality records be collected, maintained, and dispositioned.
17. Internal Quality Audits	ISO 9001 requires that audits be planned and performed. The results of audits are communicated to management, and any deficiencies found are corrected.
18. Training	ISO 9001 requires that training needs be identified and that training be provided, as selected tasks may require qualified personnel. Records of training are maintained.
19. Servicing	ISO 9001 requires that servicing activities be performed as specified.
20. Statistical Techniques	ISO 9001 states that, where appropriate, adequate statistical techniques are identified and used to verify the acceptability of process capability and product characteristics.

Assurance in Design/Development, Production, Installation, and Servicing, is for use when conformance to specified requirements is to be assured by the supplier during several stages. In the ISO 9000 series, it is the standard that is pertinent to software development and maintenance (Paulk).

The specific ISO standard that provides for assessing software development processes is the Software Process Improvement and Capability Determination (ISO 15504). The objective is to assist the software industry in making significant gains in productivity and quality, while reducing the risk associated with large software projects and purchases. The standard ISO/IEC TR 15504 provides a comprehensive reference framework for the assessment of software processes. The model is designed as a baseline to perform process capability determination in an organization. It was developed under the auspices of the ISO with the intention to harmonize the key concepts contained in the SEI's CMM, BOOTSTRAP, ISO 12207, and TickIT. This framework can be used by organizations involved in planning, managing, monitoring, controlling, and improving the acquisition, supply, development, operation, evolution, and support of software.

Exhibit 4. Overall Product Quality Defects Found

Requirements Gathering and Analysis/Architectural Design	Coding/Unit Test	Integration and Component/RAI SE System Test	Early Customer Feedback/Beta Test Programs	Post-Product Release
1X	5X	10X	15X	30X

	Where Errors Are Found				
Where Errors Are Introduced	**Requirements Gathering and Analysis/Architectural Design**	**Coding/Unit Test**	**Intergation and Component/RAISE System Test**	**Early Customer Feedback/Beta Test Programs**	**Post-Product Release**	**Total**
Requirements Gathering and Analysis/Architectural Design	3.5	10.5	35	6	15	70
Coding/Unit Test		6	9	2	3	20
Integration and Component/ RAISE System Test			6.5	1	2.5	10
Total	3.5	16.5	50.5	9	20.5	100%

Note: X is a normalized unit of cost and can be expressed in terms of person-hours, dollars, etc.

Source: From The Economic Impacts of Inadequate Infrastructure for Software Testing — Final Report, prepared by RTI for NIST. May 2002. With permission.

How Maturity Correlates to Quality

Identifying the relationship between maturity and quality involves looking at facts. Significant data supports maturity that brings numerous benefits, such as:

- Increased predictability
- Reduced defects
- Reduced rework
- Increased delivery on schedule
- Reduced risk of exceeding cost/budget
- Increased metrics and measurement
- Increased process improvement

Ultimately, maturity enables a company to achieve quality by eliminating steps that introduce error or by introducing steps to eliminate error. Although many studies can be cited, one of the most comprehensive in the area of software development is from the Boeing Corporation. They have maintained detailed statistics on their software development from 1991 to 1999, while conducting 175 maturity assessments. A summary of benefits they identified are shown in Exhibit 5.

Raytheon's Example

Results from several companies have been released to the public. One of the early companies to address a maturity initiative was Raytheon. Their initiative began in 1988 and, seven years later, results were released.

In addition to numerous companies that have addressed maturity initiatives, third-party reviews have also been conducted and made available. Several years ago, Carnegie Mellon University conducted a study of 13 entities that had ongoing maturity initiatives. They included:

- Motorola
- Northrop
- Schlumberger
- Bull HN
- Texas Instruments
- GTE Government Systems
- Hewlett Packard
- Siemens
- U.S. Air Force
- Hughes Aircraft
- U.S. Navy
- Loral Federal Systems
- Lockheed

Exhibit 5. Boeing Corporation's Maturity Assessments

Benefits	Level 1 to 2	Level 2 to 3	Level 3 to 4
Reduce Defects	12%	40%	85%
Reduce Time	10%	38%	63%
Reduce Cost	8%	35%	75%
Schedule Variances	145%	24%	25%

Other benefits include:
• Focused investments make significant benefits possible.
  Investments are focused on those areas that can be expected to
  deliver the best possible results.
• Strong correlation between practice and performance: Studies have
  shown that the adoption of Best Practices correlates strongly with
  the achievement of highest levels of performance.

Exhibit 6. Improvements

Category Improvements	Average Results	Results Range
Productivity (gain)	35%	9%–67%
Early defect detection (gain)	22%	6%–25%
Time to market (reduction)	19%	15%–23%
Post-release defects (reduction)	39%	10%–94%
Business value (savings/costs)	5:1	4:1–8.8:1

Source: Paulk, M., Carnegie Mellon University, 1994. With permission.

Results from the university's study were documented (see Exhibit 6) regarding how the maturity initiatives were contributing to key quality measurements within each organization.

After the Carnegie Mellon study, Capers Jones, a well-known research analyst on quality, conducted a review to determine achievements in quality at various CMM maturity levels (see Exhibit 7).

Approaches to Software Development

There are various approaches to software development: traditional information systems development, purchasing and modifying a packaged system (discussed in Chapter 9), prototyping and rapid application development, and less formal end-user development. Although each approach is unique, they all have similar steps that must be completed. For example, each approach will have to define user requirements, design programs to fulfill those requirements, verify that programs work as intended, and implement the system. Auditors need to understand the different approaches, the risks associated with a particular approach, and help ensure that all the necessary components are included in the development process.

Exhibit 7. Defects

	Defects per Function Point	Defect Removal Efficiency	Delivered Defects per Function Point
Industry Average	5.25	83%	0.89
CMM Level 2	4	90%	0.40
CMM Level 3	3	85%	0.15
Best in Class	2.75	97%	0.08
CMM Level 4	2	97%	0.06
CMM Level 5	1	99%	0.01

Source: Capers Jones, 1999. With permission.

Software Development Process

A formal systems development process provides an environment that is conducive to successful systems development. This includes: (1) an information systems strategy that guides developers in building systems that are consistent with the organization's technical and operational goals, (2) standards that guide in the selection of hardware, software, and developing new systems, (3) policies and procedures that support the organization's goals and objectives, and (4) project management that ensures projects are completed on time and within budget. Auditors can assist organizations by reviewing the systems development process to ensure that developed systems comply with the organization's strategy and standards.

Software Development Phases

The systems development process can be broken down into four phases:

- Planning
- Development
- Implementation
- Maintenance

The planning phase sets the stage for the success of the development effort. If not done properly, the budget and schedule may not be sufficient, the problem may not be adequately defined, the final project may not solve the business problem, and the right people may not be involved. The planning phase of systems development includes the following activities:

- *Needs analysis:* a study to determine whether a new system should be developed
- *Current system review:* a study of the current system to identify existing processes and procedures that will continue in the new system

- *Conceptual design:* preparation of the proposed system flow and other information illustrating how the new system will operate
- *Equipment requirements:* hardware configuration needed to process and use the new systems (e.g., processing speed, storage space, and transmission media)
- *Cost/benefit analysis:* detailed financial analysis of the cost to develop and operate the new system, the savings or additional expense, and the return on investment
- *Project team formation:* identify people from programming, user departments, and support departments to develop and implement the new system
- *Project plan:* an overall project plan with defined tasks and deliverables to monitor actual results and ensure successful progress

Auditing can be involved in the planning process to develop an understanding of the proposed system, make sure time is built into the schedule to adequately define controls, and verify that all the right people are involved.

There is a definite correlation between a well-managed systems development process and a successful system. The use of a proven system development methodology increases the probability that the system's internal controls will be effective and reliable. As discussed under the traditional development approach, systems development includes the following phases:

- *Analysis:* Define what is required of the new system.
- *Design:* Define how to build the new system to satisfy the requirements.
- *Construction:* Build the new system using the design information.
- *Testing:* Verify that the completed system meets the users' needs and functions without fault.
- *Implementation:* Deliver the completed system to the end users; obtain satisfactory feedback.
- *Maintenance:* Modify the system as needed to correct problems or meet changing needs.

Auditing can review the development process to ensure the software is designed with user requirements documented, that management approves the design, and that the application is tested before implementation. An additional focus is ensuring that the end user is able to use the system based on a combination of skills and supporting documentation.

Analysis. In the analysis phase, the users and systems analysts define the system requirements in terms that can be measured. These same measurable terms will be the basis for the functional testing that will occur later in the development process. The functionality of the existing system is matched with the new functionality and the requirements are defined and validated with the user so that they can become the basis for the design phase.

Design. In the design phase, the systems analyst defines all system interfaces, reporting, and screen layouts, and specific program logic. At this time, controls should also be defined for input points and processing. Screen layouts, controls, and reports should be reviewed and approved by the user before moving on to the next phase. Programmers will use the detailed specifications from the design phase for the construction phase.

Construction. The construction phase is complete once the programmer completes the program construction and validates the construction through individual unit testing. The program is tested for both syntax and logic flow. All paths are exercised to ensure error routines work and the program terminates processing normally.

Testing. During the testing phase, the system is tested to verify that it works as intended and meets design specifications. An overall testing strategy should be developed to define the individual test events, roles and responsibilities, test environment, problem reporting and tracking, and test deliverables. Although each project may define different test events, in general, test events include unit testing, integration testing, technical testing, functional testing, and acceptance testing (see Exhibit 8).

Each test event should have a plan that defines the test scope resources (people and environment) and test objectives with expected results. It should provide test case documentation and a test results report. It is often desirable to have the end-user participate in the functional testing.

System Documentation. System documentation helps maintenance programmers to understand the system, correct problems, and make enhancements. Documentation builds at each phase in the development process. The initial justification defines the application functionality, which is converted into program specifications for creating test cases and is used for implementation training. Documentation can be created as flowcharts, graphs, tables, or text for organization and ease of reading. Documentation may include:

- Source of the data
- Data attributes
- Input screens
- Data validations
- Data selection criteria
- Security procedures
- Description of calculations
- Program design
- Interfaces to other applications

Exhibit 8. Testing Events

Test Event	Objectives
Unit Testing	Unit testing verifies that stand-alone programs match specifications. Test cases should exercise every line of code
Integration Testing	Integration testing verifies that all software and hardware. components work together. Data is passed from one program to the next. All programs and subroutines should be tested during this phase. Test cases should cover all components (e.g., hardware and software).
Functional Testing	Functional testing verifies that the application meets user requirements. Test cases should cover screens, navigation, function keys, on-line help, processing, and output (reports, files, and screens).
Technical Testing	Technical testing verifies that the application works in the production environment. Test cases should include error processing and recovery, performance, storage requirements, hardware compatibility, and security (e.g., screens, data, and programs).
Acceptance Testing	Acceptance testing verifies that acceptance criteria defined during the project definition stage are tested. Test cases should include system usability, management reports, performance measurements, documentation and procedures, training (e.g., users, help desk, production support, and operations), and system readiness (operations/systems sign-off).

- Control procedures
- Error handling
- Operating instructions
- Archive, purge, and retrieval
- Backup, storage, and recovery

Implementation. The final step to implementing the system includes conversion, documentation, training, and support. To ensure smooth implementation, it is important that users and technical support people receive adequate training. To facilitate this training, both system and user documentation need to define the functionality of the system. Components of implementation include:

- *Strategy:* covers who, what, when, where, and how of the implementation process
- *Conversion:* defines the procedures for correcting and converting data to the new application
- *Documentation:* includes both user and system support procedures
- *Training:* includes end users, computer operators, and maintenance programmers
- *Support:* includes help desk and problem reporting

Strategy. An implementation strategy should be documented to guide the implementation team and users in the implementation process. The strategy should cover resources required, roles and responsibilities, the means of communication between the implementation team and users, the methods of training, and a schedule of the various events.

Conversion. Unless a process is new, existing information will need to be converted to the new system. Conversion is the process where this information is either entered manually or transferred programmatically from the old system to the new system. In either case, the existence of procedures should verify the conversion of all records and the accuracy of data entered into the new system.

Documentation. Documentation consists of descriptions of procedures, instructions to personnel, flowcharts, data flow diagrams, display or report layouts, and other materials that can describe an overall system. System documentation should provide maintenance programmers with enough information to understand how the system works to decrease the learning cycle and speed up analysis of program changes. User documentation should include both automated and manual workflow for initial training and ongoing reference. In both cases, documentation should be updated as the system is modified.

Training. Training is an important aspect of any project implementation. According to a Gartner Group study, the cost of not training will far exceed the investment organizations will make to train both end users and information systems (IS) professionals in new technologies. One reason for this paradox is that users who are forced to learn on their own take as much as six times longer to become productive with the software product. The Gartner Group study also showed that an effective training program reduces support costs by three to six times because users make fewer mistakes and have fewer questions (Gartner).

Support. Along with training, ongoing user support is another important component needed to ensure a successful implementation. The previously mentioned Gartner Group study found that the need for support is inelastic, and the gap between "needed" support and "formal" support will be filled by "underground support." This underground support, which is informal support by peers or department-purchased outsourcing, accounts for as much as 30 percent of user computing costs (Gartner).

Traditional Information Software Development

The traditional approach to systems development is a sequential process with defined phases beginning with the identification of a need and ending with implementation of the system. The traditional approach uses a structured systems development life cycle (SDLC) that provides a framework for planning and developing information systems. Although there are many variations of the traditional SDLC, they all have the following common phases in one form or another.

- *Feasibility:* Identify a need and decide whether to make, buy, or do nothing.
- *Analysis:* Define what is required of the new system.
- *Design:* Define how to build the new system to satisfy the requirements.
- *Construction:* Build the new system using the design information.
- *Testing:* Verify that the completed system meets the user's needs.
- *Implementation:* Deliver the completed system to the end users.
- *Maintenance:* Modify the system to correct problems as found or meet changing needs.

Although the traditional development process provides structure and organization to systems development, it is not without risks. The traditional approach can be a long development process that is costly due to the amount of resources and length of time required. The business environment may change between the time the requirements are defined and when the system is implemented. The users may have a long delay before they see how the system will look and feel. To compensate for these challenges, a project can be broken down into smaller subprojects where modules are designed, coded, and tested. The challenge in this approach is to bring all the modules together at the end of the project to test and implement the fully functional system.

Prototypes and Rapid Application Development (RAD)

In general, prototyping information systems design includes the transformation of the user's basic requirements into a working model, the revision and enhancement of the model, and the decision to accept the model as the final simulation of the actual system to be built. The model should show how the design would work in real life and provide insight into why the design is successful. The prototype can facilitate interaction between the users, system analysts, and the auditor. These techniques can be applied to production report development, a specific application module, or the entire support system. Advantages of prototyping include:

- Models can be viewed and analyzed before commitment of large funding for systems.
- User approval and final satisfaction is enhanced because of increased participation in the design of the project.
- The cost of modifying systems is reduced because users and designers can foresee problems earlier and are able to respond to the users' rapidly changing business environment.

- A rudimentary prototype can be redesigned and enhanced many times before final form is accepted.
- Many systems are designed "from scratch" and no current system exists to serve as a guide.

Because prototypes appear to be complete when presented to the users, programmers may not be given adequate time to complete the system and implement the prototype as the final product. Often the user will attempt to use the prototype instead of the full delivery system. The user must understand the prototype is not a completed system. Risks associated with prototyping and RAD include:

- Incomplete system design
- Inefficient processing performance
- Inadequate application controls
- Inadequate documentation
- Ineffective implementations

End-User Development (EUD)

End-user developed (EUD) applications are created, operated, and maintained outside of the Information System organization. There are many factors that have led the end user to build their own systems. First, and probably foremost, is the shift in technology towards personal computers and fourth-generation programming languages. This shift has been due, in part, to the declining hardware and software costs that have enabled individuals to own computers. Because of this, individuals have become more computer literate. At the same time, users are frustrated with the length of time that it takes for traditional systems development efforts to be completed. Fourth-generation programming languages have provided users with the tools to create their own applications. Examples of end-user development include the following:

- *Mainframe-based query tools* that enable the end user to develop and maintain reports. This includes fourth-generation languages such as EZ-TRIEVE and SAS or programmer-developed report generation applications using query languages.
- *Vendor packages* that automate a generic business process. This includes accounting packages for generating financial statements and legal packages for case management.
- *End-user developed applications* using PC based tools, databases, or spreadsheets to fulfill a department or individual information processing need.

Because PCs seem relatively simple and are perceived as personal productivity tools, their effect on an organization has largely been ignored. In many organizations, end-user developed applications have limited or no formal procedures. End users may not have the background knowledge to develop applications with adequate controls or maintainability. This becomes an issue as organizations begin to rely on user-developed systems for day-to-day operations and important decision making. Coupled with this is the fact that end-user systems are becoming more complex and are distributed across platforms and organizational boundaries. Risks associated with end-user computing include:

- Weak security
- Limited backup
- Inefficient use of resources
- Inadequate training
- Inadequate support
- Incompatible systems
- Redundant systems
- Inconsistent reporting across departments
- Reliance on inaccurate information
- Ineffective implementations

The Auditor's Role in the Development Process

Auditor involvement may vary from project to project and auditors may not be involved in every systems development project. Each system development project will need to be risk assessed to determine the level of audit's involvement. The type of review will also vary depending on the risks of a particular project. Auditors may only be involved in key areas or the entire development project. In any case, auditors need to understand the development process and application controls to add value and ensure adequate controls are built into the system. Auditors can take on two different roles in a systems development project: control consultant or independent reviewer. As a control consultant, the auditor becomes a member of the development team and works with analysts and programmers to design application controls. In this role, the auditor is no longer independent of the development team. As an independent reviewer, the auditor should have no design responsibilities and not report to the project team, but can provide recommendations to be acted on or not by the project manager.

Software development audits are performed to evaluate the administrative controls over the authorization, development, and implementation of new applications and review the design of the controls/audit trails of the proposed system.

The scope of a systems development audit can include an evaluation of the software development life cycle or an evaluation of the quality of the deliverables from each system development and implementation phase (e.g., an evaluation of the controls design and audit trails, systems test plan and results, user training, and systems and program documentation, etc.).

Recommendations from systems development audits might include improvements in user requirements, application controls, or the need to document test plans and expected test results.

Developing new systems can be a costly and time-consuming endeavor. A well-controlled environment with an overall strategy, standards, policies, and procedures helps ensure the success of development efforts. There are many processes that need to be well controlled to ensure the overall success of an application: analysis, design, testing, and implementation. Because of the cost to implement controls after a system has already gone into production, controls should be defined before a system is built.

There are many opportunities for auditor involvement in the development process. Auditors need to develop the skills and relationships to work with the development team to ensure that controls are built into the system. Auditors can assist organizations by reviewing the systems development environment, evaluating standards for systems development, and evaluating phases in the systems development process. Auditors can assist management by reviewing critical systems for input, processing, and output and verifying that the new system provides an adequate audit trail. The auditor's role in a systems development project depends on the organization's culture, maturity of the information systems function, and philosophy of the auditing department.

Auditing systems development requires specific knowledge about the development process and application controls. Understanding the development process allows the auditor to identify key areas that would benefit from independent verification. Understanding application controls allows the auditor to evaluate and recommend controls to ensure complete and accurate transaction processing.

By becoming involved at strategic points, the auditor can ensure that a system is well controlled and auditable. The following list highlights some of the key tasks the auditor may perform during a system's development:

- Review user requirements.
- Review manual and application controls.
- Check all technical specifications for compliance with company standards.
- Perform design walkthroughs at the end of each development phase.
- Submit written recommendations for approval after each walkthrough.
- Ensure implementation of recommendations before beginning the next phase.
- Review test plans.

- Present findings to management.
- Maintain independence to remain objective.

These tasks can help minimize control weaknesses and problems before the system becomes operational rather than after it is in use.

To determine the level of involvement, the auditor should first complete a risk assessment of the systems development process and determine the amount of time to allocate to a particular development project. Next, the auditor should develop an audit plan that includes a schedule for the specific review points tied to the development schedule. Finally, the auditor needs to communicate the scope of involvement and any findings to development, users, and management.

Risk Assessment

Depending on the organization, auditors may not have enough time to be involved in all phases of every development project. Involvement will depend on the risk assessment of the process risks and the system risks.

- Process Risks:
  - Lack of strategic direction
  - Lack of development standards
  - Lack of a formal systems development process
  - Negative organizational climate
- Application Risks:
  - Application complexity and magnitude
  - Inexperienced staff
  - Lack of end-user involvement
  - Lack of management commitment

The level of risk may be a function of the need for timely information, complexity of the application, the degree of reliance for important decisions, the length of time the application will be used, and the number of people who will use it.

The scope defines which aspects of a particular application are covered by the audit. Depending on the risk, the scope may include requirements, design and testing deliverable reviews, application controls, operational controls, security, problem management, change controls, or post-implementation review.

Audit Plan

The audit plan will detail the objectives and the steps to fulfill the audit objectives. As in any audit, a systems development audit will begin with a preliminary analysis of the control environment by reviewing existing standards and procedures. During the audit, these standards and procedures should be assessed for completeness and operational efficiency. The preliminary survey should identify the organization's strategy and the responsibilities for managing and controlling applications. The auditor can provide reasonable assurance that the following tasks are performed with regard to the system development:

- Compliance with standards and procedures
- Efficient and economical operation
- Conform systems to legal requirements
- Include the controls necessary to protect against loss or serious error
- Provide the controls and audit trails needed for management, auditor, and operational review
- Document the system: provide an understanding of the system that is required for appropriate maintenance and auditing

Software Development Controls Review

A software development controls review would assess the adequacy of the control environment for developing effective systems. The following areas would be covered:

- Development standards
- Testing strategy
- Implementation and training
- Problem management
- Change management

The review points listed represent checkpoints in the systems development process. Auditors can use these checkpoints to determine both the status of the application control system and the status of the development project itself. These reviews eliminate the necessity of devoting large amounts of audit resources to the development effort. As long as the development process is well controlled, the need for audit involvement is minimized.

Software Development Life Cycle

For any kind of a partnership involving auditors, users, and information systems management, it is important that the organization establish a formal procedure for the development of a system. Without a formal SDLC, complete with defined phases of development and specified points for review and evaluation, the auditor's job is much more difficult and recommendations are not as readily accepted.

- Auditor influence is significantly increased when there are formal procedures and required guidelines identifying each phase and project deliverable in the SDLC and the extent of auditor involvement.

- Auditors will be able to review all relevant areas and phases of the SDLC, identify any missing areas for the development team, and report independently to management on the adherence to planned objectives and procedures.

- Auditors can identify selected parts of the system and become involved in the technical aspects based upon their skills and abilities.

- Auditors can provide an evaluation of the methods and techniques applied in the systems development process, as defined earlier.

Analysis

The project team should expend considerable effort toward the analysis of the business problem and what the system is to produce without initially attempting to develop the design of the system. The auditor should observe that the primary responsibility is not to develop a product but to satisfy the user. Often, the user does not understand what is truly needed. Only by understanding the user's business, its problems, goals, constraints, weaknesses, and strengths can the project team deliver the product the user needs. Auditor's can participate by reviewing requirements, and verifying user understanding and sign-off.

Design

The auditor may review the design work to make sure that the user's requirements are met. The system's design may also be reviewed for any possible exposures or forgotten controls and for adherence to company standards (company standards should be documented as part of the SDLC methodology and defined before the beginning of the project). If an exposure is found, the auditor should recommend the appropriate controls or procedures.

A technique that brings users and project team members together for an intensive workshop in which they create a system proposal into a detail design is called Joint Application Design (JAD). Usually a trained JAD facilitator, having some claim to neutrality, takes the group through formatted discussions of the system. The auditor may be an active participant in this process. The result of the JAD session is a user-view of the system for further development. This is an excellent setting for the discussion of the advantages and cost effectiveness of controls. In addition, analysis time is compressed, discrepancies resolved, specification errors reduced, and communications greatly enhanced. Auditor's can review deliverables and recommend application controls. Application controls are discussed in more detail in Chapters 9 through 12.

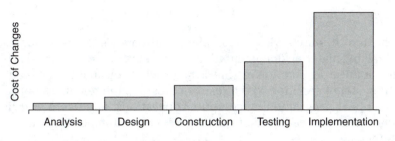

Exhibit 9. Cost Comparison of Changing a Program

Construction

The auditor may review the new system's programs to verify compliance with programming standards (see Exhibit 9). These standards help ensure that all the code has a similar structure, tracking dependencies and making maintenance easier. The auditor may review a sample of programs to verify that the standards are being followed and that the programs conform to systems design. In addition, programs may be checked for possible control exposures and for the placement of proper controls per design. If it is determined that controls are needed, the auditor should make recommendations, following the same criteria that were used during the design phase. During this phase, however, cost and time factors must be carefully considered because the cost of changing programs to include controls increases as the project progresses.

Testing

The auditor may be called on to assure management that both developers and users have thoroughly tested the system to ensure that it:

- Possesses the built-in controls necessary to provide reasonable assurance of proper operation
- Provides the capability to track events through the systems and thus supports audit review of the system in operation
- Meets the needs of the user and management

If the level of testing does not meet standards, the auditor must notify the development team or management who will then take corrective action.

Documentation

The auditor may review system, user, or operating documentation for completeness and accuracy. The maintenance programmers and users should easily understand the documentation. For instance, diagrams of information flow and samples of possible input documents/screens and output reports enhance understanding of the system.

Implementation

The auditor may review the implementation strategy, communication and training material, documentation, conversion procedures, and production readiness. Production readiness may include evaluating the readiness of the system in relation to the results of testing, the readiness of production support programmers, computer operations, and users in terms of training, and the readiness of the help desk with trained staff and a problem-tracking process.

Post-Implementation

Once the system is in production, the auditor may survey users to evaluate the effectiveness of the application from a workflow perspective, review error detection and correction procedures to confirm they are working as intended, or perform tests of data to confirm completeness of transaction processing and audit trail.

Change Control

Changes to a system in production come from two sources: problems not detected during testing and changes in user requirements. A change control review would evaluate whether problems are reported, tracked, prioritized, and resolved, and whether changes are authorized, tested, documented, and communicated. The following areas would be covered:

- Authorization
- Testing (system and user acceptance)
- Documentation
- Communication

Application Controls

When reviewing the system development phases, the auditor examines application and manual control points. The user department is responsible for specifying the needed controls and the systems analysts and programmers are responsible for implementing these controls. Although the responsibility for the auditability and controls in the new system lies with the user departments, systems analysis, and programmers, these groups may not have the expertise to design adequate controls into the new system. The auditor should interact with each of these groups during the development process to ensure the adequacy of audit and control provisions. The completion of each of the phases usually corresponds to the key points for auditor involvement.

Auditing Quality Assurance

The goal of Quality Assurance is to provide management with appropriate visibility into the processes being used to manage projects and products. To accomplish this objective requires regular reviews and audits of the software products and activities to verify that they comply with the applicable procedures and standards. Standards and procedures need to be established for valid quality assurance measurement processes in every project and operation. Quality assurance begins with the definition of a new project or product. Project activities and work products throughout the project life cycle need to comply with established plans, standards, and procedures. These processes must be documented and controlled (see Exhibit 10).

Communication

The first area to communicate is the auditor's role in the systems development project. It is very important to make sure that the management and development teams' expectations of the auditor's role are understood and communicated to all participants. To influence the systems development effort, the auditor must develop an open line of communication with both management and users. If a good relationship between these groups does not exist, information might be withheld from the auditor. This type of situation could prevent the auditor from doing the best job possible. In addition, the auditor must develop a good working relationship with analysts and programmers. Although the auditor should cultivate good working relationships with all groups that have design responsibilities, the auditor must remain independent.

Recommendations

Throughout the development project, the auditor will be making control recommendations. Depending on the organization's culture, these recommendations may need to be handled informally by reviewing designs with the project team or formally by presenting recommendations to the steering committee. In either case, the auditor must always consider the value of the control recommendation vs. the cost of implementing the control. Also, recommendations should be specific, identifying the problem and not the symptom. This allows the proper controls to be implemented and tested.

Recommendations are often rejected because of a time and cost factor. Managers may sometimes feel that implementing an auditor's recommendations will put them behind schedule. The auditor must convince management that if the recommendations are not implemented, more time and money will be spent in the long run (see Exhibit 3). Informing management

Exhibit 10. Auditing Quality Assurance

Goals

Quality Assurance activities are planned and documented.

Adherence of project activities and products to applicable standards, procedures, and requirements is verified objectively.

All impacted groups are aware of and cooperative with Quality Assurance activities.

Noncompliance issues are addressed with senior management.

Commitments

The SQA functions are in place on all software projects.

The SQA group has a reporting channel to senior management that is independent of all project related groups.

Senior management periodically reviews SQA activities and results.

Abilities

The SQA group exists and is active.

Adequate resources and funding are provided.

SQA personnel are adequately trained.

Project team members understand and support the SQA function within their project.

Activities

An SQA plan is prepared according to a documented procedure.

The SQA plan is reviewed by all impacted groups.

The SQA plan is managed and controlled (i.e., change control).

SQA activities are performed according to the SQA plan that covers responsibilities and authority, resource requirements, schedule and funding, role in establishing software development plans, standards, and procedures, evaluations to be performed, audits and reviews to be conducted, project standards and procedures to be used in audits, and procedures for documenting and reviewing findings.

The SQA function participates in the preparation and reviews of the project development plan, standards, and procedures.

The SQA function reviews the software engineering activities to verify compliance.

The SQA function audits designated software work products to verify compliance with standards, procedures, and contractual obligations and identifies, documents, and tracks deviations and corrections.

The SQA function periodically reviews its findings with the customer SQA function and IT senior management.

Measurements

Measurements are devised and utilized to determine the cost, schedule, and effectiveness of SQA activities.

Verification

SQA activities are reviewed periodically with senior management.

Subcontractor management activities are reviewed periodically with project management.

Independent experts periodically review Quality Assurance activities and work products.

of the cost of implementing a control now, rather than shutting down the system later to repair it or leaving possible exposures open, will help convince management of the need to spend time and money now.

Audit Report

Depending on the audit scope and the length of the project, interim reports may be needed at the completion of major phases in the development process. Key reporting points include:

- *Planning:* adequacy of the project plan and cost/benefit analysis
- *Design:* adequacy of the controls and auditability of the design
- *Testing:* adequacy of the test strategy and completeness of the test objectives
- *Implementation:* readiness of the system and user components for production
- *Post-Implementation:* effectiveness and efficiency of the live system and whether the initial system criteria were met

If the auditor becomes part of the development team, the team manager would become the auditor's management, and the auditor's reports and recommendations might be modified before being sent to higher management. To remain objective, the auditor should issue reports independent of the project team.

Conclusion

Developing new systems can be a costly and time-consuming endeavor. A well-controlled environment with an overall strategy, standards, policies, and procedures helps ensure the success of development efforts. There are many processes that need to be well controlled to ensure the overall success of a project and system: project management, analysis, design, testing, and implementation. Because of the cost to implement controls after a system has already gone into production, controls should be defined before a system is built.

There are many opportunities for auditor involvement in the development process. Auditors need to develop the skills and relationships to work with the development team to ensure that controls are built into the system. Auditors can assist organizations by reviewing the systems development environment, evaluating standards for systems development, monitoring project progress, and evaluating phases in the systems development process. Auditors can assist management by reviewing critical systems for input, processing, output, and verifying that the new system provides an adequate audit trail.

Review Questions

1. What are the primary benefits of systems development standards?
2. In which testing event are the user requirements validated?
3. During the development process, how can the auditor ensure a system is well controlled and auditable?
4. What technique is used to bring users and project team members together to create a detail design?
5. What are the key properties in a quality system?
6. The COBIT 11th process lists 19 control objectives within the Planning and Organization Domain. Explain what four of them are?
7. What is ISO 9000? What is the ISO?
8. How does maturity correlate to quality?
9. What does the Raytheon example show? Explain.
10. How can prototypes be controlled?

Multiple Choice Questions

1. The intent of the Planning Phase is to:
   a. Develop the project budget and gain approval from senior management.
   b. Develop the project budget, schedule, and staffing.
   c. Develop the business requirements for the design phase.
   d. Develop the communication plan for the project.
2. Standards that govern software development include all of the following, except:
   a. Capability Maturity Model (CMM)
   b. Quality Management and Quality Assurance Standards (ISO 9000)
   c. Capability Maturity Model Integration (CMMI)
   d. Control Objectives for Information Technology (COBIT)
3. Which of the following is not a test event?
   a. Functional testing
   b. Negative testing
   c. Unit testing
   d. Acceptance testing
4. Auditors must have the following skills to provide a quality audit on a systems development project:
   a. Experience in programming applications
   b. Understanding of software quality assurance standards
   c. Understanding of the software development process and key controls
   d. Experience in managing software development projects
5. A development controls review would include all of the following processes, except:
   a. Project management
   b. Problem management

   c. Software acquisition

   d. Change management

6. The risks associated with prototypes and Rapid Application Development are:
   a. Incomplete system design
   b. Inefficient processing performance
   c. Inadequate documentation
   d. All of the above

7. The following are examples of end-user development, except:
   a. Mainframe-based query tools
   b. Vendor packages that automate a generic business process
   c. Operating systems
   d. End-user developed applications

8. Which of the following is a risk associated with end-user computing:
   a. Weak security
   b. Inadequate support
   c. Inadequate training
   d. All of the above

9. Key tasks an auditor might perform during systems development are:
   a. Reviewing user requirements
   b. Checking all technical specification for compliance with organizational standards
   c. Reviewing test plans
   d. All of the above

10. Application risk may include all of the following, except:
    a. Application complexity and magnitude
    b. Experienced staff
    c. Lack of end-user involvement
    d. Lack of management commitment

Exercises

1. List and describe key tasks that should be included in a project plan. Consider phases in the development process as well as support tasks that are needed for implementation and maintenance.
2. Describe possible approaches to a systems development effort and the advantages and disadvantages of each approach.
3. Describe the general phases of a systems development life cycle and what activities are completed in each phase.
4. Describe the different test events and what aspects of the system are covered during each event.
5. List and describe ten possible review areas that auditors may be involved in during the development process.

AUDITING IT PLANNING AND ORGANIZATION

Answers to Multiple Choice Questions

1 — b; 2 — d; 3 — b; 4 — c; 5 — b; 6 — d; 7 — c; 8 — d; 9 — d; 10 — b

References

1. Allen, S., F. Gallegos, and D. Manson. *Audit Concerns for End-User Computing and Application Development.* EDP Auditing, Auerbach Publishers, Boca Raton, FL. 1996
2. Brotbeck, G., T. Miller, and J. Statz. A Survey of Current Best Practices and Utilization of Standards in the Public and Private Sectors. Tera Quest Metrics, Inc., December 1999.
3. Dow, D.P. and F. Gallegos. *Key Review Points for SDLC Audits.* EDP Auditing, Auerbach Publishers, Boca Raton, FL. 1987
4. Dow, D.P. and F. Gallegos. *Auditing Systems Maintenance: A How-to Approach.* EDP Auditing, Auerbach Publishers, Boca Raton, FL. 1986
5. Gallegos, F. *CIS Auditors Role in Systems Development.* EDP Auditing, Auerbach Publishers, Boca Raton, FL. 1998
6. Gallegos, F. *Auditing DSS: Review Points for IS Managers.* EDP Auditing, Auerbach Publishers, Boca Raton, FL. 1998
7. Gallegos, F. *Software Tools and Techniques.* EDP Auditing, Auerbach Publishers, Boca Raton, FL. 1985
8. Gallegos, F. and S. Schneider. *The Audit Process and the Information Center.* EDP Auditing, Auerbach Publishers, Boca Raton, FL. 1988
9. Gartner Group. *Managing Distributed Computing: Stabilizing an Exploding Universe.* 1995 Western Region Briefing. April 18, 1995, Universal City, CA.
10. Gaston, S.J. *Managing and Controlling Small Computer Systems Including LANs.* The Canadian Institute of Chartered Accountants, 1992.
11. Gaston, S.J. *Audit of Small Computer Systems Including LANs.* The Canadian Institute of Chartered Accountants, 1993.
12. King, D. *Current Practices in Software Development.* Yourdon Press, New York, 1984.
13. Lientz, B.P., E.B. Swanson, and G.E. Tompkins. Characteristics of Application Software Maintenance. *Communications of the ACM* 21(6): 466–471, 1978.
14. Lientz, B.P. and E.B. Swanson. Problems in Application Software Maintenance. *Communications of the ACM* 24(11): 763–769, 1981.
15. Paulk, M. et al. The Capability Maturity Model for Software; SEI, Carnegie Mellon University, Pittsburgh, PA., 1994. http://www.sei.cmu.edu/cmm/papers/cmm.pdf.
16. Paulk, M. A Comparison of ISO 9001 and the Capability Maturity Model for Software Technical Report CMU/SEI-94-TR-12 ESC-TR-94-12, 1994. http://www.sei.cmu.edu/pub/documents/94.reports/pdf/tr12.94.pdf
17. Swanson, E.B. and C.M. Beath. Departmentalization in Software Development and Maintenance. *Communications of the ACM* 33(6): 658–667, 1990.
18. The Capability Maturity Model Integration. SEI, Carnegie Mellon University, Pittsburgh, PA. December 2001. http://www.sei.cmu.edu/pub/documents/02.reports/pdf/02tr001.pdf
19. Williams, P.B. *Getting a Project Done on Time: Managing People, Time, and Results.* American Management Association, 1996.
20. Working Council for Chief Information Officers. Software Quality Assurance Metrics. May 2001. Corporate Executive Board 2001. Catalog No.: 1-766GM.

Part III
Auditing IT Acquisition and Implementation

Chapter 9 through Chapter 12

The third part of this text examines auditing IT acquisition and implementation. This section discusses risks and controls in terms of the life cycle of application systems. Specifically, it includes acquiring new systems, implementing new systems, and applications risks, as well as change management.

This area emphasizes the importance of identifying issues and concerns while they still can be corrected before the system becomes operational. Ideally, auditor involvement provides the most significant value during the acquisition and implementation phase. IT and general auditors as well as other IT security professionals give risk and control expertise to these project teams. The auditor can ensure that risks are evaluated up front and controls are integrated within the system as opposed to after the fact. However, many companies marginalize their auditors to scheduled programmed audits that negate the ability of the auditor to be a partner in the process. Conversely, involving auditors in the acquisition and implementation can infer to others that the auditor's independence is compromised. The auditor and audit management must manage this perception through the use of objective audit tools and their professionalism.

Once applications are purchased and implemented, they must be maintained. Application maintenance can introduce risk to a once stable and secure system. Additionally, maintaining applications involves costs to the organization and should be effectively managed. Auditors often review maintenance procedures and change control procedures to ensure that the application is meeting its stated objectives and performing as intended by management.

Chapter 9 provides an overview of the software acquisition process as well as the associated risks and controls. Organizations acquire software so that they can support their business needs in an automated, effective, and efficient fashion. This chapter provides an overview of the software acquisition process as well as defines some related terms and processes in the software selection process. It also discusses suggestions for an auditor in performing a review of the software acquisition process.

Chapter 10 reviews the phases of the system implementation process. The purpose of the system implementation process is to verify that the solution meets its intended purpose. Implementing a system consists of configuring the system, testing functionality, converting data, training users, and preparing for production support. An auditor's role in system implementations is to ensure that risks are identified and proper controls are considered during the implementation process. Auditors are encouraged to participate in system implementations so that they can provide security and control expertise. Additionally, identifying risks or recommending controls after a system is implemented is more costly and may limit the organization's ability to implement the most effective controls.

Chapter 11 provides an overview of risks and controls associated with application systems and their associated maintenance. Applications represent a significant investment for organizations as well as being critical for conducting business. Computer-based applications provide automated functions, which effectively support the business process. Applications also introduce risks to organizations in the form of increased costs, loss of data integrity, weaknesses in confidentiality, lack of availability, or poor performance. Assuming that these risks were addressed during the implementation phase, applications also need to be changed. Maintaining these applications costs money, introduces problems, becomes inconsistent with business or IT strategies, degrades performance, and can monopolize the resources of an organization. Due to the significant investment that companies make in applications systems as well as the significant investment of funds, the auditor's role is critical in reviewing the risk, effectiveness, and efficiencies associated with application systems.

Chapter 12 provides an introduction to change management, both in terms of IT as well as organizational change. IT change management is one of the single most important controls to ensure the integrity, availability, reliability, security, confidentiality, and accuracy of an organization or IT system supporting the organization. Organizational change also deserves consideration by the IT auditor due to its potential impact to the organization and the increased relationships with changes in the IT environment. Organizational change is impacted by limitations introduced by the technology and the organization's culture. Research debates whether the technology is a product of the culture or whether the organization's practices are dictated by technology. Regardless, it is safe to say that they are interdependent. Consequently, auditors should expand change management to include those related to the organization.

For an auditor, member of the management team, or significant user of a company's application systems, it is beneficial to understand the goals of the system and the associated risks that could impede those expectations. Consequently, risks can be managed through controls, which will ensure the success and security of the application.

Chapter 9
Software Acquisition

An organization's reason for acquiring software is to effectively and efficiently support one or more business processes. Prior to acquiring software, the requirements of these processes should have already been identified. Once the business objectives have been identified for the solution being sought, the process for acquiring software can begin. Both the IT auditor and management need to be aware of the importance of this area and the critical control processes that need to be in place to support and protect the organization.

Software Acquisition Process

There has been much written in this area. The software acquisition process should include the identification and analysis of alternative solutions that are each compared with the established business requirements. In general, the acquisition process consists of the following:

- Defining the information and system requirements
- Identifying various alternatives
- Performing a feasibility analysis
- Conducting a risk analysis
- Defining ergonomic requirements
- Carrying out the selection process
- Procuring the selected software
- Completing final acceptance

Defining the Information and System Requirements

One of the greater challenges in procuring or developing any information system is to define its requirements. System requirements describe the needs or objectives of the system. They define the problem to be solved, business and system goals, system processes to be accomplished, and the deliverables and expectations for the system. It includes defining the information being given to the system to process, the information to be processed within the system, and the information expected out of the system. Each should be clearly defined so that later gaps in requirements and expectations are avoided.

Information and system requirements can be captured via interviews, deriving requirements from existing systems, identifying characteristics

215

from related system, and discovering them from a prototype or pilot system. Generally speaking, gathering requirements is accomplished by:

- Interviewing management to understand their expectations for the system as well as to understand the business context within the industry and the company itself
- Interviewing those expected to use the information produced by the system as well as those expected to produce the information input into the system
- Reviewing related paper and electronic forms and reports
- Observing related business processes
- Meeting with IT management and support staff regarding their expectations and constraints for implementing and supporting the system
- Researching other companies in a related industry, of similar company size, and with a similar technical environment to identify best practices and lessons learned

Prototypes and Rapid Application Development (RAD). In general, prototyping information systems design includes the transformation of the user's basic requirements into a working model, the revision and enhancement of the model, and the decision to accept the model as final simulation of the actual system to be built. The model should show how the design would work in real life and provide insight into why the design is successful. The prototype can facilitate interaction between the users, system analysts, and the auditor. These techniques can be applied to production report development, a specific application module, or the entire support system. Advantages of prototyping include:

- Models can be viewed and analyzed before commitment of large funding for systems.
- User approval and final satisfaction are enhanced because of increased participation in the design of the project.
- The cost of modifying systems is reduced because users and designers can foresee problems earlier and are able to respond to the user's rapidly changing business environment.
- A rudimentary prototype can be redesigned and enhanced many times before final form is accepted.
- The prototype serves as a guide because many systems are designed "from scratch" and no current system exists to serve as a guide.

The Requirements Document. A "requirements document" is intended to record the requirements and expectations of the system. Though system requirements documents vary in design, each, in general, provides the following information:

- *The intended users of the system.* The users of the system include those who actually interact with it as well as those who use the information that it produces.
- *The scope and objectives for the system.* The scope should be "holistic," incorporating both the technical environment as well as a business perspective.
- A statement of the *problem* needing to be solved by the system.
- *The system goals and objectives.* Be sure to include goals and objectives from a technical as well as a business perspective.
- *Feasibility analysis.* Feasibility analysis defines the constraints or limitations for the system from a technical as well as a business perspective. Feasibility should be assessed in the following categories: economic, technical, operational, schedule, legal or contractual, and political. Feasibility can include those things that are tangible, intangible, one-time, or recurring.
- *Other assumptions* made regarding the system, such as compliance with existing business practices.
- *Expected system functions* to be provided, such as authorizing payments, providing account status, etc.
- *System attributes,* such as ease of use, fault tolerance, response time, and integration with existing platforms, etc.
- *The context or environment in which the system is expected to operate.* This includes a description of the system that is expected to fit or interface within the environment (industry context, company culture, technical environment, etc.).

Identifying Various Alternatives

Many options exist in procuring software solutions, which include any combination of the following: purchasing an off-the-shelf product, contracting for development, developing the system in-house, or outsourcing a system from another organization.

Off-the-Shelf Solutions. Purchasing commercially available products requires that the organization's business adapt to the functionality of the system. This business adaptation process require that the organization could also customize the software product and subsequently maintain those customizations within the processes that have been modified and changed. The advantages of using off-the-shelf products are shorter implementation time, use of proven technology, availability of technical expertise from outside the company, availability of maintenance and support, and easier-to-define costs. The disadvantages include incompatibility between packaged system capabilities and the company's requirements, long-term reliance on a vendor for maintenance and support, specific hardware or software requirements, and limitations on the use or customization of the software.

Purchased Package. Vendors develop packaged systems for wide distribution that satisfy a generic business problem. For example, a payroll system is somewhat generic for most organizations. Often, a purchased package can satisfy the business needs for much less than developing a system internally. If various packages are available, organizations will develop a Request for Proposal that defines the system requirements and asks for the vendor's solution to those requirements. Organizations then weigh how well each package meets the business requirements and whether a purchased application makes sense. When selecting a vendor package, organizations should consider the following:

- Stability of the vendor company
- Volatility of system upgrades
- Existing customer base
- Vendor's ability to provide support
- Required hardware or software in support of the vendor application
- Required modifications of the base software

Although packaged applications may appear to be less costly to implement than building a new system internally, there are risks to consider before selecting this option. A packaged application may not meet the majority of the business needs, resulting in extensive modification or changes to business processes. Also, any future releases of this software may require extensive programming to retrofit all of the company-specific code. Because packaged systems are generic by their nature, the organization may need to modify its business operations to match the vendor's method of processing. Changes in business operations may be costly due to training and the new processes may not fit into the organization's culture or other processes.

Contracted Development. Contracted development requires that the organization procure personnel to develop a new system or customize an existing system to the company's specifications. Contracting for systems development can provide increased control over costs and implementation schedules, legal and financial leverage over the contractor, additional technical expertise, and the ability to adhere to company policies, processes, and standards. Disadvantages associated with contracting for development include higher labor costs as compared to in-house staff, turnover of contract staff, business viability of the contracted company, exclusion of maintenance in development costs, and a lack of organizational understanding by the contractor.

Outsourcing a System from Another Organization. Many companies choose to outsource system functionality from another organization. Outsourcing allows the company to cost-effectively remain focused on their core competencies and quickly respond to business needs as well as take advantage of the expertise of another organization. Outsourcing provides increased control over costs without the need to acquire or maintain hardware, software, and related staff. However, outsourcing systems increases reliance on the outsourcer, limits the company to what is provided by the outsourcer, and decreases the ability of the company to acquire related experience and expertise.

Performing a Feasibility Analysis

A feasibility analysis defines the constraints or limitations for each alternative from a technical as well as a business perspective. Feasibility analysis includes the following categories: economic, technical, operational, schedule, legal or contractual, and political. Feasibility can include those matters that are tangible, intangible, one-time, or recurring.

Economic feasibility analysis provides a cost-benefit justification. The expenses of a system include procurement, start-up, project-specific, and operations. It includes one-time and recurring costs. Sample of costs include: consultants, start-up infrastructure, support staff, application software, maintenance contracts, training, communications, data conversion, and leases. Benefits include cost reduction or avoidance, error reduction, increased speed, improved management decisions, improved response to business needs, timely information, improved organizational flexibility, better efficiency, and better resource utilization.

Technical feasibility analyzes the technical practicality of the proposed system. It evaluates the consistency of the proposed system with the company's technical strategy, infrastructure, and resources. It answers the question of whether the organization has the resources to install and support the solution. Technical feasibility evaluates whether the company has the necessary hardware, software, and network resources to support the application as well as whether it provides reliability and capacity for growth. It also assesses the technical expertise requirements and compares it with those provided by the organization.

Operational feasibility examines how well the proposed system solves business problems or provides opportunities to the business. It also evaluates the extent of organizational changes required to accommodate the system. These changes can include personnel, business processes, products or services offered, etc.

Legal and contractual feasibility reviews any related legal or contractual obligations associated with the proposed system. Legal constraints include federal or state law as well as industry-related regulations. In addition to any new contract obligations introduced by the new system, existing contracts are also reviewed to ensure that there are no preexisting commitments that regulate the installation or use of the proposed system. Corporate or organization legal counsel should be involved in this process and one of the critical points for IT auditors to review. Note that the underlying theme is protection of the company and the establishment of the remedy process should the contractor fail to perform or deliver as promised. Organizations looking for assistance in this area should refer to their legal counsel or an organization such as the Computer Law Association whose members specialize in this area.

Political feasibility evaluates how the internal organization will accept the new system. This includes an assessment of the desirability of the system within the organization as well as its fit with the organization's corporate culture.

Conducting a Risk Analysis

A risk analysis reviews the security of the proposed system. It includes an analysis of security threats and potential vulnerabilities and impacts, as well as the feasibility of other controls that can be used to reduce or eliminate the identified risks. Controls include systematic or automated methods as well as audit trails. Risks, as discussed in other chapters of this text, affect control objectives in the areas of confidentiality and privacy of information, integrity and accuracy of the data, timeliness of the information for decision making, ability to access the system, as well as staff organization and knowledge required to support the system.

Defining Ergonomic Requirements

The goal of ergonomics is to provide a work environment that is safe and efficient for the employee. In the context of a computer system, ergonomics includes the design of the computer workstation and human interface components such as the monitor, keyboard, or mouse. Repetitive motion injuries and eyestrain are two of the most common ergonomic considerations in computer-related systems. A company's risk management or occupational safety department may provide guidelines for ergonomic requirements.

Carrying Out the Selection Process

The selection process includes identifying the best match between the available alternatives and the identified requirements. The selection process consists of soliciting proposals from interested providers, evaluating the proposals in terms of the identified requirements, and selecting the best available alternative. The selection process should be structured to ensure that the process would be completed diligently and in a timely manner. If done correctly, the selection process promotes buy-in for the selected solution.

There are various ways to solicit responses from providers to the needs of an organization. The most standard methods include: request for information

(RFI), request for bid (RFB), and request for proposal (RFP). We also provide more discussion and key audit review points on the process of contracting for IT Services (Hardware, Software, and Services) in Chapter 18, Legal Environment and its Impact on Information Technology Reviews.

Request for Information (RFI). An RFI seeks information from vendors for a specific purpose. However, neither the company nor the vendors are obligated by the response to the RFI. The RFI serves as a tool for determining the alternatives or associated alternatives for meeting the organization's needs. An RFI often asks vendors to respond to questions that will assist the organization in obtaining additional relevant information. Information from the RFI may then be used to prepare an RFP.

Request for Bid (RFB). An RFB is used to purchase specific goods or services. RFBs are used in cases where multiple vendors are capable of meeting all of the technical and functional specifications or only one supplier can meet them. In either case, the selection process is solely determined based on cost and schedule requirements. In these cases, contract terms and conditions are more likely to be nonnegotiable or fixed.

Request for Proposal (RFP). An RFP is a document that specifies the minimally acceptable requirements (functional, technical, and contractual) as well as the evaluation criteria used in the selection process. An RFP offers flexibility to respondents to further define or explore the requested requirements. RFPs may lead to a purchase or continued negotiation.

Potential vendors are supplied with copies of the RFP and are requested to submit proposals by a specified date. After a vendor has submitted a proposal, the response cannot be changed. The RFP should be communicated to as many prospective bidders as possible. It should contain the selection criteria that will be used. The criteria should be written with enough detail that it prevents any misunderstanding or misinterpretation. Any specific criterion that will influence the selection must appear in the RFP. The RFP should also describe the members of the selection committee. Any calculations that are required in the submittal should also be included, such as equipment, software, communications, utilities, site preparation, system conversion, file conversion, training, and continued operation of the system.

All questions from bidders should be answered in writing and made available to all bidders. Verbal answers to questions should be avoided. All questions should be received with enough time before the deadline so that answers can be incorporated in the proposal. Public meetings such as "bidder conferences" are used as a means to receive and respond to questions from all prospective bidders.

The basic components of an RFP are:

- Background information about the company, business problem, and the computing environment. It may also include results of any needs assessment performed.
- Schedule of important dates such as when the vendor's RFP response is due, when the decision is expected, when the actual purchase is expected, and when implementation is expected.
- Contact names and sources for answering questions for the RFP.
- Instructions for formatting the response to the RFP. Some RFPs include an explicit description of what the vendor should and should not include in their response.
- Specific requirements being sought.
- Technical requirements for the system, such as specifications for an operating system or a network environment.
- List of documents required as attachments, such as sample reports and standard contract language.
- Additional requirements for the selection process such as vendor presentations, vendor demonstrations, or on-site installation and testing.

The entire process listed above must be followed to the letter before the next step can be performed. If it is not followed as the company has specified, a "bid protest" could be filed by one of the potential vendors. Again, this is another audit/management/legal counsel review point before the evaluation process can begin.

Evaluating Proposals. A selection committee of one or more key stakeholders evaluates submitted proposals using a list of objective selection criteria. A list of the objective selection criteria is used as a means for identifying the best match between the product's features and functionality and the identified requirements. The basis for the selection criteria is the user and system requirements. Features and functionality are normally the most significant factors in the decision-making process.

Selection criteria may also include evaluating the consistency of the proposal with the company's business and IT strategy, the breadth of the vendor's products and services, vendor's relevant experience, vendor's customer support, scalability of the solution, vendor viability, total cost of ownership, integration and growth capabilities, and reliability. Vendor viability is one of the most critical factors identified by companies in the selection process.

Participants in the selection process often include representatives from key stakeholders such as management and anticipated users as well as the information technology department. The selection committee should consist of representatives that are impartial to any one provider or solution, have knowledge of best practices, and knowledge of the market. However, the participants should not have any conflict of interest and should sign a statement before they serve on the selection committee, indicating that they do not. If they do, they must be replaced by someone who meets the qualifications warranted and does not have a conflict of interest.

Procuring the Selected Software

The procurement process sounds simple but is actually the most complicated of all the acquisition steps. It requires that the purchase price and conditions be stipulated and agreed upon. These agreements take the form of contracts.

When procuring software, IT managers complain about unpredictable license fees, pressured sales methods, poor technical support, and unclear pricing for ongoing maintenance fees.

Software Contracts and Licenses Agreements are used to document agreements for development, marketing, distribution, licensing, maintenance, or any combination. Contracts can specify a fixed price or a price based on time and materials. Contracts based on time and materials state that the fees charged are directly attributable to actual expenses of time (hourly) or materials. These contracts place more financial risk on the buyer if the initial definition of pricing, the scope or desired requirements are unclear or poorly defined.

Contract terms and conditions normally include the following:

- A functional definition of the work to be performed
- Specifications for input or output designs, such as interfaces, screens, or reports
- Detailed description of the necessary hardware
- Description of the software systems or tools required for development or implementation
- Terms or limitations with the use of any related trademark rights or copyrights
- Requirements for the conversion or transfer of data
- System performance or capacity, such as speed, throughput, or storage
- Testing procedures used to identify problems and the results expected to define acceptance. Information and system requirements serve as the basis for defining the acceptance tests
- Vendor staffing and specified qualifications
- Contact and relationship protocols between the buyer and the vendor
- Expected schedules for development, implementation, and delivery
- Methods for providing progress reports, such as meetings or reports

- Definition of deliverables, which includes a clear description of each item to be delivered or provided by the vendor, when it is to be delivered, and any consequences for missed deliverables
- Explicit criteria for defining acceptance of each deliverable as well as for final acceptance
- Requirements and expectations for installation
- Documentation expected to be provided to the vendor or by the vendor as well as any intellectual property rights needed to maintain or customize the documentation
- Training expected to be provided as part of the product or service
- Any applicable warranties or maintenance including provisions for future versions currently in development
- Any requirements for indemnity or recovery for losses, such as insurances or bonding requirements
- A statement of future support that is to be provided as well as anticipated costs
- Clear definition of ownership or licensing of relevant copyrights and patents
- Terms and conditions related to confidentiality or trade secrets for either party
- Terms or limitations related to staff changing employers from one party to another (e.g., raiding staff)
- Description of payment terms
- Process for accepting changes to contract definition, such as changes in terms, scope, or deliverables

Other Considerations for Software Contracts and Licenses

Software contracts should also address the following:

- Flexibility and choice for upgrades and updates. Some contracts specify required upgrades in order to receive updates or maintenance.
- Service level agreements (SLAs) for defining expectations for support and maintenance.
- Annual maintenance costs. Should be fixed at the time of purchase and should not vary.
- Provisions for protecting the company against unforeseen problems such as software interoperability.
- Intellectual property rights for modifications. Customer may not be granted the rights for modifications.
- Terms and conditions for termination options such as what transfer process will take place when the license ends, length of the transition period, and impacts from the termination.
- Assignment clauses requiring consent. Assignment clauses allow the vendor to segregate the customer's payments from that of the service

provider. Under an assignment clause the vendor can transfer the customer's financial obligations to another firm or ongoing service components to a third party. With the payment and service separated, the vendor's motivation to perform to the terms of the contract may be reduced.

- Verification of any export or import restrictions by customers. Specifically, the export of the specified technology should be allowed by U.S. legal restrictions and the import allowed by the foreign government. The license should specify responsibility for any costs or duties.

- Regulatory approvals that may be required. Some governments, such as Japan, require that they approve the license. If the approval is not sought, the license can be considered void. The license should specify which party is responsible for obtaining the approval.

- Review of competition or antitrust laws to ensure compliance with any related legal requirements.

- Consideration of currency exchange regulations. Some countries place restrictions on the transfer of foreign currencies. Currency exchange considerations should be included in the contract.

- In the case of outsourcing, specification in the contract for the financial and legal interests in the company's software now being supported by the outsourcer. For example, in some cases, the software license may transfer to the outsourcer, which will require relicensing its own software if the company later chooses to discontinue outsourcing. The other option is to allow the outsourcer to use the software with the company retaining responsibility for all license agreements.

Completing Final Acceptance

An acceptance plan should be agreed upon and defined in the contract. This plan defines the terms and condition for acceptance. Normally, final payment is withheld until all acceptance tests have been completed and the software and equipment meet all specifications in the contract.

Reviewing Software Acquisitions

A purchased software solution should effectively and efficiently satisfy user requirements. It is also a situation where IT audit may be called upon to provide an external evaluation of the processes and procedures in place and whether the acquisition was in compliance with institutional processes and operating procedures. IT can also be a place where these procedures are lacking and the IT auditor can offer help and suggestions for improvement.

The most common risks associated with acquiring software are that the selected solution does not satisfy the intended purpose or is not technically feasible. The consequences of a poor software purchase are increased costs, missed deadlines, or neglected requirements. To offset these risks, the IT auditor should evaluate the following controls:

- Alignment with the company's business and IT strategy
- Definition of the information requirements
- Feasibility studies (cost, benefits, etc.)
- Identification of functionality, operational acceptance, and maintenance requirements
- Conformity with existing information and system architectures
- Adherence to security and control requirements
- Knowledge of available solutions
- Understanding of the related acquisition and implementation methodologies
- Involvement and buy-in from the user
- Supplier requirements and viability

Alignment with the Company's Business and IT Strategy

Any system development project, whether the system is developed by the organization or purchased elsewhere, should support the organization's business and IT strategy. The business requirements associated with the solution being sought should link to goals and objectives identified in the company's business and IT strategy. For further information about IT alignment with the business, see Chapter 5.

Definition of the Information Requirements

System and information requirements should be evaluated to determine if they are current and complete. Due to the fast pace of business, requirements can change quickly. Consequently, requirements that are gathered too far in advance of the actual purchase may not capture any changes in business requirements or newly available technical features.

The biggest challenge with defining system requirements is getting them to be complete. The requirements for a system can never be 100 percent complete. Conversely, revising requirements throughout the system acquisition process can result in change in scope, expectations, cost, and consequently, success.

Prototypes. Because prototypes appear to be complete when presented to the users, expectations, requirements, and feasibility may be misaligned. If users are shown a prototype, they may view the prototype as a final product and not understand the "back end" work that needs to be done to make it a complete system. Often, the user will want to use the prototype instead of the full delivery system. Programmers may not be given enough time to complete the system and are expected to implement the prototype as the final product. The user must understand that the prototype is not a completed system.

Risks associated with prototyping and other rapid application development (RAD) approaches include:

- Incomplete system design
- Inefficient processing performance
- Inadequate application controls
- Inadequate documentation
- Ineffective implementations

Feasibility Studies (Cost, Benefits, Etc.)

Feasibility studies should be reviewed to ensure that the selected solution not only meets the requirements but also is compared and contrasted with the feasibility of the other solutions. Related controls and risks are illustrated below using economic and technical feasibility as examples.

Economic feasibility should be reviewed and approved by an involved and knowledgeable sponsor prior to the final decision to ensure that the "make versus buy" question is effectively evaluated. Management should formally sign off on the cost–benefit analysis. In one circumstance, a government agency purchased a software solution without traceable documentation of the alternatives reviewed and the related cost–benefits associated with each. Consequently, regulators scrutinized the competency of senior management and the fairness of the selection process.

There are multiple examples of companies that prepare misleading cost–benefit studies that are based on immeasurable benefits and incomplete costs. Benefits are often presented in terms of functions that are not measured in the current environment. Consequently, it is difficult to prove benefit in the new environment. Indirect or in-kind costs are often excluded from cost estimates. Examples include staff costs associated with reassigning staff from their regular duties to the implementation project. These costs can include fees for temporary staff, loss of revenue associated with reduced service due to reduced staff, or changes in employee compensation resulting from increased job responsibilities or expected skills.

Technical feasibility should be reviewed and approved by an involved and knowledgeable sponsor prior to the final decision to ensure the organization's ability to implement and support the selected solution. In one example, a company's chief financial officer (CFO) purchased a financial enterprise resource planning (ERP) package without consulting the company's technology division in advance. The technology division was placed in the position of scrambling to incorporate the package into the existing architecture following the purchase. Consequently, changes were required to the design of the technical infrastructure resulting in unplanned hardware and software purchases.

Identification of Functionality, Operational, Acceptance, and Maintenance Requirements

Requirements need to extend beyond end-user expectations. They should include the internal functionality of the system with consideration for operational and maintenance requirements. Examples of functionality that can be missed include printing requirements or the business-specific algorithms for calculations. In one example, a company unexpectedly had to change its check printing process due to the implementation of a software package. Because the checks were now completely laser printed, the printed check had to include the account information in optical characters as well as the associated bar code. The banking information on the new check had to be reviewed and approved by the bank. Additionally, the font size had to be adjusted appropriately for the post office to systematically sort the mail. Lastly, the checks were jamming in the mail sorter at the post office. Because the check was now a self-enclosed mailer without a separate envelope, the paper used to print and mail the check became stressed from being passed through the folding machine, postage meter, and the mail sorter. The company subsequently purchased a different folding machine and implemented other alternatives to apply the postage.

Acceptance criteria should be specific with detailed measures. Acceptance plans should include inspections, functional tests, and workload trials. Without acceptance guidelines, the selected solution may not comply with user requirements, performance expectations, or the terms of the contract. There are many cases where inadequate acceptance guidelines have resulted in business interruptions from inadequate system performance or nonworking functions.

Conformity with Existing Information and System Architectures

This control is directly correlated with the evaluation of technical feasibility and the business's information elements. As mentioned in the technical feasibility section, conformity with the existing system architecture is critical.

In one case, a company selected a software package that did not accommodate the company's method for recording the commission for its sales agents in the general ledger. Consequently, the company chose to modify the software's structure for the chart-of-accounts structure, which resulted in changes and maintenance to the basic data structure of the product as well as all the associated code and screens.

Adherence to Security and Control Requirements

A complete understanding of the company's security and control requirements is needed to ensure that the selected solution is appropriate. Company security policies and applicable regulations need to be reviewed during the selection process to ensure that security and control requirements are considered in the selection process. The company security officer should be involved in defining the security and control requirements as well as participate in the selection process.

System acquisitions and implementations become more difficult when these requirements are not well understood or documented. The results will be missed security functionality or poorly implemented security. In instances where the security policy or requirements are not well documented, it would be wise to have them documented and approved by senior management prior to the selection process to ensure that security and control requirements are met.

In situations where there are gaps in security between requirements and the evaluated solutions, cost and benefits of controls should be evaluated to ensure that the costs do not exceed the benefits. This provides an opportunity for risks and controls to be revised and updated to reflect changes in business and technology. The security officer and management should participate in and approve any changes to security requirements or selected controls.

Knowledge of Available Solutions

Often, system development and acquisition efforts become more focused on a specific solution due to the knowledge or experience of the participants. By focusing on a specific end result, other alternatives are not considered. By not considering other alternatives, the selected solution may increase cost, scope, or the timeline for the project because they did not meet basic requirements such as incompatibility with the current company infrastructure or business practices. Specifically, it takes additional time and resources to integrate the selected solution into company technical infrastructure or business practices.

Understanding of the Related Acquisition and Implementation Methodologies

Acquisition methods of an organization can be very specific or general based on a variety of factors such as government regulations. As an example, government acquisition guidelines require that equal opportunity be provided to all potential providers. Consequently, there are specific requirement for advertising RFPs, evaluating bidders, as well as awarding contracts. If these guidelines are not followed, agreements may not be considered valid.

229

Selected implementation methods may be inadequately understood, and this may introduce risk to the deadlines, scope, and costs of the project. As an example, a company selected an implementation partner to assist it in converting its legacy billing system into a state-of-the-art system using object-oriented technologies. The company's experience and culture was based on traditional mainframe technologies and the traditional waterfall system development methodologies. The staff was ill-equipped to understand and participate in the rapid application development (RAD) approaches employed by the selected implementation partners. The company actually experienced failed contracts with several implementation partners and there were subsequent lawsuits filed by the company and implementation partners.

Involvement and Buy-In from the User

User involvement and buy-in is critical. Without user involvement, requirements will be missed and they will not support new systems. There is an increased awareness of the criticality of user support and buy-in. As a means for increasing user support, many projects are now including communication and business change management as part of their project plans.

Change management, in this context, includes people, organizations, and culture. A culture that shares values and is open to change contributes to success. To facilitate the change process, users should be involved in the design and implementation of the business process and the system. Training and professional development supports this as well.

System-implementation success relies on effective communication. Expectations need to be communicated. Communication, education, and expectations need to be managed throughout the organization. Input from users should also be managed to ensure that requirements, comments, and approvals are obtained. Communication includes the formal promotion of the project team as well as the project progress to the organization. Employees should also know the scope, objectives, activities and updates, and the expectation for change in advance.

Supplier Requirements and Viability

The acquisition process should ensure that the selected vendor meets the vendor requirements of the organization as outlined in the proposal. As mentioned previously, these requirements include:

- Stability of the vendor company
- Volatility of system upgrades
- Existing customer base
- Vendor's ability to provide support
- Required software in support of the vendor application
- Required modifications of the base software

To determine the viability of the vendor, the following elements should also be evaluated:

- Financial condition
- Risk of acquisition
- Likelihood of exiting the market
- Reputation for responsiveness during problems

Other Resources for Help and Assistance

In this area, there is quite a bit of published literature and studies available to help organizations. The U.S. General Accounting Office (GAO) has published a number of reports on software acquisition problems within the federal government. Using the training and resources of Carnegie Mellon's Software Engineering Institute (SEI), GAO IT auditors have helped organizations and individuals to improve their software engineering management practices. Carnegie Mellon's SEI has developed very good information about software engineering management, SEI projects, and software engineering. Some of the products they have developed have been applied in commercial environments. Some of their products listed below focus on increased efficiency and quality in software acquisition or development:

- Organizations using good product-line practices can exploit commonalities across software systems to reduce costs and increase quality in software product lines.
- Small organizations, especially small manufacturing enterprises (SMEs), are using techniques from the technology insertion demonstration and evaluation (TIDE) program to improve and expand their businesses by acquiring and adopting commercially available information technology.
- The COTS-Based Systems Initiative provides techniques for assembling and evolving software-intensive systems based on commercially available software components.
- Software engineers trained in the Personal Software Process^{SM} (PSP) routinely produce work on schedule with reduced development time and significantly reduced numbers of defects in delivered code.
- PSP-trained engineers work together using the Team Software Process^{SM} (TSP^{SM}). The TSP was developed to help integrated engineering teams more effectively develop software-intensive products. This process method addresses many of the current problems of developing software-intensive products and shows teams and their management explicitly how to address them.
- An "open systems" approach can help you efficiently acquire and maintain high-quality systems that are technically up-to-date.

Other organizations such as National Institute of Standards and Technology (NIST), Association of Computing Machinery (ACM), Association of Information Technology Professionals (AITP), and others have materials that may be of help as identified in Appendix II and Appendix III.

Conclusion

Software acquisitions are often thought to be faster, easier, and cheaper for companies to meet their business needs. Though acquiring software can be very successful, it can also miss the mark. Purchased software can miss user requirements, exceed implementation goals or implementation costs, as well as introduce delays in business or project schedules.

This chapter discussed the basic steps in the software acquisition process:

- Defining the information and system requirements
- Identifying various alternatives
- Performing a feasibility analysis
- Conducting a risk analysis
- Defining ergonomic requirements
- Carrying out the selection process
- Procuring the selected software
- Completing final acceptance

In participating in a software acquisition process or reviewing it after-the-fact, the auditor should evaluate processes and evidence related to the following:

- Alignment with the company's business and IT strategy
- Definition of the information requirements
- Feasibility studies (cost, benefits, etc.)
- Identification of functionality, operational, acceptance, and maintenance requirements
- Conformity with existing information and system architectures
- Adherence to security and control requirements
- Knowledge of available solutions
- Understanding of the related acquisition and implementation methodologies
- Involvement and buy-in from the user
- Supplier requirements and viability

Review Questions

1. Name and describe the eight basic steps of a software acquisition process.
2. Name and describe the methods that can be used in gathering information and system requirements.

3. What are the advantages and disadvantages of prototyping?
4. Name and describe the components of a requirements document.
5. Compare and contrast the various options that exist for acquiring software.
6. In purchasing a software solutions provided by a vendor, what should be considered?
7. What are the advantages and disadvantages for contract development?
8. What are the advantages and disadvantages for outsourcing a system from another organization?
9. Name and describe the various categories of feasibility analysis.
10. Describe the areas covered as part of a risk analysis.
11. Describe the importance of defining the ergonomic requirements.
12. Compare and contrast the various methods to solicit vendor response to the needs of an organization.
13. What are the basic components of an RFP?
14. What are the basic steps and components needed to evaluate submitted proposals?
15. In a contract for software or programming services, name and describe the terms and conditions that should be included.
16. In evaluating a software acquisition process, name and describe the areas that the auditor should include in his or her review.
17. What criteria should be evaluated to determine the viability of the proposed vendor?

Multiple Choice

1. One of the basic steps in the software acquisition process is:
   a. Identifying a single alternative
   b. Defining the information and system requirements
   c. Performing user and site surveys
   d. Replacing existing hardware platforms
2. What is the most important step in the software acquisition process?
   a. Defining information requirements
   b. Identifying alternatives
   c. Performing the feasibility analysis
   d. Conducting risk analysis
3. As a means of increasing user support, many projects are now including as part of their project plans:
   a. Infrastructure diagrams
   b. Outsourcing
   c. Communication and business change management
   d. Sales and marketing

4. Gathering information and system requirements can be accomplished by all of the following except:
   a. Interviewing those expected to use the information produced by the system as well as those expected to produce the information input into the system
   b. Interviewing the software vendor to find the best-selling software in the market
   c. Developing a prototype of the proposed system
   d. Researching other companies
5. The system requirements documents do not provide the following information:
   a. Intended users of the system
   b. Feasibility analysis
   c. System attributes
   d. System cost
6. A document that specifies the minimal acceptable requirements as well as the evaluation criteria for a solution is called a:
   a. Request for bid
   b. Request for information
   c. Request for proposal
   d. Request for quote
7. Participants in the selection process may not include representatives from:
   a. Management
   b. Anticipated users
   c. IT department
   d. Vendor
8. Contract terms and conditions normally do not include the following:
   a. An organizational chart of the customer's IT department
   b. A functional definition of the work to be performed
   c. Vendor staffing and specified qualifications
   d. Methods of providing progress reports
9. What is not an advantage of purchasing off-the-shelf solutions?
   a. Shorter implementation time
   b. The ability to use the company's existing IT infrastructure
   c. Use of proven technology
   d. Easier to define costs
10. When selecting a vendor package, organizations should consider all of the following except:
    a. Stability of the vendor company
    b. Vendor's ability to provide support
    c. Required modifications to the base software
    d. Sales and marketing literature

Exercises

Scenario: *You work in your company's payroll department and are asked to acquire software that will automate the process for employees to submit their timesheets to the payroll department. Timesheets are the means by which hourly employees submit their time. Timesheets are approved by managers and then processed by the payroll department for payment. Using the new system, employees will input their time weekly into a computer system. Once employees complete their time sheets, managers will be able to view and approve them when they log into the system.*

Using the scenario described above, answer the following:

1. What methods would you use and why to gather the requirements for the system?
2. Document the information and system requirements using the outline of the requirements documented provided in the chapter.
3. Describe two or three alternatives solutions that should be considered.
4. Using the categories provided in the text and one of the alternatives that you described in Exercise two, perform a feasibility analysis.
5. Perform a risk analysis for the proposed system.
6. Who would you recommend be on the acceptance testing team?
7. In the acceptance plan, what tests would you recommend to ensure that information requirements are met?
8. In the acceptance plan, what tests would you recommend to ensure that the system performance requirements are met?
9. In the acceptance plan, what tests would you recommend to ensure that the system requirements are met?
10. How can a resource such as NIST or Carnegie Mellon's SEI be helpful in the software acquisition process?

Answers to Multiple Choice Questions

1 — b; 2 — a; 3 — c; 4 — b; 5 — d; 6 — c; 7 — d; 8 — a; 9 — b; 10 — d

References

1. Applegate, L.M., F.W. McFarlan, and R.D. Austin. *Corporate Information Strategy and Management: Text and Cases.* 6th ed., McGraw-Hill Irwin, New York, 2002.
2. Bachelor, B. Implementation Imperative. *Information Week.* April 28, 2003.
3. Burgunder, L. *Legal Aspects of Managing Technology.* 3rd ed., Thomson Corporation–South-Western, Mason, OH, 2004.
4. Corporate Executive Board. Case Studies of Software Purchasing Decisions. Working Council for Chief Information Officers. February 2003.
5. Corporate Executive Board. Negotiating Global Licensing Agreements. Working Council for Chief Information Officers. June 2001.
6. Davison, D. Assessing the vendor's viability. *ZDNet.* January 24, 2002. http://techupdate.zdnet.com/techupdate/stories/main/0,14179,2841191-2,00.html. (Accessed on January 8, 2003.)

7. Ferrera, G.R. et al. *Cyberlaw: Texts and Cases*. 2nd ed., Thomson Corporation–South-Western, Mason, OH, 2004.

8. Hoffer, J.A., J.F. George, and J.S. Valacich. *Modern Systems Analysis and Design*. 2nd ed., Addison Wesley, Reading, MA, 1999.

9. Information Systems Audit and Control Foundation. CoBiT Audit Guidelines. Information Systems Audit and Control Foundation, July 2000.

10. Kroemer, K. Ergonomics: Definition of Ergonomics. National Safety Council. http://www.nsc.org/issues/ergo/define.htm. (Accessed on July 28, 2003.)

11. Larman, C. *Applying UML and Patterns: An Introduction to Object-Oriented Analysis and Design*. Prentice-Hall, New York, 1998.

12. Markus, M.L. and C. Tanis. The enterprise systems experience — from adoption to success. In. *Framing the Domains of IT Research: Glimpsing the Future through the Past*, R.W. Zmud, Ed. Pinnaflex Educational Resources, Inc.,Cincinnati, OH, 2000.

13. Nah, L.K. Critical factors for successful implementation of enterprise systems. *Bus. Proc. Manage. J.* Vol. 7, No. 3, 2001.

14. National Consortium for Justice Information and Statistics. Court Technology Model Request for Proposals. SEARCH. http://www.search.org/courts/modelrfp/intro.htm. (Accessed on July 25, 2003.)

15. Pereira, B. A customer-centric software contract. *Network Magazine*. September 2002.

16. Watson, H., J. Frolic, and N. Mark. Determining Information Requirements for an EIS. MISQ, Vol. 17, No. 3, September 1993.

Chapter 10
System Implementation

The purpose of the system implementation process is to verify that the solution meets its intended purpose. Implementing a system consists of configuring the system, testing functionality, converting data, training users, and preparing for production support. It is another key IT audit review point because implementation is often where critical controls may be overwritten or deactivated to bring the system up and operational to meet organizational needs and requirements. Good planning and requirements definitions, management support, end-user involvement and support, and management of the configuration are the elements that contribute to successful implementation. Search any of the GAO reports as shown in Appendix II, news magazines such as *InfoWorld, Computer World, and Network World*, Auerbach Publications, and other sources where you can read about those system implementations that are successful and those that fail, and the lessons to be learned.

The System Implementation Process

The implementation phase not only includes implementing the system itself but guarantees that it meets its purpose, it works, and that the necessary process and procedures are in place for production. To ensure a well-controlled system implementation, the following controls should be included in the system implementation process:

- Implementation approach
- System testing
- User processes and procedures
- Management reports and controls
- Problem management/reporting
- User-acceptance testing
- Help desk and production support training and readiness
- Data conversion and data correction processes
- Operational procedures and readiness
- Security

A well-controlled implementation phase minimizes production issues such as system bugs, performance issues, misunderstood expectations, and misaligned staffing.

Implementation Approach

An implementation approach should be documented to guide the implementation team and users in the implementation process. The strategy should cover the implementation schedule, the resources required, roles and responsibilities of the implementation team, the means of communication between the implementation team and users, decision processes, issue management procedures, and a training plan for the implementation team and end users.

System Testing

Testing is by far the most critical part of any system implementation. However, it is also the first to get short-changed when go-live dates get challenged. The primary purpose of testing is to validate that the system works as expected and to identify bugs at an early stage because bugs discovered later are costly to fix. The testing plan should address the effects on online help functions and user manuals, as well as installation and operational guidelines.

An overall testing strategy should be developed to define the individual test events, roles and responsibilities, test environment, problem reporting and tracking, and test deliverables. The testing process should be based on existing testing methodologies established by the organization. An effective testing process allows for documentation that will prevent duplicate testing efforts.

A testing plan should be made in accordance with the organization's standards and should include test scenarios, the role of the test participants, acceptance criteria, and testing logistics. All types of users should perform testing and they should not be developers. The testing plan should also identify responsibility for documentation, review, and approval of tests and test results. End users and system owners should sign off that appropriate testing was performed with expected results for all requirements. Senior management sign-off is required when programs are promoted to production with known errors.

Although each application may define different test events, in general, test events include unit testing, integration testing, technical testing, functional testing, and acceptance testing (see Exhibit 1).

The test scenarios, associated data, and the expected results should be documented for every condition and option. Test data should include data that is representative of relevant business scenarios, which could be real

Exhibit 1. Test Events

Test Event	Test Objectives
Unit testing	Unit testing verifies that stand-alone programs match specifications. Test cases should exercise every line of code.
Integration testing	Integration testing verifies that all software and hardware components work together. Data is passed from one program to the next. All programs and subroutines should be tested during this phase. Test cases should cover all components (e.g., hardware and software).
Functional testing	Functional testing verifies that the application meets user requirements. Test cases should cover screens, navigation, function keys, online help, processing, and output (reports, files, and screens)
Technical testing	Technical testing verifies that the application works in the production environment. Test cases should include error processing and recovery, performance, storage requirements, hardware compatibility, and security (e.g., screens, data, and programs).
Acceptance testing	Acceptance testing verifies that acceptance criteria defined during the project definition stage are tested. Test cases should include system usability, management reports, performance measurements, documentation and procedures, training (e.g., users, help desk, production support, operations), and system readiness (Operations/Systems sign-off).

or generated test data. Regardless of the type of test data chosen, it should represent the quality and volume of data that is expected. However, controls over the production data used for testing should be evaluated to ensure that the test data is not misused or compromised.

Performance and load testing defines and tests the performance expectations in advance. It ensures that the application is scalable (functionally and technically). It also ensures that applications can be implemented without disruption to the business. The entire infrastructure should be represented in performance and load testing to ensure capacity and throughput at all levels: central processing, input and output media, networks, etc. The test environment should reflect the live environment as much as possible.

User Processes and Procedures

User reference materials and procedures should be included as part of the development and maintenance of associated applications. They should be reviewed and approved as part of acceptance testing. User reference materials should be designed for all levels of user expertise and should instruct them on the use of the application. The documentation should be kept current as changes are made to the dependent systems.

Management Reports and Controls

The development of management reports and their associated controls needs to be included within the scope of the system implementation. The reports generated should be aligned with business requirements. The reports should be relevant to ensure effectiveness and efficiency of the report development effort.

In general, report specifications should include its recipients, usage, required details, and frequency, as well as the method of generation and delivery. The format of the report needs to be defined so that the report is clear, concise, and understandable. Each report should be validated to ensure that it is accurate and complete. The control measures for each report should be evaluated to ensure that the appropriate controls are implemented so that availability, integrity, and confidentiality are assured.

Problem Management/Reporting

No matter how well a system is tested, there will always be problems discovered after implementation. There needs to be a way for the users to report system problems to the programmers, and in turn for the programmers to communicate to the users when the problem has been fixed. It ensures that problems are resolved and the causes are investigated to prevent their reoccurrence.

A problem management system should consist of audit trails for problems and their solutions, timely resolution, prioritization, escalation procedures, incident reports, accessibility to configuration, information coordination with change management, and a definition of any dependencies on outside services.

The problem management process should ensure that all unexpected events (errors, problems, etc.) are recorded, analyzed, and resolved in a timely manner. Incident reports should be established in the case of significant problems.

Escalation procedures ensure that problems are resolved in the most timely and efficient way possible. Escalation procedures include prioritizing problems based on the impact severity as well as the activation of a business continuity plan when necessary.

Problems should be traceable from the incident to the source cause (e.g., new software release, emergency change, etc.). The problem management process should be closely associated with change management.

User Acceptance Testing

User acceptance testing is a key to application controls. It ensures that the application fulfills the agreed-upon functional expectations of the users, meets established usability criteria, and satisfies performance guidelines prior to being implemented into production. Acceptance testing minimizes the risks that the new application will cause business interruptions or be disjointed with business processes. Acceptance testing should include all components of the system (facilities, application software, procedures, etc.).

Acceptance Team. The process owner should establish the acceptance team. The team is responsible for developing and implementing the acceptance process. The acceptance team should be comprised of representatives from various functions including developers, IT operations, technical support, capacity planning, the help desk, and database administration.

Agreed-Upon Requirements. Requirements for acceptance testing need to be identified, prioritized, and agreed upon. Indirectly, the acceptance requirements become the criteria for making go/no-go decisions for determining if the system satisfies the critical requirements prior to being implemented.

Acceptance criteria should be specific with detailed measures. Acceptance plans should include inspections, functional tests, and workload trials. Ideally, users should use actual samples of their work in designing and executing acceptance tests.

Management Approval. Acceptance plans and test results need to be approved by the affected functional department as well as the IT department.

To avoid surprises, users should be involved in system testing throughout the development processes. This minimizes the risk of key functionality being excluded or having it not work.

Help Desk and Production Support Training and Readiness

Help desk and production support processes ensure that any problems experienced by the user are appropriately resolved in a timely manner. A help-desk function should provide first-line support to end users. It should provide the ability for customers to ask questions and receive effective answers. Help requests should be monitored to ensure that all problems are resolved in a timely manner. Trend analysis should be conducted to identify patterns in problems or solutions. Problems should be analyzed to identify root causes. Procedures need to be in place for escalating problems based on inadequate response or level of impact. Questions that cannot be immediately resolved should be escalated to higher levels of management or expertise.

All problems should be recorded with the help desk to allow for their complete analysis and resolution. Problems should be monitored to ensure that they are resolved in a timely manner. The help desk function should work closely with the problem management function.

Organizations with established help desks will need to staff and train help-desk personnel to handle the new application. Good training will minimize the volume of calls to the help desk and thereby keep support costs down. Help desks can be managed efficiently with the use of problem management software, automated telephone systems, expert systems, e-mail, voicemail, and fax.

Training is an important aspect of any project implementation. According to a Gartner Group study, the cost of not training will far exceed the investment organizations will make to train both end users and IS professionals in new technologies. One reason for this paradox is that users who are forced to learn on their own take as much as six times longer to become productive with the software product. The Gartner Group study also showed that an effective training program reduces support costs by three to six times because users make fewer mistakes and have fewer questions (Gartner, p. 9).

Ongoing user support is another important component needed to ensure a successful implementation. The previously mentioned Gartner Group study found that the need for support is inelastic, and the gap between needed support and formal support will be filled by "underground support." This underground support, which is informal support by peers or department-purchased outsourcing, accounts for as much as 30 percent of user-computing costs (Gartner, p. 9). Ongoing support materials can include quick reference guides, access to answers to commonly asked questions, or the ability to call a subject matter expert.

Data Conversion and Data Correction Processes

Unless a process is new, existing information will need to be converted to the new system. Conversion is the process whereby this information is either entered manually or transferred programmatically from the old system to the new system. In either case, the existence of procedures should verify the conversion of all records and the accuracy of data entered into the new system.

A data conversion plan defines how the data is collected and verified for conversion. Prior to conversion, the data should be "cleaned" to remove any inconsistencies that introduce errors during the conversion or when the data is placed in the new application.

Tests to be performed include comparing the original and converted files and checking the compatibility of the converted data with the new system, and ensuring transactions affecting both converted and not-yet unconverted data. This will keep the data current during the period between initial conversion and final implementation. A detailed verification of the processing with the converted data in the new system should be performed to confirm successful implementation. The system owners are responsible for ensuring that data is successfully converted.

The data conversion process often gets intermingled with data cleanup. Data cleanup is a process that companies embark upon to ensure that the most accurate and complete data gets transferred into the new system. A common example is company names in a vendor file. A company can be input into a vendor file multiple times in multiple ways. For example, "ABC Manufacturing" can be "ABC mfg" or "abc Mfg.," etc. Many of these data cleanup changes can be dealt with systematically because many errors happen consistently.

Ideally, the data cleanup effort should happen prior to the planning for data conversion. This allows the conversion programmers to focus on converting the data as opposed to coding for data differences. However, in reality, the exemptions from data conversion become issues for the data cleanup team to deal with. Data conversion and data cleanup teams should work closely with each other to ensure that the most accurate and complete data is converted. Management should sign off on test results for converted data as well as approve changes identified by the data cleanup team.

Operational Procedures and Readiness

System documentation ensures maintainability of the system and its components and minimizes the likelihood of errors. Documentation should be based on a defined standard and consist of descriptions of procedures, instructions to personnel, flowcharts, data flow diagrams, display or report layouts, and other materials that describe the system. System documentation should provide maintenance programmers with enough information to understand how the system works to ensure effective and efficient analysis of program changes and troubleshooting. Documentation should be updated as the system is modified.

The processing logic should be documented in a manner that is understandable, using pseudocode, flowcharts, etc., while containing sufficient detail to allow programmers to accurately support the application. The software must also include documentation within the code, with descriptive comments embedded in the body of the source code. These comments should include cross-references to design documentation and requirements documents. The documentation should describe the sequence of programs and the steps to be taken in case of a processing failure.

System documentation helps maintenance programmers understand the system to correct problems and make enhancements. Documentation builds at each phase in the development process. The initial justification defines the application functionality that is converted into program specifications and used to create test cases. Test cases are used for implementation training and exercises. Documentation can be created as flowcharts, graphs, tables, or text for organization and ease of reading. Documentation may include:

- Source of the data
- Data attributes
- Input screens
- Data validations
- Data selection criteria
- Security procedures
- Description of calculations
- Program design
- Interfaces to other applications
- Control procedures
- Error handling
- Operating instructions
- Archive, purge, and retrieval
- Backup, storage, and recovery

IT Disaster/Continuity Plans

This is another key review point for both management and the IT auditor and security personnel. As part of the system implementation, requirements for its recovery in the event of a disaster or other disruption should be accounted for. IT continuity plans should be reviewed to ensure that the company plans incorporate the resources necessary to recover the new application. Significant upgrades to existing applications may also require modification to disaster recovery requirements in areas such as processor requirements, disk storage, or operating system versions. Recovery procedures related to the new application should be tested as soon as possible after it is put into production.

In the rush to implement a system, documentation and procedures can be the first to "slide." However, the price is paid when decisions to address problems become reactionary. Formalizing documentation and procedures is the difference between delivering a technology versus delivering a service. This plan should be in place at the point of implementation and carried through into operations. Later in Chapter 16 we discuss thoroughly the importance and execution of the plan.

Security

When new systems are developed, appropriate security access controls need to be developed. Additionally, existing security processes, procedures, and controls may need to be reviewed. The goal of application security is to safeguard information against unapproved disclosure or modification, and damage or loss.

Logical access controls are used to ensure that access to systems, data, and programs is limited to appropriate users and IT support personnel. Application security should consider privacy and confidentiality requirements, authorization and authentication processes, business access requirements, user training, and monitoring.

In one case, a packaged ERP (enterprise resource planning) software implementation caused a company to revisit its authentication process and standards, security management process, and information access practices. Authentication was previously provided by each application. As a consequence of implementing a package, the company decided to consolidate authentication from many systems into one system using LDAP (Lightweight Directory Access Protocol). Based on that decision, the process for approving access needed to be consolidated to ensure consistency in policies and practices. Lastly, information access practices needed to be revisited due to the combination of various types of data and users into one system. Data that was once specific to only one group in its individual application was now contributed to and needed by multiple departments.

Case Example: GMA Business Overview and Profile

General Mercantile of America, also know as GMA, is the premier importer and distributor of chinaware in the United States. Founded in 1985, GMA has been able to secure, maintain, and grow its market share by offering the largest selection of products available from a single distributor resource to the various channels of distributors. By stocking more than 1100 individual items, GMA serves its dealers and its suppliers by providing each of them with a virtually uninterrupted flow of well-designed, well-manufactured, and well-priced products. This is accomplished via its network of four strategically located warehouses whose total square footage exceeds 400,000. There are plans currently in place to add one new branch in New York in 2001.

GMA is headquartered in the Los Angeles suburb of City of Commerce, which has convenient access to several major freeways and the ports of Los Angeles and Long Beach. This location has the capacity to handle more than 5000 ocean containers annually, 3000 of which are piggybacked to branch locations. The commitment to depth and breadth of inventory makes GMA the logical, one-stop source for full-line chinaware dealers or specialty retailers who require a narrow selection of merchandise.

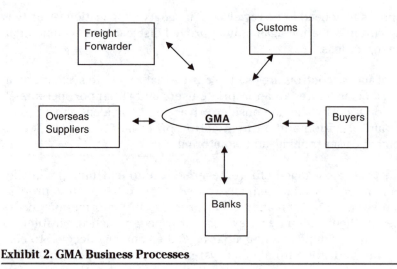

Exhibit 2. GMA Business Processes

International trade is complex because it involves suppliers and import-ers, customer services, port storage companies, and transportation com-panies. GMA operates in a highly competitive environment along with hun-dreds of other chinaware importers and distributors in the United States. In this market, large amounts of information flow among several trading partners and support services. This information includes orders, billings, status query, contracts, payments, etc. The problem faced by GMA is how to effectively manage the information at competitive prices and how to uti-lize current IT to effectively support its business operation process and meet the business objective.

The external business operations actively involve parties from overseas manufacturers (suppliers), transportation forwarding companies, cus-toms, and banks. (See Exhibit 2.)

IT Solutions for GMA

Based an an evaluation of GMA's business process, trading partner pref-erences, and requirements, GMA launched E-commerce solutions for its international trading business. The company believes that E-commerce is the trend in doing business in the future and this is why it started its Web site in 1998. At the same time, GMA started Web-based EDI to conduct its import business with overseas supplies and major vendors in the United States, such as Nordstrom Department Store and Sears. The management of GMA believes that the effective way of doing business equates poten-tially to saving time and saving money. Normal business transactions require large amounts of paper, phone calls, and printing among other things. All of these can be replaced with the use of Web-based electronic data interchange (EDI). By performing electronically the same transactions done on paper, not only is time saved but the chance of error is reduced as well. Much of the error that occurs during such transactions includes human typographical errors. A user may enter in an extra zero, changing 10,000 to 100,000. With EDI, having to reenter data is no longer an issue. Moreover, EDI can reduce business expenses such as shipping and handling by providing added support to manufacturers in terms of just-in-time inventory and third-party warehousing.

At the same time, GMA is using the extranet to open their networks to provide access for business partners, distributors, and customers. When deploying extranets, transactions between companies becomes less and less complicated. The extranet has become the ideal medium for B2B transactions. They are fast becoming vital business tools, providing a cross between the openness of the Internet and the security and privacy of the intranet. On a basic level, the extranet allows for routine transactions via the Internet within a trading community, assuring security through built-in measures appropriate to the user and task at hand. A much broader perspective envisions collaborative communities where partnering companies readily share data, knowledge, systems, goals, and issues.

Major E-Commerce Security Implementation Issues at GMA

The issues of identification, privacy, and overall security are compounded within GMA as it engages in commerce on the Internet on a global basis. There are several main risks of utilizing E-commerce, which could impact GMA's business operations. For instance, extranets are not without caveats. For one thing, the security may be rudimentary. Most extranets, for instance, do not encrypt the passwords and user IDs sent across the network. Customers may not protect their user IDs and passwords as well as they should. In each case, the result could be unauthorized use. Based on an awareness assessment prior to implementation in GMA, we can locate some crucial risks facing international trading companies that are deploying E-commerce. The most threatening risk facing organizations like GMA is the leakage of business-sensitive data. Such sensitive data can be customer data, credit card data, contracts between supplier and vendor, supplier information, etc. In addition, data inaccessibility and lack of data integrity are also major threats to organizations that conduct international trading business.

Awareness Assessment. The following questions are intended to gauge the level of data sensitivity involved in the E-commerce solution being deployed in international trading businesses. Data sensitivity is a vulnerability that must be addressed in a B2B and B2C solution.

1. Is there or will there be financial data being transmitted?
2. Is there or will there be customer information begin transmitted?
3. Is there or will there be contract information being transmitted?

The following questions assess the level of communication that has taken place between trading partners using a B2B solution. It is critical to communicate and agree upon policies and procedures, as well as how and what business will be conducted in a B2B deployment.

1. Are there standards set and communicated between trading partners in regards to security architecture and policies?
2. Is there a recovery plan shared between partners if one or more system's security is compromised?
3. Is there an agreed-upon access control policy between trading partners?

The following questions raise the issue of physical and logical security. Again, are the trading partners involved aware and comfortable with the others' security measures?

- Is your enterprise systems' architecture protected with firewalls? At what levels are firewalls deployed and what risks have been identified but not addressed?
  - WAN/LAN level
  - Operating systems level
  - Server level (DNS servers)
  - Application level
  - Database level
- What is the physical access level policy for your systems? Are all stakeholders aware and in agreement with this policy?

The following questions are intended to point out the importance of development standards within an organization and across trading organizations for the sake of security. It is important that all stakeholders understand the development process of B2B solutions in terms of security policy adherence at development, maintenance, and support.

1. Are your systems' solution development projects centralized or decentralized?
2. Do developers of B2B solutions in your organization and trading partners adhere to security and architecture standards? How are these policies communicated and enforced?
3. Will the development, support, or maintenance of the B2B solution be outsourced? If so, what are the security policies and controls deployed by the outsource partner?

The objective of the above assessment is not to measure the risks present in a current E-commerce solution in GMA but to get the business entities behind an E-commerce solution asking the right questions prior to implementation. The goal is awareness. The assessment is a gauge as to how aware the business entity is of the risks and controls that must be considered along with the return on investment analysis of an E-commerce solution. The assessment is comprised of questions that are, also, intended to raise level of awareness. Each question should be followed by a small explanation of the question's value.

Implementing Risk Analysis and Controls at GMA. Three main areas of concern to address the risks of compromising E-commerce solution securities involve the method of capturing and formatting data for Internet communication through Extensible Markup Language (XML), the data transport security involved in virtual private networks, and policies revolving around security measures for a B2B solution.

With the use of B2B solutions predicted to rise to a $2.8 trillion business by 2003, according to the Boston Consulting Group, most of that being in the use of the Internet rather than EDI, we cannot ignore the fundamental steps of the E-commerce solutions and the security risks they introduce. For the sake of this discussion, let us use an order entry in GMA Web site as our example. The GMA Company manufactures ceramic cups that are sold in department stores. These department stores enter their orders for the ceramic cups on the GMA Web site, which is protected by a username and password. The GMA Company does not extend credit to its customers, which means a VISA or MasterCard number must accompany each order. Payment for the orders is verified and transacted at the time the orders are confirmed by the GMA system.

The first thing a GMA customer must do is log on to the GMA Web site, which requires a username and password that is unique to each one of its customers. The authentication information is then verified by the GMA system and access is either granted or denied. Let us assume the customer is granted access. The order entry screen is shown with the customer's name, address, phone and shipping information, and compliments of the GMA system. Next, an order must be entered for the ceramic cups; again, this order must be accompanied by a VISA or MasterCard number. The customer provides the information and clicks a button to submit the order. This information is transmitted to the GMA system for confirmation. Confirmation is granted when the GMA inventory has been checked for product availability and the customer credit card transaction is successful. Again, let us assume the order is confirmed, which allows for the GMA system to send a confirmation message back to the waiting customer. The cups are then picked, packed, and shipped to the customer. All this business was performed paper-free and just in time. This scenario is the ideal behind a B2B solution. What are the concerns?

Were risks involved in that scenario? Yes. The GMA Company systems and customer systems were opened to the worldwide network and the customer's financial data was transmitted across open lines. From a business perspective, the main risks here are the risks that an attack from an intruder could take the ordering system down and customer information confidentiality could be compromised, causing the loss of a potentially large amount of business. Before we begin the discussion of how to address these risks, let us state the scope of this discussion. As stated, the risks involved extend across the entire network of systems connected to the systems involved in the E-commerce solution as well as the data being transmitted across the systems. The three overriding concerns are confidentiality, authenticity, and data integrity. This section will concentrate on the preservation of the data confidentiality and the authenticity. Again, the loss of business can be attributed to an intruder who gains access to the systems via capturing of authentication information and "takes down" the systems, or by an intruder capturing customer financial information for malicious use. Both vulnerabilities are exposed when the data passes from one system to another via untrusted transport. The scope of the controls to combat or manage these risks will revolve around the securing of the transport of this confidential data rather than the deploying of firewalls that can be deployed to either detect intruders or slow them down.

What controls are available for improving the security of vulnerable data passing through the open pipes of the network? Before we can answer this question we must understand where and how the data is vulnerable. Let us take data entry as an example. In the case of our example this would be at the order entry screen. Most likely, the screen was written in XML because of its ability to provide the programmer with the flexibility to represent any number of forms such as invoices and order entry. The problem with this is that it depends on further standards development to ensure security. Key security issues include authentication and nonrepudiation of XML documents.

Summary

Identification of risks and controls in E-commerce is not intended to defer the deployment of a B2B and B2C solution. It is this technology that will catapult a business into competitiveness in tomorrow's market. The intent of this is to provide an understanding that will lead to proper deployment of security technology and policy to provide a safe environment for conducting business in the E-commerce realm. To what extent does a company or client have to deploy the available solutions or be concerned about the risks involved? Again, the answer is that it depends. The GMA Company is at a high risk of losing business if the data confidentiality in their B2B system is compromised due to the sensitivity of the data being transmitted. On the other hand, if the GMA Company continued to provide online ordering to their customers but implemented a manual billing system for financial reconciliation of the business transactions taking place between themselves and their customers, the risks dramatically depreciate. Each situation or B2B solution must evaluate its risks and the controls reasonable for its situation.

Conclusion

The purpose of the system implementation process is to verify that the solution meets its intended purpose. As indicated in the GMC case, implementing a system consists of configuring the system, testing functionality, converting data, training users, and preparing for production support. A number of questions have to be asked prior to implementation to ensure that a successful and secure transition takes place minimizing any vulnerabilities.

In this chapter, the following controls for system implementation were reviewed:

- Implementation approach
- System testing
- User processes and procedures
- Management reports and controls
- Problem management/reporting
- User-acceptance testing
- Help desk and production support training and readiness
- Data conversion and data correction processes
- Operational procedures and readiness
- Security

An auditor's role in system implementations is to ensure that risks are identified and proper controls are considered during the implementation process. In some organizations, auditors are members of the implementation team and participate like any other member. In some cases, auditors review documentation at key stages of the implementations. If organizations do not have the resources to include auditors during the implementations, auditors then do postimplementation reviews to test for implemented controls after-the-fact. In those cases, there is no assurance that the controls implemented were completed or all the risks accounted for. Consequently, identifying risks or recommending controls after a system is implemented is more costly and may limit the organization's ability to implement the most effective controls.

Review Questions

1. Name and describe the ten controls for the system implementation process.
2. What risks are minimized with a well-controlled system implementation process?

3. Explain the purpose of defining the implementation approach.
4. What should be included in an overall testing strategy?
5. What is the purpose of a testing plan? What should be included in a testing plan?
6. Describe the purpose of test data. Compare and contrast the difference between real or generated test data.
7. Describe the purpose of developing user processes and procedures as part of the system implementation. What type of procedures should be included?
8. What is included in a report specification?
9. What controls should be included as part of the report development process?
10. Explain why a problem management system is important.
11. What should be included as part of user-acceptance testing?
12. Why is a help desk and production support critical to system implementations? Discuss its interrelationship with the problem management and reporting system.
13. What risks are associated with data conversion? What controls should be considered in a data conversion process?
14. Compare and contrast data cleanup with data conversion.
15. Name and describe items that should be included as part of operation procedures and documentation.
16. Why is it necessary for maintenance programmers to have good documentation?
17. Why should continuity plans be addressed during an implementation as opposed to after?
18. Define logical access controls.
19. Describe the benefit of having an IT auditor as part of the system implementation team.

Multiple Choice

1. All of the following are types of controls to include in a system implementation except:
   a. System testing
   b. User procedures
   c. Job descriptions
   d. Management reports
2. Testing that verifies that a stand-alone program meets the specifications is:
   a. Unit testing
   b. Functional testing
   c. Technical testing
   d. Acceptance testing

3. Testing that verifies that the application can be implemented without interruption to business and that there is enough capacity is:
   a. Unit testing
   b. Functional testing
   c. Technical testing
   d. Performance and load testing

4. Using a video store scenario, the store uses an application that helps manage the video store. The following are examples of user processes that need procedures except:
   a. Checking videos out
   b. Store closing
   c. Adding new customers
   d. Restocking video tapes

5. End-user acceptance testing ensures that the system:
   a. Fulfils the agreed-upon functional expectations
   b. Meets established usability
   c. Satisfies performance guidelines
   d. Meets state regulations

6. Documentation included in a software implementation includes of the following except:
   a. User procedures
   b. Error handling procedures
   c. Training materials
   d. Job descriptions

7. Conversion is defined as the process of:
   a. Cleaning data in the legacy system
   b. Testing data
   c. Transferring data from the legacy system to the new system
   d. Testing data during an implementation

8. Which one of these in not part of user-acceptance testing?
   a. Acceptance team
   b. Agreed-upon requirements
   c. Management approval
   d. Legal requirements

9. What is not considered a form of documentation in a system implementation?
   a. The sequence of programs and steps to be taken in case of processing failure
   b. Code with comments embedded
   c. IS strategy
   d. Pseudocode and flowcharts

10. A well-controlled implementation minimizes the following risks except:
    a. Staff turnover
    b. System bugs

c. Misaligned staff
d. Performance issues

Exercises

For the exercises below, refer to the following scenario:

A video store has a cash register application used to total a customer's order and receive cash payments. The company now wants to accept credit cards. Consequently, the cash register company comes to the store and enables the credit card feature within the cash register software.

1. Outline a user process/procedure that should be developed for this system.
2. Give an example of a unit test and an integration test.
3. Write three test scenarios that should be included in the test plan.
4. Describe an example of when performance and load testing would be important.
5. Describe three system implementation controls that you would recommend for this system. What risks will occur if they are not in place?
6. Describe the major components of a help desk/end-user assistance plan for this system.
7. What groups of people should receive training as part of this system implementation? For each defined group, describe the training that they should receive.
8. What application security risks exist with this application? Describe the controls that you would recommend for each.
9. Develop report specifications for a management report delivered as part of this system.

Answers to Multiple Choice Questions

1 — c; 2 — a; 3 — d; 4 — b; 5 — a; 6 — d; 7 — c; 8 — d; 9 — c; 10 — a

References

1. Allen, S., F. Gallegos, and D. Manson. *Audit Concerns for End-User Computing and Application Development.* EDP Auditing, Auerbach Publishers, Boca Raton, FL. 1996.
2. Dow, D.P. and F. Gallegos. *Auditing Systems Maintenance: A How-to Approach.* EDP Auditing, Auerbach Publishers, Boca Raton, FL. 1986.
3. Dow, D.P. and F. Gallegos. *Key Review Points for SDLC Audits.* EDP Auditing, Auerbach Publishers, Boca Raton, FL. 1987.
4. F. Gallegos, *CIS Auditors Role in Systems Development.* EDP Auditing, Auerbach Publishers, Boca Raton, FL. 1998.
5. Gallegos, F. and S. Schneider. *The Audit Process and the Information Center.* EDP Auditing, Auerbach Publishers, Boca Raton, FL. 1988.
6. Gallegos, F. *Auditing DSS: Review Points for IS Managers.* EDP Auditing, Auerbach Publishers, Boca Raton, FL. 1998.

7. Gallegos, F. *Software Tools and Techniques*. EDP Auditing, Auerbach Publishers, Boca Raton, FL. 1985.
8. Gartner Group. *Managing Distributed Computing: Stabilizing an Exploding Universe.* 1995 Western Region Briefing. April 18, 1995, Universal City, CA.
9. Gaston, S.J. *Audit of Small Computer Systems Including LANs*. The Canadian Institute of Chartered Accountants 1993.
10. Gaston, S.J. *Managing and Controlling Small Computer Systems Including LANs*. The Canadian Institute of Chartered Accountants 1992.
11. Information Systems Audit and Control Foundation. IT Control Practice Statement: AI-2 Acquiring and Maintaining Application Software. Information Systems Audit and Control Foundation, February 2002.
12. Information Systems Audit and Control Foundation. CoBiT Audit Guidelines. Information Systems Audit and Control Foundation, July 2000.
13. King, D. *Current Practices in Software Development*. Yourdon Press, New York, 1984.
14. Lientz, B.P. and E.B. Swanson. Problems in Application Software Maintenance. *Communications of the ACM* 24(11): 763–769, 1981.
15. Lientz, B.P., E.B. Swanson, and G.E. Tompkins. Characteristics of Application Software Maintenance. *Communications of the ACM* 21(6): 466–471, 1978.
16. Markus, M.L. and C. Tanis. The enterprise systems experience — from adoption to success. In: *Framing the Domains of IT Research: Glimpsing the Future through the Past,* R.W. Zmud, Ed. Pinnaflex Educational Resources, Inc., Cincinnati, OH. 2000.
17. Schiesser, R. Guaranteeing Production Readiness Prior to Deployment. Prentice Hall PTR, New York. http://www.informit.com/isapi/product_id~%7B0CF23CBC-CDCC-4B50-A00E-17CBE595AA31%7D/content/index.asp. (Verified on August 1, 2003).
18. Swanson, E.B. and Beath C.M. Departmentalization in Software Development and Maintenance. *Communications of the ACM* 33(6): 658–667, 1990.
19. Williams, P.B. *Getting a Project Done on Time: Managing People, Time, and Results*. American Management Association. 1996.

Chapter 11
Application Risks and Controls

Computer-based applications provide automated functions, which effectively support the business process. Applications also introduce risks to organizations in the form of increased costs, loss of data integrity, weaknesses in confidentiality, lack of availability, or poor performance.

Assuming that these risks were addressed during the implementation phase, applications need to be changed and these risks can be reintroduced. Once an application is implemented, programs will need to be periodically modified to correct program errors or implement system enhancements. However, maintaining these applications costs money, introduces problems, becomes inconsistent with business or IT strategies, degrades performance, and can monopolize the resources of an organization.

Application Risks

The risks in a computer-based system include both the risks that would be present in any manual processing system and those that are unique to an automated environment. In a manual system, errors are made individually, but in computer systems errors are made in quantity because automated systems apply rules (good and bad) consistently. Additionally, automated systems can contain errors that can trigger errors in an unrelated part of the system and so on. This cascading effect can occur between applications when they become more integrated, which magnifies the potential risks.

In a manual system, data is voluminous and stored in many places. Conversely, in automated systems, the data is concentrated and is in a format that can be easily accessed. The concentration of data can also increase the risks by placing greater reliance on a single piece of data or on a single computer file or database table. If the data entered is erroneous, the more applications that rely on that piece of data and the greater the impact of the error. Further, the more applications that use the concentrated data, the greater the impact when that data becomes unavailable because of problems with either the hardware or software used for processing it.

257

Information systems (IS) professionals need to consider the levels of risk associated with an application and establish appropriate controls. Risks associated with automated applications include:

- Weak security
- Unauthorized access to data
- Unauthorized remote access
- Inaccurate information
- Erroneous or falsified data input
- Misuse by authorized end users
- Incomplete processing
- Duplicate transactions
- Untimely processing
- Communications system failure
- Inadequate training
- Inadequate support

Weak Security

Information systems security should be a concern of IT, users, and management. However, security, for many companies, is not a top priority. In a 1994 survey conducted by Ernst and Young and a 1996 report by Price Waterhouse, organizations were found to be more concerned with budgets and staff shortages than security. When resources are tight, it is difficult to sell management on spending money for the intangible benefits of security efforts. Respondents to the survey identified obstacles to reducing security risks as lack of human resources, lack of funds, lack of management awareness, and lack of tools and solutions. However, the survey did discover that organizations have increased their security staff. Advanced technology and increased end-user access to critical information has fueled the increase in security risks. According to an *Infosecurity News* survey, the primary concern regarding security involves a lack of end-user awareness.

Unauthorized Access or Changes to Data or Programs

Applications should be built with various levels of authorization for transaction submission and approval. Once an application goes into production, programmers should no longer have access to programs and data. If programmers are provided access, all activity should be logged, reported, and reviewed by an independent group. Risks of unauthorized access to data include the possibility of information leaks that would permit outsiders to assess the present state and characteristics of an organization.

Unauthorized Remote Access

More and more users are demanding remote access to a company's computer resources. The easiest method to provide security is to eliminate modem access completely. With weak access controls, a modem allows virtually anyone access to an organization's resources. To protect against unauthorized access, remote dial-up access could have a callback feature that identifies the user with a specific location. A more complicated solution is to have key cards with encrypted IDs installed on the remote terminal and a front-end server on the host. At a minimum, user IDs and passwords should be encrypted when transmitted over public lines. In addition, confidential data that is transmitted over public lines should be encrypted. The security solution depends on the sensitivity of the data being transmitted.

Inaccurate Information

Accurate information is an issue whether the end user is accessing a database on the mainframe or a departmental database on a PC. End users may be asked to generate reports without their fully understanding the underlying information or they may not be sufficiently trained in the reporting application to ask the appropriate questions. Additional complications occur when end users download information from the mainframe for analysis and reporting. Departmental databases may have redundant information with different timeframes. The result is waste of time in reconciling two databases to determine which data is accurate. Another major area of concern is that management may fail to use information properly. The reasons for such neglect include:

- Failure to identify significant information
- Failure to interpret the meaning and value of the acquired information
- Failure to communicate information to the responsible manager or chief decision maker

Erroneous or Falsified Data Input

This is the simplest and most common cause of undesirable performance by an application system. Vulnerabilities occur whenever data is collected, manually processed, or prepared for entry to the computer.

Misuse by Authorized End Users

The system is designed for use by end users but can also be misused by them. It is often difficult to determine whether end users are operating the system in accordance with the legitimate performance of their job.

Incomplete Processing

This includes transactions or files that are not processed due to an error. Incomplete processing may occur in batch processing when a file is not present or during online processing when a transaction trigger fails to kick off a transaction.

Duplicate Transaction Processing

This includes transactions that are processed more than once. Duplicate transactions can occur during batch processing if files are run multiple times or during online processing when a transaction trigger kicks off a transaction more than once.

Untimely Processing

This includes delayed processing due to production problems or missing a time cutoff. For example, financial processes must occur at month-end closing to ensure that the detailed transactions processed in one system match the transaction posting to the general ledger. In addition, when online systems post transactions to a batch system, there is usually a cutoff time where processing ends on day one and begins for day two.

Communications System Failure

Information that is routed from one location to another over communication lines is vulnerable to accidental failures and to intentional interception and modification by unauthorized parties.

Inadequate Testing

Independent testing is important to identify design flaws that may have been overlooked by the developer of a system. Often, the individual who creates the design will be the only one testing the program and so he or she is only confirming that the system performs exactly as it was designed to be. The end user should develop acceptance criteria that can be used in testing the development effort. An acceptance criterion helps to ensure that the end users' system requirements are validated during testing. For example, the National Institute of Standards and Technology (NIST) has created a forum of developers and users to exchange testing and acceptance criteria on new IT security products. Examples of the types of tests that need to be performed are shown in Exhibit 1.

Inadequate Training

Organizations may decide not to invest in training by only looking at the up-front costs. According to one study by the Gartner Group and a study by the U.S. National Institute of Standards and Technology, the cost of not training will far exceed the investment organizations will make to train

Exhibit 1. Test Events

Test Event	Objectives
Unit testing	Unit testing verifies that stand-alone programs match specifications. Test cases should exercise every line of code.
Integration testing	Integration testing verifies that all software and hardware components work together. Data is passed from one program to the next. All programs and subroutines should be tested during this phase. Test cases should cover all components (e.g., hardware and software).
Functional testing	Functional testing verifies that the application meets user requirements. Test cases should cover screens, navigation, function keys, online help, processing, and output (reports, files, and screens).
Technical testing	Technical testing verifies that the application works in the production environment. Test cases should include error processing and recovery, performance, storage requirements, hardware compatibility, and security (e.g., screens, data, and programs).
Acceptance testing	Acceptance testing verifies that acceptance criteria defined during the project definition stage are tested. Test cases should include system usability, management reports, performance measurements, documentation and procedures, training (e.g., users, help desk, production support, operations), and system readiness (operations/systems sign-off).

both end users and IT professionals in new technologies. One reason for this paradox is that end users who are forced to learn on their own take as much as six times longer to become productive with the software application. Self-training is also inefficient from the standpoint that end users tend to ask their colleagues for help, which results in the loss of more than one individual's time, and they may also be learning inappropriate or inefficient techniques. Both studies also showed that an effective training program reduces support costs by a factor of three to six because end users make fewer mistakes and have fewer questions.

Inadequate Support

The increasing complexity of technical environments and more sophisticated technical tools has fueled the increased demand for end-user support. Because traditional IT departments do not have the staffing or advanced technical knowledge to help end-user departments, end users have turned to "underground support" (i.e., support by peers or department-purchased outsourcing) to fill the gap. The previously mentioned studies found that the need for support is inelastic, and the gap between needed support and formal support is filled by underground support. This underground support accounts for as much as 30% of end-user computing costs. End users need *focal points* that are local for assistance. A focal point is a functional support person. Many times, the functional support person is an accomplished end user. However, without a central support organization, there may be limited coordination between end-user departments, which ensures that procedures are consistent and applications are compatible.

Insufficient Documentation

End users typically focus on solving a business need and may not recognize the importance of documentation. Any program that is used by multiple users or has long-term benefits must be documented, particularly if the original developer is no longer available. Documentation also assists the developer in solving problems or making changes to the application in the future, in addition to facilitating testing and familiarizing new users to the system.

End-User Computing (EUC) Application Risks

End-user computing has resulted in the need to extend the scope of audits outside the central information systems environment to include end-user computing environments or groups. The level of risk and the required level of controls depend on the criticality of the application. Three key questions should be asked to determine the importance of an application:

- Does the application yield information that affects the direction or goals of the company?
- Is the application's data considered to be sensitive or important to the company?
- Does the application access other critical or sensitive applications located on other computers?

If the answer is yes to any of these questions, the validity, integrity, and accuracy of the data from these applications must be protected and ensured. For example, an application that consolidates data from several departments that will later be input into the financial reporting system is a prime target for an audit.

In addition to determining which applications should be audited, each end-user computing group must be evaluated to determine the audit approach required for that specific environment. The following four basic end-user environments require different audit approaches: stand-alone microcomputers, local area networks (LANs), wide area networks (WANs), corporate client/server, and a departmental mainframe or microcomputer server. In addition to various audit approaches, the inherent risks in each of these environments must be evaluated and the appropriate matching

controls must be tested. Standalone PCs, LANs, and client/servers are probably the most complex environments because of the variety of ways in which
they can be configured, and each requires a different auditing approach.

The IT auditor must be aware of additional threats or risks common to
microcomputers configured within a LAN environment. For example, there
is the possibility of unauthorized users monitoring, duplicating, modifying,
or altering the message or process that may be flowing across the network.
These types of threats emphasize the need for developing an audit approach
that considers the additional controls required in a LAN environment.

The WAN environment is a centralized area designed to provide users
access to computerized tools with assistance and guidance from knowledgeable IT personnel. Although this information center is controlled,
users can still develop their own applications, applications that will
require appropriate attention by IT auditors to ensure that proper controls
are in place.

The client/server environment is one of considerable growth and evolution, especially in the area of Internet, intranet, and extranet support.
Development and application controls must be assessed and validated.

Another environment is the departmental mainframe, which is the least
common and probably the most difficult to audit. In this case, the computer is used for a special purpose. Its users are typically more technically
sophisticated, and they frequently ignore corporate internal controls.

Sometimes risks in end-user computing are not readily identified
because of lack of awareness and the absence of adequate resources.
Because PCs seem relatively simple and are perceived as personal productivity tools, their effect on an organization has largely been ignored. In
many organizations, end-user computing has limited or no formal procedures. The control or review of reports produced by end-user computing is
either limited or nonexistent. The associated risk is that management may
be relying on end-user-developed reports and information to the same
degree as those developed under traditional centralized IT controls. Management should consider the levels of risk associated with end-user applications and establish appropriate levels of control. The risks associated
with end-user computing include:

- Inefficient use of resources
- Incompatible systems
- Redundant systems
- Ineffective implementations
- Absence of separation of duties
- Unauthorized access to data or programs
- Copyright violations
- The destruction of information by computer viruses

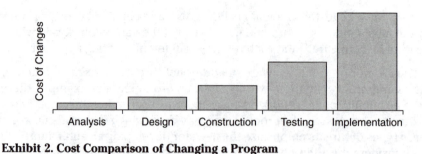

Exhibit 2. Cost Comparison of Changing a Program

Inefficient Use of Resources

End-user development may at first appear to be relatively inexpensive compared to traditional IT development. However, a number of hidden costs are associated with end-user computing that organizations should consider. In addition to operation costs, costs may increase due to lack of training and technical support. Lack of end-user training and their inexperience may also result in the purchase of inappropriate hardware and the implementation of software solutions that are incompatible with the organization's systems architecture. End users may also increase organizational costs by creating inefficient or redundant applications. The cost of change to an existing or new application in the latter stages can be expensive, as shown in Exhibit 2.

Incompatible Systems

End-user-designed applications that are developed in isolation may not be compatible with existing or future organizational IT architectures. Traditional IT systems development verifies compatibility with existing hardware and related software applications. The absence of hardware and software standards can result in the inability to share data with other applications in the organization.

Redundant Systems

In addition to developing incompatible systems, end users may be developing redundant applications or databases because of the lack of communication between departments. Because of this lack of communication, end-user departments may create a new database or application that another department may have already created. A more efficient implementation process has end-user departments coordinating their systems application development projects with IT and meeting with other end-user departments to discuss their proposed projects.

264

Ineffective Implementations

End users typically use fourth-generation languages such as database or Internet Web development tools to develop applications. In these cases, the end user is usually self-taught. However, they lack formal training in structured applications development, do not realize the importance of documentation, and omit necessary control measures that are required for effective implementations. In addition, there is no segregation of duties because one person acts as the end user, systems analyst, developer, and tester. Because of insufficient analysis, documentation, and testing, end-user developed systems may not meet management's expectations.

Absence of Segregation of Duties

Traditional systems application development is separated by function, and tested and completed by trained experts in each area. In many end-user development projects, one individual is responsible for all phases such as analyzing, designing, constructing, testing, and implementing the development life cycle. There are inherent risks in having the same person creating and testing a program because he or she may overlook his or her own errors. He or she will ensure the system works just as it was designed to. It is more likely that an independent review will catch errors made by the end-user developer, and such a review helps to ensure the integrity of the newly designed system.

Incomplete System Analysis

Many of the steps established by central IT departments are eliminated by end-user departments. For example, the analysis phase of development may be incomplete and all facets of a problem may not be appropriately identified. In addition, with incomplete specifications, the completed system may not solve the business problem. End users must define their objectives for a particular application before they decide to purchase existing software, to have IT develop the application, or to use their limited expertise to develop the application. Incomplete specifications will ensure system deficiencies.

Unauthorized Access to Data or Programs

Access controls provide the first line of defense against unauthorized users who gain entrance to a system's programs and data. The use of access controls, such as user IDs and passwords, are typically weak in user-controlled systems. In some cases, user IDs and passwords may be shared or easily determined. This oversight can subject applications to accidental or deliberate changes or deletions that threaten the reliability of any information generated. Programs require additional protection to prevent any unexpected changes. To prevent any accidental changes, the user should be limited to execute only.

Copyright Violations

Software programs can easily be copied or installed on multiple computers. Most organizations do not specifically address software piracy in training, in policy and procedures, or in the application of general internal controls. Many organizations are in violation of copyright laws and are not even aware of the potential risk. Organizations are responsible for controlling the computing environment to prevent software piracy and copyright violations.

The Copyright Act of 1976 makes it illegal to copy computer programs except for backup or archival purposes. Any business or individual convicted of illegally copying software is liable for both compensatory and statutory damages of up to $100,000 for each illegal copy of software found on the premises. Software piracy is also a federal crime that carries penalties of up to five years in jail. The Software Publishers Association (SPA) was established in 1988 to promote, protect, and inform the software industry regarding copyright issues. In 1993, the SPA had a staff of 23 people, a budget of $3.8 million, and represented 792 software companies. The SPA receives information from disgruntled employees and consultants about organizations that use illegal software. In 1994, the SPA filed 197 lawsuits for damages of $100,000 per violation.

An organization faces a number of additional risks when they tolerate software piracy. Copied software may be unreliable and carry viruses. Litigation involving copyright violations is highly publicized, and the organization is at risk of losing potential goodwill. In July 1998, the Los Angeles Unified School District was one of the largest school systems targeted by the Washington-based Business Software Alliance. It spent $5 million a year to replace the unlicensed software. Furthermore, tolerating software piracy encourages deterioration in business ethics that can seep into other areas of the organization.

The key to controlling the use of illegal software rests with the end user. Organizations should inform end users of the copyright laws and the potential damages that result from violations of those laws. When users are given access to a personal or desktop computer, they should sign an acknowledgment that lists the installed software, the individual's responsibilities, and any disciplinary action for violations. In addition, written procedures should detail responsibility for maintaining a software inventory, auditing compliance, and removing unlicensed software.

The Destruction of Information by Computer Viruses

Most end users are knowledgeable about virus attacks, but the effect of a virus remains only a threat until they actually experience a loss. The 2003 CSI/FBI Computer Crime and Security Survey reported that 82 percent of the respondents had suffered virus attacks and 99 percent use anti-virus software.

A virus is the common term used to describe self-reproducing programs (SRP), worms, moles, holes, Trojan horses, and time bombs. In today's environment, the threat is great because of the unlimited number of sources from which a virus can be introduced. For example, viruses can be copied from a diskette in a floppy drive or downloaded from a remote connection through a modem.

A virus is a piece of program code that contains self-reproducing logic, which piggybacks onto other programs and cannot survive by itself. A worm is an independent program code that replicates itself and eats away at data, uses up memory, and slows down processing. A mole enters a system through a software application and enables the user to break the normal processing and exits the program to the operating system without logging off the user, which gives the creator access to the entire system. A hole is a weakness built into a program or system that allows programmers to enter through a "back-door," bypassing any security controls. A Trojan horse is a piece of code inside a program that causes damage by destroying data or obtaining information. A time bomb is a code that is activated by a certain event such as a date or command.

The boot sector of a disk is the most susceptible to virus infection because it is accessed every time that the computer is turned on, providing easy replication of the virus. When a virus is activated, it copies code to the hard drive, and it can spread to additional floppies by executing a common application such as a word processor or mail program. The floppies that contain the virus will continue to infect other computers and spread the virus throughout an organization.

Viruses can also spread among computers connected within a network (local, Internet, etc.). They can spread when infected files or programs are downloaded from a public computer bulletin board via attachments to e-mails via codes hidden within hyperlinks, etc. Viruses can cause a variety of problems such as:

- Destroy or alter data
- Destroy hardware
- Display unwanted messages
- Cause keyboards to lock (i.e., become inactive)
- Slow down a network by performing many tasks that are really just a continuous loop with no end or resolution
- Produce spam
- Launch denial-of-service attacks

A virus can consume processing power and disk space by replicating itself multiple times. The risk to organizations is the time involved in removing the virus, rebuilding the affected systems, and reconstructing the data. The cost to remove viruses periodically exceeds $1.5 billion, in addition to the costs in lost data and downtime, which translates into a total of $5 to $10 billion worldwide. In addition, organizations should be concerned about sending virus-infected programs to other organizations. Viruses cause significant financial damage, and recipients may file lawsuits against the instituting organization.

Electronic Data Interchange (EDI) Application Risks

Auditors, management, developers, and security consultants need to be aware of the business risks associated with EDI as they provide a framework for placing appropriate security and control mechanisms within an EDI application or in an EDI environment. Risks include the following:

- *Loss of Business Continuity/Going-Concern Problem:* Inadvertent or deliberate corruption of EDI-related applications could affect every EDI transaction entered into by an organization, impacting customer satisfaction, supplier relations, and possibly business continuity eventually.
- *Interdependence:* There is increased dependence on the systems of trading partners, which is beyond the control of the company.
- *Loss of confidentiality of sensitive information:* Sensitive information may be accidentally or deliberately divulged on the network or in the mailbox storage system to unauthorized parties including competitors.
- *Increased exposure to fraud:* Access to computer systems may provide an increased opportunity to change the computer records of both a single organization and that of its trading partners by staff of the trading parties or by third-party network staff. This could include the introduction of unauthorized transactions by user organization or third-party personnel.
- *Manipulation of payment:* A situation where amounts charged by or paid to suppliers are not reviewed before transmission. Therefore, there is a risk that payments could be made for goods not received, payment amounts could be excessive, or duplicate payment could occur.
- *Loss of transactions:* Transactions could be lost as a result of processing disruptions at third-party network sites or en route to the recipient organization, which could cause losses to the organization and inaccurate financial reporting.
- *Errors in information and communication systems:* Errors in the processing and communications systems, such as incorrect message

repair, can result in the transmission of incorrect trading information or inaccurate reporting to management.

- *Loss of audit trail:* EDI eliminates the need for hard copy. There will be less paper for the auditors to check. The EDI user may not provide adequate or appropriate audit evidence, either on hard copy or on magnetic media. The third-party vendor may not hold audit trails for a significant length of time, or audit trails could be lost when messages are passed across multiple networks.

- *Concentration of control:* There will be increased reliance on computer controls where they replace manual controls, and they may not be sufficiently timely. The use of EDI with its greater reliance on computer systems concentrates control in the hands of fewer staff, increases reliance on key people, and increases risk.

- *Application failure:* Application or EDI component failures could have a significant negative impact on partner organizations within the respective business cycles, especially for just-in-time inventory management, production, and payment systems. In addition, there is a possibility of error propagation across other systems due to integration with other business applications.

- *Potential legal liability:* A situation where liability is not clearly defined in trading partner agreements, legal liability may arise due to errors outside the control of an organization or by its own employees. There is still considerable uncertainty about the legal status of EDI documents or the inability to enforce contracts in unforeseen circumstances.

- *Overcharging by third-party service providers:* Third-party suppliers may accidentally or deliberately overcharge an organization that is using their services.

- *Manipulation of organization:* The information available to the proprietors of third-party networks may enable them or competitors to take unfair advantage of an organization.

- *Not achieving anticipated cost savings:* Happens where the anticipated cost savings from the investment in EDI are not realized for some reason by an organization.

The ICAEW (Institute of Chartered Accountants in England and Wales) Working Party on EDI (1992) classifies EDI risks into general, internal, and external categories. General risks are those inherent in using EDI and that occur throughout the trading cycle. Internal risks are those within the territory and control of the organization using EDI. External risks are those under the control of another party, such as other trading parties, Value Added Network (VAN) providers, or network management services organizations. These categories can be further subdivided into existing risks and new risks.

Implications of Risks in an EDI System

Implications arising from the above-mentioned potential risks include:

- *Potential loss of transaction audit trail,* thereby making it difficult or impossible to reconcile, reconstruct, and review records. This could possibly be a breach of legislation and result in prosecution and fines.
- *Increased exposure to ransom, blackmail, or fraud* through potential disruption of services or increased opportunities to alter computer records in an organization and its trading partners' information systems.
- *Disruption of cash flows* when payment transactions are generated in error or diverted or manipulated.
- *Loss of profitability* occurring through increased interest charges or orders going to a competitor due to lack of receipt of EDI messages.
- *Damage to reputation* through loss of major customers, especially if EDI problems are widely publicized.
- *Financial collapse* (the repudiation of EDI orders after manufacture and delivery of a product) where, for example, errors occur in order quantities for high value products — for instance, 500 instead of 50 — so when the goods are manufactured and delivered, the recipient refuses to accept responsibility for sending the inaccurate order. This could cripple smaller manufacturing firms. This is a new implication and risk arising from the implementation of EDI.

Application Controls

To minimize application risks, various functional and operational requirements need to be included as part of a company's control structure, such as:

- Application controls and security requirements
- Functional testing and acceptance
- Documentation requirements
- Application software life cycle
- System development methodology
- User–machine interface
- Package customization

Application controls can be described as the manual or automated techniques used to control input, processing, and output of information in an application. As discussed in the previous section, the purpose of application controls is to ensure the complete processing and integrity of data. Application controls can be broken down into three main categories: input, processing, and output.

Input Controls

Input controls are meant to minimize risks associated with data input into the system. Defining input requirements ensures that the method of capturing the data is appropriate for the type of data being input and how it is subsequently used. Performance problems and accuracy issues can be introduced with nonappropriate methods for capturing data.

Input requirements should specify all valid sources for data as well as the method for validating the data. Input controls prevent invalid transactions from being entered and prevent invalid data within valid transactions. These controls ensure that any errors identified are captured and effectively resolved.

Input controls ensure the authenticity, accuracy, completeness, and timeliness of data entered into an application. Authenticity is ensured by limiting access at the screen and field level and requiring secondary approvals of transactions above a defined threshold. Accuracy is ensured by edit checks that validate data entered before accepting the transaction for processing. Completeness is ensured through error-handling procedures that provide logging, reporting, and correction of errors. Timeliness is ensured through monitoring transaction flow, logging, and reporting exceptions.

Interfaces

Interfaces can be considered a means of providing input into a system. Controls over interfaces should be carefully reviewed because of the volume of transactions and the automated methods used for interfaces. An inventory of all interfaces should be compiled and reviewed for systems. The interface definitions include the source, format, structure, content, and support requirements. In the instance of one company, a general ledger application had over 80 interfaces providing input of journal entries from the company subsidiary units. In this situation, the company chose to develop interface standards to minimize the number of interface formats as well as the effort in coding interfaces, which in turn reduced risk. The company designed five different interface formats that the 80 interfaces needed to adapt. Consequently, the auditors needed to only audit five interface mechanisms as opposed to 80 different interfaces.

Authenticity

Authenticity ensures that only authorized users have access to entering transactions. During the development process, business users should define the authorized users of the application and the security levels for data access. This information can be used when designing input screens to limit screens or fields to particular user groups. Controls can also be designed to enforce separation of duties. For example, a user may be able to enter a transaction, but a supervisor may need to approve the transaction before it is submitted for processing.

All authentication needs to be considered when automated applications interface to other applications. Often, scheduled batch jobs operate under the authority with specified access privileges to the database. Risks associated with these access accounts as well as the access privileges need to be reviewed. Generic accounts should not be used. The batch jobs should be given minimal privileges and system-level accounts should not be used.

Accuracy

Accuracy ensures that the information entered into an application is consistent and complies with procedures. This is accomplished by designing input screens with edits and validations that check the data being entered against predefined rules or values.

The accuracy of transactions processed can be ensured by having all transactions entered into the application go through data validation checks, whether coming from an online screen, an interface from another application, or generated by the system. Programs that automatically generate transactions (e.g., time triggered) should have built-in edits that validate transaction accuracy similar to transactions entered by a user. It is also important to track transaction volume and frequency against expected trends to ensure that transactions are triggered properly. Missing and duplicate checks should also be installed in case an error occurs in the triggering logic.

Edit and validation routines are generally unique to the application system being used, although some general-purpose routines may be incorporated. These routines may include checking the validity of codes, recording length, range, sequence, number of fields in a record, reasonability of values, authorization and approval codes, check digits, transactions, amounts, calculations, missing and extra data, signs, etc.

Edit and validation routines are placed in a system to aid in ensuring the completeness and accuracy of data. Therefore, overriding edit routines should not be taken lightly. In most systems the user is not provided this capability. Overriding edit routines is allowed only by privileged user IDs belonging to user department managers or supervisors, and from a master terminal. Overrides should be automatically logged by the application so that these actions can be analyzed for appropriateness and correctness.

Processing Controls

Processing controls ensure the accuracy, completeness, and timeliness of data during either batch or online processing. These controls help

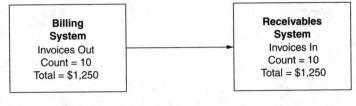

Exhibit 3. Batch Balancing Totals

ensure that data is accurately processed through the application and that no data is added, lost, or altered during processing.

Jobs scheduled within an application should be reviewed to ensure that the changes being made are appropriate and do not introduce risk. As an example, in an ERP application, an SQL program can be written to modify data directly against the database, avoiding the controls within the application and operating against the database with system administrator privileges. However, from the screen, this program can look like a report if the underlying code is not evaluated.

Completeness

Completeness can be ensured in batch processing by balancing transactions going in with transactions going out of a predecessor. Balancing steps should occur in major processing points. The following control points are examples of major processing points:

- *Input points:* programs that accept transactions from input processing.
- *Major processing modules:* programs that modify the data.
- *Branching points:* programs that split or merge data to transactions in and out.
- *Output points:* balance total records in with total records out.

Designed properly, balancing totals for transaction count and amount can detect missing or duplicate transactions (see Exhibit 3).

In addition to balancing between jobs within an application, balancing should also occur between applications that share common data. This can be achieved by creating a reconciliation report that lists data from both systems and reports on any differences for a user group (e.g., accounting) to review and follow up on any exceptions (see Exhibit 4).

Balancing totals should include a transaction count and totals for all amount fields for each type of transaction, and cross-foot totals for detail fields to total fields. In Exhibit 5, for example, the total quantity and price for parts A, B, and C should equal the total order amount.

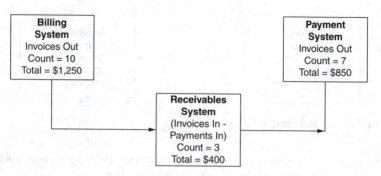

Exhibit 4. Cross-Application Balancing Totals

Exhibit 5. Sample Balancing Totals

Order	Quantity	Part Number	Unit Price	Total
Part A	100	1288543	$1.20	$120.00
Part B	80	0982374	$0.60	$48.00
Part C	200	5436682	$0.45	$90.00
Total	**380**	**7707599**		**$258.00**

In files where there are no meaningful totals, hash totals can be created that add all of the figures in a column to verify that the same total is accepted by the next process. For example, totaling part numbers does not mean anything, but this total can be used to verify that all the correct part numbers were received. Transaction flows should be balanced on a daily basis and cumulatively to monthly jobs before the register closes. Balancing totals should also take into consideration both error transactions leaving and entering the processing flow. In Exhibit 6, for example, total transactions entered less transactions written to an error file should equal transactions written out to the next job step.

Error Correction

Logging error activity, reporting open errors, and recording error correction as part of the transaction's audit trial can ensure transaction completeness. As part of ensuring accuracy, programs should be built with logic to detect and correct errors. Error handling procedures should include:

- Approval of error correction and resubmission
- Defined responsibility for suspense files
- Reports of unresolved errors
- Aging and prioritization of unresolved errors (COBIT)

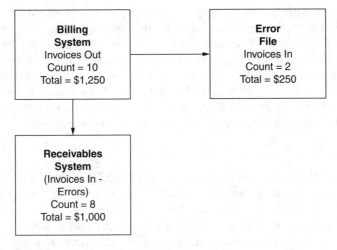

Exhibit 6. Balancing Totals with Error Transactions

Output Controls

Output controls ensure the integrity of output and the correct and timely distribution of output produced. To be useful, information must be accurate and received in time to benefit decision making. Output controls include procedures to verify data is complete, accurate, and properly recorded, procedures for report distribution and retention, and procedures for correct output errors. If outputs are produced centrally, conventional controls such as a security officer and distribution logs may be appropriate. If output is distributed over a data communication network, control emphasis shifts to access controls for individual workstations. Access to reports should be based on confidentiality.

Reconciliation

Output should be verified against an independent source to verify accuracy. For example, transaction totals posted to the general ledger should be reconciled against the detailed balance due in the accounts receivable system. As mentioned earlier, data that is common to two or more applications should be reconciled to verify consistency. Often, applications are developed over time that use the same information for different purposes. For example, an inventory system may use purchasing information to know when to reorder, an accounting system for financial statements, and a billing system for invoices.

Distribution

Distribution of output is clearly defined and physical and logical access is limited to authorized personnel. The need for output should be regularly reviewed as reports may be requested at the time an application is developed but may no longer be useful. Also, the same information may be used for more than one system with different views, organization, and use. For example, the marketing department may use sales information to pay commission and monitor sales quotas while the accounting department uses the same information for financial statements. These two systems should be reconciled to make sure that the amount reported for paying sales staff is the same as the amount reported on the financial statements.

Retention

Because storage space (computer and physical) is expensive, retention periods and storage requirements should be defined for programs, data, and reports. Critical information should be stored securely (e.g., encrypted), its destruction should be permanent, and destruction should be conducted in such a way as to prevent unauthorized viewing.

Functional Testing and Acceptance

Functional testing and acceptance testing is a key to application controls. It ensures that the application fulfills the agreed-upon functional expectations of the users, meets established usability criteria, and satisfies performance guidelines prior to being implemented into production. Acceptance testing minimizes the risks that the new application will cause business interruptions or be disjointed with business processes. It should include all components of the system (facilities, application software, procedures, etc.)

Acceptance criteria should be specific with detailed measures. Acceptance plans should include inspections, functional tests, and workload trials. Users should be involved in system testing throughout the development processes. This minimizes the risk of key functionality being excluded or having it not work. Ideally, users should use actual samples of their work in designing and executing acceptance tests.

Management Approval

Functional and acceptance plans and the respective test results need to be approved by the affected functional department as well as the IT department.

Documentation Requirements

Documentation ensures maintainability of the system and its components and minimizes the likelihood of errors. Documentation should be based on a defined standard and consist of descriptions of procedures, instructions to personnel, flowcharts, data flow diagrams, display or report layouts, and other materials that describe the system. System documentation should provide maintenance programmers with enough information to understand how the system works to ensure effective and efficient analysis of program changes and troubleshooting. Documentation should be updated as the system is modified.

The processing logic should be documented in a manner that understands using pseudocode, flowcharts, etc., while containing sufficient detail to allow programmers to accurately support the application. The software must also include documentation within the code, with descriptive comments embedded within the body of the source code. These comments should include cross-references to design documentation and requirements documents. The documentation should describe the sequence of programs and the steps to be taken in case of a processing failure.

Additional documentation includes a recovery plan for the application, service-level agreements with user departments, training plans, inventory of system components, interfaces, development tools, and third-party components.

Application Software Life Cycle

The software life cycle encompasses the development, acquisition, implementation, and maintenance of software. Further related information regarding each of these various phases is incorporated within various chapters in this text. Specifically, the software life cycle is described in Chapter 8. Chapter 9 discusses the acquisition process. Chapter 10 discusses implementation, and this chapter covers application maintenance.

System Development Methodology

A formal system development process provides an environment that is conducive to successful system development. A system development methodology obtains the control and security requirements from the users as well as their functional requirements. These include: (1) an information systems strategy that guides developers in building systems that are consistent with the organization's technical and operational goals, (2) standards that guide in the selection of hardware, software, and in developing new systems, (3) policies and procedures that support the organization's goals and objectives, and (4) project management which ensures that projects are completed on time and within budget. This is discussed in more detail in Chapter 8 and Chapter 10.

User Interface

The *user interface* is the means by which the user interacts with the system. In most cases, this is the screen mouse and keyboard. An effective interface for the users will help reduce desk costs and improve accuracy and efficiency. Additionally, a user interface should provide a means for the user to obtain context-sensitive help.

Application Maintenance

Organizations often feel that once an application is put into production, all the work is done. However, applications require maintenance and changes over time, and changes provide an opportunity for risk.

Application Maintenance: Defined

Software maintenance is an important phase in the systems development life cycle. Maintenance can be separated into the following three categories:

- *Corrective maintenance:* emergency program fixes and routine debugging
- *Adaptive maintenance:* accommodations of change
- *Perfective maintenance:* user enhancements, improved documentation, and recoding for efficiency

Corrective Maintenance. Corrective maintenance involves resolving software errors, commonly known as *bugs*. The purpose of corrective maintenance is to correct functionality that should be working as opposed to providing new functionality. This type of maintenance can occur at any time during software use and usually is a result of inadequate software testing. Corrective maintenance can be required to accommodate a new type of data that was inadvertently excluded or to modify code related to an assumption of a specific type of data element or relationship.

As an example of the latter, it was assumed in a report that each employee's employment application had an employee requisition (request to hire) associated with it in the system. However, when users did not see a complete listing of their entire employee applications listed, they discovered that not every employee application had an associated hiring request. In this case, the requirement for each application to be associated with a hiring request was a new system feature provided in the latest software release. As a result, employee applications entered into the system previous to the installation of the new release did not have hiring requests associated with them.

Adaptive Maintenance. Adaptive maintenance results from regulatory and other environmental changes. The purpose of adaptive maintenance is to adapt to some change in business conditions as opposed to providing new functionality. An example of adaptive maintenance is modifications to accommodate changes in tax law. Annually, federal and state laws change, which requires changes to financial systems and their associated reports.

Another example could be the Y2K (Year 2000) problem. Many software programs were written to handle dates up to 1999 and were rewritten at significant costs to handle dates beginning January 1, 2000. While these changes cost organizations many millions of dollars in maintenance effort, the goal of these changes is not to provide users with new capabilities but simply to allow users to continue using programs the way they are using them today. Some people argue that fixing code to accommodate Y2K was actually corrective maintenance as software should have been designed to accommodate years beyond 1999. However, due to the expense and limitations of storage, older systems used two digits to represent the year as a means to minimize the cost and limits of storage.

Perfective Maintenance. Perfective maintenance includes incorporation of new user needs not met by the current system. The goal of perfective maintenance is to adapt software to support new requirements. Perfective maintenance can be relatively simple, such as modifying the layout of an input screen or adding new columns to a report. Complex changes can involve sophisticated new functionality. In one example, a university wanted to provide its students with the ability to pay for their fees online. A requirement for such a system involves a number of complexities including the ability to receive, process, and confirm payment. These requirements include additional requirements such as ability to secure the information and protect the student and institution by maintaining the integrity of the data and information. Along with this, additional requirements are necessary to protect the process in its ability to recover and continue processing, as well as the ability to validate, verify, and audit each transaction.

Measuring Risk for Application Maintenance

The following metrics should be reviewed to evaluate the effectiveness and efficiency of the application maintenance process:

- The ratio of actual maintenance cost per application versus the average of all applications
- Requested average time to deliver change requests
- The number of change requests for the application that were related to bugs, critical errors, and new functional specifications
- The number of production problems per application and per respective maintenance changes
- The number of divergence from standard procedures, such as undocumented applications, unapproved design, and testing reductions
- The number of returned modules returned to development due to errors discovered in the acceptance fee
- Time elapsed to analyze and fix problems
- Percent of application software effectively documented for maintenance

Conclusion

Applications represent a significant investment for organizations as well as being critical for conducting business. Additionally, applications are a point of risk to organizations. Specifically, applications introduce the following risk:

- Weak security
- Unauthorized access to data
- Unauthorized remote access
- Inaccurate information
- Erroneous or falsified data input
- Misuse by authorized end users
- Incomplete processing
- Duplicate transactions
- Untimely processing
- Communications system failure
- Inadequate training
- Inadequate support

Due to these risks, controls need to be employed to reduce the risk as well as to ensure that the application continues to meet the business needs in an effective and efficient manner. The following is a list of components in a control structure for applications:

- Definition of the application's control and security requirements
- Definition and use of functional testing and acceptance plans
- Development of system documentation
- A documented application software life cycle
- A documented system development methodology
- A well-designed user–machine interface

Applications require maintenance in order to correct errors, adapt the application to a new requirement, or perfect the application through additional functionality to meet a business need.

Maintenance also introduces risk. An auditor assigned to evaluate the risk, effectiveness, and efficiency of application maintenance associated with application should review various metrics. The metrics look at actual performance and issues related to the application, as compared to the established thresholds. Additionally, maintenance issues need to be traced back to their source causes.

Chapter Review Questions

1. List and explain five application risks.
2. How can applications become incompatible systems?

3. What are the key questions an IT auditor can ask in helping determine which end-user applications have top priority in an organization?
4. What are the four basic end-user environments?
5. In preparation for the audit of an end-user-developed application, what are the important questions the auditor can ask about the data that can help in assessing application risk?
6. In end-user developed applications, list three reasons why new applications may fail.
7. Why are copyright violations an area of application risk with end-user-developed applications?
8. Name and describe three potential risks associated with viruses.
9. Name and describe three potential risks areas associated with EDI applications.
10. Name and describe five application controls.
11. Define an interface.
12. Describe the importance of functional testing.
13. Name and describe the three types of application maintenance.

Multiple Choice

1. The following are examples of application risks except:
   a. Inaccurate data
   b. Incomplete data
   c. Repeated data
   d. Duplicate data
2. Within a convenience store register system used to total orders and receive payment from customers, which of the following has the highest risk?
   a. Duplicate transactions
   b. Communications failure
   c. Unauthorized remote access
   d. Misuse by authorized users
3. The following are examples of application controls except:
   a. Testing the data-entry screen
   b. User ergonomic requirements
   c. Documentation of backup procedures
   d. A list of valid sources of input data
4. A company allows data from their sales tracking system to be extracted to spreadsheets by all users. Which of the following is the highest risk associated with this practice:
   a. Copyright violations
   b. Inefficient user of resources
   c. Unauthorized access to data
   d. Incompatible systems

5. Which one of the following is an example of a risk associated with end-user computing?
   a. Employees make copies of software to work at home.
   b. Employees enter time into company timesheet system.
   c. Employees can view all sales data within the company's sales tracking system.
   d. Employee can modify his timesheet data after he has entered it into the timesheet system.

6. Below are examples of misuse of resources associated with end-user computing except:
   a. Employees can purchase their own computer equipment for their work.
   b. Employees can purchase their own software to be used at work.
   c. Employees can purchase their own computer training.
   d. Employees create their own end-user procedure manuals.

7. A department employee creates and maintains a spreadsheet for the employees in that department to enter their time worked. The spreadsheets are subsequently used to load the employees' time into the system. Which of the following is the highest risk associated with the specific use of the spreadsheet?
   a. The timesheet does not accurately compute the total time worked.
   b. Employees may see the time worked by their fellow employees.
   c. Employees do not enter their time correctly.
   d. The spreadsheets are not signed by the employee.

8. Viruses pose all of the following risks except:
   a. Loss of data
   b. Loss of paper documents
   c. Loss of hardware
   d. Loss of performance

9. Interfaces are another form of:
   a. Output
   b. Report
   c. Input
   d. Processing

10. Which form of documentation would be the most critical to an applications programmer?
    a. Procedures
    b. Flowcharts
    c. Report layout
    d. Processing logic

Exercises

1. List and describe the five most prominent application risks associated with a spreadsheet system used to maintain a company's budget. The company uses the spreadsheet to solicit the budget from each of its departments. The budget department subsequently compiles the individual spreadsheets into on master sheet, reviews and revises the budget based on its constraints, and then uses it to load the budget values into the company's finance system where the department can then view its finalized budget.

2. A catalog company allows orders to be placed directly via their Web site. Additionally, customers can also call directly to their customer service line. Describe the three most prominent risks that could contribute to unauthorized access to a customer's order information. Identify the controls.

3. A payroll department has a timesheet application where employees enter their hours worked. Describe the three most prominent risks and respective controls.

4. A company allows data from their sales tracking system to be extracted to spreadsheets by all users. Name and describe three risks associated with this practice.

5. Each department has its own technical support person who creates and maintains applications for his or her assigned department. Name three risks associated with this practice. What three controls would you recommend to help minimize those risks?

6. Research and summarize a recent virus outbreak. Include: costs and impacts (depth and breadth).

7. A company has a centralized accounting system. Each individual department currently compiles its accounting paper transactions from its local accounting system. To eliminate the paper and increase efficiency, the company wants to implement an interface from the department accounting systems to the centralized accounting system. Name and describe the three most critical controls that you would recommend.

8. For the application controls described in the chapter, classify them as preventative, detective, or corrective.

9. Using the scenario described in Question 7, list and describe the three most critical documents that should be provided.

10. For each type of application maintenance, describe an example using the scenario described in Question 7.

Answers to Multiple Choice Questions

1 — c; 2 — d; 3 — b; 4 — c; 5 — a; 6 — c; 7 — a; 8 — b; 9 — c; 10 — d

References

1. Allen, S., F. Gallegos, and D. Manson. *Audit Concerns for End-User Computing and Application Development*. EDP Auditing, Auerbach Publishers, Boca Raton, FL. 1996.

2. Coffou, A.K. Year 2000 Risks: What are the Consequences of Information Technology Failure? Statement of Hearing Testimony, Joint Committee Hearing of the Subcommittee on Technology and Subcommittee on Government Management, Information and Technology, Washington, D.C., March 29, 1997. http://www.house.gov/science/couffou_3-20.html.

3. Computer Security Institute. 2003 CSI/FBI Computer Crime and Security Survey. 2003. http://www.gocsi.com/press/20030528.jhtml. Verified on 8/8/03.

4. Executive Office of the President, Memorandum for Agency Chief Information Officers and Senior Procurement Executives, January 9, 1998. http://www.itpolicy.gsa.gov/mks/yr2000/ombmemo.htm.

5. Federal Guidance Package, Best Practices Document. 1998. http://infosphere.safb.af.mil/~jwid/fadl/world/fedguide.htm.

6. Gallegos, F. *Auditing DSS: Review Points for IS Managers*. EDP Auditing, Auerbach Publishers, Boca Raton, FL. 1998.

7. Gallegos, F. *EDI Audit Risk Assessment*. EDP Auditing, Auerbach Publishers, Boca Raton, FL. 1999.

8. Hall, B.H. Year 2000 Risks: What are the Consequences of Information Technology Failure? Statement of Hearing Testimony, Joint Committee Hearing of the Subcommittee on Technology and Subcommittee on Government Management, Information and Technology, Washington, D.C., March 29, 1997. http://www.house.gov/science/hall_3-20.html.

9. Jamieson, R. EDI: An Audit Approach, Research Monograph Series Number 7, The EDP Auditors Foundation, USA, 1994.

10. Kanter, H.A. The Year 2000 problem: challenges for IS audit. *J. Inform. Syst. Audit Control Assoc.* Vol. 2, p. 48–55, 1997.

11. Kappelman, L.A. Solving the Year 2000 computer date problem — the critical role of IS audit and control professionals. *J. Inform. Syst. Audit Control Assoc.* Vol. 2, p. 34–44, 1997.

12. McCusker, T. How to Get More Value from EDI. *Datamation* 56–60, May 1, 1994.

13. Neo, B.S. Managing new information technologies: lessons from Singapore's experience with EDI. *Information and Management* Vol. 26, 317–326, 1994.

14. Picard, J.Y. and E. Leschiutta. The paperless chase. *CA Magazine*, 54–56, January/February 1994.

Chapter 12
Change Management

The purpose of change management is to minimize the likelihood of disruption and unapproved changes, as well as errors. A change management process is one that consists of analysis, implementation, and review of all changes. From an IT perspective, change management is thought of in terms of changes made to the existing IT infrastructure. However, changes affecting the organization are also a factor. In many cases, it is the organizational changes that introduce changes to the IT infrastructure.

This chapter provides an overview of change management in terms of the organization as well as IT. Specifically, this chapter describes control points within an IT change management process. An organizational change model is also presented and is discussed again from an operational perspective in Chapter 17.

Vulnerabilities in Software Development and Change Control

The U.S. General Accounting Office (GAO) in their Federal Information System Control Audit Manual makes change control a specific checkpoint in their review process. Application software is designed to support a specific operation such as payroll or loan accounting. Typically, several applications may operate under one set of operating system software. Controls over operating system software are discussed in Chapter 14 and Chapter 17. Establishing controls over the modification of application software programs helps to ensure that only authorized programs and authorized modifications are implemented. Instituting policies, procedures, and techniques that help make sure all programs and program modifications are properly authorized, tested, and approved and that access to accomplish this and distribution of programs is carefully controlled. Without proper controls, there is a risk that security features could be inadvertently or deliberately omitted or "turned off" or that processing irregularities or malicious code could be introduced. For example:

- A knowledgeable programmer could surreptitiously modify program code to provide a means of bypassing controls to gain access to sensitive data.
- The wrong version of a program could be implemented, thereby perpetuating outdated or erroneous processing that is assumed to have been updated.

- A virus could be introduced, inadvertently or on purpose, that disrupts processing.

The primary focus of this section is on controlling the changes that are made to software systems in operation, as operational systems produce the financial statements and a majority of program changes are made to maintain operational systems. However, the same risks and mitigating controls apply to changes associated with systems under development, once both user management and the project development team have formally approved their baseline requirements. Assessing controls over application software development and modification involves evaluating the entity's success in performing each of the critical elements listed below.

In a presentation before the Federal Information Systems Educators Conference in March 2002, a GAO representative stated that the overall impact of inadequate change control found in audits of federal agencies were that:

- Operational costs were increased.
- The usefulness of risk assessments and security plans was diminished.
- Logical controls to prevent or detect unauthorized access were hard to establish.
- It was difficult to monitor access, investigate apparent security violations, and implement effective security patches.

They believe that organizations need to implement good change controls and configuration management. Configuration management is the process that is used to monitor the installation of and updates to system hardware, operating system software, and software to ensure that hardware and software function as expected and that a historical record of application changes is maintained.

Software Configuration Management

The National Institute of Standards and Technology defined the process of software configuration management in its Publication 500-223, "A Frame Work for the Development and Assurance of High Integrity Software." The major objectives of the software configuration management (SCM) process are to track the different versions of the software and to ensure that each version of the software contains the exact software outputs generated and approved for that version. It must be established before software development starts and continue throughout the software development processes. SCM is responsible for ensuring that any changes to any software outputs during the development processes are made in a controlled and complete manner.

The SCM process produces a software configuration management plan (SCMP). When the software is integrated with system components, system configuration management begins. However, any changes to the software necessitates that SCM be invoked.

Exhibit 1 lists activities of the SCM process.

IT Change Management

An IT change control system ensures that there is segregation of duties between who initiates the change, who approves the change, and who implements the change so that unauthorized changes cannot be implemented into a production environment. Each change made to any component of an IT infrastructure or system within should be:

- Identified
- Categorized
- Prioritized
- Assessed for impact
- Authorized

Changes can be introduced to fix a bug or to add new functionality. Changes can also be introduced from new software releases and the distribution of new software. Additionally, changes can result from configuration management and business process redesign. Large enterprises employ automated tools to help ensure effective change management.

Change Management System

A change management system consists of the following controls:

- Process for requesting changes
- Assessment of impact by the change
- Control process over changes
- Process for emergency changes
- Revisions to documentation and procedures
- Authorization of maintenance changes
- Policy for new software releases
- Process for distributing software

Change management should be documented in the form of an organizational policy. Exhibit 2 is an example of such a policy suggested.

Change Request Process

A change request process ensures that only authorized changes are made. It requires that a record is kept of all changes to the system, appropriate resources are allocated, and changes are prioritized. Changes should be prioritized in terms of benefit, urgency, and effort required, as

Exhibit 1. Activities of the SCM Process

• Generate a Software Configuration Management Plan

Software Configuration Identification

• Identify configuration items (CIs), i.e., select the most significant and critical functions that will require constant attention and control throughout software development.
• Assign a unique identifier/number to each CI.
• Establish baselines for the following CIs, i.e., documents that have been formally reviewed and agreed upon, (1) that serve as the basis for further development, and (2) that can be changed only through formal change control procedures.
  – *Functional baseline* (the completion and acceptance of the system requirements specification): the prerequisite for the development of the software requirements specification (SRS) for each CI
  – *Allocated baseline* (the review and acceptance of the SRSs): the prerequisite of the development of the software design description (SDD) for all components making up a CI
  – *Developmental configuration* (developer-controlled "rolling" baseline): all of the documents and code accepted and committed for configuration control up to the establishment of the product baseline
  – *Product baseline* (established with the successful conclusion of a configuration audit): prerequisite to the operation and maintenance of the software

Problem Reporting, Tracking, and Corrective Action

• Document when a software development activity does not comply with its plan, output deficiency, or anomalous behavior and give the corrective action taken.

Change Control

• Document, evaluate, resolve, and approve changes to the software.

Change Review

• Assess problems and changes, implement approved changes, and provide feedback to processes affected by changes.

Traceability Analysis

• Trace forward and backward through the current software outputs to establish the scope of impacted software.

Configuration Control

• Delegate authority for controlling changes to software; determine method for processing change requests.

Configuration Status Accounting

• Keep records detailing the state of the software product's development, e.g., record changes made to the software, status of documents, changes in process, change history, and release status, etc.

Exhibit 1. Activities of the SCM Process (Continued)

Configuration Audits and Reviews

- Audit configuration items before release of product baseline or updated version of product baseline; review to determine progress and quality of product.
  - *Functional configuration audit:* prove that a CI's actual performance agrees with its software requirements stated in the SRS.
  - *Physical configuration audit:* ensure that the documentation to be delivered with the software represents the content of the software product.

Archive, Retrieval, and Release

- Archive software outputs (with backups) so it cannot be changed without authorization and it will not deteriorate data to ensure it can be retrieved if necessary; describe software being released to ensure it is authorized.

---

well as possible impact on existing operations. The process should also manage coordination between changes to account for any interdependencies that may exist.

Change management procedures should be documented and require:

- A record of change requests to be kept for each application and system.
- A definition of the authority and responsibility of the IT department, as well as the user.
- Approval by management after all the related information is reviewed.
- A schedule for changes as well as allow for changes outside of the schedule. This allows changes made outside of the schedule to receive specific management approval.
- A notification process included in the procedures so that requesters are kept informed regarding the status of their requests.

Impact Assessment

Each change requires an impact assessment which ensures that potential negative consequences of a change are identified and planned for. Changes can introduce risk to the availability, integrity, confidentiality, and performance of a system.

Each change request needs to include supporting evidence of the impact assessment. The impact analysis should include specific measures compared with prescribed limits. This enables the extent of the impact to be evaluated. Changes should also be reviewed to determine the effect on compliance with existing policy, procedures, and processes.

Exhibit 2. Draft Agency Configuration Management Policy

XX Agency
INTERIM POLICY DOCUMENT

XX Agency Configuration Management

1. **Purpose.** This Interim Policy Document (IPD) establishes XX Agency procedures for maintaining a standard configuration of the XX Agency network and at the client desktop.
2. **Objective.** The objective is to comply with the XX Agency guidelines and "standard push" to maintain a proper level-of-standard configuration on XX Agency network and client desktop.
3. **Reference**
   A. Computer Security Act of 1987 (PL 100-235)
   B. OMB Circular A-130, Appendix III, Security of Federal Automated Information Resources
4. **Policy.** It is XX Agency policy to protect information and corporate assets. One way of facilitating this requirement is to formally manage and control hardware and software configuration.
5. **Responsibilities**
   A. The Council of Management Officials (CIMO) is responsible for:
      1. Ensuring coordination among program area offices on IRM issues (including the Network) and activities
   B. Client Work Group (CWG) is responsible for:
      1. Maintaining desktop design, development, and maintenance
      2. Developing procedures for software change control and synchronized software distribution
      3. Evaluating, recommending, and coordinating the implementation of desktop solutions consistent with XX Agency strategic and technical plans
      4. Providing updates to XX Agency desktop software; resolving Tier 1 and Tier 2 issues and problems among XX Agency offices
   C. The Security Working Group (SWG) is responsible for:
      1. Approving or coordinating on documents prepared by the Bureau Chief Information Systems Security Manager for the purpose of maintaining network security and for Director, XX Agency signature
   D. Bureau Information Technology Security Manager (BITSM) is responsible for:
      1. Ensuring that IT resources are adequately safeguarded throughout the Bureau
      2. Developing and implementing an overall network security plan for XX Agency systems
      3. Issuing guidelines and procedures for the Bureau
      4. Providing oversight for XX Agency network security
      5. Maintaining current inventory of sensitive systems and a schedule for testing system contingency plans
   E. XX Agency Program Information Technology Security Manager (PITSM) is responsible for:
      1. Ensuring IT resources are adequately safeguarded throughout XX Agency
      2. Implementing the overall XX Agency network security plan for XX Agency systems
      3. Issuing guidelines and procedures
      4. Providing oversight for XX Agency network security and standard configurations
      5. Maintaining current inventory of sensitive systems and a schedule for testing systems contingency plans

Exhibit 2. Draft Agency Configuration Management Policy (Continued)

Scope

Involved Persons: Every worker at the XX Agency — no matter what their status (employee, contractor, consultant, temporary, etc.) — must comply with the information security policies found in this and related information security documents.

Involved Systems: This policy applies to all computer and network systems owned by or administered by the XX Agency. Similarly, this policy applies to all platforms (operating systems), all computer sizes (personal computers through mainframes), and all application systems (whether developed in-house or purchased from third parties). The policy covers only information handled via computers or networks.

Procedures

With the exception of emergency situations, all changes to XX Agency computer networks must be: (1) documented in a work order request and (2) approved in advance by the authorized XX Agency officials. All emergency changes to XX Agency networks must only be made by persons who are authorized by the respective XX Agency officials. This process prevents unexpected changes from inadvertently leading to denial of service, unauthorized disclosure of information, and other problems. This process applies not only to workers as defined in the Scope section of this policy but also to vendor personnel.

XX Agency has formally established a consistent, cross-organizational Configuration Management process for the architecture and its components. Configuration management involves identifying the configuration of a network system at given points in time, systematically controlling changes to the configuration, and maintaining the integrity and traceability of the configuration throughout the life cycle. The items placed under configuration management include the software and hardware products that comprise the network, as well as items required to create or maintain these products. Proper configuration management enables an organization to answer the following questions:

• What is the process for making changes to the network and its components?
• Who made a change to the network and its components?
• What changes were made to the network and its components?
• When were the changes made?
• Why were the changes made?
• Who authorized the changes?

The following sections present the configuration change control activities for the XX Agency network.

At a high-level, the XX Agency change control process consists of the following basic steps:
• Identifying and classifying a change to the network
• Evaluating what components in the current network configuration need to be changed
• Testing or modeling the impact of the change upon the current network
• Implementing the change if it is approved

Misuse: XX Agency management reserves the right to revoke the system privileges of any user at any time. Workers who deliberately violate this and other information security policy statements will be subject to disciplinary action up to and including termination.

Controls over Changes

The control over changes is enabled via the processes and automated tools that are needed to ensure the integration of changes requests, software changes, and software distribution. These controls would ensure not just that only authorized changes were made but also the detection of unauthorized changes, reduction of the errors due to system changes, and an increase in the reliability of changes.

Controls over the change control process include an independent verification of the success or failure of implemented changes. Another control is the update to the infrastructure or system configuration. By formally updating the configuration record, it allows for the detection of unauthorized changes that are not in the record.

Emergency Change Process

Emergency changes are changes that are required outside of the prescribed schedule. Normally, emergency changes are required to fix errors in functionality that adversely affect system performance or business processes. Emergency changes may also be required to fix discovered imminent vulnerabilities to availability, integrity, or confidentiality. Conversely, emergency changes should not compromise the integrity, availability, reliability, security, confidentiality, or accuracy of the system. Because of the consequences that can occur with emergency changes, they should only be implemented in declared emergencies.

Emergency change procedures should not only describe the process for implementing emergency changes but should also include description of what constitutes an emergency change. The definitive parameters and characteristics of an emergency change need to be clearly described. Emergency changes should be documented like regular changes but the documentation may not occur until after the change is made due to the nature of the emergency. Emergency changes do require formal authorization by those responsible for the system as well as by management before implementation. In some cases, backups before and after the change are retained for later review.

Emergency changes, by their nature, pose increased risk as they bypass some of the formal analyses and processes of the traditional change control process. As a result, audits of change control procedures should play particular attention to emergency changes.

Revisions to Documentation and Procedures

In most cases, changes to production environments will require that existing documentation and procedures be updated to reflect the nature of the change. Current documentation ensures the maintainability of the system by any assigned staff member and minimizes reliance on individual staff.

Change control procedures should include a task for updating documentation, operational procedures, help-desk resources, and training materials. Changes to business processes should also be considered. Documentation, procedures, and business processes should actually receive the same consideration and testing as other components impacted by the change.

Authorized Maintenance

Maintenance updates are also considered changes and should be accounted for in the change control procedures. Maintenance tasks should be described to the level of detail necessary to ensure appropriate controls. Maintenance actions should be logged and the log reviewed to ensure appropriateness. Access controls should be used to limit the actions of personnel performing the maintenance to only the access required. An example of a routine maintenance task is defragmenting a hard disk to remove fragmented files or lost clusters.

Software Release Policy

Like any change, new software releases require management approval to ensure that the change is authorized, tested, and documented before the new software release is applied to production environment.

The following controls need to be applied specifically to new software releases:

- Appropriate backups of the system's data and programs should be made before the change.

- Version control should be accounted for in the process. Version control is the manner in which the set of files associated with a version is tracked. It also defines the coordination between the developers working on various aspects of the system. There are automated systems that contain databases to store the various versions of files.

- Software releases should only be considered received from the prescribed central repository.

- A formal hand-over process is also required so that authorized personnel are involved in the process, the implemented software is unchanged from what was tested, and software media is prepared by the appropriate function based on the formal build instructions.

Software Distribution Process

The purpose of a software distribution process is to ensure that all copies of software are distributed in accordance with their license agreements. A software distribution process minimizes the risk of multiple versions of the software being installed at the same time. Multiple versions of a software package increase support costs. Staff then needs to be trained and skilled in the features, functionality, and issues with each version.

A software distribution process should also account for a verification of the software's integrity, as well as verification for compliance with software license agreements. License agreements normally grant permission to use the specified software based on limitations, number of users, location, type of use, etc. Software licenses can be for unlimited use by a specifically named person, for concurrent use by an unlimited number of simultaneous users, a site license for unlimited use on one site, or an enterprise license for unlimited use by the enterprise.

Violating software agreements has legal ramifications for companies, including costs for installed copies not licensed, damages and legal fees, and loss of corporate reputation. News stories about software piracy mainly focus on court cases related to someone's setting up a Web site distributing software illegally. However, the unprinted stories are those settled out of court with companies. The Software and Information Industry Association (SIIA) is an organization comprised of companies of the software and information industry. One of their objectives is to protect the intellectual property of their members. SIIA is instrumental in influencing laws to protect intellectual property and taking action to combat software piracy. SIIA's Corporate Anti-Piracy Program identifies, investigates, and resolves software piracy cases on behalf of its members.

Software distributions practices should include the following controls:

- Distribution is made in a timely manner only to those authorized.
- A means is in place for ensuring verification of integrity, and this is incorporated into the installation.
- A formal record exists of who has received software and where it has been implemented. This record should also match with the number of purchased licenses.

Some examples of change control software products in this category are listed below:

- **KONFIG® Configuration Management (KONFIG CM)** by Auto-trol Technology Corporation is a comprehensive Web-based information, configuration, and data management solution that includes the core components of fully integrated configuration management, data/document management, product data management, workflow, and change management. KONFIG CM is designed to be an enterprise solution.

- **Kintana Accelerators for Oracle, PeopleSoft, SAP, and Siebel** by Kintana, Inc. Accelerators simplifies the complex activities required to maintain large enterprise applications like Oracle, PeopleSoft, SAP, and Siebel. This can help reduce an application's total cost of ownership.
- **TurnOver™ Change Management** by SoftLanding Systems, Inc. is an AS400 and iSeries change management package. TurnOver™ gives a software management strategy and a strong, flexible foundation. Much more than just source and object management, it organizes and automates an entire development cycle from change request to risk-free installation.
- **IBM Tivoli® Configuration Manager** by IBM Corporation. IBM Tivoli Configuration Manager helps gain control over software and hardware installations, deploys complex mission-critical applications to multiple locations from a central point, and automatically scans for and collects configuration information from diverse computer systems for rapid, centralized application deployment and management.
- **MKS Code Integrity Enterprise Edition** by MKS, Inc. helps regain control of source code and increase developer productivity by increasing understanding of software systems. It graphically tracks the progress of software projects throughout their life cycles and identifies potential defects earlier in the development life cycle, saving time and expense.

Change Management Example

The following are possible areas to consider in developing a change management procedure.

Objectives

Below is a list of possible objectives to consider for change management procedures:

- Document the reason for change.
- Identify who is requesting the change.
- Formalize who will make the change.
- Define how the change will be made.
- Document back-out procedures should the need arise.
- Assess the risk of failure and impact of the change.
- Aid in communicating with those affected by the change.
- Identify disaster recovery considerations.
- Identify conflicts between multiple changes.
- Enhance management's awareness of all of the above.

Scope

The scope for these procedures can include the following:

- Hardware (Unix, NT, Client, Sun)
- System software (Unix, NT, Oracle, Client)
- Database instances
- Application software
- Third-party tools
- Telecommunications (circuits)
- Firewalls
- Network (LAN, WAN, routers, servers, software delivery, etc.)
- Facilities environment (UPS, electrical, etc.)

Change Management Boards or Committees

These are common entities to deal with coordinating the communication of changes within an organization. Below are possible source for members of a change management board:

- Application development/support teams (finance, human resources, etc.) who can provide leads
- Data center operations
- Networks/telecommunications
- Help desk
- Key user representatives

The individuals on the change board should be selected based on their in-depth perspective and broad knowledge of the areas they represent as well as their awareness for other functional areas involved. The goal is to ensure that the decisions made are objective as these changes have the potential of affecting the organization.

Change committees meet daily or weekly. The following types of changes are often considered during daily change review meetings:

- Emergency releases, fixes, etc. These are normally related to circumstances in which production is down.
- Database clones, restores, links, or new instances.
- "Fast-tracked" requests that cannot wait for the normally scheduled dates for updates. Fast-tracked requests can be associated with new functionality to meet a business need by a published deadline.
- Oracle account maintenance.
- Upgrades to development tools.

The following topics are often covered during weekly meetings:

- Migrations of new releases
- Upgrades to production or development tools
- Environment setup for migrations

- Environment setup for tools
- Third-party upgrades
- Configuration changes
- Hardware changes

Criteria for Approving Changes

Approval can be based on the following criteria:

- *State of the production environment:* Before determining if a change should be approved, the change board should evaluate the performance and availability of each system in the production environment during the previous week. In general, if the production environment has performed well and has been available to the users, the change board is more likely to approve changes that provide new functionality or changes that might have a higher risk of failure. Conversely, if the state of the production environment during the previous week has been poor, the change board is more likely to approve only those changes designed to correct problems.
- *Change level:* As part of the approval process, the change level is examined along with the detail information and instructions attached to the change request. The attachments should detail the associated risk and impact of the change. Particularly important are the subjective comments provided by the change author indicating the reasons for the assigned change level. The change level can be based on six factors: risk, impact, communication requirements, install time, documentation requirements, and education or training requirements.
- *Cumulative effect of all proposed changes:* The change board is one place where all of the changes requested for the week come together. The change board has the ability to examine several changes, each of which may appear to carry a reasonable risk if taken independently, but when all changes proposed for a particular week are considered as a group, the composite effect may result in too much change activity — hence, risk. When the change board reaches this conclusion, its responsibility is to prioritize the various changes, approve the most significant ones, and recommend that the others be rescheduled.
- *Resource availability:* The change board evaluates the availability of people, time, and system resources when considering the scheduling and approval of changes.
- *Criticality:* There are issues that may affect the impact of the change as viewed by the requester. For example, the change author may feel that the impact is relatively low because his change affects a small percentage of the user community. However, the change board may view the criticality to be high because that small percentage of

users is a critical client or user. An example might be the finance department during a year-end close process.

Post-Implementation

Following a change, the following items need to be evaluated.

- Were the change procedures followed?
- Did the change adequately meet its objectives?
- Were the implementation and back-out procedures adequate? (Any problems encountered can be addressed during future planning.)
- The status is updated and identified as to be complete, not complete, in progress, failed, or cancelled.

Organizational Change Management

Organizational change relates to the organization's ability and methods for adopting, managing, and adapting to change. Factors for evaluating change vary based on the scope of the change (i.e., changes to work habits as opposed to changes to the organization itself). Regardless of how IT is managed, it is still enacted by organizations in order to realize their expected monetary results. Consequently, an IT project can actually be considered a product of the organization's culture.

There are many studies to support the assertion that many IT projects fail due to the inability of the organization to adapt to the change necessary to take advantage of IT. Organizations find it difficult to change their practices and structures, especially if the application is perceived to be in conflict with the company's culture.

Organizational Culture Defined

According to Robert Kling and Roberta Lamb, organizational culture is comprised of structures for incentives, politics, support for interorganizational relationships, and social repercussions.

Incentives offered by the organization can impact the success of the organization in adapting to change because users do not necessarily see the "natural" advantages of adopting the change. As a point of caution, incentives should not conflict with other rewards or incentives or the culture. For example, if employees are told that they will be offered training to learn a new state-of-the-art system, but they will risk losing their bonus due to their increase in nonbillable time, the employee will see the training as a punishment as opposed to being considered an incentive.

Company politics can have significant effects on the success of a new IT system or change in the organization. Most models of organizational change exclude recognition for the importance of political influences over organizational change. For example, a new IT system can shift the power of information. In one case, it provided the corporate office direct online access to the live sales activity in each sales office. Prior to the new system, the field offices were able to determine how and when to present their sales figures to the corporate office. In some cases, the sales office would modify actual sales data with sales that were not yet realized. This enabled the sales offices to present their "best" sales figures. With direct access to the sales information, the corporate office was empowered to see the data when and how they wanted, allowing them insight into the volatility of the sales for a given office. Because it transferred control over the information to the corporate offices, the system was perceived to transfer decision power to the corporate office away from the sales offices. Subsequent power struggles ensued between the sales offices and the corporate office.

Organizational and technical support is critical for the effective use of IT. A supporting infrastructure includes organizational practices, key support staff, and access to technical and organizational skill sets. In this model, individual and organizational learning are considered a subset of the IT system. Many major IT system implementations are now including business process review sessions within their implementation scope. This enables the organization to review their business process in terms of the change that will be introduced into the system. This fit-gap analysis identifies gaps in functionality, which is integral to business processes. Subsequent plans can be made to accommodate for these gaps in redesigned business process, changes in business services, or modifications to the system itself.

Interorganizational relationships and social networks are supported and impacted through the use of IT. The influence of relationships and social networks are believed to explain why some technologies are supported and others are not. Looking at online communities and electronic market places — Is it the influence of technology on relationships and networks that created online communities and electronic market places or vice versa?

An example of a successful online community is E-Bay. E-Bay defines itself as an online community. Its community is comprised of individual buyers and sellers as well as large and small companies. Member relationships are supported with discussion boards. The sense of community is used to ensure that E-Bay guidelines are followed with a "neighborhood watch" philosophy. The E-Bay community has also joined together to support social causes such as fundraising for victims of September 11, 2001.

Managing Organizational Change Management

Culture and structure change should be managed through the life cycle. It includes people, organization, and culture. A culture that shares values and is open to change contributes to success. To facilitate the change process, users should be involved in the design and implementation of the business process and the enterprise resource planning (ERP) system. A communications plan and training and professional development plans also support this.

The business processes associated with a software implementation need to be aligned. In adapting packaged software packages, organizations face the question of whether to adapt the organization to the software or vice versa. To minimize maintenance of the software, the company should consider changing the business process to fit the software and the software should be modified as little as possible. Reducing customization reduces errors and improves the ability to utilize newer releases.

Organizational change relies on effective communication. Expectations need to be communicated. Communication, education, and expectations need to be managed throughout the organization. Input from users should also be managed to ensure that requirements, comments, and approval are obtained. Communication includes the formal promotion of the implemented change as well as the organization's progress with adopting the change. Employees should also know the scope, objectives, activities, and updates and the expectation for change in advance.

Training and professional development plans should be incorporated into any effort to introduce change into an organization. Employees need to be trained in the new processes and procedures. Additionally, the team assigned to implement the change requires special training in the process and procedures. Training in adapting to change is also beneficial to all employees.

Some organizations adopt formal change management programs as a means of assisting employees to adapt to major changes. *Who Moved My Cheese,* by Spencer Johnson, M.D. and Kenneth Blanchard, is a popular book being adopted by major organizations to introduce the concept of changes and why change is important to the organization, as well as how change is beneficial for the employee. Cheese is used as a metaphor for the things that people want out of their lives. There are four characters in the book. Each character represents different approaches to adapting to change. The characteristics of each mouse are observed as they embark on a journey through a maze in search of the cheese that has been moved.

Conclusion

Change management is one of the single most important controls to ensure the integrity, availability, reliability, security, confidentiality, and accuracy of an organization or IT system supporting the organization. As discussed in this chapter, a well-controlled IT change management program is enabled by:

- Process for requesting changes
- Assessment of impact by the change
- Control process over changes
- Process for emergency changes
- Revisions to documentation and procedures
- Authorization of maintenance changes
- Policy for new software releases
- Process for distributing software

Many IT change control systems are not only documented but also automated. These automated systems enable the systematic implementation and control of the change control process. Additionally, automated change control systems also enable an auditor to perform an effective and efficient review through the evaluation of rule sets, access lists, and log files.

Organizational change also deserves consideration by the IT auditor due to its potential impact on the organization and the increased relationships with changes in the IT environment. Organizational change is impacted by limitations introduced by the technology and the organization's culture. An organization's culture is comprised of its structures for incentives, politics, and relationships with other organizations and the community.

Review Questions

1. Identify and describe the five goals of an IT change management system.
2. Name and describe the eight controls of a change management system.
3. Describe the risks associated with maintenance.
4. Name and describe the four controls associated with the software release process.
5. Name and describe three risks associated with the software distribution process.
6. Describe the responsibilities of a change management board.
7. Name and describe five criteria for approving changes.
8. Name and describe the components of organizational culture.
9. Name and describe the components of an organizational change management plan.

Multiple Choice

1. In classifying the importance of each of the goals for change management, which one is the most important?
   a. Identification
   b. Categorization
   c. Prioritization
   d. Authorization

2. In the change request process, the following information should be obtained except:
    a. User contact and responsibility
    b. List of future changes
    c. IT contact and responsibility
    d. Management approval
3. In an emergency change control process, which of the following is the highest risk?
    a. Unauthorized changes are made
    b. Emergency change introduces performance problems
    c. Changes are approved after they are implemented
    d. Lack of analysis
4. In the following list of criteria for approving changes, select the one that is most important:
    a. Criticality
    b. State of the production environment
    c. Resource availability
    d. Effect of all proposed changes
5. Following a change, the condition of which of the following should be evaluated?
    a. Requester
    b. Change objectives
    c. Technical support
    d. Staffing
6. The following are components of organizational culture that affect the success of IT except:
    a. Incentives
    b. Company politics
    c. Interorganizational relationships
    d. Government politics
7. Managing organizational change would include all of the following except:
    a. Marketing plans
    b. Training and professional development plans
    c. User involvement in design
    d. Communication plans
8. Business process review sessions review:
    a. Requests for system changes
    b. Requests for business process changes
    c. Changes introduced by the new system
    d. Training requests
9. An IT system that now allows the corporate office to view data from their individual sales offices introduces the most change to:
    a. Social relationships
    b. Technical support

    c. Interorganizational relationships

    d. Company politics

10. In auditing an automated change control system, an auditor would review all of the following except:

    a. License agreements

    b. Rules

    c. Access lists

    d. Log files

Exercises

1. Discuss the impact if all changes are not identified.

2. Develop a high-level flowchart for an emergency change process. On the flow chart, label the control points. If there are residual risks, make note of those as well.

3. Discuss why revising documentation is an important part of change management.

4. Discuss the importance of why system maintenance activities need to be approved.

5. Discuss the importance of violating software agreements for a publicly traded company?

6. Research a news story related to software license agreements. What controls would prevent or minimize an outbreak within a company?

7. A company would like to include facilities management in the change management board. Describe the benefits associated with including facilities management in the change management board.

8. Describe the interdependencies between IT change management and organizational change management.

9. From your experience, describe a situation where IT affected the distribution of power within the organization.

10. A university currently provides the ability to register for classes via a telephone registration system. However, the university is in the process of modifying its student registration system so that it allows registration via the web. The university is evaluating whether it should discontinue the phone service or continue it once the online service is available. Perform a fit-gap analysis of this scenario considering organizational/social changes as well as IT changes.

11. From your experience, describe a situation where the success of a new IT system was impacted by the organization.

Answers to Multiple Choice Questions

    1 — d; 2 — b; 3 — a; 4 — b; 5 — b; 6 — d; 7 — a; 8 — c; 9 — d; 10 — a

References

1. Brynjolfsson, E. and Hitt, L. Beyond the productivity paradox: computers are the catalyst for bigger changes. *Communications of the ACM*, 41(8). August 1998.
2. Corporate Executive Board. Change Management Models. Working Council for Chief Information Officers. January 2003.
3. Ebay. Ebay Community. http://www.ebay.com/aboutebay98/community/. Verified on August 8, 2003.
4. Information Systems Audit and Control Foundation. *IT Control Practice Statement: AI-6 Manage Changes*. Information Systems Audit and Control Foundation. February 2002.
5. Information Systems Audit and Control Foundation. *CobiT Audit Guidelines*. Information Systems Audit and Control Foundation. February 2002.
6. Johnson, S. and Blanchard, K. *Who Moved My Cheese*. Putnam Publishing, New York. September 1998.
7. Kling, R. and Lamb, R. IT and Organizational Change in Digital Economies: a Sociotechnical Approach. *Organizational Change*. 2001.
8. Software & Information Industry Association (SIIA). About SIIA. http://www.siia.net/glance/default.asp. Verified on August 8, 2003.
9. U.S. Department of Commerce and the National Institute of Standards and Technology. A Framework for the Development and Assurance of High Integrity Software. SP 500-223, 1994.
10. U.S. General Accounting Office. Federal Information System Controls Audit Manual: Vol. 1. Financial Statement Audits. AIMD-12.19.6. June 2001.

Part IV
Auditing IT Operations: From Standalone to Global

AUDITING IT OPERATIONS: FROM STANDALONE TO GLOBAL

Chapter 13 through Chapter 17

The fourth part of this text examines the auditing of information technology (IT) operations from the stand-alone to global environment. This section focuses on the IT operations environment. Computer applications operate within this environment and are very dependent on the general controls that protect the applications. It is the operations environment that is an integral component and helps control stand-alone PCs and sophisticated network applications. The domain can encompass worldwide activities supported by wide area network architectures.

Chapter 13 provides discussion on the types of IT operations that exist and their complexities and approaches being used today by practitioners in successfully auditing the operational environment and varied platform configurations.

Chapter 14 covers important IT audit and control issues of the varied complexities of the platforms and their impact on the application. The focus of this chapter is the key control points in operation of which the IT auditors must be cognizant in conducting their review. Several different operations environments will be addressed, such as general controls over operating systems, production, networks, and enterprise operations. Approaches and techniques used by practitioners will be examined.

Chapter 15 discusses the process of assessing risk and controls in IT operations. What are the successful characteristics of a risk assessment process as it pertains to IT operations? What are the standards of practice for risk assessment in this area? Examples are given of risk assessment practices used in varied environments.

Chapter 16 discusses IT audit methods and techniques used in the review of operations. Several emerging areas of importance will be examined, such as end-user computing, EDI, Internet, intranet, and extranet operations issues.

Chapter 17 looks at the multitude of support tools available to IT auditors in assisting them in auditing IT operations over varied environments. As this chapter suggests, the auditor's tool kit is a critical component in his or her ability to audit control processes through today's complex information technology environment. The chapter will provide examples of uses of computer-assisted audit tools and techniques (CAATT) and the lessons learned as they pertain to audits of operations and issues of efficiency and effectiveness. The use and application of IT forensics is also addressed.

Chapter 13
IT Operations Environments: Complexities and Control Issues

Historically, organizations have perceived several advantages in centralizing computer operations. A major advantage relates to economies of scale. It was widely accepted that a large computer was more cost-effective than a small computer. Advances in processor technology and vendor pricing policies, however, have made this belief obsolete. It is now possible for a microcomputer to connect "seamlessly" through a local area network (LAN) to a host file server, mid-range, or mainframe computer which, in turn, may be connected to other remote computers. Exhibit 1 illustrates the five most common topologies for networked distributed processing systems. Most distributed or wide area networks (WANs) use a hierarchical or tree topology (although mesh topologies are becoming increasingly popular).

A great deal has been written about how well-suited the virtual corporation will be for competition in the 21st century and how critically this business organization will depend upon the reliable and timely communication of information for its success. The virtual corporation employs a mass customization strategy in which both quality products are tailored to specific needs and low cost is achieved. In addition, the virtual corporation is exceedingly agile and flexible, linking a variety of organizations in an ever-changing network in which partner firms contribute to the overall enterprise based upon their core competencies. Work is performed by teams composed of members from across the functions and across the organizations in the network. Members of these teams collaborate wherever they are and whenever they are able to do so. The authority to make decisions does not reside only at the top but is distributed throughout the organization. Finally, and very important, is the fact that the venture is based on openness, cooperativeness, and trust.

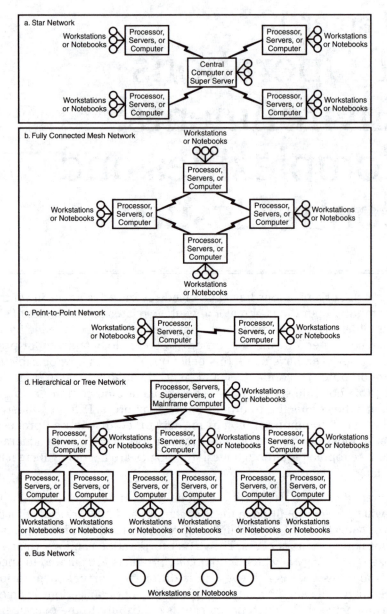

Exhibit 1. Network Topologies

The Virtual Environment

The virtual corporation's dynamic global multienterprise organization and team-oriented collaborative approach to work will place very stringent requirements on the venture's telecommunications network. The design of such systems is complex and management will be very difficult. As the name implies, the virtual corporation is critically dependent on the timely flow of accurate information throughout the organization. A good way to view how stringent the network requirements are is to analyze them in terms of the quality of telecommunications service. Most telecommunication experts believe that the network must be able to reach anyone anywhere in the world and be capable of supporting the sharing of a wide range of information, from simple voice, data, and text messages to cooperative transactions requiring the information updating of a variety of databases. The CEO and CIO want to meet or exceed their business objectives and attain maximum profitability through an extremely high degree of availability, fast response time, extreme reliability, and a very high level of security.

This means that the products, where IT provides consumer feedback, will also be of high quality, rich in information content, and come packaged with a variety of useful services to meet the changing business conditions and competition. Flexible manufacturing and improvement programs such as Just in Time (JIT), "lean manufacturing," and Total Quality Management (TQM), will enable low-cost production. Flexible manufacturing will permit products to be produced economically in arbitrary lot sizes through modularization of the production process.

The unpredictability of customer needs and the shortness of product life cycles will cause the mix of production capabilities and underlying resources required by the virtual corporation to change constantly. The virtual corporation must be capable of assembling its capabilities and resources quickly, thereby bringing a product to the market swiftly. To achieve the high degree of organizational flexibility and value chain coordination necessary for quick market response, excellent product quality, and low cost, the virtual corporation will employ a network, team-oriented, distributed decision-making organizational approach rather than a more traditional hierarchical, vertically integrated, command-and-control approach.

The virtual corporation will possess a dynamic network organization, synthesizing the best available design, production, supply, and distribution capabilities and resources from enterprises around the world and link them and the virtual corporation's customers together. Its multienterprise nature will enable the virtual corporation to respond to a competitive opportunity quickly and with the requisite scale, while, at the same time, enabling the individual network participant's cost and risk to be reduced. The network will be dynamic because participant identities and relationships will change as the capabilities and resources required change. The global scope of the network will enable virtual corporations to capitalize on worldwide market opportunities. Work will be performed by multidisciplinary and multienterprise teams, which will function concurrently and, to reduce production time, be granted significant decision-making authority. Team members will be able to work collaboratively, regardless of location and time zone. Openness, cooperativeness, and trust will characterize the relationships among the organizations in the network and their personnel.

Aside from reach, range, and service responsiveness, the network must be highly interconnective so that people, organizations, and machines can communicate at any time, regardless of location. Also, the network must be very flexible, because the organization is constantly changing. Finally, the network must be cost-effective because low cost is one of the ingredients in the mass-customization strategy. In addition, a control structure must be designed, developed, and implemented that provides assurances of integrity, reliability, and validity.

So, how can this be accomplished? The ability to reach anyone anywhere in the world requires global area networks. Clearly, the Internet and global carrier services, such as Concert, will be crucial. Also, because the intended receiver need not be in the office or even at home, wireless networks will play a part. This will be true on-premise, such as with the use of wireless private branch exchanges (PBXs) or LANs, and off-premise, with the use of cellular networks and global satellite networks such as Iridium and Personal Communications. To support the sharing of a wide range of voice, data, and video information, bandwidth-on-demand will be required all the way to the desktop as well as the mobile terminal. Also, various collaborative service platforms such as Lotus Domino will be necessary. Finally, perfect service will have to be designed into the network. Speed can be achieved through broadband networking: locally via fast Ethernet, gigabit, and Asynchronous Transfer Mode (ATM) LANs, and over a wide area via Switched Multimegabyte Data Services (SDMS) and ATM services.

Areas of Control and Risk Issues

The competitive success of the virtual corporation will depend heavily on information and its timely, reliable, and secure communication. Backups and redundancy will increase the network's availability. The use of firewalls and encrypted communication can increase security. Increased interconnectivity can be achieved by using broadly accepted standards. Designs should be modular and Open Architectures such as TCP/IP and ISDN should be employed. Finally, flexibility can be achieved by using software-driven solutions, such as virtual LANs and common carrier or Internet virtual private networks (VPNs) in which intranet, extranet, or other network reconfigurations are easily made through the software rather than the hardware. Similarly, public networks, which can be reconfigured easily, are preferable to harder-to-reconfigure private networks.

Currently, some of these building blocks are not entirely capable of meeting the virtual corporation's stringent requirements. In a recent survey of network managers in Fortune 1000 firms, over 75 percent reported that they would not send sensitive traffic over the Internet because of lack of faith in its security. In addition to security problems, response time is suffering from congestion on the Internet and it is likely to get worse.

Although today greater reliability is available through wired rather than wireless solutions, wireless networking is fast becoming a network connection of choice for individual users and organizations. Wireless technology is the ability of computing devices to communicate on a network without the need of a physical connection to that network. Wireless popularity means that organizations can no longer choose not to deploy wireless LANs (WLANs). However, with a wireless network, the network signal is transmitted in the air, thus posing a greater risk of abuse. Business should control wireless through the use of sanctioned WLANs and user authentication, and take steps to prevent employees creating WLANs using unauthorized access points.

Even if technology permits it, there is a question whether or not these requirements can be satisfied due to the complexity of the management problem. In addition to the ordinary network management headaches, such as user demands for higher levels of security, shrinking budgets, inadequate training, etc., network managers in virtual corporations will have new challenges. First is the mission-critical nature of the network to the firm. It is the lifeblood of the firm. Second is the fact that these requirements are very stringent. Complexity is a major problem now for network managers and it will get worse as the industry becomes more deregulated, competition intensifies, and technology offers more choices. It is especially difficult in the virtual corporation because the network is a multienterprise one. Not only that but also it is one that is continually changing.

IT Operations Issues in Network Installation

The IT operations issues focus on the planning, implementation, and operation of networks. The following list provides a quick reference identifying the installation issues most relevant to the subject:

- *Wiring and cabling:* Many articles and case studies have shown that approximately 80 percent of network problems are due to improperly installed or poor-quality cabling. When quality is sacrificed for cost, operations may be detrimentally affected once the network is put into service, resulting in retrofit costs.
- *Throughput or traffic:* This is an area in which effective planning and visits to organizations that have implemented a similar network can pay off. Major decisions include specifying the type of file servers needed to support the desired application and determining

connectivity with other networks and peripherals. An assessment of the organizations' current and planned applications is important input to this process.

- *Layout:* To facilitate enhancements and the ability to adapt to organizational change, layout should be part of the planning process. This can save the organization money in the long run and help identify control concerns.
- *Measuring performance:* Tools that help monitor performance and analyze change can be very valuable to the network manager. In addition, network analysis products can assist in diagnosing data bottlenecks as well as system and control failures.

Because a network represents a substantial business investment in microcomputer equipment, network equipment, network operating software, shared software, individual user software, data, personnel, administration, and training, the network or the information contained in the network files may represent an organization's major assets. Therefore, an organization must evaluate the major controls to be used in the Network Architecture.

LANs have become commonplace in most medium and large companies and their capabilities extend to the smaller enterprises. Now, WANs and WLANs have become the next communications frontier. However, WANs and WLANs are much more complicated than LANs. In most WAN environments, the more devices an individual has to manage, the more time-consuming is the process of monitoring those devices. Complexity also increases very rapidly because each new device on the network invariably has to interface with many existing devices.

WLAN protocols are a moving target for organizations today. Although 802.11b was for several years considered a wireless standard, many protocols have been created. The most recent standard is 802.11g. As we will discuss later, IEEE 802.11i is forthcoming as an improved security measure. Organizations considering WLANs must consider trade-offs between frequency, modulation, and data rate in addition to security and compatibility issues. A list of the most common wireless network standards is shown in Exhibit 2.

To get a further understanding of WANs, it is useful to explore the differences between WANs and LANs. LANs are defined as communications networks in which all components are located within several miles of each other and communicate using high transmission speeds, generally 10 bps or higher. They are typically used to support interconnection within a building or campus environment.

WANs connect system users who are geographically dispersed and connected by means of public telecommunications facilities. WANs provide

Exhibit 2. Most Common WLAN Standards

Protocol	Author	Frequency	Modulation	Data Rate	Comments
802.11	IEEE	900 MHz ISM	FHSS	~ 300 Kbps	Original standard of the series (Obsolescent)
802.11a	IEEE	5 GHz UNII	OFDM	Up to 54 Mbps	Emerging standard not backward compatible with 802.11
802.11b	IEEE	2.4 GHz ISM, 900MHz legacy	DSSS FHSS legacy	1 to 11 Mbps	Most popular as of this writing
802.11e	IEEE	5 GHz UNII	OFDM	Up to 54 Mbps	Adds QoS capability to 802.11h (Not yet available)
802.11g	IEEE	2.4 GHz ISM	DSSS FHSS	Up to 54 Mbps	Intended to maintain backward compatibility with 802.11b. (Not yet available; expected to be ratified third quarter 2002)
802.11h	IEEE	5 GHz UNII	OFDM	Up to 54 Mbps	Adds transmit power control dynamic freq. selection to 802.11a to counter EU area interference issues
802.11i	IEEE	5 GHz UNII	OFDM	54 Mbps or beyond	Intended to specifically include security and authentication (In process; probably years in future)
802.11j (5UP — 2003)	IEEE, ETSI	5 GHz UNII	OFDM, GMSK	54 Mbps or beyond	Effort to converge 802.11 and HiperLAN standards to permit interoperation in the 5 GHz band (Committee forming)
HiperLAN	ETSI	5.15–5.30 GHz or 17.1–17.3 GHz	GMSK	23.529 Mbps	European Community backed standard, expected to appear by mid 2002
HiperLAN/2	ETSI	5.15–5.30 GHz or 17.1–17.3 GHz	GMSK	54 Mbps	European Community developed standard, expected to appear in 2002
HomeRF™	HomeRF™ Industry group	2.4 GHz	FHSS	Up to 10 Mbps	Integrated voice, data, and entertainment for home networking
Bluetooth	Bluetooth Consortium	2.4 GHz	FHSS	1 Mbps	Cable replacement, not comparable to 802.11 or HiperLAN

system users with access to computers for fast interchange of information. Major components of WANs include CPUs, ranging from microcomputers to mainframes, intelligent terminals, modems, and communications controllers. WANs cover distances of about 30 miles and often connect a group of campuses.

WANs are usually static in nature. Changes to them require rerouting telephone lines and installing modems. LANs on the other hand can be quickly reconfigured; communications lines are set up and rerouted more easily and gateways to host computers can be quickly added.

Types of WANs

There are two basic types of WANs: centralized and distributed. Centralized WANs consist of a mainframe or minicomputer that serves remotely distributed dumb terminals. Network managers lease communications channels from a common long-distance carrier and tie together terminals and the central computer using a star (or other) topology. (WAN topologies are described in more detail later in this chapter). Communications are fairly straightforward; the smart computer polls the dumb terminals to find out if they have anything to transmit, and then it controls data transmission so that there are no collisions.

Distributed networks provide an environment that allows independent computers to have equal levels of control in the communications architecture. Distributed networks have grown as smart computers have increased throughout organizations. Today's packet WAN technologies are capable of supporting worldwide transmission at rates that are less than LAN transmission rates (LANs transmission rates of 100 MB and higher over relatively short distances).

Another recent addition to the variation of network support infrastructures is the virtual private network (VPN). This has proven to be an exploding market in recent years as organizations move toward decentralized facilities that can provide secure remote access to company data for their mobile workforces. VPN is a private data network that utilizes public communication infrastructures such as the Internet, while ensuring privacy through the use of Tunneling Protocols and security procedures. VPNs essentially eliminate the costs of a real private network, where companies can own or lease their own private lines.

There are two main categories of VPNs that utilize the Internet as their public telecommunications infrastructure. VPNs that operate at the network layer (Layer 3) of the Open System Interconnection (OSI) Network Architecture Model are called Internet Protocol Security (IPS) VPNs. VPNs that function at the application levels (Layers 4–7 of OSI) are called Secure Sockets Layer (SSL) VPNs.

Elements of WANs

WANs differ according to their access methods, connective hardware and software, Communications Protocols, types of network services, and network topologies. These differences affect network installation, growth, and operating costs. In addition, WANs depend on the network management system for efficient and reliable operation. The following sections describe these elements.

Access Methods

Connections to remote networks may be accomplished over public data networks or private lines provided by long-distance and interexchange telephone carriers. The Internet requires the use of 32-bit addresses, which are administered by the network information center. Locally administered private networks should encourage use of addresses that are compatible with Internet addresses to facilitate connection to the Internet.

Connective Devices

Information is transmitted over WANs in packets. In addition to user data, these packets contain information necessary for network management and protocols that permit local and remote devices on the network to recognize one another. For example, each packet contains address information, which is necessary to ensure the correct routing of the packet. Bridges and routers are the primary connective devices used to handle these transmissions.

Bridges. A bridge is a hardware and software device used to connect networks using various media and signaling systems. Bridges operate at the data-link layer of the OSI Model. Bridges read and filter data packets and frames, passing traffic only if the address is on the same segment of the network cable as the originating station. Frames contain information that is necessary for reassembling the messages contained in packets after they reach their destination. There are two types of frames: control frames for link management and information frames for the transfer of information.

Routers. A router is a sophisticated hardware and software device that connects LANs and WANs. It serves packets or frames containing certain protocols and it routes packets using Network Layer Protocols. Multiprotocol routers can operate in heterogeneous environments by simultaneously using multiple protocols.

Protocols. WAN Protocols are designed to provide connections for many devices within a wide area. Their purpose is to support a peer network of terminals, microcomputers, and hosts. A number of WAN Protocols are available, including TCP/IP (which is the combined acronym for a pair

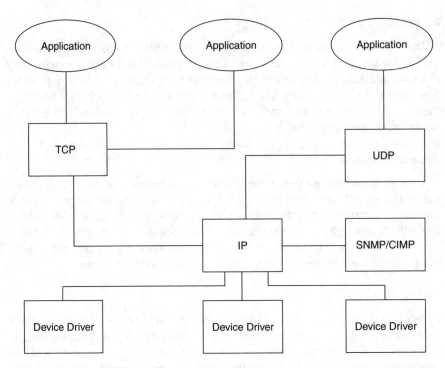

Exhibit 3. A Schematic Diagram of Different Types of Layers Involving TCP/IP

of Networking Protocols: the Transmission Control Protocol [TCP], and the Internet Protocol [IP]). The TCP/IP provide the primary communications procedures for the Internet. IBM's Systems Network Architecture (SNA) is designed to provide communications compatibility among microcomputers, minicomputers, and mainframes. For example, it can be used to connect IBM token-ring LANs to a host environment (see Exhibit 3).

Network Services

Frame relay and ATM are technologies used to support network traffic. Their method of operation is described in the following paragraphs. There are a number of vendors of frame relay and ATM products.

Frame Relay Network Services. Frame relay is an extremely flexible and cost-effective technology that supports variable network traffic. Service bandwidth is scalable from 56 Kbps to 2.048 Mbps, and it offers a variable-length frame size from 262 bytes to 8 kB.

Frame relay allows users to gain the advantages of high-speed circuits without having to run dedicated links between all the endpoints on a private network. The other major advantage of frame relay is its minimal packet overhead.

Asynchronous Transfer Mode Network Services. Asynchronous Transfer Mode (ATM) refers to a high-bandwidth, low-delay switching and multiplexing technology. ATM network services provide a foundation for high-speed digital transmission, LAN connectivity, imaging, and multimedia applications. ATM is based on cell switching technology that is equally effective at transmitting voice, video, and data at high speeds.

ATM is better suited than packet switching to real-time communications (e.g., video) because it uses standard length cells with small headers containing packet and address information. ATM supports transmission speeds of up to 622 Mbps. It supports services requiring both circuit-mode information transfer capabilities (characterized by a constant bit rate) and packet-mode capabilities (characterized by a variable bit rate).

The Network Management System

Every major business wants to have the most efficient and economical operation of the corporate network. In order for a business to achieve this, it must effectively manage the computer and communications resources over the WAN. Because most businesses buy their networking products from more than one vendor, network management systems must be able to support a wide variety of equipment on the same network. This diversity makes the task of management and troubleshooting more challenging. (Network management software is discussed later in this chapter.)

Network Topologies

Although the star topology is the most popular WAN topology, a number of other network topologies are available and depicted earlier in Exhibit 1. Each of the topologies has consequences with respect to reliability and availability.

Star Topology. The star topology is highly reliable; loss of one node results only in loss of a single line. Loss of that line prevents communication between the hub and the affected node, but all other nodes continue to operate normally.

This topology is more limited in regard to ensuring availability. The network can only support the level of traffic that can be handled by the hub. In some cases, the hub is only able to handle one request at a time, which can cause serious delays during peak workloads.

Ring Topology. The ring topology uses link segments to connect adjacent nodes; each node is actively involved in the transmission of tokens to and from other nodes. The loss of a link causes operation of the entire network to cease. Therefore, this topology is not considered very reliable.

The ring topology is less effective than the mesh topology at ensuring availability of network services, but it is more effective than the star topology. Its effectiveness is limited because each node on the ring waits to receive the token before transmitting data.

Bus Topology. The bus topology is also not considered reliable. If the link fails, the entire segment connected to that link also fails. However, if the node fails, the rest of the network will continue to operate.

The availability of network resources using this topology depends on the Access Control Protocol used, the length of the bus, and the transmission load. Under a light load, availability is virtually assured, but as the load increases so too does the chance of collisions among transmissions. The chance of collisions also increases with greater bus length.

Mesh Topology. This kind of topology is highly reliable because it provides a diverse set of transmission routes. If one segment of the line fails, the rest of the line is not affected. Because of its multiple transmission paths, mesh topology also provides a high level of availability.

Hybrid Topology. The hybrid topology is highly reliable; the failure of one node does not affect the operation of other nodes. It also provides a high degree of availability because it provides a large number of connections to users.

Tools for Network Monitoring

A number of automated tools can assist the security specialist in identifying risks to network security. These include:

- Protocol analyzers
- Network monitors
- Network management software
- General statistical tools
- Hybrid tools

The following sections describe each of these types of tools.

Protocol Analyzers

Protocol analyzers can be used to observe data packets as they travel across a network, measure rates of line use, and simulate traffic to gauge changes in the network configuration. They are designed to capture and decode data packets, breaking traffic down according to the Seven-Layer OSI Reference Model; the device is physically connected to the network segments being monitored. Wandell and Goltermann's DA-30C is an example of a protocol analyzer. As described next, a WAN protocol analyzer is a specialized type of protocol analyzer.

WAN Protocol Analyzers. High-speed WAN protocol analyzers can be used to help network and security specialists plan and maintain multiple LANs linked to WAN services. With their unparalleled packet-filtering capabilities, these instruments are able to monitor overall network activity, view organizational data traffic patterns, simulate new circuits, and pinpoint problems. WAN analyzers allow the user to track exactly how much of a leased line is being used for a particular protocol. These analyzers can also capture and store data samples and filter out specific data packets for scrutiny. WAN analyzers are being developed with capabilities to provide fault management filters and rule-based judgments, performance trend analysis, and reports that identify problems and assign responsibility for their diagnosis and tracking.

For efficient monitoring and diagnosis, it is vital that the analyzer be able to filter out specific packets from the overall data stream. This requires that the analyzer keep pace with system line speeds so that it does not overlook packets that may be critical to the network. In practice, most high-speed WAN protocol analyzers do not really filter data at the full rate of a T1 line, and the filtering and decoding processes further slow down the analyzer's operation.

Because of this, most vendors of protocol analyzers specify a frame rate for their products, indicating the number of packets or frames per second that the analyzer can process. The vendors also specify the size of frames for which rates are given. Most analyzers come with simulation programs that allow network managers to gauge the possible effects of specific types of data traffic on WAN circuits. With this software, sample packets are actually launched onto the network so that the analyzer can measure the effects of adding different types of protocol loads. (Running simulation applications may require shutting down network traffic.) Because most analyzers already have sophisticated packet filtering and time-stamping capabilities, it is relatively easy to add statistical software for data sampling and analysis. Such statistical packages can generally be run without interfering with network traffic.

Network Monitors

Network monitors track and statistically analyze traffic on network segments. As with protocol analyzers, the device is physically connected to the segments being monitored. Sample products include Bay Mountain's IT Appliance and DPS Telecom's Network Alarm Management System.

Network Management Software

Network management software and workstations are designed to monitor and report on the conditions of network elements such as bridges, routers, and hubs, typically displaying information using multicolored icons on a map. These products typically use the Simple Network Management Protocol (SNMP). A number of products are available, including Hewlett-Packard's HP-OpenView, Sun Microsystems' SunNet Manager, IBM's Net-View/6000, and Compuware Corporation's Application Expert 2.1. Their products offer reliable network security and data integrity services.

General Statistical Tools

These tools are designed primarily to provide statistical information about network performance. They typically track CPU and memory levels of use, free disk space, and network 1/0. Among the available products is Hewlett-Packard's PerfView.

Hybrids. It should be noted that many products are actually hybrids that offer elements of two or more of the proceding categories of monitoring tools. For example, many network management stations include the statistical analysis capabilities of network monitors; some network monitors provide basic protocol analysis capabilities. Among hybrid products that combine traffic monitoring, protocol analysis, and network mapping are the InfraTool Network Discovery 4.0, Peregrine Systems, Spectrum 6.0 from Aprisma Management Technologies, and OpenView NetWork Node Manager release B.06.10 from Hewlett-Packard.

The Internet, Intranet, and Extranet

The Internet was started in the 1960s by the U.S. Defense Department's Advanced Research Projects Agency to link the department with its suppliers. Today, the Internet is a worldwide collection of millions of computers tied together by means of high-speed communications lines to form an apparently single network. The Internet provides an electronic forum in which people can share information and ideas, exchange e-mail and data, use remote computers, and access public-domain information and software.

Corporate customers now represent the fastest growing segment of the overall Internet user population. They use the Internet for many reasons, including file transfers, electronic mail, system maintenance, and interactive sessions. For example, one chemical company uses the Internet to disseminate the results of its research; the company prefers using Internet because it is available 24 hours a day, everyday. An oil company uses the Internet to transmit maps and land surveys to remote locations for oil and gas exploration; the Internet is able to reach nearly all countries. Users can connect to the Internet in several ways: dialing into a personal account on an Internet-connected computer, connecting through a commercial gateway, or subscribing to a commercial service.

Today, an intranet is an internal company network. The intranet uses the Internet standards of HTML (Hypertext Markup Language), XML (Extensible Markup Language) and HTTP (Hypertext Transfer Protocol), and the TCP/IP Communication Protocol along with a graphical Web browser to support business applications and provide departmental, interdepartmental, and companywide communication solutions. An intranet uses a Web server that is only connected to a company's LAN. Intranets can also use news and mail servers to create private newsgroups for the company's intranet and to send and receive e-mail among the company's users.

The term intranet was introduced in late 1995. Before that they were called "enterprise Internets." Even though the prior name better describes its functionality, the intranet term is used more frequently because of its closeness with the Internet.

The four main components of an intranet are:

- *TCP/IP:* This is the primary protocol of an intranet. Within this environment, information travels in discrete units called IP packets. TCP/IP software attaches each computer to the network; it hides the router and different Network Architectures and makes everything seem as one large, integrated network.
- *Information services:* These are any software application that enables data manipulation (receive, store, and send) over an intranet. Examples of information services are e-mail, newsgroups, remote log-in, File Transfer Protocol (FTP), database search engines, electronic commerce, intranet systems management, security, gateways, and firewalls.
- *Clients:* Clients are the applications needed to access the information services. The most common intranet client is the Web browser.
- *Authoring tools:* These are applications (Dreamweaver, Flash, MS FrontPage, etc.) that create, edit, alter, or manipulate the data handled by an information service's server.

Intranets are redefining the way the corporate world communicates. Intranets are expanding to extranets, or two or more intranets, which belong to different enterprises, and are bound into one virtual network.

The media, especially the Internet and network-focused publications, and general and business news, has played a major role in disseminating and making intranets hot and extranets hotter. Below are some urging reasons that move intranet implementation in corporations.

- Internet technology can be transferred fairly easy to intranets and most companies already have experience with the Internet.
- The tools used on intranets by users are similar to those used on the Internet. Therefore, the learning curve is not too high.

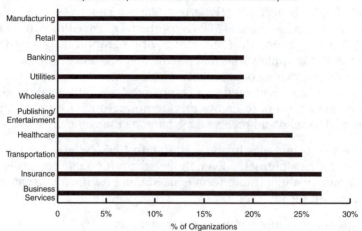

Adapted from http://www.internetwk.com/cwi/netcentral/study.html

Exhibit 4. Next Wave of Intranet Demand

- New tools such as scheduling tools, workflow, database-query applications, etc., have been developed rapidly. Also, Web fronts can usually interface with old legacy systems, giving old applications longer life span.

- The cost and complexity of building intranets is usually significantly less than other in-house development efforts. One of the more compelling reasons to deploy intranets is to reduce costs. A good example on how companies are saving money on intranets is Hewlett-Packard (HP). HP created and deployed a corporate intranet called InfoNet. The initial goal of InfoNet was to make general information, such as personnel policy manuals, available to its 105,000+ employees on the company's internal TCP/IP network. Encouraged by the success of publishing its personnel policies electronically, HP's management decided to provide all major forms electronically to reduce distribution costs, printing costs, and e-mail traffic to personnel [Tittle and Stewart 1997].

The statistics show that the growth in intranets is steady and magazines such as the *Intranet Journal* indicate that the evolution and development of intranet with companies has evolved into actuaries of internal knowledge assets, external information resources, and content engineering management.

Several studies have shown that intranet adoption has gone beyond leading edge companies and now is penetrating traditional companies. Exhibit 4 shows how the next wave of intranet will be in traditional companies distributed by industry type.

Exhibit 5. Functional Uses of Intranets by Corporations

Development of Internal Knowledge Assets, External Information Sources, and Content Engineering in the following areas:

- Retrieval of product and market information
- Retrieval of best practices and lessons learned
- Retrieval of employee and organizational information
  - Manuals
  - Procedures
  - Job opportunities
  - Personnel announcements
  - Department or employee Web page
- Design, development, review, implementation, and revision or updating of project or organizational documentation
- Retrieval of information from organizational databases
  - Statistics (overall and by areas)
  - Graphics
  - Trends and forecasts
  - Status of goods, services, and suppliers/vendors
- Time Management Support
  - For scheduling meetings and conferences
  - Attending events
  - Meeting due dates and reporting dates

Another interesting aspect of intranets is how are they being used. There are many ways corporations are using intranets today (see Exhibit 5). This illustration provides some functional examples of how they are deployed in corporate setups in today's environment.

Personal Accounts

With this first alternative, service is limited to certain levels of access, for example, access to USENET (an Internet-based news service), e-mail services, or FTP services. In addition to obtaining statistical information about an account on one of these systems, the user must implement a modem and communications package. A monthly connect-time fee is charged; the telephone carrier also charges the user for any long-distance calls.

With this approach, the computer is not actually on the Internet — it is just acting as a terminal for another computer with a direct Internet connection. The user does not need to run any Internet-Protocol software with this approach. But any files the user transfers to server accounts using the Internet FTP must be downloaded using the selected communications software, which can be very expensive. To simplify the downloading process and reduce connection costs, a software access package (e.g., WS_FTP) can be used to obtain an interface to Internet file transfer services.

Commercial Gateways

With this approach, users must obtain an official Internet membership for their systems; in effect, they become official Internet nodes. This can be accomplished in several ways.

If the user does not need to support a heavy traffic load, he or she might get by with a 28,800-bps connection using a standard modem and a public telephone line. If faster connection is required (for example, for regularly downloading files), a 56-Kbps Tl dedicated access line might be necessary. (A less expensive alternative is to use a dedicated X. 25 or ISDN communications method.) A 2-Mbps Tl line might be necessary to support extremely heavy loads involving the frequent transfer of vast quantities of data. In addition to installing the T1 connection, the gateway provider would also install a router at the user's site; the computers at the user's site would need to be on an Ethernet network running a version of the Internet's TCP/IP.

Commercial Services

Private users and businesses can subscribe to such commercial communications services as America Online and an Internet mail drop. Use of this method is extremely popular and represents a significant source of growth in Internet accounts.

LAN Security Issues: Wired versus Wireless

Both the wired LAN and WLAN are subject to substantial security risks and issues. These include:

- Threats to the physical security of the network
- Unauthorized access and eavesdropping
- Attacks from within the network's (authorized) user community

In fact, a WLAN has all of the properties of a wired LAN, and thus security measures taken to ensure the integrity and security of data in the wired-LAN environment are also applicable to WLANs as well. The only difference between a wired LAN and a WLAN is at the physical layer and super high frequency (SHF); all other network services and vulnerabilities remain. WLANs in fact include an additional set of unique security elements that are not available in the wired world, leading to the proposition that wireless LANs are actually more secure than their wired counterparts — an opinion that is shared by many industry analysts and experts.

What Can Be Done to the Wired LANs?

Physical Security: Site Control and Management. Given the obvious reliance of wired LANs on a wired physical plant, anyone gaining access to that wire can damage the network or compromise the integrity and security of information on it; therefore, physical access to network wires needs to be protected. However, the vast amount of wire inherent in most LANs provides many points for unauthorized access.

User Authentication. One of the big concerns of LAN technology relating to user authentication is access. Remote access products that allow traveling sales and marketing people to dial in for their e-mail, remote offices connected via dial-up lines, intranets, and extranets that connect vendors and customers to a network can all leave the network vulnerable to hackers, viruses, and other intruders. Firewall products offering packet filtering, proxy servers, and user-to-session filtering add additional protection, but hackers seem to get smarter all the time.

Eavesdropping Countermeasures. The most difficult threat to detect is someone just looking at and likely copying raw data on the LAN. Inexpensive and readily available programs let anyone with physical access to the network to read, capture, and display any type of packet data on the net, especially when the network administrator does not have some kind of "packet sniffer" or LAN-traffic analyzer for troubleshooting the network. And even wired LANs have an unintended wireless component. Many types of LAN cabling, particularly the unshielded twisted pair, radiate significant energy. This leads to the possibility that anyone can sit in the parking lot outside a building and actually intercept wired Ethernet data packets without detection. Data encryption is the only line of defense against this kind of threat. Unfortunately, a sense of complacency among network managers has resulted in the limited use of in-building encryption, often with unforeseen and unknown results.

Why WLANs Are More Secure

As can be seen from the above discussion, data security considerations impact the entire Network Architecture and also apply equally to WLANs. In addition to this, the various standards in place and the many professionals across the world working on improving the IEEE standards give hope to improved security measures being developed now. The very different physical layer of WLANs actually increases overall network security as discussed below.

Spread-Spectrum Technology

Most WLANs use spread-spectrum radio transmission techniques. Spread-spectrum technology was first introduced about 60 years ago by the military for improving both message integrity and security. Spread-spectrum systems are designed to be resistant to noise, interference, jamming, and unauthorized detection. Spread-spectrum transmitters send their signals out over a broad range of frequencies at very low power, in contrast to narrowband radios that concentrate all of their power into a single frequency. There are two common ways to implement spread-spectrum transmission: they are direct sequence (DS) and frequency hopping (FH). Then we should know the basics in the DS and FH transmission module, which makes it extremely difficult for an eavesdropper to obtain the data being transmitted in the air. In the case of DS, an eavesdropper must know the chipping code. Someone trying to intercept an FH transmission must know the hopping pattern. In both cases, the specific frequency band and modulation techniques in use must also be known. Radio systems also use a form of data scrambling for purely technical reasons, which is to assist in managing the timing and decoding of radio signals. An unintended receiver would also need to know this scrambling pattern. In addition to the secure features embedded in DS and FH techniques, they also allow the use of encryption. Indeed, many WLAN products include encryption features as a standard or optional component. The IEEE 802.11 standard, for example, includes a security technique known as wired equivalent privacy (WEP), which is based on the use of 64-bit keys and the popular RC4 encryption algorithm. Other emerging developments such as the possibility of including better encryption capability and key management techniques are being developed under new IEEE initiatives.

Station Authentication

Most WLAN products have the ability, as an authentication management function, to specifically authorize or exclude individual wireless station. Thus, an individual wireless user can be either included in the network or locked out. More importantly, users need to know a wide variety of information, including radio domains, channels (specific frequencies or hopping patterns), subchannels, security IDs, and passwords. Other information, such as in-building roaming, also needs to be known. Combining all of the above-mentioned aspects, the network administrators can make unauthorized network access extremely difficult for hackers even when they possess the specific wireless equipment being used at a given site. Certainly, the work being done on the development of IEEE 802.11i offers greater assurances of this being achieved soon.

Physical Security

Compared to the wired LANs, which have a significant amount of wire being exposed to the outsiders, the WLANs eliminate the possible mass physical contact points. Although wireless LANs usually involve the use of a wired backbone network for access-point interconnection, the amount of wire is quite small, and extra steps can be taken to safeguard its physical integrity without inordinate cost. Moreover, because the access points used in WLANs function as bridges, individual wireless users are isolated from the majority of LAN traffic, again limiting user access to raw network packets.

Network Management Control Issues

Perhaps the most vulnerable area for CIOs and CEOs to review is the structure of network management within IT operations. In August 2003, the northeast area of the United States up through Canada experienced a massive electrical outage that hampered many IT facilities. Cell stations used for transfer of wireless communications had no power. Also, the recent 22-hour outage of a major AT&T frame relay is reason enough for executives to ask if it could happen to them and the potential losses incurred as a result of one procedural error and two software routines not working as planned. Where were the network management controls in place to quickly identify and resolve the problem?

The question is that after the network has been designed and implemented, will it be manageable in terms of the ability to respond and recover from any possible interruption of quality service? Challenging as network management is for today's enterprises, it could be even more challenging for virtual corporations. First, network expectations will be higher, involving both wired and wireless topologies. Although telecommunications networks can be a source of competitive advantage to many firms in the 21st century, they will be mission-critical to virtual corporations. Next, network management will be a complex problem in virtual corporations. As stated earlier, network managers face a variety of interconnectivity, integration, policy setting, control and coordination, and security issues in their enterprise networks. Network managers in virtual corporations will face the same problems, but in a more challenging multi-enterprise network context. Last, the network management environment in virtual corporations will be much more dynamic than it is in today's companies. Because the virtual corporation's business requirements and organizational structure will be changing constantly, the telecommunications network that supports them will be in a continual state of flux.

In some respects, however, managing telecommunications networks in virtual corporations could be less challenging. Because network management systems are improving, by the next century a really effective integrated system could be available. In addition, telecommunications are likely to have greater senior management support in virtual corporations than in many conventional organizations because the virtual corporations depend on telecommunications so critically for their success. Also, given the heavy emphasis that virtual corporations place on the need for compatibility and complementary capabilities among venture partners, venture partners are likely to have compatible networks and complementary telecommunications capabilities. Venturing with partners whose telecommunications platforms, policies, and organizations are compatible would reduce the interconnectivity problem immensely. Similarly, an organization possessing experience in designing and managing telecommunications networks

327

would fit well in a partnership with organizations lacking such capabilities. The final reason that the network management job could be less challenging in virtual corporations is that the structure of the telecommunications organization and the caliber of its personnel will be ideally suited for the dynamic and complex environment of telecommunications.

Development of a National Information Infrastructure Policy and assurances that it addresses the Global Information Infrastructure are ways in which the CEO and CIO can strategically plan for the coming of the virtual enterprise. The organizational philosophy of the virtual corporation, the telecommunications organization, will be lean, close to the users, and opportunistic, making it exceedingly adaptable to change. Knowledgeable, trained, empowered, team-oriented personnel, enabling it to respond quickly and surely to problems as they arise, will staff this function.

Importance of National Information Infrastructure

The events of September 11, 2001, excelled the need to develop a National Information Infrastructure. The National Telecommunications and Information Administration (NTIA), an agency of the U.S. Department of Commerce, is the Executive Branch's principal voice on domestic and international telecommunications and IT issues. NTIA works to spur innovation, encourage competition, help create jobs, and provide consumers with more choices and better-quality telecommunications products and services at lower prices. By the 21st century, telecommunications and information-related industries will account for approximately 20 percent of the U.S. economy.

The NTIA is the primary federal agency working toward the definition and development of the National Information Infrastructure (NII), commonly referred to as "the information superhighway." The NII will be a network linking people, businesses, schools, hospitals, communities, and governments, allowing them to communicate and exchange information using voice, video, and data with computers, telephones, radios, and other devices. The concept of the NII encompasses a wide range of telecommunications equipment, services, and transmission media. The technology encompassed by the NII includes, among other things, electronic cameras, computers, televisions, optical fiber transmission lines, microwave links, satellite systems, wireless networks, car telephones, pagers, and facsimile machines. The NII will integrate and interconnect these physical components to provide a nationwide information conduit accessible by everyone. Although the NII is not a discrete telecommunication service, the increase in information flow, particularly to and from mobile users, will ultimately result in an increased requirement for radio spectrum to support the various mobile and fixed service interconnections.

In February 1998, the National Computerization Agency of South Korea published its views regarding the importance of a national information infrastructure, global information infrastructure, and electronic government. Countries worldwide are recognizing the importance of establishing such guidance to assist their movement into the world of electronic commerce. A communications and information infrastructure is comprised of many components, two key components of which are the telecommunications network linking its users, whether human or machine, and the services provided by the networks to its users. Some specific communication services which will be useful in a virtual corporate environment include basic voice and data communications services; messaging services, such as electronic mail, voice mail, facsimile, and EDI; bulletin board services; electronic conferencing services, such as videoconferencing; services that promote information sharing, such as Lotus Notes; and specialized services that facilitate collaboration over WANs. Verizon DSL and SprintLink Plus are examples of specialized services that facilitate collaboration over the Internet. The remainder of this South Korean paper analyzes the network that will support such services.

Conclusion

Although there is little doubt that companies small and large in the 21st century will be competing in a turbulent environment, the virtual corporation, with its mass-customization strategy, dynamic global network organization, and team-oriented collaborative approach to work seems particularly well suited for the task. This chapter has identified the requirements, design, and management of IT operations network as high-risk areas that are critical to the success of the organization. Examples are the need for stringent network requirements; very flexible networks; heavy reliance on the Internet, intranet, and extranet; collaborative services/platforms; broadband networks, open Network Architectures; compatible partner networks; and network management approaches consistent with the companies' overall management philosophies.

The CEO and CIO must continually ask the hard questions. Doing so would provide an answer to the important question of how virtual corporations respond to such factors as growth, competition, security, and new technology when making their telecommunications network design and management decisions. Perhaps through funded research with universities and the sampling of larger, more broadly based samples of virtual corporations the impact on network decisions of such factors as company size, age, industry, and location can be investigated more thoroughly.

The IT auditor has a very important role in assuring management that general controls are being followed in all aspects. IT operations controls help ensure that programmed procedures are consistently and correctly applied to the transmission, processing, and storage of data. Computer operations and network software advances have provided improvements in data center management. Vendors that used to compete with each other in marketing their products are now working together to provide a common routing protocol. This protocol will give customers the ability to implement an open computing environment using components from multiple vendors. Customers will no longer have to rely on a single vendor to meet their networking requirements, which will provide them greater flexibility and efficiency and help reduce network-operating costs.

Questions

1. What is a virtual corporation?
2. Why are IT operations, especially networks, important to virtual corporations?
3. What are some of the key areas of control and risk issues associated with IT operations, especially in the virtual environment?
4. What are the four areas of installation issues most relevant to IT operations?
5. What are the two basic types of WANs?
6. List and describe the different network topologies. As an IT auditor, why is it important to understand these aspects of IT operations?
7. What are network-monitoring tools? What do they do?
8. What is the Internet? What is an intranet? What is an extranet?
9. What are management's concerns with IT operations?
10. What is an NII? Why is it important?

Multiple Choice

1. Which of the following is not a virtual corporation business objective?
   a. Availability
   b. Response
   c. Downtime
   d. Security
2. Virtual corporation products, where IT provides consumer feedback, will be rich in:
   a. Bells and whistles
   b. Features
   c. Bugs
   d. Information content
3. IT operations issues in network installation include all of the following except:
   a. Wiring and cabling
   b. Customer service
   c. Throughput or traffic
   d. Measuring performance

4. Which of the following WLAN standards is not backward compatible?
   a. 802.11a
   b. 802.11b
   c. 802.11g
   d. 802.11
5. Which wireless standard is not compatible with Bluetooth?
   a. 802.11a only
   b. 802.11b only
   c. 802.11g only
   d. All of the above
6. VPNs are:
   a. Mainframes or minicomputers that serve remotely distributed dumb terminals
   b. An environment that allows independent computers to have equal levels of control in the Communications Architecture
   c. A private data network that utilizes public communication infrastructures such as the Internet, while ensuring privacy through the use of Tunneling Protocols and security procedures
   d. Capable of supporting worldwide transmission at rates that are less than LAN transmission rates
7. Which of the following is not a tool for network monitoring?
   a. Connective devices
   b. Protocol analyzer
   c. General statistical tools
   d. Network management software
8. Which of the following is not a main component of an intranet?
   a. Peer-to-peer software
   b. TCP/IP
   c. Information services
   d. Authoring tools
9. The most vulnerable network area for CIOs and CEOs to review is the structure of:
   a. Telecommunications equipment standards
   b. Firewall policies
   c. Network management within IT operations
   d. Wireless standards
10. Corporate customers use the Internet for all of the following except:
    a. File transfers
    b. Illegal software downloads
    c. Electronic mail
    d. Interactive sessions

Exercises

1. The National Institute of Standards and Technology, a federal government agency, provides information that can assist IT managers and users on current IT topics. The Association of Computing Machinery is another IT organization that provides information to the IT community in general. Visit the Web sites of both of these organizations and identify five reports or information that can be beneficial to an IT manager.
2. From an auditor's perspective, which network topology do you believe would be the easiest to audit? Why? Which network topology would be the most difficult to audit? Why?
3. What types of audit software could be used to audit a LAN?
4. Why would audit weaknesses potentially be more serious when an organization uses a WAN than a LAN?
5. Why are virtual organizations difficult to audit in terms of assessing responsibility and liability for control weaknesses?

Answers to Multiple Choice Questions

1 — c; 2 — c; 3 — b; 4 — a; 5 — d; 6 — c; 7 — a; 8 — a; 9 — c; 10 — b

References

1. Author unknown, 802.11b Wireless LAN Security FAQ from Internet Security Systems, at http://documents.iss.net/whitepapers/wireless_LAN_security.pdf, Oct. 2002.
2. Author unknown, Industry Embraces 802.1x WLAN Standard and EAP-TTLS Security Protocol, from Funk Software. http://www.funk.com/News&Events/8021x_partner.asp, May 6, 2002.
3. Author unknown, The Wireless LAN ROI/Cost-Benefit Study, from RF Smart. http://www.rfsmart.com/downloads/R_WP_ROI.PDF, June 2003.
4. Author unknown, Wireless LANs: Growing, but Slowing Down, from MobileInfo.com at http://www.mobileinfo.com/News_2002/Issue32/WLAN_growth.htm, August, 2002.
5. Gallegos, F., *Security and Control over Intranets and Extranets: Part 1*, #75-10-35, EDP Auditing, Auerbach Publishers, Boca Raton, FL. pp. 1–12, February 2002.
6. Gallegos, F., *Security and Control over Intranets and Extranets: Part 2*, #75-10-36, *EDP Auditing*, Auerbach Publishers, Boca Raton, FL. pp. 1–20, February 2002.
7. Gallegos, F. and S.R. Powell, Is the Virtual Corporation a Reality, Volume III, IS Audit & Control Assn., *IS Audit & Control J.*, pp. 26–28, 1997.
8. Gallegos, F. and S.R. Powell, *Strategies For Securing Wide Area Networks, Data Security Management,* Auerbach Publishers, Boca Raton, FL, 87-01-46.1, 1997, pp. 1–24.
9. Gallegos, F., *Wireless LANs: Technology and Security Issues,* Enterprise Operations Management, # 46-40-65, Auerbach Publishers, Boca Raton, FL, November 2001, pp. 1–16.
10. Gallegos, F. and S.R. Powell, *Securing Local Area Networks, Information Management: Strategy,* Systems and Technologies Series, # 1-06-25, Auerbach Publishers, Boca Raton, FL, January 2001 issue, pp 1–20.
11. Gallegos, F. and J.U. Kim, Policy of GII (Global Information Infrastructure) Standardization and Security Control Auditing of NII (National Information Infrastructure) and EG (Electronic Government), National Computerization Agency (NCA), Republic of South Korea, NCA III — RER-98-002/1998.2, February 1998.

12. Goldman, S.L., R.N. Nagel, and K. Preiss, *Agile Competitors and Virtual Organizations*, Van Nostrand Rheinhold, New York, 1995.
13. Kabara, J., P. Krishnamurthy, and D. Tipper, Information Assurance in Wireless Networks, University of Pittsburgh [electronic journal; cited September 04, 2001]. Available http://www.cert.org/research/isw/isw2001/papers/Kabara-31-08.pdf
14. Karygiannis, T. and L. Owens, Wireless Network Security, National Institute of Standards And Technology [electronic journal; Publication 800-48, 2000]. Available http://www.nist.gov/
15. Kennard, L., Cordless and Cable-Free: The Risks and Rewards of Going Wireless, Novell Connection [electronic journal; cited July 2001, pp. 6–21]. Available http://www.nc-mag.com/2001_07/wireless71/
16. Keen, G.W. Peter, and J.M. Cummins, *Networks in Action: Business Choices and Telecommunications Decisions,* Wadsworth Publishing Company, Belmont, CA, 1994.
17. Lannerstrom, S., Wireless Enterprise PC Security, Smart Trust [electronic white paper; cited September 12, 2002]. Available http://www.smarttrust.com/whitepapers/.
18. Liebmann, L., Are Intranets Safe? *Communications Week Interactive*, August 1996; Here comes the intranet, *BusinessWeek*, September 1997.
19. McCollum, T., Wireless Security, *Internal Auditor Magazine* [electronic magazine; cited October 2002]. Available http://www.theiia.org/ecm/magazine.cfm?doc_id=3951
20. Sage Research, Intranet trends second wave, *Network Computing*, May 1997.
21. Saita, A., The Wild Wireless West, *Information Security* [electronic magazine; cited January 2002]. Available http://www.infosecuritymag.com/2002/jan/cover_case_study.shtml
22. Stanley, R.A., Wireless LAN Risks and Vulnerabilities, Information Systems Audit and Control Foundation, Vol. 2, pp. 57–61, 2002.
23. Tate, P., Internet security: can best practices overcome worst perils? *Computerworld*, 32, 18, May 1998. Special Supplement.
24. Tittel, E. and J. Stewart., *Intranet Bible*, IDG Books Worldwide, Foster City, CA, 1997.
25. Van Cleve, B. and M. Brittton, *Discover Intranets*, IDG Books Worldwide, Foster City, CA, 1997.
26. Vaughan-Nichols, S., The Internet, Extranets and Intranets: Oh My! *Sm@rtReseller*, May 1998.
27. Winkler, C., Opportunities Knock, *InformationWeek*, November 1996. Available www.techweb.cmp.com/iw/606/06opp.htm

Chapter 14
Operational Control Issues

In the operations area, general controls implement the reliability designed into computerized systems during the application development process. Within an IT installation, operations controls are in place that implement organizational policy and organization controls. Operations controls focus on protecting data files and programs as well as assuring the security of the computer installation itself. Computer installation controls can be classified as physical security and access controls, environmental controls, software and data security controls, and administrative security controls. Each of these is discussed in the following sections.

Organizational Policy and Organization Controls

Every computer installation should have specific standards and procedures manuals covering operations. Although most operations have some type of standards and manuals covering them, having policies and procedures in place is much easier than actively enforcing policies and procedures. The weakness with many operations policy and procedures manuals is their lack of use.

In other cases, problems arise because procedure manuals have been prepared on the basis of the capabilities of highly experienced, competent operators. These people may feel they do not have to refer to the documentation. Often, they regard their specialized knowledge as a kind of job security. Having these people available can become a rationale for not supplying more detail. However, apart from the inherently poor practice that this attitude represents, situations may arise when these operators are not available for consultation. New hires may have to be trained during peak operational periods. For example, systems may have to be restarted by less-experienced personnel in the event of a major disaster that injures or incapacitates key operations personnel. In this situation, systems analysts who are unfamiliar with the systems may need to use the manuals to gain an overview. Manuals generally fall short of guiding people in such situations.

The manager or auditor should regard operating standards and procedures manuals as highly important controls. Accordingly, these controls should be tested periodically. This can be done through observation to determine if the standards and procedures described in the manuals actually are being followed in the day-to-day operation of the computer center.

An important element of any set of standards or manuals should be the requirement that operators maintain logs on which any unusual events or failures are recorded, according to time and in detail. If such logs do not exist or are not kept faithfully, a major control weakness is indicated.

Data Files and Program Controls

Each computer installation should have a data library and procedures that control access to programs, data files, and documentation.

One important data library control centers on assurance that all file media are clearly and accurately labeled. That is, external labels must be affixed to or marked upon the data media themselves. On tape cartridges and disk packs, pressure-sensitive labels usually are affixed to identify both the volume and the file content. Procedures should be in place to assure that all labels are current and that all information they contain is accurate.

Library procedures should assure that only authorized persons receive files, programs, or documents, and that these persons acknowledge their responsibility at the time of each issuance. Each time a file is removed for processing, controls over data files should assure that a new file would be generated and returned to the library. If appropriate to the backup system in place, both the issued and the new files should be returned together, with the prior version serving as backup.

Control is enhanced by the practice of maintaining an inventory of file media within the data library. That is, an inventory record should exist for each tape cartridge or disk pack.

The record should note any utilization or activity. After a given number of users, the file medium or device is cleaned and recertified. Further, if any troubles are encountered in reading or writing to the device, maintenance steps are taken and noted.

Ideally, a full-time person independent of computer operations will be assigned as the data librarian. In smaller installations, however, such assignment might not be economically feasible. When an installation cannot afford a full-time librarian, this custodial duty still should be segregated from operations. That is, for adequacy of control, the function of librarian must be assigned as a specific responsibility to someone who does not have access to the computer.

Backup/Restart and Disaster Recovery Controls

Control planning must be based on the assumption that any computer system is subject to several different types of failures. In particular, procedures must exist and must be tested for recovery from failures or losses of equipment, programs, or data files.

In the case of equipment failures, each installation might have a contractual agreement covering the use of an alternate site with a comparable computer configuration, if one is available. In most cases, such agreements will be reciprocal, with two or more computer users agreeing to come to one another's aid in the event of a catastrophe.

Backup and restart capabilities for both programs and data files require specific retention cycles and the storage of backup copies or programs and files at remote, protected locations. Copies of system documentation, standards, and procedure manuals also should be protected through remote, off-site storage.

Physical Security and Access Controls

The objective of physical security and access controls is to prevent or deter theft, damage, and unauthorized access, and to control movement of network-related equipment and attached devices. Some physical controls also prevent unauthorized access to data and software.

General physical controls that can be used to protect office equipment and personal computer networks include personnel badges, which help employees identify authorized personnel, and alarms and guards, which deter theft of network equipment. In addition, placement of the network equipment and office design will further secure the network. For example, network equipment should be placed in areas where office traffic is light. If possible, the microcomputers, printers, and other equipment should be placed behind locked office doors. Data center operations managers may want to use combination locks to prevent duplication of keys; another alternative is to use a locking device that operates on magnetic strips or plastic cards — a convenient device when employees regularly carry picture identification (ID) badges.

Network equipment should be attached to heavy immovable office equipment, permanent office fixtures, special enclosures, or special microcomputer workstations. The attachment can be achieved with lock-down devices, which consist of a base attached to permanent fixtures and a second interlocking base attached to the microcomputer equipment. The bases lock together, and a key, combination, or extreme force is required to remove the equipment. All network equipment must be locked down to prevent unauthorized movement, installation, or attachment.

337

Many microcomputers and other equipment attached to the network may contain expensive hardware and security-sensitive devices. The removal of these devices not only incurs replacement costs but also could cause software to fail and may be a means of circumventing security or allowing for unauthorized disclosure of such company-sensitive information as customer lists, trade secrets, payroll data, or proprietary software. Internal equipment can be protected by lock-down devices, as previously discussed, and special locks that replace one or more screws and secure the top of the equipment. These special locks are called CPU locks because they prevent access to the CPU area.

Cabling enables the various users and peripheral equipment to communicate. Cabling is also a source of exposure to accidental or intentional damage or loss. Damage and loss can occur from the weather or by cutting, detaching, or attaching to and from equipment and other incidents. In many networks, if the cable is severed or damaged, the entire system will be impaired.

Cabling should not be accessible to either the environment or individuals. The communications manager may want to route and enclose cabling in an electrical conduit. If possible and if the exposure warrants the cost, cabling can also be encased in concrete tubing. When the cable is encased, unauthorized access through attachment is lessened. In addition, unauthorized movement of the cabling will not occur easily, and this situation will enable the network manager to more efficiently monitor and control the network and access to it.

To alleviate potential downtime, cable may be laid in pairs. In this arrangement, if one set is damaged, the alternate set can be readily attached. The second pair is usually protected in the same manner as the original but is not encased in the same tubing, thus preventing the same type of accident from damaging both cables.

Notebook microcomputers should also receive the same care and attention as cited above. These are even more vulnerable in that they can be taken and used off site by employees and then brought back into the office and attached to the network. Off site vulnerability to theft and sabotage such as viruses or theft of programs and data is reduced when protected in a secure off-site storage location.

Environmental Controls

All network equipment operates under daily office conditions (e.g., humidity, temperature, smoke, and electrical flow). However, a specific office environment may not be suited to a microcomputer because of geographical location, industrial facilities, or employee habits. A primary problem is the sensitivity of microcomputer equipment to dust, water, food, and other contaminants. Water and other substances not only can damage the keyboard, CPU, disk drive, and diskettes but also may cause electrocution or a fire. To prevent such occurrences, the network manager should adhere to a policy of prohibiting food, liquids, and the like at or near the microcomputer.

Although most offices are air conditioned and temperatures and humidity are usually controlled, these conditions must nonetheless be evaluated by the network manager. If for any reason the environment is not controlled, the network manager must take periodic readings of the temperature and humidity. If the temperature or humidity is excessively high or low, the microcomputer equipment and the network should be shut down to prevent loss of equipment, software, and data. When microcomputer equipment is transported, either within the building or especially outdoors to a new location, the equipment should be left idle at its new location for a short time to allow it to adjust to the new environmental conditions.

Airborne contaminants can enter the equipment and damage the circuitry. Hard disks are susceptible to damage by dust, pollen, air sprays, and gas fumes. Excessive dust between the read/write head and the disk platter can damage the platter or head or cause damage to the data or programs. If there is excessive smoke or dust, the microcomputers should be moved to another location. Small desktop air filters can be placed near smokers' desks to reduce smoke, or the responsible manager can limit smoking to specific locations, away from microcomputer equipment.

Static electricity is another air contaminant. Using antistatic carpeting can reduce static electricity, as well as pads placed around the microcomputer area, antistatic chair and keyboard pads, and special sprays that can be applied to the bottoms of shoes. Machines can also be used to control static electricity in an entire room or building.

Major causes of damage to network equipment are power surges, blackouts, and brownouts. Power surges, or spikes, are sudden fluctuations in voltage or frequency in the electrical supply that originates in the public utility. They are more frequent when the data center is located near an electrical generating plant or power substation. The sudden surge or drop in power supply can damage the electronic boards and chips, as well as cause a loss of data or software. If power supply problems occur frequently, special electrical cords and devices can be attached to prevent damage. These devices are commonly referred to as power surge protectors. Staff who take notebook microcomputers off site should be issued appropriate support peripherals such as surge protectors and electric connectors (should they be traveling to Europe or other countries that do not have U.S. voltage standards).

Exhibit 1. The 13 Processes for the Delivery and Support Domain

Domain	Process
DS 1	Define and manage service levels
DS 2	Manage third-party services
DS 3	Manage performance and capacity
DS 4	Ensure continuous service
DS 5	Ensure systems security
DS 6	Identify and allocate costs
DS 7	Educate and train users
DS 8	Assist and advise customers
DS 9	Manage the configuration
DS 10	Manage problems and incidents
DS 11	Manage data
DS 12	Manage facilities
DS 13	Manage operations

Blackouts are caused by a total loss of electrical power and can last seconds, hours, or days. Brownouts occur when the electrical supply is diminished to below-normal levels for several hours or days. Although brownouts and blackouts occur infrequently, they are disruptive to continuing operations. If microcomputer use is essential and the organization's normal backup power is limited to necessary functions, special uninterruptible power supply (UPS) equipment can be purchased specifically for the microcomputer equipment. UPS equipment can be either battery packs or gas-powered generators. Battery packs are typically used for short-term tasks only (e.g., completing a job in progress or supporting operations during a transition to generator power). Gas-powered generators provide long-term power and conceivably could be used indefinitely.

CoBiT **Operational Controls**

The Control Objectives for Information Technology (CoBiT) addresses operational controls in the 13 processes for the delivery and support domain, as shown in Exhibit 1.

As all of the above domain processes affect operational controls, it is worth considering control objectives for each process. The control objectives are shown in Exhibit 2.

Comparing CoBiT and General Controls for Operational Auditing

Exhibit 3 provides a cross-reference between traditional general controls used in operational information systems auditing and operational controls from CoBiT. Following are sample descriptions of three audits that

Exhibit 2. Control Objectives of Domain Processes

DS 1 Define and Manage Service Levels

Control objectives

1. Service level agreement framework
2. Aspects of service level agreements
3. Performance procedures
4. Monitoring and reporting
5. Review of service level agreements and contracts
6. Chargeable items
7. Service improvement program

DS 2 Manage Third-Party Services

Control objectives

1. Supplier interfaces
2. Owner relationships
3. Third-party contracts
4. Outsourcing contracts
5. Continuity of services
6. Security relationships
7. Monitoring

DS 3 Manage Performance and Capacity

Control objectives

1. Availability and performance requirements
2. Availability plan
3. Monitoring and reporting
4. Modeling tools
5. Proactive performance management
6. Workload forecasting
7. Capacity management of resources
8. Resource schedule

DS 4 Ensure Continuous Service

Control objectives

1. IT continuity framework
2. IT continuity plan, strategy, and philosophy
3. IT continuity plan contents
4. Minimizing IT continuity requirements
5. Maintaining the IT continuity plan
6. Testing the IT continuity plan
7. IT continuity plan training
8. IT continuity plan distribution
9. User department alternative processing backup procedures
10. Critical IT resources
11. Backup site and hardware

Exhibit 2. Control Objectives of Domain Processes (Continued)

12. Off-site backup storage
13. Wrap-up procedures

DS 5 Ensure Systems Security

Control objectives
1. Manage security measures
2. Identification, authentication, and access
3. Security of online access to data
4. User account management
5. Management review of user accounts
6. User control of user accounts
7. Security surveillance
8. Data classification
9. Central identification and access rights management
10. Violation and security activity reports
11. Incident handling
12. Reaccreditation
13. Counterparty trust
14. Transaction authorization
15. Nonrepudiation
16. Trusted path
17. Protection of security functions
18. Cryptographic key management
19. Malicious software prevention, detection, and correction
20. Firewall architectures and connections with public networks
21. Protection of electronic value

DS 6 Identify and Allocate Costs

Control objectives
1. Chargeable items
2. Costing procedures
3. User billing and chargeback procedures

DS 7 Educate and Train Users

Control objectives
1. Identification of training needs
2. Training organization
3. Security principles and awareness training

DS 8 Assisting and Advising Information Technology Customers

Control objectives
1. Help desk
2. Registration of customer queries
3. Customer query escalation

Exhibit 2. Control Objectives of Domain Processes (Continued)

4. Monitoring of clearance
5. Trend analysis and reporting

DS 9 Manage the Configuration

Control objectives

1. Configuration recording
2. Configuration baseline
3. Status accounting
4. Configuration control
5. Unauthorized software
6. Software storage
7. Configuration management procedures
8. Software accountability

DS 10 Manage Problems and Incidents

Control objectives

1. Problem management system
2. Problem escalation
3. Problem tracking and audit trail
4. Emergency and temporary authorizations
5. Emergency processing priorities

DS 11 Manage Data

Control objectives

1. Data preparation procedures
2. Source document authorization procedures
3. Source document data collection
4. Source document error handling
5. Source document retention
6. Data input authorization procedures
7. Accuracy, completeness, and authorization checks
8. Data input error handling
9. Data processing integrity
10. Data processing, validation, and editing
11. Data processing and error handling
12. Output handling and retention
13. Output distribution
14. Output balancing and reconciliation
15. Output review and error handling
16. Security of output reports
17. Protection of sensitive information during transmission and transport
18. Protection of disposed sensitive information
19. Storage management
20. Retention periods and storage terms
21. Media library management system

Exhibit 2. Control Objectives of Domain Processes (Continued)

22. Media library management responsibilities
23. Backup and restoration
24. Backup jobs
25. Backup storage
26. Archiving
27. Protection of sensitive messages
28. Authentication and integrity
29. Electronic transaction integrity
30. Continued integrity of stored data

DS 12 Manage Facilities

Control objectives

1. Physical security
2. Low profile of the information technology site
3. Visitor escort
4. Personnel health and safety
5. Protection against environmental factors
6. Uninterruptible power supply

DS 13 Manage Operations

Control objectives

1. Processing operations procedures and instructions manuals
2. Start-up process and other operations documentation
3. Job scheduling
4. Departures from standard job schedules
5. Processing continuity
6. Operations logs
7. Safeguard special forms and output devices
8. Remote operations

Exhibit 3. General Controls versus COBIT Controls

General Control	COBIT Control
Organizational policy and organizational controls	Manage third-party services
	Manage operations
Data files and program controls	Manage performance and capacity
	Ensure systems security
	Identify and allocate costs
	Manage data
Backup/restart and disaster recovery controls	Ensure continuous service
Environmental controls	Manage the configuration
	Manage the facility
Physical security access controls	Ensure systems security

general and operational CoBiT controls can be applied to in the case of problem management, data center reviews, and call center reviews.

Problem Management Auditing

Problem management is a process that is used to report, log, correct, track, and resolve problems within the hardware, software, network, tele-communications, and computing environment of an organization. Problems can be anything from a customer being unable to print a report to a line connecting the computer to the controller going down (dropping). Problem management provides the framework to open, transfer, escalate, close, and report problems. It establishes procedures and standards for handling customer problems.

Effective problem management procedures are vital to the long-term control over the performance of a data processing organization. At most installations, these procedures have been developed piecemeal, as the need for recognizing and resolving specific problems in the organization has arisen. In the early stages of growth, this approach works well, but as the organization grows, this piecemeal approach limits its ability to iden-tify and solve problems effectively.

Because it is basically reactive — wait for a problem to develop and then fix it — the data processing organization creates a perception of poor per-formance in its user community. At some point in its growth, it is best to develop procedures that allow anticipation of problems. Having a reliable problem management system will allow the organization to anticipate, report, track, and solve problems in a timely and effective manner. Auditing the problem management system will bring the organization assurance of its reliability and effectiveness.

Problem Management Auditing in Action Overview

Problem management is the process of effectively managing problems that have an impact on the delivery of system service from problem iden-tification to resolution. At Acme Computing Services (ACS), problem man-agement includes resolving problems, recognizing recurring problems, problem addressing procedures, and containing or reducing the number and impact of problems that occur. Various types of records can be created in ACS's problem management. When a call is received and the caller is helped immediately, an incident record is created. The information from the call and any procedures that the help-desk consultant performed are placed in the incident record and it is closed; no follow-up is necessary.

When a customer has a problem that will take some time to solve, a problem record is created. The information is placed in the problem record and the record is kept open until the problem is resolved. A problem record can receive various status classifications, (e.g., monitor, opened, transferred, completed, and closed) and all problem records are assigned a priority code (0 = Catastrophe, 1 = Critical, 2 = Intermediate, 3 = Minor, 4 = Small Impact, 5 = No Impact).

Purpose

Problem management establishes procedures and standards to handle customer problems that are under the responsibility of ACS. These include the detection, reporting, and correction of problems that have an impact on service and processes. In this way, ACS is better able to meet service level agreements (SLAs) and to have procedures for analyzing and resolving problems and preventing their recurrence.

Scope

Problem management begins with the recognition of a problem and ends when a problem has been resolved to the customer's satisfaction. It involves all systems and applications. Within these environments, problem management includes but is not limited to:

- Local and remote hardware and software problems
- Incomplete or unavailable functions and applications
- Local and remote facility (environmental) problems
- Operational problems
- Local and remote network problems
- Process problems

Objectives

The objectives of problem management at ACS are to reduce failures to an acceptable level at an acceptable cost, help insure that SLAs are achieved, and to effectively use personnel resources. The primary objectives of problem management are to:

- Ensure that all problems are reported and recorded correctly.
- Ensure that all problems are assigned appropriate priority.
- Recognize and escalate recurring problems.
- Ensure all outstanding problems are managed to resolution.
- Identify and escalate to management problems that are not resolved within stated criteria.
- Review closed problems and validate their resolutions.
- Provide management with an overview of the problems having an impact on the delivery of applications or system service.
- Advise management on methods to prevent problem recurrence.

Key Success Factors

The success of problem management at ACS is measured against indications that include but are not limited to:

- *Problem reassignment:* When the help desk receives a problem that the help desk consultant cannot solve, the problem is reassigned to one of the support groups for resolution. The support group that is assigned the problem can reassign it to another group or resolve the problem and assign it back to the help desk for closure. Reports can be generated that detail how many times a problem has been assigned to other groups.
- *Problem duplication:* Problem management keeps track of all problems, date of occurrence, and their resolution. In this way, if the same problem appears several days or months later, it has already been documented. The old problem record can be checked for any special activities that may help solve the current problem. The old problem records are also used to report on how well equipment is working. If a piece of equipment has the same problem repeatedly over a period of time, this could indicate a major problem with the equipment.
- *Problem escalation:* At times, problems take longer to resolve than the customer, help desk consultant, or support group consultant would like. Each problem is assigned a priority when it is first opened. Each priority has an allotted time within which the problem must be resolved. If the problem is not resolved within this allotted time, it is escalated to the next-higher management level.

Introduction to Data Center Reviews

The objectives of data center audits are to identify audit risks in the operating environment and the controls in place and functioning to reasonably mitigate those audit risks in accordance with the intentions of the company's management. For each control objective, the auditor must evaluate control mechanisms and determine whether the objective has been achieved.

Pre-audit preparation is required for effective data center reviews. These include meeting with information systems (IS) management to determine possible areas of concern. At this meeting, the following information should be obtained.

- Current IT organization chart
- Current job descriptions for IT data center employees
- List of application software supported and the hardware they reside on
- IT policy and procedures manual

- Systems planning documentation and fiscal budget
- Disaster recovery plan

Audit personnel should review the above information and become familiar with the way the data center provides user services. In addition, auditors should become familiar with basic terminology and resource definition methodology used in support of the operations environment. Engagement personnel should review the audit program and become familiar with the areas assigned for completion of an audit task. The following is an example of typical audit program steps performed during a data center review.

Data Center Audit Program

A. *Administration of IT Activities*

Audit Steps

1. Review the organization chart and evaluate the established procedures for adequacy in defining responsibilities in the security administration area. Implement general control (provision for general authorization over the execution of transactions, e.g., prohibiting the IT department from initiating or authorizing transactions) and CoBiT objective (position descriptions clearly and delineate both authority and responsibility).
2. Determine who is responsible for control and administration of security. Verify that adequate security exists in the security administration function. Implement general control (prevents or detects deliberate or accidental errors caused by improper use) and CoBiT objective (information services function is in compliance with security standards).
3. Determine whether adequate direction is maintained for each IT functional area within a policy and procedures manual. Evaluate whether the manual is kept up to date by IT management. Implement general control (written manuals in support of systems and procedures) and CoBiT objective (operations staff have operations manuals for all systems and processing within their responsibility).
4. Determine if written personnel policies for the IT administration personnel exist, and if these policies stress adequate qualification and level of training and development.
5. Determine if long-range (two to five) years' system planning is maintained by IT management and is adequately considered in the fiscal budgeting process.
6. Assess the adequacy of inventory procurement and control pertaining to the administration of the LAN environment. Review available inventory documentation to determine if it is adequately maintained and complete in description and location. Compare the serial numbers

on the computer software with inventory records to determine if illegal copies of system and application software are being supported.

B. Operating Systems Software and Data

Audit Steps

1. Determine through interviews with data center personnel whether any significant modifications or upgrades were implemented during this audit year. Review authorization documentation to ensure that adequate IT management approval is obtained prior to the implementation.
2. Determine through interviews with the IT personnel the procedures implemented to ensure that adequate IT management approval is obtained prior to the implementation.
3. Evaluate access restrictions over critical system operation areas.

C. Computer Operations/Business Resumption

Audit Steps

1. Review the IT policies and procedures manual to determine if written operating instructions adequately define recovery procedures in the event of processing disruption, shutdown and restart procedures, procedures for restoration of file server data from backups, and procedures for reporting incidents.
2. Determine through interviews with IT personnel the use of tape management software or other mechanism used to prevent the erasure of data.
3. Determine through interviews with IT personnel the rotation of tapes used in storing backup data. Determine if adequate off-site storage facilities are used and that tapes are rotated to the facility daily.
4. Evaluate procedures in place to control inventory of tapes maintained both on site and off site.
5. Determine through observation the physical security of the consoles supporting backup procedures. If the console is not adequately secure, inquire as to mechanisms used to prevent unauthorized tampering during backup processing.
6. Determine through observation of computer operations facility the use of security mechanisms to provide access to authorized personnel only.
7. Evaluate procedures in place to monitor the activities of noncomputer operations personnel having access to the operations facility. Entry of unauthorized personnel should be supervised, and a log maintained and regularly reviewed by IT management.
8. Determine through observation the installation and maintenance of an automated fire-suppression system, raised-floor water sensors

below floors, installation of power conditioning units, and backup power supply.

D. Security Administration

Audit Steps

1. Determine through interviews with IT personnel if a separate security administration function has been established.
2. Determine through interviews with IT personnel, review of IT policies and procedures manuals, and/or IT job descriptions if training programs have been established for all personnel for areas such as:
   - Organizational security policies
   - Disclosure of sensitive data
   - Access privileges to IT resources
   - Reporting of security incidents
   - Naming conventions for user passwords
3. Determine if formal policies define the organization's information security objectives and the responsibilities of employees with respect to the protection and disclosure of informational resources. Agreement to these policies should be evidenced by signature of employees.
4. Determine if procedures and responsibility for the maintenance of user IDs and access privileges in the case of termination or transfer are defined and performed on a regular basis.

Software and Data Security Controls

Data and software security and access controls are the key controls over today's network-oriented business systems. These are considered operational controls in the sense that these controls function day in and day out to meet the needs of business. The administration of the network is similar to the administration and management of any information processing facility. In the information processing manager's scenario, the main objective is to prevent, detect, and correct unauthorized access to the network's hardware, software, and data, and to ensure the network's sound operation and the security of the corporate intellectual property and information.

Daily management of such an operation is required due to the reliance on the information provided that supports decision making and operations. Daily management ensures that security controls are maintained, though changes occur in the software, applications, and personnel. Daily management can be classified into various categories, which are discussed in the following sections and areas for IT auditor review and evaluation.

Physical and Environmental Controls Management. All such controls in active use must be tested periodically. Such testing includes the evaluation of the effectiveness of current controls and the implementation of additional controls as determined to be necessary. The results of the testing of physical and environmental controls should be reported to senior management.

Data Access Management. The data center operations manager, the network administrator, or the corporate IT security manager, whoever assigned this responsibility, must perform it in a very responsible manner. This person must accurately maintain user IDs and passwords and associated file and data access schemes, as well as receive computer-generated reports of attempted unauthorized accesses. Reports on data access and traffic analysis should be reviewed. Such reports will allow the administrator to manage network growth and help foresee future security needs.

Policy and Procedures Documentation. The objectives here are to provide standards for preparing documentation and ensuring the maintenance of documentation. The IT operations manager must set documentation standards so that when employees change jobs, become ill, or leave the organization, replacement personnel can adequately perform the task of that employee. The IT operations manager must periodically test the documentation for clarity, completeness, appropriateness, and accuracy.

Data and Software Backup Management. Backup media must be labeled, controlled, and stored in an appropriate manner. The IT manager must maintain control logs of all backups as well as provide documentation on how to recover files, data, directories, and disks.

Other Management Controls. The internal audit department, external auditors, contingency or disaster recovery planning, personnel background checks, and user training are included in this category. The IT auditor can aid in establishing proper testing requirements and in reviewing, testing, and recommending the proper controls to establish the necessary safeguards. Contingency planning and disaster recovery is essential to proper maintenance of the network and supporting systems. The contingency plan establishes the steps to recover from the destruction of hardware, software, and data.

Operational controls include such items as periodic personnel background checks on all employees who have access to key organizational information directly or through support functions. The background check should involve a review of credit history, financial health, personal problems, and other areas that may identify potential risks. This information can establish potential integrity breaches before they occur.

User training must be established for all network functions. End users must be trained in microcomputer/workstation use, general computer knowledge, security, policies and procedures, consequences of noncompliance, and general network use. In addition, users should undergo more specific training for the different software on the network as required. Such user training can prevent many problems from occurring.

The Call Center (CC) Concept

Functionally, a call center (CC) offers technical support to the user community. Organizationally, the CC may act as a separate department or a support component of the information systems department. It may even be outsourced by an organization with locations in foreign countries such as India, China, Philippines, and others. The objective of the CC is to respond to questions and/or problems that may occur with applications, thereby helping users and enabling them to retrieve, manipulate, and format data to fit their own specifications. Users can develop their systems or reports or tools by using the technical support available from the CC's experienced staff. Working with a CC means that users can:

- Keep data confidential and maintain privacy
- Remain independent of information systems schedules
- Develop their applications
- Use their business skills to define their needs and expected results
- Have questions answered by competent support staff

Call centers are very critical to keeping customers satisfied, especially in today's E-commerce environment. The extent to which these functions are performed depends on the business objectives and the philosophy of the organization. For example, online merchants must work hard to eliminate the kinds of problems that plagued consumers during the 1999 Holiday shopping season. More than five million online purchases went undelivered, and shoppers could not get answers and abandoned their shopping carts.

One of the keys to solving those kind of problems is offering CC services that can not only handle telephone inquires but inbound and outbound e-mail, online chat, and even Internet telephony. This function can be handled internally or outsourced to an application service provider (ASP). Some of the benefits that have been reported by organizations using outsourcing are trouble-free maintenance, quicker implementation time, productive use of systems, and lower training costs. On the other hand, some companies have reported less-than-satisfactory support from ASPs and do not like the thought of sharing or shipping out their customer data beyond their firewall protection.

The relationship between the user and the CC is critical to establishing the credibility of support and the quality of assistance given. For this reason, fourth-generation languages (4GLs) (e.g., JAVA, VS_BASIC, MAPPER, and FOCUS) are an important development in the computer industry (see Exhibit 4). In the past, programmers in the information systems department

Exhibit 4. Fourth-Generation Languages and Other Support Software

Product	Environment					Application-Generation Function									Human Factor					Database Support						
	IBM Environment	Server Environment	Tool Available on PC	Micro-to-Mainframe Link	Full PC Implementation	Query Language	Report Generator	Screen Painter/Data Entry	Graphics Generator	Decision-Support Tools	Subset for End Users	Information Systems Professionals	Procedural Language	Interface to Action Diagrams	Well-Structured Code	Provable Specifications	Heavy-Duty Computing	Full COBOL Replacement	Recommended for Call Centers	HELP Facility	Computer-Aided Instruction	Computer-Aided Thinking	Support to Data Base Management	Standard of Data Base Management	Data Dictionary	Data-Modeling Tool
MS-Office	×	×	×	×	×	×	×	×	×	×	×	×		×						×	×	×	×	×	×	×
SQL	×	×	×		×	×	×	×	×	×	×	×		×					×	×		×	×	×	×	×
Perl	×	×	×	×	×	×	×	×	×	×	×	×							×	×			×	×	×	×
Oracle	×	×		×	×	×	×	×	×	×	×	×		×					×		×		×	×	×	
DB2	×	×	×			×	×	×	×	×	×	×	×		×	×	×		×				×	×	×	×
QMF	×	×	×	×	×	×	×	×	×	×	×	×	×		×			×	×	×			×	×	×	×
Java	×	×	×	×	×	×	×	×	×		×	×	×		×	×	×	×	×	×	×		×	×	×	×
C++	×	×		×	×	×	×	×	×	×	×	×		×	×		×		×	×	×		×	×	×	×
Nomad	×	×	×		×				×			×	×	×	×	×	×						×	×		×
VS Basic	×	×		×	×							×	×		×								×	×		×
DMS	×					×	×	×		×	×	×		×	×		×	×	×	×	×		×	×	×	
Informix		×		×		×	×	×			×	×					×						×	×	×	
Application Factory	×	×				×	×	×			×	×	×		×	×	×	×	×	×		×	×		×	×
Sybase	×	×	×			×	×	×	×		×	×	×	×	×	×	×	×	×	×		×	×	×	×	
FlexTool	×	×	×	×	×	×	×	×	×	×	×	×	×	×	×	×	×	×	×	×		×	×	×	×	×
AI RoboForm			×	×	×		×	×		×		×	×		×	×	×	×	×	×		×	×		×	×

who implemented user requests used such procedural languages as COBOL, FORTRAN, Pascal, and Ada. A nonprocedural language specifies what is to be accomplished, whereas a procedural language specifies how (step by step) it is to be accomplished. Technical expertise is essential to the successful application of procedural languages, but those with little or no technical expertise can effectively use nonprocedural languages. Some of the major characteristics of nonprocedural languages are:

- Nonprocedural instructions
- Easily developed user proficiency
- An online mode or processing
- No requisite knowledge of data formats
- The rapid modification of existing routines

In addition, because many nonprocedural languages do not warn the user of errors, the CC is vital in providing the user with the training to know when a valid relational statement is initialized and when plausible results are in fact erroneous.

New Audit Responsibilities

The information systems auditor must be aware of the goals of the CC, how it interrelates with other departments, the data stores it uses, the services it provides, and its structure within the organization. The auditor must know what languages are available and what each language's capabilities and limitations are. Furthermore, the auditor should be aware of any threats, both internal and external, to the CC. The auditor should know the CC's operations and assist in the development of security, control procedures, and standards.

The information systems auditor should be trained in several high-level languages. By knowing one or more languages, the auditor can best understand applications under review while possessing the skills to develop applications for the auditing department. Auditors, therefore, must also stay current with high-level computer languages and the CC and thus track the future concerns of the organization.

Developing Audit Software in the CC

In the past, auditors developed and maintained many of their own applications using languages such as COBOL. This development activity caused some additional backlog in the information systems department; the applications required were too complex for the auditor to develop, and because auditors had to spend a long time creating applications, staff resources were limited and scheduled audit assignments went begging. Languages such as FOCUS, IDEA, ACL II, JAVA, C++, Perl, and MAPPER can be used to speed development and to lend flexibility of application to the audit tool.

The relative ease of use of 4GLs helps greatly decrease the amount of time needed to maintain and create an application. Even the MS Suite (Word, Excel, Access, etc.) can be a useful tool for extracting and retrieving data for trend analysis and statistics.

In addition to the time saved in the development of computer-assisted audit techniques (CAATs), high-level languages allow the audit department, rather than the information systems department, to create additional audit applications. This shift increases the independence of audit departments and creates a greater amount of objectivity in the auditing of information systems facilities. The auditor can now design routines that effectively evaluate the information systems department without having information systems involvement in the design of those tools. This enables the auditor to make investigations and write checking programs without information systems programmers knowing the details of what the auditor is doing or looking for.

Auditing the CC

Because the CC is a relatively new function at many organizations, the standards that applied to the organization as a whole and in the information systems department in particular may either not apply directly or have to be modified. The call center serves the internal and external customer. If the CC is internal, then metrics must be established to monitor the efficiency and effectiveness of its operations. Thus, the number and types of calls for assistance and the ability to provide the customer (internal or external) a quality answer must be captured, collected, analyzed, and evaluated. This can be done by selective monitoring of calls or requesting feedback from customers after servicing their questions. Collection instruments could be surveys, questionnaires, online questionnaires, email surveys, etc.

Call centers can be configured as self-hosting, multi- or single-tenant host, or Web-based. In a single-tenant system, individual customers own their own servers, databases, and applications. Call centers can be staffed internally or they can be outsourced. In an outsource situation, the contract should hold the application service provider (ASP) accountable to appropriately run, manage, and maintain the system. In a multi-tenant environment, the application gives the customers a generic template-driven product provided by the ASP. Thus, you are running on the ASP resources. In a Web-based call center/customer relations management product, user agents must access the server (and customer data) via a Web browser and the Internet, not a stand-alone, PC resident application in a client/server environment.

Web-based CC support systems are slower in providing screen updates of customer information than a client/server-based system. This often can result in delays, which are frustrating to the customer and agent. However, this environment is much easier to maintain. All software updates occur at the server level, with users only concerned about browser enhancements. Such browser-based systems reduce the training time of support agents. According to several studies, call centers experience high agent turnover rates, 60–70 percent annually.

The decision to outsource the call center cannot be based on cost alone, even though the cost of building a call center is highest in the mind of management. Costs not only include the physical space — a separate office where agents can work 24 hours a day/seven days a week — but also buying the hardware and software mentioned earlier. Hardware includes interactive voice response systems, which route the call to the correct agent and servers for running the software required. Software includes license fees for the help desk, e-mail management, customer relationship management (CRM), and workforce management applications. People who maintain these systems can be internal or outsourced from external companies. Support agents can be internal or outsourced from external support resources. Depending on the type of CC established and the number of agents and the type of support services desired, costs have been estimated to approximately $40,000 per agent (licenses, hardware, and training) to high-end packages that cost hundreds of thousands of dollars to license and deploy.

Even audit techniques that are commonly used have to be adjusted to the new environment. Although the areas of concern for the CC are similar to those of larger applications and systems, they do vary. For example, the auditor must decide which of the small, user-developed systems require auditing. This decision may be limited to only those systems that modify organizational data.

Another factor that needs to be considered is the sensitivity of the data being retrieved by the user application. In addition, these audits are concerned both with the applications used in the main computer and with the sensitive materials that are stored on microcomputers.

The System Development Life Cycle

High-level languages seriously alter the applicability of standard SDLC concepts. The construction of a prototype is especially different from the SDLC. Auditors should find less documentation regarding the requirements of the system because in an iterative development activity involving both the user and technical consultant there is less need to write things down. Thus, the CC can assist in documentation of the problem or issue and help incorporate those changes or corrections into the code of the application if necessary. The modified SDLC should take the following into account:

- Experience of the user
- Computer-generated code
- Need for thorough testing
- Protection of applications
- Need of source documentation
- Need for formal modification request

This modified SDLC helps evaluate systems that were developed according to certain stated criteria and ensures that the user, management, and the CC support staff will adhere to control review points.

Data Integrity

Data integrity is a reflection of the accuracy, correctness, validity, and currency of the data. The primary objective in ensuring integrity is to protect the data against erroneous input from authorized users. The auditor should be concerned with the testing of user-developed systems; changes or the release of data, unknown to the user, could occur because of flawed design. The user may assume that the visible output is the only system activity. The possibility that erroneous data could infest the system is strong. A person other than the designer or user should test any application that has access to the organization's data in more than a read-only format. Again, this is a critical area if the CC is outsourcing to an application service provider. Release of customer information to such an entity must be controlled through contractual requirements with stiff remedies or penalties if data is compromised.

Data Security

Data security entails the protection of data against accidental or intentional disclosure to unauthorized persons as well as the prevention of unauthorized modification and deletion of the data. Many levels of data security are necessary in a CC environment; they include database protection, data integrity, and security of the hardware and software controls, physical security over the user, and organizational policies. Because the main objective of a CC is to give rapid, flexible access to information and help solve the problem, the security precautions in place should be as stringent as traditional applications. The auditor must ask the following questions when reviewing the adequacy of data security controls:

- Who is responsible for the accuracy of the data?
- Who is permitted to update data?
- Who is permitted to read and use the data?
- Who is responsible for determining who can read and update the data?
- Who controls the security of the data?

- If the CC is outsourced, what security controls and protection mechanism does the ASP have in place to secure and protect data?
- Contractually, what penalties or remedies are in place to protect the tangible and intangible values of the information?

The disclosure of sensitive information is a serious concern to the organization and must be high on the auditor's list of priorities.

Physical Security and Recovery Procedures

Physical security is most obvious and critical in preventing unauthorized access to data, hardware, and systems. Access identification and log-on procedures should be evaluated and a secure physical site for equipment and data should be determined. As with the information systems department, proper backup and recovery procedures should be implemented. Auditors should work with personnel involved in contingency planning and security activities to ensure that proper safeguards and procedures for the CC are implemented. The auditor must assess the criticality of the data accessed in the CC when drafting these procedures.

Computer Resources

The use of 4GLs in the development process often requires much machine time. Fourth-generation languages that must be translated into conventional third-generation languages and then into machine-executable code use the most system resources. The auditor must determine how much computer time is consumed for each application. This may cause the auditor to recommend an alternative processing mode. The efficiency rate of the CC as a whole can be determined when it is compared with the rest of the information systems organization.

Department Standards

Because the CC is a relatively new addition to most organizations, its standards and policies must be reviewed and recast according to the following guidelines of accepted policy formulation:

- Compatibility with organizational standards
- Sensitivity to the needs of end users
- Clarity of written and oral notices
- Consistency of application

The auditors should be involved in the initial development of departmental standards for the CC. These procedures need to specify the responsibilities of the users in protection of information, systems design, and documentation. It is the auditor's responsibility to ensure that the standards and project controls used in the information systems department are applied to the call center.

Conclusion

We have provided an in-depth overview of operational controls and their importance. Operational controls, like application controls, can be complex. The IT auditor has to be aware of these controls in their review and audit of the IT activity. Many of these controls are designed to prevent, detect, and/or correct any anomalies that may impact the quality or reliability of corporate information.

We have provided some approaches and techniques that IT auditors can use to evaluate the effectiveness of the controls. These general controls are extremely important in protecting the applications and support systems. Any breakdown in their effectiveness can have catastrophic impact to the applications and systems.

Such controls are costly because many of them involve human interaction. But they are necessary in giving the user, management, and the customer assurances that they are protected, and assurances that they can rely on the information provided to make sound business decisions. Operational controls are the first line of protection.

Review Questions

1. What are operational controls? What purpose do they serve?
2. Why are policies, procedures, and standards viewed as examples of operational controls?
3. Provide two examples of data files and program controls.
4. Backup and Restart — why is this control important?
5. What are environmental controls? List and explain three examples.
6. What problems can power surges cause to computer systems?
7. How and where does COBIT address operational controls?
8. What is problem management? What does it do?
9. In conducting a data center review, list information that an IT audit should request or obtain at the pre-audit meeting? Why is this information important in auditing operational controls?
10. What might be the components of a data center audit program?
11. Operational controls play a key role in protecting intellectual property of a company. Why is intellectual property so important in today's business world?
12. List and explain three areas of daily management that IT auditors need to review.
13. What are other management control areas IT auditors may need to review with regard to testing operational controls?

Multiple Choice

1. Backup/recover and disaster recover procedures must exist and be tested for recovery from failures or losses of equipment, programs, or:
   a. Operating systems
   b. Critical paper documents
   c. Electronic mail
   d. Data files
2. Copies of system documentation, standards, and procedure manuals should be protected through:
   a. Local backup
   b. Off-site storage
   c. Antivirus software
   d. Firewalls
3. Which of the following is not a major cause of damage to network equipment ?
   a. Flooding
   b. Power surges
   c. Blackouts
   d. Brownouts
4. The COBIT control objective of chargeable items falls under the domain of:
   a. Define and manage third-party services
   b. Manage performance and capacity
   c. Ensure continuous service
   d. Ensure systems security
5. The COBIT control objective of the help desk falls under the domain of:
   a. Manage problems and incidents
   b. Manage the configuration
   c. Assist and advise customers
   d. Educate and train users
6. In a data center audit program, the administration of IS activities includes all of the following except:
   a. Reviewing the organization chart
   b. Determining if written policies by IS administration personnel exist
   c. Determining if short-range planning is maintained by IS management
   d. Assessing the accuracy of inventory procurement
7. Problem management is a process that is used to report, log, correct, track, and:
   a. Find problems
   b. Create problems

    c. Allow problems

    d. Resolve problems

8. An audit of security administration should determine through interviews with IS personnel if a separate security administration function has been:

    a. Resolved

    b. Documented

    c. Reported

    d. Established

9. The results of testing of physical and environmental controls should be reported to:

    a. Supervisors

    b. Auditors

    c. Senior management

    d. Outside agencies

10. Operational controls are costly because many of them involve:

    a. Human interaction

    b. Technology

    c. Auditors

    d. Software

Exercises

1. You are an internal auditor assigned to perform an operations audit of a data center. On reviewing the operations policy and procedures manuals, you find that the manuals appear to be fairly complete and up-to-date. Describe three audit tests you would perform to test whether the manuals are actually used and followed.

2. Describe five required capabilities for effective auditor use of tape management software.

3. Your organization is considering signing a contract with a company to provide off-site storage. You have been asked to review the contract to see if backup and recovery needs have been addressed. List five areas that you would look for in the contract related to backup and recovery needs.

4. You have been asked to write an audit program to review the problem management function for a software vendor that provides technical support over the Internet. Prepare a scope, objective, and a list of ten audit steps to be performed.

5. A previous audit of your company recommended a disaster recovery plan. In performing your follow-up review, you find that although a plan is in place, it has not been tested. Write your audit finding regarding the weakness of an untested disaster recovery plan.

Answers to Multiple Choice Questions

1 — d; 2 — b; 3 — a; 4 — a; 5 — c; 6 — c; 7 — d; 8 — d; 9 — d; 10 — a

References

1. Briones, J.R., Problem identification, reporting, and resolution in the data center, *Data Center Management*, Auerbach Publishers, Boca Raton, FL. 1988.
2. Gallegos, F., D.R. Richardson, and A.F. Borthick, *Audit and Control of Information Systems*, Thomson Corporation–South-Western Publishing Co., Cincinnati, OH, 1987.
3. Gallegos, F. and S. Powell, Security & Control of Wide Area Networks: Part 1, 87 -01-45, Data Security Management, October 1994.
4. Gallegos, F. and S. Powell, Security & Control of Wide Area Networks: Part 2, 87-01-46, Data Security Management, October 1994.
5. Gallegos, F. and D. Manson, DBMS Recovery Procedures, 4-06-60, Information Management: Strategy, Systems, and Technologies, December 1994.
6. Gallegos, F. and S. Powell, Microcomputer network controls, *Handbook of Communications Management*, Auerbach Publishers, Boca Raton, FL. 1996.
7. Gallegos, F. and S. Powell, Security & control of wide area networks, *Handbook of Communications Systems Management — 1996-97 Yearbook*, Auerbach Publishers, Boca Raton, FL. (s-48:56), 1998.
8. Gallegos, F. and S. Powell, Microcomputer computer security & controls, *Netware Managers Handbook*, Auerbach Publishers, RIA Group, Boca Raton, FL. 1997, pp. 351–276.
9. Klosky, M., V. Klosky, and F. Gallegos, Information protection and security: a perspective, *IS Audit Control J.*, Nov–Dec 1995, pp. 6–9.
10. Legner, D., F. Gallegos, J.M. Klosky, and V. Klosky, An Analysis of Documentation Sufficiency for PC and LAN Based Database Applications, presented and published in the South East Decision Sciences Conference Proceedings — Savannah, GA, pp. 64–66, Spring 1992.
11. Information Systems Audit and Control Foundation. CoBIT Control Objectives, Information Systems Audit and Control Foundation, July 2000.
12. Perry, W.E., Data center auditing overview, *Data Center Operations Management*, Auerbach Publishers, Boca Raton, FL. 1987.
13. Powell, S. and F. Gallegos, Is the virtual corporation a reality, *IS Audit Control J.*, Volume III, 1997, pp. 26–28.
14. Woods, M.L., Auditing Problem Management at Hughes Aircraft Company, Business Research Project, California State Polytechnic University, Pomona, CA, 1993.

Chapter 15

Assessing Risk
in IT Operations

This chapter discusses the process of assessing risk and controls in information technology (IT) related operations. What are the successful characteristics of a risk assessment process as it pertains to IT operations? What are the standards of practice for risk assessment in this area? What are some examples of risk assessment practices used in varied environment?

This chapter begins by defining risk assessment and briefly discusses organizations that provide standards related to IT risk assessment. Following this discussion are in-depth examples of three areas of IT risk assessment related to Enterprise/Operational Risk Management (ERM/ORM), use of the World Wide Web and Java, and IT insurance.

Risk Assessment

Risk assessment is both a tool and technique that can be used to self-evaluate the level of risk of a given process or function. The audit process must be thorough and complete; otherwise, the element of risk can be judged to be extremely high. Therefore, management must evaluate the quality of an audit, especially in today's world of ever-changing technology with increasing complexity. Credibility and thoroughness of audit work in validating and verifying the controls at all levels is extremely important. Managers and auditors should perform risk assessment in their self-evaluation process on an ongoing basis within the IT environment.

Available Guidance

We have several professional standards documents in place that provide guidance to auditors and managers involved in risk assessment. Standards assist in the development of technology and provide consistent quality measurement if adopted, maintained, and supported by the organization. The following are standards related to assessing risk in IT operations. By no means is this area limited to U.S. issues. Operational review encompasses the global business community. One of the most recent endeavors is the International Standards Organization (ISO) and its effort to develop ISO Guide 73 on risk management terminology. It also has a number of projects under the technical program JTC 1 Committee on IT.

U.S. National Institute of Standards and Technology (NIST)

A major focus of NIST activities in IT is providing measurement criteria to support the development of pivotal, forward-looking technology. NIST standards and guidelines are issued as Federal Information Processing Standards (FIPS) for use government-wide. NIST develops FIPS when there are compelling federal government requirements for IT standards related to security and interoperability and there are no acceptable industry standards or solutions. It supports a very fine Web site at www.nist.gov and provides very useful information and tools. For example, its Computer Security Resource Center (CSRC) has a package called Automated Security Self-Evaluation Tool (ASSET) and another called Webmetrics, Version 3.0, found in the Information Access Division.

One of the first of several federal documents issued by NIST and still in force today is FIPS 31, "Guidelines for Automatic Data Processing Physical Security and Risk Management." This standard provides guidance to federal organizations in developing physical security and risk management programs for information systems (IS) facilities. FIPS 73, "Guidelines for Security of Computer Applications," describes different security objectives for a computer application, explains control measures that can be used, and identifies decisions that should be made at each stage in the life cycle of a sensitive computer application. The next major FIPS in this domain is FIPS 87, "Guidelines for ADP Contingency Planning," and then FIPS 102, "Guidelines for Computer Security Certification and Accreditation." These documents are a very good starting point for understanding the basis and many approaches one can use in assessing risk in IT today. The current list of FIPS that applies to IT can be found in Appendix III.

Government Accounting Office (GAO)

The GAO is a nonpartisan agency within the legislative branch of the government. GAO conducts audits, surveys, investigations, and evaluations of federal programs. GAO work is done at the request of Congressional committees or members, or to fulfill specifically mandated or basic legislative requirements. GAO's findings and recommendations are published as reports to congressional members or delivered as testimony to congressional committees. GAO has issued numerous reports on computer security, IT vulnerabilities, and risk assessment. Its Web site can be found at www.gao.gov. Several of these reports are located in Appendix III.

Several Government Accounting Standards (GAS) and Information Management and Technology (IMTEC) reports relate to risk assessment. For example, GAS 4.29, "Safeguarding Controls," is used to help auditors recognize risk factors involving computer processing. IMTEC 8.1.4, "Information Technology: An Audit Guide for Assessing Acquisition Risk," is used in planning and conducting risk assessments of computer hardware and software, telecommunications, and system development acquisitions. In 1999, it issued a very good report titled "Information Security Risk Assessment: Practices of Leading Organizations," GAO/AIMD-00-33. Recently, in October 2002, it issued an outstanding document titled "Assessing the Reliability of Computer-Processed Data," supplement to the GAS (Yellow Book) — External Version, GAO–03-273G, October 2002.

The latter report above identifies the process of assessing the reliability of computer-processed data and how one might approach it from an audit or management review process. The following is an illustration of the process that IMTEC recommends. Exhibit 1 is an overview. Exhibit 2 recommends the key steps one must consider when assessing the reliability of computer-generated information. Exhibit 3 does a very fine job of showing the depth necessary when assessing the reliability of computer-generated information.

These processes are well reviewed by GAO and certainly provide fine guidance for those wanting to learn the mechanics and details of this process.

American Institute of Certified Public Accountants (AICPA)

Statements on Audit Standards (SAS) are issued by the Auditing Standards Board (ASB) of the AICPA and are recognized as interpretations of the ten generally accepted auditing standards. SAS 47, "Audit Risk and Materiality in Conducting an Audit," relates to risk assessment. In SAS 47, control risk is defined as the possibility of misstatement occurring in an account balance or class of transactions that (1) could be material when aggregated with misstatements in other balances or classes and (2) will not be prevented or detected on a timely basis by the system of internal control.

SAS 65 requires that, in all engagements, the auditor develop some understanding of the internal audit function (EDP audit, if available) and determine whether that function is relevant to the assessment of control risk. Thus, if there is an internal audit function, it must be evaluated. The evaluation is not optional. In 1996, AICPA issued SAS 80, which is directly aimed at improving auditing in the EDP environment. This SAS was published in the same year and has made a profound impact on the auditing profession. An excerpt from SAS 80 states: "In entities where significant information is transmitted, processed, maintained, or accessed electronically, the auditor may determine that it is not practical or possible to reduce detection risk to an acceptable level by performing only substantive tests for one or more financial statement assertions. For example, the potential for improper initiation or alteration of information to occur and not be detected may be greater if information is produced, maintained, or

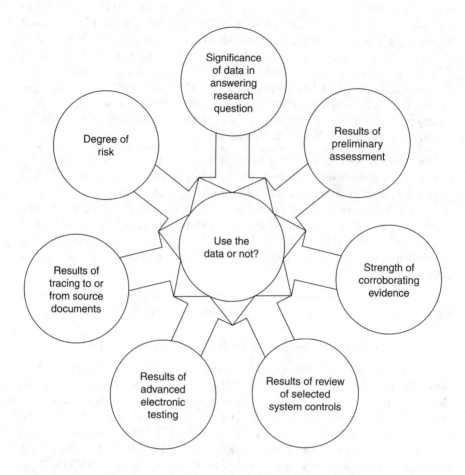

Exhibit 1. Factors to Consider in Making the Decision on Using the Data Recommended by GAO
Source: Assessing the Reliability of Computer-Processed Data, Supplement to the Government Auditing Standards (Yellow Book) — External Version, GAO–03-273G, October 2002.

accessed only in electronic form. In such circumstances, the auditor should perform tests of controls to gather evidential matter to use in assessing control risk, or consider the effect on his or her report." The GAO process illustrated earlier is the federal government guide to implementation of this SAS.

SAS 94 was adopted in 2001. This SAS provides guidance to auditors about the effect of IT on internal control and on the auditor's understanding of internal control and assessment of control risk. SAS 94 amends SAS 55, "Consideration of Internal Control in a Financial Statement Audit."

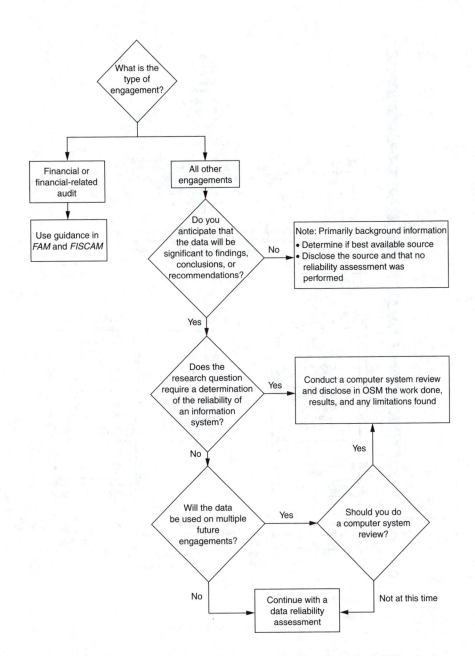

Exhibit 2. The Decision Process to Determine Whether Data Reliability Assessment Is Required
Source: Assessing the Reliability of Computer-Processed Data, Supplement to the Government Auditing Standards (Yellow Book) — External Version, GAO–03-273G, October 2002.

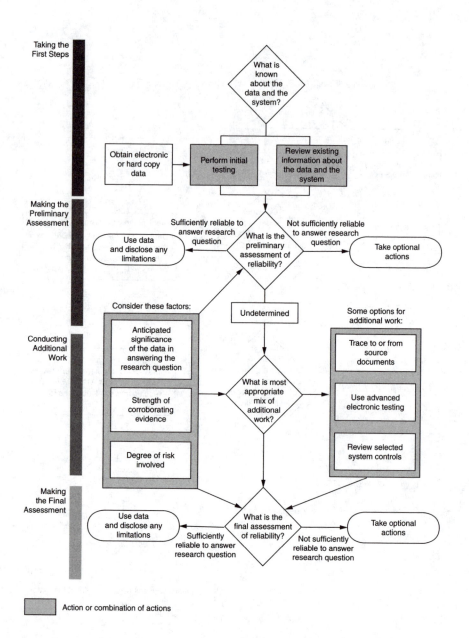

Exhibit 3. GAO's Recommended Data Reliability Assessment Process
Source: Assessing the Reliability of Computer-Processed Data, Supplement to the Government Auditing Standards (Yellow Book) — External Version, GAO–03-273G, October 2002.

Information Systems Audit and Control Association (ISACA)

ISACA is a worldwide not-for-profit association of more than 28,000 practitioners dedicated to IT audit, control, and security in over 100 countries. The Information Systems Audit and Control Foundation (ISACAF) is an associated not-for-profit foundation committed to expanding the knowledge base of the profession through a commitment to research. The ISACA standards board has updated and issued several Information System Audit Guidelines (ISAG); these are recognized as system auditing standards.

ISACA's recent updated guideline titled "Use of Risk Assessment in Audit Planning" specifies the level of audit work required to meet a specific audit objective; it is a subjective decision made by the IT auditor. The risk of reaching an incorrect conclusion based on the audit findings (audit risk) is one aspect of this decision. The other is the risk of errors occurring in the area being audited (error risk). Recommended practices for risk assessment in carrying out financial audits are well documented in auditing standards for financial auditors, but guidance is required on how to apply such techniques to IT audits.

Management also bases its decisions on how much control is appropriate upon assessment of the level of risk exposure it is prepared to accept. For example, the inability to process computer applications for a period of time is an exposure that could result from unexpected and undesirable events (e.g., data center fire). Exposures can be reduced by the implementation of appropriately designed controls. These controls are ordinarily based upon estimation of the occurrence of adverse events and are intended to decrease such probability. For example, a fire alarm does not prevent fires but is intended to reduce the extent of fire damage.

This guideline provides guidance in applying IT auditing standards. The IT auditor should consider it in determining how to achieve implementation of the above standards, use professional judgment in its application, and be prepared to justify any departure.

Institute of Internal Auditors (IIA)

Established in 1941, IIA serves more than 85,000 members in internal auditing, governance and internal control, IT audits education, and security in more than 120 countries. Statements on Internal Auditing Standards (SIAS) are issued by the Professional Standards and Responsibilities Committee, the senior technical committee designated by IIA to issue pronouncements on auditing standards.

IIA has in place Performance Standard 2110 titled "Risk Management," which specifies that the internal audit activity should assist the organization by identifying and evaluating significant exposures to risk and contributing to the improvement of risk management and control systems. It provides additional guidance in the form of Implementation Standard 2110.A1 (Assurance Engagements), with which the internal audit activity should monitor and evaluate the effectiveness of the organization's risk management system. Implementation Standard 2110.A2 (Assurance Engagements) stipulates that the internal audit activity should evaluate risk exposures relating to the organization's governance, operations, and IS regarding:

- Reliability and integrity of financial and operational information
- Effectiveness and efficiency of operations
- Safeguarding of assets
- Compliance with laws, regulations, and contracts

Its last performance standard addresses consulting engagements in Implementation Standard 2110.C1 (Consulting Engagements). The IIA recommends that during consulting engagements, internal auditors should address risk consistent with the engagement's objectives and should be alert to the existence of other significant risks.

Committee of Sponsoring Organizations of the Treadway Commission (COSO)

COSO was formed in 1985 as an independent, voluntary, private sector organization dedicated to improving the quality of financial reporting through business ethics, effective internal controls, and corporate governance. COSO consists of representatives from industry, public accounting agencies, investment firms, and the New York Stock Exchange. The first chairman of COSO was James C. Treadway, Jr., executive vice president and general counsel, Paine Webber Inc., and a former commissioner of the U.S. Securities and Exchange Commission; hence the name Treadway Commission. The current chairman is John Flaherty, chairman, retired vice president and general auditor for PepsiCo Inc.

Recently, the COSO board assigned PriceWaterhouseCoopers to lead a project to develop a framework for ERM. In July 2003, a draft ERM framework document was released for a 90-day review process with the final framework estimated for release in early 2004. The next section offers a detailed review of ERM and ORM.

Introduction to ERM/ORM

The COSO Enterprise Risk Management Framework defines ERM as follows:

Enterprise risk management is a process, effected by an entity's board of directors, management and other personnel, applied in strategy setting and across the enterprise, designed to identify potential events that may affect the entity, and manage risks to be within its risk appetite, to provide reasonable assurance regarding the achievement of entity objectives.

Mismanagement of risk can carry an enormous cost. In recent years, business has experienced numerous risk-associated reversals that have resulted in considerable financial loss, decrease in shareholder value, damage to company reputations, dismissals of senior management, and, in some cases, the very dissolution of the business. This increasingly risky environment in which risk mismanagement can have dire consequences mandates that management adopt a new more proactive perspective on risk management.

What Is ERM/ORM?

Clearly, there is a correlation between effective risk management and a well-managed business. Over time, a business that cannot manage risk effectively will not prosper and will perhaps fail. A product recall could be disastrous and the company's end. Rogue traders without oversight and adequate controls have destroyed old, well-established institutions in a very short time. Historically, risk management in even the most successful businesses has tended to be in "silos" — the insurance risk, the technology risk, the financial risk, and the environmental risk — all managed independently in separate compartments. Coordination of risk management has usually been nonexistent, and identification of emerging risks has been sluggish.

Enterprise/Operational Risk Management

At first glimpse, there is much similarity between ORM and other classes of risk (e.g., credit, market, liquidity risk, etc.) and the tools and techniques applied to them. In fact, the principles applied are nearly identical. Both ORM and ERM must identify, measure, mitigate, and monitor risk. However, at a more detailed level, there are numerous differences, ranging from the risk classes themselves to the skills needed to work with operational risk.

ORM is just beginning to define the next phase of evolution of corporate risk management. Should firms be able to develop successful ORM programs, the next step will be for these firms to integrate ORM with all other classes of risks into truly enterprisewide risk management frameworks. See Exhibit 4 for an example of an ERM/ORM organizational structure representative of the banking industry.

Why ERM/ORM?

There are many reasons ERM/ORM functions are being established within corporations. The following are a few of the reasons.

Organizational Oversight. Two groups have recently emphasized the importance of risk management at the organization's highest levels. In October 1999, the National Association of Corporate Directors released its

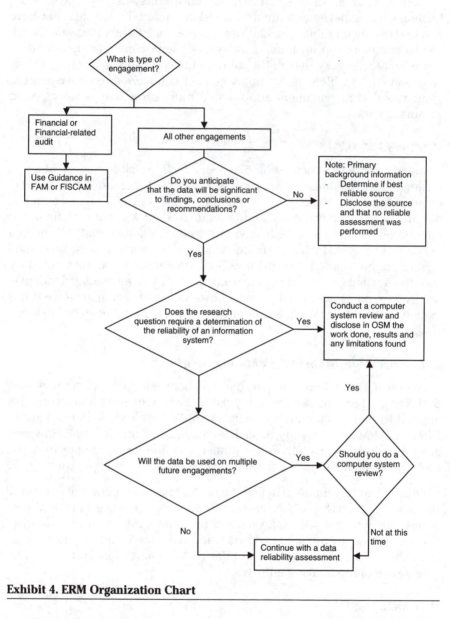

Exhibit 4. ERM Organization Chart

"Report of the Blue Ribbon Commission on Audit Committees," which recommends that audit committees "define and use timely, focused information that is responsive to important performance measures and to the key risks they oversee." The report states that the chair of the audit committee should develop an agenda that includes "a periodic review of risk by each significant business unit."

In January 2000, the Financial Executives Institute released the results of a survey on audit committee effectiveness. Respondents, primarily CFOs and corporate controllers, ranked key areas of business and financial risk as most important for audit committee oversight.

In light of events surrounding recent corporate scandals (e.g., Enron, etc.), and the increasing executive and regulatory focus on risk management, the percentage of companies with formal ERM methods is increasing and audit committees are becoming more involved in corporate oversight. The U.K. and Canada have set forth specific legal requirements for audit committee oversight of risk evaluation, mitigation, and management, which are widely accepted as best practices in the United States.

Magnitude of Problem. The magnitude of loss and the impact of operational risk and losses to date are difficult to ignore. Losses by large operational, risk-related financial services losses have averaged well in excess of $15 billion annually for the past 20 years, according to public records. This reflects just the large public and visible losses. Research has yielded nearly 100 individual relevant losses greater than $500 million each and over 300 individual losses greater than $100 million each.[1] Exhibit 5 is a listing of major operational losses. Interestingly enough, the majority of these losses have occurred in financial services, which explains the industry's leading focus on ORM, especially in the area of asset–liability modeling and treasury management models to manage risks in the highly volatile capital markets' activity of derivative trading and speculation.

Increasing Business Risks. With the increasing speed of change for all companies in this new era, senior management must deal with many complex risks that have substantial consequences for the organization. A few forces currently creating uncertainty are:

- Technology and the Internet
- Increased worldwide competition
- Free trade and investment worldwide
- Complex financial instruments
- Deregulation of key industries
- Changes in organizational structures from downsizing, reengineering, and mergers
- Increasing customer expectations for products and services
- More and larger mergers

Collectively, these forces are stimulating considerable change and creating an increasing risk in the business environment.

Regulatory Issues. The international regulators clearly intend to encourage banks to develop their own proprietary risk measurement models to assess regulatory as well as economic capital. The advantage for banks

Exhibit 5. Some Examples of Top Operational Risk Losses

Company	Loss Amount	Date	Description
Numerous financial institutions and others	$20 billion initial estimates	2001	Terrorists hijacked four commercial airliners and crashed two of them into the World Trade Center. Over 2000 lives lost. Countless businesses impacted
BCCI	$16 billion	1991	Regulators seized about 75 percent of The Bank of Credit and Commerce International's $17 billion in assets in a major fraud
Sumitomo Corporation	$2.8 billion	1996	Sumitomo Corporation incurred huge losses through excessive trading of copper
Tokyo Shinkin Bank	$2.2 billion	1990–1991	The manager of the Imasato branch forged 19 deposit certificates, which were used to raise money for stock deals
Banca Nazionale del Lavoro	$1.7 billion	1992	Former employees plead guilty to conspiring to arrange $5 billion in unauthorized loans to Iraq
Nonfinancial institutions: LTCM	$4 billion	1998	Huge market losses due to inadequate model management and inadequate controls at Long Term Capital Management
Texaco, Inc.	$3.1 billion	1984	Pennzoil sued Texaco alleging that Texaco "wrongfully interfered" in its merger deal with Getty
Cendant Corporation	$2.8 billion	1985–1998	Largest and longest-running accounting fraud in history. Former executives conspired to inflate earnings
Dow Corning	$2 billion	1994	The company agreed to pay settlements to 18 women who indicated breast implants made them ill
St. Francis Assisi Foundation	$2 billion	1999	Insurance fraud case in which Martin Frankel allegedly stole as much as $2 billion from this foundation
Owens Corning Fiber Glass	$1.6 billion	1980s–1990s	Settlement of asbestos-related claims
Orange County	$1.6 billion	1994	Largest people risk class case in financial history. Largest investment loss ever registered by a municipality
Kashima Oil	$1.5 billion	1994	Disguised losses on FX forward contracts
Prudential Securities	$1.4 billion	1994	Settled charges of securities fraud with state and federal regulators
Drexel Burnham Lambert	$1.3 billion	1988 –1993	Former employees filed a class action suit charging the company with fraud, breach of duty, and negligence
General Motors	$1.2 billion	1996	Heavy losses suffered due to three strikes
Phar Mor	$1.1 billion	1992	A former president of the firm defrauded in an embezzlement scheme

should be a substantial reduction in regulatory capital and a more accurate allocation of capital vis-à-vis the actual risk confronted.

In December 2001, the Basel Committee on Banking Supervision submitted a paper "Sound Practices for the Management and Supervision of Operational Risk," for comment by the banking industry. In developing these sound practices, the committee recommended that banks have risk management systems in place to identify, measure, monitor, and control operational risks. While the guidance in this paper is intended to apply to internationally active banks, plans are to eventually apply this guidance to those banks deemed significant on the basis of size, complexity, or systemic importance and to smaller, less complex banks. Regulators will eventually conduct regular independent evaluations of a bank's strategies, policies, procedures, and practices, addressing operational risks. The paper indicates that an independent evaluation of operational risk will incorporate a review of the following six bank areas[2]:

- Process for assessing overall capital adequacy for operational risk in relation to its risk profile and its internal capital targets
- Risk management process and overall control environment effectiveness with respect to operational risk exposures
- Systems for monitoring and reporting operational risk exposures and other data quality considerations
- Procedures for timely and effective resolution of operational risk exposures and events
- Process of internal controls, reviews, and audit to ensure integrity of the overall risk management process
- Effectiveness of operational risk mitigation efforts

Market Factors. Market factors also play an important role in motivating organizations to consider ERM/ORM. Comprehensive shareholder value management and ERM/ORM are very much linked. Today's financial markets place substantial premiums for consistently meeting earnings expectations. Not meeting expectations can result in severe and rapid decline in shareholder value. Research conducted by Tillinghast–Towers Perrin found that, with all else being equal, organizations that achieved more consistent earnings than their peers were rewarded with materially higher market valuations.[3] Therefore, for corporate executives, managing key risks to earnings is an important element of shareholder value management. The traditional view of risk management has often focused on property and liability related issues or internal controls. However, traditional risk events such as lawsuits and natural disasters may have little or no impact on destroying shareholder value compared to other strategic and operational exposures such as customer demand shortfall, competitive pressures, and cost overruns. One explanation for this is that traditional risk hazards are relatively well understood and managed today — not that they do not matter. Managers now have the opportunity to apply tools and techniques for traditional risks to all risks that affect the strategic and financial objectives of the organization.

For nonpublicly traded organizations, ERM/ORM is valuable for many of the same reasons. Rather than from the perspective of shareholder value, ERM/ORM would provide managers with a comprehensive overview of other important items such as cash flow risks or shareholder risks. Regardless of the organizational form, ERM/ORM can be an important management tool.

Corporate Governance. The strongest defense against operational risk and losses resides and flows from the highest level of the organization — the board of directors and executive management. The board, the management team that they hire, and the policies that they develop, all set the tone for a company. As guardians of shareholder value, the board of directors must be acutely attuned to market reaction to negative news. In fact, they can find themselves castigated by the public if the reaction is severe enough. As representatives of the shareholders, the board of directors are responsible for policy matters relative to corporate governance, including but not limited to setting the stage for the framework and foundation for ERM.

Right now, ORM is a hot topic of discussion for regulators and in boardrooms across the United States. In the wake of the 2001 releases from the Basel Risk Management Committee, banks now have further insight as to the regulatory position on the need for regulatory capital for operational risk. Meanwhile, shareholders are aware that there are means to identify, measure, manage, and mitigate operational risk that add up to billions of dollars every year and include frequent, low-level losses and also infrequent but catastrophic losses that have actually wiped out firms such as Barings and others. Regulators and shareholders have already signaled that they will hold directors and executives accountable for managing operational risk.

Best Practice. Senior managers need to encourage the development of integrated systems that aggregate various market, credit, liquidity, operational, and other risks generated by business units in a consistent framework across the institution. Consistency may become a necessary condition to regulatory approval of internal risk management models. An environment where each business unit calculates its risk separately with different rules will not provide a meaningful oversight of firmwide risk. The increasing complexity of products, linkages between markets, and potential benefits offered by overall portfolio effects are pushing organizations toward standardizing and integrating risk management.

Concluding Thoughts on ERM/ORM

It seems clear that ERM/ORM is more than another management fad or academic theory. It is believed that ERM/ORM will become part of the management process for organizations in the future. Had these processes been in place during the past two decades, a number of the operational risk debacles that took place may not have occurred or would have been of lesser magnitude.

These are thoughts on what will happen in the ERM/ORM environment in the next five years.

- It is likely that companies will no longer view risk management as a specialized and isolated activity — for instance, the management of insurance or foreign exchange risks. The new approach will keep managers and employees at all levels sensitized to and concerned about risk management. Risk management will be coordinated with senior management oversight and everyone in the organization will view it as part of his or her job. The risk management process will be continuous and broadly focused. All business risks and opportunities will be covered.
- The use of bottom-up risk assessments will be a standard used to identify risks throughout the organization. Self-assessment will involve everyone in the company and require individual units to focus and report on the threats to their business objectives. Through this the organization will be able to understand loss potential and risk control by business, profit center, and product. The individual line manager will begin to understand the loss potential in his or her own processing system.
- The use of top-down scenario analysis will be another standard method used to identify risks throughout the organization. This analysis will determine the risk potential for the entire firm, business, organization, or portfolio of business. By its very nature, it is a high-level representation and cannot get into the bottom-up transaction-by-transaction risk analysis.

For example, Microsoft has a campus of more than 50 buildings in the quake-prone Seattle area and therefore earthquakes are a risk.[4] In the past, the company looked at silos of risk. It would have looked at property insurance when considering the risks of an earthquake and how to protect equipment and buildings. However, using scenario analysis, it is now taking a more holistic perspective in considering the risk of an earthquake.

The Microsoft risk management group has analyzed this disaster scenario with its advisors and has attempted to quantify its real cost, taking into account how risks are correlated. In the process, the group identified risks in addition to property damage such as the following:

- Director and officer liability if some people think management was not properly prepared
- Key personnel risk
- Capital market risk because of the firm's inability to trade
- Worker compensation or employee benefit risk
- Supplier risk for those in the area of the earthquake
- Risk related to loss of market share because the business is interrupted
- Research and development risks because those activities are interrupted and product delays occur
- Product support risks because the company cannot respond to customer inquiries

By using scenario analysis, the management has identified a number of risks that it might not have otherwise, and Microsoft is now in a better position to manage these risks. The future ERM/ORM tools such as risk assessment and scenario analysis will assist companies in identifying and mitigating the majority of these risks.

In the next five years, companies will be using internal and external loss databases to capture occurrences that may cause loss to the company and the extent of the loss. This data will be used in quantitative models that will project the potential losses from the various risk exposures. It will be used to manage the amount of risk a company may be willing to take.

Companies will allocate capital to individual business units based on operational risk. By linking operational risk capital charges to the sources of that risk, individuals with risk optimizing behavior will be rewarded and those without proper risk practices will be penalized.

Internal audit will become even more focused on how risks are managed and controlled throughout the company on a continuous basis. Internal audit will be responsible for reporting on integrity, accuracy, and reasonableness of the company's entire risk management process. In addition, internal audit will be involved in ensuring the appropriateness of the company's capital assessment and allocation processes. Audit will also influence continual improvement of risk management and controls through the sharing of best practices.

Management will be looking for individuals who are skilled in risk management. Professional designations such as the Bank Administration Institute's Certified Risk Professional (CRP) and the Information and Audit and Control Association's Certified Information Security Manager (CISM) will demonstrate proficiency in the risk management area and will be in demand.

External auditors will be required to report on the efficiency and effectiveness of a company's risk management program. These companies will be required to disclose the scope and nature of risk reporting and measurement systems in their annual reports.

Overall, companies will be better positioned in the next five years to deal with the broad scope of enterprisewide risks. By implementing the ERM/ORM process now, companies will begin to maximize their overall risk profile for competitive advantage.

We now will discuss the second area of risk assessment related to IT operations, the World Wide Web and Java.

Web and Java Risk Issues

The Internet has been around for years, but private industry became interested in its commercial possibilities only after the graphical World Wide Web emerged during the early 1990s. The Web version of the Internet offered a potentially inexpensive and platform independent network over which to conduct business and disseminate information. In addition, companies grew excited about the possibility of developing intranets (internal Internets) that would give them access to all of their legacy data via one simple Internet browser interface.

All of this was to be enabled by a programming language, Java, that would work on any operating system (OS) or computing platform. This language could also be used to deliver to client machines the program and data elements (in the form of a Java applet) that the client needed to use at any given time. Companies envisioned desktops equipped with "internet appliances" that would not need to contain expensive copies of application programs such as word processors and spreadsheets. It is little wonder that corporations were ready to embrace both the Internet and Java and to build such high expectations about these technologies. These expectations have not died. Many corporate executives and managers expect these technologies to drive economic growth well into the next century.

Perceived Risks

However, the Internet and its most promising language, Java, present an interesting mix of opportunities and risks to organizations. On the one hand, organizations want to stay competitive and embrace technologies that provide so much promise. On the other, both corporations and individuals still perceive the Internet as insecure and the use of Java applets as unsafe. Corporations are wary of the very serious security threats from outside hackers to which a connection to the Internet might expose them. Individual users of the Internet are wary of the possible destructive use of Java applets that they download to their computers over the Internet. Thus, while the promise of the Internet and Java pushes companies toward expectations of free and open communication over the Internet, fear pushes companies toward isolation because they want to protect their information assets from theft, corruption, or destruction.

Internet Security

Security tools and procedures exist right now to reduce risk when a company gives its customers access to business resources over the Internet. Security measures are available to provide *access security* to protect the company's own computers, disks, memory, and other computing equipment from outside interference, and *transaction security* to ensure that two individuals or organizations on the Internet can privately and safely execute a transaction.

Properly implemented, these security mechanisms will:

- Protect the company from intruders who attempt to enter the internal network through the Internet
- Provide authorized users with access to Internet services such as HTTP, FTP, Telnet, and Gopher
- Deliver required Internet applications from the internal network to the Internet
- Deliver SMTP and Netnews services to the internal network from the Internet
- Prevent unauthorized use of resources on the internal network
- Give users an easy way to understand network security status without being Internet security experts
- Assure expert round-the-clock, seven-day-a-week (7×24) monitoring and response to security events
- Maximize protection from the Internet and minimize the cost of operating and monitoring protective devices such as the application proxy firewall

Security Tools and Technologies

Effective security solutions rely on several tools and technologies designed to protect information and computers from intrusion, compromise, or misuse, such as encryption technologies, security policies and procedures, and various types of firewalls.

Encryption Technologies. Encryption technologies electronically store information in an encoded form that can only be decoded by an authorized individual who has the appropriate decryption technology and authorization to decrypt. Encryption provides a number of important security components to protect electronic information:

- *Identification:* Who are you?
- *Authentication:* Can you prove who you are?
- *Authorization:* What can you do?

- *Auditing:* What did you do?
- *Integrity:* Is it tamper proof?
- *Privacy:* Who can see it?
- *Nonrepudiation:* Can I prove that you said what you said?

When information is encoded, it is first translated into a numerical form and then encrypted using a mathematical algorithm. The algorithm requires a number or message, called a key, in order to encode or decode the information. The algorithm cannot decode the encrypted information without a decode key.

Security Policies and Procedures

In the rush to establish an Internet presence, many companies have overlooked perhaps the most important foundation piece in an effective security solution: a sound security policy that identifies who has access to a company's electronic resources and under what circumstances they have access. Thus, security policies in some companies are almost nonexistent and in others not clearly defined. For example, the use of stateless filters means that the organization is relying on defaults set by the vendor of the security package, whereas the use of state-maintained filters means the organization is ensuring that certain types of activities or patterns are reviewed to prevent possible intrusion or loss.

Security policies fall along a continuum that ranges from promiscuous at one end to paranoid at the other. The promiscuous policy allows unchecked access between the Internet and the organization's internal network to everyone. The paranoid policy refuses access between these two networks to everyone. In between are two more palatable alternatives — the permissive policy and the prudent policy.

The permissive policy allows all traffic to flow between the internal network and the Internet except that which is explicitly disallowed. Permissive policies are implemented through packet filtering gateways, where stateless filters prevent individual packets of data from crossing the network boundary if the packet is coming from or going to a specific computer, network, or network port. However, there are two major drawbacks to a permissive policy. First, it requires an exhaustive set of filters to cover all possible addresses and ports that should be denied access. Second, it is virtually impossible to block certain undesirable packets without also blocking other desirable and necessary packets because network protocols are dynamic and often change network port numbers, depending on the protocol state.

A prudent policy, on the other hand, selectively allows traffic that is explicitly allowed by the protocol and excludes any other. Prudent policies are implemented by a set of application proxies that understand the underlying application protocol and can implement a set of state-maintaining filters that allow specific application data to pass from one network to the next. Because the filters can follow the state of the protocol, they can change dynamically when the protocol changes state. This way, rules allow only properly authorized data to flow across the network boundary. Prudent policies are implemented through application proxy firewalls. Because prudent and permissive policies act as the network boundaries, they are referred to as *perimeter security solutions.*

Once a company selects the appropriate security policy, it can be implemented according to a strict set of procedures with the support of software systems. These security procedures — which include a documented set of rules governing the management and administration of the security system and its generated events — record a trail of all modifications to the security system (auditing) and set off signal alarms when someone attempts to violate the policies. Properly followed, they protect an organization from all types of security violations, including accidental administrative mistakes, human factor attacks (i.e., people characteristics), and unauthorized modifications to the security policy. To reduce the risk of "inside" break-ins, many companies also require a background check of security systems personnel, and separate security management and auditing to prevent an administrator from altering the audit of management actions.

Internet Firewalls

Internet application proxy firewalls are a prudent perimeter security solution. These systems sit between the Internet and the organization's internal network (see Exhibit 6) and control the traffic flow between the Internet and a company's internal resources. A firewall provides application proxies for most popular Internet applications as well as support for a more restrictive prudent policy. This policy might restrict the establishment of network connections from within the company outward to the Internet. In addition, rather than forwarding packets between networks, the firewall can require the application client to establish an application service connection to the firewall. The firewall then maintains the connection with the outside server. The firewall will only pass data for applications that it currently supports, which eliminates most security "holes."

Security holes created by incorrectly configured computers on the internal network are not visible to the Internet and therefore cannot be exploited by external Internet users. The organization's own Internet application servers then sit outside the firewall in what is called the "demilitarized zone." This eliminates the need for outside traffic to travel through the firewall into the organization's internal network when it is using Web, FTP, or Telnet services.

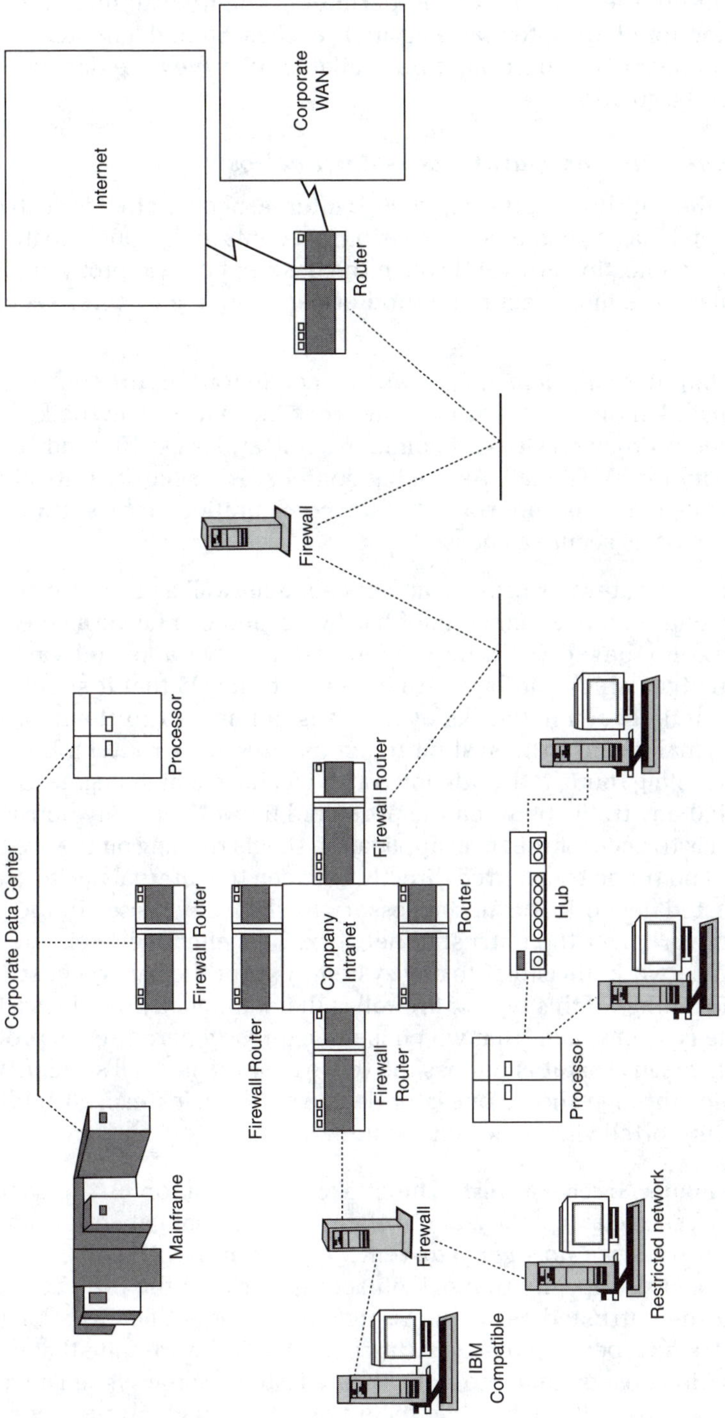

Exhibit 6. Firewall Placement within an Organization's Intranet/WAN

To maintain the integrity of the perimeter, the firewall must be constantly monitored for potential security breaches. Should a breach occur, an Internet security expert must be available to survey the damage and recommend a solution.

Internet Firewall Configurations — Bastion Host

This is the only host on the customer's internal network that is visible to the Internet. It has no customer-accessible accounts for logging into it. Customer communications travel through the bastion host via proxy applications. This is the most secure method of performing perimeter security today.

In the popular *dual-homed bastion host* configuration, the toolkit software is installed on a host with two network interfaces. The toolkit software provides proxy services for common applications like FTP and Telnet, and security for SMTP mail. As the bastion host is a security-critical network strong-point, it is important that the configuration of the software on that system be as secure as possible.

Dual-homed gateways provide an appealing firewall as they are simple to implement, require a minimum of hardware, and can be verified easily. Most Berkeley-based UNIX implementations have a kernel variable **_ipforwardign,** which can be set to indicate to the OS that it should not route traffic between networks even if it is connected to them (which would normally cause the system to act as a gateway router). By completely disabling routing, the administrator can have a high degree of confidence that any traffic between the protected network and any untrusted network has to occur through an application that is running on the firewall. As there is no traffic transferred directly between the internal network and the untrusted network, it is not necessary to show any routes to the protected network over the untrusted network. This effectively renders the protected network "invisible" to any systems except the bastion host. The only disadvantage of this type of firewall is that it implicitly provides a firewall of the type in which "that which is not expressly permitted is prohibited." This means that it is impossible to weaken the firewall's security to let a service through should one later decide to do so. Instead, all services must be supported via proxies on the firewall.

Choke Router/Screened Host. The choke router reinforces the bastion host, enforces security policy, and isolates the internal network from the Internet. A *screened host gateway* relies on a router with some form of packet screening capacity to block off access between the protected network and the untrusted network. A single host is identified as a bastion host and traffic is permitted only to that host. The software suite that is run on the bastion host is similar to a dual-homed gateway; the system must be as secure as possible, as it is the focal point for attack on the network.

Screened host gateways are a very flexible solution because they offer the opportunity to selectively permit traffic through the screening router for applications that are considered trustworthy, or between mutually trusted networks.

The disadvantage of this configuration is that there are now two critical security systems in effect: the bastion host and the router. If the router has access control lists that permit certain services through, the firewall administrator has to manage an additional point of complexity. Verifying the correctness of a screened host firewall is a bit more difficult. It becomes increasingly difficult as the number of services permitted through the router grows. Screened host firewalls also introduce management risks because it is possible to open holes in the firewall for special applications or influential users; the firewall administrator must be careful to resist pressure to modify the screening rules in the router.

In a *screened subnet firewall*, a small isolated network is placed between the trusted network and the untrusted network. Screening rules in routers protect access to this network by restricting traffic so that both networks can only reach hosts on the screened subnet. Conceptually, this is the dual-homed gateway approach applied to an entire network. The main utility of this approach is that it permits multiple hosts to exist on the "outside" network (again referred to as the demilitarized zone). An additional advantage to the screened host subnet is that the firewall administrator can configure network routing in a way that does not advertise routes to the private network from the Internet, or internal routes to the Internet. This is a powerful means to protect a large private network because it becomes very difficult for an outsider to direct traffic toward the hidden private network. If the routing is blocked, then all traffic must pass through an application on the bastion host just as it must in the dual-homed gateway.

Firewalls in a Partitioned Network

Not every network is a single, isolated network attached to an untrusted network. As the use of large-scale networks continues to increase, businesses increasingly form business partnerships and transmit corporate sensitive information over public networks. In addition, single corporations seek to establish a common security perimeter among multiple facilities connected over a public backbone. In this type of situation, a business can effectively combine a firewall with network-level encryption hardware (or software) to produce a virtual network with a common security perimeter.

A company can establish a common security perimeter between two facilities over a public Wide Area Network (WAN). The encryption is separate from the router but need not be if integrated encrypting routers are available. Currently, there are several products that act as encrypting bridges at a frame level. These products work by examining the source and destination address of all packets arriving via one interface and retransmitting the packet out via another interface. If the encrypting bridge/router is configured to encrypt traffic to a specific network, the packet data is encrypted and a new checksum is inserted into the *packet* header. Once the packet is received at the other *computer*, the peer encrypting bridge/router determines that it is from a network with which the router is encrypting traffic and decrypts the packet, patches the checksum, and retransmits it.

Anyone intercepting traffic between the two encrypting networks would see only useless cipher text. An additional benefit of this approach is that it protects against attempts to inject traffic by spoofing the source network address. Unless attackers know the cipher key that is in use, their packets will be encrypted into junk when they go through the encrypting bridge/router. If the encrypting bridge/router gets traffic for a network with which it does not have an encryption arrangement, traffic is transmitted normally. In this manner, a firewall can be configured with encrypted "tunnels" to other networks. For example, a company could safely share files via NFS or safely use weakly authenticated network log-in programs, such as rlogin over their encrypted link, and still have a strong firewall protecting access between the corporate perimeter and the rest of the world. Two companies that want to establish a business connection for proprietary information could apply a similar approach in which traffic between the firewall bastion host on one corporate network and the firewall bastion host on the other corporate network is automatically encrypted.

Practical Web Security Solutions

It is easy to see that businesses need not be intimidated into bypassing the opportunities available to them on the Internet. Several security solutions exist immediately to reduce or remove the risk involved in connecting to the Internet. A few more are listed and summarized.

A Backdoor Connection. This method connects the Internet server (Web server, list server, etc.) to other company computer systems through a dial-up link that is not made available anywhere on the Internet.

A backdoor data transfer method might include setting up a program like ProComm Plus (by Datastorm) on a computer connected to the Web server. The company's other computer systems periodically dial into that backdoor computer via ProComm to upload files that are then imported to the Web server's database via a custom import program. This same method works well for sending order or questionnaire data in batches from a Web server to other computers within the company.

In using this approach, the communications lines between the company's computers and its Internet presence are severed most of the time. Even when the link is established between computers, it does not use an insecure network protocol like TCP/IP, which is easy for hackers to penetrate. This prevents Internet hackers from drilling through to vital company systems and information.

A Network Firewall. A network firewall connects the Internet server into the company's existing computer network system via a permanent firewall router. Firewall routers are sold by a growing number of network hardware and software companies. They serve as a security barrier between network systems. By placing such a barrier between the company's Web server and the rest of the company's network, a network administrator can restrict the flow of network data packets between these segments. The firewall could restrict all inbound packets to those generated by the Web server itself; thus, only the Web server can access internal information.

A good hacker can get through a firewall although attempting to gain access beyond the firewall would require the use of sophisticated IP source-address spoofing techniques. These techniques fool the firewall into believing that the hacker's connection has the same network address as the Web server or some other privileged user. At this point, the hacker would need sufficient motivation to expend the effort and time to get through.

Any time a company plans to connect its in-house computer network directly to an Internet server, a firewall should be used to deter casual hacking and other less malicious security risks.

A Pseudo Firewall. A pseudo firewall connects the Internet server into the company's existing computer network system via standard router equipment, but segregates network traffic with different network protocols (i.e., TCP/IP and IPX/SPX). The main security problem on the Internet exists due to certain flaws in the Internet network protocol (TCP/IP). Thus, using a different protocol to connect the company's internal computers to its Internet server solves this problem.

For example, if a company's Internet server used a Pentium PC running Microsoft Windows NT as its Web server over a leased line connected to an Internet service provider (ISP), this method would entail running two network protocols on the Web server. The Web server must use TCP/IP to connect to the Internet. Yet, to access information on internal computer networks, that same Web server could be configured to use something else, such as IPX/SPX, which is native to Novell's NetWare. The hacker could spoof the TCP/IP address but would find no other network connections beyond the Web server.

This method is not proven to work more effectively than a firewall. However, its appeal is that it can provide a similar level of security to a firewall router at lower cost. Exhibit 7 provides a profile of Web protection levels (encrypted).

Next discussed is the application language Java and the risks and opportunities it provides to organizational computing.

Java Risk Issues

Another area for management review in corporate use of the World Wide Web is the use of Java. Java is an object-oriented programming language in which small programs (called applets) can be compiled and run on any computing platform. Within an intranet, applets could deliver software and data to client workstations only as needed. And the applet would only need to include the functions of a software application and the data that the client needs to accomplish a specific task. Thus, corporations could save on software licenses and workstation computing power across the enterprise. On the Internet, Java applets are downloaded by the client from a server on the Internet. However, many individuals fear the destructive potential of Java applets from unknown sources. Current browsers allow users to refuse Java applets or accept them only from trusted sources.

Although Java provides benefits and cost-effective measures to a corporation, the current versions of Java are not mature enough to satisfy the needs of corporate security. Java may be fine for building Windows applets, but it is not yet a real tool for mission critical programs that draw on legacy data. The earlier Java tools provided weak data validation and leaned too heavily on object linking and embedding (OLE). These older Java tools were geared too much towards Windows and often lacked some of the key features such as debuggers and compilers that are essential in a workbench.

Recent studies by universities and private industry groups have identified three areas that pose the most significant risks to Java applications: (1) the lack of audit trails, (2) the variances between Java language and byte-code semantics, and (3) the deficiencies in the design of the language and byte code format and the input/output object classes.

Presently, the Java environment does not provide a standard or default mechanism to produce audit trails. The developer must customize all verification into the application. Java needs built-in accountability functions to maintain protected and selective auditing information much like an audit log that identifies the parties responsible for various actions performed on the computer.

Users also need to understand that they do not control a Java applet once it is downloaded into the local environment. For example, users may

Exhibit 7. Need For Web Protection Levels (Encrypted)

Service Type	Destruction	Interference	Modification or Replacement	Misrepresentation	Reputation	Inadvertent Misuse	Unauthorized Altering/ Downloading	Unauthorized Transaction	Unauthorized Disclosure
Advertising	Basic	Basic	Strong	Basic	Basic	Strong/prevent IP spoofing	Basic	Basic	Strong[a]
Secure Internet/intranet/extranet									
1. Informational	Basic	Basic	Strong	Basic	No level	Basic	Strong	Basic	Basic
2. Transactional basic	Strong	Strong	Basic	Basic	Basic	Strong	Basic	Basic	Strong[a]
Electronic commerce	Strong	Strong	Strong	Strong	Strong	Basic	Strong	Strong	Strong[a]

[a] See State of California SB 1386

389

not necessarily know that an applet has been downloaded or may not have information on how many applets are in operation, unless they set up adequate security on their Internet browsers. A common form of malicious applet can continue running on the client and force the user to restart the system.

There are other security problems as well. Today, compiler languages such as C or Ada can produce bytecode that looks like Java bytecode to the verifier. If the verifier erroneously accepts the non-Java bytecode, it is unlikely to follow Java's language restrictions and it may allow performance of illegal procedures. For example, a hostile applet could be used to create a classloader containing unacceptable statements. The classloader, which is responsible for defining namespace seen by other classes, could then allow the attacking applet to customize the user's computer environment.

Finally, from an IT audit standpoint, Java input/output object classes are public. Even though this feature improves the usefulness of Java, it provides hackers with a way to deliver damage. This major weakness of Java makes the use of audit tools critical to safe use of Java programs.

For the average corporate IT developer accustomed to Visual Basic and similar drag-and-drop development tools, the early Java environments seemed to take two steps backwards. Therefore, Java's competitors took advantage of this weakness and prepared a second generation of Java toolsets to resolve some of the weaknesses of the Java programming language. These tools were intended to give corporate IT developers the same warm, fuzzy feeling of confidence they get from other visual development environments.

Corporate IT developers want to build Web applications for the long term. Many corporate and government IT departments are caught up in testing new Web-based development technologies primarily centered on Java-based development. These include tools such as Visix's-Eleven, and emerging technologies such as Remote Method Invocation (RMI) and object serialization. One of the documented weaknesses that most toolsets do not redress is Sun's implementation of the abstract Windowing Toolkit for building user interface features. Developers are still working to resolve this problem.

World Wide Web and Java Risk Conclusions

For CIOs and CEOs, the new millennium promises many exciting opportunities and risks in IT. As unsettling and unnerving as many of these changes are, managers must employ common sense and informed business judgment to understand both risks and benefits. Managers should understand the technical complexities and encourage decision makers to carefully weigh the investment in security against the potential risks. There are answers and solutions for many of the security issues discussed. Effective measures exist to protect both access security and transaction security over the Internet. As improvements are made to Java and as the programming language matures, it can be expected that Java will incorporate more and better security measures because Java language developers realize that security is critical to the acceptance and success of the language.

Java provides an entirely new kind of cross-platform computing environment that can be used to integrate and work with an organization's existing systems and networks. As Java matures, it may well replace costlier, less efficient elements in existing computing systems and make feasible the continued use of existing legacy systems. This is especially important today when multiple incompatible platforms and legacy systems are typical in global corporate and private IS infrastructures. The Web and Java hold great promise for organizations that want to integrate their existing, incompatible applications and make them available through one common user interface — an internet browser.

Web platforms and application platforms are incredibly complex and resource-intensive, expensive to buy and maintain, and costly to update or expand. But, as troublesome as these systems may be, the CEO and CIO have to consider whether they can afford to scrap huge corporate investments in such IS. It is very costly to replace systems, convert databases that contain invaluable information, and retrain workers in new computing environments and techniques.

Throughout the business and personal computing world, industry leaders, software vendors, and software developers are showing utmost support for Java, the programming language that they believe will transcend all barriers. Most business organizations will benefit by using adaptable application architecture. This new technology can save a company millions of corporate dollars per fiscal year on hardware, software, and systems development by converting a "custom fat client" into a "thin client."

While Web technology and Java are still somewhat immature, there is no doubt that they are here to stay. Major software developers continue to give credence to Java's future and have addressed user concerns by announcing plans to embed Java in future versions of their OS. As other higher-order tools are built up around it, Java should become one of the best enablers on the market. Those higher-order tools are on their way to the marketplace now, so sit tight and be prepared to embrace the Web and the Java revolution.

IT Insurance Risk

The third area of risk assessment related to IT operations is IT insurance. A clear understanding of insurance and risk management is necessary to review the adequacy of an organization's IT insurance. The IT management and the data security administrator must be aware of the relationship between risk and insurance to understand the reasons behind insurance choices and the types of insurance that are most applicable to the IT environment. This portfolio provides an overview of the reasons for and the methods of risk analysis, insurance alternatives, and what to look for in IT insurance coverage. As we move toward E-commerce, the need for this review becomes apparent because E-commerce spamming, denial-of-service (DOS) attacks, etc., can cost lost opportunities. Business must have a way to protect itself and recover losses.

Problems Addressed

Insurance distributes losses so that a devastating loss to an individual or business is spread equitably among a group of insured members. Insurance does not prevent loss nor reduce its cost; it merely reduces the risk. Risk is the possibility of an adverse deviation from a desired outcome (e.g., the possibility of dying before reaching age 72, a home being destroyed by fire, or an interruption in business operations, and now, an E-commerce site overloaded with invalid transactions or IT business spamming). When not managed, risks may be assumed that should be insured and vice versa. Insurance policies often provide overlapping coverage in some areas and none in other critical ones. Other problems may include lack of control over loss and premium costs, uneconomic insurance arrangements, organizational errors, and failure to adopt loss-prevention techniques.

Insurance Requirements

The following conditions must be met for insurance companies to calculate risk in monetary terms and distribute costs over enough members to cover losses and leave a profit.

- The insured objects must be of sufficient number and quantity to allow a reasonably close calculation of probable loss.
- Losses must be accidental.
- Losses must be capable of being determined and measured.
- All insured objects should not be able to be simultaneously destroyed (i.e., catastrophic hazard should be minimal).

Although there are obvious costs (i.e., premiums) involved in insurance, some economic and social values of insurance that may not be obvious to include are:

- The amount of accumulated funds needed to meet possible losses is reduced.
- Cash reserves that insurers accumulate are freed for investment purposes, effecting a better allocation of economic resources and increasing production.
- Because the supply of investment funds is greater than it would be without insurance, capital is available at a lower cost.
- The entrepreneur with adequate insurance coverage is a better credit risk.
- Insurers actively engage in loss-prevention activities.
- Insurance contributes to business and social stability by protecting business firms and their employees.

Insurance is an important means for business to handle risks; it is not, however, the only means. By insurance standards, risks are classified as insurable or uninsurable commercial risks.

Risks insurable commercially are given below.

- *Property risks.* This refers to direct or indirect loss of property.
- *Personal risks.* Loss of life or income as a result of:
  - Premature death
  - Physical disability
  - Old age
  - Unemployment
- *Legal liability risks.* Loss caused by negligent behavior resulting in injury to persons, arising out of:
  - The use of automobiles
  - The occupancy of buildings
  - Employment
  - The manufacture of products
  - Professional misconduct

The following are risks not insurable commercially.

- *Market risks.* Factors that may result in loss to property or income, including:
  - Seasonal or cyclical price changes
  - Consumer indifference
  - Style changes
  - Competition offered by a better product
- *Political risks.* Loss due to political reasons:
  - War or overthrow of the government
  - Restriction imposed on free trade
  - Unreasonable or punitive taxation
  - Restriction on free exchange of currencies

- *Production risks.* Loss related to production such as:
  - Failure of machinery to function economically
  - Failure to solve technical problems
  - Exhaustion of raw material resources
  - Strikes, absenteeism, and labor unrest

Reduction and Retention of Risks

Risks that are not insurable can be managed in other ways, and just because a risk is insurable does not mean that insurance is the only way to handle it. Risk reduction can be accomplished through loss prevention and control. If the possibility of loss can be prevented, the risk is eliminated; even reducing the chance of the loss occurring is a significant improvement. If the chance cannot be reduced, at least the severity of the loss can often be controlled. The reduction method is frequently used with insurance to lessen the premiums.

Uninsurable risks can also be reduced by risk retention, which can be voluntary or involuntary depending on the organization's awareness of the risks. The retention method, which is sometimes referred to as self-insurance, should be voluntary and should meet the following criteria.

- The risk should be spread physically so that there is a reasonably even distribution of exposure to loss over several locations.
- A study should be made to determine the maximum exposure to loss.
- Consideration should be given to the possibility of unfavorable loss experience and a decision reached as to whether this contingency should be covered by provision for self-insurance reserves.
- A premium charge should be made against operations that are adequate to cover losses and any increase in reserves that appear advisable.

Many companies, however, retain risks without estimating the future losses or reserving funds to pay for these losses. To decide what methods to use, companies must first analyze their risks. Managing the risk of significant losses is essential to protecting the interests of a business. Exhibit 8 below is the structure of that process.

Risk Management

Risk management ensures that risk losses do not prevent corporate management from seeking its goals of conserving assets and maximizing profits. The functions of risk management include the following:

- Recognizing the exposures to loss by becoming aware of the possibility of each type of loss. This is a basic function that must precede all others.

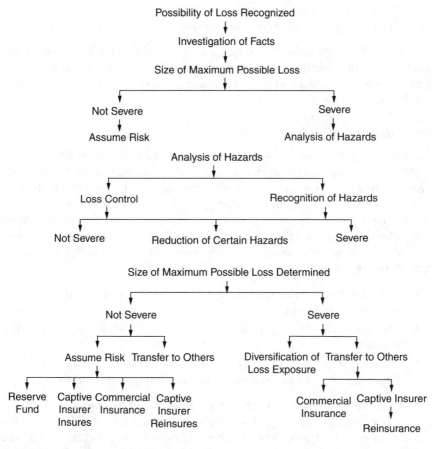

Exhibit 8. Structure of Risk Analysis

- Estimating the frequency and size of loss by determining its probability from various sources.
- Deciding the best and most economical method of managing the risk of loss, whether it is by assumption, avoidance, self-insurance, reduction of hazards, transfer, commercial insurance, or a combination of these methods.
- Administering the programs of risk management, including the tasks of constant reevaluation of the programs and record keeping.

These functions should be carried out through the following steps:

- Determining the objectives
- Identifying the risks
- Evaluating the risks
- Considering the alternatives and selecting the risk treatment device

- Implementing the decision
- Performing an evaluation and review

In following these steps, the organization should consider the odds and should not risk more than the company can afford to lose or risk a lot for a little. These rules point out that risk management is really just a series of cost/benefit decisions.

Determination of Objectives

A set of clearly defined objectives can guide those responsible for developing and administering the risk management program as well as provide a means for evaluating the program's performance. Obviously, each company has objectives specifically suited for its operation; however, some broad objectives can be defined. First, the aggregate cost of risks should be kept below the point at which a company's assets or earnings would be significantly reduced by uninsured losses. The cost of risks is defined as the sum of the following:

- The direct and consequential costs of loss-prevention measures
- Insurance premiums
- The costs of losses sustained (including expenses to curtail the losses)
- Net cost of indemnities from insurers and third parties
- Expenses of relevant management, administration, and finance

Second, the prime goals of a company should not be prejudiced. Third, a company must avoid a loss that it neither insured nor identified. Finally, the life, health, and property of others should be respected. Executive management and the board of directors should be involved in formulating the company's risk management objectives. Above all, management has to recognize that IT is an asset and it should be valued and validated continuously.

IT Risk Identification

This step is critical because unidentified risks are retained by default. As with any business, and IT is no exception, using some of the following identification tools can assure a comprehensive review:

- Audit or inspection by managers, workers, and/or independent parties of the firm's operational sites or practices.
- Operations and/or process flowchart of the firm's operations.
- Periodic use of a risk analysis questionnaire where information can be captured about the company's operations and ongoing activities. If questions are too general, unusual exposures or unique loss areas may be overlooked.

- Financial statement analysis using spreadsheet software to depict trends in revenue and cost areas, identifying asset exposure analysis.
- Insurance policy checklist — a catalog of various policies or types of insurance that identifies measurable insurable risk.

Using several tools is highly recommended in allowing the analyst or reviewer more coverage of targeted IT areas. The key is identification of those IT areas that can have a substantial impact on business operations and revenue. The use of multiple tools and techniques allows one to view the business from a different perspective, providing a more complete picture of the complexity and interrelationship of various operations and functions. Thus, IT risks can be viewed and assessed by management from different areas of assessment.

IT Risk Assessment Tools and Techniques

In view of the increased reliance on IT and automated systems, special emphasis must be placed in the review and analysis of risk in these areas. IT facilities and hardware are often included in the company's overall plant and property review; however, automated systems require a separate analysis, especially when these systems are the sole source of critical information to the business as in today's E-business movement. There are many risks that affect today's IT environment. Today's businesses face loss from traditional events such as natural disaster, accidents, vandalism, and theft, and also from similar events in electronic form. These can be from computer viruses, information or data theft of corporate data or records or files, electronic sabotage, electronic spamming of E-commerce business, etc. To assist in the identification and evaluation of these IT-related risks, the following resources for tools and techniques have been identified:

- *nist.gov:* The National Institute of Standards and Technology (NIST) has been a leader in providing tools and techniques to support IT. It has a number of support tools that can be used for risk assessment purposes.
- *gao.gov:* The U.S. General Accounting Office has provided a number of audit, control, and security resources as well as identification of best practices in managing and reviewing IT risk in many areas.
- *Expected loss approach:* A method developed by IBM that assesses the probable loss and the frequency of occurrence for all unacceptable events for each automated system or data file. Unacceptable events are categorized as:
  - Accidental disclosure
  - Deliberate disclosure
  - Accidental modification
  - Deliberate modification
  - Accidental destruction
  - Deliberate destruction

- *Scoring approach:* Identifies and weighs various characteristics of the IT systems. Uses the final score to compare and rank their importance.

IT Risk Evaluation

IT evaluation involves the quantification or ranking of the size and probability of potential loss. The risk should be categorized as follows:

- *Critical:* These exposures would result in bankruptcy.
- *Important:* These are exposures in which possible losses would not lead to bankruptcy but require the business to take out loans to continue operations.
- *Unimportant:* These are exposures that could be accommodated by existing assets or current income without imposing undue financial strain.

Assigning the identified risks to one of these categories gives it a level of significance and helps determine the proper means for treating it.

IT Risk Management

Risks can be managed using one or several of the following techniques:

- Avoidance
- Prevention
- Reduction
- Transfer
- Retention

More than one technique can be applied to a given risk (typically the case of reduction and transfer or retention). The IT risk management objectives should be used as a guide in choosing a technique. Below are some of the key questions IT and corporate management need to ask when choosing a technique.

- High severity or catastrophic loss risks:
  - Why is the business loss so severe?
  - How did the loss evolve?
  - What are the shortcomings of the existing control procedures?
- Avoidance:
  - Is it impossible to avoid?
  - Is it impractical to avoid?
  - Is it too expensive to avoid?
  - Is it too time-consuming to avoid?
- Prevention:
  - Are there any direct countermeasures to prevent the risk from occurring?
  - Are they cost-effective?

- – Do they have beneficial side effects?
- – Do they have adverse side effects?
- Reduction:
  - – Are there any direct countermeasures to reduce the risk?
  - – Are they cost effective?
  - – Do they reduce the loss occurrence?
  - – Will other risks be reduced as well?
  - – Do they have beneficial side effects?
  - – Do they have adverse side effects?
- Transfer:
  - – By insurance?
  - – By contractual agreement?
  - – By other means?
  - – Are there other benefits?
  - – Can the risk be best dealt with by a combination of controls?
  - – Can it be partially reduced and partially transferred?
  - – What are the benefits of each method?

If consideration is being given to the transfer technique and the use of insurance, in particular, the following items should be taken into account:

- *Advantage of deductibles:* Retaining a portion of the risk such as a higher deductible can greatly reduce the insurance or premium costs.
- *Tax considerations:* The impact of the tax laws on insurance costs and losses may influence the decision. In business, property and liability insurance premiums are a deductible expense, as are uninsured losses. However, contributions by a business to a funded retention program are not deductible.
- *Selection of the insurer:* Factors to consider in selecting an insurer include:
  - – Availability of coverage
  - – Cost of coverage
  - – Financial solvency, stability, and profitability of the insurer
  - – Quantity and quality of insurance services offered, both by the insurer directly and through the agency system it uses

If consideration is being given to retaining the risks, the following major financial aspects must be analyzed in assessing the value of loss retention:

- Cash flow
- Opportunity cost of funds

In general, the financial advantage of loss retention is greater when:

- The difference is small between interest rates on liquid accounts and rates of return on capital employed within a business.

- Commercial insurance rates on the risk are relatively high compared with the opportunity cost of funds.
- The firm's perceived needs for liquid loss reserve funds are low such that the firm is willing to accept more risk.

Finally, the records and documents of past losses and choices can be used as a prime information source in the process of choosing the appropriate risk handling technique. In this manner, the knowledge, experience, and patterns of the past can be used to make better decisions for the future.

Once the appropriate technique has been chosen, it must be implemented. The necessary facts and figures are now available to help negotiate insurance, set up a loss-prevention program, or establish a loss reserve fund. The risk analysis structure has been illustrated earlier. The various implemented plans must be evaluated and reviewed. This is an important process because the variables are changing constantly. Techniques that were appropriate last year may not be this year and mistakes do occur. The application of the wrong technique or coverage must be detected early and corrected.

How to Determine IT Insurance Coverage

Risk management as discussed above acts as a guide during the review of IT insurance coverage. It must be understood how the choice of insurance was arrived at. As mentioned earlier, there are fundamental steps that must be performed:

- The objectives of risk management policy must be in line with the overall goals of the organization.
- The method used to identify the risks associated with IT should provide an accurate and comprehensive list.
- Risk exposures should be properly quantified and categorized.
- The appropriate decision should be made after careful review of the options and alternatives.

After the risk management process has been reviewed, a more detailed investigation of IT-related risks can commence. The following is a list of questions that must be addressed.

- Prevention and reduction:
  - Is there a comprehensive, up-to-date disaster recovery contingency plan?
  - What efforts have been made to check that the plan is workable?
  - Are there off-site backups of the appropriate file?
  - Are the procedures and practices for controlling accidents adequate?

- Have practical measures been taken to control the impact of a disaster?
- Is physical security adequate to protect property and equipment?
- Is software security adequate to protect important or sensitive information?
- Are there appropriate balancing and control checks made at key points in the processing?
- Are there appropriate control checks on the operations?
- Are there appropriate control checks during the development and modification of systems?
- Are Network firewalls tested weekly and have firewalls been certified on a semi annual basis?
- Has E-commerce Web site been certified for business commerce by an external organization? Does the organization have credentials for certification? Does it have liability insurance and limit of losses?
- Do contracts for purchases or leases have terms and conditions and remedies that adequately protect the company if there is a problem?
- Have contracts been prepared by legal counsel who has expertise in IT and legal issues?
- Are facilities, equipment, and network maintained properly?
- Transfer:
  - Are risks handled by insurance according to risk management objectives and risk analysis?
  - Has the insurer been checked out?
- Retention:
  - Are risks retained according to risk management objectives and risk analysis?
  - Have deductibles been used judiciously in insurance policies?

Once the methods available to prevent and reduce risk losses have been examined and risks to be insured have been determined, attention can be focused on the insured risks.

In the IT environment, there are special risks that are commonly handled by insurance, including:

- Damage to computer equipment
- Cost of storage media
- Cost of acquiring the data stored on the media
- Damage to outsiders
- Business effects of the loss of computer functions

The types of insurance policies that cover these risks include property, liability, business interruption, and fidelity-bonding insurance. The review of the policies especially written for IT-related risks should examine:

- Coverage of hardware and equipment (i.e., network, mass storage devices, terminals, printers, and CPUs).
- Coverage of the media and information stored thereon. For example, a disk drive that is destroyed can be replaced at the cost of a new drive. If the drive or mass storage device contains important information, the value of the new replacement drive plus the value of the lost information must be recovered.
- Coverage of the replacement or reconstruction cost and the cost of doing business as usual (i.e., business interruption). This might involve renting time on equivalent equipment from a nearby company or outsourcing to a vendor, paying overtime wages for reconstruction, and detective work. In this area, logging of daily E-commerce business activity resulting in financial transaction is extremely important to identify business interruption or loss due to spamming or information theft.
- Noncoverage of such items as damage to media from magnets, damage from power failure (blackout) or power cut (brownout), and damage from software failure.

After it has been verified in the policies that the proper items are covered, the dollar values assigned must be checked.

Conclusion

The assessment and analysis of risk in any IT environment is not an easy process. This chapter has examined the application of risk assessment in ERM/ORM, Web and Java design and development, and IT insurance coverage. There are a number of resources available to assist IT auditors and IT professionals in this area.

Companies are beginning to see the benefit of protecting themselves from all types of potential risk exposures. By identifying and mapping risk exposures throughout the organization, a company can concentrate on mitigating those exposures that can do the most damage. With an understanding of risks, their severity, and their frequency, a company can turn to solutions, be it retaining, transferring, sharing, or avoiding a particular risk.

With regard to Web and Java operational issues, some of the security tools and procedures that exist now to reduce risk when a company gives its customers access to business resources over the Internet have been discussed. Examples have been given of security measures available to provide access security to protect the company's own computers, disks, memory, and other computing equipment from outside interference, and transaction security to ensure that two individuals or organizations on the Internet can privately and safely execute a transaction.

Finally, organizations must develop a sound risk management program to be able to determine the adequacy of their IT insurance coverage. The first step in properly developing a program is becoming aware of the limits and advantages of insurance and learning the methods of risk reduction. For the risk management program itself, objectives must be determined; risks must be identified, categorized, and evaluated, and risk-handling techniques must be chosen. Understanding insurance choices and the types of policies available is also important.

The development of a comprehensive risk management program is a long process and a lot of work. Once established, however, the benefits become invaluable. IT operations will always be at risk. The IT auditor, IT professional, and management can work together to minimize that risk.

Chapter Review Questions

1. What is risk assessment?
2. Can risk assessment be both a tool and a technique?
3. When should managers and auditors perform risk assessment?
4. What is a risk assessment related standard by NIST? GAO? AICPA? ISACA? IIA?
5. What is enterprise risk management (ERM)?
6. Why is ERM becoming more important to organizations?
7. How is ERM expected to grow in importance in the next five years?
8. What are some of the perceived risks of using the Internet and the Java programming language?
9. What is an Internet firewall?
10. What three areas pose the most significant risk to Java applications?
11. What effect does insurance have on risk?
12. How should organizations develop a sound risk management program to determine the adequacy of their IT insurance coverage?

Multiple Choice

1. NIST stands for which of the following?
   a. National Information Security Test
   b. National Institute of Standards and Testing
   c. National Institute of Standards and Technology
   d. National Institute of Security and Technology
2. The GAO conducts audits, surveys, investigations, and evaluations of:
   a. Software products
   b. Businesses
   c. State agencies
   d. Federal agencies

3. Which of the following organizations consists of representatives from industry, public accounting, investment firms, and the New York Stock Exchange?
   a. IIA
   b. COSO
   c. ISACA
   d. AICPA

4. Which of the following is not a main reason for ERM/ORM functions being established within corporations?
   a. Increasing software patches
   b. Magnitude of problem
   c. Increasing business risks
   d. Organizational oversight

5. Properly implemented, Internet security mechanisms will:
   a. Protect the company from inside employees who attempt to enter the internal network from the Internet.
   b. Provide unauthorized users with access to Internet services such as HTTP, FTP, Telnet, and Gopher.
   c. Deliver unneeded Internet applications from the internal network.
   d. Prevent unauthorized use of resources on the internal network.

6. Encryption technologies electronically store information in an encoded form that can only be decoded by an authorized individual who has the appropriate decryption technology and a:
   a. Private key
   b. Public key
   c. Authorization to decrypt
   d. Ability to decrypt

7. Internet security policies fall along a continuum that ranges from promiscuous to:
   a. Permissive
   b. Undocumented
   c. Informal
   d. Paranoid

8. Internet application proxy firewalls are:
   a. A prudent perimeter security solution
   b. A sufficient defense against hackers
   c. An inadequate use of firewall technology
   d. A way to avoid using network connections from within the company

9. A network firewall connects the Internet server into the company's existing computer network system via a permanent firewall:
   a. Router
   b. Hub
   c. Bridge
   d. Port

10. Which of the following is not a risk to Java applications?
    a. Lack of audit trails
    b. Active X security weaknesses
    c. Variances between Java language and bytecode semantics
    d. Deficiencies in the design of the language

Exercises

1. Your organization is performing an evaluation of security tools to be used to provide protection for your company intranet from unauthorized use by employees and outside intruders. Write a list of evaluation criteria for security software and hardware to be used, including client software, server software, network software, and firewall hardware and software.

2. You have been asked to audit your company security plan as it applies to acceptable employee use of the Internet and e-mail. Write a preliminary audit plan; include scope, objectives, and audit steps.

3. Your organization has recently developed criteria for a risk management program. One goal of the program is to determine the adequacy and effectiveness of the company IT insurance coverage. Describe how an effective risk management program can enable a more cost-effective use of IT insurance.

Answers to Multiple Choice Questions

1 — c; 2 — d; 3 — b; 4 — a; 5 — d; 6 — c; 7 — d; 8 — a; 9 — a; 10 — b

Notes

1. Hoffman, D.G., *Managing Operational Risk*, John Wiley & Sons, New York, 2002, p. xxvi.
2. Basel Committee on Banking Supervision, Sound Practices for the Management and Supervision of Operational Risk, Basel, Switzerland, 2001, p. 11.
3. Tillinghast–Towers Perrin, Enterprise Risk Management: Trends and Emerging Practices, The Institute of Internal Auditors Research Foundation, 2001, p. xxvi.
4. Crouhy, M., Galai, D., and Mark, R., *Making Enterprise Risk Management Payoff*, McGraw-Hill, New York, 2001, pp. 132–133.

References

1. Barton, T.L., Shenkir, W.G., and Walker, P.L., *Making Enterprise Risk Management Pay Off*, Financial Times/Prentice Hall, Upper Saddle River, NJ, 2002.
2. Basel II Mandates a Nest Egg for Banks, *U.S. Banker*, July 1, 2002, 48, http://web2. infotrac.galegroup.co
3. Berson, A. and Anderson, G., *Sybase and Client/Server Computing*, 1996, BITS Technology Risk Transfer Gap Analysis Tool, BITS, Washington, D.C., 2002.
4. Bock, J.T., *The Strategic Role of "Economic Capital" in Bank Management*, Midas-Kapiti International, Wimbledon, England, 2000.
5. Business Banking Board, RAROC and Operating Risk, Washington, D.C., Corporate Executive Board, 2001.

6. Business Banking Board, Risk Management Structure, Washington, D.C., Corporate Executive Board, 2001.

7. Carmichael, D.R., The Auditor's New Guide to Errors, Irregularities and Illegal Acts, *J. Accountancy*, September 1988.

8. Cassidy, M.J., *Introductory Guide to System Management Facilities*, 1992.

9. Chan, S., Govindan, M., Picard, J.Y., Leschiutta, E., Takach, G.S., and Wright, B., *EDI for Managers and Auditors*, Second Edition, 1993.

10. Bank for International Settlements and Basel Committee on Banking Supervision, Consultative Document Operational Risk, 2001, updated July 2002, http://www.bis. org/publ/bcbsa07.pdf

11. Crouhy, M., Galai, D., and Mark, R., *Risk Management*, McGraw-Hill, New York, 2001.

12. Dalton, G., Acceptable Risks, *Information Week*, August 31, 1998, pp. 36–48.

13. Elements of a Successful IT Risk Management Program, Gartner, May 2002, http:// www.gartner.com/gc/webletter/bindview/issue1/ggarticle1.html

14. Ernst & Young, "Integrated Risk Management Practices," Unpublished PowerPoint slides, 2000.

15. Gallegos, F., *EDI Audit Risk Assessment*, EDP Auditing Series, #74-15-05, Auerbach Publications, Boca Raton, FL, May 1998, pp. 1–12.

16. Gallagher, S., E-Commerce Needs a Paper Trail, *Information Week*, August 31, 1998, p. 114.

17. Halper, S., *Handbook of EDP Auditing*, Warren, Gorham & Lamont, Inc., Boston, MA, 1985.

18. Hernandez, P., Practical IT Auditing, *IS Audit Control J.*, Vol. 3, 1998.

19. Hively, K., Merkley, B.W., and Miccolis, J.A., *Enterprise Risk Management: Trends and Emerging Practices*, The Institute of Internal Auditors Foundation, Altamonte Springs, FL, 2001.

20. Hoffman, D.G., *Managing Operational Risk*, John Wiley & Sons, New York, 2002.

21. In Brief: Ferguson Urges Investing in Risk Control, *American Banker*, March 5, 2002, http://0proquest.umi.com.opac.library.csupomona.edu

22. Institute of Internal Auditors, Web site, http://www.theiia.org/standard/sias9-98.html

23. Information Systems Audit and Control Association, Web site, http://www.isaca. org/standard/state5.htm

24. James, C., RAROC Based Capital Budgeting and Performance Evaluation: a Case Study of Bank Capital Allocation, The Wharton School, Philadelphia, PA, 1996.

25. Jameson, R. and Walsh, J., The Leading Contenders, *Risk Magazine*, November 2000, http://www.financewise.com/public/edit/riskm/oprisk/opr-soft00.htm

26. Lam, J., Top Ten Requirements for Operational Risk Management, *Risk Management*, November 2001, http://0-proquest.umi.com.opac.library.csupomona.edu

27. Le Grand, C.H., Virtual Office: Risk Management, Security, Control, and Auditing, Institute of Internal Auditors, Altamonte Springs, FL, 1996.

28. Marcella, A., Jr., Auditing IBM's Customer Information Control System (CICS), Institute of Internal Auditors, Altamonte Springs, FL, 1991.

29. Marks, N., The New Age of Internal Auditing, *The Internal Auditor*, December 2001, http://0-proquest.umi.com.opac.library.csupomona.edu

30. McNamee, D.W., Telecommunications: Detecting and Deterring Fraud, Institute of Internal Auditors, Altamonte Springs, FL, 1993.

31. National Association of Financial Services Auditors, Enterprise Risk Management, Spring 2002, pp. 12–13.

32. Ong, M., Why bother? *Risk Magazine*, November 2000, http://www.financewise.com/ public/edit/riskm/oprisk/oprcommentary00.htm

33. The Institute of Internal Auditors, Practice Advisory 2100-3: Internal Audit's Role in the Risk Management Process, March 2001, http://www.theiia.org/ecm/guide-frame. cfm?doc_id=73

34. Santomero, A.M., Commercial Bank Risk Management: an Analysis of the Process, The Wharton School, Philadelphia, PA, 1997.
35. Schindel, M. and Gallegos, F., DP Insurance: a Management Tool, *The Handbook of MIS Management*, Second Edition, Auerbach Publishers, Boca Raton, FL, 1988, pp. 505–515.
36. Soe, L. and Gallegos, F., *Web and Java Risk Issues*, Information Management Series: Strategies, Systems, and Technologies, #1-06-50, Auerbach Publishers, Boca Raton, FL, July 1998, pp. 1–16.
37. Bank for International Settlements and Basel Committee on Banking Supervision, Sound Practices for the Management and Supervision of Operational Risk, 2002, http://www.bis.org/publ/bcbs86.htm
38. The Financial Services Roundtable, Guiding Principles in Risk Management for U.S. Commercial Banks, Washington, D.C., 1999.
39. U.S. General Accounting Office, An Audit Quality Control System: Essential Elements, GAO Report OP-4.1.6, August 1993.
40. U.S. General Accounting Office, Executive Guide: Improving Mission Performance through Strategic Information Management and Technology, GAO Report AIMD-94-115, May 1, 1994.
41. U.S. General Accounting Office, Executive Guide: Information Security Management — Learning from Leading Organizations, GAO Report AIMD-98-68, May 1998.
42. U.S. General Accounting Office, Information Technology: an Audit Guide for Assessing Acquisition Risk, GAO Report IMTEC-8.1.4, December 1992.
43. U.S. General Accounting Office, Assessing the Reliability of Computer-Processed Data, [Supplement to the Government Auditing Standards (Yellow Book) — External Version], GAO-03-273G, October 2002.
44. U.S. General Accounting Office, Information Security Risk Assessment: Practices of Leading Organizations, GAO/AIMD-00-33, November 1999.
45. U.S. General Accounting Office, Government Auditing Standards (Yellow Book) — Preliminary Edition, GAO-03-673G, June 2003.
46. U.S. General Accounting Office, Information Technology Investment Evaluation Guide, Assessing Risks and Returns: a Guide for Evaluating Federal Agencies' IT Investment Decision-Making, GAO/AIMD-10.1.13, February 1997.
47. U.S. General Accounting Office, Major Management Challenges and Risks, GAO/OCG-99-ES, February 1999.
48. Verschoor, C.C., Audit Committee Briefing — 2001: Facilitating New Audit Committee Responsibilities, The Institute of Internal Auditors, Altamonte Springs, FL, 2001.
49. Working Paper on the Regulatory Treatment of Operational Risk, 2001, Bank for International Settlements and Basel Committee on Banking Supervision, July 2002, http://www.bis.org/publ/bcbs_wp8.pdf

Chapter 16
Audit Methods and Techniques for Operations

Chapter 16 discusses IT audit methods and techniques used in the review of operations. Several emerging areas of importance will be discussed, such as contingency and disaster recovery planning, DBMS recovery, data communications, wireless operations, and end-user computing (EUC).

The first area discussed, contingency and disaster recovery planning, requires significant corporate resources to develop. Should a disaster occur, the payoff is to implement them without significant business or operations downtime and loss. Audit of such a plan should be continuous to ensure corporate viability and dependability. This section discusses the major steps an auditor should look for in such plans.

The second area covered is DBMS recovery. When a DBMS crashes, all or a portion of the data can become unusable. For an IT manager, this can be a nightmare. Appropriate procedures must be followed to restore, validate, and return the system to normal. In a client/server environment with distributed databases or where data-warehousing, data-mining, and Web-based databases are used, additional procedures are needed. Users and IT professionals must do their part to ensure the security, integrity, and validity of information and DBMS transactions. This section provides a checklist of major areas of concern to the IT manager and staff regarding DBMS recovery.

The third area reviewed is data communications. Data communications are an integral part of today's organizations, yet many auditors are not trained sufficiently in analyzing and assessing data communications controls. This section presents an overview of data communications and provides guidelines for reviewing key control areas including wireless technology.

The last area covered in this chapter is end-user computing (EUC). End-user computing groups are growing rapidly in pervasiveness and importance. The knowledge worker's application of technology to help business solve problems has been one of the major forces of change in business today. User dominance will prevail. Auditors, as knowledge workers and users, can assist departments in identifying sensitive or critical PC applications that require special attention. In organizations where controls are inadequate or nonexistent, auditors can play a key role in developing these controls for EUC groups. Once controls are in place, auditors can review them for adequacy and effectiveness. Auditing an EUC group can encompass the entire spectrum of IS reviews from systems development to disaster recovery. This section covers steps performed in auditing EUC groups.

Auditing Contingency and Disaster Recovery Planning

The contingency plan or disaster recovery plan is an important tool to business. It is a survival tool to help a business recover in the wake of an event that disrupts normal business operations. Provided management and staff support the plan, updated frequently and maintained and tested, it offers the chance for the business to survive.

Recent surveys and reports show that disasters can occur to any size business and, frequently, those that are unprepared do not survive to continue. On August 14, 2003, an enormous power failure blacked out population centers from New York City to Cleveland, Detroit, and Toronto, crippling transportation networks and trapping tens of thousands of people in subways, elevators, and trains. Computers became useless to those who did not have battery power. On September 11, 2001, after the New York Twin Towers disaster, 37 percent of the businesses that had offices there did not survive. In the Los Angeles earthquake of 1994, which occurred in the San Fernando Valley, 75 percent of the area's small businesses did not survive. Of the medium-size businesses, 50 percent did not survive. The impact was felt not only by the business but also by the supplier and the customers who relied on that business for its products and sales.

An audit of the contingency and disaster recovery plan is a check on the reliability and viability of the plan to support it when called for. It is a checkpoint for management and staff to assist them in maintaining a realistic and viable plan.

Audit of Disaster Recovery Planning Steps

Each contingency and disaster recovery plan should have major steps or processes. The following steps should be considered as important to a disaster recovery plan. In essence, it is an audit plan.

1. Steps put in writing
2. Hot site/cold site selected
3. Full and incremental system backups made on a daily or weekly basis

4. Data backed up
5. Tests and drills scheduled
6. Data and system backups stored off site
7. Disaster recovery chairperson and committee appointed
8. Emergency telephone numbers listed
9. Critical applications identified
10. Operating system, utilities, and application files backed up
11. Insurance coverage in place
12. Communication plan made
13. Up-to-date system and operation documentation confirmed
14. Employee relocation plan made for alternate work site
15. Food and water stocked
16. Key personnel positions backed up
17. CPR/first aid education in place
18. Care planned for families in an emergency
19. List made of hardware and software
20. Mission statement drawn up for disaster recovery plan
21. Manual procedures in place as a backup to automated procedures
22. Contractual arrangements signed with cleanup crew to remove debris

Written Disaster Recovery Plan. As stated earlier, a disaster recovery plan is a plan set up to enable an organization and its computer installation to quickly restore operations and resume business in the event of a disaster. Additionally, as the resources in an installation usually are in a constant state of flux — new applications are being developed, existing systems are being modified, personnel are turning over, and new hardware is being acquired — the plan must be updated on a regular basis. The objective of maintaining the plan in a continued state of readiness is to reduce the likelihood of incorrect decisions being made during the recovery process and to decrease the level of stress that may be placed on the disaster recovery team members during this process.

Once the plan is developed, members of the organization should be familiar with the plan. If an emergency occurs, it is easy for staff members to execute their roles in the plan. Efforts are not duplicated and all the necessary steps are taken.

As an auditor, you may find that the current condition is that no written disaster recovery plan exists. Many recovery procedures have been put into place, but they have not been formally documented.

Mission Statement for Disaster Recovery Plan. A mission statement and objectives should be developed for the disaster recovery plan. These objectives should be realistic, achievable, and economically feasible.

These objectives provide direction in preparing the plan and in continually reevaluating its usefulness.

Again, as an auditor, you may find that the company has not established disaster recovery objectives for the plan.

Disaster Recovery Plan Tests and Drill. Disaster simulation drills or tests are used to test the staffing, management, and decision making of both the computer- and noncomputer-related aspects of an organization's disaster recovery plan. The test reduces the opportunity for miscommunication when the plan is implemented during a real disaster. It also offers management an opportunity to spot weaknesses and improve procedures.

Unfortunately, organizations are often unwilling to carry out a test because of the disruption that occurs to daily operations and the fear that a real disaster may arise as a result of the test procedures. Therefore, a phased approach to testing would be helpful in building up to a full test. Below is a suggested phased approach:

1. Begin testing by using desk checks inspections and walk-throughs.
2. Next, a disaster can be simulated at a convenient time (during a slow period in the day). Personnel also might be given prior notice of the test so they are prepared.
3. Finally, simulate a disaster without warning.

Unless a disaster recovery plan is tested, it seldom remains usable. A practice test of a plan could very well be the difference between the success and the failure of the plan. The process is parallel to the old adage about the three things it takes for a retail business to be successful: location, location, and location. What is needed for a company's disaster recovery plan to allow it to continue to stay in business is testing, testing, and more testing.

The audit of contingency and disaster recovery planning is an important check. The major elements and areas such a plan has should be validated against recent publications on the subject. In turn, this approach can be used as a checklist to help both the auditor and management assess their plans.

Auditing DBMS Recovery

Many organizations such as banks and airlines have online computer systems that must function at all times. With the Internet, online commerce worldwide has become a reality. In most online applications, there are many application programs that access databases concurrently. Therefore, the databases must be correct and up-to-date at all times.

Yet technology is imperfect and computer systems and their supporting communications infrastructures are subject to many types of failure. When a system fails, recovery procedures must be in place to restore, validate, and return the system to normal. Information is an essential tool used by all levels of management in planning and organizing, directing, and controlling an organization. Therefore, the security, availability, and integrity of information are of utmost importance.

Technological advances have significantly influenced the way an organization's information is collected, processed, and distributed. Database management systems (DBMS) have evolved from some of these technological advances and are of primary concern to IT managers who are responsible for securing an organization's data while facilitating the efficient dissemination of information. Although DBMS can organize, process, and generate information designed to meet user needs, the integrity and security of this information are also essential to protect users.

Importance of DBMS Recovery

Recovery — the return to a fully operational environment after a hardware or software failure — is an important process in today's business world. Moreover, the effects of a system failure on the organization must be curtailed to minimize any substantial financial loss. Actions must be taken to prevent DBMS failures or resolve them quickly if they occur.

It is not always cost-effective to implement all possible DBMS controls and use all known review techniques. The choice of whether or not to review can have a direct impact on the financial consequences caused by these failures. A review of DBMS recovery ensures adherence to appropriate practices and procedures and minimizes business losses. A review further ensures that an organization can recover and return to full operational status following a disaster. For example, the 2001 New York Twin Towers disaster caused sustained interruption of business in many organizations in and around the destruction area. Those organizations that had established recovery procedures were able to more readily restore operations and minimize losses.

Developing, implementing, maintaining, and auditing the DBMS recovery controls and processes involve a considerable amount of money and company resources. Costs and benefits must be considered to ensure that company resources are expended efficiently. Systems managers who are either developing or maintaining a DBMS must understand database structures and participate in the recovery process. The following are some of the major areas in DBMS recovery and the process and techniques for reviewing DBMS recovery.

413

The Recovery Process

The DBMS recovery process is designed to restore database operations to their prefailure status. Users and IT professionals play a critical role in restoring the DBMS to operation; i.e., after the system has been successfully restored, the entire staff — IT and corporate — must participate to ensure the security, integrity, and validity of the information and its transaction properties.

Transaction Properties

The transaction is the fundamental activity of a DBMS and an area of concern for the reviewer. Transactions maintain consistency constraints or controls determined for an application. This consistency must be maintained at all times, even during a transaction failure. Concurrent processing must also be protected against adverse effects during a transaction failure.

A transaction is a command, message stream, or input display that explicitly or implicitly calls for a processing action (e.g., updating a file). Transaction processing is a sequential process that does not overlap or parallel a single application. It is started with a "Begin Transaction" and ended with an "End Transaction" identifier. The following typical transaction properties must be reviewed in assessing recovery controls:

- *Atomicity:* During a transaction, either all or none of its operations are performed on the database; atomicity ensures the preclusion of partially completed transactions.
- *Permanence:* If a transaction completes the "End Transaction" function, the results of its operation will never subsequently be lost.
- *Serialization of transactions:* If more than one transaction is executed concurrently, the transactions affect the database as if they were executed in serial order. This ensures that concurrently executing jobs do not use inconsistent data from partially completed transactions.
- *Prevention of cascading aborts:* An incomplete transaction cannot reveal results to other transactions, thereby limiting the effect of a transaction error throughout the entire system.
- *Consistency:* A transaction that reaches its usual end commits its results to memory, thereby preserving the consistency of the database contents.

Transactions are more effective when written in enterprise resource planning systems (ERPS) such as SAP, PeopleSoft, Baan, and J. D. Edwards or in DBMS languages such as Sybase, Oracle, Access, Visual Basic, MAGIC, SQL, and ASP than in legacy software such as COBOL or BASIC. They are well suited to structured programming and can help make systems development a routine process by modularizing the actions being performed in code and simplifying the treatment of failures and concurrency. These transaction properties have specific control functions that, from a review standpoint, should be organized and verified for DBMS operational validity and reliability.

Causes of DBMS Failure

There are many causes of DBMS failure. When a DBMS fails, it falls into an incorrect state and will likely contain erroneous data. Typical causes of DBMS failures include errors in the application program, an error by the terminal user, an operator error, loss of data validity and consistency, a hardware error, media failures, network transmission error, an error introduced by the environment, and errors caused by mischief or catastrophe.

Typically, the four major types of failure that result from a major hardware or software malfunction are transaction, system, communications, and media. A natural disaster, computer crime, or user, designer, developer, or operator error may cause these failures.

- *Transaction failure:* Transaction failures occur when the transaction is not processed and the processing steps are rolled back to a specific point in the processing cycle. In a distributed database environment, a single logical database may be spread across several physical databases. Transaction failure can occur when some, but not all, physical databases are updated at the same time.

- *System failure:* Bugs, errors, or anomalies in the database, operating system, or hardware can cause system failure. In each case, the transaction processing is terminated without control of the application. Data in the memory is lost; however, disk storage remains stable. The system must recover in the amount of time it takes to complete all interrupted transactions. At one transaction per second, the system should recover in a few seconds. System failures may occur as often as several times a week.

- *Communications failure:* With transactional systems now linked globally, the importance of the successful transfer of information to the DBMS is critical in maintaining the concurrency, reliability, and relevance of financial information. A formidable example is a stock exchange and its monitoring of business trading activity internationally. Transactional activities not recorded or "lost" could mean substantial losses to investors. The ability to recover is critical in this environment.

- *Media failure:* Disk crashes or controller failures can occur because of disk-write bugs in the operating system release, hardware errors in the channel or controller, head crashes, or media degradation. These failures are rare but costly.

By identifying the type of DBMS failure, an organization can define the state of activity to return to after recovery. To design the database recovery procedures, the potential failures must be identified and the reliability of the hardware and software must be determined. The following is a summary of four such recovery actions:

- *Transaction undo:* A transaction that aborts itself or must be aborted by the system during routine execution.
- *Global redo:* When recovering from a system failure, the effects of all incomplete transactions must be rolled back. This means the ability of the system to contact all linked DBMSs to retransmit missing, incomplete, or lost information across communication networks.
- *Partial undo:* While a system is recovering from failure, the results of completed transactions may not yet be reflected in the database because execution has been terminated in an uncontrolled manner. Therefore, they must be repeated, if necessary, by the recovery component.
- *Global undo:* If the database is totally destroyed, a copy of the entire database must be reloaded from a backup source. A supplemental copy of the transaction is necessary to roll up the state of the database to the present. This means the ability of the system to contact all linked DBMSs (i.e. client/server) to retransmit missing, incomplete, or lost information across communication networks.

Database Users

The four primary classes of database users are database administrators, applications and systems programmers, Web designers and developers, and end users — and each has a unique view of the data. The DBMS must be flexible enough to present data appropriately to each class of user and maintain the proper controls to inhibit abuse of the system, especially during recovery, when controls may not be fully operational.

Database Administrator. The database administrator is responsible for ensuring that the database retains its integrity and is accountable if the database becomes compromised, no matter what circumstances arise. This individual has the ultimate power over the schema that the organization has implemented. The database administrator must approve any modifications or additions to this schema. Permission to use subschemas (i.e., logical views) is given to end users and programmers only after their intentions are fully known and are consistent with organizational goals.

Because the database administrator has immediate and unrestricted access to almost every piece of valuable organizational information, an incompetent employee in this position can expose the organization to enormous risk, especially during DBMS recovery. Therefore, an organization should have controls in place to ensure the appointment of a qualified database administrator.

The database administrator must ensure that appropriate procedures are followed during DBMS recovery. The database administrator should also validate and verify the system once it has been recovered before allowing user access so that if controls are not functioning or if accessing problems continue, users will not be affected.

Applications and Systems Programmers. After recovery, programmers must access the database to manipulate and report on data according to some predetermined specification or to access whether data loss has occurred. Each application should have a unique subschema to work with. After recovery, the database administrator validates the subschema organization to ensure that it is operating properly and allowing the application to receive only the data necessary to perform its tasks.

Systems programmers must be controlled in a slightly different manner than applications programmers. They must have the freedom to perform their tasks but be constrained from altering production programs or system utility programs in a fraudulent manner.

Web Designers and Developers. This new breed of database integrators uses the Internet as their work desk and the world as their product show place. They are involved in design and development of applications to support communication and marketing of their company's products. More recently, the Internet has been the staging ground for electronic commerce and electronic data interchange (EDI). Also, products such as intranets and extranets are enhancing corporate communication. Because of the information's exposure to a worldwide audience, care in the quality, integrity, and validity as well as the professionalism of the information presented is critical.

End Users. End users are defined as all organizational members not included in the previous categories that need to interact with the database through DBMS utilities or application programs. Data elements of the database generally originate from end users. As mentioned earlier in a data warehousing application, they are often the ones who recognize data inaccuracies, inconsistencies, and duplication.

Each data element should be assigned to an end user. The end user is then responsible for defining the element's access and security rules. Every other user who wishes to use this data element must confer with the responsible end user. If access is granted, the database administrator must implement any restrictions placed on the request through the DBMS.

For example, Web site diagnostic tools are available that can detect and report errors and discrepancies such as broken links of an intranet or internet Web site, missing images, suspect pages, and suspect graphics or applets. Such software even allows the user to access the files containing errors and fix or correct problems with information.

Assigning ownership of specific data elements to end users discourages the corruption of data elements, thereby enhancing database integrity. Reviewers should ensure that this process exists and is appropriately reinstituted after the recovery process has been completed and the database administrator has provided operational approval.

After recovery, the database administrator should ensure that all forms of security practices and procedures are reinstated. These processes are a part of database security.

With data-warehousing applications, summary tables are the most powerful performance improvement technique. Summary tables are typically the most frequently used data assembled into tables. Recovery and rebuilding the summary tables is crucial. Data quality must be preserved by running the source data through cleansing tools continuously to ensure accuracy of the warehouse. Personnel responsible for entry and maintenance should be provided with incentives to ensure quality.

Backup and Recovery of the Data Warehouse

The warehouse databases must be available and up-to-date during business hours and even for a while after hours. Availability in this context means that the users must be able to access the data stored in the databases. Many factors threaten the availability of the data-warehouse databases. These include natural disasters (such as floods and earthquakes), hardware failures (like power failure or disk crash), software failures (such as DBMS malfunctions), and people failures (for example, operator errors and user misunderstanding).

Recovery is the corrective process to restore the database to usable state from an erroneous state. The basic recovery process consists of the following steps:

- Identifying that the database is in an erroneous, damaged, or crashed state
- Suspending normal processing
- Determining the source and extent of the damage
- Taking corrective action like:
  - Restoring the system resources to a usable state
  - Correcting the damage or removing invalid data
  - Restarting or continuing the interrupted process, including the reexecution of interrupted transactions
- Resuming normal processing

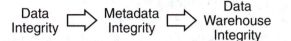

Exhibit 1. Phases of Data Integrity

To cope with failures, additional components and algorithms are usually added to the system. Most techniques use recovery data or redundant data, which makes recovery possible. When taking corrective action, the effects of some transactions must be removed, while other transactions must be reexecuted; some transactions must even be undone and redone. The recovery data must make it possible to perform these steps.

A last but extremely important aspect of backup and recovery is testing. Test the backup and recovery procedures in a test environment before deploying them in the production environment.

Data Warehouse Integrity Check List

Data warehouse integrity should be the concern of all those who will be designing and using the warehouse. There are three areas of integrity that should be considered throughout the life of the data-warehouse system. Exhibit 1 and Exhibit 2 illustrate this.

Although these are basic questions of business policy, database design, and audit procedures, they take on new meaning when asked in the environment of a data warehouse. As we are all too aware, policies change. The historical nature of a data warehouse precludes the assumption that all pieces of data have been gathered under the same policies that are in effect today or that will be in the future. IT auditors and managers will have to make certain that not only will they need to understand the impacts but decision makers using the data will also have to have access to an expanded understanding of these potential anomalies in the data.

Trends in Data Warehousing

"Data warehouses and data mining are getting more attention from organizational executives, [and] more and more companies are going into it in a big way," said Scott Kandel, a partner at Deloitte and Touché Information Risk Management in Los Angeles (March, 2003). Several studies conducted by research organizations last year indicate that the size of data warehouses maintained by Fortune 500 companies were swelling by 36 times between 1997 and 2002. The implications are that a 100GB warehouse today could weigh in at 3.6 terabytes in the not too distant future. Among the 200+ companies surveyed with warehouses of at least 100GB, estimated users would increase by 70 times — from 444 to more than 31,000.

Exhibit 2. Data Warehouse Integrity Checklist

How **stable** was the data when it was transferred?

- At what point in time should the data migrate to the data warehouse?
- Too close to the transaction, and it is still in flux and subject to change
- Too far away, and the detail is lost in an aggregation

What is the **basis** of its quantitative value?

- What operational unit holds the keys to the data's storage and definition?
- When is a "sale" considered to be completed?
- Sales: When the customer signs the order.
- Marketing: When it's invoiced.
- Finance: When the accounting period closes.
- Production: When it is ready to ship.
- Distribution: When it is shipped.
- Accounts receivable: When the check clears.
- All of these positions are valid from the perspective of each operational unit. When they are finished working with a sale, they consider it complete.

What is the **state** of the data value?

- Inventory, for example, changes its state as it moves through the firm from raw material to work-in-process to finished goods.
- Different material control policies have a diverse effect on the state of these values.
- Does the material get pushed through the system? Is the material "kited" for production and moved in lots?
- Does the material get pulled through the system? Does each operation in the cycle pull the material as needed?
- Does the material get "flushed" through the system? Is work-in-process only debited on an explosion of the bill-of-material, based on units completed at the end of the run?

Data warehouses are becoming more and more useful, and as companies realize their utility, they start adding more and more data.

Auditing Data Communications

Expanding computer use has resulted in serious abuses of data communications systems. Computer hackers and sometimes employees use an organization's data communications system to tamper with the organization's data, destroying information, introducing fraudulent records, and stealing assets with the touch of a few keys. First occurrences of this vulnerability appeared in 1981. A grand jury in Pennsylvania charged nine students (aged 17 to 22) with using computers and private telephone services to make illegal long-distance calls and to have merchandise delivered to three mail drops in the Philadelphia area without getting billed. Over a six-month period, the group was responsible for $212,000 in theft of services and $100,000 in stolen merchandise.

After 22 years, the vulnerabilities are still there. The Computer Security Institute (CSI) and the Federal Bureau of Investigation (FBI) still report that electronic commerce sites are three to ten times more likely to incur theft of data, and companies with supply chain networks are invaded more than other sites. Most staggering are the results of their most recent study. In the 2003 CSI and FBI Computer Crime and Security Survey, they reported that the dollar amount of theft of proprietary information was over $70 million, denial-of-service cost businesses over $65 million, and reported losses to viruses totaled over $27 million. These again are surveys received from 530 security practitioners.

On the government side, the GAO issued their report to the Senate Subcommittee on Governmental Affairs in September 1998, which identifies the vulnerabilities of data communications:

- Poor computer security program planning and management continue to be fundamental problems. Security planning and management deficiencies were reported for 17 of the 24 agencies included in GAO's analysis.
- Break-ins and damage of various levels of significance have been acknowledged.
- Serious weaknesses in data communications and network controls place critical federal operations and assets at risk.

In each case reported before the committee, the lack of data communications controls or insufficient testing of existing controls played a key role in the organization's vulnerability. This section describes the vulnerabilities of data communications systems and explains how auditors can successfully audit this complex field. The example used is the data communications system in a service bureau.

The results from the 2003 report (see Exhibit 3) do not show much improvement. The weaknesses identified place a broad array of federal operations and assets still at risk. For example, resources such as federal payments and collections could be lost or stolen; computer resources could be used for unauthorized purposes or to launch attacks on others; sensitive information such as taxpayer data, Social Security records, medical records, and proprietary business information could be inappropriately disclosed, browsed, or copied for purposes of espionage or other types of crime; and critical operations such as those supporting national defense and emergency services could be disrupted.

Also, the GAO recently noted some very interesting trends reported by both the FBI and the CERT. The FBI identified specifically the types of activity that are increasing, as shown in Exhibit 4. The Carnegie Mellon's Computer Emergency Response Team (CERT) Center has also been reporting increasing activity in cyber incidences (see Exhibit 5).

Along with these increasing threats, the number of computer security incidents reported to the CERT Coordination Center (Cert/CC) rose from

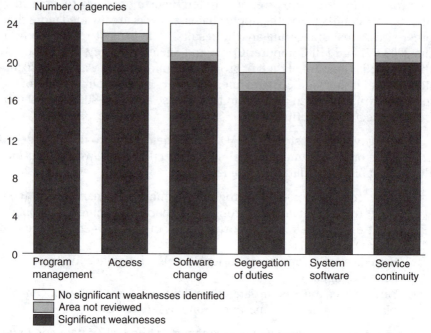

Source: Audit reports issued October 2001 through October 2002.

Exhibit 3. Information Security Weaknesses at 24 Major Agencies
GAO Report, Critical Infrastructure Protection: Challenges for Selected Agencies
and Industry Sectors, February 2003, GAO–03-233 (http://energycommerce.house.
gov/108/pubs/GAO-03-233.pdf).

9,859 in 1999 to 82,094 in 2002. So far for the first quarter of 2003, they have
recorded 42,586 incidents. If this trend continues for the year, it is estimated that the final figure for the year may be over 160,000. This is an 1800
percent or more growth from 1999. According to the GAO report, the director of the CERT Center stated that as much as 80 percent of actual security
incidents goes unreported in most cases because the organization (1) was
unable to recognize that its systems had been penetrated because there
was no indication of penetration or attack or (2) was reluctant to report the
incidents.

Data Communications Controls

Several data communications controls for protecting and recovering
data have been developed and applied successfully. These controls, which
are primarily transmission oriented, depend on human interaction and regular reviews to ensure that they are functionally sound. In addition, data
entry, computer processing, data storage, and output controls all play
interdependent roles in the protection and recovery of information. If one

Exhibit 4. Cyber Threats to Critical Infrastructure Observed by the FBI

Threat	Description
Criminal groups	There is an increased use of cyber intrusions by criminal groups who attack systems for purposes of monetary gain.
Foreign intelligence services	Foreign intelligence services use cyber tools as part of their information gathering and espionage activities.
Hackers	Hackers sometimes crack into networks for the thrill of the challenge or for bragging rights in the hacker community. While remote cracking once required a fair amount of skill or computer knowledge, hackers can now download attack scripts and protocols from the Internet and launch them against victim sites. Thus, while attack tools have become more sophisticated, they have also become easier to use.
Hacktivists	Hacktivism refers to politically motivated attacks on publicly accessible Web pages or e-mail servers. These groups and individuals overload e-mail servers and hack into Web sites to send a political message.
Information warfare	Several nations are aggressively working to develop information warfare doctrines, programs, and capabilities. Such capabilities enable an entity to have a significant and serious impact by disrupting the supply, communications, and economic infrastructures that support military power — impacts that, according to the Director of Central Intelligence, a can affect the daily lives of Americans across the country.
Insider threat	The disgruntled organization insider is a principal source of computer crimes. Insiders may not need a great deal of knowledge about computer intrusions because their knowledge of a victim system often allows them to gain unrestricted access to cause damage to the system or to steal system data.
Virus writers	Virus writers are posing an increasingly serious threat. Several destructive computer viruses and "worms" have harmed files and hard drives, including the Melissa Macro Virus, the Explore.Zip worm, the CIH (Chernobyl) Virus, Nimda, and Code Red.

Source: U.S. General Accounting Office, Homeland Security: Information Sharing Responsibilities, Challenges, and Key Management Issues, GAO-03-715T May 8, 2003.

of these controls is not functioning properly or an unauthorized intervention overrides complementary control processes, the data communications system becomes vulnerable.

These controls can be oriented toward prevention, detection, or correction of errors and abuse. Preventive controls ensure that events proceed as intended. Detective controls signal an alert or terminate a function and stop further processing when the system is violated or an error occurs. Corrective controls may perform an alert or terminate a function, but they also restore or repair part of the system to its proper state.

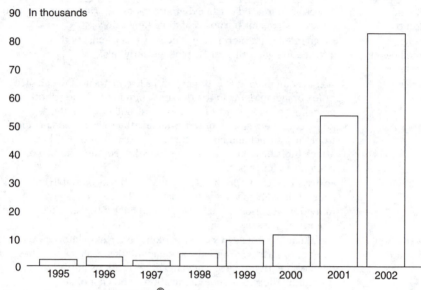

Source: Carnegie-Mellon's CERT® Coordination Center.

Exhibit 5. Carnegie Mellon CERT Report of Incidences Received 1995–2003 First Quarter
GAO Report, Critical Infrastructure Protection: Challenges for Selected Agencies and Industry Sectors, February 2003, GAO–03-233 (http://energycommerce.house. gov/108/pubs/GAO-03-233.pdf).

Errors in data communications usually occur because of the distances involved, speeds of transmission, or equipment malfunctions. To address these data communications controls, auditors should ask the following key questions:

1. Is a unique hardwired identification code, requiring no human intervention for its use, incorporated into each workstation device (PC, laptop, PDA, etc.)?
2. Is this identification code checked and validated by the computer to ensure that no unauthorized workstations are used?
3. Does the communications system avoid the general switchboard to reduce the data transmission error rate and the chance of wiretapping?
4. Are there appropriate controls for voice grade lines to reduce data transmission errors and maintain the integrity of data transmitted?
5. Are data communications lines conditioned for improved accuracy and physical security?

6. Does the system have an automatic store-and-forward capability to maintain control over messages queued for an inoperative or a busy communications device?
7. If leased lines fail, is there an automatic switch over to backup lines?
8. Is a message intercept function used to receive messages directed to inoperable or unauthorized workstations?
9. Does the system use parity checks to detect errors in data transmission?
10. Are validity checks used to compare character signals transmitted with the set of valid characters?
11. Does the system use echo checking to verify each character so that erroneous data is detected?
12. Are forward errors correcting techniques and sophisticated redundancy codes used for detecting and reporting data communications errors?
13. Are techniques available for detecting erroneous retransmissions of data?
14. Are modems equipped with loopback switches for fault isolation?
15. Is there validity checking of hardwired terminal identification codes and transmitted data characters?
16. Are there specially conditioned transmission lines to reduce noise, fading, and amplitude and frequency distortion?
17. Is parity checking done of both individual characters and blocks of characters?
18. Is echo checking done, comparing characters entered with characters received?
19. Are we using wireless technology within our infrastructure? If so, did we implement security to keep our traffic from being intercepted and analyzed?

Other hardware controls that can be incorporated into the data communications system include encryption of sensitive data to reduce the effectiveness of wiretapping and automatic storing of data at intermediary points when lines or other devices are inoperative. These controls are designed to ensure that only valid data is entered, transmitted, and received and that no data is lost, accessed, or tampered with during entry or transmission.

LAN Audit and Security Issues: Wired versus Wireless

As we mentioned earlier in Chapter 13, both the wired LAN and wireless LAN (WLAN) are subject to substantial security risks and issues. These include:

- Threats to the physical security of a network
- Unauthorized access and eavesdropping
- Attacks from within the networks' (authorized) user community

In fact, a wireless LAN has all of the properties of a wired LAN, and thus security measures taken to ensure the integrity and security of data in the wired LAN environment are applicable to WLANs as well. The only difference between a wired LAN and a WLAN is at the physical layer and special high frequency; all other network services and vulnerabilities remain. WLANs, in fact, include an additional set of unique security elements that are not available in the wired world, leading to the proposition that WLANs are actually more secure that their wired counterparts — an opinion shared by many industry analysts and experts.

What Can Be Done to the Wired LANs?

Physical Security: Site Control and Management. Given the obvious reliance of wired LANs on a wired physical plant, anyone gaining access to that wire can damage the network or compromise the integrity and security of information on it; therefore, physical access to network wires needs to be protected. However, the vast amount of wire inherent in most LANs provides many points for unauthorized access.

User Authentication. One of the big concerns of LAN technology relating to user authentication is access. Remote access products allow traveling sales and marketing people to dial in for their e-mail from remote offices connected via dial-up lines, intranets, and extranets that connect vendors and customers to a network. Use of these products leaves the network vulnerable to hackers, viruses, and other intruders. Firewall products offering packet filtering, proxy servers, and user-to-session filtering add additional protection, but hackers seem to get smarter all the time.

Eavesdropping Countermeasures. The most difficult threat to detect is someone just looking at and likely copying raw data on the LAN. Inexpensive and readily available programs let anyone with physical access to the network to read, capture, and display any type of packet data on the net, especially when the network administrator does not have some kind of "packet sniffer" or LAN-traffic analyzer for troubleshooting the network. And even wired LANs have an unintended wireless component. Many types of LAN cabling, particularly unshielded twisted pairs, radiate significant energy. This leads to the possibility that anyone can sit in the parking lot outside a building and actually intercept wired Ethernet data packets without detection. Data encryption is the only line of defense against this kind of threat. Unfortunately, a sense of complacency among network managers has resulted in the limited use of in-building encryption, often with unforeseen and unknown results.

For Wireless: Key Audit and Security Checkpoints

Indeed, many wireless LAN products include encryption features as a standard or optional component. The IEEE 802.11 standard, for example, includes a security technique known as Wired Equivalent Privacy (WEP), which is based on the use of 64-bit keys and the popular RC4 encryption algorithm. The most recent addition to the IEEE series 802.11 wireless standards due to be issued late in 2003 is 802.11i Robust Security Network (RSN).

Control Concerns with IEEE 802.11 Wired Equivalent Privacy (WEP) Protocol

At a 2002 NIST-sponsored conference on wireless technology, there were some control concerns reported by users of the IEEE 802.11 Wired Equivalent Privacy (WEP) Protocol. In their opinion, WEP lacked group-keyed access control, provided no user authentication, and encryption appeared to be flawed. Two other vulnerabilities noted were that the radio signals extended beyond the property of the user, and any interception of those signals was hard to detect. To add to this area, the Virtual Private Network (VPN) solution to this was poor and unstable. At the time of the conference there was limited availability of VPN client software to handle this type of situation, and it was found that VPNs required frequent reconnection.

Station Authentication

Most WLAN products have the ability, as an authentication management function, to specifically authorize or exclude individual wireless stations. Thus an individual wireless user can be either included in the network or locked out. More importantly, users need to know a wide variety of information, including radio domains, channels (specific frequencies or hopping patterns), subchannels, security IDs, and passwords. Other information such as in-building roaming also needs to be known. Combining all of the above-mentioned aspects, the network administrators can make unauthorized network access extremely difficult for hackers even if they possess the specific wireless equipment being used at a given site.

Physical Security

Compared to the wired LANs, which have a significant amount of wire being exposed to outsiders, the WLANs eliminate possible mass physical contact points. While WLANs usually involve the use of a wired backbone network for access-point interconnection, the amount of wire is quite small, and extra steps can be taken to safeguard its physical integrity without inordinate cost. Moreover, since the access points used in WLANs function as bridges, individual wireless users are isolated from the majority of LAN traffic, again limiting user access to raw network packets.

IEEE 802.11i Robust Security Network Standard

This standard appears to enable WLANs to be trusted within the architecture and infrastructure. It provides native per-user access control, strong authentication capability (for example, smart badges, certificates, and token cards), and strong native encryption. At the conference, it was disclosed that this technology is in testing with the standards hopefully to be released by fall 2003. Some of the preliminary findings are that the new standard supports VLANs and will require a software-only upgrade to the application and radius server. At this time, this upgrade is critical as well as a control issue due to the fact that it has to be done right. The NIST conference found that the application and radius server configurations were complex and difficult. From a business standpoint, the decision to incorporate this technology is being driven by competition and demand. In planning for this technology and its implementation, testing and maintenance are critical along with a mandatory review point. The affordability aspect of implementing this technology at this time may be an issue if a business wants to secure and use it properly. In time, as technology solutions are found, it will be affordable. In the opinion of the NIST participants, it is an evolution and not a revolution. Better software upgrades are the key, not hardware replacements. Also, this technology must be strategically incorporated into the organizational infrastructure and coexist with the corporation infrastructure strategies.

The new IEEE 802.11i data protocols provide confidentiality, data origin authenticity, and replay protection. These protocols require a fresh key on every session. The key management capability delivers keys used as authorization tokens, providing channel access is authorized. The architecture requires the key to the authentication process.

Auditing End-User Computing

Once it is determined that an audit of an EUC group is required, the IT auditor needs management's agreement as to the audit objectives, audit method, and audit scope. The audit objectives may cover specific applications, end-user support, financial issues, or provide for strategic information to be reported to the management. Depending on the control environment and audit objectives, the audit method will be either formal or informal. Defining the EUC group for a particular environment will determine the audit scope of the audit.

Preliminary Audit Planning

PC applications have grown from individuals creating personal productivity tools into critical applications that are used by the entire corporation. The management may not fully realize the importance of EUC groups to the organization to dedicate the necessary resources for a complete and thorough applications audit. However, it is essential to have the management's support to overcome any obstacles put forth by the EUC groups. End users tend to think of their PCs as personal property, and they may be resentful of an intrusion by auditors. However, the end user's cooperation can be gained, in part, by explaining the criteria that the audit will measure. In addition, management support can be gained by providing them with a risk analysis that identifies the exposures of EUC.

Defining the Audit Methodology

The method used to conduct the audit depends on the environment being reviewed and the agreed-upon audit objectives. An inventory of end-user applications can be used to gain a general understanding of the EUC group. The auditor should discuss this inventory with management to determine what type of audit should be performed. For example, a more formal audit can be used if a specific application is being evaluated for reliance on financial information, whereas a statistical audit that collects sample data from transactions or supporting logs can confirm end-user practices. Auditors could also perform a quick, informal assessment by interviewing the IT staff about their impressions of the EUC group.

Defining the Scope and Content of the Audit

The scope limits the coverage of the audit to a particular department, function, or application. The content defines what aspects of a particular area are covered. Depending on the audit objective, the content covers general controls, application controls, hardware and software acquisition, systems development controls, change controls problem management, or disaster recovery.

The Audit Plan

The audit plan details the objectives and the steps to fulfill those objectives. Like any audit, an audit of an EUC group begins with a preliminary survey or analysis of the control environment by reviewing existing policies and procedures. During the audit, these policies and procedures should be assessed for completeness and operational efficiency. The preliminary survey or analysis should identify the organization's position and strategy for the EUC group and the responsibilities for managing and controlling it. The following are the kinds of steps performed to gather the necessary evidence on which to base audit findings, conclusions, and recommendations.

- *Evidence gathering:* A review of any documentation that the end-users group uses
- *Inquiry:* Conducting interviews with end users and any IT support technicians

- *Observation:* A walkthrough to become familiar with department procedures and to assess physical controls
- *Inventory:* A physical examination of any inventoried goods or products on hand in the EUC group
- *Confirmation:* A review of the end users' satisfaction surveys that were handed out and completed during the preliminary audit planning stages
- *Analytical procedures:* A review of data gathered from statistical or financial information contained in spreadsheets or other data files
- *Mechanical accuracy:* A review of the information contained in any databases used by the EUC group through testing procedures

After the evidence is gathered, the auditor should assess control strengths and weaknesses, taking into consideration the interrelationships between compensating and overlapping controls. These controls should be tested for compliance and to ensure that they are applied in accordance with management's policies and procedures. For example, management policy states that end users should change their passwords periodically to protect information resources. To test for compliance, the auditor identifies the controls that force password changes. Substantive tests determine the adequacy of these controls to prevent fraudulent activity. For example, software piracy puts the company at risk for fines and the potential loss of goodwill. Reviewing the directories on the LAN and PC drives for unlicensed software would assess the effectiveness of controls to ensure that only property-licensed software is installed.

Reviewing the EUC Group's Procedures and Objectives

IT should have policies or guidelines that cover EUC. These should be designed to protect company data. IT should also have standards to ensure that end users are not using hardware or software that is not supported by them. There should be an EUC policy that encompasses and is applicable to all EUC groups. If only departmental policies exist, each policy should be similar to ensure continuity between departmental policies. A company-wide policy should cover:

- Assignment of ownership of data
- User accountability
- Backup procedures
- Physical access controls to PCs
- Appropriate documentation of all EUC groups applications and adequate documentation changes and modifications
- Segregation of duties

Evaluating the EUC Group's Effectiveness by Reviewing Their Documentation

Because many end users are developing their own applications, often there is little or no documentation apart from the end user's own notes. Another audit concern is that several end users may be developing the same type of application independently of each other, which is an inefficient use of computer resources. For example, if an end user in accounting is developing an application that is already in use in payroll, there should be some type of documentation or reference for end users to consult in order to prevent duplication of effort.

Another problem posed by inadequate documentation is illustrated by this example. An end user has developed several applications that have become crucial to the operation of the company. This individual has left the company without leaving any documentation on those applications, and other end users must use this application and make modifications to it. This potential exists for multiple problems because of the lack of end-user documentation.

End users must assume responsibility for the maintenance of documentation for their application and ensure that it is complete, current, and accurate. The IT auditor can perform an effective management advisory role by highlighting and emphasizing the importance of EUC documentation.

Audit Testing

The auditor must address many considerations that cover the nature, timing, and extent of testing. The auditor must devise an auditing testing plan and a testing methodology to determine whether the previously identified controls are effective. The auditor also tests whether the end-user applications are producing valid and accurate information. For microcomputers, several manual and automated methods are available to test for erroneous data. An initial step is to browse the directories of the PCs in which the end-user-developed application resides. Any irregularities in files should be investigated. Depending on the nature of the audit, computer-assisted techniques could also be used to audit the application. The auditor should also conduct several tests with both valid and invalid data to test the ability and extent of error detection, correction, and prevention within the application. In addition, the auditor should look for controls such as input balancing and record or hash totals to ensure that the end user reconciles any differences between input and output. The intensity and extent of the testing should be related to the sensitivity and importance of the application. The auditor should be wary of too much testing and limit his or her tests to controls that cover all the key risk exposures and possible error types. The key audit concern is that the testing should reveal any type of exposure of sensitive data and that the information produced by the application is valid, intact, and correct.

The Audit Report

The audit report should inform management about the results of the review of the EUC group. It can also suggest support for resources to enhance end-user controls. In addition, the audit report should recommend policies and procedures that could strengthen end-user controls. Finally, the audit report should convince end users and management of the need for controlling EUC by identifying the importance of the information and assets stored on the PCs and LANs and by pointing out the risks to those assets.

The auditor's report should also inform management of the types of controls that are needed to increase efficiency and to decrease risk and exposure. These recommended controls should be defined in a cost versus benefit manner and should be expressed in terms that management will understand: How much it will cost the company if these types of controls are not in place? or how much the company can save if such types of controls are in place? After these recommendations have been made, approved, and implemented, the auditor should reevaluate the controls to ensure that they have been implemented and that they are effective.

Conclusion

We have covered a number of operational areas to give readers and future IT auditors the varied environment the IT audit professionals face and the depth of resources and experience they must possess. There are approaches, techniques, and methods to perform reviews of these complex areas.

Under the topic of disaster recovery planning, we have presented several crucial steps that disaster recovery planning authors have written about in detail. The repetition of the same steps by several different authors proves the importance of the subject. These can be used as audit steps to check the validity and reliability of the contingency and disaster recovery plan. These steps are crucial in determining where companies are regarding their disaster recovery planning. Based on this information, the auditors are able to determine the current condition of a company and provide the recommendations for each of the disaster recovery step findings.

As for DBMS recovery, it is everyone's business, especially the IT professional. The need for review of DBMS recovery is critical in order to be responsive to business requirements. The ability to recover and continue business operations can mean the difference between business loss and business profitability. Business worldwide is highly dependent on information collection and dissemination, recording of the business transaction, and reporting of the profitability.

Finally, data communications is a critical part of an organization's business systems. In this chapter we presented some steps and suggestions to help the auditor begin to understand this area; however, the rapid technological advances occurring in this field as well as the growth of data communications systems require that the auditor be familiar with new technological areas such as wireless technology and the emerging standards being applied in business.

Finally, the importance of EUC groups has grown considerably as a reaction to the strictly controlled IT environment. Unfortunately, end-user computing groups, to their detriment, have neglected most of the controls that were developed by IT. As end users create and maintain critical information, organizations must institute controls to ensure complete and accurate information. A balance should be achieved between control and flexibility to encourage innovation in a stable environment.

The role of IT and end users continues to change as technology changes. The role of the auditor will also continue to evolve in response to these changes. IT auditors must be aware of the changing environments to respond with viable suggestions for controlling information and resources. The EUC environment provides many opportunities for IT auditors' involvement in identifying risks and educating users and management on the need for effective controls. All areas are within the purview of IT, and they are all important for the IT auditor and the business manager.

Chapter Review Questions

1. Why is a contingency plan or disaster recovery plan an important tool to business?
2. What steps are considered as important to a disaster recovery plan?
3. What are some key attributes of the mission plan or the objectives of a disaster recovery plan?
4. Why does a disaster recovery plan need to be tested?
5. Define the term DBMS recovery.
6. What is a DBMS transaction?
7. What are some of the control concerns in the backup and recovery of data warehousing?
8. Define several typical transaction properties that must be reviewed in assessing recovery controls.
9. What are the four major types of failure that result from a major hardware or software malfunction?
10. Why should each data element be assigned to an end user?

11. What are some of the consequences of a lack of data communications controls or insufficient testing of existing controls?
12. What types of intervention do data communication controls depend on to ensure that they are functionally sound?
13. What are some of the control concerns associated with wireless technology?
14. What are three reasons that errors in data communications usually occur?
15. What are some typical types of end-user audit objectives?
16. What should an EUC policy cover?

Multiple Choice

1. To be effective, which groups must support a contingency and disaster recovery plan to offer a business the best chance to survive?
   a. Auditors and management
   b. Technical personnel and management
   c. Management and staff
   d. Auditors and security officers
2. In the September 11, 2001 New York Twin Towers disaster, what percent of the businesses did not survive?
   a. 25 percent
   b. 37 percent
   c. 42 percent
   d. 50 percent
3. To be usable, a disaster recovery plan must be:
   a. Written
   b. Approved
   c. Tested
   d. Enforced
4. The first step in the DBMS recovery process is:
   a. Taking corrective action
   b. Determining the source and extent of the damage
   c. Suspending normal processing
   d. Identifying that the database is an erroneous, damaged, or in a crashed state
5. According to the CERT, what percent of actual security incidents goes unreported?
   a. 20 percent
   b. 40 percent
   c. 60 percent
   d. 80 percent
6. WLANs are actually more secure than their wired counterparts because of:
   a. Threats to the physical security of network

b. A WLAN's having all of the properties of a wired LAN
c. An additional set of unique security elements
d. Unauthorized access and eavesdropping

7. WEP is based on the use of:
    a. 32-bit keys
    b. 64-bit keys
    c. 128-bit keys
    d. 256-bit keys

8. Which of the following is not true about the IEEE 802.11i data protocol?
    a. The protocol requires a fresh key every month.
    b. The key management capability provides channel access as needed.
    c. The architecture requires the key to the authentication process.
    d. The protocol requires a 256-bit key.

9. Which of the following would not be included in a companywide policy on EUC?
    a. Wireless encryption standards
    b. Appropriate documentation
    c. Segregation of duties
    d. Backup procedures

10. To be effective, auditor recommendations should be:
    a. Made
    b. Approved
    c. Implemented
    d. All of the above

Exercises

1. List five professional organizations that provide guidance or written studies on contingency planning and disaster recovery planning.
2. List five professional organizations that have provided studies or research on DBMS recovery and/or data warehousing control concerns.
3. Using Web browsers, review two reports issued by the U.S. General Accounting Office or the National Institute of Standards and Technology on the subject of information security: http://www.gao.gov and http://www.nist.gov
4. Read Case 6 from Appendix I on Wedco Electronics, and answer.
5. Identify five Web sites that provide IT auditors with useful information on auditing end-user computing.

Answers to Multiple Choice Questions

1 — c; 2 — b; 3 — c; 4 — b; 5 — d; 6 — c; 7 — c; 8 — c; 9 — a; 10 — d

References

1. Cam-Winget, N., T. Moore, D. Stanley, and J. Walker, IEEE 802.11i Overview, Presentation at NIST 802.11 Wireless LAN Security Workshop, December 4, 2002.
2. Murphy Smith, L., Planning for disaster, *The CPA Journal*, 64 (June 1994): http://www.nysscpa.ctg/cpajournal/old/16097614.htm
3. Computer Security Institute/FBI, 2003 Computer Security Institute/Federal Bureau of Investigation Computer Crime and Security Survey Results, Computer Security Institute, 2003.
4. Computer Security and Privacy: Concepts, Issues, and Resources: An Information Sourcebook, Computer Software, Lexikon Services, 2001–2002.
5. Dalton, G., Acceptable Risks, *Information Week*, August 31, 1998, pp. 36–48.
6. Disaster recovery planning checklist, *J. Acc.*, 177 (May 1994): 6.
7. Gallegos, F. and S. Allen-Senft, Control Issues in End-User Computing and Applications, in *Handbook of IS Management*, Auerbach Publishers, Boca Raton, FL. 1999.
8. Gallegos, F. and L. Freibott, *Data Warehousing: An Audit Approach*, EDP Auditing Series, #74-15-40, Auerbach Publishers, Boca Raton, FL. December 1999 issue, pp. 1–16.
9. Gallegos, F. and L. Tyson-Dualan, SAP Implementation and Control, in *Project Management*, CRC Press, Boca Raton, FL. July 1999 issue.
10. Gallegos, F. and J. Yin, *Auditing in a Client Server Environment*, EDP Auditing Series, #74-10-25, Auerbach Publishers, Boca Raton, FL. August 2000 issue, pp. 1–20.
11. Gallegos, F. and J. Yin, *Auditing Oracle*, EDP Auditing Series, #74-15-37, Auerbach Publishers, Boca Raton, FL. August 2000 issue, pp. 1–12.
12. Gallegos, F. and A. Carlin, *Auditing Systems Maintenance — A How to Approach*, EDP Auditing Series, #74-30-25, Auerbach Publishers, Boca Raton, FL. October 2000 issue, pp 1–12.
13. Gallegos, F., *Reviewing Focus Database Applications*, EDP Auditing Series, #74-10-23, Auerbach Publishers, Boca Raton, FL. January 2001 issue, pp. 1–24.
14. Gallegos, F. and K. Seketa, *Auditing Contingency and Business Continuity Planning*, Business Continuity Planning Best Practices Series, K. Doughty, Ed., Auerbach Publishers, Boca Raton, FL. 2000.
15. Gallegos, F., *Wireless LANs: Technology and Security Issues*, Enterprise Operations Management Series, # 46-40-65, Auerbach Publishers, Boca Raton, FL. November 2001 issue, pp. 1–16.
16. Gallegos, F. and L. Preiser-Houy, *Auditing Prototypes: Approaches and Techniques*, #74-30-60, Auerbach Publishers, Boca Raton, FL, December 2001, pp. 1–8.
17. Gallegos, F. and D. Manson, *Auditing DBMS Recovery Procedures*, #75-20-45, Auerbach Publishers, Boca Raton, FL. September 2002, pp. 1–20.
18. Gallegos, F., D. Manson, and S. Allen, *Audit Concerns for End-User Computing and Application Development*, #72-30-20, Auerbach Publishers, Boca Raton, FL. 1996, pp. 1–11.
19. Gallegos, F., D. Manson, and S. Allen, *How to Audit an End-User Computing Group*, #72-30-21, Auerbach Publishers, Boca Raton, FL. 1996, pp. 1–6.
20. Gallegos, F., D. Manson, and S. Allen, *Putting Together an Audit Program for End-User Computing Applications*, #72-30-22, Auerbach Publishers, Boca Raton, FL. 1996, pp. 1–12.
21. Gallegos, F., and D. Manson, *DBMS Recovery Procedures, Database Management Series*, #24-03-61, Auerbach Publishers, Boca Raton, FL. October 1997, pp.1–11.
22. Gallegos, F., *EDI Audit Risk Assessment*, EDP Auditing Series, #74-15-05, Auerbach Publishers, Boca Raton, FL. May 1998, pp. 1–12.
23. Gallegos, F. and W.L. Treinan, Data Communication Integrity Audits, *The Handbook of MIS Management: Supplement I*, Auerbach Publishers, Boca Raton, FL, 1986, pp. 1015–1025.

24. Pescatore, J., Wireless Networks: Can Security Catch up with Business, Presentation at NIST 802.11 Wireless LAN Security Workshop, December 2002.

25. United States General Accounting Office, Information Security: Serious Weaknesses Place Critical Federal Operations and Assets at Risk, GAO/AIMD-98-92, September 23, 1998.

26. United States General Accounting Office, Information Systems: VA Computer Control Weaknesses Increase Risk of Fraud, Misuse, and Improper Disclosure, GAO/AIMD-98-175, September 23, 1998.

27. United States General Accounting Office, Critical Infrastructure Protection, GAO-03-233, February 2003.

28. United States General Accounting Office, Information Security: Progress Made, but Challenges Remain to Protect Federal Systems and the Nation's Critical Infrastructures, GAO-03-564T, April 8, 2003.

29. United States General Accounting Office, Critical Infrastructure Protection: Efforts of the Financial Services Sector to Address Cyber Threats, GAO-03-173, January 30, 2003.

30. United States General Accounting Office, Information Security: Computer Controls over Key Treasury Internet Payment System, GAO-03-837, July 30, 2003.

31. United States General Accounting Office, Information Security: Further Efforts Needed to Fully Implement Statutory Requirements in DOD, GAO-03-1037T, July 24, 2003.

32. United States General Accounting Office, Information Security: Continued Efforts Needed to Fully Implement Statutory Requirements, GAO-03-852T, June 24, 2003.

33. United States General Accounting Office, FDIC Information Security: Progress Made but Existing Weaknesses Place Data at Risk, GAO-03-630, June 18, 2003.

34. United States General Accounting Office, Information Security: Progress Made, but Weaknesses at the Internal Revenue Service Continue to Pose Risks, GAO-03-44, May 30, 2003.

35. United States General Accounting Office, Homeland Security: Information Sharing Responsibilities, Challenges, and Key Management Issues, GAO-03-715T, May 8, 2003.

36. Weber, R., *Information Systems Control and Audit*, Prentice Hall, NJ, 1999.

Chapter 17
Using Tools and Techniques in IT Operation Reviews

Chapter 17 examines the multitude of support tools available to the IT auditor, which assist him in auditing IT operations. As this chapter suggests, the auditor's tool kit is a critical component in controlling audit processes through today's complex environment. The chapter will provide examples of uses of Computer-Assisted Audit Tools and Techniques (CAATTs) and the lessons learned as they pertain to audits of operations and issues of efficiency and effectiveness.

This chapter focuses on using audit tools and techniques during system maintenance and operating system reviews. Because systems maintenance is one of the least rewarding functions in the IT department, it is also one of the most neglected and often the area where control weaknesses can be found. Through a comprehensive review of this area, the IT auditor must evaluate the organization's change management process to determine whether software fixes and changes compromise the system's integrity. We provide a sample audit program of this process in Appendix 5.

During an audit of the operating system and other system software, it is extremely important that the auditor construct a logical audit program that will enhance the evaluation of the operating system software and support the audit findings and recommendations. This chapter identifies the key control areas of operating systems and provides the auditor with a sample audit program in Appendix 5.

The final four areas presented in this chapter are operational approaches in reviewing system application products (SAP) applications in a client/server environment and performing an ISO 9001 review. SAP is a revolutionary support product being acquired and implemented by many companies worldwide. An important role for today's information systems auditor is in the design of internal controls and the definition of security measures. Issues of implementation and control of SAP must be addressed by the management, user, and auditor. In this chapter, we provide general guidelines and suggested approaches to achieving both teamwork and success. The chapter also introduces a fast-growing area of computer-assisted audit tools, called computer forensics, supporting law enforcement, security, and audit professionals in computer forensics investigations. Also, discussed is the use and application of Webmetrics as audit tools for reviewing Web design, development, and usability.

The search for quality is a goal we strive for as audit professionals. This chapter provides both an approach and experiences in attaining International Standards Organization (ISO) 9001 certification. IT auditing plays a key role in this process. It is a reflection of corporate management support, institutional cooperation, and the search for better quality in information systems (IS) operations. Sample documents and work steps are provided in Appendix 5.

Computer-Assisted Audit Tools and Techniques for Operational Reviews

In Chapter 4, we cover a number of tools and techniques used for performing tasks to support the audit of applications. As we have seen in Chapters 13 and 14, most of these tools can be used to support operational reviews as well as collect information about the effectiveness of general controls over IS operations. Exhibit 1 lists sample of tools that can be used for different areas of review and support.

However, the use of tools need not be limited to specialized packages. Computer languages can be useful in performing operational tests and collecting information about the effectiveness of general controls. Even basic tools such as Access in MS Office can be used to take an imported data file of operational data (i.e., users' account information, file accesses, rights to number of file accesses, etc.), perform analysis on the file (histograms, frequencies, summaries), and then move data into MS Excel and visually portray information for management or even forecast trends with regard to workload, growth, and other IT operational areas.

Should the IT auditor have the technical capability to "design, develop, and implement" host routines to support audit function and activities, most fourth-generation languages offer full support. Exhibit 2 outlines the capability of the support available.

The methods or techniques in use for performing the reviews in the areas of systems maintenance, operating systems, client/server applications, and ISO 9001 will be presented. Please keep in mind that the ability to perform these tasks (the techniques) is supported by tools to gather information that may help determine if controls are working.

Exhibit 1. List of Selected Operational Audit Tools and Techniques for Client/Server, CAATS, Contingency Planning, and Data Warehousing/EDI

Name of Tool	Client/ Server Control	Computer Assisted Audit Tools	Contingency Planning	Data Warehousing and EDI Commerce
AXENT™ by Axent Technologies and Safestone Technologies PLC, Princeton, NJ	X	X		
SQL<>Secure by BrainTree Security Software, Norwell, MA	X	X		
LANSleuth by LANSleuth, DejaView+, LANPanther Systems, and Synchronous, Inc., Aurora, IL	X	X		
ACL by ACL Services Ltd., Vancouver, BC, Canada		X		
Idea and DATAs by Audimation Services, Inc., Houston, TX		X		
The Number-Audit Sampling by Linton Shafer Computer Services, Inc., Frederick, MD		X		X
ADM Plus by Joseph Pleier & Associates, Mission Viejo, CA		X		
WizWhy™ and WizRule™ by Wizsoft Inc., Syosset, NY		X		
Remote Shadow by Advanced Systems Concepts, Parsippany, NJ	X		X	
Recovery PAC and Recovery PAC Web by CSCI, a Harris Recovery Group Company, Ridgefield, CT			X	X
SAM by Intra Computer, Inc., Jamaica, NY	X		X	
Disaster Recovery System (DRS) by TAMP Computer Systems Inc., Merrick, NY	X		X	X
SSA-Name3 by Search America Software, Old Greenwich, CT		X		X
C.O.D. 32, Double Check, and Achieve by IPS of Boston, Braintree, MA				X

Exhibit 2. Fourth-Generation Languages and Other Products as Support Tools

Product	Environment					Application-Generation Function															Human Factoring		Database Support			
	IBM Environment	Server Environment	Tool Available on PC	Micro-to-Mainframe Link	Full PC Implementation	Query Language	Report Generator	Screen Painter/Data Entry	Graphics Generator	Decision-Support Tools	Subset for End Users	IT Professionals	Procedural Language	Interface-to-Action Diagrams	Well-Structured Code	Provable Specifications	Heavy-Duty Computing	Full COBOL Replacement	Recommended for Information Centers	HELP Facility	Computer-Aided Instruction	Computer Aided Thinking	Support Database Management	Standard DBMS Package	Data Dictionary	Data-Modeling Tool
MS Office	×	×	×		×	×	×	×	×	×	×	×		×					×	×		×	×	×	×	×
SQL	×	×	×		×	×	×	×	×	×	×	×		×					×	×		×	×	×	×	×
Perl	×	×	×			×	×	×	×	×	×	×	×		×				×	×			×	×	×	×
SAP	×	×		×		×	×	×	×	×	×	×	×		×				×	×	×		×	×	×	
QBE	×					×	×	×			×												×	×		
QMF	×	×	×	×	×	×	×	×	×	×	×	×		×	×				×	×			×	×	×	×
ACL	×	×	×	×					×	×		×	×	×					×	×		×	×			
IDEA	×	×	×	×	×	×	×	×	×	×	×	×		×	×	×	×	×	×	×	×	×	×			
Oracle	×	×	×	×				×	×	×	×	×	×	×	×			×	×	×			×	×	×	×
WebMetrics 3.0	×	×	×		×	×	×		×	×	×	×					×			×	×					
C++	×	×	×	×		×	×	×	×	×	×	×	×	×	×		×	×	×	×		×	×	×		
SAS	×	×	×		×					×	×	×					×		×	×		×			×	
VS-Basic	×	×		×		×		×	×		×	×	×	×	×		×	×	×	×			×	×		
DMS	×		×							×	×	×					×							×	×	
SPSS	×		×														×		×	×		×			×	
Application Factory												×					×					×	×			
Asset	×	×	×																×						×	×
JAVA	×	×	×		×							×							×	×	×					×

Systems Maintenance

Systems maintenance, one of the most unnoticed and thankless jobs performed within the IT facility, carries one of the highest risks of exposure. Maintenance is rarely acknowledged when it is done right but is always noticed when something goes wrong. For newly installed systems, the job of the maintenance group is to track down and eliminate the remaining bugs in the system. Once a system is operational, the maintenance group is responsible for making the changes requested by the user until the entire system is replaced and the development cycle begins all over again.

All systems require some maintenance, but the time and expense associated with maintenance can be reduced if systems are developed and implemented in a controlled environment according to specific user requirements. We focus on postimplementation maintenance for installed, operational systems.

Definition of Systems Maintenance

Systems maintenance can be defined simply as changes made to systems or applications software to maintain an effective, efficient, operational, and up-to-date system. These changes, which are generally requested by system users or provided by vendors or programmers, are made to meet users' requirements or correct minor system errors before they become major problems. Maintenance can be applied to several areas within the IT facility, including:

- Systems hardware
- Systems software
- Database software
- Applications software
- Environmental areas
- Network software
- Network hardware

This section of the chapter addresses maintenance for systems, applications, and network software. (Because systems and network software maintenance is generally performed by the systems programming group, no distinction is made between the two types of software in this article; both are classified as systems software.) The major difference between systems and applications software maintenance is that changes to systems software can affect an organization's entire data processing capability, whereas changes to application system or program within the facility have more limited effects.

As a result, systems software changes present a higher level of risk than applications software changes. Systems software is especially vulnerable because it supports and interacts with database systems. An erroneous change or faulty link to a database system or its supporting systems software can corrupt information throughout an organization. Therefore, maintenance changes affecting such systems should be closely reviewed.

The primary focus of a systems maintenance audit is the change of control process, or how IT personnel manage change. Adequate controls must be in place to minimize, detect, and correct accidental errors and omissions and malicious or fraudulent changes to software systems. The following sections describe change management within IT organizations and detail the steps needed to audit systems maintenance.

Change Control

The most important area of control in any information processing environment is change control. Given the complexity of hardware, software, and application relationships in the operating environment, each change must be properly defined, planned, coordinated, tested, and implemented.

Effective change management reduces the risk of disruption of IT services. Once a change has been proposed, it must be evaluated for risk and impact. If a proposed change introduces significant risk to the operating environment, all parties affected must be notified, the appropriate level of management must approve the implementation schedule, and backout plans must be developed to remove the change from the system if necessary. The proposed change must be reviewed by change management personnel for potential conflicts with other systems. The change management process should be reviewed periodically to evaluate its effectiveness.

A well-defined, structured, and well-implemented change management system benefits the IT organization by:

- Reducing system disruptions that can lead to business losses
- Minimizing the number of backouts called by ineffective change implementation
- Providing consistent change implementation that permits management to allocate staff and system time efficiently and meet scheduled implementation dates
- Providing accurate and timely documentation to minimize the impact to change-related problems

The implementation of a sound change management process simplifies systems maintenance audits. The auditor obtains the necessary background information, determines the key controls, performs limited substantive testing to assess the reliability and effectiveness of the process controls, and evaluates the process.

The auditor must take the time to become thoroughly familiar with the change control process. He or she should develop a flowchart of the process in which points of origination and initiation, approval points, changes to documentation, and review points are all identified.

There are three types of changes: routine, nonroutine, and emergency. Routine changes typically have minimal impact on daily operations. They can be implemented or backed out quickly and easily. Nonroutine changes potentially have a greater impact on operations. They frequently affect many users and typically have lengthy, complex implementation and back-out procedures. An emergency change is any change, major or minor, that must be made quickly, without following standard change control procedures. Management must approve such changes before they are undertaken or implemented. The auditor should develop flowcharts documenting the procedures for emergency and nonemergency changes. Exhibit 3 is a typical flowchart for nonemergency changes. Exhibit 4 documents emergency change procedures.

Points of Change Origination and Initiation

The auditor should identify the people or groups who initiate changes. Vendors, computer operations staff, application or system programmers, or users request most changes. In addition, the auditor should ascertain that all requests are submitted on a standard change request form that contains the following information:

- Date of request
- Name of requester
- Description of the change
- Reason for the change
- Approvals of the request
- Areas that may be affected by the change

The urgency of each request should be determined and all requested changes should be filed by priority and date. The process must also provide the means for implementing emergency changes in response to an operational problem. Control points for emergency change processing should be established to record, document, and obtain subsequent approval for changes. Emergency changes should be cross-referenced to operations problem reports to help verify the proper recording and handling of the changes.

Each change request should be numbered sequentially and recorded in a change log at a central control point. Most organizations use online tools to facilitate this process. The change request is entered online and, based on the areas affected, electronically routed to those areas for approval. The responsible area's approval is also recorded online. Any and all discussions

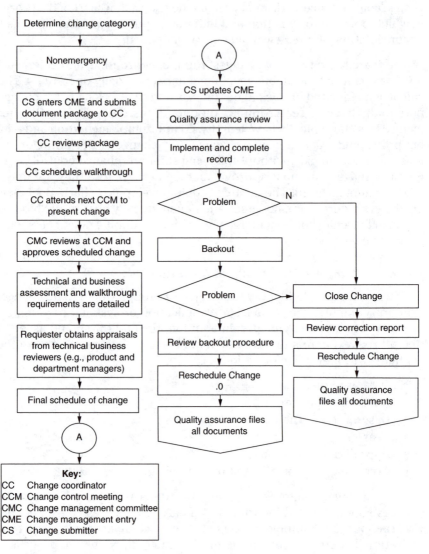

Exhibit 3. Procedure Flowchart for Nonemergency Changes

regarding that change are documented online. Once the change has been scheduled, the online system will notify users of the upcoming change; it will provide a confirmation once the change has occurred. Storing this information online allows management to perform a subsequent review of all changes for a variety of reasons. One may be the routine occurrence of the same type of emergency, indicating that the changes are fixing the symptom and not the underlying problem. Also, management could analyze what amounts of their

446

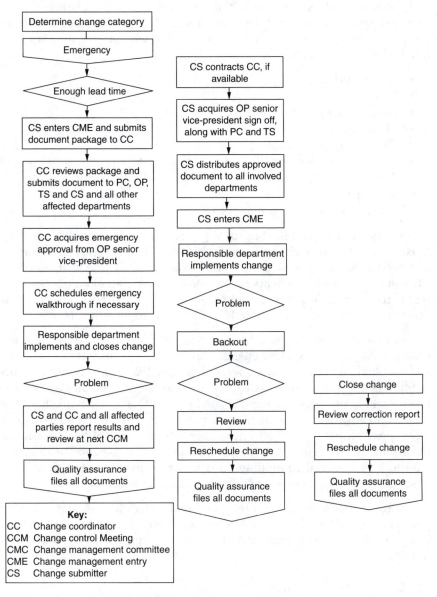

Exhibit 4. Procedure Flowchart for Emergency Changes

resources are devoted to the routine, nonroutine, and emergency changes. If one application is requiring a significant amount of resources for changes, this may be an indicator that the application is reaching the point of where replacing it may be more cost-effective.

Approval Points

Approval points should be scheduled throughout the change control process. All key people and departments affected by a change should be notified of its implementation schedule. Those who may require notification include:

- Users of the system
- Vendors
- Application programmers
- IT management
- Operations personnel
- Data control personnel
- Network management
- Auditors
- Third-party service providers

An important part of the approval process often overlooked is testing. Most system software changes cannot be tested in a safe test environment and need to be made in the production environment. These changes either work or do not work. Application changes are of a different nature than system software changes and should be verified in a test environment. Who does the testing and verification depend on the application change.

Application changes can be grouped into system or functionality changes. Application system changes are typically transparent to the end user and usually improve the speed of processing transactions. The programming support group, instead of the end users, typically tests these changes. Functionality changes are obvious to the end user and should be tested and approved by them. Functionality changes should be verified in a test environment. The test environment is a mirror of the production environment, which includes the data, programs, or objects. The data files should be expanded to include unusual or nonroutine transactions to ensure that all transaction types are used in the testing.

Approval levels should be predetermined as to who can approve what changes. Part of the change control process should ensure that the appropriate approval level is obtained before any changes are moved into production.

Changes to Documentation

As a system ages, the task of keeping track of changes and their impact on the operating system, operations environment, and application programs becomes increasingly difficult. The organization should maintain a record of all changes made to the system. Without such a record, it is impossible to determine how proposed changes will affect the system. Not only should the change be documented with the change request but also in the programmer's documentation. Programmer documentation is absolutely necessary for future maintenance.

It is also important to know when and why changes were requested but not implemented. With personnel changes, you may be revisiting an issue already deemed to be undeserving of time but it must be revisited to ensure integrity. The opposite can also be true where a previously undeserving issue could have merit due to the changing business environment.

Review Points

The change process must be carefully coordinated if changes to the system are to be successfully implemented. The auditor should determine that the following steps in the review process are followed:

- Pending changes are reviewed with key personnel in operations, application programming, network and data control, and auditing.
- Written change notification is sent to all interested parties, informing them of the nature of the change, scheduling of the change, purpose of the change, individual responsible for implementing the change, and systems affected by the change.
- Sufficient response time is provided for interested parties to examine proposed changes. The change notification should indicate the response deadline and the individual to contact for additional information.
- Periodic (e.g., weekly) change control meetings should be held to discuss changes with key personnel.
- Reports are filed on implemented changes to record postimplementation results and successes as well as problems.

Appendix V, Exhibit 1 provides a generalized audit program for use in most IT environments. Depending on the size and complexity of the organization, the program may need to be revised or expanded to obtain adequate audit coverage of the system maintenance function. Exhibit 5 illustrates program maintenance activities and controls and provides examples of errors.

Reviewing Operating Systems

As computers become more sophisticated, many manual operations are automated within the systems software. Systems software includes any program or system that helps interconnect or control the elements of input, output, processing, data, and application programs. Typically, this software is provided by outside vendors and falls into one of the following categories:

- Operating systems
- System utilities

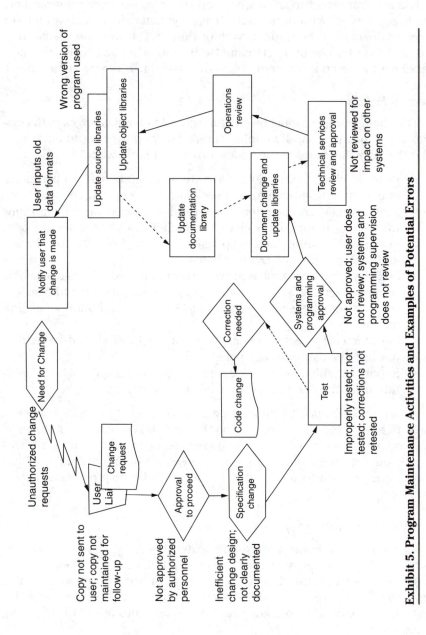

Exhibit 5. Program Maintenance Activities and Examples of Potential Errors

- Program library systems
- File maintenance systems
- Security software
- Data communications systems
- Database management systems (DBMS)

Each category usually represents a complete system and could be the basis for an individual audit. The audit program is critical in determining overall relationships between the application and the systems software and the extent to which systems software controls influence an application's accuracy and reliability. The audit program provides detailed procedures for thoroughly evaluating specific types of system software.

When evaluating system software controls, the auditor has several areas of concern, including:

- Types and uses of systems software
- Reliance on systems software to perform control processes
- Controls over access to systems software
- Controls over changes to systems software

This article examines these concerns and provides a sample audit program for an operating system.

Types and Uses of System Software

Most organizations rely on the operating system to:

- Manage computer resources with minimum operator intervention
- Help programmers and operators control the operation and allocation of peripheral devices and other computer resources
- Minimize the differences between a given manufacturer's line of computers, thus facilitating the transfer of application programs

In addition, many system utilities (e.g., copy and sort programs) are heavily used. To better understand systems software, the auditor should obtain complete technical descriptions and documentation from vendors.

In some computer centers, systems software controls application programs, tape and disk computer files, and other resources require greater security. For example, program library systems usually control all application programs, including the functions for accessing files, updating information, and converting from source to object code. Most of these packages contain an audit trail feature that records all changes made to application programs, including identification of the programmers making the changes. When properly implemented, this software promotes better security and backup of application programs.

451

File management systems perform similar functions for security and backup of tape and disk files. These software packages help reduce manual library functions and, in many cases, eliminate the need for external file labels. The audit trail feature is usually standard and shows when and by whom a particular file was created and used.

Security software packages are one of the newer methods of automating access controls. They control access to the computer system by identifying individuals who try to gain access to various system resources and verifying access legitimacy. Typically, these packages control terminals (e.g., hardwired or dial-up access); remote job entry stations; individual tape, disk, or mass storage data sets; individual application programs; and other systems software (e.g., operating systems and DBMSs). These packages usually provide an audit trail of all accesses, including authorized and unauthorized attempts.

For applications using online dial-up terminals, data communications software usually provides an interface among messages to and from terminals, the operating system, data files, and, if present, the DBMS. In addition, this system software typically:

- Controls access to and from terminal devices
- Polls and receives messages from computer terminals or other computers
- Addresses messages and sends them back to terminals or other computers
- Edits input and output messages
- Handles errors
- Reroutes messages when a particular terminal or communications line is inoperative
- Performs online formatting on visual display terminals

When data throughout an organization has been combined into a single database to eliminate redundancy and improve access, a DBMS is used to update the database, retrieve data from it, and provide controls over its use. The DBMS enables several users to share data and allows many different application programs to access the single database. The DBMS provides the interface between the application program's logical view of the database and the computer system's physical storage of the database.

Reliance on Systems Software

Organizations rely on systems software in varying degrees to control information-processing functions. The auditor should first identify the types and uses of systems software that affect the system under review and then determine the organization's level of reliance on that software.

452

Operating systems, by their nature, are heavily relied on for general operation of computer hardware. As such, they warrant further investigation. The auditor should determine whether:

- An application program can access main or data storage areas or files being used by another application program.
- Important security and accuracy features (e.g., error handling for invalid data types or formats) are fully used and are not being overridden by application programs or system programmers.
- Access to and use of privileged instructions (e.g., input and output instructions that would enable reading or writing of data from another user's file) is restricted.
- Scheduling functions are self-processing or require extensive operator intervention.

The use of system utility software varies greatly among organizations. The most commonly used utilities are copy and sort programs. Regardless of type, the auditor should determine whether:

- Utilities are properly controlled.
- Control features within the utilities are properly used.
- Utilities can be used to bypass control features of other systems or software packages.

Program library systems, when properly implemented and operated, add another level of control over an organization's application programs. Because the software packages are vulnerable to misuse and inadvertent error, the auditor should determine whether:

- Adequate manual procedures support and enhance the reliability of the program library system.
- Control features of the program library system are fully used and cannot be overridden or bypassed.
- The program library system consistently and accurately controls application programs.

File maintenance systems are similar to program library systems except that they help control automated data files instead of application programs. If implemented and operated properly, file maintenance systems increase the level of control. The auditor should determine whether:

- Adequate manual procedures support and enhance the reliability of the file maintenance system.
- Control features of the file maintenance systems are fully used and cannot be overridden or bypassed.
- The file maintenance system consistently and accurately controls automated data files.

Security software also provides an extra level of protection. To ensure that reliance on this software does not create a false sense of security, the auditor should determine whether proper security control features are being used and whether they can be bypassed or overridden.

For telecommunications applications, data communications software provides the interface between user terminals and the computer-based system. In most cases, such systems software provides additional security and reliability controls. The auditor should determine whether:

- Workstation use is restricted to authorized personnel for legitimate purposes only.
- Controls ensure that no transactions are lost, added to, or changed during transmission.
- All control procedures of the data communications software are being used and cannot be bypassed or overridden.

For applications in the database environment, a DBMS can control and maintain the organization's database. The auditor should determine whether:

- The DBMS consistently maintains accurate and reliable data.
- Security over different data elements restricts access to authorized users only.
- Proper backup is provided for the database.

Controlling Access to Systems Software

To maintain separation of duties, management must keep the responsibility for controlling and maintaining systems software separate from the responsibility for applications; that is, a distinction should be made between systems and applications programmers.

The job of systems programmers is to ensure that the systems software continues to function accurately and reliably. Systems programmers usually have access to all systems software. This concentration of functions, however, causes a control problem because the systems programmer can control the entire operation of the organization's computers. As a result, activities of systems programmers must be controlled to reduce the programmers' ability to perform unauthorized or damaging acts that could impair the accuracy and reliability of the systems. A primary control is strong supervision. Adequate supervisory procedures should be established, even though supervisors may lack the technical proficiency needed to ensure detailed scrutiny. In addition, security background investigations should be conducted periodically.

In a database environment, the database administrator usually has complete access to and control over the DBMS. This administrator is usually responsible for preserving the integrity of the database, maintaining data definitions, and preventing unauthorized use of or change to the database. Database administrators, like systems programmers, should be carefully supervised and double-checks with database users should be performed. For example, a database administrator may initiate DBMS changes that a systems programmer implements. The database administrator, however, should be the only person with complete access to the entire database and the only one who changes access levels for other database users.

Controlling Changes to System Software

Control procedures over changes to system software must be established and followed. Such controls help maintain software integrity and prevent unauthorized or inaccurate software changes. Although most changes are initiated as maintenance changes described by the software vendor, the organization should control system software changes by:

- Establishing formal change procedures and forms that require supervisory authorization before implementation
- Ensuring that all changes are thoroughly tested
- Removing critical files and application programs from the computer area while the system programmer is making the change

SAP Implementation and Control Issues

Enterprise resource planning systems (ERPS) such as SAP R/3's enterprisewide integrated system may be the answer to the needs of many organizations. After recognizing the threats, accurately assessing their ramification, and developing ways to mitigate the risks associated with R/3, auditors will be ready to begin implementation. The implementation of R/3 should be performed with its unique characteristics in mind. This section will discuss both general implementation guidelines and specific guidelines unique to the R/3 environment.

Understanding the Corporate Culture

The first factor involves understanding the corporate culture of your company in relation to the corporation's readiness and capability for change. There is a difference between seeing the necessity for change and actually making changes. ERPs such as SAP are an enterprisewide implementation that will affect many if not all of the departments. Thus, understanding each department and its issues is important. Many decentralized organizations may find that their divisions may not welcome change that affects their territory. Thus, resistance to change is common. The implementation team will need to "unfreeze the organization" or prepare the organization for the change. By educating the users about the R/3 system and involving the user departments in the decision-making process, project teams can develop stronger acceptance of the system change.

Understood and Complete Process Changes

The second critical success factor requires the completion of all business process changes. These changes must occur prior to implementation. Thus, difficult decision making can be done early. Each company should perform some level of business process reevaluation or redesign prior to implementing SAP. The cost and difficulty of changing the way a packaged system is configured after implementation is far greater than that of making the most informed decisions early. It is important to understand the structural and policy decisions that must be made.

In addition, auditors should reevaluate the controls in the newly designed processes. Emphasis should be placed on the new risks associated with the new objectives. As the controls available in the new system will differ from the previous environment, auditors can perform proactive design phase review to address exposures inherent in the new system.

Communication: Never Enough!

The third factor deals with communication. It is important to communicate continuously with new users at all levels in business other than in technical terms. Employees who are affected by the new system need to be informed of its progress so that their expectations will be set accurately. People need to be notified many times about change. Communication is the key to managing expectations. When expectations are set too high, people tend to become frustrated, upset, and disappointed with the results. When they are set too low, people may have difficulty adapting or are surprised with the extent of the change. Thus, to allow people time to accept and fully use the new system, a rigorous communication program should be adopted.

Auditors evaluating the system development phase of R/3 can ensure that the team is performing communication activities appropriately by reviewing minutes form meetings and workshops, interviewing users, and watching for behavioral problems. Lack of communication will create tension and resistance to the system change. By helping employees see their work and as part of the whole, or how it fits into the final product, the team can help to communicate that the success of project depends on the efforts of all employees.

Management Support

Acquiring superior executive support for the project is essential from the beginning. Executive management must spearhead the effort to conform to the R/3 structure. Executives need to provide active leadership and commitment during the implementation of R/3. Their efforts to personally engage in the change process will provide the support needed to gain success in this project. Many companies or divisions within an organization will be reluctant to change their business to fit the R/3 Framework. Some may become territorial and want to sabotage the project. According to a survey of executives, the initial phase is the hardest part of implementation. The organization must align its policies and processes with SAP. R/3 is a centralized, top-down, and structured approach. It works well when companies are able to operate within these limits. Executive management must encourage dedication to the reengineering effort.

R/3 requires full reengineering, not just automation to employee job tasks. Empowerment from the start will ensure success to the business process improvement efforts.

SAP Project Manager Competence

Another relevant and critical success factor deals with project management. The project manager should be capable of negotiating on even terms with the technical, business, and change management requirements. Integrated change blends both the organizational and technical solutions into one large-scale change. In this, many concerns fall between the cracks. With an enterprisewide integrated information system, there is a need to address issues from all perspectives. Thus, the project manager as well as the project team should be sensitive to the impact of the new technology, new business processes, and changes in organizational structures, standards, and procedures on the project as a whole. This will help him or her from becoming overwhelmed by the sometimes conflicting requirements of the implementation project.

The Team

A project team that includes both IT and business personnel will find the balance to be more effective. After defining project roles up front, team members should be reminded that they would be expected to shift to non-traditional roles. With R/3, many IT roles shift to the users. Customizing the R/3 software to fit the requirements of a particular function becomes a user responsibility. Users configure the systems by using the tables and functions to run their business in the new way. They are responsible for modifying and maintaining the tables. Thus, with many IT responsibilities shifting to the users, the project teams will be more effective when they are composed of not only IT personnel but also of people from the business departments that are affected by the new system. In addition, many companies are strengthening their R/3 project teams by adding outside consultants. These firms are able to provide project leadership support and R/3 and ABAP/4 expertise that are not always readily available in-house.

Project Methodology: It Is Important

Another critical success factor relates to chosen project methodology. It should act as a road map to the project team. Objectives should be clear and measurable so that progress can be reviewed at intervals. Setting measurement goals is a key aspect of reengineering. They demonstrate the effectiveness of actual improvements. System integration projects are complicated and require detailed attention. All interfaces should be documented so that any implication of change will be given the required attention. Whatever the methodology taken, auditors must keep in mind that no single approach will work best at all times. The auditor must evaluate how a particular implementation approach was chosen and assess its appropriateness to the R/3 project.

Training

It is also important to train users at all levels and provide support for all job changes. The SAP environment will change the roles of many of the employees. Current skills need to be reassessed and new skills need to be identified. The changing nature of the jobs will mean that management will need to provide support via new job definitions, rewards and recognitions, and reevaluation of pay schedules. Education reflects a financial commitment to the effort and promotes problem-solving skills. Problem-solving skills empower employees to make effective changes.

It is also important to provide the project team members with the training that will help them succeed in the project, such as training in the technology, the business, and change management issues. But training is not enough; it is only the beginning with R/3. It is difficult to master all the modules because the system is complex. Experimentation is the only way to arrive at the best choice; it also locks in the learning. Users of the system have hundreds of ways to access the same data. They will need to understand what will and will not happen with certain parameters. SAP encourages the "sandbox" approach so that users can understand in elaborate detail exactly what the system is designed to do. Even team members need to try multiple options before they choose the configuration that works best for them.

Commit to the Change

Problems will definitely arise and the project team should expect them. The project scale and complexity of R/3 renders that problems will surface throughout the implementation effort. The project leader and team, however, must continue to persevere and remain committed to the information system change. Thus, although the project team will run into resistance and problems, commitment to the change will help overcome the tides of reengineering. With management's persistence and consistency, the team will be able to overcome the pitfalls.

In today's client/server environment, corporate success with SAP requires diligence for all the critical success factors; there is little tolerance for mediocre performance. The auditors and project teams that encourage the consideration of these critical factors will set a winning course for their implementation of the R/3 system.

Establishing Security and Controls

SAP R/3 imposes on an organization a changed computer environment and a stronger reliance on networked computers. Thus, there is a need for the reassessment of the Information Security Architecture. The Security Architecture is the foundation of all diverse computing and networking elements of an organization. It is imperative that Information Security Architectures provide for consistent administration and monitoring tools and techniques, common identification and authentication processes, and an alerting capability that meets realistic needs.

In an earlier chapter, we went into SAP R/3 applications security in-depth, so we will not cover that here other than as a reminder. Lastly, we will discuss the impact of R/3's electronic data interchange (EDI) and Internet capabilities on security.

Security Features of the Basis Component

Auditors are challenged with ensuring that adequate controls are in place in information systems. Controls should reduce business risks and security exposures. Fortunately, the SAP Business Connection module has built-in security features. They provide for security-related concerns of applications, data, and resources. SAP's security and control capabilities support identification, authentication, and authorization of system users to ensure that only authorized users are able to access specific transactions, tables, modules, or the entire R/3 system. In addition, SAP programs and data are internally protected from other applications and utilities. Thus, with SAP's security and control features, the complex R/3 environment can be adequately safeguarded.

The effectiveness of the security system depends on the combination of the security measures implemented. Security measures should uniquely define individual users to the system and prove or confirm their identity. In addition, they should determine whether users are allowed access to certain resources. The IT auditor needs to review the major areas below. These are SAP's unique security components and how they work together to support the identification, authentication, and authorization of the R/3 users.

- Logon process
- User master records
- SAP
- TSTC table

- Authorization objects
- Authorization value sets
- Authorization profiles
- Additional authorization checks
- Changes

Summary of Access Control

In summary, the R/3 process for user access is very detailed. Before a user can initiate a transaction, SAP performs an access checking process. When the user enters the User ID and password, the system checks the User ID and only allows valid users with the appropriate password to gain access. After gaining access, the user can initiate a transaction. However, if the transaction is not defined or locked in the TSTC table, it is rejected. Further, if an additional authorization check has been defined, the user's authorization value set for the object is tested. It is rejected if the user is not authorized for the additional check. Lastly, the other detailed authorizations of the user (that are stored in profiles and in authorization value sets) are checked by the system to determine whether the user is authorized for the object.

In R/3, user access capabilities are managed by the user master records, authorization profiles, and authorization value sets. To ensure that all user access is consistent with management policies, procedures, and guidelines, control must be exercised over changes to user master records, profiles, and authorization value sets. The R/3 system provides standard authorization objects specifically for this purpose. Thus, they can be used to control the actions of the administrator in relation to different user groups. They can also specify the profiles an administrator is able to maintain, and the profiles a user is able to add to a user master record. Further, the authorization value sets that an administrator is able to maintain and enter into a profile can also be restricted.

Administrative Controls

Administrative controls are implemented via documented policies and procedures and are exercised by people rather than the system. These controls address access to data, system development, customization and modification, and maintenance processes. The automated control procedures offered through the SAP system are more effective when reinforced with control procedures. Business-based policies and procedures should be established to address accountability, access control, confidentiality, integrity, and security management issues.

Accountability

As users become developers of the R/3 system, they will be customizing the system through changes to the tables. Segregation of duties between

460

the users and the IT department will become imperative to ensure accountability. Thus, polices should address and monitor segregation of duties. For example, customization should be separated from the production environment and procedures should allow only properly tested and approved changes to be copied into production. Likewise, access to customization functions should be prevented in the production environment and all changes should require approval and require sign-off by users and IT management. In addition, a detailed security policy should specify the ownership of the system and data and require the documentation of all system changes. Management should review system logs for unauthorized table changes and follow up and investigate any unauthorized use of the system. Lastly, physical access to the servers and workstations should be restricted to authorized personnel.

Access Control

Access to SAP data and transactions are restricted by the SAP security system. However, standards and procedures will ensure that management has authorized access rights, users' accesses are relevant to their duties, and that access rights are not incompatible. Thus, the following segregation of duty procedures should be established:

1. Users' direct access capability should be restricted by the operating system and database.
2. Users' access rights should be approved and documented by management.
3. User master records should be assigned for each user to prevent sharing of IDs and passwords.
4. Passwords should be kept confidential and should be difficult to divulge.
5. Passwords should be changed regularly.
6. Management should regularly review and follow up on any access violations.
7. Access to the SAP system during nonworking hours should be minimized and adequately controlled.

Confidentiality, Integrity, and Security Management

The environmental controls within SAP can be compromised if access or changes to SAP programs and data from other applications and utilities are not properly restricted. Thus, the following issues should be reviewed to ensure that the security system is not negated:

1. The ability to change the system and start-up profiles should be appropriately restricted.
2. The SAP user master record should not be deleted and users should not be able to delete this record.

3. DYNPROs changes should be prohibited in the production environment and should be restricted to appropriate, authorized users.
4. Additional authorization checks for potentially dangerous transactions should be defined in the TSTC and should not be changed or deleted.
5. Review of users given access as batch administrators should be performed periodically because these users can perform any operations on all background jobs in the R/3 system.
6. Batch input session files that have been created by an interface program or an internal SAP program should not be modified prior to the release stage.
7. Changes to the ABAP/4 Dictionary should be adequately tested and authorized.
8. Standard table entries should be removed when not intended to be used for a particular installation.
9. ABAPs should be assigned to appropriate authorization groups so that users cannot execute ABAPs that are not relevant to their work functions.

EDI and Internet Security

SAP R/3 is not immune to intrusion and exploitation from outsiders. R/3 supports EDI and has recently released Internet capabilities for their R/3 processes. EDI and the Internet make security issues more critical because external intruders can degrade the integrity of the system and jeopardize company assets. Thus, security policies should accommodate the unique needs of EDI and the Internet.

Dangers threatening EDI messages include the compromise of message integrity, message repudiation, disclosure of confidential data, misrouting of messages, and delaying of messages. To ensure that EDI messages arrive at appropriate destinations and are only accessed by authorized users, security mechanisms and procedures must be employed. EDI security mechanisms available include encryption, digital signatures, key management, and sealing. Unfortunately, these tools are not all available within the R/3 system. At this time, they will need to be installed outside the R/3 environment. Therefore, auditors must ensure that the overall Security Architecture includes security mechanisms that support EDI. In addition, procedures to ensure that information transferred via EDI is complete and accurate should be established.

With the advent of the Internet, computer hackers are becoming more sophisticated. As companies combine SAP with the advantages of the Internet, security threats will continue to multiply. In an integrated system such as R/3, a hacker may be able to compromise not only a small section of the system but all the systems connected to the basic component. Thus, it is even more crucial to ensure that basic Internet security measures are applied. Examples of Internet security measures include installing internal and external firewalls, using security tools to find well-known security problems and holes, and making safe computing practices a condition for employment. Although SAP provides Internet capabilities, they do not yet provide for the encryption or encoding of TCP/IP packets over the Internet.

The ISO 9001 Review

Worldwide, the search for quality in how we do our work has advanced through many different efforts and program. The ISO 9001 review is an outcome of the process. The audit community is to be commended for its efforts and search for excellence. Moreover, professionals worldwide strive through many different programs to attain improvement in what they do and how they do it. This is a brief description of several of the major quality programs.

CRBE (Formerly Known as CTQA)

The Chairman's Recognition for Business Excellence (CRBE), formerly known as the Chairman's Total Quality Award initiative, is based on the Malcolm Baldrige National Quality Award Criteria. The first year of implementation was 1991. The applications are reviewed by teams of trained, voluntary examiners. Collective findings are presented to the applicant via a feedback report that highlights strengths (for reinforcement) and weaknesses (for advance towards world class quality). CRBE judges send teams on site visits for further investigation. There were 47 applicants with 6 site visits in 1995. Of the 25 applicants for 1994, 19 were repeats from 1993; 14 of those had applied in 1992, while 4 had applied in 1991.

SEI

Named after the Software Engineering Institute, SEI is based on the Capability Maturity Model (CMM). The purpose of SEI is to put a program in place so that the good ideas about what can be done to improve an organization could be heard and acted upon. The CMM specifies which areas need to be addressed first by identifying six key process areas to help provide a road map to go from level one (the lowest level on the scale) to a level two. These areas include:

- Requirements management
- Software configuration management
- Project planning
- Project tracking and oversight
- Subcontract management
- Software quality assurance

Each key process area (KPA) was assigned a champion and the champions meet once a month.

Companies and organizations establish quality improvement teams, which spawn working groups (WG). The working groups form a framework for the software engineering process group to address the tasks associated with the action plan that came out of the SEI assessment findings.

ISO 9000

International Organization for Standardization (ISO) accreditation is accomplished after being certified by what is known as a notified body. Accreditation itself is the act whereby the National Accreditation Council for Certification Bodies (NACCB) approves an organization to operate an assessment and registration or certification scheme approved by NACCB. This organization or notified body conducts an audit to certify adherence to the appropriate standard. If the company passes the audit criteria, it then registers with the notified body as ISO 9000 compliant and may use the ISO seal to advertise compliance.

National Standards Authority of Ireland (NSAI) and British Standards Institute (BSI) are examples of notified bodies for a registration effort. ISO 9001, also known as EN29001, Q91, and BS5750 Part 1, is the model for quality assurance in design/development, production, installation, and servicing. ISO 9001 is the specific quality system that applies to companies such as UNISYS, Hewlett Packard, INTEL, etc., because they design, manufacture, and service products that are produced here.

The most important benefit from the registration is access to markets such as the European Community (EC), which require compliance. A second benefit is competitive advantage over another supplier who cannot establish ISO 9001 compliance.

Getting Started: ISO 9000

In general, if an ISO initiative would result in a business objective that is part of a business plan, it should be pursued. Thus, a company may decide to seek ISO 9001 certification as a necessary action to remain competitive within the product area in the emerging worldwide marketplace. The first step is to hire or appoint someone to lead the effort. That person's job would be to lead the effort, determine what direction to take, select an appropriate auditing body for determining compliance and awarding registration, develop training materials for an internal auditing staff, and oversee implementation of general ISO 9001 quality initiatives. One of the primary objectives and roles of this person is to select the notified body from which to obtain certification and which would then come on site to conduct periodic conformance audits. Other responsibilities of this person are to roll out an internal auditor training program and to help establish individual quality manuals and processes that would then be used as a basis to quality for certification.

ISO 9001 is the most comprehensive standard. It states specific requirements for the following kinds of work: design, development, production, installation, and servicing. It is process oriented and not product or people oriented.

Any company wishing to sell software products or services in Europe was required to register by November 1992. Countries such as Canada, Australia, Japan, Mexico, and the U.S. Department of Defense have adopted it. ISO has come to represent good business practices.

Registration gives formal recognition that the processes used to produce, deliver, and support products meet an acceptable level of standard of control and effectiveness. Initial registration depends on passing an audit by a qualified organization like NSAI. Continued registration depends on passing continued audits. The registration is site specific.

E-Q-NET

NSAI is a member of E-Q-NET. E-Q-NET, the European Network for Quality System Assessment and certification, is the partnership of 16 European not-for-profit third-party certification bodies and five associate members — each a national leader in quality systems certification. Countries represented include: France, Belgium, Spain, U.K., Denmark, Germany, Italy, Greece, Netherlands, Ireland, Norway, Austria, Portugal, Sweden, Finland, and Switzerland. The associate members are Japan, Slovenia, Australia, Israel, and New Zealand. Surveillance audits may be performed by the local E-Q-Net partner.

More about NSAI

NSAI, a division of EOLAS and also the national standards body of Ireland, was established in 1946 and currently operates under the Industrial Research and Standards Act (1961) as well as the Science and Technology Act (1987) of Ireland and is actually a body of the Irish government. While the main office is located in Dublin, there is a branch office for North America that is located in Merrimack, New Hampshire. An additional office has been opened in Fremont, California.

NSAI has a reciprocal agreement with all the European Community countries (Belgium, Denmark, France, Germany, Greece, Ireland, Italy, Luxembourg, Netherlands, Portugal, Spain, and the U.K.) and the European Free Trade Association (EFTA) — Austria, Finland, Iceland, Norway, Sweden, and Switzerland — that recognize its certificates without payment of additional registration fees, and also has a separate bilateral agreement with the Canadian General Standards Board (CGSB). Each of the twelve EEC (European Economic Community) nations has a recognized governing body. FORFAS, a division of the government of Ireland and parent of NSAI, is that body for Ireland.

- IDA (Industrial Development Agency) Ireland is the subdivision of FORFAS, which is responsible for attracting business into Ireland.
- FORBAIRT is the subdivision of FORFAS, which is chartered to develop Irish industrial infrastructure, investments, etc.

Standards development is to go to the EEC for input to directives. Every six months, each nation meets to provide the political framework for problem solving.

Certification is provided in five groups, e.g., product certification in the food industry, pharmaceuticals, and chemicals. The rest look after other industrial segments of the country. There are 300+ such companies in Ireland from Dublin to the south. The overall goal is to result in a consistent product.

Principal Themes of an ISO 9000 Review

ISO 9000 Standards set the requirements for a quality system. Its principal themes focus on five areas: documentation, practices, records, audits, and corrective action. Documentation says what we do. Practices provides examples of what we say we do. Records are evidence of what we have done. Audits check what we do. Corrective action corrects discrepancies that are found.

The IT auditor, or any internal auditor, has the experience to perform such a review or assist in training corporate staff to perform their own self-evaluation to ISO Compliance Standards and processes.

For an ISO 9001 review, there are 20 items specifically reviewed. In Appendix 5 is an example of an Audit Analysis Worksheet to summarize the comprehensive review. Each of the major areas are identified and the outcome of the review indicates whether the area passed, was not covered, and the number of corrective action requests (CARs). Included in Appendix 5 is an example of a CAR form recently used by a software company in its ISO 9001 review.

An example of summary ISO 9001 review findings is described in Appendix 5 for a software vendor located at a New York City site and a summary of its lessons learned are detailed below.

The staff associated with the New York City review and the ISO certification effort was asked for their comments. This are a summary of their comments:

- Expect to be challenged. You will not get complete buy-in because people are being asked to go beyond the scope of what they believe they were hired to do. It is important that employees have a forum to vent their frustrations. Such comments can be a good indicator of the attitude and commitment employees are making and how well they understand why the company has chosen specific approaches to meeting its business needs.

- It was very poor planning to have another group within our facility to have its own ISO certification in the same plant with the rest of us. It increases COTS and duplicates services.

- It is much harder to achieve and maintain certification for a site which does not have a single site manager. If we could change the world we would have all organizations in New York City report up to one manager who is located here.

- We did too much work when we first started. We had people with backgrounds in Product Quality Assurance running the program and they make it a major effort. Perhaps if we had known, we would not have had these same people calling the shots. Instead, we might have quickly gone to the streamlined internal auditing system.

- ... a sitewide document control system and team ... common numbering and formats would have helped. More document templates would have helped. Developing our own on-line document control system has been a tragedy of errors. Don't do it.

In terms of the description, experience, and examples given above regarding ISO certification, the IT auditor can contribute to the training and development of internal staff in performing the audit process.

There are a number of questions the organization must ask itself before performing this function. It is an intensive effort and process that must be followed and performed to the letter. There must be a commitment to training, learning, and education if it is to succeed. Corporate management must support the process.

Computer Forensics

Computer forensics is the examination, analysis, testing, and evaluation of computer-based material, conducted to provide relevant and valid information to a court of law. Computer forensics tools are increasingly used to support law enforcement, computer security, and computer audit investigations.

A good source for evaluating computer forensics tools is the Computer Forensics Tool Testing (CFTT) Project Web site at http://www.cftt.nist.gov/index.html. CFTT is a joint project of the National Institute of Standards and Technology (NIST), the U.S. Department of Justice's National Institute of Justice (NIJ), the Federal Bureau of Investigation (FBI), the Defense Computer Forensics Laboratory (DCFL), the U.S. Customs Service, and others to develop programs for testing computer forensics tools used in the investigation of crimes involving computers.

One tool recently reviewed by CFTT was EnCase by Guidance Software, Inc. EnCase enables "noninvasive" computer forensic investigations, allowing examiners to view relevant files, including "deleted" files, file slack, and unallocated space. A screen shot of EnCase Forensic Edition is shown in Exhibit 6.

WebMetrics: An Introduction

On reviewing an organization's Web site, IT auditors can measure download time, transaction time, and availability of the Web site. In addition, IT auditors have to be aware of errors such as failed connection attempts, missing pages, missing page components, and broken links, which have to be tabulated. The IT auditor should evaluate the overall performance of the organization's Web site by obtaining or preparing comparative Web-performance statistics for several months. These statistics should be examined for significant issues and used in the assessment of the overall performance of the Web site. Moreover, IT auditors should review the Web information to ensure that all posted data is current. It is impossible for IT auditors to manually perform Web site audit. Manually checking that all posted data is current will be time-consuming. Discovering broken links, missing pages, and page components manually are almost impossible. Thus, IT auditors need CAATTs to assist them in performing this kind of audit.

WebMetrics provided by Information Technology Laboratory (ITL) of NIST is one of the Computer-Assisted Audit Tools (CAATs) that can assist IT auditors in evaluating the usability of a Web site. WebMetrics is appropriate to be one of the CAATs because it gives IT auditors the following advantages:

- Reduces the time to complete audit analysis, test, and reports
- Increases audit coverage by reducing the amount of time spent on manual processes
- Provides quality audit services by having a standard set of audit tools and procedures
- Leverages the knowledge gathered as a result of audit projects to provide immediate metric/data quality feedback to management

WebMetrics has four tools; WebSAT, WebCAT, WebVIP, VISVIP, FLUD, FLUDViz Tool, and TreeDec. How does WebMetrics assist IT auditors in performing their audit tasks regarding evaluation of Web site performance? WebMetrics helps IT auditors lessen audit time because there are lots of tasks that will be time consuming if done manually. For example:

- WebSAT helps IT auditors a check the performance of a Web site to ensure that the load time of a Web site is not slow. It checks total amounts of graphics that are 30K or less. The result of the test should be the size of graphics that have more than 30K.

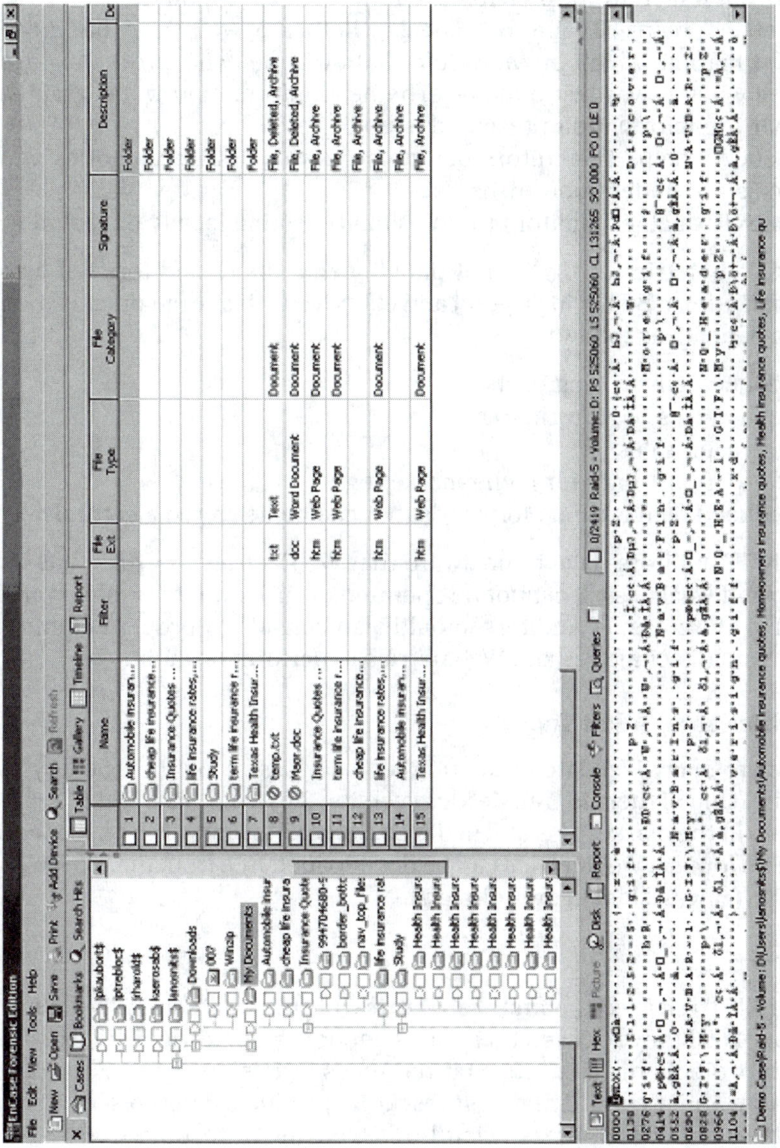

Exhibit 6. EnCase Screen Shot

- WebSAT provides IT auditors a number of images that do not have a height and width specified in the IMG tag, which could slow down the load time.
- WebSAT helps IT auditors check whether a web page has a "Send" or "Submit" button to enable users to deliver responses.
- WebSAT helps IT auditors check whether a web page has head information, which provides information about who wrote the page and when it was last updated. The head information will guarantee that the information presented is up-to-date.
- WebCAT helps IT auditors determine how well the categories and items are understood by users.
- WebVIP enables auditors to do usability testing locally or remotely.

Using WebMetrics as CAATs not only benefits the IT auditors but also the organizations. By having a good and effective Web site, an organization will gain benefits as follows:

- Reduced advertising costs
- Equal access to new markets
- Increased sales
- More opportunity for niche marketing
- Reduced delivery cost for goods that can be delivered electronically

Finally, IT auditors have to be aware that WebMetrics as CAATs has its strength and weakness. It cannot be operated on all computer systems and platforms. Moreover, IT auditors should also consider a proper combination of manual techniques and WebMetrics in performing audit.

WebMetrics as an Audit Tool

There are many Web site evaluation tools for assessing the usability of a Web site. One of them is WebMetrics (version 3.0) from NIST. WebMetrics is not sold in the market; it is still in development. However, NIST has made it available for use. WebMetrics can be downloaded free from the NIST Web site (http://zing.ncsl.nist.gov/webmet/).

Overview

ITL of NIST released the first WebMetrics 1.0 Tool Suite in August 1998. In January 2003 they released their latest version. WebMetrics is one of the research projects of ITL's Information Access Division (IAD). For more information about current and past research, products and tools, or other information about IAD, please visit IAD's web site at http://www.itl.nist.gov/iaui/index.html.

The objective of developing WebMetrics is to provide industries with current state-of-the-art technology that will allow improved usability of Web sites. Improved usability can dramatically increase the effectiveness and accessibility of a Web site, and this is critical if U.S. industry is to remain competitive in the global marketplace.

The first release of WebMetrics Tool Suite includes:

- *The Web Static Analyzer Tool (WebSAT),* which checks the html of a Web page against numerous usability guidelines. The output from WebSAT consists of identification of potential usability problems, which should be investigated further through user testing.
- *The Web Category Analysis Tool (WebCAT),* which lets the usability engineer (UE) quickly construct and conduct a simple category analysis across the Web site.
- *The Web Visual Instrumenter Program (WebVIP),* which lets the UE rapidly instrument a Web site for local or remote testing by employing visual instrumentation as well as automated techniques.

In January 2003, version 3.0 of WebMetric Tool Suite was released. The upgrades of the new version include the following features:

- The software is organized into a standard directory structure. The purpose is to provide integrated data transfer among various related software components, in particular, WebVIP, FLUD, FLUDViz, and VisVIP.
- The experimenter interface for WebVIP has been substantially revised and improved. Also, WebVIP can automatically invoke various postprocessing software such as the FLUD parser.
- A new software tool, FLUDViz, has been developed. The FLUDViz tool lets the UE visualize and analyze a single usability session.

Conclusion

In this chapter we have covered the use of CAATTs in four complex areas of IT operations. The methodology or techniques are presented with the integration of tools used to support it. Typically, these tasks are performed by experienced IT auditors or under their supervision.

The audit program provided in Appendix 5 should be expanded or revised to include specifics regarding the maintenance function under review. Systems maintenance is one of the highest exposure areas in an organization because the systems maintenance group, whether for systems or applications software, is responsible for changing how systems accept, process, and generate data. The overall objective of a systems maintenance audit should be to ascertain that adequate controls are in place to ensure that only authorized changes are made to the system and that they are implemented effectively and efficiently. Obviously, it is difficult to control the actions of IT personnel, such as systems and application programmers, who have access to a range of computer utilities and facilities and still maintain a productive environment. Nevertheless, controls must be in place to reduce the risk associated with systems maintenance to a level acceptable to management and in compliance with federal and state regulations such as the Homeland Security Act of 2002, the Sarbanes–Oxley Act of 2002, the HIPAA Act of 1996, and others discussed earlier in this book and later in Chapters 18 and 19.

Operating Systems (OSs) are also very complex area. We have seen the depths to which an audit may be taken. Appendix 5 offers a sample program for auditing an OS. This program should be tailored to the organizational environment and should cover all aspects of computer use that affect an OS. Auditors may decide to break the audit of systems software down into smaller, discrete audits as outlined in this section.

With regard to ERP systems such as SAP, people and passwords can become the weakest link in most information systems. Both must be managed effectively to ensure the protection of the R/3 system. Thus, system security features can only be effective when reinforced with policies and procedures that prevent the compromise of security in the R/3 system.

In performing the ISO 9001 review, planning and organizational support and involvement is critical. Once the process is started and tools used to collect the valuable information are being collected, a continuous monitoring effort can be implemented. From this information, the participants and stakeholders in the process can take corrective actions. A form of control self-assessment must be in place to improve the process and the organization.

Finally, recognizing the available tools that can help in assessing controls and utility of Web sites provides the IT auditor another way of independently evaluating Web operations. There are a number of support packages available from various resources to help the IT auditor evaluate control structure. Such tools also provide features to assess the efficiency, effectiveness, and economy of those sites to the business. The tool available to the IT auditor and his ability to recognize situations when the appropriate tool can be used are tremendous assets to any organization.

Review Questions

1. What role or roles do tools play in operational reviews of IT controls?
2. List two tools that can be used for a client/server controls review and two that can be used for EDI and data warehousing. What do they do?
3. How can MS Office be used as a support tool in IT operational audits?
4. What capabilities does Oracle have as a support tool?
5. Define systems maintenance; what does it involve and encompass?

6. What are the types of system changes an IT auditor should be aware of? Diagram the processes of those three types of changes. What are the control points?
7. What is an operating system? Why are audits of this area viewed as complex?
8. What is the reliance placed in system software working? And when operating systems do not work properly, what are the consequences in business terms?
9. Why is security software necessary in operating systems?
10. How does SAP impact corporate culture? How does it impact business processes?
11. If SAP is being considered for implementation in your company, list the control points you would look for in its implementation.
12. What security features does SAP BC have? List and explain five of them.
13. What security features does SAP have with regard to EDI and the Internet?
14. What is an ISO 9001 review?
15. What are some of the major quality programs?
16. What is E-Q-Net?
17. On what five areas do the ISO 9000 principal themes focus on?
18. What were some of the lessons learned from an ISO 9000 review?
19. What is computer forensics?
20. What are some commonly used computer forensics tools?

Multiple Choice

1. Which of the following is not true about systems maintenance?
   a. Maintenance is noticed when it is done right.
   b. Maintenance carries one of the highest risks of exposure.
   c. The maintenance group is responsible for making changes requested by the user.
   d. All systems require some maintenance.
2. The primary focus of a systems maintenance audit is:
   a. Systems software
   b. Network software
   c. Network hardware
   d. How IT personnel manage change
3. Which of the following information would an auditor not look for on a standard change request form?
   a. Date of request
   b. Description of the change
   c. Approvals of the request
   d. Auditor initiation of the request

4. Which of the following is not a system software category?
   a. Operating systems
   b. Documentation systems
   c. Data communication systems
   d. File maintenance systems
5. Most organizations rely on the operating system to:
   a. Maximize the difference between a given manufacturer's line of computers, thus facilitating the transfer of application programs
   b. Prevent programmers and operators from controlling the operation and allocation of peripheral devices and other computer resources
   c. Manage computer resources with minimum operator intervention
   d. Limit copy and sort programs
6. Data communications software typically performs all of the following except:
   a. Receives messages from computer terminals or other computers
   b. Edits input and output programs
   c. Handles errors
   d. Blocks messages when a particular terminal or communications line is inoperative
7. An auditor should determine whether file maintenance systems perform all of the following except:
   a. The file maintenance system consistently and accurately controls automated data files.
   b. The program library system consistently and accurately controls application programs.
   c. Control features of the file maintenance systems are fully used and cannot be overridden or bypassed.
   d. Whether manual procedures support and enhance the reliability of the file maintenance systems.
8. Communication is the key to managing expectations because:
   a. When expectations are set too low, people tend to become frustrated, upset, and disappointed with the results.
   b. When expectations are set too high, people may have difficulty adapting or are surprised with the extent of the change.
   c. A rigorous communications program is needed to allow people time to accept and fully use the new system.
   d. People need to be notified once or twice about change.
9. In SAP/R3, user access capabilities are managed by all of the following except:
   a. Encryption
   b. Authorization value sets
   c. Authorization profiles
   d. User master records

10. Which of the following is not true about ISO 9001 certification?
    a. Accreditation is accomplished after being certified by a notified body.
    b. All organizations can establish ISO 9001 compliance.
    c. The most important benefit from the registration is access to markets such as the EC that require compliance.
    d. The National Accreditation Council for Certification Bodies (NAC-CB) approves an organization to operate an assessment and registration or certification scheme.

Exercises

1. (a) Read Appendix I, Case 3, Holt Valley Hospital Services, Inc. (b) Answer the assignment. (c) Describe three tools you could use to perform work required. (d) In reviewing the transaction files, you encounter a misread at the beginning of month two data; what possibly happened? What questions or inquiries do you need to make?
2. Read Appendix I, Case 7, Amazon Industries. Answer the questions.
3. Add on to Case 7, above, the following: The system programmer has disappeared, he leaves no forwarding address, and his phone is disconnected. You are asked to perform an audit of the operating system. How would you approach it?
4. You are asked to perform an audit of SAP implementation in your company. Design an audit program for reviewing key steps or control points in this process.
5. You are asked to perform an ISO 9001 review on your corporation's software development activity, which accounts for 30 percent of the corporation profits. The president is concerned because revenue in this area is down and returns due to software errors were up 39 percent from last year.

Multiple Choice Answers

1 — a; 2 — d; 3 — d; 4 — b; 5 — c; 6 — d; 7 — b; 8 — c; 9 — a; 10 — b

References

1. Arnold, K.L. *The Manager's Guide to ISO 9000*. Simon & Schuster, New York. 1994.
2. Bates, J. What is Computer Forensics? T.J. Bates and Co. http://www.computer-investigations.com/wotis.html.
3. Berson, A. and G. Anderson. *Sybase and Client/Server Computing*. McGraw-Hill, New York. 1995.
4. Computer Forensic Tool Testing (CFTT) Project Web Site. National Institute of Standards and Technology. http://www.cftt.nist.gov/
5. Ford, W. and M.S. Baum. *Secure Electronic Commerce: Building the Infrastructure for Digital Signatures and Encryption, 2/E*. 2nd ed., Prentice Hall PTR, Upper Saddle River, NJ. 2001.

6. Gallegos, F., *Auditing Global Information Infrastructure and National Information Infra-structure*, EDP Auditing Series, #75-10-55, Auerbach Publishers, Boca Raton, FL. January 2000 issue, pp. 1–16.

7. Gallegos, F. and J. Yin. *Auditing in a Client Server Environment*, EDP Auditing Series, #74-10-25, Auerbach Publishers, Boca Raton, FL. August 2000 issue, pp. 1–20.

8. Gallegos, F. and J. Yin, *Auditing Oracle*, EDP Auditing Series, #74-15-37, Auerbach Publishers, Boca Raton, FL. August 2000 issue, pp. 1–12.

9. Gallegos, F. and A. Carlin, *Auditing Systems Maintenance — A How to Approach,* EDP Auditing Series, #74-30-25, Auerbach Publishers, Boca Raton, FL. October 2000 issue pp. 1–12.

10. Gallegos, F. and A. Carlin, *Key Review Points for Auditing Systems Development* EDP Auditing Series, #74-30-37, Auerbach Publishers, Boca Raton, FL. October 2000 issue pp. 1–24.

11. Gallegos, F., *Reviewing Focus Database Applications*, EDP Auditing Series, #74-10-23, Auerbach Publishers, Boca Raton, FL. January 2001 issue, pp. 1–24.

12. Gallegos, F., *WebMetrics: Computer-Assisted Audit Tools*, EDP Auditing Series, #73-20-50, Auerbach Publishers, Boca Raton, FL. November 2001 issue, pp. 1–16.

13. Gallegos, F. and L. Preiser-Houy, *Auditing Prototypes: Approaches and Techniques*, #74-30-60, Auerbach Publishers, Boca Raton, FL. December 2001, pp. 1–8.

14. Gallegos, F., W. Testerman, and J.M. Klosky, paper entitled, The Use and Application of Computer Performance Evaluation Tools as an EDP Audit Resource, Accepted for presentation and publication at the Decision Sciences Conference, Miami, FL. November 1991.

15. Gallegos, F. and R. Kocot, Auditing operating systems, *The Handbook of MIS Management,* Supplement I, Auerbach Publishers, Boca Raton, FL. 1986, pp. 1027–1040.

16. Gallegos, F. and M. Stegner, *Auditing Material Requirement Planning Systems*, #76-01-40, Auerbach Publishers, Boca Raton, FL. February 1988.

17. Gallegos, F. and S. Tanner, *Developing a Network Security Plan*, Information Management Series: Strategies, Systems, and Technologies, #1-06-30, Auerbach Publishers, Boca Raton, FL. April 1998, pp. 1–12.

18. Gallegos, F. and L. Tison-Dualan, *SAP Implementation and Control*, EDP Auditing Series #75-10-60, Auerbach Publishers, Boca Raton, FL. June 1998, pp. 1–12.

19. Gallegos, F., *ISO 9001 Audit: An Approach*, EDP Auditing Series, #76-20-15, Auerbach Publishers, Boca Raton, FL. 1998, pp. 1–16.

20. Guidance Software, Inc. EnCase Version 4 Demo Edition.

21. Guidance Software, Inc. EnCase Forensic Edition Version 4: Product Information http://www.guidancesoftware.com/products/software/encaseforensic/prodbrochure.shtm

22. Health, J. Internet Security Risk and Solutions, accessed October 15th, 2002, available: http://www.ecommercecentre.online.wa.gov.au/matrix/security.htm.

23. IPNet 2001. The Basic of Business-to-Business E-Commerce Security, accessed October 15th, 2002, available: http://www.ipnetsolutions.com.

24. Katsikas, S., Ed., *Communications & Multimedia Security.* Vol. 3. Kluwer Academic, Boston, MA. 1997, 328 pp.

25. Katsikas, S. and D. Gritzalis. *Information Systems Security Facing the Information Society of the 21st Century.* Kluwer Academic, Boston, MA. 1996, 520pp.

26. Morris C.A. Sr., What Every Auditor Needs to Know about E-Commerce, *Internal Auditor,* June 2000: 60.

27. National Institute of Standards and Technology, NIST Web Metrics, Version 3.0, January 2003.

28. Sherif, M.H., *Protocols for Secure Electronic Commerce.* CRC Press, Boca Raton, FL. 2000.

29. Symantec Enterprise Solutions 2000. A Comprehensive Risk Management Guide, accessed October 15th, 2002, available: http://enterprisesecurity.Symantec.com

30. Terashima, N. and E. Altman, Eds. *Advanced IT Tools.* Kluwer Academic, Boston, MA. 1996, 592 pp.
31. Tivoli System, Inc. Managing E-Business Risks, accessed October 9th, 2001, available: http://www_8.ibm.com/e-business.
32. Unknown. A Security Management Framework for Online Services, accessed October 15th, 2002, available: http://www.indtech.wa.gov.au/doit/publications.
33. Unknown. Risk Management and Security, accessed October 9th, 2002, available: http://www.asisonline.org/ITSC/library/hout99lv.html.

Part V
Emerging Issues in IT Audit

Chapter 18 through Chapter 21

The final part of this text examines the emerging issues in information technology (IT) auditing today and in the future. It focuses on the legal environment, its impact on information reviews, and the important roles IT auditors will play in examination of issues from IT contracts to compliance with Netlaw. Other major areas for IT auditors are the issues of security and privacy of IT. Demand by the public and governments have generated concern for the protection of individual rights and corporate information. Thus, career planning has become an important element for IT auditors and management. Development of the knowledge, skills, and abilities is a continuous challenge for the IT audit professional. Finally, we provide an outlook for the IS audit profession, a view of the future.

Chapter 18 provides discussion on the legal environment and the IT auditor's role in assisting management and legal counsel. Much has happened in our world and changed our views and outlook. The events of September 11th, 2001 have made us more security conscious. The financial disasters of Enron, WorldCom, and others have generated the call for new laws and federal regulation. With the services industry expanding, the importance of financial responsibility, contract compliance, and monitoring has grown proportionally, exceeding the abilities of the organization to successfully identify problems and alert management to take action before they become business disasters or frauds and end up in the courts. Recent rulings and laws have hastened organizations to examine corporations' use of electronic mail, intranets, extranets, and the Internet itself. Government's concern for protection of individual rights has generated a frenzy worldwide and global positioning for information control and dissemination. The Homeland Security Act and the Sarbanes–Oxley Act will have tremendous impact on the audit, control, and security of IT in business and our lives.

Chapter 19 covers the key IT security and privacy issues of the varied complexities of the platforms and their impact on the application. The focus of this chapter is the key control points in the examination of security and privacy that the IT auditors must be cognizant of in conducting their review. With Internet identity theft on the rise and the violation of information privacy increasing as well, such events have caused public both alarm and anger and a lack of confidence in organizations (business and government) to protect information. Several different operations environments will be discussed as we examine system and privacy issues as they pertain to business IT. Approaches and techniques used by practitioners will be discussed.

Chapter 20 discusses the process of IT audit career planning and development. As we move into the next millennium with the growth of IT services, the continued advances of new IT into business processes, and the generation of global IT competition, management must be ready to deal with the multitude of current and future IT-related control issues they will face. IT audit career planning and development will play a key role in development of new resources to meet the challenge and the retooling or advanced training of current resources. As new information technologies are integrated and become commercially profitable, so too must the skills of the IT auditor be at a level to meet the challenge and comply with professional practice standards.

Chapter 21 discusses IT auditing and provides the student and practitioner a view of the IT auditor's role in the years ahead. The audit profession has a long history of standardizing methods and techniques used in the review of operations. Although the process of performing the audit will change little, the tools to do it with and the rapidity of reporting with follow-up of management actions will change in order to be profitable, competitive, efficient, effective, and economic. Several emerging areas of importance will be studied, such as end-user computing, electronic data interchange (EDI), Internet, intranet, and extranet operations issues. The multitude of support tools available to the IT auditor in assisting them in auditing IT operations over these new and varied environments will also be covered. As this chapter suggests, auditors' tool kits are a critical component in the ability to audit control processes through tomorrow's complex IT environment. We will provide examples of the latest computer assisted audit tools and techniques (CAATTs) and the lessons learned as they pertain to audits of operations and issues of efficiency and effectiveness.

Chapter 18

The Legal Environment and Its Impact on Information Technology: From IT Crime Law to IT Contract Law to Netlaw

Information technology auditing, control, and security comprise one of the fastest growing fields in technology today. Computers are used in almost every business in America and companies want to ensure that their systems are performing optimally. In 1974, the American Institute of Certified Public Accountants published the first *Accounting and Auditing Guide* addressing internal control and the role of information systems. Since that publication, many laws, standards, and guides have been introduced into the field of IT auditing, security, and control.

In recent years, the advancements in network environment technologies have resulted in bringing to the forefront issues of security and privacy that were once only of interest to the legal and technical expert but today are topics that affect virtually every user of the information superhighway. The Internet has grown exponentially from a simple linkage of a relatively few government and educational computers to a complex worldwide network that is utilized by almost everyone from the computer specialist to the novice user and everyone in between. Common uses for the Internet include everything from marketing, sales, and entertainment purposes to electronic mail, research, and commerce, and virtually any other type of information sharing. Unfortunately, as with any breakthrough in technology, advancements have also given rise to various new problems that must be addressed. These problems are often being brought to the attention of the IT audit and control specialist. Hence, the focus of this chapter will discuss security and privacy legislation as they relate to the networked environment and the Internet. Current federal legislation and its lasting impact on the online community is discussed, along with the government's role in the networked society and the impact it has had on the networked environment in recent years.

IT Crime Issues

The IT explosion has opened up many new gateways for criminals. Since the integration of computers into business, companies have had to safeguard their intellectual assets against computer crime. The National Center for Computer Crime (NCCC) estimates that the annual cost of computer crime in the United States is in excess of $2 billion, plus 2000 personnel years, and 26 years of computer service. The Federal Bureau of Investigation (FBI) estimates that the average dollar amount of *reported* computer frauds now exceeds $1 million. Recent FBI and NCCC reports indicate that less than 10 percent of computer fraud crimes are reported. This is due largely to the public embarrassment companies face and potential negative press such incidences receive.

The latest Computer Crime and Security Survey and a sample study of large corporations and government agencies conducted by the Computer Security Institute (CSI) and the FBI have revealed the following:

- 90 percent of respondents have detected computer security breaches within the past 12 months. (In 1998 this was 64 percent.)
- 80 percent acknowledged financial losses due to computer security breaches.
- 44 percent quantified their financial losses for a total of $455,848,000 in losses among 223 respondents.
- 74 percent cited their Internet connection as a frequent point of attack.
- 33 percent cited their internal systems as a frequent point of attack.
- 34 percent reported the intrusions to law enforcement. (This has more than doubled since 1996.)

The most serious financial losses occurred through theft of proprietary information (26 respondents reported over $170 million in losses) and financial fraud (25 respondents reported more than $115 million).

484

There are three main categories of crimes involving computers. These crimes may be committed as individual acts or concurrently. The first of these is where the computer is the target of the crime. Generally, this type of crime involves the theft of information that is stored in the computer. This also covers unauthorized access or modification of records. Two specific crimes that can result directly from targeting the computer are techno-vandalism and techno-trespass. Damage resulting from unauthorized access of an information system is commonly called techno-vandalism. Techno-trespass occurs when the unauthorized access occurs. The most common ways to gain unauthorized access to an information system is for the criminal to become a "super user" through a backdoor in the system. The backdoor in the system is there to permit access should a problem arise. Being a super user is equivalent to being the system's manager and it allows the criminal access to practically all areas and functions within the system. This type of crime is of the greatest concern to industry and is the primary focus when security measures come into question.

The next general type of computer crime occurs when the computer is used as an instrument of the crime. In this scenario, the computer is used to assist the criminal in committing the crime. This category covers fraudulent use of ATM cards and machines, identity fraud, credit card fraud, telecommunications fraud, and financial fraud from computer transactions. Until 2001, the most publicized example of this type of crime was the cloning of cellular phone numbers. This crime is committed by capturing computerized billing codes during cellular transmissions. The code is then transmitted into a portable computer, and a program then allows the criminal to bill his or her cellular phone calls to other cellular phone customers. In this scenario, the computer is an instrument in two facets. First, the computer is used to illegally capture information. Then, a program inside the computer manipulates the data in order to further the crime. In this category, the computer is necessary to commit the crime. But the financial fiascos of 2001–2002 involving Enron, WorldCom, and others have cast doubts on the integrity of the financial statement and the word of the CFO and the CEO. With the Equity Funding fraud of the 1970s, the rise of the Foreign Corrupt Practices Act of 1976–77, and industry's promise that they can self regulate, we have come full circle again to misreporting and financial integrity and the lack of due professional care by the accounting profession. We enter the era of Sarbanes–Oxley, Public Law 107-204.

In the third category, the computer is not necessary to commit the crime. The computer is incidental and is used to commit the crime faster, process greater amounts of information, and make the crime more difficult to identify and trace. The most popular example of this crime is child pornography. Due to increased Internet access, child pornography is more widespread, easier to access, and harder to trace. This is law enforcement's favorite category of crime because the incriminating information is often stored in the computer. This makes criminal prosecution easier. If the criminal is savvy, the computer is programmed to encrypt the data or erase the files if it is not properly accessed. Thus, the field of computer forensics and computer security are opening new job opportunities for audit and security professionals who use their skills to capture the evidence.

Organizations such as the Computer Law Association (www.cla.org) and Association of Certified Fraud Examiners (www.cfenet.com) provide a source for those looking at career opportunities in the law and IT field. In their new book just released, Gerald R. Ferrera et al. state that cyberlaw is the law governing the use of computers and the Internet. The authors agree and believe that cyberlaw not only encompasses a combination of state and federal statutory, decisional, and administrative laws but international laws arising out of the use of the Internet as well.

Protection against Computer Fraud

In light of the lack of effective legislation in place currently, the best defense against computer fraud is a good offense. IT auditors should alert their clients to the dangers that are present, and there are several ways they can protect their clients from computer fraud. This is generally in the form of controls, firewalls, or encryption. The combined use of these methods will certainly help to reduce the risk of unauthorized access to the information system.

The FBI's National Computer Crime Squad has the following advice to help protect against computer fraud:

- Place a log-in banner to ensure that unauthorized users are warned that they may be subject to monitoring.
- Turn audit trails on.
- Consider keystroke level monitoring if adequate banner is displayed. Request trap and tracing from your local telephone company.
- Consider installing caller identification.
- Make backups of damaged or altered files.
- Maintain old backups to show the status of the original.
- Designate one person to secure potential evidence. Evidence can consist of tape backups and printouts. These pieces of evidence should be documented and verified by the person obtaining the evidence. Evidence should be retained in a locked cabinet with access limited to one person.
- Keep a record of resources used to reestablish the system and locate the perpetrator.
- Encrypt files.
- Encrypt transmissions.
- Use one-time password (OTP) generators.
- Use secure firewalls.

The explosion of the information age has created many opportunities for improving business. It has also created more opportunities for criminals. Three years ago, the International Trade Commission reported that computer software piracy is a $4 billion-a-year problem worldwide. Today, experts believe that software piracy costs the computer industry more than $11 billion a year and software thefts drain the U.S. economy of jobs and wages. Others estimate that there is one illegal copy of each computer software program for every two legitimate copies. Organizations such as the Business Software Alliance, Software Publishers Association, Institute of Internal Auditors, and the Information Systems Audit and Control have been instrumental in raising the awareness to this type of crime.

In addition to the IT auditor's primary function of auditing the computer system, he or she has obtained the additional responsibility of the security of the system. The government is passing new laws and improving existing ones to help combat computer crimes. However, the greatest aid to the safety of the information is a combination of scrutiny controls, firewalls, and encryption. The IT auditor's role is constantly expanding, and security of the data is an important concern.

The Computer Fraud and Abuse Act (CFAA)

The CFAA was first drafted in 1984 as a response to computer crimes. The government's response to network security and network-related crimes was to revise the act in 1994 under the Computer Abuse Amendments Act to cover such crimes as trespass (unauthorized entry) into an online system, exceeding authorized access, and exchanging information on how to gain unauthorized access. Although the Act was intended to protect against attacks in a network environment, it does also have its fair share of faults.

The Act requires that certain conditions needed to be present in order for the crime to be a violation of the CFAA. Only if these conditions are present will the crime fall under violation of the CFAA. The three types of attacks that are covered under the Act and the conditions that have to be met include:

- *Fraudulent trespass:* This is when a trespass is made with an intent to defraud that results in both furthering the fraud and the attacker obtaining something of value.
- *Intentional destructive trespass:* This is a trespass along with actions that intentionally cause damage to a computer, computer system, network, information, data, or program, or results in denial-of-service and causes at least $1000 in total loss in the course of a year.
- *Reckless destructive trespass:* This is when there is the presence of trespass along with reckless actions (though not deliberately harmful), cause damage to a computer, computer system, network, information, data, or program, or results in denial-of-service and causes at least $1000 in total loss in the course of a year.

Each of these three types of definitions is geared towards a particular type of attack. Fraudulent trespass was a response against crimes involving telephone fraud that is committed through a computer system, such as using a telephone company computer to obtain free telephone service. This condition helps prosecute individuals responsible for the large financial losses suffered by companies like AT&T as mentioned earlier. Telephone toll fraud has snowballed into over a billion dollars a year problem for the phone companies.

The other two usually apply to online systems and have been implemented to address problems of hackers or crackers, worms, viruses, and virtually any other type of intruder that can damage, alter, or destroy information. The two attacks are similar in many ways, but the key in differentiating the two are the words "Intentional," which would, of course, mean a deliberate attack with intent to cause damage, while "reckless" can cover an attack in which damage was caused due to negligence. Penalties under Section 1030(c) of the CFAA vary from one year imprisonment for reckless destructive trespass on a nonfederal computer to up to twenty years for an intentional attack on a federal computer where the information obtained is used for "the injury of the United States or to the advantage of any foreign nation" (i.e., cases of espionage).

The penalties are obviously less severe for "reckless destructive trespass" than for "intentional destructive trespass." The reasoning behind this is that the reckless attacker may not necessarily intend to cause damage but must still be punished for gaining access to places that they should not have access to. However, the impact of such terminology appears to possibly create some confusion in prosecuting the trespasser as it resides in such a gray area. In *Morris v. United States* it was determined that "intent" applied to access and not to damages. The implication here would be that if the "intentional" part of the violation was applied to access and not to the damage, then the culprit could possibly be prosecuted under the lesser sentence. For example, if an individual intentionally intended to release a virus over a network, it would seem difficult for prosecutors to prove the motive for the violation. What if the individual stated that he or she was conducting some type of security test (like Morris contested), and "accidentally" set off a procedure that released a virus over the network? Intentional could refer to access to a system, but it may not apply to damage. In this case, the lesser penalty of reckless destructive trespass may be applied. Obviously, this is a matter that must be contemplated on a case-by-case basis, observing the facts of each individual case. In some instances, however, it would appear that even intentional trespass could be defended by claims that the violation was due to negligence and therefore falls under the less severe of the two circumstances.

This legislation has been helpful as a legal tool for prosecuting crimes involving some of the above-mentioned intruders and violators of system security, but it also seems to have a loophole in certain cases. Unfortunately, this loophole may be large enough for a serious violator of the act to slip through and be prosecuted under a lesser penalty by virtue of having to prove intent. All states have closed a portion of that loophole through statutes prohibiting harassment or stalking including electronic mail.

Computer Abuse Amendments Act

A more specific crime that is often prosecuted is trespass. The Computer Abuse Amendments Act of 1994 qualified trespass as including "unauthorized entry onto an online system, exceeding authorized access and exchanging information on gaining authorized access." Included in the Act are three kinds of trespass and the conditions that must be met in order for the crime to be a violation of the Act. Fraudulent trespass is trespass with intent to defraud; the fraud is pursued during the trespass and the trespasser procures information that is of value. This definition of fraud was a "response to telephone fraud committed through a computer system." The other two types of trespasses were introduced to criminally prosecute the trespasser who damages, alters, or destroys information. Intentional destructive trespass is fraudulent trespass with the additional criterion of intentional action to cause damage to the computer and resulting in damages worth at least $1000 in the course of the year. This is a deliberate act with the intent to cause damage. Penalties for this crime can be up to 20 years in prison. Reckless destructive trespass is the same as intentional destructive access without the intent to damage, alter, or destroy information. Reckless actions occur that cause at least $1000 in damage to the computer system. The penalties for this crime are not as stiff. It is important to note that for intentional destructive trespass, the intent of the crime is related to the intent to damage the system, not the intent to illicitly access the system. If prosecutors can only prove intentional unauthorized access of the system, then reckless destructive trespass applies.

Sarbanes–Oxley Act (Public Law 107-204)

The world of financial auditing has changed dramatically over the past decade and will continue to rapidly change as more and more companies rely on IT to achieve their business objectives. Certainly, the passage of the Sarbanes–Oxley Act of 2002 (Public Law 107-204) will have a major impact on the internal and external auditor. Also, the IT auditor will play an integral role in assuring compliance with this Act.

It is no longer acceptable for auditors to audit around the computer, as was once the case. With the increase of fraud and ceaseless corporate scandals over the past two years, it is even more imperative now than ever before that auditors have a full understanding of both manual and automated internal control processes. The assessment of both the manual and automated internal controls of any system can provide the needed assurance auditors can use to base their professional judgment on as far as the quality of the information derived off the system. This judgment is a key element in the risk analysis process that the auditor must perform during the planning stages of any audit.

Today, external financial auditors are relying more on the process approach rather than on the traditional transaction approach. The results of an evaluation of an organization's manual and automated internal controls can either increase or reduce the amount of transaction testing needed to render an opinion on financial statements.

For internal auditors, internal controls are also very important. One of the main functions of an internal auditor is to provide assurances to the management that their approved internal controls are in place and are working effectively and efficiently, and if in fact there are problems, they are being addressed and corrected.

It is important for both the manual and automated internal controls to be operational and effective because management will base their business decisions on the financial results generated from the information system.

It is also important to external auditors that manual and automated internal controls are operational and effective because this will provide assurance to external auditors that information generated from the system is valid, accurate, and complete. Based on this assurance from the system, auditors can then place the appropriate level of reliance on the internal controls of the information system.

If the necessary controls are not in place, or if they are in place but not being applied effectively and as management intended, then the integrity of the data and information generated from the system should be called into question by both external and internal auditors.

Even though it is essential that manual controls be in place and be working effectively and efficiently to produce accurate data output, due to the broadness of the subject matter, this paper will focus on auditors' reliance on automated internal controls and the effects of this reliance on auditors' judgment in assessing business risk related to the integrity of information generated from the system.

As mentioned in the first three chapters, the Sarbanes–Oxley Act has provided the needed muscle to internal auditors to do their jobs better and added accountability to management to take action on whatever auditors may identify. Once again, financial fraud has come to the forefront of the audit community at the beginning of this decade as a result of the financial scandals of Enron, Global Crossing, and others. Just as the Equity Funding scandal of 1973 gave rise to the development of strong state and federal regulation of the insurance industries, corporate creative accounting of oil companies and the aerospace industry provided support for the development and enactment of the Foreign Corrupt Practices Act of 1977 more than 25 years before the Sarbanes–Oxley Act.

Perhaps now the Sarbanes–Oxley Act of 2002 will be a vivid reminder of the importance of due professional care and financial integrity. This act is a major reform package mandating the most far-reaching changes Congress has imposed on the business world since the Foreign Corrupt Practices Act of 1977 and the SEC Act of the 1930s. It seeks to thwart future scandals and restore investor confidence by, among other things, creating a Public Company Accounting Oversight Board, revising auditor independence rules, revising corporate governance standards, and significantly increasing the criminal penalties for violations of securities laws.

Major Points from the Sarbanes–Oxley Act of 2002. The Act discusses requirements for the Board including composition and duties. The Board must (1) register public accounting firms; (2) establish or adopt, by rule, auditing, quality control, ethics, independence, and other standards relating to the preparation of audit reports for issuers; (3) conduct inspections of accounting firms; (4) conduct investigations and disciplinary proceedings, and impose appropriate sanctions; (5) perform such other duties or functions as necessary or appropriate; (6) enforce compliance with the Act, the rules of the Board, professional standards, and the securities laws relating to the preparation and issuance of audit reports and the obligations and liabilities of accountants with respect thereto; and (7) set the budget and manage the operations of the Board and the staff of the Board.

The Sarbanes–Oxley Act of 2002 focuses on the importance of due professional care. It prohibits all registered public accounting firms from providing to audit clients, contemporaneously with the audit, certain nonaudit services including internal audit outsourcing, financial information systems design and implementation services, and expert services (e.g., tax consulting, systems design, special studies). These scope-of-service restrictions go beyond existing Security and Exchange Commission (SEC) independence regulations. All other services, including tax services, are permissible only if preapproved by the issuer's audit committee, and all such preapprovals must be disclosed in the issuer's periodic reports to the SEC.

The Act requires auditor (not audit firm) rotation. Therefore, the lead audit partner or the concurring review partner must rotate off the engagement if he or she has performed audit services for the issuer in each of the five previous fiscal years. The Act provides no distinction regarding the capacity in which the audit or concurring partner provided such audit services. Any services provided as a manager or in some other capacity appear to count toward the five-year period. The provision starts as soon as the firm is registered, so, absent guidance to the contrary, the audit and concurring partner must count back five years starting with the date in which Public Company Accounting Oversight Board registration occurs. This provision has a definite impact on small accounting firms. The SEC is currently considering whether or not to accommodate small firms in this area; currently there is no small-firm exemption from this provision.

In order to audit a public company, a public accounting firm must register with the Board. The Board shall collect a registration fee and an annual fee from each registered public accounting firm in amounts that are sufficient to recover the costs of processing and reviewing applications and annual reports. The Board shall also establish a reasonable annual accounting support fee to maintain the Board.

Annual quality reviews must be conducted for firms that audit more than 100 issuers; all others must be conducted every three years. The SEC and the Board may order a special inspection of any firm at any time. The Board of a firm can impose sanctions if it fails to reasonably supervise any associated person with regard to auditing or quality control standards. The Act also includes foreign accounting firms that audit a U.S. company for registrations with the Board. This would include foreign firms that perform some audit work, such as in a foreign subsidiary of a U.S. company, that is relied on by the primary auditor.

It is unlawful for a registered public accounting firm to provide any non-audit service to an issuer during the same time with the audit, including:

- Bookkeeping or other services related to the accounting records or financial statements of the audit client
- Financial information systems design and implementation
- Appraisal or valuation services, fairness opinions, or contribution-in-kind reports
- Actuarial services
- Internal audit outsourcing services
- Management functions or human resources
- Broker or dealer, investment adviser, or investment banking services
- Legal services and expert services unrelated to the audit
- Any other service that the Board determines, by regulation, is impermissible

The Board may, on a case-by-case basis, exempt from these prohibitions any person, issuer, public accounting firm, or transaction, subject to review by the Commission. However, the SEC has oversight and enforcement authority over the Board. The Board, in its rulemaking process, is to be treated as if it were a registered securities association.

It will not be unlawful to provide other nonaudit services if they are pre-approved by the audit committee in the following manner. The Act allows an accounting firm to engage in any nonaudit service, including tax services that are not listed above, only if the activity is preapproved by the audit committee of the issuer. The audit committee will disclose to investors in periodic reports its decision to preapprove nonaudit services. Statutory insurance company regulatory audits are treated as an audit service and thus do not require preapproval.

The preapproval requirement is waived with respect to the provision of nonaudit services for an issuer if the aggregate amount of all such nonaudit services provided to the issuer constitutes less than 5 percent of the total amount of revenues paid by the issuer to its auditor (calculated on the basis of revenues paid by the issuer during the fiscal year when the nonaudit services are performed). Such services were not recognized by the issuer at the time of the engagement to be nonaudit services, and such services are promptly brought to the attention of the audit committee and approved prior to completion of the audit. The authority to preapprove services can be delegated to one or more members of the audit committee, but any decision by the delegate must be presented to the full audit committee.

For independence acceptance, the lead audit or coordinating partner and the reviewing partner must rotate off of the audit every five years. Also, the accounting firm must report to the audit committee all critical accounting policies and practices to be used, all alternative methods to GAAP that have been discussed with the management, and ramifications of the use of such alternative disclosures and methods.

Another audit independence compliance issue is that the CEO, Controller, CFO, Chief Accounting Officer, or person in an equivalent position cannot have been employed by the company's audit firm during the one-year period preceding the audit. The CEO and the CFO of each issuer shall prepare a statement to accompany the audit report to certify the appropriateness of the financial statements and disclosures contained in the periodic report, and that those financial statements and disclosures fairly present, in all material respects, the operations and financial condition of the issuer. A violation of this section must be knowing and intentional to give rise to liability. It shall be unlawful for any officer or director of an issuer to take any action to fraudulently influence, coerce, manipulate, or mislead any auditor engaged in the performance of an audit for the purpose of rendering the financial statements materially misleading.

The Act penalizes executives for nonperformance. If an issuer is required to prepare a restatement due to material noncompliance with financial reporting requirements, the CEO and the CFO must reimburse the issuer for any bonus or other incentive-based or equity-based compensation received during the twelve months following the issuance. It prohibits the purchase or sale of stock by officers and directors and other insiders during blackout periods. Any profits resulting from sales in violation of this will be recoverable by the issuer.

Each financial report that is required to be prepared in accordance with GAAP shall reflect all material- correcting adjustments that have been identified by a registered accounting firm. Each annual and quarterly financial report shall disclose all material off-balance sheet transactions and other relationships with unconsolidated entities that may have a material current or future effect on the financial condition of the issuer.

The SEC shall study off-balance sheet disclosures to determine (1) extent of off-balance sheet transactions (including assets, liabilities, leases, losses, and the use of special purpose entities) and (2) whether generally accepted accounting rules result in financial statements of issuers reflecting the economics of such off-balance sheet transactions to investors in a transparent fashion and make a report containing recommendations to Congress. Generally, it will be unlawful for an issuer to extend credit to any director or executive officer. Consumer credit companies may make home improvement and consumer credit loans and issue credit cards to its directors and executive officers if it is done in the ordinary course of business on the same terms and conditions made to the general public. Also, directors, officers, and 10 percent owners must report designated transactions by the end of the second business day following the day on which the transaction was executed.

The Act requires each annual report of an issuer to contain an internal control report. The SEC shall issue rules to require issuers to disclose whether at least one member of its audit committee is a financial expert. Also, the issuers must disclose information on material changes in the financial condition or operations of the issuer on a rapid and current basis.

Criminal Intent. The Act identifies as a crime for any person to corruptly alter, destroy, mutilate, or conceal any document with the intent to impair the object's integrity or availability for use in an official proceeding or to otherwise obstruct, influence, or impede any official proceeding such a person being liable for up to 20 years in prison and a fine. Also, the SEC is authorized to freeze the payment of an extraordinary payment to any director, officer, partner, controlling person, agent, or employee of a company during an investigation of possible violations of securities laws. Finally, the SEC may prohibit a person from serving as an officer or director of a public company if the person has committed securities fraud.

Penalties and Requirements under Title VIII of the Act

- It is a felony to knowingly destroy or create documents to "impede, obstruct, or influence" any existing or contemplated federal investigation.
- Auditors are required to maintain "all audit or review work papers" for five years.
- The statute of limitations on securities fraud claims is extended to the earlier of five years from the fraud or two years after the fraud was discovered, from three years and one year, respectively.
- Employees of issuers and accounting firms are extended "whistle-blower protection" that would prohibit the employer from taking certain actions against employees who lawfully disclose private employer information to, among others, parties in a judicial proceeding involving a fraud claim. Whistle blowers are also granted a remedy of special damages and attorney's fees.

Penalties and Requirements under Title IX of the Act

- Maximum penalty for mail and wire fraud increased from five to ten years.
- The CEO and CFO must certify financial statements filed with the SEC. The certification must state that the financial statements and disclosures fully comply with provisions of the Securities Exchange Act and that they fairly present, in all material respects, the operations and financial condition of the issuer. Maximum penalties for willful and knowing violations of this section are a fine of not more than $5 million and imprisonment of up to 20 years.

Remedies and Effectiveness

Computer-related crimes are relatively new in law enforcement and prosecution. Criminal prosecution continues to lag behind the wave of precedence set by civil courts. Currently, individuals and companies can obtain civil or criminal justice to varying degrees of effectiveness. Some of the new aggressive remedies and financial penalties recognized by Congress are injunctive relief, seizure, impoundment, and destruction of goods. As discussed above in the passage of the Sarbanes–Oxley Act, these monetary and nonmonetary remedies are designed to prevent further wrongful activity.

Injunctive relief is available to both federal and state courts. Parties found in violation of an injunction are in contempt of court and are subject to fines or jail time. The federal courts have specific criteria for issuing an injunction:

- The movant's (party asking for injunction) likelihood of prevailing on the merits
- Lack of adequate remedy at law (irreparable harm in the absence of injunctive relief)

- Balance of hardships between movant and respondent
- Public interest

The plaintiff must start the injunctive procedures within a reasonable time period of discovering the crime. If not, the courts will deny the injunction.

Two of the most common types of injunctions are permanent and preliminary. A permanent injunction is granted after the case has been adjudicated and the court has found for the plaintiff. Preliminary injunctions are granted before the final adjudication. Before a preliminary injunction is granted, a hearing is normally held so that the defendant may oppose the motion. The purpose of a preliminary injunction is to prevent irreversible harm to the plaintiff while the case is being decided. Another type of injunction available to the courts is *ex parte*. In this situation, the defendant does not need to be present to oppose the plaintiff's motion for an injunction. This is especially useful in Internet fraud cases. An example of this type of injunction is a temporary restraining order. A temporary restraining order forces the defendant to cease the harmful activity until a hearing can be held to determine whether a preliminary injunction will be granted. If the court grants a preliminary injunction or a temporary restraining order, the movant must post a bond for the payment of damages incurred by the defendant in the case of wrongful injunction or seizure.

Another aggressive remedy within the court system is the seizure, impoundment, and destruction of property used to commit or facilitate the crime. This is much more difficult to obtain than injunctive relief as courts are much less likely to grant it. Congress determined that counterfeiters could easily destroy evidence of their crime and amended the 1984 Lanham Act. This amendment provides for seizure of goods without the presence of the defendant at the hearing. The *ex parte* provision is available when the property can be easily destroyed or erased. This is especially prevalent in cases involving Internet crime.

As always, there are concerns about Constitutional violations whenever these remedies are enacted. Some argue that freedom of speech as provided by the First Amendment is violated by injunctions, usually injunctions involving copyright infringement cases. The Fourth, Fifth, and Fourteenth Amendments are scrutinized when the seizure of property by the courts has been authorized. The Fourth Amendment does not allow search or seizure of another's property without a warrant. It also qualifies that the warrant must specify the place to be searched and the items to be seized. This poses a unique problem for law enforcement, as it is difficult to identify a specific computer that committed a crime just by looking at it. The Fifth and Fourteenth Amendments specify that neither the federal nor state governments may seize property without due *process of law*. Due process of law usually requires than an individual be given notice and an opportunity to be heard before he is deprived of his property. Therefore, *ex parte* orders are argued to be a constitutional violation. The Supreme Court has formed criteria for *ex parte* seizure orders to continue to allow them to be a useful tool to law enforcement.

Legislation Providing for Civil and Criminal Penalties

In the past 20 years, Congress has become very active in passing legislation providing penalties for computer fraud. More recently, the Sarbanes–Oxley Act has changed the audit process to ensure the practice of due professional care, integrity, and validity. Various pieces of legislation have provided essential tools in the fight against computer crime. However, as with most new laws, there are a lot of problems. Most of the laws currently in effect, with the exception of the Sarbanes–Oxley Act and the Homeland Security Act, are either not specific enough or provide enough loopholes so that it is difficult to convict. Other problems materialize with the courts implementing the laws. In some instances, the courts ignore the mandated legislation and follow their own law. In order for the fight against computer fraud to become more effective, useful and effective laws must be passed and adhered to.

The 1976 Copyright Act grants civil courts the authority to grant injunctions as well as orders for impoundment and destruction of articles used in committing the fraud in disputes involving copyright infringement. This Act also provides the definition of infringement for criminal prosecution. It requires that a person willfully infringe on a copyright for the purposes of personal or commercial financial gain. A party found guilty of criminal copyright infringement is subject to the forfeiture of profits from the criminal activity as well as the destruction of property used in the activity. The Copyright Act has not proven useful in court cases involving Internet fraud. In *United States v. LaMacchia,* an MIT student set up a Web site that uploaded programs from visitors to the site. Others could then go to another site and download free applications. This is clearly a violation of the spirit of the Copyright Act but because the premise is not clearly addressed in the legislation, the Supreme Court did not believe the student to be guilty. The 1984 amendments to the Lanham Act are similar to those provided under the civil remedies of the Copyright Act. The Lanham Act allows the courts to grant injunctions and allows seizures in cases of trademark counterfeiting.

The Federal Trademark Dilution Act signed in 1996 addresses a new form of intellectual property — domain names. Under this Act, domain names are now subject to trademark law. Many lawsuits have been filed in this area and to date few have gone to trial. Generally, a large corporation has sued a small business or individual and the individual cannot afford the legal costs of the battle. Out-of-court settlements usually result in the large corporation getting rights to the domain name they want. As you will read later in this chapter, this issue has now come up at a major International Internet Conference and for a potential World Court involvement on the issue of Internet governance.

The few cases that have been adjudicated have resulted in the courts finding the defendant in violation of the Federal Dilution Act. In *Intermatic Inc. v. Toeppen*, the court demanded that the domain name "intermatic.com" be turned over to Intermatic. There are some inconsistencies in the courts' decisions. "The federal anti-dilution of law only calls for the remedy of an order that a party cease and desist from its diluting activity. In rare cases it might allow for damages, attorney fees or the destruction of the offending goods. It does not specify that the prevailing trademark owner actually get to take possession of the diluting goods." These types of inconsistencies show that there are still many issues that need to be addressed in the field of computer legislation.

The Industrial Espionage Act is another piece of legislation to address fraud concerning intellectual property. This Act provides monetary and criminal penalties for theft, misappropriation, or copying of proprietary information. If convicted, the criminal must forfeit all the monetary proceeds from the conduct and the computer equipment used to commit the crime. The proceeds and equipment confiscated are turned over to the government, not to the parties harmed by the misconduct.

Criminal prosecution for information crimes is growing rapidly. There are associated benefits and problems with criminally prosecuting information crimes. Some of the benefits are earlier trials, greater deterrence due to the criminal penalties, and criminal penalties, including incarceration. The downside to criminal prosecution is that it is not a high priority for law enforcement officials. Some see it as a victimless crime, because no physical injury is caused. Another issue is that computer crimes are difficult to prove and evidence is easy to destroy. It is difficult to prove which person out of the numerous people that had access to the computer actually committed the crime. Also, the evidence on a computer is very easily erased. By the time law enforcement arrives with the proper warrants, the criminals have ample time to destroy all evidence of the crime. The legislation providing for the criminal penalties is usually poorly written, so it is easy for the defendant's lawyers to find loopholes for their clients.

The Computer Security Act of 1987

Although covered earlier in this book, it is important to revisit the Computer Security Act of 1987. It was drafted due to congressional concerns and public awareness on computer-security-related issues and because of disputes on the control of unclassified information. The general purpose of the Act was a declaration from the government that improving the security and privacy of sensitive information in federal computer systems is in the public interest.

The Act established a federal government computer-security program that would protect sensitive information in federal government computer systems. It would also develop standards and guidelines for unclassified federal computer systems and facilitate such protection.[2] The Computer Security Act also assigned responsibility for developing governmentwide computer system security standards, guidelines, and security training programs to the National Bureau of Standards (now the National Institute of Standards and Technology or NIST) by amending the Act of March 3, 1901, and the Federal Property and Administrative Services Act of 1949.[3] It further established a Computer System Security and Privacy Advisory Board within the Commerce Department and required federal agencies to identify those computer systems containing sensitive information and develop security plans for those systems. Finally, it provided periodic training in computer security for all federal employees and contractors who managed, used, or operated federal computer systems.

The Computer Security Act is particularly important because it is fundamental to the development of federal standards of safeguarding unclassified information and establishing a balance between national security (as well as other issues in implementing security) and privacy policies within the federal government. It is also important in addressing issues concerning government control of cryptography, which as we will learn later, has recently become a hotly contested topic.

The Act was also a legislative response to overlapping responsibilities for computer security among several federal agencies. Some level of federal computer-security responsibility rests with the Office of Management and Budget (OMB), the General Services Administration (GSA) and the Commerce Department (particularly NIST), and the National Telecommunications and Information Administration (NTIA). The OMB maintains overall responsibility for computer security policy. The GSA issues regulations for physical security of computer facilities and oversees technological and fiscal specifications for security hardware and software. The National Security Administration (NSA) is responsible for security of information that is classified for national security purposes.[4] Such overlapping responsibilities were found to impede the development of one uniform federal policy regarding the security of unclassified information.

The Act gives authority to NIST for developing standards and guidelines (see Appendix II and Appendix III), and the intent was to refrain from giving the NSA a dominant role. However, this and overall implementation of the Act has not been a simple task. The Office of Technology Assessment (OTA) found in its 1994 report on information security and privacy implementation of the Computer Security Act that it has not been without problems. It was found that although the agencies follow the rules set forth by the Act regarding security plans and training, they do not necessarily follow the intent of the act. For example, it was shown that although agencies do develop the required security plans, the Act does not require periodically reviewing or updating them as technology changes.[5] Because of this, existing security of systems may remain stagnant over time unless the agencies review them regularly. As a result, the required security plans, if not evaluated on a regular basis, can become outdated and ultimately less effective, and may not be able to properly address the new problems associated with computer security.

As was stated above, the Act also was to give NIST the lead in developing security standards and guidelines and define the role of NSA as technical advisor to NIST. NSA, however, has sought to undermine NIST's authority. In 1989, the two agencies developed and signed the controversial Memorandum of Understanding (MoU) in an attempt to clarify the role that the two agencies play in regard to standards and guidelines for information security and to create a NIST–NSA technical working group that developed the Clipper Chip (which will be discussed later). The MoU, however, has been viewed as an attempt by the NSA to undercut NIST's authority and transfer control back to NSA. OTA, as a result, has viewed NSA as the leader in the development of cryptographic standards and technical guidelines for unclassified information security, while NIST has not demonstrated leadership in this area. This could have a great impact in the area of privacy violation because if NSA is viewed as the authority on this, then guidelines and procedures are likely to favor national security and possibly weaken the mandate of the Computer Security Act. This, in turn, could possibly lead to the implementation of policies and procedures made in the name of national security and law enforcement, which could infringe on an individual's privacy rights. All the above has changed with the events of September 11 and the subsequent creation of the Department of Homeland Security.

The Homeland Security Act of 2002

With the event of September 11, 2001, fresh in our minds and the Department of Homeland Security releasing its "National Strategy for Securing Cyberspace" in 2002, it may be time for educational entities at all levels to begin rolling up their sleeves and bringing the process of establishing courses and curriculum to educate the masses in protecting its information and infrastructure. This is a tall order to begin establishing such coursework at the university level, not to mention extending this to the community colleges and K-12. The passage of the Homeland Security Act of 2002 and the inclusion of the Cyber Security Enhancement Act within that

Act makes cyber security or information assurances everyone's business (private and public).

The Cyber Security Enhancement Act (H.R. 3482) was incorporated into the Homeland Security Act of 2002. The Act demands life sentences for those hackers who recklessly endanger lives. Also, the Act included provisions that seek to allow Net surveillance to gather telephone numbers, IP addresses, and URLs or e-mail information without recourse to a court where an "immediate threat to a national security interest" is suspected. Finally, Internet Service Providers (ISPs) are required to hand users' records over to law enforcement authorities, overturning current legislation that outlaws such behavior.

The Homeland Security Act added additional phrasing that seeks to outlaw the publication anywhere of details of such tools as PGP which encode e-mails so that they cannot be read by snoops. This provision allows police to conduct Internet or telephone eavesdropping randomly with no requirement to ask a court's permission first. As mentioned earlier, this law has a provision that calls for punishment of up to life in prison for electronic hackers who are found guilty of causing death to others through their actions. Any hacker convicted of causing injuries to others could face prison terms up to 20 years under cyber crime provisions, which are in Section 225 of the Cyber Security Enhancement Act provision of the Homeland Security Act.

The Homeland Security Act of 2002 was created to prevent terrorist attacks within the United States and reduce the vulnerability of the United States to terrorism. It plays a major role in the security of cyberspace because it enforces many limitations and restrictions to users of the Internet. For example, one goal of the Act is to establish an Internet-based system that will only allow authorized persons access to certain information or services. Due to this restriction, the chances for vulnerability and attacks may decrease. The impact of this Act will definitely contribute to the security of cyberspace because its primary function is to protect the people of the United States from any form of attack, including Internet attacks.

Section 214 of the Homeland Security Act is titled "Protection of Voluntarily Shared Critical Infrastructure Information." This section states that the Act "[Protects] critical infrastructure information accompanied by an express statement protecting its disclosure ... [It] protects systems, which include physical systems, computer-based virtual systems, and information that affect national security." This section is similar to "National Strategy to Secure Cyberspace," which is discussed later; *both* promote security of the nation's infrastructures. Overall, with the implementation of these strategies, it is hoped that the United States will gradually reduce its vulnerability and, most importantly, be protected from threats and attacks. In the future, the Internet will become one of the most important assets to many companies. With this in mind, it is very important that a strong security is established today so that tomorrow's security will be indomitable.

IT Contract Issues

The increased use of computers has forced organizations to enter into more contracts for computer hardware, software, and services. Poorly informed and counseled computer buyers, however, are at a disadvantage relative to the vendors. The vendors have familiarity with the products and contract terms. The rising costs associated with upgrading equipment and keeping pace with the state of the art, the acquisition of services from vendors to design, develop, and maintain equipment and continue IT operations have generated more concern among top management. Management has recognized that its traditional posture of accepting vendor contracts without negotiation is a poor business practice. Negotiating computer-related acquisitions is being taken very seriously by management and raised to a higher priority as we have become much more dependent on information systems to support strategic and day-to-day operations. IT auditors can assist their organization in preparing for negotiating computer hardware, software, and services contracts. Within the Big Four environment, management advisory services (MAS) can help their clients contract for computer hardware, software, and services.

IT users want systems that perform as intended; resorting to litigation in response to dissatisfaction with products or services is admitting that the selection or acquisition process has failed. IT users need the protection of having systems that meet their needs, not lawsuits. Some examples are companies like Catamore Enterprises, a 30-year-old business, which hired a major computer firm to automate its production control system. The system failed to match incoming orders with inventory records. The computer company, IBM, disclaimed responsibility for the software because the contract did not include it. The court awarded the business over $11 million in damages and it settled with IBM out of court for an undisclosed amount. In another case, Triangle Underwriters, a 40-year-old insurance business, filed for bankruptcy three years after converting to a new computer system that never worked to meet their needs.

IT auditors can help their companies avoid similar predicaments, especially those lacking in-house computer contracting expertise in such areas as first-time purchases, contract services for computer maintenance, custom applications, and multiple vendor procurements. Many times the evidence gathered by auditors can help or assist the organization in specifying both performance standards and remedies for nonperformance.

Exhibit 1. Types of Standard Vendor Contract Clauses

Standard Vendor Contract Clause	Effect on Customer Assumption of Risk
Integration into writing	Precontract promises are negated by vendor
Defect-free media warranty	Only the physical media, not the software on the media, is warranted
Warranty disclaimer	No expressed or implied warranties
Abbreviated time for filing suit	Too short a period to confirm failure
Limitation of remedies	Remedy limited by vendor to price of goods, excludes ancillary damages incurred
Shrinkwrap contract	Buyer bound without signature

Borthick and Massingale identify three areas where IT auditors and Big Four management advisory services consultants can be very helpful in their review of IT-related contracts. These areas are:

- Review of vendor contract terms that limit vendor liability

- Review of contract objectives and performance measurements to ensure objectives have been met

- Review and inclusion in future contracts of contract clauses for protecting customer interests

In many instances, the auditor will review the contract if the scope of the audit encompasses activities or actions they are to audit. This is done in the gathering of background or detailed information phase of an audit. Several types of standard vendor contract clauses to look for are listed in Exhibit 1.

In the development or review of any IT contract, the objectives of the contracting process should focus on preparing or examining the acceptance criteria. There are three key goals to achieve in contracting for computer goods and services. The first is the preparation of explicit criteria that can be used for acceptance, and the criteria will clearly allow the customer to see that their requirements have been either met or exceeded. Next is the process of negotiating the contract and the inclusion of clauses that assure vendor compliance. Finally, the process of monitoring contract compliance is the responsibility of the entire organization if they wish to protect their rights and leverage. For an IT auditor, this is an area that often is to be identified as a major control weakness, and as a result of the audit process, problems and contract issues are identified that many times require immediate management and organizational attention.

In reviewing the procurement and contract negotiation process, the IT auditor can look for the following tasks to be accomplished:

- Does the contract accurately reflect the organization's requirements and have they been verified by appropriate levels within the organization?
- Have the requirements been translated into measurable acceptance criteria that can be monitored and verified?
- Ensure that the request for proposal (RFP) contains the needs and requirements.
- The process for evaluating the contractor bids includes thorough evaluation of how they will meet requirements.
- Review the negotiation process:
  - Was legal counsel or contracting officer present at all meetings and documentation of proceedings recorded?
  - What changes or agreements were reached in refining contract terms and were they verified with management?
- The contract has been executed and monitored to assure customer's rights.
- Acceptance tests are performed on all products or services provided and tests are documented and reviewed by management.
- Acceptance tests are documented, evaluated, and the results are reviewed and signed off by customers at affected levels including management.
- Your organization exercises its right to accept or decline the contract, and documentation from above supports its decision.

In contracting for IT services, it is very important that the requirements be stated in terms of business needs. For example, a savings and loan supporting customer transactions with online terminals might require 98 percent uptime to avoid customer dissatisfaction. Such a requirement means that the need to ensure its being stated in terms of functional performance or specified as on time and within budget is critical. Also, another important provision to include is identifying the need for maintainability over the useful life of the systems or services provided. The integration of wording to this effect into the contract during the negotiation process can provide some assurance of protecting the customers' rights. Exhibit 2 lists some sample clauses that can provide this level of protection.

The above types of clauses used in the contract, especially IT-related contracts, can be effective instruments for providing a minimum level of assurance. As you are aware, these are clauses that vendors do not like to see in contracts, and in negotiation they will try to eliminate them from the contract language. This is where corporate legal counsel with information technology experience and past audit evidence and research can assist in getting them into the contract. One company was awarded over $3 million because they had included such clauses into their contract for systems development effort that did not meet their requirements and that lacked

Exhibit 2. Sample Clauses Providing Protection

Clause	Functional Performance	Installation on Time within Budget	Maintainability over Useful Life
Warranty against latent defects			X
Guarantee of reliability and exercise of "due professional care"			X
Operation of system "as a whole" required for acceptance		X	
Continuation and access rights			X
Incremental payments to maintain vendor incentive		X	
Performance warranty to guarantee sustained functional performance	X		
Warranty again limiting routines			X
Right to make backups			X
Right to unrestrained use			X
Customer-determined acceptance to permit rejection of unworkable products	X		

"due professional care." Many professional organizations have established standards of practice for their profession and membership in the form of a code of ethics and define due professional care (see Appendix III).

The IT auditor can play an important role in IT contract planning, formulation, and monitoring. The IT auditor provides management with information when they conduct their independent reviews, examining the various sources of information that can be of value to management and the organization. Contract nonperformance often end up in the court. The cost in time and resources can be great as mentioned earlier.

Netlaw: Privacy on the Information Superhighway

Private Information Available for the Taking

Now that we have had an opportunity to view some issues associated with computer security, we need to examine how the issue of privacy is impacted when computer security is breached. As we all know, there is a tremendous amount of information that companies and agencies are able to retrieve on any individual. People, corporations, and government are active in trading personal information for their own gain. Thankfully, the Federal Trade Commission (FTC), an agency within the federal government, has increased its monitoring and review of the Internet for consumer fraud and identity theft. Unfortunately, understaffed for this assignment, their Web site should be one to bookmark for current information about such issues at www.ftc.gov.

In a televised broadcast on CSPAN on July 21, 2003, on the subject of Identity Theft, officials from Earthlink, FBI, and FTC spoke on this crisis. Online identity theft is a major concern regarding E-commerce security. Striking millions of people every year, identity theft is carried out when someone uses another's name or personal information (such as a credit number) in a fraudulent manner and without the other's consent. Such action can be carried out on purchasing products, taking out loans, accessing bank accounts, and much more. The most common way personal information is stolen is through stealing business records, but other ways such as "Dumpster diving" or stealing information found in the trash, stealing mail, and simply snatching someone's wallet or purse have been found as tools to gain private information. Other tools include IP spoofing and spoofing or spam e-mail soliciting donations, funds, deals, etc.

This type of crime is a big threat and a growing concern for Internet users. According to a July 2002 U.S. General Accounting Office report, 2633 victims said they lost money or paid out of pocket as a result of identity theft. Credit card information theft accounts for the major portion of identity theft. This problem has been a big worry for the insecure commerce Web sites. Hackers broke into these sites and stole social security and card numbers as well as other personal information that is useful to them. In February 2003, the *Los Angeles Times* reported that a security breach recently occurred at a company that processes transactions of up to 8 million credit card accounts — including Visa, MasterCard, and American Express. Unidentified hackers broke into this company's database and obtained its customers' account information. There are 3.4 million Visa and 2.2 million MasterCard cardholders being affected. According to the Department of Justice, identity theft has affected up to 700,000 Americans each year. On the average, tens of thousands of credit card numbers have been stolen every week. Credit card information theft has caused a loss of billions of dollars for credit card companies and their merchants. Two major companies, Visa and MasterCard, reported that in the year 2000 fraud cost them about $1 billion. Just a card replacement costs them about $35. Other factors account for the losses including time and effort to enforce the new security system, money spent on security tools such as encryption, and money and labor for developing new security practices.

Research firm Celent and the FTC estimate that identity theft will likely reach 1.7 million cases by 2005. However, statistics gathered by the FTC suggests that credit card fraud will likely be the most common type of identity theft (invasion of the data snatchers). Visa International, most known for Visa credit card products, reported that half of all credit card disputes in 1999 were over Internet transactions even though E-commerce transactions made up only 2 percent of their total business. The study also found that 5 percent of consumers across the European Union (EU) trust E-commerce, and even when there is no credit card fraud, goods correctly ordered and paid for never arrive. We know that individuals share private information on a daily basis, but how has it affected the network world and the Internet?

The large number of users on the Internet has resulted in the availability of an enormous amount of private information on the network. This information unfortunately seems to be available for the taking by anyone who might be interested. A person's sexual orientation, bank balance, Social Security number, political leanings, and an individual's medical record and much more are there for anyone who may want it.

In 1995, it was revealed that somebody had developed a list of 250,000 Internet addresses showing what chat groups people visited, along with the Web sites users logged onto. The list was then put up for sale to anyone who was interested in this information. Some people have been collecting information on the Internet and making it available for use, and a large number of these individuals seem to be refusing to follow any sort of fair information practice. These are some examples:

- *Cellular telephones:* Your calls can be intercepted and your access number cribbed by eavesdroppers with police scanners.

- *Registering to vote:* In most states, voter-registration records are public and online. They typically list your birth date, phone number, and address.

- *Supermarket scanners:* Many grocery stores let you register for discount coupons that are used to track what you purchase.

- *Browsing on the Web:* Many sites mark visitors with "magic cookies" that record what you have been looking for and when you do it.

Are they entitled to your information? What is the government's policy regarding privacy of an individual and keeping strong security policy? Ideally, we would like to limit the amount of monitoring that the government is allowed to do on us, but is the government in a position to monitor our communications on the information superhighway? How will this affect our right to privacy as guaranteed by the U.S. Constitution? The focus of the following section will then be to address these issues paying especially close attention to the security-based measures that have affected the ideal of individual right to privacy. Later in this chapter we will discuss new and emerging laws that impact such issues.

Exhibit 3. Roles and Responsibilities in Securing Cyberspace

	Priority 1	Priority 2	Priority 3	Priority 4	Priority 5
	National Cyberspace Security Response System	National Cyberspace Security Threat and Vulnerability Reduction System	National Cyberspace Security Awareness and Training Program	Securing Government's Cyberspace	National Security and International Cyberspace Security Corporation
Home user/ small business		X	X		
Large enterprises	X	X	X	X	X
Critical sectors/ infrastructures	X	X	X	X	X
National issues and vulnerabilities	X	X	X	X	
Global					X

Source: From U.S. government, author unknown, *Cyberspace Threats and Vulnerabilities*. Available at: http://www.whitehouse.gov/pcipb/case_for_action.pdf.

The National Strategy for Securing Cyberspace

Over the years, the government has drastically changed its operations, and businesses have not been able to function the way they used to. These activities now rely on IT infrastructures called cyberspace. President Bush believes that over the years cyberspace threats have increased dramatically. His goal is to eliminate these threats before they affect the nation's critical infrastructures. However, securing cyberspace is not a simple task. It involves a coordinated effort by the government, businesses, and the American people. Exhibit 3 represents some of the roles and responsibilities in securing cyberspace. Bush plans to implement a strategy called the "National Strategy to Secure Cyberspace," which provides a framework for protecting the nation's infrastructures that are essential to the country's economy, security, and way of life. However, the government alone cannot apply this strategy. It needs the help and effort of the entire nation. Bush states, "The federal government invites the creation of, and participation in, public–private partnerships to implement this strategy. Only by acting together can we build a more secure future in cyberspace." If cyber attacks were to occur, U.S information networks could have serious consequences. Some of the consequences include losing revenue and the destruction of property. For example, if terrorists were able to penetrate into the U.S information networks, they could obtain confidential information that exploits the United States' most vulnerable areas for attack.

As technology continues to emerge, new vulnerabilities emerge as well. The strategy to eliminate all threats and vulnerabilities is almost impossible these days. Although it is difficult to eliminate these occurrences, another strategy would be to reduce them. Bush says that the United States plans to:

- Reduce threats and deter malicious hackers through effective programs to identify and punish them.
- Identify and remediate those existing vulnerabilities that could create the most damage to critical systems if exploited.
- Develop new systems with less vulnerability and assess emerging technologies for vulnerabilities.

Currently, there are approximately 3500 vulnerabilities reported annually. Exhibit 4 represents the number of vulnerabilities reported as well as the number of incidents handled within the past few years. This amount will continue to grow if these strategies fail or are not implemented properly. Overall, if the nation fails to work together, cyberspace will remain unsecured. Personally, we believe that President Bush is taking the right approach by utilizing the National Strategy to Secure Cyberspace because Internet security is a serious issue. Bringing the nation together with the intention to prevent threats and vulnerabilities is a good idea because it allows people to work as one for the betterment of society. However, due to the unending growth in technology, the nation must be aware of the possible cyberspace threats and have a good understanding of these technologies and their implications for security. In addition to the National Strategy to Secure Cyberspace, the Homeland Security Act of 2002 was also created to reduce threats and vulnerabilities.

An interesting side note to this plan is the cooperation of big business. On March 5, 2003, TechNet announced a CEO Cybersecurity Task Force formation. According to their Web site, "TechNet is a bipartisan network of CEOs that promotes the growth of Technology Industries and the Economy by building long-term relationships between Technology Leaders and Policymakers and advocating a targeted policy agenda." The Cybersecurity Task Force, made up of chief executives from leading computer companies such as 3Com, Cisco, Netegrity, RSA Security, and VeriSign, have agreed to devote time and resources in targeted initiatives to inform cybersecurity policymaking, promote best practices in network security, and support public–private efforts to protect the Internet.

"We represent the companies who created the Internet and whose hardware and software power the Internet on a daily basis, and we pledge our continued support in this public–private partnership to reduce our vulnerability to cyber attacks," stated Barry Bycoff, co-chair of TechNet's CEO Cyber Security Task Force and CEO of Netegrity, Inc. "The White House's National Strategy to Secure Cyberspace builds a strong foundation for

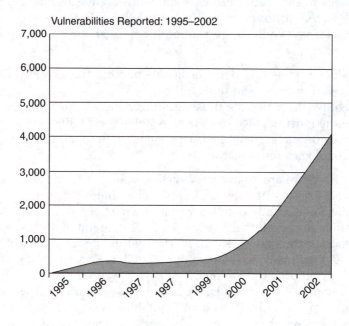

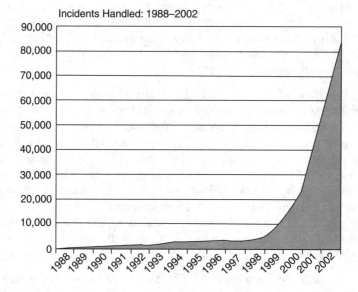

Exhibit 4. Vulnerabilities Reported and Incidences Handled
Source: U.S. Government, author unknown, *Cyberspace Threats and Vulnerabilities*.
Available at: http://www.whitehouse.gov/pcipb/case_for_action.pdf.

what we must accomplish as a nation. It is now time to begin implementing the recommendations," said Eric Benhamou, Co-Chairman of TechNet's CEO Cyber Security Task Force and Chairman of 3Com and Palm. "If our goal is to encourage enterprises in every sector to rapidly adopt known cybersecurity best practices, we believe that a privately led, voluntary initiative is preferable to a government mandate. This task force of TechNet CEOs is uniquely qualified to lead the way."

Specifically, the mission of the TechNet CEO Cybersecurity Task is to:

- Support public–private efforts to protect America's information infrastructure by providing expertise, advice, and resources for selected initiatives
- Promote awareness and best practices in cybersecurity
- Develop policy statements on key topics in cybersecurity
- Monitor IT industry participation in the various public–private partnerships, including the NIAC, NSTAC, PCIS, NRIC, IPv6 Task Force, and others.

Methods that Provide for Protection of Information

Multiple pieces of legislation have been passed that allow for the protection of information. Through amendments to the original legislation, intellectual property rights and computer-related issues have been addressed. The acts that are currently included in law fall into two applications, commercial and government. Some of the acts provide criminal penalties but are only applicable if the criminal accessed a federal computer or entered a federal system. These acts tend to have stiffer penalties as all the information in a federal computer is deemed "sensitive."

The Trade Secrecy and Protection Act establishes security for sensitive information in federal government computer systems. This act only covers information on federal computers but is viewed as a precursor to the same type of law for a commercial setting. The Computer Security Act of 1987 and the Computer Security Enhancement Act of 1997 enhance the Trade Secrecy and Protection Act by establishing minimum-security standards for guarding federal systems. Few of the acts applicable to commercial purposes allow criminal penalties. Generally, civil prosecution is the only remedy allowed.

The Web Copyright Law

The Copyright Law pertains to violations of copyright infringement. In order to prosecute a successful claim in court, it must be proven that the material was copied from a Web site or computer and that the owner has ownership of a valid copyright. Penalties for infringement of copyright valued of at least $1000 include fines ranging from $100,000 to $250,000. For infringements against property valued at more than $2500, an additional sentence may include a jail term of up to three years. Repeated offenses may result in a jail term of up to six years and fines.

The Copyright Law allows intellectual property to be copyrighted and is subject to all the same privileges and penalties that tangible property is provided under this law. The Electronic Communications Privacy Act prohibits the interception and divulgence of wire, oral, or electronic communications or the use of these intercepted communications as evidence. The Encrypted Communications Privacy Act provides encryption as a legal form of data transmission and authorized criminal and civil penalties to a party releasing the key to the code without consent. This act also permits the sale of encryption within the United States. These acts and other pending legislation attempt to curb the crime wave that is infecting information systems (IS) technology.

Privacy Legislation and the Federal Government Privacy Act

One of the major pieces of federal legislation to come out of the 1970s to augment the basic right to privacy that an individual is entitled to under the U.S. Constitution is the Privacy Act of 1974. The purpose of this act is to provide certain safeguards for an individual against an invasion of personal privacy. This act places certain requirements on federal agencies, some of which include:[7]

- Permitting an individual to determine what records pertaining to him or her are collected and maintained by federal agencies
- Permitting an individual to prevent records pertaining to him or her obtained for a particular purpose from being used or made available for another purpose without consent
- Permitting an individual to gain access to information pertaining to him or her in federal agency records and to correct or amend them
- Requiring federal agencies to collect, maintain, and use any personal information in a manner that assures that such action is for a necessary and lawful purpose, that the information is current and accurate, and that safeguards are provided to prevent misuse of the information

In light of the provision mentioned above, it would seem that the Privacy Act would protect many individuals against distribution of private information on the part of any agency. This, however, may not be the case as the Act outlines various general and specific exemptions. Because of these exemptions, it would seem that law enforcement agencies as well as other commercial agencies may have some rights to private information according to the Act.

Under Section (j), "General Exemptions," information maintained by agencies like the Central Intelligence Agency (CIA) is exempt from the above provision for national security reasons. In addition to the CIA, information maintained by an agency that performs any activity pertaining to the enforcement of criminal laws is also exempt from the provisions of the Act. This seems to implicate that these agencies can make inquiries for the sake of national security whenever they wish. Section (k), "Special Exemptions," further makes exempt from the provision certain information in regard to positions, appointments, and promotions in federal service jobs or positions in the armed forces.

The point of this seems to be that even though the Privacy Act is an important part of safeguarding individual privacy rights, there are many exemptions under which it may be lawful for certain information to be disclosed. This could in some cases allow for various agencies, both federal and nonfederal, means by which they can obtain and disclose information on any individual simply because they may fall under one of the many exemptions that the Privacy Act allows.

Electronic Communications Privacy Act

The Electronic Communications Privacy Act is one of the leading legislations against violation of private information applicable to online systems. Before analyzing some of the implications that the Act has had on the network community, let us briefly analyze some of the provisions defined by the Act as they seem to be quite complicated in giving privacy protection in some instances and not others.

Section 2511 of the Act makes interception and disclosure of wire, oral, or electronic communications prohibited, and prohibits the manufacture and possession of intercepting devices prohibited under Section 2512. Section 2516, however, seems to transcend these two as it authorizes and makes exceptions for the interception of wire or electronic communications under certain circumstances. In spite of the exceptions under Section 2516, Section 2515 prohibits the use of intercepted wire or oral communications as evidence. Even if evidence is intercepted and collected, it would seem that agencies cannot introduce that evidence in court! Does that make sense?

To continue with our analysis, we come to a very important provision in the sense of government intervention in online privacy. Under Section 2701, it is unlawful for anyone (including the government) to access stored communications without proper authority (i.e., a warrant). Once again, however, an exception is made in this provision. Under Section 2701(c)(a)(1) it is stated that the person or entity providing a wire or electronic communications service can intercept communications with prior user consent. Under Section 2702 (b)(6)(B) on disclosure, such a person can then report the information to a law enforcement agency if such contents appear to pertain to the commission of a crime (again with prior consent). Upon reading this, most people may think that clearly anyone desiring privacy would not give prior consent. But what about cases where consent is given when the contract is agreed upon? Some services will include fine print on the terminal screen at the time the user first joins the service, which indicates the role of the system operator or system administrator. This can contain statements regarding privacy rights as they apply to that specific service. If people do not scrutinize the fine print closely enough, then they may be setting themselves up and having their private information intercepted by and disclosed to others. For these reasons, one must take special care to read the policy guidelines when signing up for an online service.

The point of seizure of private information stored on computer without a warrant was made clear in the landmark case of *Steve Jackson Games Inc. v. U.S. Secret Service*.[8] Secret Service officials raided the office of Steve Jackson Games as part of a nationwide investigation of data piracy in 1990. The agents first violated privacy rights by searching and seizing messages without proper authority and without a warrant. It was found when the gaming company did receive a copy of the Secret Service warrant affidavit that it was unbelievably flimsy. It seems as though the author of the game GURPS Cyberpunk was suspected to be guilty by "remote association"! The author had corresponded with a variety of people, from computer security experts to computer hackers. That was enough to put him on a federal list of "dangerous hoodlums."[9] More than three years later, a federal court awarded damages over $50,000, plus over $250,000 in attorney's fees, ruling that the raid had been careless, illegal, and completely unjustified. This was an important case on the topic because it was the first step toward establishing that online speech is entitled to constitutional protection and that law enforcement agents cannot seize and hold a Bulletin Board Service (BBS) with impunity.

In summary, the Electronic Communications Privacy Act, although very good in its intentions to protect privacy rights, may have too many exceptions to be fully effective. This would hold true for the user and law enforcement agencies alike. Ideally, we would like to keep any information regarding our private affairs from being shared by others, but as we have observed, this is not always easy to do. In addition, even though law enforcement officials may get access to private information, it would appear to be difficult at times for authorities to base their prosecution solely on electronic communication.

Communications Decency Act of 1995

Another act passed by the Congress, the Communication Decency Act (CDA), bans the making of "indecent" or "patently offensive" material available to minors via computer networks. The Act imposes a fine of up to $250,000 and imprisonment for up to two years. The CDA does specifically exempt from liability any person who provides access or connection to or from a facility, system, or network that is not under the control of the person violating the Act. Also, the CDA specifically states that an employer shall not be held liable for the actions of an employee unless the employee's conduct is within the scope of his or her employment.

Encrypted Communications Privacy Act of 1996

This act contains a general declaration that the use of encryption by a U.S. person, domestically or abroad, regardless of algorithm selected, with or without key escrow function, and with or without third-party key escrow holder is lawful. The Act provides for criminal penalties and civil liabilities for a key holder (escrow agent) who releases the key to other than either the consent of the key owner or to authorized investigative or law enforcement officers. Another provision would make all sales of encryption within the United States legal, no matter how strong the technology.

Health Insurance Portability and Accountability Act of 1996 (HIPAA)

The first-ever federal privacy standards to protect patients' medical records and other health information provided to health plans, doctors, hospitals, and other healthcare providers took effect on April 14, 2003. Developed by the Department of Health and Human Services (HHS), these new standards provide patients with access to their medical records and more control over how their personal health information is used and disclosed. They represent a uniform, federal floor of privacy protections for consumers across the country. State laws providing additional protections to consumers are not affected by this new rule.

The Health Insurance Portability and Accountability Act of 1996 calls for stringent security protection for electronic health information, both while maintained and while in transmission. For IT directors, complying with HIPAA's privacy requirements is primarily a matter of computer security protecting the privacy and confidentiality of medical patient information and standardizing the reporting and billing processes for all health and medical related information.

National standards for electronic healthcare transactions will encourage electronic commerce in the healthcare industry and ultimately simplify the processes involved. This will result in savings from the reduction in administrative burdens on healthcare providers and health plans. Today, healthcare providers and health plans that conduct business electronically must use many different formats for electronic transactions. For example, about 400 different formats exist today for healthcare claims. With a national standard for electronic claims and other transactions, healthcare providers will be able to submit the same transaction to any health plan in the United States and the health plan must accept it. Health plans will be able to send standard electronic transactions such as remittance advices and referral authorizations to healthcare providers. These national standards will make EDI a viable and preferable alternative to paper processing for providers and health plans alike.

HIPAA Compliance

- Any connection to the Internet or other external networks or systems occur through a gateway or firewall.
- Strong authentication is used to restrict the access to critical systems or business processes and highly sensitive data.
- Assessments of vulnerability, reliability, and the threat environment are made at least annually.

The U.S. Health and Human Services Department has given the healthcare industry until August 2002 (October 2003 for small health plans) to comply and set substantial penalties for noncompliance.

Risk Assessment and Communications Act of 1997

This act coordinates federal information policy including privacy and information access under ONM, develops privacy and computer security policies and standards, and creates a Government Information Locator Service (GILS).

Gramm–Leach–Bliley Act of 1999

The **Gramm–Leach–Bliley Act,** which signed into law on November 12, 1999, **requires financial institutions to assess risk, manage and control risk,** oversee service providers, and adjust security programs as needed based on changing risk. One specific provision requires the business to "identify reasonably foreseeable internal and external threats that could result in unauthorized disclosure, misuse, alteration, or destruction of customer information or customer information systems."

Current Pending Bills and Other Legislative Material

Several pending bills are currently being evaluated by our government, which would affect the issues of personal privacy protection. At this time it would be worthwhile to examine a few of them and see how they may affect an individual's right to privacy.

The Notification of Risk to Personal Data Act (NORPDA) was introduced to the U.S. Senate on June 26, 2003, by Senator Diane Feinstein. This law is modeled on California's SB 1386 and requires all U.S. businesses and government agencies to notify customers in the event of a network security breach. Penalties are $5,000 per violation or up to $25,000 per day.

Due to the number of exemptions, exceptions, and overall confusing content of both the Privacy Act and the Electronic Communication Privacy Act, the latter two bills may be helpful in resolving some of the problems associated with the Acts. General standards need to be implemented so that there may be a uniform method of conduct as it applies to the Acts. The meaning of this is, with so many exemptions, it seems that certain organizations could violate privacy laws by finding ways of being exempt from the confines of the laws. Applying standards and enforcement of the laws, however, may be a step towards the right direction in assuring rights to individual privacy as guaranteed in the Constitution.

In California, the California Civil Code, SB 1386 was effective from July 1, 2003. The new California Data Security Law, SB 1386, will require organizations to notify Californian residents of breaches in the security of the personal information held about them by that organization. This will apply not just to businesses resident in California but also to any entities that conduct online business in California.

Only specific types of information trigger the notification requirements. The security breach has to involve an individual's first name or first initial and last name combined with one or more of the following:

- Social Security number
- Driver's license number or California identification card number
- Account number, credit or debit card number, in combination with any required security code, access code, or password that will permit access to an individual's financial account

Notification requirements will only be triggered in situations where this personal information has not been encrypted. The definition of a security breach under this new California law is very broad. A breach is "unauthorized acquisition of computerized data that compromises the security, confidentiality, or integrity of personal information maintained by the agency, person, or business." Notification has to be in writing or electronically and must be notified "in the most expedient time possible and without unreasonable delay."

Notification requirements comply with the Federal Electronic Signatures in Global and National Commerce Act 2000. Where the cost of providing the requisite notice would exceed $250,000, the number of people to be notified exceeds 500,000, or where there is no sufficient contact information available, the organization may provide substitute notice, which would consist of providing all of the following:

- E-mail notice if e-mail addresses are available
- Web site notice, provided there is a Web site that can be used to post such notice
- Notification to major statewide media

There are no criminal sanctions for noncompliance with the Act, but residents of California may enforce them through civil actions for damages.

Internet Governance

At the Annual Convention of the Internet Society held in Geneva, more than 1500 participants attended representing nearly every country in the world. This conference has produced some controversy and debate, focusing mostly on reforming the way the Internet domain names are created and registered. For example, recently, a Canadian firm was ordered to relinquish the "avery.net" and "dennison.net" domain names to business supplies maker Avery Dennison Corporation by a U.S. district judge. Legal experts say the decision could have a far-reaching impact on the way the trademark law is applied to the Internet. Other countries expressed dissatisfaction with the U.S. dominance in assigning domain names and have argued for this function being assigned to a nonprofit international governance board. Legal experts say that these cases and a growing number like them underscore future issues, which may ultimately end up in the World Court as international giants battle for the right to domain names.

Perhaps the most far-reaching was the fact that the ISO issued its Standard 17799 and soon to be implemented is the Organization for Economic Cooperation and Development (OECD) (see www.OECD.org) guidance for providing Internet security.[11] Also, the International Federation of Accountants (IFAC) and the International Association of Supreme Audit Organizations (INTOSAI) have issued their directive and guidance for Internet governance and controls. This issue will be a very important one in the coming years. Internationally, especially in Europe, privacy of personal information has been a very important and sensitive issue since the end of World War II. In the United Kingdom, the Data Protection Act of 1998 provides very firm guidance to organizations wishing to do business in the country. The Act has financial and criminal penalties for violation.

Conclusion

In summary, it appears that traditional as well as new security methods and techniques are simply not working. Although many products are quite efficient in securing the majority of attacks on a network, no single product seems to be able to protect a system from every possible intruder. Current security legislation, although addressing the issues of unwanted entry onto a network, may also allow for ways by which some criminals can escape the most severe penalties for violating authorized access to a computer system.

Moreover, some legislation in effect does not require periodic review, thus allowing for various policies and procedures to become outdated. The computer networking industry is continually changing. Because of this, laws, policies, procedures, and guidelines must constantly change with it; otherwise, they will have a tendency to become outdated, ineffective, and obsolete.

On the subject of privacy, we have seen that in the online world, private information has begun to leak out of systems as though it were a running faucet. Even though some of today's legislation does protect the user against invasion of privacy, some of the laws we have observed contain far too many exceptions and exclusions to the point that their efficiency suffers. In addition, the government continues to utilize state-of-the-art techniques for the purpose of getting to our information for the sake of national security. New bills and legislation continue to attempt to find a resolution to these problems, but new guidelines, policies, and procedures need to be established, and laws need to be enforced to their full extent if we are to enjoy our right to privacy as guaranteed under the Constitution.

For the IT auditor entering the new millennium, the need to keep current of new laws and changes in existing laws and Cyberlaw is critical. They can provide leverage in helping organizations understand the risks they face and the potential for consequences. Such consequences could even be decided at the International level as IT issues such as Internet governance begin to appear before the World Court. The potential for lawsuit through computer crime, invasion of privacy, copyright, patent and trademark infringement, and IT contract nonperformance is very high. The cost is even greater in dollars and resources if the case goes to court and the company, business, or industry receives negative exposure from the incident.

Review Questions

1. According to the National Center for Computer Crime, what is the annual cost of computer crime?
2. According to the FBI, what is the average dollar amount of reported computer fraud?
3. According to the NCCC and the FBI, what is the estimated percentage of computer crimes not reported? Why are these crimes not reported?
4. What advice does the FBI provide in protecting against computer fraud?
5. What is software piracy? How big a problem is it? Who is the Software Publishers Association or the Business Software Alliance?
6. What is the Computer Fraud and Abuse Act?
7. What is "reckless destructive trespass"?
8. What is the Sarbanes–Oxley Act?

9. What is the Copyright Act? How is this being used in IT issues?
10. What impact has the Federal Trademark Dilution Act had on corporate users of the Internet?
11. What is the Computer Security Act? Who does it impact? What problems has the Act encountered?
12. What are the potential ramifications of poorly written IT contracts? What is the IT auditor's role? How can IT auditors or management advisory services staff assist?
13. What is the Homeland Security Act? Can hackers who cause injury or death to others be prosecuted under this Act?
14. When a vendor includes a contract clause such as "Defect Free Media Warranty," what is the effect on the customer's assumption of risk?
15. What are the steps in negotiating a contract? What should the IT auditor look for?
16. When a customer, during the negotiation process, is able to get the vendor to accept a clause such as "guarantee of reliability and exercise of due professional care," what does that mean?
17. What kind of information is out there, available for the taking?
18. What is the Privacy Act? What does it protect?
19. What is the Electronic Communications Privacy Act? What does it protect?
20. What is the Communications Decency Act? What does it protect?
21. What is the U.S. plan for securing cyberspace?
22. List and explain two other bills Congress has under consideration.
23. Why is it important for IT auditors to know about the legal environment of information systems?

Multiple Choice

1. According to a recent Computer Security Institute and FBI study:
   a. 90 percent of respondents have detected computer security breaches within the last 12 months.
   b. 74 percent cited their Internet connection as the frequent point of attack.
   c. 80 percent acknowledged financial losses due to computer security breaches.
   d. All of the above.
2. Cyberlaw is:
   a. State law
   b. Federal law
   c. Law governing use of the computer and the Internet
   d. International law
3. Software Piracy costs the computer industry more than:
   a. $1 billion per year
   b. $4 billion per year

    c. $9 billion per year
    d. More than $10 billion dollars per year
4. The Computer Fraud and Abuse Act covers:
    a. Fraudulent trespass
    b. Intentional destructive trespass
    c. Reckless destructive trespass
    d. All of the above
5. The Sarbanes–Oxley Act requires that the board of an organization must:
    a. Register public accounting firms
    b. Establish or adopt, by rule, auditing, quality control, ethics, independence, and other standards related to preparation of the audit reports for issuers
    c. Conduct inspections of accounting firms
    d. All of the above
6. The Cyber Security Enhancement Act as incorporated into the Homeland Security Act of 2002:
    a. Demands life sentences for those hackers who recklessly endanger lives
    b. Does not require ISPs to hand over records
    c. Does not outlaw publications such as details of PGP
    d. None of the above
7. Key areas to look at in IT contracts are:
    a. Vendor contract terms that limit vendor liability
    b. Contract objectives and performance measurements to ensure objectives have been met
    c. Review and inclusion in future contracts specific clauses for protecting customer interests
    d. All of the above
8. A federal agency that protects consumers and has increased its monitoring and review of the Internet for consumer fraud and identity theft is the:
    a. NSA
    b. CIA
    c. FTC
    d. None of the above
9. The National Strategy for Securing Cyberspace:
    a. Applies only to defense area
    b. Applies only to medical records
    c. Provides a framework for protecting the nation's infrastructures that is essential to the economy, security, and the way of life
    d. None of the above
10. This Act is the first-ever federal privacy standard to protect patient's medical records:
    a. Encrypted Communications Privacy Act of 1996
    b. Privacy Act of 1974

    c. Health Insurance Portability and Accountability Act of 1996

    d. All of the above

Exercises

1. Using an Internet Web browser, perform a search on the topic "Computer Crime." Examine five Web sites and summarize the information they provide.
2. Using an Internet Web browser, perform a search on the topic "Computer Privacy." Examine five Web sites and summarize the information they provide.
3. Using an Internet Web browser, perform a search on the topic "Computer Law." Examine five Web sites and summarize the information they provide.
4. Using an Internet Web browser, perform a search on the topic "Computer Security Act." Examine five Web sites and summarize the information they provide.
5. Using the Internet Web browser, look up the Software Publishers Association. Who are they? What help or assistance can they provide?
6. Answer Case 8 in Appendix I, OHMY Corporation.

Answers to Multiple Choice Questions

1 — d; 2 — c; 3 — d; 4 — d; 5 — d; 6 — a; 7 — d; 8 — c; 9 — c; 10 — c

Notes

1. Lance Rose, Netlaw, p. 191.
2. Office of Technology Assessment, Issue Update on Information Security and Privacy in Networked Environments, p. 105.
3. House of Representatives, Computer Security Act of 1987 Public Law 100-235 (H.R. 145).
4. Office of Technology Assessment, Issue Update on Information Security and Privacy in Network Environments, p. 108.
5. Office of Technology Assessment, Issue Update on Information Security and Privacy in Network Environments, p. 115.
6. Murray Peck, A Review of Computer Privacy Handbook, p. 3.
7. CSR Privacy/Information Archive, Privacy Act of 1974 and Amendments.
8. *Steve Jackson Games v. U.S. Secret Service,* 36F. 3d 457 (5th Cir. 1994).
9. *Steve Jackson Games v. U.S. Secret Service,* 36F. 3d 457 (5th Cir. 1994).
10. Proceedings from the 19th National Information Systems Security Conference, p. 781.
11. "Privacy Online: OECD Guidance on Policy and Practice," Nov. 14, 2003.

References

1. Author unknown, Cyberspace Threats and Vulnerabilities, available at: http://www.whitehouse.gov/pcipb/case_for_action.pdf
2. Author unknown, A National Cyberspace Security Threat and Vulnerability Reduction, available at: http://www.whitehouse.gov/pcipb/priority_2.pdf

3. Author unknown, A Letter from the President, available at: http://www.whitehouse. gov/pcipb/letter.pdf

4. Borthick, A.F. and C.S. Massingale, MAS Opportunity: Helping Clients Negotiate Computer Contracts, University of Tennessee, College of Business Administration, 1986.

5. Brewer, E., P. Gauthier, I. Goldberg, and D. Wagner, *Basic Flaws in Internet Security and Commerce*, http://http.cs.berkeley.edu/-gauthier/endpoint-security.html.

6. Carter, D.L., Computer Crime Categories: How Techno-Criminals Operate, FBI Law Enforcement Bulletin, http://nsi.org/Library/Compsec/crimecom.html.

7. Clyde, R., *Exposing the Future of Internet Security*, available at: http://www.extremetech .com/article2/0,3973,1009679,00.asp

8. *Commercial Key Escrow/NIST Notices on Commercial Key Escrow*, Compiled by Electronic Privacy Information Center, http://www.epic.org

9. CSPAN, Televised briefing on Identity Theft by officials from FBI, FTC, and Earthlink on 7/21/03.

10. DeGidio, A.J., Jr., Internet Domain Names and the Federal Trademark Dilution Act: A Law for the Rich and Famous, http://www.lawoffices.net/tradedom/sempap.htm

11. Federal Anti-Dilution Act, 15 USC 1125.

12. Ferrera, G.R. et al., *CyberLaw: Text and Cases*, 2nd ed., Thomson/South-Western West 2004.

13. Gallegos, F., Federal *Laws Affecting IS Audit and Control Professionals,* EDP Auditing Series #72-10-20, Auerbach Publishers, Boca Raton, FL, January 2001, pp. 1–20.

14. Graff, M.G., Sleepless in 2021: The Future of the Internet, available at: http://www.tnty. com/newsletter/futures/archive/v01-02technology.html

15. Keyes, J., *Internet Management*, CRC Press LLC, Boca Raton, FL, 2000.

16. Overview of 104th Congress: Electronic Privacy and Civil Liberties Legislation, Compiled by the Electronic Privacy Information Center 1995. http://www.epic.org/privacy/ legislative_update.txt.

17. Privacy Act of 1974 and Amendments, Document from the CPSR Privacy/Information Archive, http://www.cpsr.org./lib/htdocs/home.html.

18. Privacy Guidelines for NII Review of Proposed Principles of the Privacy Working Group, Compiled by Electronic Privacy Information Center, http://www.epic.org.

19. The Copyright Act, 18 USC 506.

20. The Lanham Act, 15 USC 105.

21. U.S. Congress, Computer Security Act of 1987, Compiled by Electronic Privacy Information Center, http://www.epic.org/crypto/csa.

22. U.S. General Accounting Office, U.S. General Accounting Office, GAO-02-766, Identity Theft: Greater Awareness and Use of Existing Data Are Needed, July 2002.

23. Xie, J., Summary of the Homeland Security Act of 2002. Copyright 2002. Available at: http://www.uslawnet.com/Englishhome/News/messages/35.htm

Other Internet Sites

1. Journal of Online Law, http://www.law.comell.edu/jol/jol.table.htrffl

2. Forum of Incident Response and Security Teams, http://csrc.ncsl.nist.gov/firs/

3. CIPHER — Electronic Newsletter of the Technical Committee on Security & Privacy, A Technical Committee of the Computer Society of the IEEE, http://www.itd.nrl.naby. @Uitd/5540/ieee/cipher

4. Rutgers University Network Services — www Security, http://www-ns.rutgers.edu/ www-security/index.html

5. Cornell Law Review, http://www.law.comell.edu/clr/clr.html.

6. House of Representatives Internet Law Library, http://www.pls.com:8001/his/95.html.

7. *Netsurfer Focus on Online Commerce*, http://www.netsurf.com/nsf/vOl/02/nsfOl.02a. htn-d

8. State of California, S.B. 1386, http://info.sen.ca.gov/pub/01-02/bill/sen/sb_1351-1400/sb_1386_bill_20020926_chaptered.html

9. The Web Copyright Law, U.S. Copyright Office, http://www.copyright.gov/title17/circ92.pdf — Provides a full text version of the Copyright Law.

10. U.S. Department of Health and Services, Office for Civil Rights — HIPAA.

11. Medical Privacy — National Standards to Protect the Privacy of Personal Health Information, http://www.hhs.gov/ocr/hipaa/

12. U.S. Department of Justice, Overview of the Privacy Act of 1974, May 2002, http://www.usdoj.gov/04foia/04_7_1.html.

13. U.S. Government Resources, http://www.1l.mit.edu/links/usgov.html.

14. West's Legal Directory, http://www.wid.com/htbin/htimage/wld.conf7l99,177

15. D. Fisher, Cyber Plan's Future Bleak, http://www.eweek.com/article2/0,3959,901382,00.asp

16. D. Fisher, Cyber Plan Hitting Home, http://www.eweek.com/article2/0,3959,901382,00.asp

17. D. Fisher, Fizzer Worm Has More Lessons for Enterprise, http://www.eweek.com/article2/0,3959,1094570,00.asp

18. Author unknown, http://www.iso-17799-security-world.co.uk/

19. Author unknown, http://www.articsoft.com/iso17799.htm

20. Author unknown, http://www.oecd.org/EN/about/0,,EN-about-43-nodirectorate-no-no-no-29,00.html

21. Author unknown, http://www.securitystats.com/reports/Riptech-Internet_Security_Threat_Report_vlI.20020708.pdf

22. Author unknown, Computer Security Spending Statistics, http://www.securitystats.com/sspend.asp

23. Houle, K.J. and G.M. Weaver, Trends in Denial of Service Attack Technology, http://www.cert.org/archive/pdf/DoS_trends.pdf

24. Griffiths, A., Cost of Hacking, http://dag.unifiedcomputing.com/costs.pdf

25. Associated Press, Intruder Breaches Credit Card Security, *Los Angeles Times,* February 19, 2003: C5.

26. Author unknown, Site Clues Consumers into Identity Theft, www.usatoday.com/tech/2002/06/26/identity-theft-site.htm, June 2002.

27. Author unknown, Credit Card Theft, www.theftlibrary.com/tl.nsf/html/cctheft.html.

28. Author unknown, www.wired.com/news/privacy/0,1848,57823,00.html, February 2003.

Chapter 19

Security and Privacy of Information Technology: From the Individual to the Extranet/Intranet/ Internet

The development of Internet technology has originated a surge of new application solutions to improve business practices in corporations and E-government. For corporations, this technology has allowed companies to be more competitive and profitable from a global perspective and has changed the way people do business. For E-government, the Internet serves as a way of providing better services and information to the public. In the previous chapter, we examined some of the major IT-related legal issues impacting business and the need for IT audit awareness and understanding of their impact to the business. In this chapter, we take one step further in examining security and privacy issues in information systems (IS). Maintaining security and privacy requires corporate planning, training, implementing controls properly, monitoring the effectiveness of controls, and taking necessary corrective action.

To get an understanding of how profitable conducting E-commerce business is today, the U.S. Census Bureau conducted research that showed that the total E-commerce sales for 2002 were estimated at $45.6 billion, an increase of 26.9 percent (±3.1 percent) from 2001. The total retail sales in 2002 increased by 3.1 percent (±0.2 percent) from 2001. E-commerce sales in 2002 accounted for 1.4 percent of the total sales compared to those in 2001, which accounted for 1.1 percent of the total sales. The outlook for the year 2003 looks even more encouraging according to analysts. Researchers have estimated that 2003 will bring in more than $50 billion in business-to-consumer retail revenue, excluding travel. This could represent more than 97 million consumers or greater than 58 percent of the online population. A recent survey conducted by the Center for Communication Policy at the University of California at Los Angeles and published in the 2002 UCLA Internet Report found out from consumers that, when asked if their online buying is likely to increase, 71.2 percent of the 2002 respondents answered affirmatively, compared to 66 percent in 2001 and 54.5 percent in 2000.

Due to the nature of E-commerce, the Web applications that were created utilized electronic interfaces that often replaced human relationships. As these interfaces become standard to customers and business partners, the challenge for companies is that they need to provide the same level of trust and confidence from their E-commerce site compared to businesses that run without them. The security technology that underlies these E-commerce applications is crucial in building this trust, enabling clients to deal with the company with confidence and security. Security is the most important factor for E-commerce businesses because it is the bind for strengthening the relationships and tying the company more closely to its customers and partners. As business success depends largely on the close ties with clients, the security technology needed for E-commerce differs from the tools that are often used to secure corporate networks.

Information Systems Security and Privacy in 1998

In their September 1998 report, the U.S. General Accounting Office (GAO), the watchdog of Congressional spending, provided a status report to the U.S. Senate Committee on governmental affairs. In their past audit work and reports generated between March 1996 through August 1998, they identified significant information security weaknesses in each of the 24 federal agencies covered by the analysis. Poor control over access to sensitive data and systems was the most widely reported type of security weakness. Poor access controls in today's environment can expose an agency's information and operations to attacks from remote locations all over the world by individuals with minimal computer or telecommunications resources and expertise.

Such weaknesses can place a broad range of critical operations and assets at risk to fraud, misuse, and disruption of services. The report provides examples of weaknesses in such agencies as the Department of Defense, Department of Treasury, Internal Revenue Service, Social Security Administration, Health Care Financing Administration, and others. In GAO's 1997 report on the Health Care Financing Administration, which is responsible for processing healthcare claims for over 38 million patients, it was found that at least 60 contractors were not adequately protecting confidential patient information. The Social Security Administration, which is responsible for distributing $390 billion in payments to more than 50 million beneficiaries, reported similar problems.

In March 1998, a study published by the Computer Security Institute (CSI) and the Federal Bureau of Investigation (FBI) found that 64 percent of the 520 private and public agencies surveyed reported a security breach within the last 12 months. This study showed a 16 percent increase over a similar study. *Information Week*/PricewaterhouseCoopers in their 1998 Global Information Systems Security Survey of approximately 50 countries and more than 1600 IT and security professionals reported some very comparable statistics.

- At least one or more security breaches was reported by 59 percent of the Web sites selling products or services in the past year.
- Those that reported information loss totaled 22 percent.
- Theft of data or trade secrets was reported by 12 percent of E-commerce Web sites.
- Losses of between $1000 and $100,000 were incurred by 84 percent, and 16 percent experienced heavier losses.

In essence, all surveys had losses.

As both governments and businesses worldwide place increasing reliance on interconnected systems and electronic data, a corresponding rise is occurring of risks in fraud, inappropriate disclosure of sensitive data, and disruption of critical operations and services. The same factors that benefit business and government operations also make it possible for individuals and organizations to inexpensively interfere with, or eavesdrop on, these operations from remote locations for purposes of fraud or sabotage, or other mischievous or malicious purposes.

Information Systems Security and Privacy Today

Since the 1999 edition, this area has remained dynamic, and the public is more conscious and aware of their vulnerabilities. Cyber-crime continues to bleed U.S. corporations as surveys show; financial losses from attacks climbed for the third year in a row, and 44 percent of 503 computer practitioners reported financial losses of $455,848,000. Of these 503 respondents, 74 percent reported that their Internet connection was the point of attack, according to the 2003 CSI and FBI reports.

The GAO continued its review of the original agencies surveyed in 1998. As a follow-up, the results of their study found that not much had changed. Exhibit 1 shows that vulnerabilities still exist.

Recent developments have come to the attention of President Bush and caused him to take steps. The President along with Congress has passed an Act in an effort to secure cyberspace. The Act, known as the Homeland

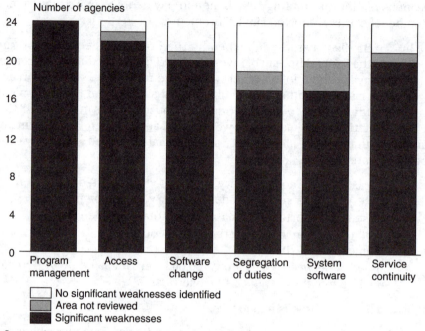

Source: Audit reports issued October 2001 through October 2002.

Exhibit 1. Information Security Weaknesses at 24 Major Agencies
Source: Information Security: Progress Made, but Challenges Remain to Protect Federal Systems and the Nation's Critical Infrastructures, GAO-03-564T, April 8, 2003. (http://www.gao.gov/new.items/d03564t.pdf)

Security Act, is a government strategy that is supposed to help protect our nation from terrorist attacks. Covering the topic of Internet security, it has been noted that terrorism has come in the form of Internet vandals. The President has derived another strategy to help secure cyberspace. Known as the "National Strategy to Secure Cyberspace," it is supposed to be a national effort to help secure the information that flows in and out of cyberspace. The purpose of President Bush's plan " ... is to engage and empower Americans to secure the portions of cyberspace that they own, operate, control, or with which they interact."[1] This means that each company or individual will be responsible for any information that leaves its systems and gets into cyberspace. Also, businesses need to work with government agencies in order to help secure cyberspace and to create a national cyberspace security response system.

In order for a national cyberspace security response system to function properly, "the United States needs a partnership between the government and industry to perform analyses, issue warnings, and coordinate response efforts."[2] Overall, the impact of the Homeland Security Act is

Exhibit 2. The 10 Areas Covered by the ISO 17799 Standard

1. **Security policy:** Adopting a security process that outlines an organization's expectations for security, which can then demonstrate management's support and commitment to security
2. **Security organization:** Having a management structure for security, including appointing security coordinators, delegating security management responsibilities, and establishing a security incident response process
3. **Asset classification and control:** Conducting a detailed assessment and inventory of an organization's information infrastructure and information assets to determine an appropriate level of security
4. **Personnel security:** Making security a key component of the human resources and business operations. This includes writing security expectations in job responsibilities (IT administrators and end users), screening new personnel for criminal histories, using confidentiality agreements when dealing with sensitive information, and having a reporting process for security incidents
5. **Physical and environmental security:** Establishing a policy that protects the IT infrastructure, physical plant, and employees. This includes controlling building access, having backup power supplies, performing routine equipment maintenance, and securing off-site equipment
6. **Communications and operations management:** Preventing security incidents by implementing preventive measures such as using anti-virus protection, maintaining and monitoring logs, securing remote connections, and having incident response procedures
7. **Access control:** Protecting against internal abuses and external intrusions by controlling access to network and application resources through such measures as password management, authentication, and event logging
8. **Systems development and maintenance:** Ensuring that security is an integral part of any network deployment or expansion and that existing systems are properly maintained
9. **Business continuity management:** Planning for disasters — natural and man-made — and recovering from them
10. **Compliance:** Complying with any applicable regulatory and legal requirements such as the Health Insurance Portability and Accountability Act (HIPAA), the Gramm–Leach–Bliley Act (GLBA), and cryptography export controls

making businesses, corporations, and individuals responsible for information that they possess. Because the Internet is not owned by a single entity, the responsibility of securing the information is also not placed on a single entity. The National Strategy to Secure Cyberspace correlates to the practices and efforts that were mentioned above in the sense that companies must implement their own policies and procedures in order to try to keep the information that they possess safe and secure.

The National Strategy to Secure Cyberspace mentions that five different levels of users are interconnected within the global problem of securing cyberspace. Exhibit 2 shows the five different levels along with the five different priority levels for each item. The five levels range from the home user/small business to the global sector. Since there is a lack in trained personnel who know how to secure the information, the likelihood of a breach is high. Having some of the different solutions mentioned above such as firewalls, encryption devices, and intrusion detection systems is not enough. "The mere installation of a network security device is not a substitute for maintaining and updating a network's defenses."[3] Administrators must be able to maintain and operate the system being implemented. Also, administrators must make sure that the system solutions must be operating properly and that regular updates and patches are installed in order to keep the software or device current.[4]

President Bush has asked Congress to increase the funds to secure federal computers by 64 percent.[5] The increases in the federal sector will then be passed down to the public sector. With the different implementation being placed on cyberspace security, it seems as if the amount of money spent in order to secure the information stored in cyberspace is large. However, comparing the cost to secure the Internet or cyberspace to the return on the investment, it is seen that the public would have greater trust in placing information on the Internet and the return on the investment would outweigh the cost of implementing the system.

In a May 2003 briefing by the Office of Management and Budget (OMB) staff on OMB-11A compliance, IT management, and reporting, the agency specifically identified the actions federal managers will have to take to comply with the directions stated. The guidance given was that in the area of IT security, OMB-11A reports must state security costs per system, associate spending with level of performance, identify if they have no security controls, and provide additional information where necessary. In answer to what security costs should consist of, the agency stated that it included all products, procedures, personnel, etc., that are primarily dedicated to or used for provision of security controls. Also, it will include employee training, security inspections and audits, vulnerability and penetration testing of, especially, those products, procedures, personnel, etc., that have, as an integral component, a quantifiable benefit to security and privacy training, and system/program evaluations. This amendment will support homeland security and the means to federal agencies and their programs and those who contract with the federal government for IT investments that support the homeland security mission areas of intelligence and warning, border and transportation security, defending against catastrophic threats, protecting critical infrastructure and key assets, emergency preparedness and response, and other areas of security and privacy. For example, federal managers will have to answer privacy questions such as, "Was a privacy impact assessment performed for this IT investment?"

Interconnected Systems and Electronic Commerce: Global Issues

An area of great attention under this topic and mentioned in earlier chapters is the Internet. After corporations used the Internet to do business externally, they realized the great potential in using it internally as well. That is how the conception of the intranet or corporate intranet began to change the way people work.

Intranet technology allows employees to accomplish tasks more effectively by sharing the company's information easily. Some of these tasks are online search, distribution of documents and policies, electronic mail, and a help desk, among others.

Network managers thought that because intranets are not open to the public, they are just networks within a corporation and so there were no security concerns. However, several recent surveys have shown that nine out of ten break-ins come from inside the organization. In essence, intranets are prime targets for disgruntled employees, hackers, and competitors. Internal networks are now taking on all the properties of the public networks that frighten us — openness, complexity, and flatness. Another factor is that user-controlled intranets can leave security to the clueless. Now, with communication links moving to wireless technologies, network vulnerabilities have expanded to another level. Certainly, the international community has not stood still and has taken action.

International Organization for Standardization and ISO 17799

Besides the government's having a hand in securing E-commerce, there are organizations such as the International Organization for Standardization (ISO) that list a comprehensive set of controls comprising the best practices in IT security. Their latest standard, ISO 17799, is an internationally recognized generic information security standard. Within these are the detailed statements that comprise the standard. Since the compilations of these standards have been through rigorous analyzing, ISO 17799 is a great way for better risk management. According to their Web site, "(ISO 17799) is also being used in some sectors as a market differentiator, as organizations begin to quote their ISO 17799 status within their individual markets and to potential customers … another factor to ensure much wider uptake of the standard."

There are two parts to ISO 17799: a code of practice and a specification for an information security management system (see Exhibit 3). It is intended to serve as a single reference point for identifying a range of controls needed for most situations where information systems are used in industry and commerce. First published as the DTI Code of Practice in the United Kingdom, it was rebadged and published as Version 1 of BS7799, which was published in February 1995. It is not widely embraced because

Exhibit 3. Roles and Responsibilities in Securing Cyberspace

	Priority 1	Priority 2	Priority 3	Priority 4	Priority 5
	National Cyberspace Security Response System	National Cyberspace Security Threat and Vulnerability Reduction System	National Cyberspace Security Awareness and Training Program	Securing Government's Cyberspace	National Security and International Cyberspace Security Corporation
Home user/ small business		X	X		
Large enterprises	X	X	X	X	X
Critical sectors/ infrastructures	X	X	X	X	X
National issues and vulnerabilities	X	X	X	X	
Global					X

Source: From U.S. government, author unknown, *Cyberspace Threats and Vulnerabilities.* Available at: http://www.whitehouse.gov/pcipb/case_for_action.pdf.

it is not flexible, has a simplistic "key control" approach, and has various other issues such as Y2K compliancy. Version 2 of BS7799 was published in 1999 with formal certification and accreditation schemes following. In 2002, Part 2 of the ISO standard was published, and in the same year the ISO17799 Toolkit was published.

An enterprise that is ISO 17799-certified could win business over competitors who are not certified. If a potential customer is choosing between two different services, and security is a concern, they will usually go with the certified choice. In addition, a certified enterprise will realize:

- Improved enterprise security
- More effective security planning and management
- More secure partnerships and E-commerce
- Enhanced customer confidence
- More accurate and reliable security audits
- Reduced liability

So, the purpose of this chapter is two-fold. The first objective is to address the most common security issues for intranets that corporations and E-governments encounter today, a new and dynamic area for IT auditors. The second is to enumerate recommendations to improve intranet security, which IT auditors need to look for as they assess and evaluate controls within these environments.

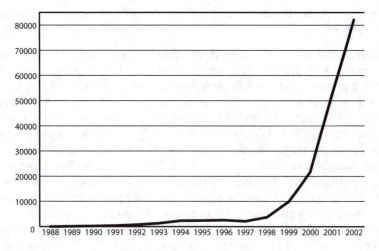

Exhibit 4. Number of Incidents Reported

The first part covers intranet definition, benefits, problems, and background. The second part discusses in detail current trends, intranet security, threats, tips, products, and the future of the intranet.

The Battleground: The Internet

How well have we done? The problems are there and growing, if you consider that the CERT's 1995 annual report indicated some 12,000 sites that had experienced some form of network-security violation. The CERT also reported at least 732 known break-ins and an equal number of probes of other instances of suspicious activity. Exhibit 4 shows that in the first quarter of 2003, the number of incidents reported was 42,586, and they project that 170,344 incidences will be reported by the year-end. This is a reported growth of more than 1400 percent since 1995.

The CERT Coordination Center (CERT/CC) is located at the Software Engineering Institute (SEI), a federally funded research and development center at Carnegie Mellon University in Pittsburgh, Pennsylvania. For IS auditors and IT security personnel, it has been an excellent resource on information. Following the Internet Worm incident which brought 10 percent of Internet systems to a halt in November 1988, the Defense Advanced Research Projects Agency (DARPA) charged the SEI with setting up a center to coordinate communication among experts during security emergencies and to help prevent future incidents. Since then, the CERT/CC has helped to establish other response teams while maintaining leadership in analyzing vulnerabilities and threats.

More than 69 incident response teams around the world have adopted the incident handling practices of the CERT/CC. The time to both resolve computer security incidents and repair computer system vulnerabilities has decreased.

Similarly, the use of practices developed by the CERT/CC has resulted in improved resistance to attacks on networked computers and, thus, improved protection for the information stored on or transmitted by those computers. This upward trend, as shown in Exhibit 4, is particularly disturbing as Internet attacks cost companies millions of dollars a year. In 2002, the annual CSI/FBI Computer Crime and Security Survey showed that 233 companies that were willing and able to calculate their losses due to Internet attacks reported a loss of over $455 million, with the most serious losses coming from the theft of proprietary information and financial fraud.[6] It is also important to note that Internet attacks are not just a problem for businesses but have far wider-reaching consequences. The general public and, in some cases, even countries can be affected by Internet attacks. One of the more destructive Internet attacks in recent memory occurred early this year. In January 2003, the Slammer worm caused the Internet to slow to a crawl and cost Internet-related companies to lose millions of dollars. The worm also caused bank ATM machines throughout the nation to crash. Some experts even believed that the Slammer worm was responsible for the drop in the South Korean stock market. All this only serves to reinforce the importance of businesses implementing reliable Internet security systems.

The GAO has made recommendations suggesting a clearinghouse that will provide the Congressional committee an incentive to support the Fed-CIRC, the Federal Computer Incident Response Capability, which is the CERT/CC incident response team. It was established in 1996 as a joint effort of the National Institute of Standards and Technology (NIST), the CERT/CC, and the Computer Incident Advisory Capability (CIAC). The FedCIRC provides incident response and other security-related services to federal civilian agencies.

The Tools

In the early days on the Internet, personal computers were scarce. Access to the Internet was limited primarily to university students with UUCP accounts. Today, the sheer size of the Internet makes it vulnerable to attacks from anywhere in the world. Tools used by IT designers, developers, and system maintainers are also tools of the hacker. And as mentioned earlier in Chapter 5 and Chapters 13 to 17, they are also tools of the IT audit, security, and control professional.

Scanners

Scanners comprise a major category of attacking tools used by crackers. Scanners are mainly TCP scanners that probe weaknesses by launching attacks against the targeted host's TCP/IP ports. The response from the targeted host is recorded. Valuable information such as probing results for anonymous user log-in is recorded. Some scanners are merely operating system utilities. For instance, "fingers" are UNIX utilities that scan for users who are currently logged on. Most scanners currently run on UNIX operating systems. However, movement to port scanners to Windows NT has become increasingly popular as NT gains popularity as an Internet server. Creating scanners is relatively easy. Anyone with an extensive knowledge of TCP/IP routines and any UNIX shell languages like C, C++, or Perl can create a scanner.

Scanners are important to Internet security because they reveal weaknesses in the network. System administrators can use scanners to help strengthen security. These tools are often found in the public domain. Scanners provide the following capabilities:

- Finding a machine or network
- Finding the type of services that is being run on the host
- Testing those services for holes

Still one of the most controversial scanners is the Security Administrator's Tool for Analyzing Networks, or SATAN. The authors of SATAN, Dan Farmer and Weitse Venema, are both security experts who have created other security tools. SATAN primarily runs on UNIX. It ports poorly to Linux platform. SATAN scans remote hosts for most known holes, including:

- FTPD vulnerabilities and writable FTP directories
- NFS vulnerabilities
- NIS vulnerabilities
- RSH vulnerabilities
- Sendmail
- X server vulnerabilities

Password Crackers

Password crackers are tools that use brute-force tactics to guess user passwords. For the security administrators, these tools check for weak passwords that are easy to crack. Programs can be run as parallel processes to speed up the cracking. Since a cracking program utilizes large quantities of system resources, a cracker running distributed cracking processes is easily detected. If Randal Schwartz ran his password cracking only on a single machine, other security administrators may not have caught him.

Password crackers are very simple in concept. The program uses a word in a predefined wordlist or dictionary and submits the list through the encryption process. This process repeats itself until a match is found. If the output matches the encrypted password, the password is cracked.

Another technique of password cracking takes the entire list and submits it through the password encryption process. Using the encrypted word list, each password is match against the wordlist. If a match is found, the password is found. This second technique is much faster because the wordlist is encrypted once. The success level of the password depends on the completeness of the wordlist. The COAST project at Purdue University has one of the most comprehensive dictionary listings. At the Purdue COAST site, password listings are available in English, German, Italian, Swedish, Chinese, Japanese, etc. Wordlists are also available by categories such as sports, cartoons, places, etc.

For crackers to make full use of the password crack program, the user listing must be obtained. In the UNIX environment, the fingers and rusers should be disabled to stop the outside world to obtain a password listing. Holes that leak user listings should be fixed. For instance, Kerberos 4 has a bug that allows the capture of user names. It turns out that upon receiving a malformed User Datagram Protocol (UDP) packet, the Kerberos 4 server returns a packet containing an error string and the principle from some unsanitized data structures. A perfect example is the UDP packet containing a null. Because not as much data is handed in as it is expecting, the pointer to the reused structure references the unpurged principle information. This unsanitized data contains the name of the last user to request a TGT and the Kerberos realm name. Needless to say, this is all the information you need to then request a TGT for that user and dictionary to attack the response.

Several crack programs are currently available. By far, Crack, written by Alec Muffet, is the most popular UNIX password cracker. CrackerJack by Jackal is another program often exchanged at the alt.2600 usenet. Exhibit 5 lists Internet sites that contain password crack programs.

Trojan Horse

As the name implies, Trojan horse is an unauthorized computer program within possibly an authorized computer program, which performs a function or series of functions unknown to the user. Internet Request for Comment 1244 defines Trojan horse as:

> One of the ruses used by attackers to gain access to a system is by the insertion of a so-called Trojan horse program. A Trojan horse program can be a program that does something useful, or merely something interesting. It always does something unexpected, like steal passwords or copy files without your knowledge. Imagine a Trojan log-in program that prompts for username and password in the usual way, but also writes that information to a special file that the attacker can come back and read at will. Imagine a Trojan editor program that, despite the file permissions you have given your files, makes copies of everything in your directory space without you knowing about it.

Exhibit 5. Sites with Password Crack Programs

Site	Program Name	Platform
http://www.fc.net/phrack/under/misc.html http://tms.netrom.com/~cassidy/crack.htm	CrackerJack	UNIX, OS2, DOS
http://tms.netrom.com/~cassidy/crack.htm	PaceCRACK95	Windows 95
http://tms.netrom.com/~cassidy/crack.htm	Qcrack	Linux, MS-DOS, Windows 95
http://tms.netrom.com/~cassidy/crack.htm	John the Ripper	UNIX (Relatively new), Linux, Windows 95
http://tms.netrom.com/~cassidy/crack.htm	Pcrack (PerlCrack)	UNIX, NT (Required porting)

One hacker suggested a Trojan horse attack to a gain password. The attacker sends garbage to a remote terminal while a user is logged on to the point that the user logs off. While the person remains logged off, the attacker runs a script to simulate the log-in screen. When the user attempts to log in again, the script records the password and sends it to the attacker. The script then displays an error message before deleting itself.

Insiders who devise elaborate nondestructive programs to collect intelligence write the most dangerous Trojan horses type computer programs. The discovery of such programs is mostly accidental. The infamous security tool, SATAN, fell victim to the attack. A programmer gained physical access to the computer that housed a Linux version of SATAN. The programmer modified the main ( ) function and altered a fping file so that when users ran SATAN, a special entry would be placed in the password file. The attacker hoped to compromise the servers that ran this utility. Due to poor programming, the Trojan version could not handle systems that used password shadow files. Only two known servers were compromised.

A technique known as object reconciliation protects the system against Trojans. Objects within the system are compared against an earlier recorded time stamp (i.e., from system backup). If the time stamp changes, possible attacks may be staged. Another method is examining the file size. However, both techniques are extremely unreliable. Since time stamps can be easily changed, reconciliation is not a good technique. Comparing file size does not always work. The really devious programmers may carefully consider the date, time stamp, and file size to minimize discovery.

One technique that works against file modification is digital fingerprinting. Algorithms like MD5 generate a digital signature of a file. MD5 belongs to a family of one-way hash functions called message digest algorithms. The algorithm produces a 128-bit fingerprint of the file. According to RFC 1321, producing the same key using different files is "infeasible."

Sniffers

Sniffers are devices that grab information traveling along a network. By placing network interfaces (i.e., Ethernet adapter) into a promiscuous mode, a sniffer captures the network traffic. Normally, network devices listen only to their own traffic (nonpromiscuous) while ignoring others. When placed in the promiscuous mode, network devices listen to all traffics on the network. Information such as IP datagrams can be captured in this manner. A sniffer is nothing more than a hardware or software that hears all packets sent across the wire. Information captured is then stored and archived for later viewing. Virtually any machine in a network can be used as a sniffer.

For crackers, the strategic placement of sniffers is important. One of the best points to place a sniffer is anywhere adjacent to a computer that receives many passwords. Connections to other networks (i.e., Internet) are especially of interest because capturing authentication procedures between two networks allows the cracker to expand his or her activity.

Sniffers represent a high level of risk. The simple existence of an unauthorized sniffer in the network is a telltale sign that the network is already compromised. As early as February 1994, CHIPS advisory notices from Naval Computer and Telecommunications Area Master Station, LANT Advisory, issued this warning:

> An unidentified person installed a network sniffer on numerous hosts and backbone elements collecting over 100,000 valid user names and passwords via the Internet and Milnet. Any computer host allowing FTP, Telnet, or remote log-in to the system should be considered at risk.

To defeat a sniffer attack, encryption is one of the best tools. By providing link encryption, information disclosed is minimized. Good network topology also helps. A network should be designed to trust other networks only if there is a reason. The design of the network should center on the trust relationships among the staff, not what the hardware needs.

Destructive Devices

There are two major types of destructive devices: harassment and data destruction. These tools are often readily available off the Internet. This availability means that anyone with a devious intent can launch an attack without much technical knowledge. Both large and small networks under the attack can come to a halt when enduring an e-mail attack. In general, these devices can be grouped into four major categories:

1. E-mail bombs and worms
2. Flash bombs and war scripts
3. Denial-of-service (DoS) tools
4. Viruses

E-Mail Bombs and Worms. The concept of the e-mail bomb is based on anonymous e-mail writing via port 25 on the Internet. Anyone running Windows NT or Windows 2000 can open a Telnet session from the DOS command prompt while logging on to any Internet service. Once logged on to port 25, any anonymous e-mail can be composed with falsified addresses (E-Hack, KwAnTAM_PoZeEtroN's Hacking Pages). The e-mail bomber simply automates the process.

The most famous e-mail bomber is Up Yours 3.0©. This application is freely distributed among hacking pages. The Up Yours mail-bombing program is extremely efficient with a friendly user interface. The features of the program include being able to specify times of day to start and stop as well as the number of messages with which it will hammer the victim. A variation of the e-mail bombing is list linking. List servers are e-mail servers on the Internet that distribute mail messages collected from various sources, usually for special interest groups. The attacker forges subscription to the list server using the victim's e-mail address. Tools like Kaboom are a variation of the e-mail bomber that automates this process.

The most common way that the worm achieves this is by infecting the system's e-mail program and sending itself to everyone in the host system's e-mail address book. In August 2003, the Blaster worm penetrated a number of Windows-support systems worldwide and created havoc among end users infested with strains of the virus. The MS Blaster worm is a piece of malicious software that unscrupulous persons place on other people's computers in order to gain unauthorized access to that computer. If a computer is infected, it can be used as part of a distributed denial-of-service (DoS) attack against a Web site by flooding the site with requests for pages from that computer and others across the Internet. The worm exploits vulnerability in some versions of Microsoft's Windows operating system, including Windows NT, Windows 2000, and Windows XP. (It does not affect Win95, 97, ME, or MacOS.)

Another example of a particularly effective worm was the Sircam worm, which infected many Windows systems. The Sircam worm had its own SMTP engine and would attach itself to a random document from the infected system and e-mail that document and itself to other systems. The Sircam worm also had a one–in-twenty chance of deleting files and folders in the C: drive of any system that was dated October 16 that were using the D/M/Y date format. Viruses, in turn, are also malicious self-replicating programs. Unlike worms, however, viruses are unable to spread themselves and depend on humans to unintentionally infect other systems. Viruses can cause a number of different negative effects in a system, ranging from the loss of files and information to lags in system performance to crashing of the entire system.

Flash Bombs and War Scripts. Flash bombs are specifically aimed at the Internet Relay Chat (IRC). IRC tends to be uncontrolled. People can chat from virtual channel to virtual channel. Flash bombs and war scripts are pranks that kick users off the IRC line. The following site contains vast repository on different types of "weapons" available: http://web.cyber-street.com/quake/files/weapons/

Denial-of-Service Attacks. The U.S. Air Force's CERT group defines DoS as "action(s), which prevent any part of an AIS (Automated Information Service) from functioning in accordance with its intended purpose." This technique does not involve an intruder gaining access to the network. The DoS attack exploits holes in the Protocol or operating system. The attacker simply invokes remote procedures that render a portion or the entire target inoperable.

One of the simplest methods is the ancient Chinese "Ping of Death." This attack is targeted at Windows NT 3.51. The attacker simply issues the PING -l 65527 -s 1 <target computer> command and the victim server will hang. The latest Windows NT service pack contains the fix for this problem (Q132470, MS Online).

Besides the current MS Blaster worm mentioned earlier, which can be used to launch DoS attacks, another famous case of DoS attacks occurred in February 2000 and affected many major companies. This DoS incident targeted many popular Web sites such as Yahoo Inc., eBay Inc., Amazon.com Inc., CNN.com, Buy.com Inc., and ETrade and resulted in huge damages for these companies. The total loss of money caused by the attack was estimated in excess of $1 billion. This figure was calculated based on the estimated revenue losses at the affected Web sites ($100 million), market capitalization losses on the days of the attack ($1 billion), and the amount needed to be spent on security upgrades after the incident ($100 to $200 million). The assaults were categorized as distributed DoS (DDoS) type, in which the hackers used multiple compromised computer systems to launch their attacks. During the incident, the companies experienced slowdowns in services ranging from two hours, forty-five minutes to five hours. Besides money losses, these companies also suffered other consequences such as loss of consumer confidence, damaged public images, loss of business opportunities, etc.

Viruses. According to the International Computer Security Association (ICSA), more than 10,000 viruses have been identified, and around 500 new ones are created almost every month. Viruses have become a major concern for many businesses because virus attacks result in a variety of devastating consequences for them. They can destroy valuable confidential information, cause lost productivity and operation disruptions, and bring about huge financial losses. The typical virus attacks include the following:

- In May 2000, the "I Love You" virus swept around the world infecting more than 45 million e-mail users. The Virus exploited a flaw in Microsoft Outlook and took over the e-mail address books of those using this e-mail software and sent itself to those listed. The damages caused by this virus were estimated at about $10 billion.
- The Code Red worms were released in July and August 2001, and their attacks were considered the biggest worm attack incidents in the history of the Internet. These worms took advantage of the loopholes in the Microsoft operating systems and broke into the Internet networks of many service providers and other major companies. They caused hundreds of thousands of computers to be vulnerable to hijacking. The hackers could easily take control over these fainted machines and steal any data they contained. The economic cost of the Code Red worms was estimated at $2 billion.
- The Melissa virus attack occurred in 1999 and cost the U.S. economy $1.2 billion in damages. This virus also exploited a loophole in Microsoft Outlook to penetrate a computer, replicated itself, and sent e-mail to other addresses listed in the user's e-mail address book. This virus acted very quickly and infected the e-mail systems of as many as 300 corporations.

This area is a huge topic in itself and much has been written about it in a number of publications.

Exploiting the TCP/IP Holes

Like IP spoofing, DoS attacks exploit vulnerabilities in the TCP/IP (Transmission Control Protocol/Internet Protocol). The UDP denial-of-service attacks can be staged by anyone who is on the network. No authentication is necessary. The UDP denial-of-service from one host can cause poor performance. If the attack is staged from a different host, both networks will experience heavy congestion. The attacker often exploits chargen and filter services. CERT made these following recommendations to avoid such attacks:

- Disable unnecessary UDP server. Chargen and filter are usually not used. Disable these two services. Use firewall instead.
- Use proxy gateway when using UDP. If UDP server must be used, proxy mechanism can protect the system from DoS attacks.
- Ensure the system is not subjected to IP spoofing. The UDP often follows after the initial break-in.

In 1996, a New York-based Internet service provider called Public Access Networks Corporation (Panix.com) came under attack from the unknown. The method used is known as syn_flooder. The syn_flooder attack is a DoS technique that exploits the Three-Way Handshake Protocol in TCP/IP, as shown in Exhibit 6.

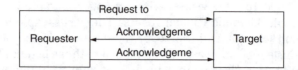

Exhibit 6. Three-Part Handshake

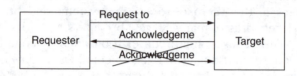

Exhibit 7. The syn_flooder Attack

In three-way handshaking, the requesting machine sends a packet requesting connections. The target machine responds with an acknowledgment. The requesting machine then returns its own, as shown in Exhibit 7.

In the syn_flooder attack, the attacker sends a series of connection requests but fails to acknowledge the target's response. The target never receives an acknowledgment and waits for the answer. Eventually the target's port becomes useless because the target is waiting for the response. The Panix.com attack in New York rendered the Internet service provider (ISP) out of service for more than a week.

The syn_flooder attack creates a high number of half-open connections. Because each connection opened must be processed, the system awaits the acknowledgment from the attacking machine. This is an inherent problem in the design of the TCP/IP suite. However, acceptable remedies are not available. The CERT advisory made this comment:

> *There is, as yet, no generally accepted solution to this problem with the current IP technology. However, proper router configuration can reduce the likelihood that your site will be the source of one of these attacks.*

— CERT Sept. Advisories

Any system that is connected to a TCP/IP-based network (Internet or intranet) and offers TCP-based services is vulnerable to the syn_flood attack. The attack does not distinguish between operating systems, software version levels, or hardware platforms; all systems are vulnerable. CERT recommends packet filtering to protect the network against the syn_flood attack.

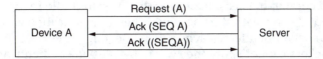

Exhibit 8. Sequence Numbering in Three-Way Handshaking

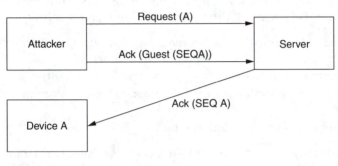

Exhibit 9. IP Spoofing Technique

IP Spoofing

IP spoofing was made famous by Kevin Mitnick's 1996 Christmas break-in of UC San Diego. The technique is also known as the sequence number attacks. This technique was discovered in 1984 and not addressed until 1996. The IP spoofing attack exploits the three-way handshaking. As mentioned before, three-way handshaking requires both the requester and the server to acknowledge. Upon receiving the request, the host acknowledges by using a sequence number; the requester receives the information and sends back the acknowledgment with the sequence number. The sequence number is generated based on random sequence routine (see Exhibit 8).

The assumption here is that if the receiver sends a response back, the response is from a valid address. However, a flaw in the randomized algorithm and the restriction of the protocol allows the attacker to guess the sequence number.

The attacker penetrates the system by guessing the sequence number of a valid node during the authentication process known as the three-way handshaking. If the guess is successful and no other authentication takes place, the attacker succeeds in the attack (see Exhibit 9).

Kerberos can address problems like IP spoofing. Authentication is performed using ticket-granting services. The node requesting the service must establish a session with the Kerberos server. The Kerberos server then sends an encrypted session key to the requesting node and a key to the ticket-granting server. The ticket-granting server then sends an encrypted copy of the session keys with a user ID. If the requesting node can decrypt the key with the password, then authentication is successful. Kerberos must authenticate each node requesting the service. In this situation, attackers cannot spoof the system by guessing authentication.

On July 21, 2003, EarthLink, FBI, and FTC made a joint presentation, which was televised by CSPAN, on the subject of Internet Identity Theft. They presented information on the Phisher site case they were currently prosecuting. The basics of the process are highlighted below:

- Thief sends e-mail to customer claiming to be a legitimate company that has lost the customer's personal information
- Customer reads e-mail and goes to the fake Web site
- Customer enters credit card or other personal information on Web site
- Thief steals personal information

The individual had attempted to impersonate (spoof) Earthlink to gain information for identity fraud purposes.

Recommendation to IT Auditors, Security, and IT Professionals

Hacking is simple: hackers exploit security holes. The security administrator should look for these holes in four major areas:

- *Physical security holes:* Giving unauthorized persons physical access to the system causes potential problems. Flaws in hardware may give way to the break-in.
- *Software security holes:* These are flaws in operating systems and protocols (i.e., TCP/IP) that allow the breach of security.
- *Incompatible usage:* Occurs when hardware and software may not be set up properly.
- *Lack of security:* Absence of security and weak security policies allow hackers to break into the system. One hacker noted that default passwords in hardware such as routers are often not changed.

Security administrators should constantly check for these types of flaws. Here are some recommendations:

- Regularly check for security advisories such as CERT advisories and vendor advisories.
- Review security policies on a regular basis.
- Report security breaks to authorities and organizations such as CERT. This helps other security administrators to prevent the same type of attack.
- Conduct security audit on a regular basis. This will uncover security weaknesses.

- Check for hacking sites to gain a better understanding on hacking methods.
- Think like a hacker. Look for security holes. Apply methods such as password crackers and tools like SATAN to uncover security holes.

Hackers are here to stay. Regardless of how they see themselves in the society, hackers are a threat to the information asset. With the fast-changing world of IT, security administration should be an active process. As security holes are fixed, new ones are being implemented. In a very unusual way, hackers help the development of security measures. However, good tools are only good when the administrator uses them.

Intranet Definition and Components

There is a tight relationship between the Internet and the intranet because intranets incorporate the protocols, processes, and standards found in the Internet. Intranets are more than a hybrid of network and Internet technologies; they improve on the capabilities of both. The Internet is an immense network that connects innumerable smaller networks and their individual resources, the heart of which is the TCP/IP. In its simplest form, an intranet can be defined as Internet services and sharing provided within an organization.

An intranet is an internal company network that uses the Internet standards of HTML (Hyper Text Markup Language) and HTTP (Hyper Text Transfer Protocol) and the TCP/IP communication protocol along with a graphical Web browser to support business applications and provide departmental, interdepartmental, and companywide communication solutions. An intranet uses a Web server that is connected only to a company's local area network (LAN). Intranets can also use news and mail servers to create private newsgroups for the company's intranet and to send and receive e-mail among the company's users.

The term intranet was introduced in late 1995. They were previously called "enterprise Internets." Even though the former name better describes its functionality, the term intranet is used more frequently because of its closeness with the Internet. An exact definition of the Internet and intranet is difficult, as Internet experts have not agreed on what exactly it is. For intranet, it is difficult because many kinds of intranets exist with different purposes.

The four main components of an intranet are:

- *TCP/IP:* This is the primary protocol of an intranet. On a TCP/IP intranet, information travels in discrete units called IP packets. TCP/IP software makes each computer attached to the network a sibling to the others; in essence, it hides the routers and underlying network architectures and makes everything seem like one big network.

- *Information services:* These are any software application that enables data manipulation (receive, store, and send) over an intranet. Examples of information services are e-mail, newsgroups, remote log-in, File Transfer Protocol (FTP), database search engines, E-commerce, intranet systems management, security, gateways, and firewalls.
- *Clients:* They are the applications needed to access the IS. The most common intranet client is the Web browser.
- *Authoring tools:* These are applications that create, edit, alter, or manipulate the data handled by an information service's server.

Intranet Benefits and Obstacles

There are many advantages to an intranet, including easy access and immediate delivery, cross-platform, reduced distribution costs, scalability, and increased internal communication among others.

- *Easy access and immediate delivery:* The intranet is available to anyone connected to the company's network whether at the local site or remotely via direct dial-up or the Internet. In general, intranets are available 24 hours a day, seven days a week. Authorized personnel can update it anytime and the information becomes available instantaneously throughout the entire organization.
- *Cross-platform:* Employees can use the tools of their choice on any major platform (PC, Mac, and UNIX) to create and manage information. This is one of the greatest benefits of intranets in which the exchange of information across multiple platforms is crucial.
- *Reduced distribution costs:* The traditional mechanisms of corporate communication, memos, printed documents, flyers, booklets, etc., are no longer necessary with an intranet. All these printed material can be published electronically on the company's intranet, saving printing costs and time. Typically, all this printing, duplicating, and distributing costs $25 to $100 per employee per year. In a company like Hewlett-Packard, with more than 105K employees, this represents a huge saving. Also, it can be used to deliver software upgrades.([www.pathfinder.com/fortune/specials/intranets)
- *Scalability:* Intranets can grow as necessary according to the company's needs. Starting small could be a good strategy due to the rapidly emerging intranet technologies and price changes within very little timeframe. Later, based on the company's needs, the system can grow easily.
- *Increased internal communication:* Communication in a worldwide company can sometimes be problematic; time differences and the expense of long-distance communication can impede collaboration between branches. Intranets help employees from all over to communicate easily using e-mail, sending documents electronically, creating online forums or training sessions, and videoconferencing.

Despite all the benefits that intranets provide, there are some problems or obstacles to overcome. They include controls, inertia, performance, and costs:

- *Controls:* These are needed when developing an intranet and include content proliferation, security, and conformity.
- *Inertia:* This refers to the following areas: training users, integrating legacy applications and documents, and overcoming the fear of new technology.
- *Performance:* Depending on the company's network structure the adoption of the new technology can impact the network performance, which may degrade. This is mainly due to the network's bandwidth. Also, company managers worry about employee productivity because employees will spend time surfing the Net, causing their work activities to suffer.
- *Costs:* Intranets are not free. Funds are needed to buy software and hardware. Even though intranets create costs, they also save money by conserving paper and ink, as well as reducing transportation costs.

Current Intranet Trends

The media, especially the Internet and network-focused publications, and general and business news, has played a major role in disseminating and making intranets hot. The intranet phenomenon is not artificial. Below are some compelling reasons that move intranet implementation in corporations.

- Internet technology can be transferred fairly easily to intranets, and most companies already have experience with the Internet.
- The tools used on intranets by users are similar to those used on the Internet. Therefore, the learning curve is not too high.
- There is rapid development of new tools such as scheduling tools, workflow, database-query applications, etc. Also, Web fronts can usually interface with old legacy systems giving old applications a longer life span.
- The cost and complexity of building intranets is, usually, significantly less than other in-house development efforts. One of the more compelling reasons to deploy intranets is to reduce costs. An early example of how companies are saving money on intranets is taken from the history of Hewlett-Packard (HP). HP created and deployed a corporate intranet called InfoNet. The initial goal of InfoNet was to make general information such as personnel policy manuals available to its 105K+ employees on the company's internal TCP/IP network. Due to the success of publishing its personnel policies electronically, HP's management decided to provide all major forms electronically to reduce distribution costs, printing costs, and e-mail traffic to personnel. Another example is found at Cisco Systems. Its

intranet is called the Cisco Connection Online, and it has saved the company $90 million a year through lowered operating costs, improved productivity, and better information flow. Managers like to see numbers come into play when the benefits of having an intranet include saving them a lot of money. For example, E-PeopleServe estimates that moving human resources information to a company's intranet can save it approximately 40 percent. Moreover, eliminating the paper for reports on travel and expenses can save a company as much as 93 percent in processing and administration.

Another interesting aspect of intranets is how are they being used. There are many ways corporations are using intranets today. How intranets are deployed in corporate environments has been a creative process. In addition, the market for Internet and intranet-related technologies and products exceeded $20 billion. Intranet and extranet projects have been growth areas for business and will reach up to $15 billion by 2005. In 1995, the market for Web authoring tools (the software used to create Web pages) was $2 million; it has exceeded $1 billion by 2002. The entire market for Internet software grew due to the demand coming from E-payment systems, and intranet and extranet development.

Intranet/Extranet Security

The responsibility for network security and intranet/extranet security is a task of the network administrator, and has to do with ensuring not only that authorized persons use the network but also that they use it in authorized ways. Intranet security includes making the network hardware, software, and data available whenever the authorized users need it.

Based on the current trends explained in the previous sections, most major corporations are already providing Internet access from each employee's PC or workstation. Most of the Internet access is gained from the corporate LAN, which raises some security concerns. But with employees being on the move, the use of their notebooks or PDAs now provide communication linkage with the corporate office. This can be wired or wireless in communication form. The major concern is that the Internet was developed for interoperability and communication, not for impenetrability. Therefore, connecting the corporate intranet to the outside world will bring a whole new set of potential problems. Corporations must define clearly security policies to protect their information. However, before establishing policies it is important to understand the risks or problems that can attack a company's intranet or network. Internal problems are the most common. This is when a disgruntled employee breaks the network to get confidential information from the company. As stated in an earlier chapter, a CSI/FBI report indicated that most break-ins come from inside organizations.

Other risks are computer viruses and an outsider attempting to break in or intercept confidential information such as credit information. The external threats are the most problematic because it is difficult to determine who was the intruder and what he was trying to do. There are many cases of outsiders easily gaining access to systems that were once assumed to be under the protection of their control systems. For example, the U.S. Department of Defense (DoD) admits that its computer systems were attacked more than 250,000 times in 1995. Understand that today the DoD has well over 2.1 million computers, over 10,000 LANs, and over 100 long-distance networks. They have established the Web Risk Assessment Team under direction by the Joint Task Force for Computer Network Defense. This team is made up of reservists who spend one weekend each month scanning DoD Web sites for classified or sensitive material. As a result of this proactive security initiative, a major survey of 800 major DoD sites on the Internet recently revealed as many as 1300 "discrepancies," some of them involving highly classified information. Also, the team uncovered more than 10 instances where information on Pentagon war plans was posted.

The security policy that a corporation puts into place depends on the degree of security desired on its network system. This degree may range from full restriction to complete public access. This should be a top priority in any organization. Management will be extremely concerned about how security is implemented and administered. There are four major areas in need of protection. The first area is the corporate information traveling over intranets and should have the greatest protection. The next area is the extranet applications, which connect corporate users with their suppliers or vendors. This information has to cross two security areas. The third area is the Web site. Here, information traveling to and from the corporate center needs to pass four security areas and has to meet the access requirements of each area. The last area is the mode of access, wired or wireless. Each has special considerations and levels of protection, which needs to be implemented, tested, maintained, and monitored.

Technology Tactics Used to Protect Networks

- *Firewalls:* These are protective software and hardware that block unwanted users and activities from the intranet. The firewall sits between the private local network and the Internet, and all the traffic from one to the other must flow through the firewall. There are several firewall categories, which are application gateways, packet-filtering systems, and circuit-level gateways. Firewalls are not only most often found in the form of stand-alone hardware devices but can also be entirely built into a piece of software that is loaded on the gateway server in a company's network. It also allows user authentication and traffic information log and report generation. A firewall can be used as the main mechanism of a company's security policy or plan. However, there are some shortcomings in using firewalls. The cost and performance tradeoffs protecting Internet firewalls may not be practical for high-traffic intranets because many firewalls impose severe performance penalties. On a network infrastructure, a traffic cop versus a roadblock approach is needed. Try to allow the traffic to flow, but be in a monitoring and execution position to shut it down if something bad happens.

- *Proxy servers (PS):* PS is a program that handles traffic to external host systems on behalf of client software running on the protected network; this means that users of the intranet can access the Internet through the firewall. Proxy servers hide the true address of the client workstation.
- *Encryption:* This is the process of encoding information in a special way so that it is secure from unauthorized access; the reverse process is called decryption. Encryption allows the communication to be secure over an unsecured communication channel. Secure Web servers use public key encryption techniques for different purposes such as user authentication, encryption, and digital certificates. To set up a secure server, first a digital certificate must be obtained. This depends on the server the company is using; for example, Microsoft and Netscape servers use VeriSign as the certifying authority. Once the certificate and the encryption keys are obtained, the Secure Sockets Layer (SSL) can be used to add security to the intranet as well as secure HTTP to make sure that all the company's documents and forms are fully encrypted.
- *Auditing systems (AS):* These systems record and track events that occur in the organization's network. They help to discover a potential intruder before the intruder succeeds. It is indispensable that all corporate networks have a good auditing system in place.
- *Access Control:* This is the capability to control who accesses what on the network. It is related to user authentication whether local or remote. Security experts talk about three factors for authentication:
  - What you know (user name and password)
  - What you have (a security key of some sort)
  - Who you are (a fingerprint, signature verification, or retinal scan — physical authentication)

Most likely the third option is the best but we are not there yet. Today the most widely accepted way of making sure who is logging into a network is a combination of the first two options. Requiring a digital signature like the one provided by VeriSign, Inc., in addition to username and password, provides some additional assurances. This type of key is being used largely for securing electronic commerce and e-mail transmissions but can also be used to verify intranet access rights. Yet, somebody could gain unauthorized access to the computer where the authentication key is stored.

Exhibit 10. Types of Common Internet Security Technology and Techniques

Technology/Technique
Authentication for users
Authentication for messages
Authentication for servers
Business contingency plan
Digital certificates
Disaster recovery plan
Encryption
Firewalls
Key recovery or escrow
Risk assessment/management
Single sign-on
Tunneling
Virtual private connections
Virus protection

Therefore, a network log-in in addition to the authentication provided is a better choice. However, with more than 10 million people communicating with the office and wanting access to the corporate intranet, the authentication key needs to be a moving target. Several companies have developed and manufactured devices that can be embedded in a PC, PDA, or notebook that looks like a credit-card calculator and generates a new mathematical key every 60 seconds according to a formula that the company's security server recognizes. By integrating a security service of this sort with the firewall, dial-up access and applications security are greatly improved.

Internet security products must be implemented at multiple levels within an organization. Corporation security policies should include continuous monitoring at each security layer. Although many companies have implemented firewalls, virus protection, and user authentication technologies for the Internet, other technology and techniques are being used in combination with other security measures on the intranet (see Exhibit 10). There has been additional development in authentication technologies, such as digital certificates, single sign-on, tunneling, virtual private networks (VPNs), and key recovery systems.

Management Tactics

It is important to know the technology available to protect networks, especially intranets and extranets. However, the most important factor to implement a security policy in an organization is to do an assessment of security needs. This is achieved by first understanding the organization's business needs and second by establishing security goals. There are some common questions that have to be answered. For example:

- What information is critical to the business?
- Who creates that critical information?
- Who uses that information?
- What would happen if the critical data were stolen, corrupted, or lost?
- How long can the company operate without access to the critical data?

Intranet security starts with a written policy. These guidelines should state Web and e-mail usage ethics and procedures, and discuss access limitations, confidentiality policy, and any other security issue. Good policies give employees exact instruction as to how events are handled and recovery escalated if necessary. The policy should be available online and be distributed to all intranet users. Other recommendations to minimize intranet security are:

- Frequently monitor areas where information is uploaded and downloaded to detect any unusual file formats.
- Evaluate regularly the content of posted material to be alert for any strangely worded postings.
- Revoke access immediately to the corporate intranet to all employees that leave the company.
- Ensure that the server is physically secure from theft and damage.
- Schedule and make frequent backups and ensure that they contain what they should. Store backups in an off-site location.
- Control access to sensitive files and directories such as human resources or financial data. Ensure that the proper access rights (read, write, and execute) on all contents, files, and directories are on the intranet.
- Provide virus protection for all users and scan file servers and workstations daily.

In summary, having well defined security goals, written policies, the right technology, and careful administration and monitoring of user access rights is the best way to control intranet security.

Network Security Products

There are plenty of security applications available. What is selected depends on the company's security needs and what the vendor's product offers. Exhibit 11 lists the major network security products available today. Most of them are applicable to intranets.

Over the past 10 years we have seen software security vendors pursuing partnership opportunities with server hardware and software manufacturers

Exhibit 11. Security Products

Product	Vendor	Elements	Enhanced Security Services
OmniGuard	AXENT Technologies	Firewall	Centralized management complete systems control
Gauntlet	Trusted Information Systems	Firewall, virus checking	Complete system control, encryption
E-Trust Firewall	Computer Associates	Firewall	Complete system control, access and password controls, encryption
Guardian	NetGuard LTD	Firewall	Session controls, terminal security, complete systems control
Sunscreen EFS	Sun Microsystems	Firewall	UNIX System Control
LANGuard	Gfi Software Limited	Auditing, intrusion detection, network management	Scans entire network, IP by IP, and provides information such as service-pack level of the machine, missing security patches, open shares, open ports, services/applications active on the computer, key registry entries, weak passwords, users, and groups, and more. Scan results are output to an HTML report, which can be customized/queried, enabling proactive securing of the network — for example, by shutting down unnecessary ports, closing shares, installing service packs and hotfixes, etc.
Intruder Alert	Symantec	Intrusion detection	Monitors systems and networks in real-time to detect and prevent unauthorized activity. Enables the creation of powerful, customizable intrusion detection policies and responses. Enables policy enforcement with the automatic deployment of new policies and updated detection signatures. Delivers networkwide responses to security breaches from a central management console. Provides audit data for incident analyses and generates graphical reports for both host and network intrusion detection activity. Complements firewalls and other access control systems with no impact on network performance
Intrusion Detection E-Trust	Computer Associates	IDS, real-time monitoring, internet content blocking	A complete session security solution that incorporates three key security capabilities into one package — a comprehensive network intrusion detection system, real-time session monitoring, and Internet content blocking. These solutions work together to address specific security requirements, forming a complete network defense without the high cost, administrative overhead, and nonintegrative approach associated with separate products from different vendors. Key-based access control

because customers in general do not perceive security as a separate product. The need for external access has driven the increased adoption of security products and the percentage of companies gaining access to the Internet.

There are also available tools that a network administrator can use to test the effectiveness of the security established at their companies. These tools can actually do little to catch any outsiders, but what they can do is highlight the security weaknesses in a company's network. The first one is SATAN for UNIX systems. SATAN collects data from each host in the specified network and creates reports for each host by type, service, vulnerability, and trust relationship. SATAN is free and available on the Internet, and for this reason many critics have argued that SATAN lets potential intruders take advantage of the information it contains to learn how to infiltrate systems more effectively. The second one, KSA (Kane Security Analyst) is for Windows NT servers and soon for UNIX and Novell NetWare systems. KSA examines the system and displays a bar chart with the following information:

- *Account restrictions:* Evaluates password controls, use of log-on scripts, and password-expiration dates
- *Password strength:* Rates password policies
- *Access control:* Checks user rights and removable drive allocations
- *System monitoring:* Collects a set of security-related concerns
- *Data integrity:* Checks uninterruptible power supply (UPS) installation and configuration
- *Data confidentiality:* Tests to see if passwords are stored in clear text or in encrypted form

A New Challenge: Wireless Technology

Wireless technologies have become more popular in our everyday business and personal lives. New technologies such as personal digital assistants, or PDAs, allow individuals to access calendars, e-mail, phone number lists, and the Internet. Others offer capabilities that can pinpoint the location of the device anywhere in the world, such as global positioning system or GPS. Wireless technologies promise to offer even more features and functions in the next few years.

Wireless technology enables devices to communicate without physical connections and utilizes radio frequency transmissions as a way to transmit data, whereas the traditional wired technology uses cables. Wireless networks serve as the means of transport between devices and among devices and wired networks such as the Internet. It is categorized into three groups based on the coverage range. They are Wireless Wide Area Networks (WWANs), Wireless Local Area Networks (WLANs), and Wireless Personal Area Networks (WPANs).

Several groups of computer security specialists have discovered security problems that let malicious users compromise the security of IEEE 802.11 WLAN's standard, such as passive attacks, to decrypt traffic and trick the access point. Active attacks inject new traffic from unauthorized mobile stations to decrypt traffic. Also, a well-known security vulnerability includes the use of static keys, where users in a wireless network share identical keys for long periods of time. If a computer such as a laptop were to be lost or stolen, the key could become compromised along with all the other computers sharing that key.

Wired Equivalent Privacy (WEP) for encryption is used for most IEEE 802.11a and b wireless products today. The problem without WEP is that, for example, with a laptop and a high-gain antenna, someone can sit in a parking lot and tap the traffic crossing that wireless WLAN. Having WEP encryption, the traffic will have the security that will be equivalent to that of the regular CAT5 Ethernet network. Unfortunately, the standard has security flaws (but at the same time it is better than nothing), and one should still consider any traffic that crosses a WLAN link to be compromised. Another answer may come in the form of IEEE 802.11i, discussed in the earlier chapters.

A good example of a business solution that copes with the security problem associated with owning a wireless LAN has been developed by Strix Systems, Inc. This company recently unveiled a new system technology that provides secure WLAN networks. Strix Systems, Inc., has implemented 802.11x authentication and authorization, along with standard protection schemes such as WEP, WPA (Wireless Protected Access), and TKIP (Temporal Key Integrity Protocol). They have built-in AES encryption and transparently support any VPN selected by the customer. The company's technology also includes system-level security features that prevent physical intrusion and detect and block rogue access points.

The government will continuously expand as it furthers its mission-central networks with new E-government applications and intranets. Thus, network security technologies will become very important in preventing intrusions.

Identity Theft

Online identity theft is another major concern regarding E-commerce security. Striking millions of people every year, identity theft is carried out when someone uses another's name or personal information (such as a credit number) in a fraudulent manner and without the other's consent. Such action can be carried out on purchasing products, taking out loans, accessing bank accounts, and much more. The most common way personal information is stolen is through stealing business records, but other ways such as "dumpster diving" or stealing information found in the trash, stealing mail, and simply snatching someone's wallet or purse have been exploited as ways to gain private information.

The research firm Celent and the FTC estimate that identity theft will likely reach 1.7 million cases by 2005. However, statistics gathered by the FTC suggest that credit card fraud will likely be the most common type of identity theft (invasion of the data snatchers). Visa International, most known for Visa credit card products, reported that half of all credit card disputes in 1999 were over Internet transactions even though E-commerce transactions made up only 2 percent of their total business. The company also found that 5 percent of consumers across the European Union (EU) trust E-commerce, and even when there is no credit card fraud, goods correctly ordered and paid for sometimes never arrive.

There are various ethical, legal, and business issues, and each require businesses to conduct specific levels of privacy protection while at the same time track changes to a consumer's personal information. One such tactic popular among businesses is to publicly declare their privacy policy. This is a way of assuring customers that their information is safe, and it also lets them know how the company will utilize their information. To be effective, these policies must be consistent throughout the company in order to ensure data integrity when it is being transmitted. The primary goal of the security is to provide access to specific information for those who request it and at the same time make sure that it only allows and ensures that the people who receive the information are the people who have the right level of access.

To encourage Internet growth and participation, a number of government and private organizations are trying to track and fight electronic crimes. However, because many businesses are reluctant to provide law enforcement officials with sufficient information to pursue possible criminals, legal action over Internet concerns has been limited. FBI officials believe companies "often fear that they will lose business if security breaches become public or that they will become the target of revenge attacks."[16]

Regardless of advancements in security and encryption, consumer fears continue to hurt the ability of companies to conduct transactions and documentation via the Internet. In June 2000, ITAA conducted a survey which found that "72 percent of respondents would not feel safe using a secure digital signature to sign a legal document." Terriorism fears have also increased uneasiness over Internet security, especially after the September 11, 2001 terrorist attacks. In another ITAA survey, it was found that "70 percent of respondents were concerned about cyber security and 74 percent worried that their personal information could be stolen online." These terrorist attacks have created legitimate reasons for internet security anxiety.

As mentioned earlier in this chapter, the statistics are overwhelming as the Federal Trade Commission (FTC) (see Exhibit 12 and Exhibit 13) and the FBI pursue criminal activity in this area. In their presentation before a national audience via CSPAN on 7/21/03, they provided information on the growth of cyber-crime.

The Future of Intranets and Other Networks

One approach to sense the future direction of intranets is to study the marketing of products and technology that support the intranets. Intranets will expand to extranets — two or more intranets that belong to different enterprises that are bound into one virtual network. This expansion consists of including suppliers and customers in making a frictionless economy where there is no paperwork, communications delays, or other obstacles to efficiency.

Some companies such as Wal-Mart, Home Depot, Staples, Nordstrom's, and Boeing already have developed extranets and provided their suppliers/vendors external access to enable simple information exchanges and database searches for product availability, pricing, and shipment data.

Despite all the new technology offerings and advances, security fears have prevented many companies from linking the Internet to their intranets, and even avoiding extranets. However, the proponents in favor of extranets say that extranets will increase revenues, reduce time to market and improve customer service, and otherwise fulfill every CEO's income-statement dreams as they have in Wal-Mart's case.

Other vision for intranets is to include the use of audio and video to enhance communication and inspire corporate employees in novel ways. For example, in the past, Sun Microsystems used the intranet to broadcast their CEO's monthly briefing to employees. Other companies are experimenting with extending audio over their intranet to remote and mobile users.

Conclusions

For businesses worldwide, the benefits of intranets have greatly exceeded the problems predicted. In addition to all the benefits mentioned in this chapter, there is a significant value to corporations, especially those geographically dispersed, in bringing people together regularly and at a low cost to solve problems, train, or do many other business and personal tasks.

The rapid growth of intranets is imminent; surveys and research made by a number of different firms have corroborated this. In fact, these estimates do not include all the applications packages, programming tools, and other items that go along with this technology.

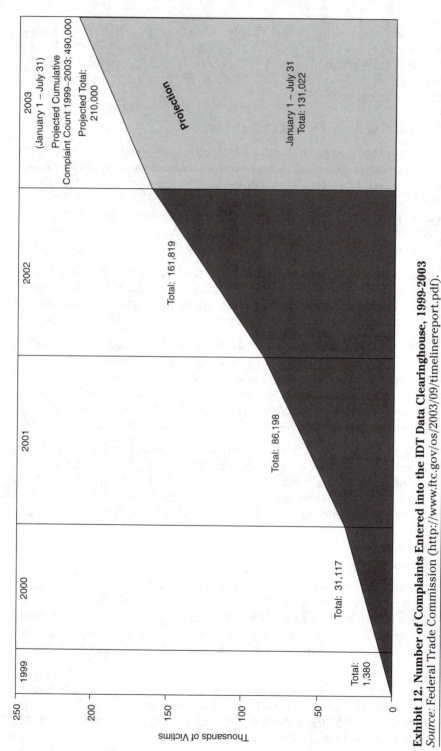

Exhibit 12. Number of Complaints Entered into the IDT Data Clearinghouse, 1999-2003
Source: Federal Trade Commission (http://www.ftc.gov/os/2003/09/timelinereport.pdf).

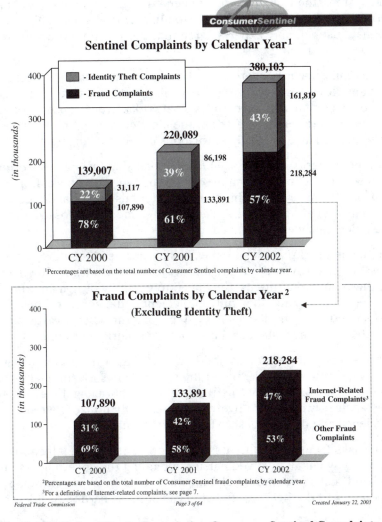

Exhibit 13. The Federal Trade Commission Consumer Sentinel Complaints
Source: Consumer Sentinel (http://www.consumer.gov/sentinel/sentinel-trends/page8.pdf).

The harnessing of Internet technologies within a corporate environment is the most important development to emerge in the computer industry in the 90s. The power of the intranet will transparently deliver the immense information resources of an organization to each individual's desktop with minimal cost, time, and effort.

However, both the organization and audit have a joint responsibility if security is a priority. The more absolute the security requirement is for a given system, the less it will be connected to any network, let alone the Internet. But the price to pay for absolute security is minimal access for legitimate users. Many experts agree that there is no perfect answer on where to draw the line.

Concerning security, there is no 100 percent guarantee for a network to be secure. However, there are security tools that offer several alternatives to the open communication of today's networks. Even if it is not connected to the Internet, internal threats are the most common. Good policies and procedures in place are the best weapons in this ongoing fight.

Internet security has had significant impacts on businesses worldwide. The emergence of new and more dangerous types of attacks from cyber-criminals continues to pose big challenges for businesses and security professionals. Cyber-attacks have caused huge monetary losses and other devastating damages to many companies.

As the online threats keep rising, businesses need to address the security issue seriously and quickly find ways to cope with it. To effectively fight these potential threats, they need to carefully design and develop a good security plan and then fully implement and enforce it. They need to consider and value its effectiveness in the long run when investing in security rather than the instant savings from the security investments.

The security professionals and IT auditor must understand that they play a very important role in battling cyber-crimes. Despite facing many difficulties that seem very frustrating and discouraging, these IT professionals must always try to overcome them, fully utilize their knowledge and talents, and do their best to fight security intrusion.

The risks from cyber threats can be prevented or significantly minimized only when all involved parties, including the governments, understand and realize the potential dangers caused by cyber-criminals, fully cooperate, and do their best to fight against these hard-to-beat law breakers.

Future studies in the following areas can be helpful in addressing Internet security issues:

- *Return on investments (ROI) in security:* Although investing in security can bring businesses many benefits in that it helps protect their valuable information assets and prevent other devastating consequences, many companies have not spent enough on security expenditures. According to many chief security officers, it is very hard to prove the value of the investments in security unless a catastrophe has occurred. A thorough understanding of the benefits brought by the investments in security will be a strong motivation in encouraging businesses to devote adequate money in security expenditure.

- *The trends of intrusion methods:* Cyber threats continue to present big challenges for businesses and security professionals. More sophisticated methods of attacks have become more common. The intruders have shown that they are moving from exploiting well-known vulnerabilities to exploring the weaknesses in software programs to launch the attacks. The study of this area will help recognize the patterns of the attack methods and thus enable businesses to prepare appropriate defense strategies.
- *Wireless networking technology — Wi-Fi:* Wireless networks have become more and more common. However, the wireless technology used in these networks, Wi-Fi, still has some serious security weaknesses. There are still many wireless networks so open or unprotected that confidential information from those can be easily intercepted and stolen. Many of these networks belong to major companies and to other companies that have already spent a lot of money to secure their information systems. A study of this area will be helpful in detecting major vulnerabilities of wireless networks and finding appropriate solutions to fix them.

The organization, management, and staff and the IT audit, control, and security professionals must work together to establish, maintain, and monitor the organization's security policy. Important elements of such a policy include end-user awareness, business contingency (such as the World Trade Center Disaster) and continuity plan, security audits, security practices, training of management and staff, use of tools, techniques and encryption, and the formation of an Incident Response Team. The only consistent way to establish security in environments with intranets, extranets, and Web sites that transport corporate data over public and private networks is to make security a top priority and move to implement the best practices for all phases of the security policy life cycle.

Review Questions

1. What were the findings of a 1998 GAO Report to the U.S. Senate Committee on governmental affairs regarding information security?
2. What were the findings of a March 1998 study published by the Computer Security Institute and the Federal Bureau of Investigation?
3. What were the findings of an Information Week/PricewaterhouseCooper study on global information systems security?
4. What is the Internet? What is an intranet? What is an extranet? Why do these areas pose risk to businesses and governments worldwide?
5. What were the findings of the CERT's 1995 report? Based on that report and findings from recent reports, are information security problems getting any better?
6. What is CERT? Where is the CERT coordination center? What is FedCIRC?

561

7. What are scanners? What are password crackers? What are Trojan horses?
8. What are sniffers? And how can perpetrators use them?
9. What are the two major types of destructive devices?
10. What is denial-of-service (DoS)? Give an example.
11. Does TCP/IP have security holes? How can systems be protected?
12. What is a syn_flood attack?
13. What is IP spoofing?
14. What is hacking? In what four major areas are there security holes?
15. What are the components of an intranet? What are the benefits and obstacles?
16. What does intranet security entail? What are the major areas of concern?
17. What are some of the major technology tactics used to protect networks?
18. What are some management tactics used to protect networks?
19. What are some security products to help secure intranets?
20. After reading this chapter, what is your opinion of today's state of information systems security and privacy?

Multiple Choice

1. According to a 2003 CSI/FBI study:
   a. There have been no security breaches within the last 12 months.
   b. Financial losses from attacks climbed for the third year in a row.
   c. The Internet as the point of attack was less than 20 percent.
   d. All of the above.
2. International Organization for Standardization (ISO) 17799 covers:
   a. Security policy
   b. Security organization
   c. Asset classification and control
   d. All of the above
3. CERT reported in 1995 that some 12,000 sites had experienced some form of network security violation. During the first quarter of 2003, the number of incidents reported were:
   a. 12,000
   b. 20,000
   c. 31,566
   d. More than 40,000
4. Which is the major attacking tool used by hackers?
   a. Scanners
   b. Trojan horses
   c. Sniffers
   d. All of the above

5. Destructive devices are:
   a. E-mail bombs and worms
   b. Flash bombs and war scripts
   c. Denial-of-service tools and viruses
   d. All of the above
6. IP spoofing is:
   a. An e-mail bomb
   b. Where the attacker impersonates a value site for purposes of gaining information that may be used in identity fraud
   c. A virus
   d. None of the above
7. Which are technology tactics used to protect networks:
   a. Firewalls
   b. Proxy servers
   c. Auditing systems
   d. All of the above
8. One of the fastest growing crimes on the Internet reported by the FTC and GAO is:
   a. IP spoofing
   b. Denial-of-service
   c. Identity fraud
   d. None of the above
9. SATAN is:
   a. A report generation tool
   b. A computer language
   c. A security administrator tool for analyzing UNIX networks
   d. None of the above
10. If not protected, a wireless LAN can be vulnerable to :
    a. Active attacks such as injecting new traffic from unauthorized mobile stations to decrypt traffic
    b. Passive attacks to decrypt traffic and trick the access point
    c. Rogue access points
    d. All of the above

Exercises

1. List 10 GAO reports in the last two years that have identified information security weaknesses in federal agencies (www.gao.gov).
2. Using a Web browser, search for the term "CERT." List and describe what is available at five Web sites?
3. Besides what is listed in Exhibit 10, what other products can you find out about via the Net or reports?
4. Using a Web browser, what information can you find if you search on the topic "network security"? List three sites that you think would be important.

5. Universities worldwide have done important research in the areas of computer security and privacy. Using the Internet, identify five that have done research or faculty who have published on this topic.

Answers to Multiple Choice Questions

1 — b; 2 — d; 3 — d; 4 — a; 5 — d; 6 — b; 7 — d; 8 — c; 9 — c; 10 — d

Notes

1. Author unknown. *The National Strategy to Secure Cyberspace*. http://www.whitehouse. gov/pcipb/cyberspace_strategy.pdf. May 2003.
2. Author unknown. *The National Strategy to Secure Cyberspace*. http://www.whitehouse. gov/pcipb/cyberspace_strategy.pdf. May 2003.
3. Author unknown. *The National Strategy to Secure Cyberspace*. http://www.whitehouse. gov/pcipb/cyberspace_strategy.pdf. May 2003.
4. Author unknown. *The National Strategy to Secure Cyberspace*. http://www.whitehouse. gov/pcipb/cyberspace_strategy.pdf. May 2003.
5. Author unknown. *The National Strategy to Secure Cyberspace*. http://www.whitehouse. gov/pcipb/cyberspace_strategy.pdf. May 2003.
6. Cyber Crime Bleeds U.S. Corporations, Survey Shows; Financial Losses from Attacks Rise for Third Year in a Row, CSI, April 7, 2002, April 29, 2003 http://www.gocsi.com/ press/20020407.html.
7. Author unknown, *The National Strategy to Secure Cyberspace*. http://www.whitehouse. gov/pcipb/cyberspace_strategy.pdf, May 2003.

References

1. Anthes G., Intranet firewalls offer no protection against enemy within the enterprise, *Computerworld*, November 1996. www.computerworld.com
2. Author unknown, Generic Enterprise Security Solutions, http://www.its.state.ms.us/ et/security/firewall.htm, April 2003.
3. Author unknown. The National Strategy to Secure Cyberspace, http://www.whitehouse. gov/pcipb/cyberspace_strategy.pdf, May 2003.
4. Author unknown, What is Kerberos? http://web.mit.edu/kerberos/www/#what_is, October 2002.
5. Author unknown, Cyber-crime bleeds U.S. Corporations, Survey Shows; Financial Losses from Attacks Climb for Third Year in a Row, http://www.gocsi.com/press/ 20020407.html, May 2003.
6. Author unknown, W32.Sircam.Worm@mm, http://www.symantec.com/avcenter/venc/ data/w32.sircam.worm@mm.html, January 22, 2003; April 29, 2003.
7. Author unknown, Studies See Internet Attacks Rising, *Business Standard*, February 10, 2003, April 27, 2003, http://www.business-standard.com/archives/2003/feb/50100203. 045.asp
8. Bradley, T., What is a firewall? *What You Need to Know About*, April 13, 2003, http:// netsecurity.about.com/library/weekly/aa030503b.htm.
9. Biggs, M., Invasion of the data snatchers, ComputerUser.com, May 2003: 24.
10. Burton, T., ITAA poll finds almost three of four Americans concerned about cyber security, Information Technology Association of America, December 11, 2001; Information Technology Association of America, June 8, 2003, http://www.celcee.edu/ abstracts/c20021706

11. Carr, D., Intranet Advisor: Weighing Options for Improved Security, *Internetworld*, December 1997. www.internetworld.com/print/1997/12/01/advisor/1997/12015/8/98. html.

12. CERT, 2000–2003, Number of Incidents Reported, CERT/CC Statistics 1988–2003, http://www.cert.org/stats/cert_stats.html, April 29, 2003. (From Table)

13. Cimino, J., *Intranets: The Surf Within*, Charles River Media, Inc., Rockland, MA, 1997.

14. Clyde, R., Exposing the Future of Internet Security. http://www.extremetech.com/print_article/0,3998,a=39857,00.asp, May 2003.

15. Costello, S., Internet attacks up 28 percent in 2002, *InfoWorld*, July 8, 2002; April 27, 2003. <http://archive.infoworld.com/articles/hn/xml/02/07/08/020708hnriptech.xml>

16. CSPAN, Internet Identity Theft, Joint presentation by Earthlink, FBI, and FTC 7/21/03.

17. Dalton, G., Acceptable risks, *Information Week*, August 31, 1998, pp. 36–48.

18. DeLong, D.F., Code Red Virus: Most Expensive in History of Internet, *Newsfactor*, August 9, 2001, April 27, 2003. http://www.newsfactor.com/perl/story/12668.html#story-start.

19. Dyson, P., Coleman, P., and Gilbert, L.,*The ABCs of Intranets*, Sybex, Alameda, CA, 1997.

20. Ferrera, G.R. et al., *CyberLaw: Text and Cases*, 2nd ed., Thomson/South-Western West, 2004.

21. Gallegos, F. and Jae Up, K., Policy of GII (Global Information Infrastructure) Standardization and Security Control Auditing of NII (National Information Infrastructure) and EG (Electronic Government), NCR — RER-98-002/1998.2, National Computerization Agency, Republic of South Korea, February 1998.

22. Gallegos, F., *Security and Control over Intranets and Extranets: Part 1*, #75-10-35, Auerbach Publishers, Boca Raton, FL, February 2002, pp. 1–12.

23. Gallegos, F., *Security and Control over Intranets and Extranets: Part 2*, #75-10-36, Auerbach Publishers, Boca Raton, FL, February 2002, pp. 1–20.

24. Greengard, S., The Real Cost of Cybersecurity, BusinessFinanceMag.com., April 2003; Penton Media, May 25, 2003, http://www.businessfinancemag.com/archives/appfiles/Article.cfm?IssueID=373&ArticleID=13957

25. Hatcher, T., Survey: Costs of Computer Security Breaches Soar, http://edition.cnn.com/2002/TECH/internet/03/12/csi.fbi.hacking.report, March 2001.

26. Huffman, L. and Hamilton, J., Employee revenge, Tech TV, November 5, 2002, May 2, 2003. < http://www.techtv.com/cybercrime/viceonline/story/0,23008,3386967,00.html.

27. Hunter, J.M.D., *An Information Security Handbook*, Springer, New York, 2001.

28. Jasper, M.C., *Identity Theft and How to Protect Yourself,* Oceana Publications, New York, 2002.

29. Levitt, J., The Keys to Security, *Information Week*, August 31, 1998, pp. 51–60.

30. Liebmann, L., Are Intranets Safe? *CommunicationsWeek Interactive*, August 1996. http://pubs.cmpnet.com/cw/080596/622impact.htm

31. Longstaff, T.A. et al., Security of the Internet, *The Froehlich/Kent Encyclopedia of Telecommunications*, Vol. 15, Marcel Dekker, New York, 1997, pp. 231–255.

32. McCarthy, L., *IT Security: Risking the Corporation*, Prentice Hall PTR/Sun Microsystems Press, February 24, 2003.

33. McClearn, M., Firms Wage War on Industrial Espionage, http://www.landfield.com/isn/mail-archive/1999/Jan/0083.html, January 18, 1999; April 29, 2003.

34. McGraw-Hill Companies, Here Comes the Intranet, *BusinessWeek*, September 1997, www.businessweek/1996/09/b34641.htm.

35. Mead, C., The opportunities and challenges of Implementing Internet Security Services, http://www.net.com/products/broadband/pdf/security_serwp_rev3.pdf, April 2003.

36. Norton, P. and Stockman, M., *Network Security Fundamentals*, SAMS, Indianapolis, IN, 2000, pp. 20–23.

37. Olsen, G., Secure Your Web Services, *Net Magazine*, March 2003: 41.

38. Saddat, M., *Network Security Principles and Practices*, Cisco Press, Indianapolis, IN, 2002, 5–12.

39. Sage Research, Intranet trends: second wave, *Network Computing*, May 1997. www.nwc.com/online/intranet0597.html.
40. Sarty, E., Internet Security Concerns Affect E-Commerce and Small Businesses, *Celcee*, May 2002; *Celcee*, May 23, 2003. http://www.celcee.edu/publications/digest/Dig02-02.html.
41. Tate, P., Internet Security: Can Best Practices Overcome Worst Perils? *Computerworld*, 32, 18, May 1998, Special Supplement.
42. Tittel, E. and Stewart, J., *Intranet Bible*, IDG Books Worldwide, Foster City, CA, 1997.
43. Tyson, J., How Firewalls Work, How Stuff Works, http://computer.howstuffworks.com/firewall.htm/printable. April 2003.
44. Tyson, J., How Encryption Works, How Stuff Works, http://computer.howstuffworks.com/encryption.htm/printable. May 7, 2003.
45. United States General Accounting Office, Information Security: Serious Weaknesses Place Critical Federal Operations and Assets at Risk, GAO/AIMD-98-92, September 23, 1998.
46. United States General Accounting Office, Information Systems: VA Computer Control Weaknesses Increase Risk of Fraud, Misuse, and Improper Disclosure, GAO/AIMD-98-175, September 23, 1998.
47. Van Cleve, B. and Brittton, M., *Discover Intranets*, IDG Books Worldwide, Foster City, CA, 1997.
48. Vaughan-Nichols, S., The Internet, Extranets and Intranets: Oh My!, *Sm@rtReseller*, May 1998. www.zdnet.com/sr/techwatch/980504/internet.html
49. Winkler, C., Opportunities Knock, *InformationWeek*, November 1996, www.techweb.cmp.com/iw/606/06opp.htm

Internet References

1. Attacks per Company per Week, Cyber Attack Activity, Symantec Internet Security Threat Report. http://www.securitystats.com/reports/Symantec-Internet_Security_Threat_Report_vIII.20030201.pdf, April 29, 2003.
2. New Vulnerabilities per Month,<http://www.securityfocus.com/vulns/stats.shtml>, April 29, 2003.
3. Attack Activity by Type, Cyber Attack Activity, Symantec Internet Security Threat Report. http://www.securitystats.com/reports/Symantec-Internet_Security_Threat_Report_vIII.20030201.pdf May 5, 2003.
4. Top 20 Scans, Attacker Platform, Symantec Internet Security Threat Report, <http://www.securitystats.com/reports/Symantec-Internet_Security_Threat_Report_vIII.20030201.pdf>, May 5, 2003.
5. Typical Firewall Layout, How Firewalls Work, Ivaldi Information Security Solutions for Your Business, < http://www.ivaldi.co.uk/firewalls_how_they_work.html>, May 12, 2003.

Chapter 20

IT Auditing: Career Planning and Development, Evaluating Audit Quality, and Best Practices

A career development plan is essential to developing and retaining information technology (IT) auditing expertise in an organization. Career development planning involves an integrated consideration of the individual's and the organization's needs. An organization can successfully develop its own IT auditor through training and development of knowledge, skills, and abilities and provide a career path for this professional. Chapter 20 presents a method for planning and establishing the career development process for the IT auditor and gives guidelines for formulating and implementing a career development plan to fit the needs of a particular organization.

A related key area is the quality of an IT auditor's performance. Managers are constantly searching for better methods of evaluating staff performance. Performance management, counseling, and career development planning require effective performance evaluation practices. Through total quality management, auditors are being challenged today to provide a more customer-oriented focus. Because of the complex technical nature of IT auditing, audit managers require effective methods for assessing individual and group performance. This article discusses techniques for assessing the quality of IT audits and the auditors conducting them.

The concept of "Best Practices" is to share ideas among IT audit professionals in their own domain. Best Practices of IT audit management is relaying to others some ideas they can use for their companies. Some ideas may help some professionals develop much needed policies, procedures, and practices for their organizations. New ideas can aid IT professionals in their quest to become more efficient and productive in their work.

IT Auditor Career Development and Planning

An IT auditor's career development is as important to the individual as to the company who commits training and resources to this position. A career development plan and path offers the professional such as an IT auditor the opportunity to grow and upgrade the level of services provided to an organization. If a career path and development program does not exist, the chances of poor performance and turnover are high. An organization must recognize that an IT auditor with the proper mix of training (formal and on-the-job), development of designated skills, and increased level of knowledge and abilities provides a valued resource for potential managerial positions in corporate, financial, and other operational areas.

Among the various types of incentives for a professional, career advancement is one of the most effective. In recent surveys, some professionals rank career advancement higher than a monetary reward. In the IT audit profession, a large percentage of the professionals who go into this field do so because they recognize the management visibility they receive from this position. Experience and exposure in the audit profession can often provide opportunities in management.

In today's environment, most organizations' career development planning for IT audit staff is insufficient. This is due largely to pressures of time and job performance. In most instances, individuals do not receive the appropriate mix of training and experience for them to adequately develop their knowledge, skills, and abilities and to progress within the organization. Thus, the career ladder and options open to an individual are not planned or formally defined, resulting in turnover and losses to outside organizations. In a recent sample of 227 IT audit professionals from various companies (government and private), approximately 31 percent of the respondents indicated the lack of an established career path for IT auditors. Of these, many stated that they had considerable problems in the hiring and retaining of IT auditors.

How does an audit manager or organizational management design, develop, and implement a career development plan? The process of matching individual career paths with organizational objectives is not easy. Career development is an important element to any organization; it should not be overlooked. The key components of such a plan are a defined career path with experiential development, training, and expected knowledge, skills, and abilities to be achieved as a person progresses up the career ladder.

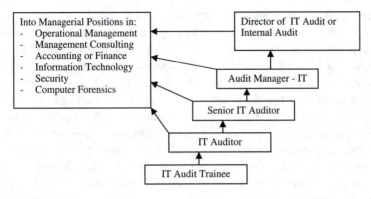

Exhibit 1. IT Audit Career Path

A key point that management needs to remember is that a career development plan must be a viable, workable, management-supported concept. It should not be another sales pitch to the potential employees or a false promise to the staff. Employee motivation and trust will be impacted in a negative manner if they find out that the plan, in reality, cannot be actualized. This is where organizational management can lose their credibility with their staff.

Establishing a Career Development Plan

A functional and fully successful career development plan consists of six major elements, which must be integrated into an established process within the organization. These elements are:

- Career path planning with management support
- Definition of knowledge, skills, and abilities
- Performance assessment
- Performance counseling and feedback
- Training
- Professional development

Each of these elements becomes necessary components of an effective career development plan. Exhibit 1 displays more information on each of these elements as related to the IT auditor.

Career Path Planning Needs Management Support

The establishment of the career development planning process must begin with the support of the management in the organization. It requires a commitment from the management to acknowledge and define horizontal and vertical career path opportunities within the organization (see Exhibit 1). The IT audit career path as illustrated offers the professional tremendous diversity in their career. Management gains by supporting such diversity and job opportunity. Often, management can help infuse an organization with knowledge, skills, and abilities to implement change. Without management support, career opportunities will be viewed with mixed emotions and doubt by IT audit staff. This can cause the eventual loss of employees to outside concerns because the opportunities are similar. An example would be an IT audit professional who started with a Big Four CPA firm, after four years moved to an IT audit manager position in a private firm, then after, say three to four years, moved to an audit director position with another firm. Those external opportunities are there if the employee is not satisfied with his or her own career development or advancement such as in corporation operations, IT security, and IT. Also, another field of growing opportunity is computer forensics.

The organization must ask itself a very serious question. Can it continue to bring new staff into these critical positions, train, and develop them and then lose these resources to opportunities outside the organization? With a good career development plan, a company builds resources that are knowledgeable about the lifeblood systems of the organization and have strong skills in information technologies and auditing methods, as well as excellent communication and administrative skills. Such people are ideal candidates for managing and integrating new technology into the operating environment of an organization.

Knowledge, Skills, and Abilities

Definition of the level of knowledge, skills, and abilities needed at each position level is a key step to a career development plan. This establishes the organization's expectation for an employee's performance in specified areas of responsibility and duties. Also implied is the level of skill one must attain to perform at a proficient level. Usually a job or position description identifies these critical elements; however, job descriptions in an organization tend to stagnate and do not adequately reflect the change of increased responsibilities and technology. Therefore, it is recommended that job descriptions be reassessed on an annual basis to ensure relevancy in the performance assessment process.

When an employee and supervisor sit down to develop a career development plan, the employee must be given specific objectives or goals from which his or her performance and acquisition/development of knowledge and abilities can be adequately assessed. Further, the plan should provide an integrated focus on both yearly performance and career aspirations beyond the immediate future. This will allow the staff to take a more active role in their own career progress within the organization.

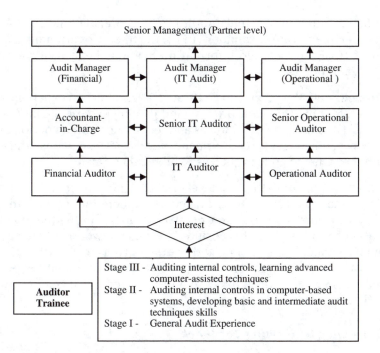

Exhibit 2. Career Path for IT Auditor within Audit Organization

Performance Assessment

The next step is to begin structuring a career development plan that integrates organizational goals and objectives. Keep in mind that an individual career development plan requires the individual's and management's participation. Further, the individual must understand that progression up the career path of IT audit (see Exhibit 2) does not guarantee horizontal or vertical movement within the organization. In order to advance, he or she must effectively demonstrate through strong performance and the successful attainment of knowledge, skills, and abilities, the traits to successfully make the transition. The assessment must incorporate organization and individual goals, any deviations to those goals that occurred as a result of workload changes, and the individual's accomplishments and contribution.

Like the financial auditor, the IT auditor can go through a period of gaining knowledge about the entire audit function and process. Typically, in later years in their careers they become more specialized, but some organizations allow transition across areas for purposes of career development and enriching traditional areas with new methods and techniques. Some of these staff that make such transitions may have multiple certifications such as Chartered Accountant (CA), Certified Public Accountant (CPA),

Certified Information Systems Auditor (CISA), Certified Internal Auditor (CIA), Certified Fraud Examiner (CFE), Certified Government Financial Auditor (CGFM), Certified Information Systems Security Professional (CISSP), and others.

For new staff, they typically go through a learning and experience cycle in understanding the audit process and gaining experience in new computer-assisted audit methodologies and techniques. After a period of time, experience, and sustained performance level, they can choose the area in which they wish to concentrate, as Exhibit 2 illustrates.

For advancement to the next level or lateral movement into other areas, a determination of level of performance expected must be made. This assessment must incorporate organizational and individual goals, any deviation to those goals that resulted because of workload changes, the individual's accomplishments, and overall corporate contribution. However, if the organization does not provide the training and experience promised, IT auditors can move to another firm that has a need for the experience and skills they possess.

Performance Counseling/Feedback

Management feedback is a very important component of the career development process. Interim feedback on a quarterly or semiannual basis as well as the annual review will provide the necessary level of employee performance counseling to assess progress within the career path. If more training or experience is needed to better develop employee knowledge, skills, and abilities, it can be effectively planned for in this process.

Training

Training is another key component within the career development planning process. One of the major reasons given by IT auditors for leaving an organization is not receiving the training originally promised to them. A carefully staged, integrated, phased training program is very important to IT audit staff, both new and experienced.

The training plan should identify formal education to be given as progress is made along the career path. As depicted in Exhibit 3, the training plan identifies the specific types of training required to adequately develop IT auditors. Note that the program is modular to allow expansion, substitution, and ease in updating. Training focuses on audit methodology development, communication development, and technical development. If an individual has equivalent training or expertise in his or her prior education or through related work experience, then other relevant, developmental courses can be substituted or training requirements can be identified as already met.

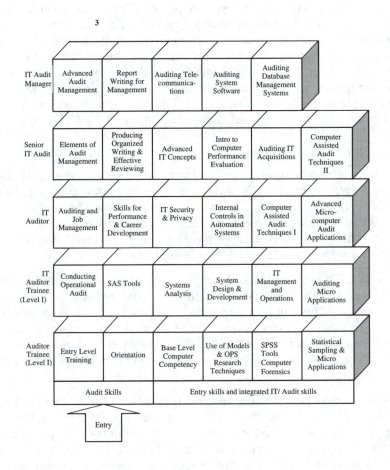

	Audit Skills		Entry skills and integrated IT/ Audit skills			
IT Audit Manager	Advanced Audit Management	Report Writing for Management	Auditing Tele-communica-tions	Auditing System Software	Auditing Database Management Systems	
Senior IT Audit	Elements of Audit Management	Producing Organized Writing & Effective Reviewing	Advanced IT Concepts	Intro to Computer Performance Evaluation	Auditing IT Acquisitions	Computer Assisted Audit Techniques II
IT Auditor	Auditing and Job Management	Skills for Performance & Career Development	IT Security & Privacy	Internal Controls in Automated Systems	Computer Assisted Audit Techniques I	Advanced Micro-computer Audit Applications
IT Auditor Trainee (Level I)	Conducting Operational Audit	SAS Tools	Systems Analysis	System Design & Development	IT Management and Operations	Auditing Micro Applications
Auditor Trainee (Level I)	Entry Level Training	Orientation	Base Level Computer Competency	Use of Models & OPS Research Techniques	SPSS Tools Computer Forensics	Statistical Sampling & Micro Applications

Entry

Exhibit 3. IT Auditor Model Curriculum

The formal training plan can be supplemented by specific on-the-job training. This type of training should be identified and integrated into the individual's career development plan. This will give IT audit supervisors and staff members guidance on how formal training may be applied to practical on-the-job experience. Of course, the training course selected for audit managers and supervisors will be at an advanced level to help them better prepare for technology changes or new IS audit methodologies, or concentrate on developing their managerial skills.

One problem that commonly occurs, especially with a small IT audit staff, is that the reality of assignment deadlines often overrides the need for training. Thus, the employee is either canceled out of the course or rescheduled for the course at "a later, more convenient time." The management must understand the consequences of not sending someone to a relevant, developmental training course; especially a course that is directly applicable to an ongoing work or may add to the staff's knowledge in future planned work. Before an audit team ever starts an assignment and milestones are agreed to, the management should plan for these developmental interruptions and allow for both on-the-job and formal training to take place as planned. A training chart (see Exhibit 4) can be extremely helpful to managers in identifying and minimizing potential conflicts.

Professional Development

Another component of any career development plan is continual professional development of the IT auditor. In IT auditing, there are a number of professional organizations that can support the varied professional interests of the IT auditor. Also, many of these organizations support professional certification as a method of establishing measures of professional competence for a specific discipline (see Exhibit 5).

The IT auditor should be encouraged to continue his professional development and seek certification to enhance his professional status and development. This can be a developmental goal set between management and the individual as well as a performance goal. Once achieved, the staff member can be rewarded with a bonus or quality step increase to present salary as a means of organizational recognition of a professional accomplishment.

Besides certification, the individual may want to develop himself through continued education beyond the bachelor's degree level. Many local colleges and universities throughout the country offer postbachelor certificate programs or advanced degrees at the master's or Ph.D. level in business administration, accountancy, computer information systems, etc. which provide more formal development of a person's knowledge, skills, and abilities.

Several universities have offered training courses and curriculums in IT auditing, i.e., a Master of Science in business administration (Option — IT Auditing) offered by California State Polytechnic University, Pomona, CA; Arizona State University; Bowling Green State University; Bentley College; Eastern Michigan University; Florida Atlantic University; and Georgia State University's Master's Degree in accounting (the latter with emphasis in IS Auditing). In Europe, several academic institutions under ERASMUS have joined together to offer a postgraduate program in IS security, safety, and dependability. Some non-U.S. universities active in educational offerings in this field are University of Queensland (Australia), Curtin University (Australia), National University (Singapore), and Chung-An University (South Korea), to name a few. Such training-related goals should be part of a career

Exhibit 4. IT Auditors Development Plan

Name _____ Position _____ Certifications _____ Date of Plan _____

Skill Category	Course #	Course Title	Month Offered												Prerequisite	*	Accepted
			J	F	M	A	M	J	J	A	S	O	N	D			
Basic																	
Intermediate																	
Advanced																	

*Needed for professional certification maintenance (check if applicable).

Exhibit 5. Professional Certifications

Designation	Title	Professional Affiliate
CPA	Certified Public Accountant	American Institute of Certified Public Accountants
CA	Chartered Accountant	Canadian Institute of Chartered Accountants
CISA	Certified Information Systems Auditor	Information Systems Audit and Control Association
CCP	Certified Computer Professional	Association of Information Technology Professionals
CIA	Certified Internal Auditor	Institute of Internal Auditors
CFE	Certified Fraud Examiner	Association of Certified Fraud Examiners
CGFM	Certified Government Financial Manager	Association of Government Accountants
CMA	Certified Management Accountant	Institute of Management Accountants
CQA	Certified Quality Analyst	Institute for Quality Assurance
CDE	Certified Data Educator	International Association of Computer Information Systems Educators
CBE	Certified Bank Examiner	Bank Administration Institute
CISSP	Certified Information Security Professional	Information Systems Security Association

development plan and performance contract. Such integration will provide accountability to both the individual and the company he works for.

Lastly, activity in professional associations is another measure of professional development. An individual's active commitment to serve on professional association boards and take an active role in the development of a professional association often goes unnoticed and is seldom rewarded. Again, a career development plan could include a requirement for enhancing the individual's professional knowledge, skills, and abilities through his involvement in external professional associations. Such involvement can be very beneficial to an individual as well as his company. For example, involvement in professional associations builds management skills and professional contacts that share information of mutual concern. For the company, an IT auditor who is amply recognized by an external professional organization for professionalism and expertise transfers that intangible benefit to the organizations he works for.

Evaluating IT Audit Quality

To ensure the value of audit assessments, audit management should implement a standard method for evaluating the quality of audits and auditors. Many companies have adopted "total quality management" (TQM).

In a TQM environment, internal auditors are measured against customer needs as well as traditional audit objectives. This section of the chapter discusses the role of the auditor in defining specific control objectives and in assessing whether the audit on completion has satisfactorily addressed those objectives. An assessment form is included as a tool for evaluating both the quality of the audit and the performance of the auditor; a list of suggested assessment criteria is provided for each audit area. How audit managers can use the assessment form as a tool to communicate audit results to senior management, evaluate audit methodology, and develop a training program for staff members has been described in this section.

Scope and Objectives of an IT Audit

To evaluate whether an IT audit has been successful, the auditor must have first clearly identified the intended scope and objectives of the audit. The IT audit may focus on one or more of the review areas discussed in the following sections.

Computerized Systems and Applications

The audit should verify that systems and applications are appropriate to the users' needs, efficient, and adequately controlled to ensure valid, reliable, timely, and secure input, processing, and output at current and projected levels of system activity.

Information Processing Facilities

The information processing facility must be controlled to ensure timely, accurate, and efficient processing of applications under normal and potentially disruptive conditions.

Systems Development

An IT audit should ensure that systems under development meet the objectives of the organization, satisfy user requirements, and provide efficient, accurate, and cost-effective systems and applications. The audit should also ensure that these systems are written, tested, and installed in accordance with generally accepted standards for systems development.

Management of IT and Enterprise Architecture

IT management must develop an organizational structure and procedures to ensure a controlled and efficient environment for information processing. This plan should also specify the computers and peripheral equipment required to support all functions in an economic and timely manner. With enterprise systems being very critical to medium-size and large businesses today, the need to monitor and validate operational integrity of an enterprise resource planning system (ERPS) is an important process. IT audit plays an important role in maintaining and monitoring the Enterprise Architecture.

Client/Server, Telecommunications, Intranets, and Extranets

Many companies are decentralizing their traditional mainframe information processing facilities into local area networks (LANs), wide area networks (WANs), value added networks (VANs), virtual private networks (VPNs), and client/server and Internet/intranet/extranet systems. In a client/server environment, all applications that can be dedicated to a user are put on the client. All resources that need to be shared are put on the server. Auditors must ensure that controls are in place on the client (computer receiving services) as well as the server (computer providing services) and on the network (i.e., the supporting WANs and VANs) connecting clients and servers. In an Internet/intranet/extranet environment, the networks provide both applications and data to clients from the intranet or extranet server. Auditors must provide the same level of control assurance in an Internet/intranet/extranet environment as in the client/server environment with emphasis on two key intranet protocols: Transmission Control Protocol/Internet Protocol (TCP/IP) and Hypertext Transfer Protocol (HTTP).

The IT Auditor's Role

The IT auditor is responsible for establishing control objectives that reduce or eliminate potential exposure to control risks. After the objective of the audit has been established, the auditor must review the audit subject and evaluate the results of the review to determine areas that require correction or improvement. In a report to the management, IT auditors should recommend actions that will provide a reasonable level of control over the assets of the entity. To ensure that the purpose of the IT audit is fulfilled and that auditors are meeting their objectives, audit management must conduct standard evaluations of both subjects on a regular basis.

Terms of Assessment

Senior management must be able to trust that the IT auditor's report and recommendations are based on a complete and thorough investigation. The findings must be documented in detail in the audit workpaper files associated with the IT audit and audit report.

To ensure that audit results are accurate, each IT audit should be reviewed. The review must assess the completeness, accuracy, and pertinence of the audit conclusions, findings, and recommendations. The IT audit management should review the results of the audit after the audit working papers and audit reports have been completed but before the audit report is issued and the closing meeting is held. Performing the review at this point allows identified weaknesses to be reviewed and corrected before audit conclusions are formally issued to senior management.

Any deviations from an acceptable audit product disclosed in the audit report and working papers must be resolved before the audit report is released. Effective communication between audit management and the auditor during this phase can be productive, not only in ensuring an acceptable audit product but in providing on-the-job training and career development.

Another important phase is the audit follow-up. This process may sometimes be conducted six months to a year after the audit report was issued. It is also important to conduct follow-up as a way for both management and the auditor to assess how successful the audit process has been.

The IT Audit and Auditor Assessment Form

Exhibit 6 presents an assessment form that can be used for evaluating both the IT audit and the performance of the auditor in charge of that audit. The evaluation form is designed to be completed by both the audit management and the auditee, the auditor's primary customer. In a TQM environment, meeting customer needs from the customer's viewpoint is critical to the success of the audit function. The evaluation of the auditor should help to indicate the auditor's strengths and list the areas in which the auditor requires further training or improvement. In addition, this review should indicate the auditor's readiness for accepting more difficult audit assignments or other career path choices.

This form is designed for use with a variety of scoring systems. A simple binary system might be used to indicate whether a specific criterion was satisfied, and a more complex scoring system might be used if it is necessary to indicate how well or to what degree the criterion was satisfied. For example, a plus sign could be used to indicate that the audit work was done well, a blank space to mean the work was adequate, and a minus sign to indicate that the work was below an acceptable level of performance. The scoring method may also be adjusted to satisfy the requirements of the firm administering the evaluation. When further information is required to clarify a specific assessment, the evaluator should add a footnote to the score, referencing the additional information. These footnotes should be attached to the assessment form.

It is not necessary to score all assessment criteria for each audit area on the form. The evaluator should select only the degree of scoring required to produce a meaningful and complete appraisal. To a large extent, the scope and complexity of the audit determine the criteria to be assessed.

Exhibit 6. Audit and Auditor Assessment Form

Audit: _____

Date Started: _____
Date Completed: _____
Assessment Date: _____

Assessment Criteria grouping:
- **Audit Management Assessment**
  - *Audit Assessment:* Completeness, Pertinence, Accuracy, Appropriateness of Findings, Conclusions, and Recommendations, Audit Follow-Up
  - *Auditor Assessment:* Timely, Inquisitive, Decisive, Initiative, Resourceful, Communication Skills, Judgment, Tact, Auditing Knowledge
- **Auditee Assessment**
  - *Audit Assessment:* Completeness, Pertinence, Appropriateness of Findings, Conclusions, and Recommendations, Accuracy, Audit Follow-Up
  - *Auditor Assessment:* Timely, Inquisitive, Decisive, Initiative, Resourceful, Communication Skills, Judgment, Tact, Auditing Knowledge

Audit Areas	Completeness	Pertinence	Accuracy	Appropriateness of Findings, Conclusions, and Recommendations	Audit Follow-Up	Timely	Inquisitive	Decisive	Initiative	Resourceful	Communication Skills	Judgment	Tact	Auditing Knowledge	Completeness	Pertinence	Appropriateness of Findings, Conclusions, and Recommendations	Accuracy	Audit Follow-Up	Timely	Inquisitive	Decisive	Initiative	Resourceful	Communication Skills	Judgment	Tact	Auditing Knowledge
Audit preparation																												
Audit objective																												
Fact gathering																												
Audit program																												
Audit tests																												
Use of audit tools																												
Conclusions																												
Documented																												
Supported																												
Findings																												
Documented																												
Supported																												
Recommendations																												
Documented																												
Supported																												
Audit report																												
Working papers																												
Organization																												
Cross-reference																												
Readability																												
Relations with auditee	NA	NA	NA	NA	NA	NA	NA	NA	NA	NA	NA	NA	NA	NA														
Relations w/audit management															NA	NA	NA	NA	NA	NA	NA	NA	NA	NA	NA	NA	NA	NA

Audit Statistics

Planned Elapsed Time: _____ Months _____ Days

Actual Time: _____ Months _____ Days

Planned Staff Resources (Audit): _____ Staff Days

Actual Staff Resources (Audit): _____ Staff Days

Planned Follow-Up Date: __/__/__

Actual Follow-Up Date: __/__/__

Follow-Up Analysis by Audit Management:

_____

_____

_____

_____

Date: __/__/__ Initials _____

Follow-Up Assessment by Auditee:

_____

_____

_____

_____

_____

Date: __/__/__ Initials _____

Future Action: _____ Reaudit Area _____ Reaudit in 2 Years _____ Reaudit in 4 Years _____

Benefits

Check Applicable Boxes

_____ Measurable

_____ Estimated Savings _____ per annum

_____ Cost Avoidance _____ per annum

_____ Improved Control

_____ Improved Efficiency, Effectiveness, and Economy

The following section of this article describes each audit area and assessment criterion that appears on the assessment form.

The second page of this form is used for the audit follow-up process (six months to a year after the audit report). It allows the management or the auditor to perform a follow-up of the audit recommendations and assess their effect on operations. This must be done in an objective, independent manner. In some cases, quantitative measurements can be taken, such as improvements in productivity, dollar savings in staff time, etc.

IT Audit Areas

Audit Preparation

Audit preparation comprises all work that is involved in initiating an audit. The functions include audit selection, definition of audit scope, initial contacts and communication with auditees, and audit team selection. In preparation for the audit, for example, the auditor should become familiar with prior audit reports on the financial accounting systems to be audited.

Audit Objectives

Audit objectives are formal statements that describe the purposes of the audit. By defining appropriate objectives at the outset, management can ensure that the audit will verify the correct functioning and control of all key audit areas. The objectives are derived from control objectives pertinent to the audit scope and the purpose of the application, activity, or installation under review. For example, to define the audit objective, the auditor should examine the organization's control objectives with regard to systems development projects.

Fact Gathering

Fact gathering comprises all activities that help the auditor understand the audit subject. Such audit activities include a review of computer information systems and human interface practices, procedures, documents, narratives, flowcharts, and record layouts. Fact gathering requires observing, interviewing, flowcharting, and documenting each activity. If the auditor is using an electronic document management support system, how well this support tool is used to capture facts gathered should be determined.

Audit Program

An audit program is a formal plan for reviewing and testing each significant audit subject area disclosed during fact gathering. The auditor should select subject areas for testing that have a significant impact on the control of the application, activity, or installation and those that are within the scope defined by the audit objectives.

Audit Tests

Audit tests are designed and conducted to verify the functional accuracy, efficiency, and control of the audit subject. During the audit of an IS application, for example, the auditor would build and process test data to verify the processing steps of an application.

Use of Audit Tools

The auditor selects and uses computer-aided audit tools to gather information and conduct the planned audit tests. The appropriate selection of audit tools and their effective and accurate use are essential to adequate audit testing. For example, if the performance of an application requires analysis, a computer program analyzer or instrumentation package would be an appropriate choice for use as an audit tool. In addition, if the audit staff uses an electronic document management system to capture their audit work (e.g., interviews, electronic documents, and schedules), how well does the auditor use this support tool?

Conclusions

Conclusions are auditor opinions, based on documented evidence, that determine whether an audit subject area meets the audit objective. All conclusions must be based on factual data obtained and documented by the auditor as a result of audit activity. The degree to which the conclusions are supported by the evidence is a function of the amount of evidence secured by the auditor.

Findings

Findings are formal statements, usually issued by the audit report, that identify and describe inaccurate, inefficient, or inadequately controlled audit subjects. For example, an auditor found that changes made to an application were implemented without authorization. The auditor then discovered that the organization's procedures manual did not include instructions to seek management permission before making changes to applications.

Recommendations

Recommendations are formal statements that describe a course of action that should be implemented to restore or provide accuracy, efficiency, or adequate control of audit subjects. A recommendation must be provided for each audit finding for the report to be useful to the management.

The Audit Report

The formal communication issued by the audit department describing the results of the audit is called an audit report. The report should include (at a minimum) the audit scope and objectives, a description of the audit subject, a narrative of the audit work activity performed, conclusions, findings, and recommendations.

Working Papers

Working papers are the formal collection of pertinent writings, documents, flowcharts, correspondence, results of observations, plans for tests, results of tests, the audit plan, minutes of meetings, computerized records, data files or application results, and evaluations that document the auditor activity for the entire audit period. Typically, the final audit report is included in the working papers. A complete, well-organized, cross-referenced, and legible set of working papers is essential to support the findings and recommendations as stated in the audit report and to achieve concurrence by an audit management. Again, a review of electronic document organization and maintenance can be used to support this process.

Relations with the Auditee

An effective relationship between the auditor and the auditees is essential to the success of the audit. Appropriate relationships foster cooperative auditees. Such relations include those with such technical personnel as programmers, systems analysts, and information systems managers and those with such nontechnical personnel as users, functional supervisors, and managers.

Relations with Audit Management

The auditor must keep audit management apprised of the progress of the audit and alert the managers to significant problems that may require intervention. For example, proper communication might involve providing progress reports to an audit manager on a weekly basis with direct contact when necessary.

Follow-Up of Audit Recommendations

The value of an audit can be immediate, and its effects can be short- or long-term. The value can be quantifiable in tangible or intangible terms. The follow-up process is often ignored because of time or resource constraints. For example, IT audit recommendations might involve the change of a process or implementation of a control that can help the company monitor a problem area more effectively, results of which could be immediate, or it may take time to collect the necessary data to determine the effect as a result of the audit recommendations.

Examples of situations in which recommendations can be quantified are: (1) unnecessary rework occurring due to a control flaw that, once changed or corrected, resulted in staff resources assigned to that issue being reduced and fewer complaints from both customers and employees, and (2) identifying an error in a computer algorithm that causes reordering or inventory problems. In the first situation, the staff time spent in handling the existing problem can be quantified in terms of salary and overhead costs. Savings can be expressed as a cost avoidance per month or per annum. In the next situation, computational processing errors, if caught in production, can be traced historically to show how much the company lost per month or per annum. In these two examples loss can be shown in projected terms.

Criteria for Assessing the Audit

The audit methodology, supervisory review, and working papers are critical to the audit process. Working with evidence that is in transparent form (e.g., magnetic tapes, magnetic disks, and optical disks) requires complete, pertinent, and accurate reports. The audit and working papers should be evaluated on the basis of the following criteria.

Completeness

An audit must cover every element of the audit subject. For example, the IT auditor should ensure that all applications currently in use by end users are examined during the audit.

Pertinence

The audit should be free of extraneous or unnecessary elements. For example, the IT auditor should examine only key fields and records that directly relate to the audit objective.

Accuracy

All elements of the audit must be precise and error free. The auditor must verify that all procedures and computerized processes produce correct results and that the measures used to evaluate these processes are error free. When developing computer-assisted audit routines, for example, the auditor must test and validate all program codes and algorithms before the routine is actually used.

Appropriate Conclusions, Findings, and Recommendations

The audit must present appropriate conclusions and findings that lead to recommendations reflecting cost-conscious, workable, and timely solutions to audit objectives.

Follow-Up of Findings and Recommendations

The value of the audit must be assessed to ensure that the findings and recommendations reflect that cost-conscious, workable, and timely solutions have been achieved in some manner.

Criteria for Assessing the Auditor

To objectively assess the performance of an IT auditor, the manager can use the standard criteria listed on the assessment form. The auditor can use this form to identify key performance areas and evaluation criteria; when the evaluation is complete, the form will help the auditor identify areas for improvement or further training. The following list explains the criteria shown in Exhibit 1 for the auditor assessment:

- *Timely:* The auditor is punctual and finishes work within time objectives.
- *Inquisitive:* The auditor questions, tests, and investigates to gain relevant facts. The auditor demonstrates a need to understand all aspects of the system under investigation.
- *Decisive:* The auditor is willing and able to make timely decisions.
- *Initiative:* The auditor is self-reliant and works well with minimal supervision.
- *Resourceful:* The auditor seeks alternative paths when initial plans are precluded or impeded.
- *Communication skills:* The auditor writes, speaks, and relates to others clearly and effectively.
- *Judgment:* The auditor chooses proper and timely courses of action and makes sound decisions based on the best data available.
- *Tact:* The auditor is helpful and respectful toward others and encourages their help and cooperation in the successful completion of audit tasks.
- *Auditing knowledge:* The auditor understands and conducts the audit according to generally accepted audit techniques and procedures.

Metrics and Management

If management has given its full support to the measurement process, it should be consulted on the types of measures it feels would be beneficial to the organization. Management will be most supportive when it sees the metrics applied to the areas that it feels are most in need of improvement. A critical metric set — the few key metrics that are critical to the successful management of the function — must be identified and applied to the environment.

Once the critical metric set has been identified, the individuals in the areas that are to be measured should be consulted, and a set of measurements that will provide meaningful data should be devised. The individuals responsible for doing the work should select the best means to measure the quality and productivity of their work. Metrics that are developed should only be applied to data that is both measurable and meaningful. The individuals in the area can best identify these areas. It is useless to waste time on developing measures on areas that do not fall within the critical metric set as these measures will not satisfy the needs of management.

After the initial implementation of the first measurements, it is important to show results. Data should be compiled over a predefined period, and results should be provided to the management on a regular basis. As the metrics database grows, the reliability of the data will increase and the usefulness of the reports to the management will increase.

The presentation of the data to the management must be on a professional level. Handwritten charts and reports will not do here. The auditor should use any automated tools available to make the presentation of the collected data as professional as possible in both appearance and format. Spreadsheet programs such as MS-Excel and presentation packages such as MS-PowerPoint come in handy. It may take a little longer to get the results to management, but the impact of a well-prepared and presented report is far better than the impact of a hand-drawn or poorly presented report. In addition, auditors should use color if at all possible. Color can be used to highlight those areas of special concern to management, and it is pleasing to the eye.

The reports to the management must stress the progress in those areas selected by management for measurement. This is a key point in that it shows short-term results in the long-term measurement process. Areas of improvement must be stressed to show management that the process is working.

Although it is quite an easy task to get management to support metrics if management is informed as to what metrics are and the impact they can have, it is difficult to get support from management if management has not been educated or if it is skeptical. In this situation, a different tack should be taken. First, management must be made to realize that it is next to impossible to manage what cannot be or is not measured. The easiest way to strengthen this argument is to back it up with some sample metrics.

Second, survey data from other companies can be compiled and presented to management to encourage it into adopting a metrics frame of mind. For the sample metrics, identify several areas that can be measured and provide management with reports on these areas. Again, it is important to provide short-term payback to show results and to continue to produce reports to management, showing progress in those areas. Once it sees that the areas being measured are improving, it may provide its full support. The support will come soon, but constant reminders will most definitely pay off, and management will look like heroes to the customers and to their bosses when the improvements start appearing.

As soon as management has been convinced that the metrics process has many benefits, it will be more than happy to identify the critical metric set. After this takes place, the remaining steps outlined previously can be completed.

Implementation of Measurements

When management has accepted the concept of metrics, it is time to begin implementing some measurements in the critical areas. During this step of the measurement process, it is crucial not to step on anyone's toes. The implementation of metrics causes uneasiness and fear in the ranks. There are good ways and there are bad ways to design and implement the measures. If the metrics process is to succeed, safe metrics implementation techniques must be used.

The most important rule to remember in the design and implementation of metrics is that in all cases the area that is to be measured must help in the development of the metrics. This will create a sense of ownership over the measurements and will ease the resistance to their implementation. The group should be informed as to the needs of management and should then be empowered to develop the metrics to meet the need. This will result in more relevant data being produced and an increase in quality in that area.

The second important rule to remember in the design and implementation of metrics is that it is absolutely vital that the measures are applied to events and processes, never individuals. If people get the idea that their performance is being measured, they will be less likely to comply with the metrics process. It must be explicitly stated that the results of the metrics will not be used to measure the productivity or effectiveness of individuals but of the processes used by the individuals to create their products or services.

Keeping these two rules in mind, the next step is to identify the attributes of an effective measure. An effective measure must be able to pass tests of reliability and validity. Reliability defines consistency of a measure, and validity determines the degree to which it actually measures what it was intended to measure. The measure must be meaningful; the data provided by it must have some use to the management and should satisfy a condition of one of the critical metrics set. The auditor should be sure that all of the measurements installed in the organization meet these requirements.

Applying the Concept

The audit manager must address the challenge of effectively coordinating human skills and talents. The form presented in Exhibit 1 helps the audit manager assess specific audit areas. The manager can evaluate staff performance for these areas on the basis of both objective and subjective criteria. The second page of this form provides a mechanism to reexamine the audit recommendations and determine what effect the audit recommendations have had on organizational controls and processes over a specific period of time. Benefits from audits are not always immediate, but over time, they can be assessed and measured in different ways.

The manager can adjust or substitute audit areas and assessment criteria on this form to meet the special requirements of the audit environment. The manager may choose to adapt the assessment method so that it conforms to the mandates of the company's IT audit charter. Adjustments can also be made to accommodate areas of emphasis from senior management or the board of directors.

The finalized standard for measuring performance should be clearly communicated to staff members to ensure that they understand the process and can provide feedback. Any changes must also be communicated to staff members so that they know what is expected of them and understand how their performance will be measured. As part of this process of communication, managers should:

- Gather and respond to feedback properly.
- Prevent misconceptions about assessment policy and methods.
- Maintain and continuously improve communications.
- Develop an effective, participative assessment system.

These characteristics are critical if the assessment process is to work effectively.

Evaluation of IT Audit Performance

As mentioned earlier in this chapter, a variety of scoring methods can be used with this assessment form. A consistent application of the selected method, however, is important. The standards for assessment should be clearly communicated to those being evaluated.

The following example illustrates the application of an assessment. An organization requires as policy that, before an audit is conducted, the following tasks be performed:

- Define the audit objectives.
- Prepare the audit program.
- Conduct an initial meeting with managers responsible for the area under audit.

Evaluation of this process assesses both compliance with official company policy and the quality of work performed. Compliance with organizational policy and procedures requires a yes or no evaluation. The managers conducting the evaluation must apply their own judgment, knowledge, skills, and experience to determine how well the work was done. It is recommended that this evaluation be based on the experience and work of a group rather than that of an individual.

In evaluating scores, the manager should be most concerned with poor scores, especially if they affect the conclusions, findings, and recommendations of the audit. On the basis of the evaluation, managers should develop training plans to improve the IT audit methodologies used and to train the staff in proper audit techniques and tools. The follow-up of the audit recommendations is another way of assisting the evaluation process. Even though the activity takes place at a later date, it may reconfirm an earlier evaluation and provide a basis for additional training requirements.

What Is a Best Practice?

What works well for others must work well for me! This is a misconception of some auditors. Unfortunately this is not always the case. There are many subfactors that auditors must take into consideration before adopting a new set of auditing standards for their firms or businesses. First, what is the environment to be audited (i.e., entertainment, financial, and industrial)? Second, how big is the business that one is auditing (i.e., employees, assets, size, and locations)? Third, what are the policies and procedures generally accepted within the organization that is being audited (i.e., personnel rules and regulations, training memos, organization charts)?

Listed below are samples of the types of responses typically received from IT audit professionals in this field today regarding their interpretation of what Best Practices means to them:

- The ability to choose and use the appropriate techniques and tools to accomplish a specific objective or set of objectives within a given circumstance or context
- The identification of those kinds of processes, procedures, and controls that will meet the business needs of an organization most effectively
- The methods that any organization uses to achieve its business objectives in the most effective and cost-efficient way while achieving the highest quality product

- The integration of business processes with technology and people to provide a practice that is both efficient and effective and can provide value to the organization

As you will note, there are a variety of different answers to the same question. However, almost all professionals polled indicated that Best Practices should provide value-added concepts to the customer.

Why Is It Important to Learn about Best Practices?

There are many reasons why people should learn about Best Practices, some of which are as follows:

- To improve efficiency
- To add value to client/auditee or organization
- To aid in the advancement of technology
- For insight into learning how others are performing audits faster and more efficiently and easily

In order to keep up good relations with the client/auditee, an effective auditor will present to the auditee some sound advice on how to correct his problem. In a sense, a good auditor comes up with a solution to the problem.

Overview of Best Practices in IT Audit Planning

To succeed in auditing, IT audit managers must have a well thought out plan as to how they will conduct their audit. A well thought out plan gives the IT auditor a checklist of important issues that must be covered, thus, giving auditors their blueprints for a successful audit if, and only if, the checklist is correct. One of the most important steps in determining the correct approach in planning an audit of a large or small organization is to obtain an in-depth understanding of the area to be audited and its organization. The auditor's understanding should include data processing environments, operating practices, and assigned responsibilities. Lastly, the auditor should thoroughly understand the business issues associated with management risks.

The audit plan should have a purpose for each task that was to be completed in a sequential order. This provides an easy-to-use reference when it is time to present the findings and recommendations to the auditee or management. A well thought out plan can also be an answer to possible questions by the client/auditee.

There is nothing worse than going into a closing meeting with your client/auditee and having them ask you a question about your finding that you cannot answer. It is for this reason the audit manager or supervisor should insist that the audit is planned to a "T."

The audit manager or supervisor should make sure that all risks have been accounted for before the audit has started. With their audit experience, they may narrow down the objective and the context for which the audit will be performed. The scope of the audit should be consistent with the task at hand and the objective of the audit. All that is needed is adequate cooperation from the client/auditee. What this teaches is that every client/auditee is important, and the audit is a representation of the audit manager, the company, and the way in which job duties are performed.

Research

Another Best Practice technique used in IT audit planning and extremely valuable to IT audit managers is research. Everywhere one looks, someone is doing research. Research has become easier now than ever before. A modem capable of handling high-speed transmissions, a connection to the Internet, and an up-to-date computer with adequate RAM are all you need to find what you are looking for on the information super-highway.

The Internet is a vast storehouse of knowledge with a wide range of information covering a massive variety of different areas and topics. Most IT audit managers understand the importance the Internet brings to the forum of information systems auditing. With the use of the Internet, staff, senior auditors, and audit managers can locate information on a new client/auditee. This information becomes very important when one is competing to be the sole auditing firm of a corporation or, as an internal auditor, seeks to know all about a company to make a good impression on management. Knowing the client/auditee or the company for whom one works for is a necessity in today's dynamically changing environment. It seems the world is getting smaller and smaller with technology. This is all the more reason why IT auditors should research the company they are auditing to see if any mergers or buyouts are on the way which could impact financial statements.

The Internet, intranet, or extranet also offers auditors the ability to pose questions to people or persons they have never met or even heard of before. What makes this so advantageous is that auditors from around the world can communicate with each other on the latest techniques in information systems (IS) auditing. This is all made possible by the use of electronic mail or chat rooms provided on a local Point-to-Point (PPP) carrier. Another added bonus is that it strengthens the use of Best Practices between IT audit managers around the world. A couple of buttons pushed, a password submitted, and a few words typed to compose a question and one is in business. Another good aspect of research is coming across benchmarks for the environment in which one is auditing.

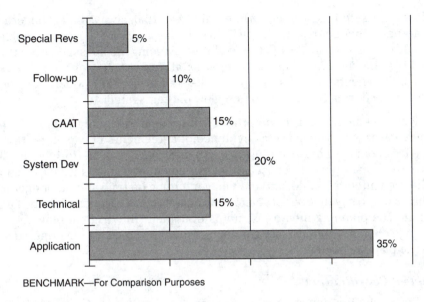

BENCHMARK—For Comparison Purposes

Exhibit 7. Benchmark Planning Guideline

Benchmarking

This is a practice that has been used to define what has worked well in other environments. This frequently mentioned tool is designed to present to individuals an idea of what to expect if they implement a certain concept into their audit approach. As defined in the dictionary, a benchmark is a point at which all measurements can be referenced back.

For example, the network security system is being audited and the goal is to verify that the service the security system is providing is adequate. One good way to measure such a task is to benchmark it against other leading brands (i.e., RACF, TOP Secret, ACF2) to see how it ranks in comparison to its leading competitors. One best practice, as shown in Exhibit 7, is where a partner of a computer audit group uses benchmarking to help aid him in the goals of his audits. In this example, the partner is looking at the types of audits being performed by staff to assess experience levels and complexity. Also, this illustrates that not all benchmarking has to be a comparison of performance.

Planning Memo

Another Best Practice technique mentioned is the planning memo. This document sets the tone or course of action IT audit managers plan to take with clients/auditees. The memo is good because it outlines for the client/auditee the areas in which one is most likely to spend time analyzing. This also gives a client/auditee the opportunity to voice concerns, if any.

Most clients/auditees, whether internal or external, always have concerns that they either address themselves, would like addressed, or are planning to address as soon as they get time. With a planning memo issued from the auditor, the client/auditee can prepare staff for a review of their operations. The clients/auditees can inform the staff to give full cooperation and assistance during the IT auditor's review of their system.

Planning memos serve the primary purpose of documenting plans. In some cases, this will serve as evidence of agreements between multiple parties about the nature, timing, and extent of work to be performed. In all cases, the plans provide a basis for measurement of results (i.e., did you do what you intended to do, and did you get it done on time and on budget?). That is not to say that people cannot change their minds once they start an audit. The planning memo just helps document the original plans. Any change of plan would usually get documented in some sort of supplement to the planning memo.

Budget Coordination

Before the first question is ever asked, first inquiry made, or an observation commenced, a well thought out budget must be completed and adhered to by the IT audit manager. The managers must know the capabilities of the staff at their disposal. The importance of knowing the associates involved is extremely vital when one is working with sensitive material, a sensitive auditee, or technologically complex software and systems. Most managers know that in today's market personnel resources for this field are scarce. When negotiating the audit, the manager should consider adding a little more time for training and error-correction purposes. After all, if the manager trains the staff right the first time the staff will eventually become another added bonus to the audit team. Most, if not all, audits the authors have conducted involved some sort of training, and the time allotted to that training was given.

Risk Analysis

Another Best Practice found is that of risk analysis. Estimation of risk is a must in any business during any type of audit. Risk is so important to understand that the Information Systems Audit and Control Association asks questions relating to many IT audit, security, and control issues during the Certified Information Systems Auditor Examination. Most IT audit managers complete what is called a risk analysis of the business to see what threats to the business exist, either externally or internally. Some of the techniques used to do this are listed below.

Reasons for a risk analysis are as follows:

- Loss or corruption of information and information systems assets
- Impaired and ineffective management decision making

- Disruptions to customer service and other critical operations
- Cost overruns, delays, and reduced quality in new systems development
- Loss of disclosure of confidential or proprietary information

For example, audit risk can be assessed in three areas: **total exposure**, **risk**, and **time since last audit**. Exhibit 8 displays a table with which to chart these areas. The **total exposure** component provides insight regarding the impact to the organization if control weaknesses exist. The **risk** component identifies the various factors that tend to increase the probability that control weaknesses may exist. The **time since last audit** component allows you to elevate the immediacy or lower the frequency of individual projects. To make sure that the risk analysis test is accurate, it is suggested that the factors used in the original risk analysis be verified with the organization's management personnel at the beginning of each project.

Business risk is a concern for all IT audit professionals, internal and external. What the chart above can do is help to alleviate some of that concern, provided the auditor takes the time to examine all steps thoroughly and exercises extreme caution when evaluating critical risks. Some risks, if not examined carefully, could bring a company to its knees. Thus the theory of examining risks as part of the planning procedure has been a Best Practice for many auditors in the past.

While most organizations and corporations view risks as being resident only in daily financial dealings, business risks live and lurk in all corners, waiting to strike and cripple. A risk must be redefined as any event or action that stops an organization from achieving its goals or business objectives. From the boardroom to the boiler room, proactive risk controls must be accepted for survival and should be embraced for success.

Kick-Off Meeting

Another Best Practice has to do with how one conducts the first meeting as an IT auditor with one's client/auditee. This is the most important aspect of the audit. From this meeting the auditor will know if the audit will go as planned or if interruptions will supersede the progress of the audit. The first meeting sets the tone of the audit and establishes the auditor's rapport with the client/auditee. It is important to keep in mind that this is just as equally important between internal auditors as it is with external auditors.

Good client/auditee relations are a necessity for productive and efficient audit results to occur. Conduct and professionalism are primary attributes, with respect to the auditee, even when they are difficult to work with. The main impression the auditor wants to give his or her client/auditee is that the auditor is there to help and not to find all their mistakes. Nobody

Exhibit 8. Components of Risk Analysis

Subject	Description	Low	Medium	High
		0 = Low	1 = Medium	2 = High
1. Total exposure factor	Dollar value or equivalent controlled by system			
A. Total asset value		Less than $2 million	$2–$9 million	More than $9 million
B. Transaction volume		Hundreds per month	Hundreds per week	Hundreds per day
C. Business impact		Minor business impact, company non-critical	Management focus, departmental critical	Legal/Regulatory compliance, mission critical, potential impact to goodwill, reputation, public standing
2. Institutional or organizational risk factor				
A. Previous audit results	History of control weaknesses, system failure, operational problems	Few minor findings	Some medium control weaknesses or previously limited scope review	Many significant control weaknesses
B. Assets/liabilities controlled by system		Fixed assets — not readily disposable	Confidential data or readily disposable assets	Financial Assets
C. System maturity		More than five years old	2–5 years old	Less than 2 years old
D. Enhancements/changes to system	Program/platform change, organizational restructure	Minor	Average	Major (include use of new technology, client/server)
E. System complexity	Consider: stand-alone, enterprisewide, number of interfaces, number of processes, technical operating environment	Small noncomplex or stand-alone	Moderately complex	Enterprisewide system, complex operations or complicated database
F. Enterprise	Transactions	International	U.S. only	Small business
3. Time since last audit	Critical area? audit follow-up?	More than 3 years	1–3 years	Less than 1 year

enjoys being told they are wrong, especially from an outsider who is just visiting for a short while.

Speaking from experience, if auditors have a client/auditee that is reluctant to help them through the audit, it may become harder for the auditors to meet all the demands of their audit managers. It will also be equally difficult to meet the desired budget set for the audit engagement. If an auditor encounters such a problem, contact the audit manager as soon as possible. The manager will appreciate the alert and will most likely take care of the situation for the auditor.

Staff Mentoring

Again, part of the planning process is knowing when to be a mentor for one's staff and seniors to follow. This is a necessary duty that must be performed by all IT audit managements. After all, managers have to instruct their staff on the fine art of IT auditing and what better way to do that than to teach by example. In addition, the mentoring process provides the manager the opportunity to stay current on new issues that pop up before the everyday staff or seniors working in the trenches. It also allows the manager to be more proactive when building a team from the ground up. Most managers like to mold their people to conform to their style of auditing and client/auditee relationships. Along with the concept of mentoring comes a new concept called coaching.

Coaching

Another Best Practice technique is coaching, which has been around since the early days of sports and probably before then. Time must be allocated to allow for coaching. The concept of coaching is relatively simple. The coach is someone who knows all about the subject and is willing to spend the time to pass on his or her knowledge. Often, managers are now reviewing the work of staff before the work is due to make sure all aspects of the audit are covered and are correctly stated. In the event the work is not correct, managers now take the time to explain in full detail how they would approach the issue. This approach to auditing seems to be working because there are fewer and fewer review notes that are handed out after the engagements. Thus the engagement runs more smoothly, accurately, and within budget.

Lunch Meetings

The lunch meeting has been around for years. This is a chance to meet with staff and supervisors and discuss issues and new developments. Managers frequently mention that they hold such a meeting once a month and name a supervisor or staff member to identify a topic to be covered and to run the meeting. This facilitates sharing of information among members of the staff and generates new techniques or approaches to audits.

Managers often include members of the client's staff who might have a special interest or experience in an area. Audit managers take advantage of all opportunities they get to establish a greater rapport with their client/auditee. The times they work in are highly competitive and so their number one priority is their client/auditee and getting to know them as well as possible.

Understand Requirements

Another critical process for the audit manager to understand, especially within audit planning, is the audit objectives and requirements. Clients/auditees for the most part are all the same; they all have needs and concerns for their businesses that must be addressed. Clients/auditees may come to IT auditors with concerns about a certain operating system or application. Even if the concern is not within the scope of their audit, they must adhere to the client/auditee on a request. Most requests are simple and take but a few minutes to complete. The auditee will appreciate the communication of the potential delay and at the same time have more confidence in the auditor's ability to provide them with quality analytical skills, thus giving added value to a client/auditee.

Conclusion

The IT audit career development process should be institutionalized and supported by corporate management. The process itself involves (1) the establishment and integration of career path planning; (2) the definition of career path knowledge, skills, and abilities; (3) performance measurement; (4) performance counseling; (5) training; and (6) professional development. Each element requires institutional support and commitment to make it work. Like any process, it will require time, refinement, and improvement to make it work effectively.

The investment in establishing such a process in an organization is small compared to the long-range benefits it can bring. An example of such a benefit can be in the form of an experienced management cadre who can effectively understand, use, and manage the information systems flows within the organization. This cadre was formerly IT auditors who capably developed their individual knowledge, skills, and abilities to successfully make the transition into a financial, operational, or corporate management position.

The IT auditor handles a great deal of responsibility within an organization. To develop controls that reduce the company's threat of exposure, IT auditors must understand the objectives of the audit, which is to conduct thorough, accurate, pertinent, and complete reviews that yield effective recommendations to senior management. To ensure that the audit and the auditor are meeting these goals, the audit management must provide evaluations regularly.

Evaluating audits and the auditors who perform them poses a substantial challenge to the audit management. For an evaluation to be effective, the management must be sure that every audit is reviewed and that its findings are clearly communicated to the auditor.

The IT audit and auditor assessment form can serve as a standardized testing system. It should indicate an auditor's strengths and weaknesses and provide guidance for career objectives. Scoring systems and assessment criteria can differ according to the level of detail required; however, it is essential that one scoring system and one set of criteria be consistently applied to every evaluation. Furthermore, evaluating IT audits should be an ongoing process to ensure audit quality and adjust to the organizational changes placed on the IT audit function.

Audit planning is a critical component of the audit process. A number of Best Practices that have been successfully used by audit management, supervisors, and staff in performing this process have been shared in this chapter. The audit plan itself is a guide to performing the steps of the audit process.

It has been shown how research, benchmarking, planning memos, budget coordination, risk analysis, kick-off meetings, staff mentoring and coaching, lunch meetings, and understanding requirements are all components of the planning process. Examples of these components have been provided as a way of showing how others have used them in being successful in their audit planning.

A Best Practice is a technique or method used that proves successful in practice. The ability to transfer these practices depends on the operating environment of the recipient. The sharing of Best Practices provides information to those who want to continue to improve their operations and are looking for those elements that help make others successful.

Review Questions

1. What is a career development plan? What is the IT audit career path? What options and alternatives does it provide?
2. How does an audit manager or organizational management design, develop, and implement a career development plan?
3. Why is performance assessment and performance counseling and feedback an important component within a career development plan?
4. What does professional development consist of?

5. Why is evaluating audit quality important?

6. What criteria can be developed for assessing the audit process? What are the critical steps in the audit process that can be evaluated?

7. What criteria can be developed for assessing the auditor? What are metrics?

8. What are two very important rules in the development of metrics?

9. How can audit follow-up assist in the evaluation process?

10. What is a Best Practice? Why should auditors learn about Best Practices?

11. What are some Best Practices in IT audit planning?

12. What are some of the major reasons for using risk analysis in audit planning?

13. What roles do mentoring or coaching play in audit planning Best Practices?

14. What are the skills needed to be an IT auditor? What skills do you have? What weaknesses do you need to build on?

Multiple Choice

1. Some of the following elements should be included in a career development plan:
   a. Career path planning with management support
   b. Definition of knowledge, skills, and abilities
   c. Performance assessment and counseling
   d. All of the above

2. Which professional certification can be helpful to an IT auditor's career?
   a. CISA
   b. CISSP
   c. CPA
   d. All of the above

3. Which IT audit area involves audit selection, definition of audit scope, initial contacts and communication with auditees, and audit team selection?
   a. Fact gathering
   b. Audit tests
   c. Audit preparation
   d. Audit objectives

4. Which IT audit area involves a formal plan for reviewing and testing each significant audit subject area disclosed during fact gathering?
   a. Audit objectives
   b. Audit program
   c. Audit tests
   d. Use of audit tools

5. Which IT audit area involves formal statements that describe a course of action that should be implemented to restore or provide accuracy, efficiency, or adequate control of audit subject?
   a. Audit tests
   b. Findings of the audit reports
   c. Recommendations of an audit report
   d. Conclusion of an audit report

6. IT audit assessment is very important and, at a minimum, consists of reviewing:
   a. The completeness of the audit
   b. The pertinence of the information presented
   c. The accuracy of the audit work and supporting working papers
   d. All of the above

7. Some of the areas that one can assess for the IT auditor's individual performance are:
   a. Communication skills
   b. Judgment
   c. Auditing knowledge
   d. All of the above

8. Why is it important to learn about Best Practices?
   a. Efficiency
   b. Add value to client/auditee or organization
   c. Advancement in technology
   d. All of the above

9. This Best Practice consists of a document that sets the tone or course of action you plan to take with your client/auditee:
   a. Benchmarking
   b. Planning memo
   c. Risk analysis
   d. None of the above

10. The reasons for risk analysis are:
    a. Loss or corruption of information and information systems assets
    b. Impaired and ineffective management decision making
    c. Disruption to customer service or other critical operations
    d. All of the above

Exercises

1. Interview an IT auditor and gather the following information:
   - Position and company
   - Number of years of experience in IT auditing
   - Degree(s) and professional certifications
   - Career path
   - Why did he or she get into this field? What do they like about IT auditing? What do they dislike?

- What do they feel about the future of this field? Where do they see themselves in five years?

2. Using Web browsers, find general information about the Information Systems Audit and Control Association.

3. Using a Web Browser, find general information about the Institute of Internal Auditors.

4. Using a Web browser, find general information about the Association of Government Accountants.

5. Using a Web browser, find what universities offer graduate education in this field.

Answers to Multiple Choice Questions

1 — d; 2 — d; 3 — c; 4 — b; 5 — c; 6 — d; 7 — d; 8 — d; 9 — b; 10 — d

References

1. Cangemi, M. and Gallegos, F., CIS auditing: a career plan, *New Accountant*, pp. 27–30, February 1991.

2. Cotter, R., Checklists and forms for quality control in system development, *CIS Auditing*, Auerbach Publications, Boca Raton, FL, 1989.

3. Curts, R.J. and Campbell, D.E., A Systems Engineering Approach to Information Assurance Operations, 2002 Command and Control Research and Technology Symposium, Conference Proceedings, Monterrey Naval Post Graduate School, CA, June 2002.

4. Gallegos, F., Richardson, D.R., and Borthick, A.F., *Audit and Control of Information Systems*, Thomson Corporation–South-Western Publishers, Cincinnati, OH, 1987.

5. Gallegos, F., Computer information systems audit career development, *CIS Auditors J.*, Vol. 1, pp. 37–40, 1991.

6. Gallegos, F., Due professional care, *IS Control J.*, Vol. 2, pp. 25–28, 2002.

7. Gallegos, F., *Educating Auditors for the Twenty First Century*, Accepted for presentation and publication at the EDPAC96 Conference, Perth, Australia, May 1996.

8. Gallegos, F., *IS Audit Career Development Planning*, RIA/Auerbach Publishers, Boca Raton, FL, 1997.

9. Gallegos, F., IT auditor careers: IT governance provides new roles and opportunities, *IS Control J.*, Vol. 3, pp. 40–43, 2003.

10. Gallegos, F., IT audit career development plan, *IS Control J.*, Vol. 2, pp. 16–17, 2003.

11. Gallegos, F., Maintaining IT audit proficiency: the role of professional development planning, *IS Control J.*, Vol. 6, pp. 20–23, 2002.

12. Gallegos, F., The audit report and followup: methods and techniques for communicating audit findings, *IS Control J.*, Vol. 4, pp. 17–20, 2002.

13. Information Systems Audit and Control Foundation, Model Curriculum for Undergraduate and Graduate Education in IS Auditing, Carol Stream, IL, March 1998.

14. Katsikas, S.K., A Proposal for a Post-Graduate Curriculum in Information Security, Dependability and Safety, ERASMUS New Technologies Publications, Greece, 1994.

15. Kneer, D. et al., Information systems audit education, *IS Audit Control J.*, ISACA, ILL, Vol. 4, pp. 1–10, 1994.

16. Looho, A. and Gallegos, F., IS Audit Training Needs for the 21st Century: A Selected Assessment, Accepted for presentation and publication at International Association for Computer Information Systems Conference, Las Vegas, NV, October 4–7, 2000. Published in the issues in *Information Systems*, Vol. 1, pp 147–153, 2000, ISSN 1529-7314. Referred paper was selected by IACIS as their Year 2000 recipient of the Best Research Paper Award.

17. Manson, D. and Gallegos, F., *Evaluating the Quality of an IS Audit*, RIA/Auerbach Publishers, Boca Raton, FL, 1997.

18. McIntosh, E., *Internal Auditing in a Total Quality Environment*, The Institute of Internal Auditors, Altamonte Springs, FL, 1992.

19. Menkus, B. and Gallegos, F., Introduction to IT Auditing, #71-10-10.1, Auerbach Publishers, Boca Raton, FL, February 2002, pp. 1–20.

20. Quality Assurance Institute, *Survey on Function Point Measurement*, QAI, Orlando, FL, 1991.

21. Rubin, H.A., Measurements in the 1990s — shifting focus to business value: the key indicators that you need to track, *J. Qual. Assurance*, QAI, Orlando, FL, January 1992.

22. Smith, W., The Critical Metric Set: Speaking the Language of Executive Management, Presentation at the 1991 International Conference on Information Systems Quality Assurance, QAI, Orlando, FL, April 17–19, 1991.

23. Stephan, B.A., Metrics for CASE: A Case for Metrics, Presentation at the 1991 International Conference on Information Systems Quality Assurance, QAI, Orlando, FL, April 17–19, 1991.

Chapter 21
IT Auditing in the New Millennium

The new millennium has brought with it much change since the 1999 edition of this book. September 11, 2001 changed the U.S. view and perception of the meaning of terrorism. The financial debacles of Enron, WorldCom, and others provided a more realistic and fragile view of the U.S. economic infrastructure. The downfall of Arthur Andersen LLP offers a vivid reminder of the responsibility of auditors to the public, stockholders, and taxpayers and that ethics and the practice of due professional care have both meaning and substance to the auditors' practice.

With the passage of the Homeland Security Act and the Sarbanes–Oxley Act, the role of the auditor (internal and external) will be more critical to the verification and validation of the U.S. financial infrastructure. It will also be a valued process for supporting the security of the United States against terrorist activities. The profession of information technology (IT) auditing can provide a person with exposure to the way information flows in an organization and give its members ability to assess its validity, reliability, and security. IT auditing involves people, technology, operations, and systems. It is a dynamic and challenging profession, a profession with a future. In addition, the field brings growth into new areas such as IT security and computer forensics.

Today, IT auditors interact with managers, users, and technicians from all areas of most organizations. They must have interpersonal skills to interact with multiple levels of personnel and technical skills to understand the variety of technology used in information processing activity — especially that technology that impacts the company's financial statements. Also, he or she must gain an understanding of and a familiarity with the operational environment in order to assess the effectiveness of internal control. Finally, the IT auditor must understand the technological complexities of existing and future systems and the impact they have on operations and decisions at all levels.

IT auditing involves using computers to verify the integrity of computer-based systems. This process includes the examination, testing, and evaluation of internal controls within and around computer-based systems. The

IT auditor is the technical expert who provides guidance to the audit staff or performs this function. Also, the IT auditor may be involved in assessing efficiency, effectiveness, and risks associated with the use of computers in the organization. IT auditing is a relatively new profession. IT audit employment opportunities are in all sectors of private industry, public accounting, and government worldwide.

Nevertheless, what of tomorrow? What does the profession hold for us? What new challenges do we face? For example, at the end of Chapter 1 we mentioned the study by George Washington University on emerging technology and its impact on industry. What controls will need to be in place? How will we educate the IT auditor of the future to deal with the changes the new millennium brings? This chapter is intended to provide thoughts toward the future of an exciting field and profession.

IT Auditing Trends

Computing has become indispensable to organizations' activities. The CobiT Framework (IS Audit and Control Foundation, 1995) emphasizes this point and substantiates the need to research, develop, publicize, and promote up-to-date, internationally accepted information technology control objectives. In earlier documents such as the 1993 discussion paper "Minimum Skill Levels in Information Technology for Professional Accountants" and their 1992 final report "The Impact of Information Technology on the Accountancy Profession," the International Federation of Accountants (IFAC) acknowledges the need for better university-level education to address growing information technology control concerns and issues.

Around the world, reports of information theft, computer fraud, information abuse, and other information/technology control concerns are being heard more frequently. Organizations are more information-conscious, people are scattered due to decentralization, and computers are used more extensively in all areas of commerce. Due to the rapid diffusion of computer technologies and the ease of information accessibility, knowledgeable and well-trained IT auditors are needed to ensure more effective controls are put in place to maintain data integrity and to manage access to information. The need for better controls over IT has been echoed in the past by prior studies such as the AICPA's Committee of Sponsoring Organizations of the Treadway Commission (COSO), ISO 9000, the Institute of Internal Auditors' (IIA) Systems Auditability and Control Report, Guidelines for the Security of IS by the Organization for Economic Cooperation and Development (OECD), and the U.S. President's Council on Integrity and Efficiency in Computer Audit Training curriculum. The most recent additions to these major studies are *Control Objectives for Information and Related Technology (CobiT): Framework 3rd Edition*, the United States' National Strategy for Securing Cyberspace released in 2002, and ISO 17799.

Even the AICPA has a committee in place to identify and examine broad macro-market trends and forecast the future evolution of existing trends impacting the assurance services business. There were nine trends identified by the AICPA's Special Committee on Assurances Services, which they believe to have the most effect on CPA's services and practices. These trends, ranked in largest to smallest effect, are:

- Information technology
- Competition
- Corporate structure
- Accountability
- Investment capital
- Aging of the U.S. population
- Globalization
- Education
- Changes in the legal environment

With the Enron case being pursued in the courts and the demise of Arthur Andersen LLP, the profession's legal environment may be much more impacted. The effect of the Sarbanes–Oxley Act will create change as far as the future of assurance service liability and limited liability partnership is concerned. This is an area that is very hard to predict with certainty. The opportunities basically fall into three areas: providing needed information to companies, providing assurances on new accountabilities including criteria for measurement, and providing intermediary services on behalf of the principals. The threats are in areas such as potential damage to profession's image or reputation, increased competition, liability, and discontinuities caused by difficulty in adapting to new conditions.

Other areas mentioned for future growth are electronic commerce, health care performance measurement, elder care, policy compliance, outsourced internal audit, trading partner accountability, mergers and acquisitions, ISO 9000, and World Wide Web assertions. These and the previously mentioned areas provide a glimpse of the impact of technology on business processes and the need for information assurances to audit, control, and secure. The AICPA's two reports, "Megatrends Affecting Future Assurance Services" and "Effect of Information Technology on the Assurance Services Market Place," are well worth reading at www.aicpa.org.

The theory and methodologies of IT auditing are integrated from five areas: a fundamental understanding of business, traditional auditing, IT management, behavioral science, and IT sciences. Business understanding and knowledge are the cornerstones of the audit process. Traditional auditing contributes knowledge of internal control practices and overall control philosophy within a business enterprise. Information systems management provides methodologies necessary to achieve successful design and implementation of systems. Behavioral science indicates when and why information systems are likely to fail because of people problems. IT sciences contribute to knowledge about control theory and the formal models that underlie hardware and software design as a basis for maintaining data integrity.

IT auditing is an integral part of the audit function because it supports the auditor's judgment on the quality of computer systems. IT auditors are the technological resource for the audit staff. The audit staff often looks to them for technical assistance. Within IT auditing, there are organizational IT audits (management control over information technology), technical IT audits (infrastructure, data centers, data communication), application (business/financial) IT audits, and compliance IT audits involving national or international standards. Ever since the Information Systems Audit and Control Association (ISACA) [formerly the EDP Auditors Association (EDPAA)], was formed in Los Angeles in 1969, there has been a growing demand for well-trained and skilled IT audit professionals.

IT auditing is a profession with conduct, aims, and qualities that are characterized by worldwide technical and ethical standards. It requires specialized knowledge and often long and intensive academic preparation. Most accounting, auditing, and IT professional societies believe that improvements in research and education will definitely provide a "better-developed theoretical and empirical knowledge base for the IT audit function." They feel that emphasis should be placed upon education obtained at the college level.

The breath and depth of knowledge required to audit IT is extensive. For example, IT auditing involves the application of risk-oriented audit approaches; the use of computer-assisted audit tools and techniques (e.g., EnCase, CaseWare, Idea, ACL, Guardant, eTrust, CA-Examine); the application of standards (national or international) such as ISO 9000/3 and ISO 17799 to improve and implement quality systems in software development; the auditing of systems under development involving complex Systems Development Life Cycle (SDLC) or new development techniques (e.g., prototyping, end-user computing, rapid systems development); and the auditing of complex technologies involving electronic data interchange, client servers, local and wide area networks, data communications, telecommunications, and integrated voice/data/video systems.

The New Dimension: Information Assurances

As a result of September 11, 2001, IT audit in the private section must expand its domain of review to information assurances. Our country (military and nonmilitary) has increasingly relied upon critical digital electronic information capabilities to store, process, and move essential data in planning, directing, coordinating, and executing operations. Powerful and sophisticated threats can exploit security weaknesses in many of these systems. Outsourcing technological development to countries that could have terrorists on their development staff causes speculation that the potential exists for code to be implanted that would cause disruption, havoc, embezzlement, theft, etc. These and other weaknesses that can be exploited become vulnerabilities that can jeopardize the most sensitive components of information capabilities. However, we can employ deep, layered defenses to reduce vulnerabilities and to deter, defeat, and recover from a wide range of threats. From an information assurance perspective, the capabilities that we must defend can be viewed broadly in terms of four major elements: local computing environments, their boundaries, networks that link them together, and their supporting infrastructure.

The term *information assurance* is defined as information integrity (the level of confidence and trust that can be placed on the information) and service availability. It means safeguarding the collection, storage, transmission, and use of information. The ultimate goal of information assurance is to protect users, business units, and enterprises from the negative effects of corruption of information or denial-of-services. For example, if the personnel data in a human resource database is valid in the sense that it could be but is not, in fact, correct, there may be no negative impact on the information system but the enterprise may suffer when people get the wrong amount of money in their paychecks or when the money is sent to the wrong address. Similarly, if an order for an engine part in a supply and logistics system is lost in the part of the system that should have dictated which pallets get loaded onto which boat to which destination, the information system continues to operate but the supply service is denied to the person requiring the parts. Naturally, if the information system's processing, storing, or communicating information becomes corrupt or unavailable, the enterprise may also be affected as a whole. However, simply protecting the systems without protecting the information, processing, and communication is not adequate.

As the nation's information systems are being tied together (government and business), the points of entry and exposure increase, and thus risks increase. The technological advancement toward higher bandwidth communication and advanced switching systems has reduced the number of communications lines and further centralized the switching functions. Survey data indicates that the increased risk from these changes is not widely recognized. Efforts have been made by U.S. defense organizations such as the Defense Information Systems Agency (DISA) to promulgate standards for the Defense Information Infrastructure (DII) and the Global Information Grid (GiG), which should have a positive impact on information assurance that will extend beyond the U.S Department of Defense (DoD) and impact all segments of the national economy.

IT Audit: The Profession

IT auditing is a relatively new profession for a new generation. A profession is more than just an occupation. A profession has certain special characteristics: it is supported by a common body of knowledge, certification, continuing education, code of ethics and standards, an educational curriculum, and a professional association. Since 1975, there have been various studies identifying a common body of knowledge for the IT audit profession. With regard to certification, the Certified Information Systems Auditor (CISA) provides a level of accreditation for the profession. Certification requires continuing education so that those who are certified maintain a level of proficiency and continue their certification.

The audit profession, as shown in Appendix III, is supported by a code of ethics and professional standards that has been developed by several professional associations that support audit professionals. As mentioned in the previous chapter, there are a number of additional certifications that can benefit one seeking to enter the IT audit, control, and security field. A number of universities provide education in auditing computer systems and several are in the process of developing IT audit curricula and information assurances curricula. Finally, there are a number of professional associations involved in IT audit, control, and security community, as noted in Appendix III.

As for the future, the profession will continue as information technology impacts the business process and shrinks our global communication structure. As several studies mentioned in earlier chapters have stated, new standards and practices will evolve. The terms mobility, flexibility, efficiency, effectiveness, and economy will be commonplace in the method of work. The ability to use technology in accomplishing assigned tasks and responsibilities, reporting, and follow-up will continue to evolve.

A Common Body of Knowledge

A common body of knowledge consists of clearly identified areas in which a person must attain a specific level of understanding and competency necessary to successfully practice within the profession. These areas are categorized into core areas. Organizations such as ISACA, AICPA, IIA, the Canadian Institute of Chartered Accountant (CICA), Information Systems Security Association (ISSA), INFOSEC, and others around the world have issued major studies and papers on the topic of the knowledge, skills, and abilities needed to audit computers. Students, especially business and computer majors, receive a degree of base-level training in (1) auditing concepts and practices, (2) management concepts and practices, (3) computer systems, telecommunications, operations, and software, (4) computer information processing techniques, and (5) understanding of business on local and international scales. These are some of the major core areas of competency identified by the various independent studies for the individual who enters the IT audit, control, and security field.

Certification

Certification is a vital component of a profession. As you prepare for entry into your profession, whether it is accounting, information systems, or other business fields, certification will be the measure of your level of knowledge, skills, and abilities in the profession. For example, attainment of the Certified Public Accountant (CPA) designation is an important career milestone for the practicing accountant. In IT auditing, CISA, is the level of recognition and attainment.

A CISA must pass a rigorous written examination and have at least five years of experience and education. The CISA examination covers such areas as information systems security and control practices, information systems organization and management, information systems process, information systems integrity, confidentiality, and availability, and information systems development, acquisition, and maintenance. Thus, university education plays an important part in providing the groundwork toward the certification process.

Certification is important and a measure of skill attainment. Proficiency in skill application comes from experience and continuing education. The dynamic changes in business (commerce), information technology, and world events continue to shape the future.

Continuing Education

Another critical element for the next millennium is continuing education. It is an important element for career growth. As graduates enter their profession, they will find that their academic education is the foundation for continued development of career-enhancing knowledge, skills, and abilities. A continuing education requirement exists to support the CISA program. The IT auditor of the 21st century will constantly face change to existing systems and the dynamics of the environment (i.e., reorganization, new technology, operational change, changing requirements, etc.).

Because the organizational environment in which the IT auditor operates is a dynamic one, it is important that new developments in the profession be understood so that they may be appropriately applied. Thus, the continuing education requirement helps the CISA attain new knowledge and skills in order to provide the most informed professional opinion. Training courses and programs are offered by a wide variety of associations and organizations to assist in maintaining the necessary skills that they need continue to improve and evolve. Methods for receiving such training may even be global with video teleconferencing and telecommuting and with the Internet playing a major role in training delivery.

A Code of Ethics and Professional Standards

A code of ethics and professional standards provides the foundation for a profession even into the next millennium. Professional associations establish codes of ethics to guide the conduct of their members in their professional and personal activities. The image of a professional is an important characteristic in establishing creditability.

Professional standards determine how the profession should be practiced and the goals toward which the practitioner strives. As a professional of the future, you should become familiar with the code of ethics and professional standards of your profession. Further, IT audit professionals need to become involved in the development of those standards and best practices. Again, technology is a tool in the dissemination of lessons learned and best practices.

Educational Curricula

The academic communities both in the United States and abroad have incorporated portions of the common body of knowledge and the CISA examination domains into courses taught at the university level. Several recent studies indicate the growth of computer audit courses emerging in university curricula worldwide. A model curriculum for undergraduate and graduate education in information systems audit education was issued in March 1998 by the IS Audit and Control Association and Foundation (see Exhibit 1 to Exhibit 4). In Exhibit 5 and Exhibit 6, we look at how that model relates to areas of emphasis for the CISA exam of 2003.

Also, several universities have developed curricula tailored to support the profession of IT auditing. These prototypes exist at such institutions as Arizona State University, California State Polytechnic University (Pomona), the University of West Florida (Pensacola), the University of Houston, the University of Minnesota, Georgia State University, Florida Atlantic University, the University of Nagoya (Japan), Queensland University of Technology and Curtin University of Technology (Australia), and others. IT auditing is a profession that provides opportunity and challenge. As an important stepping-stone in one's career, it can open many opportunities.

Also, the area of information assurances has grown and evolved. As mentioned in the next section, INFOSEC, through U.S. federal support, has developed criteria and training standards for IT security professionals. The United States in its passage of the Cyber Security Research and Development Act has pledged almost a billion dollars for the development of curriculum, research, and skills for future professionals needed in this field.

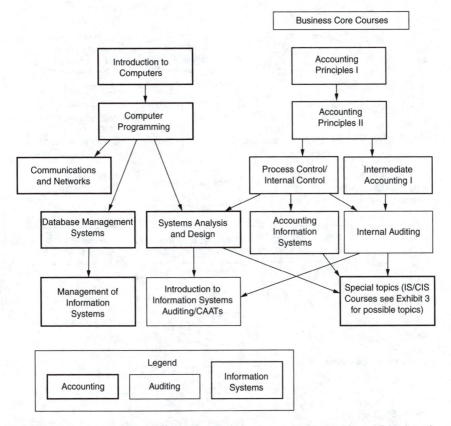

Exhibit 1. Structure of the Model Curriculum for an Undergraduate Program in Information Systems Auditing

New Trends in Developing IT Auditors and Education

The 2000 survey results from a study completed at California State Polytechnic University, Pomona, in support of the article "IS Audit Training Needs for the 21st Century: A Selected Assessment," in the *Journal of Computer Information Systems* (International Association of Computer Information Systems, Volume XXXXI, Number 2, Winter 2000–2001, pp. 9–15), confirmed that the main venues used to train IT auditors are seminars/workshops (94 percent). Almost 40 percent of respondents indicated that seminars/workshops are the only type of training they received in the past five years. About 26 percent of respondents received a combination of seminar/workshop and vendor software training.

In the past five years, almost 37 percent of IT auditors attended a university as part of their training program. Many indicated that they would like to see universities offer more training directed at information systems

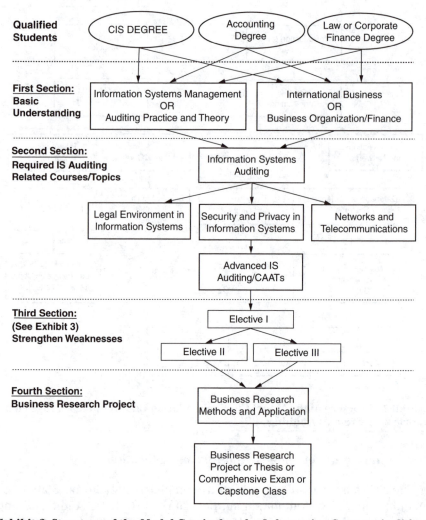

Qualified Students
- CIS DEGREE
- Accounting Degree
- Law or Corporate Finance Degree

First Section: Basic Understanding
- Information Systems Management OR Auditing Practice and Theory
- International Business OR Business Organization/Finance

Second Section: Required IS Auditing Related Courses/Topics
- Information Systems Auditing
- Legal Environment in Information Systems
- Security and Privacy in Information Systems
- Networks and Telecommunications
- Advanced IS Auditing/CAATs

Third Section: (See Exhibit 3) Strengthen Weaknesses
- Elective I
- Elective II
- Elective III

Fourth Section: Business Research Project
- Business Research Methods and Application
- Business Research Project or Thesis or Comprehensive Exam or Capstone Class

Exhibit 2. Structure of the Model Curriculum for Information Systems Auditing at Graduate Level

audit, control, and security professional. This is a result of ISACA's effort to identify and support a model curriculum. The first was published by ISACA in 1998 and is found at www.isaca.org/modelc1.htm. Under the direction of Dr. Alan T. Lord of Bowling Green University, international efforts are underway to update the first version.

The IT audit training can be at two levels — development of professionals for entry and follow-up training for professionals in the field. Of the respondents, 11 percent were able to receive a combination of all three

**Exhibit 3. Sample Undergraduate or Graduate Course
Topics for Special Topics or Directed Electives**

Rapid systems development
Information systems planning
Executive information systems
Computer forensics
Encryption, cryptographic, and biometrics
Advanced systems analysis and design
Wide area/voice networks
Information assurance
Software quality assurance
Business systems analysis
Network management
Human factors in systems design
Business economics
Advanced office systems/directed study
Managerial accounting for decision making
Database design and processing
Executive development
Professional presentations using technology/directed study
Management science/directed study
Advanced financial management/directed study
Accounting for decisions and control/directed study
IS integrity, confidentiality, and availability

methods indicated on the survey (seminar/workshops, vendor software, and university).

In the information assurances community, INFOSEC has made significant strides in gaining support from the U.S. universities. The National INFOSEC Education and Training Program (NIETP) operates under national authority and its initiatives provide the foundation for a dramatic increase in the population of trained and professionalized security experts. Activities in this area directly support government efforts to professionalize and certify system administrators and associated network positions. There is no single vehicle to accomplish this task. NIETP initiatives are multifaceted and strive to address all aspects of its role in education, training, and awareness by creating partnerships among government, academia, and industry. Through these partnerships, the NIETP can assess current offerings in INFOSEC courses, from a variety of sources to identify gaps and to determine how to fill those gaps. As of 2003, 50 U.S. universities have been identified as centers of excellence in information assurances education, and 66 have had their courses certified to meet U.S. federal standards. The U.S. National Security Agency is continuing in its leadership role with national level programs via the National Security Telecommunications and

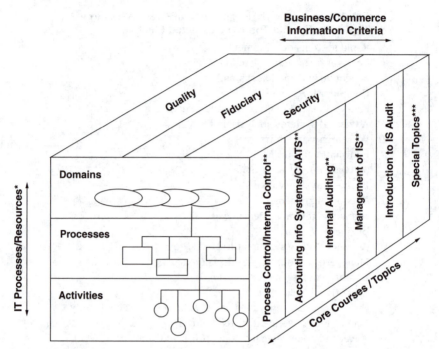

* IT Resources involve people, application systems, technology, facilities, and data
** Courses offered within most universities may have different name or course title
*** See Attached VI

Exhibit 4. Relevance of Undergraduate IS Audit Model

Information Systems Security Committee (NSTISSC) for ensuring the finest preparation of professionals entrusted with securing the U.S. National Security Systems.

Worldwide, universities have been responding to the needs of the IT audit and information assurances profession. At the undergraduate level, IT courses have begun to be integrated into accounting programs and accounting or finance courses into IT programs. At the graduate level, several universities have successfully implemented and maintained IT audit programs. These universities have attempted to meet the growing demand for entry-level knowledge, skills, and abilities. A partial list of such universities recognized by ISACA can be found at www.isaca.org/univ1.htm.

Although predicting future trends is always problematic, the need for qualified people to deal with these developments is critical. Some future trends could be:

- More applications will be purchased or outsourced, and fewer applications will be developed in-house, including audit software.

Exhibit 5. Relevance of IS Audit Undergraduate

Percent of Exam	2003 CISA Examination Content Areas to 1998 Model Curriculum (Undergraduate) Title and Description	Process Control/Internal Control	Accounting Info Systems/CAATS	Internal Audit	Management of IS	Introduction to IS Auditing
11%	**Management, Planning, and Organization of IS** Evaluate the strategy, policies, standards, procedures, and related practices for the management, planning, and organization of IS	X		X	X	X
13%	**Technical Infrastructure and Operations Practices** Evaluate the effectiveness and efficiency of the organization's implementation and ongoing management of technical and operational infrastructure to ensure that they adequately support the organization's business objectives	X	X		X	X
25%	**Protection of Information Assets** Evaluate the logical, environmental, and IT infrastructure security to ensure that it satisfies the organization's business requirements for safeguarding information assets against unauthorized use, disclosure, modification, damage, or loss	X	X	X	X	X
10%	**Disaster Recovery and Business Continuity** Evaluate the process for developing and maintaining documented, communicated, and tested plans for continuity of business operations and IS processing in the event of a disruption	X	X	X	X	X
16%	**Business Application Systems Development, Acquisition, Implementation, and Maintenance** Evaluate the methodology and processes by which the business application system development, acquisition, implementation, and maintenance are undertaken to ensure that they meet the business organization's objectives	X	X	X	X	X
15%	**Business Process Evaluation and Risk Management** Evaluate business systems and processes to ensure that risks are managed in accordance with organization's business objectives	X		X	X	X
10%	**The IS Audit Process** Analyze and evaluate information systems (IS) development, acquisition, and maintenance	X	X	X	X	X

Exhibit 6. Relevance of IS Audit Graduate

	2003 CISA Examination Domain to 1998 Model Curriculum (Graduate)	IS Audit/CAATS	Legal Environment of IS	Security and Privacy of IS	Network/Telecommunication	Advanced IS Audit
Domain	Title and Description					
11%	**Management, Planning, and Organization of IS** Evaluate the strategy, policies, standards, procedures, and related practices for the management, planning, and organization of IS	X	X	X	X	X
13%	**Technical Infrastructure and Operations Practices** Evaluate the effectiveness and efficiency of the organization's implementation and ongoing management of technical and operational infrastructure to ensure that they adequately support the organization's business objectives	X	X	X	X	X
25%	**Protection of Information Assets** Evaluate the logical, environmental, and IT infrastructure security to ensure that it satisfies the organization's business requirements for safeguarding information assets against unauthorized use, disclosure, modification, damage, or loss	X	X	X	X	X
10%	**Disaster Recovery and Business Continuity** Evaluate the process for developing and maintaining documented, communicated, and tested plans for continuity of business operations and IS processing in the event of a disruption	X	X	X	X	X
16%	**Business Application Systems Development, Acquisition, Implementation, and Maintenance** Evaluate the methodology and processes by which the business application system development, acquisition, implementation, and maintenance are undertaken to ensure that they meet the business organization's objectives	X	X	X	X	X
15%	**Business Process Evaluation and Risk Management** Evaluate business systems and processes to ensure that risks are managed in accordance with organization's business objectives	X		X	X	X
10%	**The IS Audit Process** Analyze and evaluate information systems (IS) development, acquisition, and maintenance	X	X	X	X	X

- The use of communication facilities will increase, providing greater interaction between personnel and computers, migration to virtual corporations, and businesses as a whole. The global, national, and business information infrastructure must be secure.
- More sophisticated auditing techniques will emerge, permitting the auditor to make more use of the computer in auditing the computer.
- Quality assurance groups will become more effective in the performance of their responsibilities. As these groups become more effective, auditors will be able to rely on their work and perform fewer audit tasks.
- Organizations will begin to incorporate artificial intelligence and expert systems into day-to-day business processing. As this occurs, auditors will need to become more involved in ensuring the adequacy of controls in these systems. Tests of such controls will extend beyond the physical borders of the country because business (commerce) is global.
- Less reliance will be placed on the centralized information group to manage and control information within the organization.
- More use will be made of the exchange of information electronically throughout the organization in assessing and improving the totality and quality of business processes.
- There will be a rapid reduction in the cycle time of introducing both new technology and new business applications.

If most of these predictions are accurate, auditors, as representatives of management, will become more involved in the daily operations of the computer department. To build controls into the computer systems, IT auditor, control, and security personnel must develop a high degree of competence in IT and become involved in the complete life cycle of information technology.

Perhaps the most revealing of trends is the work done at George Washington University and their "Forecast of Future Technology" and its impact to industry. One looks at this forecast with apprehension, wondering how it will be possible to audit, control, and secure this technology and its application within business and society as a whole.

Career Opportunities in the 21st Century

IT audit, control, and security offer a variety of career opportunities. This profession can be a career in itself or it can lead to other careers that utilize the knowledge, skills, and abilities gained as an IT audit professional. Today's IT auditors are employed by public accounting firms, management consulting firms, private industry, and government. The career path can be what one wants it to be. The IT auditor, IT security professional, and IT forensic professional for the 21st century will continue to be in demand. Internationally, the need is growing.

Public Accounting

Public accounting firms offer individuals an opportunity to enter into IT auditing and IT forensics. Although these firms may require such individuals to begin their careers in financial audits to gain experience in understanding the organization's audit methodologies, after initial audit experience the individual who expresses interest will be transferred to this specialty for further training and career development. Many who have taken this career path have been successful, and several have advanced to partnership level of the firm. The primary sources for most CPA firms are college recruitment and development within. However, it is not uncommon for a firm to hire from outside for specialized expertise (i.e., computer forensics, telecommunication, database systems, etc.). As mentioned earlier in the AICPA report, opportunities exist in the assurance services marketplace.

Private Industry

Like public accounting, private industry offers entry-level IT audit and IT security professional positions. In addition, IT auditors gain expertise in more specialized areas (i.e., telecommunications, systems software, systems design, etc.), which can make them candidates for IT operations and security positions. Many chief executive officers view audit experience as a management training function. The IT auditor has particular strengths of educational background, practical experience with corporate information systems, and understanding of executive decision making. Some companies have made a distinction between IT auditors and operational and financial auditors. Others require all internal auditors to be capable of auditing IT systems. The sources for persons to staff the IT audit function within a company generally may come from these areas: college recruitment, internal transfers or promotions, and outside hiring.

Management Consulting

Another area of opportunity for IT audit, control, and security personnel is management consulting. This career area usually is available to IT auditors with a number of years' experience. Many management consulting practices, especially those that provide services in the computer information systems environment, hire experienced IT audit, control, and security personnel. This career path allows these candidates to use their particular knowledge, skills, and abilities in diagnosing an array of computer and management information issues and then to assist the organization in implementing the solutions. The usual resources for such positions are experienced personnel from CPA firms, private industry, and government. IT forensics is another growing area in management consulting services.

Government

Government offers another avenue for one to gain IT audit experience. In the United States, federal, state, county, and city governments employ staffs that conduct IT audit-related responsibilities. Worldwide, governments employ staff that conduct IT audits. Such government positions offer training and experience to staff responsible for performing this function. The sources for government IT auditors are college recruits and employees seeking internal promotion or transfer. There are occasions when experienced resources may be hired from the outside as well.

As cited above, there are a number of career opportunities available to the individual seeking an opportunity in IT audit. For the college graduate with the appropriate entry-level knowledge, skills, and abilities, this career provides many paths for growth and development. Further, as a career develops and progresses, IT audit can provide mobility into other areas as well. Federal organizations such as the NSA, FBI, Department of Justice, and CIA employ personnel who have IT audit experience, computer security experience, and IT forensics experience. Career paths may vary substantially within different organizations and countries.

The Role of the IT Auditor in IT Governance

It is time to revisit the role of the IT auditor mentioned in the earlier part of this book. The role of the IT auditor is critical to the success of IT governance and the audit, control, and security of information systems of the future. Ensuring the quality, integrity, and authenticity of the information of tomorrow is of the utmost importance. The auditor evaluating today's complex systems must have highly developed technical skills to understand the evolving methods of information processing. Contemporary systems carry risks such as noncompatible platforms, new methods to penetrate security through communication networks (e.g., the Internet), and the rapid decentralization of information processing with the resulting loss of centralized controls.

Auditing the processing environment is divided into two parts. The first and the most technical part of the audit is the evaluation of the operating environment with major software packages (e.g., the operating and security systems) representing the general or environmental controls in the automated processing environment. This part is usually audited by the IT audit specialist. The second part of the processing environment is the automated application, which is audited by the general auditor who possesses some computer skills.

621

As the use of IT in organizations continues to grow, auditing computerized systems must be accomplished without having in place many of the guidelines established for the traditional auditing effort. In addition, new uses of IT introduce new risks, which in turn require new controls. IT auditors are also in a unique position to evaluate the relevance of a particular system to the enterprise as a whole. Because of this, the IT auditor often plays a role in senior management decision making.

The role of IT auditor can be examined through the process of IT governance and the existing standards of professional practice for this profession. As mentioned earlier, IT governance is an organizational involvement in the management and review of the use of IT in attaining the goals and objectives set by the organization.

Because IT impacts the operation of an entire organization, everyone should have an interest and role in governing its use and application. This growing awareness has led organizations to recognize that if they are to make the most of their IT investment and protect that investment, they need a formal process to govern it.

Reasons for implementing an IT governance program include:

- Increasing dependence on information and the systems that deliver the information
- Increasing vulnerabilities and a wide spectrum of threats
- Scale and cost of current and future investments in information and information systems
- Potential for technologies to dramatically change organizations and business practices, create new opportunities, and reduce costs.

As long as these factors remain a part of business, there will be a need for effective, interdependent systems of enterprise and IT governance.

An open-standard IT governance tool that helps nontechnical and technical managers and auditors understand and manage risks associated with information and related IT was developed by the IT Governance Institute and the Information Systems Audit and Control Foundation. Control Objectives for Information and Related Technology (CobiT) is a comprehensive framework of control objectives that helps IT auditors, managers, and executives discharge fiduciary responsibilities, understand their IT systems, and decide what level of security and control is adequate. CobiT provides an authoritative, international set of generally accepted IT practices for business managers and auditors.

CobiT can be downloaded on a complimentary basis from www.isaca. org. It includes a publication containing detailed management guidelines to bridge the gaps among business risks, control needs, and technical issues. These new tools help businesses monitor processes by using critical success factors (CSFs), key goal indicators (KGIs), key performance indicators (KPIs), and maturity models (MMs). Additional resources and information are available at www.ITgovernance.org.

The IT Auditor as Counselor

In the past, users have abdicated responsibility for controlling computer systems mostly because of the psychological barriers that surround the computer. As a result, there are few checks and balances except for the IT auditor. Therefore, auditors must take an active role in developing policies on auditability, control, testing, and standards. Auditors also must convince users and IT personnel of the need for a controlled IS environment.

An IT audit staff in a large corporation can make a major contribution to computer system control by persuading user groups to insist on a policy of comprehensive testing for all new systems and all changes to existing systems. By reviewing base-case results, user groups can control the accuracy of new or changed systems by actually performing a complete control function.

Insisting that all new systems be reviewed at predefined checkpoints throughout the system's development life cycle also can enhance control of IT. The prospect of audit review should prompt both user and systems groups to define their objectives and assumptions more carefully. Here, too, IS auditors can subtly extend their influence.

The IT Auditor as Partner of Senior Management

Although the IT auditor's roles of counselor and skilled technician are vital to successful company operation, they may be irrelevant if the auditor fails to view auditing in relation to the organization as a whole. A system that appears well-controlled may be inconsistent with the operation of a business.

Decisions concerning the need for a system traditionally belonged to senior management, but because of a combination of factors (mostly the complex technology of the computer), computer system audits had not been successfully performed. When allocating funds for new systems, management has had to rely on the judgment of computer personnel. Although their choices of new and more effective computer systems cannot be faulted, computer personnel have often failed to meet the true business needs of the organization.

Management needs the support of a skilled computer staff that understands the organization's requirements, and IT auditors are in a position to provide that information. They can provide management with an independent assessment of the effect of IT decisions on the business. In addition, the IT auditor can verify that all alternatives for a given project have been considered, all risks have been accurately assessed, the technical hardware and software solutions are correct, business needs will be satisfied, and costs are reasonable.

Educating the Next Generation on IT Audit and Control Opportunities

Many have prospered from their experiences in the profession of IT auditing. Hopefully, more will choose to become involved in the future of IT auditing by the involvement of their organization in supporting research efforts at the university level and taking the time to be a "professor-for-a-day" to share their experiences and knowledge level with faculty and students. This is valuable opportunity to educate the next generation.

Many more opportunities in IT auditing will continue to open in this new millennium. Career profiles of alumni who have chosen IT auditing provide a good example of career paths. Also, professional associations such as the IIA, Association of Government Accountants (AGA), and ISACA chapters may have student-related activities and information. Typically, many ISACA chapters sponsor such activities as a "Student Night," "Best Student Paper Contest," or provide speakers to colleges to discuss IT audit-related topics.

Participation by the professional, faculty, and student is a necessary element in this process. Certainly, if one is interested in a profession, necessary steps should be taken to educate others about it. Many ISACA chapters provide students with opportunities to learn more about this dynamic and challenging profession.

Conclusion

The events of September 11, 2001, have changed the nation in many ways, much like the event of December 7, 1941. Both days will "live in infamy." This event is still being felt in all parts of the world. IT control and audit processes and procedures will be of highest priority in safeguarding our businesses, government, and citizens. Security of the homeland is of top national importance and priority.

Where there are computer systems and information generated by this technology to support decision making, there will be a need to assess the reliability, validity, and internal controls of such systems. There will be a need to secure them. Such technology affects everyone's future regardless of profession — law, medicine, education, social work, etc. As an IT auditor or IT control professional, one is and will continue to be on the forefront of this change and aid one's employer in successfully preparing for the business environment of the new millennium. This is a dynamic profession constantly facing change and challenges — a continuous learning environment.

Opportunity for careers in this challenging and dynamic field has never been better as the new millennium begins. IT governance, new technology, E-business, and legal issues have opened a new frontier and the need for new skills and common sense in applying good business practices. Corporate integrity, institutional integrity, and business integrity are under constant review by the public and government. Audit as an institutional process can be a major player in reestablishing the public's confidence in business. Thanks to the Sarbanes–Oxley Act, the audit report has more value today than ever before. As a result of the Homeland Security Act and the U.S. National Strategy for Securing Cyberspace, information assurances (audit, control, and security) are now everyone's business.

As organizations rely more on information technology for day-to-day processing and decision making, the need for auditor involvement will increase accordingly. The introduction of new information technology brings with it new risks. Management, as part of the governance process, needs assurance that risks are under adequate control. Auditors, as part of the IT governance, must become involved in the introduction of new technology. In addition, the responsibility for IT is being distributed from information systems personnel to end users. Thus, information assurances (audit, control, and security) will become a more important part of all audits.

Review Questions

1. What knowledge, skills, and abilities must an IT auditor have?
2. Where are IT auditors employed?
3. What were the findings of the AICPA's Special Committee on Assurance Services?
4. What professional standards and guidance exist for the auditor, for the IT auditor, and for the government auditor?
5. Will the audit profession continue? How will it keep pace with change to technology, business practices, government regulation, and international events?
6. What is a common body of knowledge?
7. What professional certifications exist for the audit professional and for the IT auditor?
8. What are the CISA exam domains? What is the CISA exam?
9. In 1998, the ISACA issued its "Model Curriculum for Graduate and Undergraduate Education in Information Systems Auditing." What guidance does this document provide?
10. Where are the career opportunities for an IT auditor in the next century?

Multiple Choice

1. IT auditing involves:
   a. People
   b. Technology
   c. Operations and systems
   d. All of the above
2. CoBiT was developed and issued by:
   a. AICPA
   b. IIA
   c. ISACA
   d. ACFE
3. The SAC reports were issued by:
   a. IIA
   b. ISSA
   c. ISACA
   d. AICPA
4. Information assurance is defined as:
   a. Information integrity
   b. The level of confidence and trust that can be placed on the information
   c. The level of trust and confidence that can be placed on service availability
   d. All of the above
5. The following U.S. federal act has pledged almost a billion dollars toward curriculum, research, and skill development in IT audit, control, security, and information assurances issues:
   a. Computer Fraud and Abuse Act of 1984
   b. Computer Security Act of 1987
   c. Cyber Security Research and Development Act
   d. HIPAA Act of 1996
6. Which organization operating under U.S. national authority and its initiatives provides the foundation for a dramatic increase in the population of trained and professionalized security experts?
   a. AICPA
   b. ISACA
   c. NIETP
   d. None of the above
7. Standards for information security officers have been issued by:
   a. CIA
   b. FBI
   c. GAO
   d. NSTISSC
8. A new field of opportunity and career growth is:
   a. Business systems analyst

    b. Computer forensic analyst

    c. Network administrator

    d. None of the above

9. The number of universities within the United States identified as Centers of Excellence in Information Assurances is:

    a. 10

    b. 25

    c. 40

    d. Greater than 49

10. The IT auditor role in IT governance can be as:

    a. A counselor

    b. A partner of senior management

    c. An educator

    d. All of the above

Exercises

1. Do you believe that IT auditing is a career opportunity for you? If so, what are your strengths and do they match the knowledge, skills, and abilities needed to perform in this profession?

2. What do IT auditors do? What are their roles and areas of responsibilities?

3. Obtain five position announcements for IT auditors and summarize the five key skills wanted of them.

4. List three universities that provide graduate education in this field.

Answers to Multiple Choice Questions

1 — d; 2 — c; 3 — a; 4 — d; 5 — c; 6 — c; 7 — d; 8 — b; 9 — d; 10 — d

References

1. Accounting Education Change Commission, 1990, Position Statement No. 1: Objectives of education for accountants, *Issues in Accounting Education* (Fall): pp. 307–312.
2. American Institute of Certified Public Accountants (AICPA), IIS Spring 1987, SAS 48 and SAS 55, *Consideration of the Internal Control Structure in a Financial Statement*, Audit April 1988.
3. American Institute of Certified Public Accountants (AICPA), 1990, *Consideration of the Internal Control Structure in a Financial Statement Audit: An Amendment to SAS 55* (SAS 78).
4. American Institute of Certified Public Accountants (AICPA), 2001, *The Effect of Information Technology on the Auditor's Consideration of Internal Control in a Financial Statement Audit* (SAS 94).
5. American Institute of Certified Public Accountants (AICPA), 2002, *Consideration of Fraud in a Financial Statement Audit* (SAS 99).
6. American Institute of Certified Public Accountants (AICPA), Special Committee on Information Assurances, "MegaTrends Affecting Future Assurance Services," April 2003.

7. American Institute of Certified Public Accountants (AICPA), Special Committee on Information Assurances, "Affect of Information Technology on the Assurance Services Marketplace," April 2003.
8. Wiederkehr, B., IT Security Programme, *IS Control J.*, Vol. 3, 2003, pp. 30–33.
9. Cangemi, M.P. and F. Gallegos, CIS auditing: a career plan, *New Accountant* (February 1991), pp. 27–30.
10. Cerullo, V. and M.J. Cerullo, Impact of SAS No. 94 on computer auditing techniques, *IS Control J.*, Vol. 1, 2003, pp. 53–57.
11. Gallegos, F., IT audit careers: IT governance provides new roles and opportunities, *IS Control J.*, Vol. 3, 2003, pp. 40–43.
12. Gallegos, F., IT audit career development plan, *IS Control J.*, Vol. 2, 2003, pp. 16–17.
13. Gallegos, F., I.W. Mason, R. Guthrie, and D. Manson, Using Internet in computer information systems, *In Celebration of Teaching: Reflections of Cal Poly Pomona Professors*, Faculty Center for Professional Development, Spring 1995 issue, pp. 25–27.
14. Gallegos, F. and S. Curl, Audit considerations for EIS, *IS Audit Control J.*, Vol. 2, 1995 issue, pp. 36–42.
15. Gallegos, F., I.W. Mason, R. Guthrie, and D. Manson, Using Internet in CIS security and audit education to examine a business problem, *IS Audit Control J.*, Vol. 3, 1994 issue, pp. 14–19.
16. Gallegos, F., I. Mason, and V. Deokar, Teaching CIS auditors how to review data communications, June 1992, *EDP Auditor's J.*, Vol. 2, 1992 issue, pp. 29–41.
17. Gallegos, F., D. Ireland, and M. Hunt, Automating assessments of internal controls: a GAO perspective, *Gov. Accountants J.*, Vol. 40, No. 4, Winter 1992, pp. 33–39.
18. Gallegos, F., Computer information systems audit career development, *EDP Auditors J.*, Vol. 1, 1991, pp. 23–28.
19. Gallegos, F., A decade of excellence in EDP audit education, *EDP Auditors J.*, Vol. 1, 1991, pp. 37–40.
20. Gallegos, F., Educating Auditors for the Twenty First Century, *EDPAC96 Conference Proceedings*, Perth, Australia, May 1996.
21. Gallegos, F., Information Systems Audit Model Curriculum, *EDPAC96 Conference Proceedings*, Perth, Australia, May 1996.
22. Information Systems Audit and Control Foundation, *COBIT 3rd Edition*, Information Systems Audit and Control Foundation, Rolling Meadows, IL, 2002.
23. Information Systems Audit and Control Association, 2003 CISA *Examination Domain*, ISACA Certification Board, Rolling Meadows, IL, 2002.
24. International Federation of Accountants, Minimum Skill Levels in Information Technology for Professional Accountants, Discussion paper issued by IFAC, November 1993.
25. International Federation of Accountants, The Impact of Information Technology on the Accountancy Profession, IFAC, September 1992.
26. Katsikas, S.K. and D.A. Gritzalis, Eds., *A Proposal for a Postgraduate Curriculum in Information Security, Dependability and Safety*, New Technology Publications, Athens, Greece, September 1995.
27. Kneer, D., J. Vyskoc, D. Manson, and F. Gallegos, Information systems audit education, *IS Audit Control J.* (1994), Vol. 4, pp. 11–20.
28. McCombs, G. and M. Sharifi, Meeting the market needs: an undergraduate model curriculum for information systems auditing, Publication pending, in *ISACA J.*, 1996.
29. Menkus, B. and F. Gallegos, *An Introduction to IT Auditing*, #71-10-10.1, Auerbach Publishers, Boca Raton, FL, February 2002, pp. 1–16.
30. Singleton, T. and D.L Flesher, The developments of EDP auditing education research and literature in North America: 1977 to 1994, *IS Audit Control J.* (1994), Vol. 4, pp. 38–47.
31. Weber, R., *Information Systems Control and Audit*, Prentice Hall, New York, 1999.

Part VI
Appendices

Appendix I
Information Technology Audit Cases

Computer-Assisted Audit Cases

Case 1: Wooback City

Part 1. The computerized human resource system of Wooback City is undergoing an audit. Audry Wilson is the senior member of the audit team reviewing the payroll component of this system. Audry has heard how helpful computer-assisted audit procedures can be, and she has asked you to suggest how some of these procedures can be used in the audit.

Wooback has two types of payroll disbursements: Employee, which is part of the Human Resources System, and Welfare, which is maintained on a separate system. Audry has been informed by the IT manager that transactions for the last three years are available, however the programmer/analyst responsible for this area was terminated and funding was not budgeted for a replacement.

Your assignment: identify and describe potential computer-assisted audit procedures that could be used in this situation.

Part 2. Upon examination of files, you find that no transaction files exist for either the Welfare or Employee distributions for the last year. However, updated master files of the employee payroll exist for each pay period for the last year. Master files for prior periods can be obtained from the IRS on multifile backup tapes retained under a record retention agreement. Per discussion with the IT manager, the record layout for the file was last revised in 2001. Print files were found on the welfare payments for the last three years. These files are used to print the actual checks.

Your assignment: What do you do now?

Case 2: Ready or Not Auto Insurance

As an IT auditor for the state insurance commission you have been asked to assist field auditors. The commission's audit team would like to verify the company's total revenue from policy premiums by direct confirmation with policyholders. However, the company's computer records do not show cumulative premiums by customers. The president of the company does not want to use his staff to regenerate this information, stating that their time is valuable.

The company retains all transactions for one year on their client server. Each transaction is recorded in an Access database, one per record, with the customer number being the primary key. There are close to three million records in the file, and backup copies of the record are made in random order and copied to a zip drive. The insurance company also keeps another Access file that contains the name, address, and customer number for each policyholder. The senior auditor would like you to assist in obtaining the transaction data for a sample of policyholders and preparing the confirmations.

Your assignment: Describe the steps you would take to generate the data and produce the desired confirmations. You may either write a narrative or use a flow diagram to describe the process.

Case 3: Holt Valley Hospital Services, Inc.

Holt Valley Hospital Services, Inc., is a large health care services company that acquired W. Wilson Hospital, an acute-care hospital, this past year. This is a large facility with a typically long collection cycle for its patients' accounts receivable. During the annual audit, the "Big Four" auditors supplied a year-end aged accounts receivable trial balance to the internal audit staff. Now, three months later, the internal audit team needs to determine subsequent collections on 22,567 patient accounts.

Your assignment:

1. State the audit objective in determining subsequent collections and discuss two functions in which use of a computer would be helpful to the auditors in meeting that objective.
2. Describe the process, using transaction files that are also available, in narrative or flowchart form to summarize subsequent activity on each account.
3. Determine if the hospital is in compliance with the Health Insurance Portability and Accountability (HIPAA) Act of 1996. How do you approach this?

Case 4: Acme Insurance Corporation

The Acme Insurance Corporation is presently undergoing an audit by the state insurance commission. The commissioner's audit team would like to verify the company's total revenue. The revenue transaction file contains 30 million transactions. Each transaction is recorded individually with a summary field indicating premium paid year to date. Their tax year ends 12/30/XX, and the file is sequentially arranged by account number.

They also have another file that contains the names, addresses, and account numbers of active and inactive policyholders. The senior auditor would like you to assist in obtaining transaction data for a random sample of policyholders and in preparing the confirmations.

1. The auditors, prior to sampling, would like a profile of the number of transactions that occurred during each month of the tax year as well as the range and frequency of dollar value. How would you meet this requirement?
2. Describe in detail the steps you would take to generate the transaction data, produce the desired confirmations, and meet the auditors' additional requests.
3. Flowchart the solution to this problem.

Controls

Case 5: OnTheRise Corporation

The OnTheRise Corporation wants to automate its decision support model for organizational change. To obtain inputs for the model, corporate managers wish to download information directly from the corporate personnel files. Personnel files are maintained on the corporate human resources system. The basic worksheet for this application is the Organizational Change Model Calculation Sheet (See Exhibit 1). They are considering using Excel and importing data from the human resources system, which is in Oracle.

Your assignment:

1. What type of a decision support model do we have?
2. List and describe the major controls to look for in this type of model.
3. What computer-assisted audit tools and techniques (CATTs) can be used in auditing this application? List and explain in detail at least three techniques and three tools that could be used.

Case 6: Wedco Electronics

As a result of an inventory audit, it was found that electronic supplies worth over $1 million were stolen from the company due to control weaknesses in the equipment ordering system. Also, employee information was

Exhibit 1. All Degreed Employees: Year 1

Age	Start	Losses	Hires	Hires Rate	Part-Time Hires	Turn-Over Rate	Final Group
(1)	(2)	(3)	(4)	(5)	(6)	(7)	(8)
20–27							
28–35							
36–45							
46–50							
51–55							
56–60							
61–65							
Total							

Column # Instructions Projection Processing

1. For age groups Step Column #
2. Number of employees by age group at beginning year 1 2
3. Employees who left company, calculate T/O 2 7
4. Employees who entered company, calculate hiring rate 3 5
5. Derived for past year, a constant in projection 4 4
6. Hires part-time 5 6
7. Derived from past year, a constant in projections 6 8
8. Column 2 plus column 4 minus (Total * Column 7)

compromised. The perpetrator was able to access the inventory budget data, economic order quantities, and the equipment ordering system via the network. This corporation is located in California, and the state recently passed SB 1386.

1. How would you conduct the audit of this system and the event?
2. What controls would you test in this situation?
3. What key steps would you look for to see if they are in compliance with SB 1386?

Case 7: Amazon Industries

As a CPA, CIA, and CISA, you have been asked to perform an audit of company records in support of the Attest function to verify the annual statements. The inventory balances from the computerized system are reported to be $121 million but reports from field auditors show that balances are severely overstated. In discussions with employees and managers you find some overlap in functions with certain personnel authorized to perform functions in other departments. Also, several personnel have not taken vacations in over three years. In compliance with the Sarbanes–Oxley Act of 2002, what do you do?

1. How would you deal with this situation as an internal auditor?
2. How would you deal with this situation as an external auditor?
3. What general control weaknesses might you test and examine? And what audit evidence would you gather?
4. What application tests might you perform?

Legal Issues

Case 8: OhMY Corporation

Your company, OhMY Corporation, hires a Big Four firm to recommend a turnkey system. Your company states that it does not want to go through the hassle of customizing a system or invest in extensive training of employees to run a system. It wants a system that is ready to run. Your company has specified this in written contractual terms signed by the CPA firm's partner. The system you got is difficult to operate and does not meet your company's needs. The president of the company would like internal audit and legal counsel input to the following questions:

1. What evidence must your company provide to prove negligence on the part of the CPA firm?
2. How did the CPA firm owe duty of care?
3. How could the "reasonable person" test enter into the outcome of a potential lawsuit?
4. Where could you go to determine who is liable for damages?

Case 9: Ideal Financial

You have been asked to audit the development of Ideal Financial Integrated Systems (IFIS). In reviewing background information about the system, you find the contract, which has an integration clause written by your company's president that the contractor, AZ Consulting Services, would honor the target budget. It was signed by the AZ representative. Six weeks into the contract and systems development, the contractor appears to be overrunning his initial estimates by 50 percent. The overrun appears to be due to requirement changes, which both the contractor and your company have agreed to, and technology issues. The project is approximately 24 weeks away from completion date.

Your report is due. What do you report?

It is now 15 weeks into the project and the contractor is still 50 percent over budget and demands that the contract be renegotiated. The system is desperately needed to replace systems that have Year 2000 problems. It will cause significant problems to customers being promised these new services and may cost the company at least $20 million in new sales. What is the likely outcome of this situation?

If the decision for renegotiations was given, what additional clauses would you recommend be added to the contract to protect your company?

Security Issues

Case 10: Real-Wire

Real-Wire is a public electronic funds transfer network with its head office and major computer switch based in Chicago. It is currently under contract to the Department of Treasury to assist in E-commerce and electronic funds transfer (EFT) initiatives when federal systems are overloaded. They have handled overload processing, which has increased their workload by 15–20 percent on occasions. The company has computer switches in each capital city throughout the United States, including Alaska and Hawaii, that are linked into a national communications network. Approximately 200 financial institutions (banks, building societies, and credit unions) use the network to provide automatic teller machine and point-of-sale services to their customers.

Real-Wire has only been in operation for 15 years, but during that time it has been very successful. When the United States began to deregulate its financial markets in 1985 and foreign banks began to enter the marketplace, Real-Wire obtained substantial new business because it could offer these financial institutions immediate EFT services.

As a consultant specializing in computer controls and audit, you have been hired by the managing director of Real-Wire to examine the state of controls within the EFT system. She explains to you that an increasing number of potential customers are requesting some type of independent assurance that controls within the system are reliable. Accordingly, she has decided to initiate a controls review of the entire system so that a third-party "letter of comfort" can be provided to potential customers.

The initial part of your controls review focuses on the main switch in Chicago. As part of your review, you examine the status of disaster recovery planning for the switch. In terms of short-term recovery, controls appear to be in place and working. Backup tapes for all data and programs are stored both on site and off site to enable recovery if programs and data are lost for some reason. In addition, protocols for short-term recovery are well documented, and operators seem familiar with and well-trained in these protocols. From time to time they have to exercise these protocols because some temporary system failure occurs. Real-Wire claims to offer its customers 24-hour service. The director states that its personnel recognize the criticality of being able to perform efficient, effective system recovery in a timely manner.

When you examine controls over long-term disaster recovery, however, the situation is different. There is no long-term disaster recovery plan, nor are operators and other personnel trained in recovery protocols for a major disaster. For example, it is uncertain how Real-Wire would recover from a fire that destroyed the switch or an event that caused major structural damage to the switch.

As a result of your findings, you meet with the managing director to find out why controls in this area are so weak when controls in other areas seem strong. She is surprised by your concern about long-term disaster recovery. She argues that for three reasons it is not cost-effective to prepare a long-term disaster recovery plan and to practice recovery protocols on a regular basis. First, she believes a plan is useless because, in the event of a major disaster, timely recovery is impossible anyway. She points out that it would take several days for the telephone company to reconfigure all the data communications lines to another site. Even if Real-Wire had another switch available immediately, it could not operate during this period. Second, she argues that Real-Wire's customers would not tolerate a decrease in their service levels while disaster recovery exercises were carried out. Unless the recovery protocols are practiced regularly, she argues, they are useless. Third, she contends that eventual recovery will not be a problem anyway. Operations can simply be transferred to another switch in one of the other capital cities. While the telephone company reconfigures data communications lines to the other switch, backup files can be flown to the site with plenty of time to spare. She argues that the customers of Real-Wire recognize they will not be able to use their EFT facilities during the recovery period, but they accept this situation as a risk of doing business. The only other alternative, she argues, is to replicate all switching facilities in each capital city, and this clearly is not cost-effective.

Required

1. Outline how you intend to respond to the managing director's comments in your report to the board of directors on the state of controls in Real-Wire computer operations.
2. What federal laws apply to Real-Wire? List and explain each applicable law and describe how it could be used to support your audit.
3. Do they have an intranet that uses TCP/IP heavily? Do they have any security software installed? What would be your major security concerns?
4. The office of the comptroller of the currency plans to review them next year. What would you recommend?

Appendix II
Bibliography of Selected Publications for Information Technology Auditors

Today's information technology (IT) auditor is often confronted with situations in which accurate information is needed urgently. In the past 35 years, many works have been published that provide such information. This updated bibliography lists many of these publications and identifies significant works released since 1996. It comprises publications from government agencies and professional associations as well as relevant textbooks and reference books.

Government Publications

During the last seven years, various governmental organizations have published a variety of studies and reports on IT audit-related topics. Publications can be ordered directly from the governmental agencies for a nominal fee. Most can also be ordered through the Internet or accessed online.

Department of Justice of the United States

Publications can be ordered from the Department of Justice of the United States, 950 Pennsylvania Avenue, NW, Washington, D.C. 20530-0001. They can also be ordered, and some retrieved, through the Web at URL address http://www.usdoj.gov/05publications/.

- From the Computer Crime and Intellectual Property Section:
  - *Cyberstalking: A New Challenge for Law Enforcement and Industry*, http://www.usdoj.gov/criminal/cybercrime/cyberstalking.htm, August 1999
  - *Electronic Commerce: Legal Issues*, http://www.usdoj.gov/criminal/cybercrime/ecommerce.html, March 2001

- *The Electronic Frontier: The Challenge of Unlawful Conduct Involving the Use of the Internet* — A Report of the President's Working Group on Unlawful Conduct on the Internet, http://www.usdoj.gov/criminal/cybercrime/unlawful.htm, March 2000
- *Encryption and Computer Crime*, http://www.usdoj.gov/criminal/cybercrime/crypto.html, May 2000
- *Frequently Asked Questions and Answers About the Council of Europe Convention on Cybercrime* (Draft 24REV2), http://www.usdoj.gov/criminal/cybercrime/COEFAQs.htm, December 2000
- *International Aspects of Computer Crime*, http://www.usdoj.gov/criminal/cybercrime/intl.html, February 2002
- *Investigating and Prosecuting Computer Crime*, http://www.usdoj.gov/criminal/cybercrime/compcrime.html, April 2001
- *Legal Considerations in Designing and Implementing Electronic Processes: A Guide for Federal Agencies*, http://www.cybercrime.gov/eprocess.htm, November 2000
- *Privacy Issues in the High-Tech Context*, http://www.usdoj.gov/criminal/cybercrime/privacy.html, March 2001
- *Prosecuting Crimes Facilitated by Computers and by the Internet*, http://www.usdoj.gov/criminal/cybercrime/crimes.html, February 2002
- *Protecting Critical Infrastructures*, February 1999
- *Protecting Intellectual Property Rights*, http://www.usdoj.gov/criminal/cybercrime/ip.html, April 2001
- *Searching and Seizing Computers*, http://www.usdoj.gov/criminal/cybercrime/searching.html, December 2001
- *Speech Issues in the High-Tech Context*, http://www.usdoj.gov/criminal/cybercrime/speech.html, March 2000
- *Assessment of the Increased Risk of Terrorists or Other Criminal Activity Associated with Posting Off-Site Consequence Analysis Information on the Internet*, http://www.usdoj.gov/criminal/april18final.pdf, April 18, 2000
- From the Civil Right Division:
  - *Information Technology and People with Disabilities: The Current State of Federal Accessibility,* http://www.usdoj.gov/crt/508/report/content.htm, April 2000
  - *Federal Guidelines for Searching and Seizing Computers*, March 20, 1998
  - *Federal Prosecution of Violations of Intellectual Property Rights*, September 2, 1997
- From the Federal Bureau of Investigation Division:
  - *The FBI's Combined DNA Index System Program*, http://www.fbi.gov/hq/lab/codis/brochure.pdf, April 2000
  - *A Parent's Guide to Internet Safety*, http://www.fbi.gov/publications/pguide/pguidee.htm, March 2001

- From the Justice Management Division:
  - *Information Technology Strategic Plan,* http://www.usdoj.gov/jmd/ irm/imss/2002itplan/index.html, July 2002
  - *The Department of Justice Systems Development Life Cycle Guidance Document,* http://www.usdoj.gov/jmd/irm/lifecycle/table.htm, January 2003

General Accounting Office of the United States (GAO)

Publications can be ordered from the GAO, P.O. Box 37050, Washington, D.C. 20013. They can also be ordered through the Web at URL address http://www.gao.gov/index.htm.

1. Business Process Reengineering Guide, AIMD-10.1.15, April 1997
2. Protecting Information Systems Supporting the Federal Government's and the Nation's Critical Information, GAO High Risk Series, GAO-03-121, January 2003
3. Executive Guide: Information Security Management, Learning from Leading Organizations, GAO Report AIMD-98-68, May 1998
4. Executive Guide: Maximizing the Success of Chief Information Officers, GAO/AIMD-00-83, March 2000
5. Executive Guide: Measuring Performance and Demonstrating Results of Information Technology Investments, GAO Report AIMD-99-89, March 1998
6. Federal Information System Controls Audit Manual, AIMD-12.19.6, 2000
7. Government Auditing Standards (Yellow Book), Preliminary Edition, GAO-03-673G, June 2003
8. Information Security Risk Assessment: Practices of Leading Organizations, GAO/AIMD-00-33, November 1999
9. Information Technology Investment Evaluation Guide, Assessing Risks and Returns: A Guide for Evaluating Federal Agencies' IT Investment Decision-Making, GAO/AIMD-10.1.13, February 1997
10. Major Management Challenges and Risks, GAO/OCG-99-ES, February 1999
11. Financial Management Service: Significant Weaknesses in Computer Controls Continue, GAO-02-317, http://www.gao.gov/new.items/ d02317.pdf, January 31, 2002
12. Federal Reserve Banks: Areas for Improvement in Computer Controls, GAO-02-266R, http://www.gao.gov/new.items/d02266r.pdf, December 10, 2001
13. European Security: U.S. and European Contributions to Foster Stability and Security in Europe, GAO-02-174, http://www.gao.gov/new. items/d02174.pdf, November 28, 2001

14. Computer Security: Improvements Needed to Reduce Risk to Critical Federal Operations and Assets, GAO-02-231T, http://www.gao.gov/new.items/d02231t.pdf, November 9, 2001

15. Homeland Security: Challenges and Strategies in Addressing Short- and Long-Term National Needs, GAO-02-160T, http://www.gao.gov/new.items/d02160t.pdf, November 7, 2001

16. Homeland Security: A Risk Management Approach Can Guide Preparedness Efforts, GAO-02-208T, http://www.gao.gov/new.items/d02208t.pdf, October 31, 2001

17. Lost Security Holders: SEC Should Use Data to Evaluate Its 1997 Rule, GAO-01-978, http://www.gao.gov/new.items/d01978.pdf, September 28, 2001

18. Critical Infrastructure Protection: Significant Challenges in Safeguarding Government and Privately Controlled Systems from Computer-Based Attacks, GAO-01-1168T, http://www.gao.gov/new.items/d011168t.pdf, September 26, 2001

19. Education Information Security: Improvements Made but Control Weaknesses Remain, GAO-01-1067, http://www.gao.gov/new.items/d011067.pdf, September 12, 2001

20. Information Security: Code Red, Code Red II, and SirCam Attacks Highlight Need for Proactive Measures, GAO-01-1073T, http://www.gao.gov/new.items/d011073t.pdf, August 29, 2001

21. Information Technology Management: Social Security Administration Practices Can Be Improved, GAO-01-961, http://www.gao.gov/new.items/d01961.pdf, August 21, 2001

22. Information Security: Weaknesses Place Commerce Data and Operations at Serious Risk, GAO-01-751, http://www.gao.gov/new.items/d01751.pdf, August 13, 2001

23. Information Security: Weaknesses Place Commerce Data and Operations at Serious Risk, GAO-01-1004T, http://www.gao.gov/new.items/d011004t.pdf, August 3, 2001

24. Information Systems: Opportunities Exist to Strengthen SEC's Oversight of Capacity and Security, GAO-01-863, http://www.gao.gov/new.items/d01863.pdf, July 25, 2001

25. Information Security: Weak Controls Place Interior's Financial and Other Data at Risk, GAO-01-615, http://www.gao.gov/new.items/d01615.pdf, July 3, 2001

26. Social Security Administration: Information Systems Could Improve Processing Attorney Fee Payments in Disability Program, GAO-01-796, http://www.gao.gov/new.items/d01796.pdf, June 29, 2001

27. Computer-Based Patient Records: Better Planning and Oversight by VA, DOD, and IHS Would Enhance Health Data Sharing, GAO-01-459, http://www.gao.gov/new.items/d01459.pdf, April 30, 2001

28. Computer Security: Weaknesses Continue to Place Critical Federal Operations and Assets at Risk, GAO-01-600T, http://www.gao.gov/archive/2000/d01600t.pdf, April 5, 2001

29. Information Security: Challenges to Improving DOD's Incident Response Capabilities, GAO-01-341, http://www.gao.gov/new.items/d01341.pdf, March 29, 2001

30. Information Security: Safeguarding of Data in Excessed Department of Energy Computers, GAO-01-469, http://www.gao.gov/new.items/d01469.pdf, March 29, 2001

31. Information Security: Advances and Remaining Challenges to Adoption of Public Key Infrastructure Technology, GAO-01-277, http://www.gao.gov/new.items/d01277.pdf, February 26, 2001

32. Information Security: IRS Electronic Filing Systems, GAO-01-306, http://www.gao.gov/new.items/d01306.pdf, February 16, 2001

33. Information Security: Weak Controls Place DC Highway Trust Fund and Other Data at Risk, GAO-01-155, http://www.gao.gov/new.items/d01155.pdf, January 31, 2001

34. FAA Computer Security: Actions Needed to Address Critical Weaknesses that Jeopardize Aviation Operations, T-AIMD-00-330, http://www.gao.gov/archive/2000/ai00330t.pdf, September 27, 2000

35. Information Security: Progress Made but Challenges Remain to Protect Federal Systems and the Nation's Critical Infrastructures, GAO-03-564T, http://www.gao.gov/new.items/d03564t.pdf, April 8, 2003

36. Technology Assessment: Using Biometrics for Border Security, GAO-03-174, November 14, 2002

37. Border Security: Challenges in Implementing Border Technology, GAO-03-546T, http://www.gao.gov/new.items/d03546t.pdf, March 12, 2003

38. Homeland Security: Information Sharing Activities Face Continued Management Challenges, GAO-02-1122T, http://www.gao.gov/new.items/d021122t.pdf, October 1, 2002

39. Homeland Security: OMB's Temporary Cessation of Information Technology Funding for New Investments, GAO-03-186T, http://www.gao.gov/new.items/d03186t.pdf, October 1, 2002

40. Mass Transit: Challenges in Securing Transit Systems, GAO-02-1075T, http://www.gao.gov/new.items/d021075t.pdf, September 18, 2002

41. Critical Infrastructure Protection: Significant Homeland Security Challenges Need to Be Addressed, GAO-02-918T, http://www.gao.gov/new.items/d02918t.pdf, July 9, 2002

42. National Preparedness: Integrating New and Existing Technology and Information Sharing into an Effective Homeland Security Strategy, GAO-02-811T, http://www.gao.gov/new.items/d02811t.pdf, June 7, 2002

43. Security Breaches at Federal Buildings in Atlanta, Georgia, GAO-02-668T, http://www.gao.gov/cgi-bin/ordtab.pl?Item0=GAO-02-668T, April 30, 2002

44. National Preparedness: Technologies to Secure Federal Buildings, GAO-02-687T, http://www.gao.gov/new.items/d02687t.pdf, April 25, 2002

45. Diffuse Security Threats: Technologies for Mail Sanitization Exist, but Challenges Remain, GAO-02-365, http://www.gao.gov/new.items/d02365.pdf, April 23, 2002

46. Homeland Security: A Framework for Addressing the Nation's Efforts, GAO-01-1158T, http://www.gao.gov/new.items/d011158t.pdf, September 21, 2001

47. Critical Infrastructure Protection: Significant Challenges in Protecting Federal Systems and Developing Analysis and Warning Capabilities, GAO-01-1132T, http://www.gao.gov/new.items/d011132t.pdf, September 12, 2001

48. Critical Infrastructure Protection: Significant Challenges in Developing Analysis, Warning, and Response Capabilities, GAO-01-1005T, http://www.gao.gov/new.items/d011005t.pdf, July 25, 2001

49. Critical Infrastructure Protection: Significant Challenges in Developing National Capabilities, GAO-01-323, http://www.gao.gov/new.items/d01323.pdf, April 25, 2001

50. FAA Computer Security: Recommendations to Address Continuing Weaknesses, GAO-01-171, http://www.gao.gov/new.items/d01171.pdf, December 6, 2000

51. Critical Infrastructure Protection: Challenges to Building a Comprehensive Strategy for Information Sharing and Coordination, T-AIMD-00-268, http://www.gao.gov/archive/2000/ai00268t.pdf, July 26, 2000

52. Critical Infrastructure Protection: Comments on the Proposed Cyber Security Information Act of 2000, T-AIMD-00-229, http://www.gao.gov/archive/2000/ai00229t.pdf, June 22, 2000

53. Critical Infrastructure Protection: 'ILOVEYOU' Computer Virus Highlights Need for Improved Alert and Coordination Capabilities, T-AIMD-00-181, http://www.gao.gov/archive/2000/ai00181t.pdf, May 18, 2000

54. Critical Infrastructure Protection: National Plan for Information Systems Protection, AIMD-00-90R, http://archive.gao.gov/f0302/163238.pdf, February 11, 2000

55. Assessing the Reliability of Computer-Processed Data, (Supplement to the Government Auditing Standards [Yellow Book] — External Version), GAO-03-273G, October 2002

56. Electronic Law Enforcement: Introduction to Investigations in an Electronic Environment, GAO-01-121G, February 2001

57. Executive Guide: Maximizing the Success of Chief Information Officers: Learning from Leading Organizations, GAO-01-376G, February 2001
58. Executive Guide: Measuring Performance and Demonstrating Results of Information Technology Investments, GAO/AIMD-98-89, March 1998
59. Human Services Integration: Results of a GAO Cosponsored Conference on Modernizing Information Systems, GAO-02-121, January 2002
60. Information Technology: An Audit Guide for Assessing Acquisition Risk, IMTEC-8.1.4, December 1992
61. Electronic Law Enforcement: Introduction to Investigations in an Electronic Environment, GAO-01-121G, February 2001
62. Information Technology Investment Management: A Framework for Assessing and Improving Process Maturity (Exposure Draft), AIMD-10.1.23, May 2000.
63. Information Technology Investment Management: An Overview of GAO's Assessment Framework (Exposure Draft), AIMD-00-155, May 2000.
64. Critical Infrastrucure Protection: Challenges for Selected Agencies and Industry Sectors, GAO-03-233, February 2003

National Institute of Standards and Technology (NIST)

Publications can be ordered from the NIST, Information Technology Laboratory, Building 820, Room 562, Gaithersburg, MD 20899-0001. They can also be ordered through the Web at URL address http://www.nist.gov/itl/div897/pubs/.

1. *Electronic Data Interchange (EDI)*, FIPS PUB161-2, May 22, 1996
2. *Secure Hash Standard (SHS)*, FIPS PUB180-1, April 17, 1995
3. *Digital Signature Standard (DSS)*, FIPS PUB186-2, January 27, 2002
4. *Security Requirements for Cryptographic Modules*, FIPS PUB 140-2, June 2001
5. *Secure Hash Standard (SHS)*, FIPS PUB 180-2, August 2002
6. *Entity Authentication Using Public Key Cryptography*, FIPS PUB196, February 18, 1997
7. *Data Encryption Standard (DES)*. Specifies the use of Triple DES. FIPS 46-3, October 1999
8. *Entity Authentication Using Public Key Cryptography*, FIPS-196, February 1997
9. *Advanced Encryption Standard*, FIPS-197, November 2001
10. *The Key-Hash Message Authentication Code*, FIPS-198, March 2002
11. Ammann, P.E. et al., *A Specification-Based Coverage Metric to Evaluate Test Sets*, NISTIR 6403, October 1999
12. Ammann, P.E. et al., *Abstracting Formal Specifications to Generate Software Tests via Model Checking*, NISTIR 6405, October 1999

13. Bace, R. and Mell, P., *Intrusion Detection Systems (IDS)*, NIST Special Publication 800-31, November 2001

14. Black, P.E. et al., *Model Checkers for Software Testing*, NISTIR 6777, February 2002

15. Burr, W., Dodson, D., Nazario, N., and Polk, T., *Minimum Interoperability Specification for PKI Components*, NIST Special Publication 800-15, January 1998

16. Chernick, M., *Federal S/MIME V3 Client Profile*, NIST Special Publication 800-49, November 2002

17. Cugini, J., *The FLUD Format: Logging Usability Data from Web-Based Applications*, NIST Special Publication 500-247, January 2001

18. Cugini, J. and Laskowski, S., *Design of a File Format for Logging Website Information*, NIST Special Publication 500-248, April 2001

19. De Zafara, D., Paitcher, S., Tressler, J., and Ippolito, J., *Information Technology Security Training Requirements: A Role- and Performance-Based Model*, NIST Special Publication 800-16, April 1998

20. Dray, J., Goldfine, A., Iorga, M., Schwarzhoff, T., and Wack, J., *Government Smart Card Interoperability Specification (GSC-IS), v2.0*, NIST IR 6887, June 2002

21. Dworkin, M., *Recommendation for Block Cipher Modes of Operation — Methods and Techniques*, NIST Special Publication 800-38A, December 2001

22. Grance, T., Hash J., Peck, S., Smith, J., and Korow-Diks, K., *Security Guide for Interconnecting Information Technology Systems*, NIST Special Publications 800-47, September 2002

23. Jansen, W., Mell, P., Karygiannis, T., and Marks, D., *Applying Mobile Agents to Intrusion Detection and Response*, NIST IR 6416, September 1999

24. Jansen, W. et al., *Mobile Agent Security*, NIST Special Publication 800-19, October 1999

25. Jansen, W., *Guidelines on Active Content and Mobile Code*, NIST Special Publications 800-28, October 2001

26. Keller, S., *Modes of Operation Validation Systems for the Triple Data Encryption Algorithm (TMOVS)*, NIST Special Publication 800-20, November 1999

27. Keller, S. and Smid, M., *Modes of Operation Validation System (MOVS): Requirements and Procedures*, NIST Special Publication 800-17, February 1998

28. Karygiannis, T. and Owens, L., *Wireless Network Security: 802.11, Bluetooth, and Handheld Devices*, NIST Special Publication 800-48, November 2002

29. Kuhn, R., *PBX Vulnerability Analysis: Finding Holes in Your PBX before Someone Else Does*, NIST Special Publication 800-24, August 2000

30. Kuhn, R., Tracy, M., and Frankel, S., *Security for Telecommuting and Broadband Communications*, NIST Special Publication 800-46, September 2002

31. Kuhn, R., Hu, V., Polk, T., and Chang, S.-J., *Introduction to Public Key Technology and the Federal PKI Infrastructure*, NIST Special Publication 800-32, February 2001

32. Lee, A., *Guideline for Implementing Cryptography in Federal Government*, NIST Special Publication 800-21, November 1999

33. Lyons-Burke, K., *Federal Agency Use of Public Key Technology for Digital Signatures and Authentication*, NIST Special Publication 800-25, October 2000

34. Mell, P. and Grance, T., *Use of the Common Vulnerabilities and Exposures (CVE) Vulnerability Naming Scheme*, NIST Special Publication 800-51, September 2002

35. Mell, P. and Tracy, M., *Procedures for Handling Security Patches*, NIST Special Publication 800-40, September 2002

36. Roback, E., *Guideline to Federal Organizations on Security Assurance and Acquisition/Use of Tested/Evaluated Products*, NIST Publication 800-23, August 2000

37. Rukhin, A., Soto, J., Nechvatal, J., Smid, M., Barker, E., Leigh, S., Levenson, M., Vangel, M., Banks, D., Heckert, A., Dray, J., and Vo, S., *A Statistical Test Suite for Random and Pseudorandom Number Generators for Cryptographic Applications*, NIST Special Publication 800-22, October 2000

38. Sies, R., *A Manager's Guide for Monitoring Data Integrity in Financial Systems*, NIST Special Publication 500-233, February 1996

39. Snoufeer, R., Lee, A., and Oldehoeft, A., *A Comparison of the Security Requirements for Cryptographic Modules in FIPS 140-1 and FIPS 140-2*, NIST Special Publication 800-29, June 2001

40. Soto, J. and Basham, L., *Randomness Testing of the Advanced Encryption Standard Finalist Candidates*, NIST IR 6483, March 2000

41. Stoneburner, G., CSPP. *Guidance for COTS Security Protection Profiles*, NIST RI 6462, December 1999

42. Stoneburner, G., CSSP. *Underlying Models for Information Technology Security*, NIST Special Publication 800-33, December 2001

43. Stoneburner, G. et al., *Risk Management Guide for Information Technology Systems*, NIST Special Publication 800-30, January 2002

44. Stoneburner, G., Hayden, C., and Feringa, A., *Engineering Principles for Information Technology Security (A Baseline for Achieving Security)*, NIST Special Publication 800-27, June 2001

45. Swanson, M., Wohl, A., Pope, L., Grance, L., Hash, J., and Thomas, R., *Contingency Planning Guide for Information Technology Systems*, NIST Special Publication 800-34, June 2002

46. Swanson, M., *Security Self-Assessment Guide for Information Technology Systems*, NIST Special Publications 800-26, November 2001

647

47. Swanson, M., *Guide for Developing Security Plans for Information Technology Systems*, NIST Special Publication 800-18, December 1998
48. Swanson, M. and Guttman, B., *Generally Accepted Principles and Practices for Securing Information Technology Systems*, NIST Special Publication 800-14, September 1996
49. Wack, J. et al., *Guidelines on Firewall and Firewall Policy*, NIST Special Publication 800-41, January 2002
50. Wallace, D.R. and Kuhn, D.R., *Software Quality Lessons from Medical Device Failure Data*, NISTIR 6407, November 1999
51. Wallace, D., Ippolito, L., and Cuthill, B., *Reference Information for the Software Verification and Validation Process*, NIST Special Publication 500-234, April 1996
52. Watson, A. and McCabe, T., *Structured Testing: Methodology Using Cyclomatic Complexity Metric*, NIST Special Publication 500-235, August 1996

National Technical Information Service (NTIS)

Publications can be ordered from the NTIS, 5285 Port Royal Road, Springfield, VA 22161. They can also be ordered through the Web at URL address http://www.ntis.gov/index.asp

1. Advanced Technology Institute. Defense Healthcare Information Assurance Program. Final Report, 2001
2. Dam, K.W. and Lin, H.S. *Cryptography's Role in Securing the Information Society,* 1996
3. Department of Defense. Information Assurance for Auditors and Evaluators, April 1999
4. Department of Defense. Implementation of National Defense Center for Environmental Excellence Projects. Audit Report, 2001
5. Department of Defense. Information System Security: DoD Web Site Administration, Polices, and Practices, 2002
6. Department of Defense. Controls Over Electronic Document Management, 2001
7. Department of Defense. Controls for the Electronic Data Interchange at the Defense Finance and Accounting Service Columbus. Audit Report, 2001
8. Department of Defense. Summary of Security Control Audits of DoD Finance and Accounting Systems. Summary Report, 2001
9. Department of Defense. Defense Joint Military Pay System Security Functions at Defense Finance and Accounting Service Denver. Audit Report, 2001
10. Department of Industrial and Management Systems, University of Arizona. Process Control and Diagnosis Approach to Indications and Warning of Attacks on Computer Networks. Final Technical Report, 2001

11. GAO. Financial Management Service. Significant Weaknesses in Computer Controls Continue. Report to the Congress, 2002

12. GAO. Information Security: Weak Controls Place DC Highway Trust Fund and Other Data at Risk, 2001

13. GAO. Information Systems: Opportunities Exist to Strengthen SEC's Oversight of Capacity and Security, 2001

14. Heuler, R.R. *Strategic Approach to Information Systems Protection,* April 1999

15. Indian & Northern Affairs of Canada. Audit of Informatics and EDP Consolidation Report, December 1996

16. Operational Information Systems Security, Vol. 1 and 2, August 1998

17. Information Policy Committee. Options for Promoting Privacy on the National Information Infrastructure — Draft for Public Comment, 1998

18. Information Security. Weak Controls Place Interior's Financial and Other Data at Risk, 2001

19. Office of the Secretary of Defense. Management of Information Technology Equipment. Audit Report, 2001

20. Pipe, G.R., Charles, C., and Visser, S. *Assessing Data Privacy in the 1900's and Beyond,* August 1997.

21. Maida, P. *Freedom of Information Act Guide and Privacy Act Overview,* September 1997

22. Swanson, M. *Computer Security — Guide for Developing Security Plans for Information Technology Systems,* December 1998

23. Swanson, M. and Guttman, B. *Computer Security — Generally Accepted Principles and Practices for Securing Information Technology Systems,* September 1996

24. U.S. Working Group on Electronic Commerce. Emerging Digital Economy II, 1998

25. Wilson, T.A. and Orr, D. *Electronic Village — Policy Issues of the Information Economy,* 1999

Publications Available from Professional Association

Many professional associations are very active in the publication and distribution of IT audit and security literature. Some of these associations are based in the United States but many are international in concept and scope. Most groups are willing to share their information for a nominal fee even with nonmembers of their association.

American Institute of Certified Public Accountants (AICPA)

Publications can be ordered from the AICPA, 1211 Avenue of the Americas, New York, NY 10036. They can also be ordered through the Web at URL address http://www.cpa2biz.com/CS2000/Home/default.htm.

APPENDICES

1. Accounting for the Costs of Computer Software Developed or Obtained for Internal Use, 1998
2. CPA's Handbook of Fraud and Commercial Crime Prevention, 1999
3. CPA WebTrust — Assurance Services Alert, 1999
4. CPA WebTrust Practitioner's Guide for Business to Consumer Electronic Commerce, 2000
5. Information Technology Age: Evidential Matter in the Electronic Environment, 1998
6. Professional Ethics, 2000
7. Software Revenue Recognition, 1997
8. Strategic Management Series — 8 Volume Set, 2000.
9. Graves, J. and Justice, J. *CPA's Guide to Document Image Processing*, 2000
10. CPA's Guide to Navigating Online, 2000
11. Designing and Implementing an Information Security Plan, 2000
12. Bradley, S. *Terror Defenses Begin at Home with Your Own Computer System,* October 2001
13. Curtis, M. and Viator, R. Summary #5: An Investigation of How EDP Auditors' Thought Processes Affect Their Work, February 2001
14. Graves, J. and Torrence, K.H. *CPA's Guide to Workflow Technologies*, 2000
15. Johnston, R. and Fleenor, W. *Remote Computing: Security Options*, August 2001
16. Johnston, R. *Time to Upgrade*, December 2002
17. Mascha, M. and Miller, C. *Stop E-Mail Snoops*, July 2002
18. Phelan, S. and Hayes, M. *Before the Deluge — and After,* April 2003
19. Quinn, L. *Risky Business*, June 2002
20. Reinhold, J. *Do You Know Who Is Snooping Around Your Computer Right Now?* February 2001
21. Rose, J. and Rose, A. *The Automated Spreadsheet*, April 2001
22. Simms, D. *Creating a Digital Environment,* March 2003
23. Stambaugh, C. and Chamberlain, D. *Ready to Pull the Plug*, August 2001
24. Thomas, C. and Duarte, M. *VISA Puts the "Security" in Their CISP Program*, August 2001
25. Zarowin, S. *Hot Stuff: What You Need and What You Don't,* April 2003

Association for Computing Machinery

Publications can be ordered from the Association for Computing Machinery, One Astor Plaza, 1515 Broadway, New York, NY 10036. They can also be ordered through the Web at URL address http://www.acm.org/catalog/books/homepage.html.

1. Castano, S., Martella, G., Samarati, P., and Fugini, M. *Database Security*, 1994
2. Crawford, D. *Intellectual Property in the Age of Universal Access,* 1999

3. Denning, D.E. *Information Warfare and Security,* 1999
4. Denning, D.E. and Denning, P.J. *Internet Besieged: Countering Cyberspace Scofflaws,* 1995
5. Denning, P.J. and Metcalfe, B. *Beyond Calculation: The Next Fifty Years of Computing,* 1997
6. Fewster, M. et al. *Software Test Automation,* 1999
7. Gong, L. *Inside Java 2 Platform Security,* 1999
8. Jackson, M. *Business Process Implementation,* 1997
9. Leveson, N.G. *Safeware: System Safety and Computers, A Guide to Preventing Accidents and Losses Caused by Technology,* 1997
10. Miller, S. *Civilizing Cyberspace: Policy, Power, and the Information Superhighway,* 1995

The Canadian Institute of Chartered Accountants (CICA)

Publications can be ordered from the CICA, 277 Wellington Street West, Toronto ON M5V 3H2, Canada. They can also be ordered through the Web at http://www.cica.ca/cica/cicawebsite.nsf/public/ServicesProducts.

1. Avey, K.L. *The Accountant's Handbook of Fraud and Commercial Crime,* 2000
2. *Audit Implications of EDI,* 1995
3. Audit Implications of Electronic Document Management, 1997
4. Electronic Filing of Information: Control and Audit, 1995
5. Information Security: Strategies for Successful Management, 1996
6. Information Technology Control Guidelines, 3rd Edition, 1998
7. Management Practices in Information Technology, 1998
8. Mining Data for Knowledge — Successful Management Strategies for Creating the Knowledge-Oriented Organization, 1997
9. Security for Wireless Systems, March 2003
10. Audit and Control Implications of XBRL, May 2002
11. 20 Questions Directors Should Ask about IT, January 2002
12. A Guide for Organizations and Assurance Practitioners, February 2002
13. 20 Questions Directors Should Ask about Privacy, 2002
14. 20 Questions a Small Business Should Ask about Privacy, 2002
15. Trites, G. *The Impact and Technology on Financial Business Reporting,* October 1999

The Information Systems Audit and Control Association & Foundation (ISACA)

Publications can be ordered from the ISACA, 135 South LaSalle, Chicago, IL 670674-1055. They can also be ordered through the Web at URL address http://www.isaca.org/pubshome.htm.

1. Adams, J. The Next World War: Computers Are the Weapons and the Front Line Is Everywhere, 1998
2. Allen, J. The CERT Guide to System and Network Security Practices, 2001
3. Applegate, L.M., McFarlan, F.R.W., and McKenney, J.L. *Corporate Information Systems Management,* 5th Edition, 1999
4. Barcus, S.W., III. Financial Information Systems Manual, 1999
5. Barman, S. Writing Information Security Policies, 2001
6. Beaver, K. *Healthcare Information Systems,* 2nd Edition, 2002
7. Bhatia, M. Auditing in a Computerized Environment, 2002
8. Boni, W.C. and Kovacich, G.L. *I-Way Robbery: Crime on the Internet,* 1999
9. Boni, W.C. and Kovacich, G.L. *Netspionage: The Global Threat to Information,* 2000
10. Bort, R. and Bielfeldt, G.R. *The Handbook of EDI,* 2000
11. Bragg, R. *Windows 2000 Security,* 2001
12. Braithwaite, T. Securing E-Business Systems — A Guide for Managers and Executives, 2002
13. Brin, D. The Transparent Society: Will Technology Force Us to Choose between Privacy and Freedom? 1998
14. Canavan, J.E. Fundamentals of Network Security, 2001
15. Cangemi, M.P. *Managing the Audit Function: Corporate Audit Department Procedures Guide,* 3rd Edition, 2003
16. Champlain, J.J. Auditing Information Systems: A Comprehensive Reference Guide, 1998
17. Champlain, J.J. *Practical IT Auditing,* 2002
18. Chapman B.D., Cooper, S., and Zicky, E. *Building Internet Firewalls,* 2nd Edition, 2000
19. Clements, R.B. IS Manager's Guide to Implementing and Managing Internet Technology, 1999
20. Coderre, D.G. CAATTS and Other Beasts for Auditors, 1996
21. Coderre, D.G. *Fraud Toolkit for ACL,* 2001
22. Cole, E. Hackers Beware: Defending Your Network from the Wiley Hacker, 2001
23. Fraud Detection: Using Data Analysis Techniques to Detect Fraud, 1999
24. Curran, T.A., Keller, G., and Ladd, A. SAP R/3 Business Blueprint: Understanding the Business Process Reference Model, 1998
25. Crume, J. Inside Internet Security — What Hackers Don't Want You to Know, 2000
26. Deloitte & Touche and ISACF. E-Commerce Security: A Global Status Report, 2000
27. Denmark Chapter. Audit Guidelines for DB2, 2002
28. E-Commerce Security: Enterprise Best Practices, 2000
29. Edwards, M.J. Internet Security with Windows NT, 1998

30. Erbscloe, M. Information Warfare — How to Survive Cyber Attacks, 2001
31. Freiss, M. Protecting Networks with SATAN, 1998
32. Fogie, S. and Peikari, C. Windows Internet Security: Protecting Your Critical Data, 2002
33. Garfinkel, S. *Web Security & Commerce,* 1997
34. Garfinkel, S. and Spafford, G. *Practical UNIX and Internet Security,* 2nd Edition, 1996
35. Garfinkel, S. Web *Security, Privacy, and Commerce,* 2nd Edition, 2001
36. Gelinas, U.J. and Oram, A.E. *Accounting Information Systems,* 5th Edition, 2002
37. Ghosh, A.K. E-Commerce Security: Weak Links, Best Defenses, 1998
38. Hadfiled, L., Hatter, D., and Bixler, D. *Windows NT Server 4 Security Handbook,* 1997
39. Hahn, M.A. Guide to SYS1.PARMLIB, 1996
40. Hartley, D., Slade, R., and Gattiker, U.E. *Viruses Revealed: Understand and Counter Malicious Software,* 2002
41. Hickman, J.R. *Practical IT Auditing,* 1996
42. Practical IT Auditing: 1999 Supplement, 1999
43. ISACA. *The CobiT: 3rd Edition,* 2001
44. Digital Signatures: Security and Controls, 1999
45. ISACA IS Audit Benchmarking Study, 1998
46. ISACA Denmark Chapter. Instructions for Auditing the MVS Operating System, 1996
47. Procedure Manual for Audit of the Customer Information and Control System (CICS), 1999
48. Procedure Manual for Audit of LANs, 1999
49. Jones, K., Shema, M., and Johnson, B.C. *Anti-Hacker Toolkit,* 2002
50. Jumes, J.C. and PricewaterhouseCoopers. Microsoft Windows NT 4.0 Security, Audit and Control: In-depth Techniques and Guidelines to Ensure System Security, 1999
51. Kalakota, R. and Robinson, M. *E-Business 2.0: Roadmap for Success,* 2001
52. Kempis, R.-D. et al. *Do IT Smart — Seven Rules for Superior Information Technology Performance,* 1999
53. Kind, C., Dalton, C., and Osmanoglu, E. *Security Architecture-Design, Deployment and Operations,* 2001
54. Krause, M. and Topton, H.F. *Handbook of Information Security Management,* 4th Edition, 1999
55. Krist, M.A. A Standard for Auditing Computer Applications, 1999
56. Effective Use of Teams for IT Auditors, 1999
57. Lanza, R.B. 101 ACL Applications: A Toolkit for Today's Auditor, 1997
58. Lewin, R. and Regine, B. *The Soul at Work,* 2000
59. Madden, W. and Woodbury, C. *Implementing AS/400 Security,* 3rd Edition, 1998

60. Mandia, K. and Prosise, C. Incident Response — Investigating Computer Crime, 2001

61. Meyers, K.N. Manager's Guide to Contingency Planning for Disasters: Protecting Vital Facilities and Critical Operations, 1999

62. Moody, G. The Internet with Windows, 1996

63. Moeller, R.R. *Brink's Modern Internal Auditing,* 5th Edition, 1999

64. Morin, T. et al. Information Leadership: A Government Executive Guide, 1999

65. Musaji, Y. Auditing and Security: AS/400, UNIX, NT, Networks, and Disaster Recovery, 2001

66. Nair, M. Activity-Based Information Systems: An Executive's Guide to Implementation, 1999

67. Nakano, R. Web Content Management — Collaborative Approach, 2001

68. Nigrini, M. Digital Analysis Using Benford's Law: Tests and Statistics for Auditors, 2000

69. Northcutt, S., Zeltser, L., Winters, S., Frederick, K.K., and Ritchey, R.W. Inside Network Perimeter Security — The Definitive Guide to Firewalls, VPNs, Routers, and Intrusion Detection Systems, 2002

70. Northcutt, S., Cooper, M., Fearnow, M., and Frederick, K. *Intrusion Signatures and Analysis,* 2001

71. Northcutt, S. *Network Intrusion Detection,* 2nd Edition, 2000

72. Parker, D.B. Fighting Computer Crime: A New Framework for Protecting Information, 1998

73. Pinto, J. and Millet, I. *Sucessful Systems Implementation — The Human Side,* 2nd Edition, 1999

74. Pikover, Y. and Drake, J., and the ISACA. *Security Provisioning: Managing Access in Extended Enterprises,* 2002

75. Piper, F. and Murphy, S. Cryptography: A Very Short Introduction, 2002

76. PricewaterhouseCoopers LLP and the ISACA. *Risks of Computer Relationship Management — A Security, Audit and Control Approach,* 2003

77. Ross, S., Allison, S., DeFeo, S., Barnes, J., Deloitte & Touche LLP, and the ISACA. *E-Commerce Security — Business Continuity Planning a Technical Reference Guide,* 2002

78. Handbook of IT Auditing: 2000, Supplement, 2000

79. Sackman, R.B. Achieving the Promise of Information Technology, 1998

80. Salmi, H. and Vahtera, P. Internet and EDI in Effective Accounting, 1997

81. SANS Institute. Computer Security Incident Handling: Step-by-Step, 1998

82. Intrusion Detection: Shadow Style — A Primer for ID Analysis, 1998

83. *Windows NT Security: Step-by-Step,* 2nd Edition, 1999

84. Scambray, J., McClure, S., and Kurtz, G. *Hacking Exposed: Network Security Secrets and Solutions,* 4th Edition, 2003
85. Schneier, B. *Applied Cryptography,* 2nd Edition, 1996
86. Schultz, E. Windows NT/2000 Network Security, 2000
87. E-Mail Security: How to Keep Your Electronic Messages Private, 1995
88. Shaw, J. Surviving the Digital Jungle, 2000
89. Shim, J.K., Siegel, J.G., and Chi, R. *The Vest-Pocket Guide to Information Technology,* 1997
90. Spencer, R. and Johnston, R. *Technology Best Practices,* 2002
91. Smith, G.E. Network Auditing: A Control Assessment Approach, 1999
92. Sriram, R. *Systems Audit,* 2000
93. Sutton, S.A. Windows NT Security Guide, 1997
94. Theriault, M. *Oracle Security,* 1998
95. Tiller, J.S. A Technical Guide to IPSec Virtual Private Networks, 2001
96. Toigo, J.W. Disaster Recovery Planning for Computers and Communications Resources, 1996
97. Tudor, J. Information Security Architecture: An Integrated Approach to Security in the Organization, 2000
98. Van Wyk, K.R. and Forno, R. *Incident Response,* 2001
99. Weber, R. Information Systems Control and Audit, 1999
100. Winkler, I. Corporate Espionage: What It Is, Why It's Happening in Your Company, What You Must Do about It, 1997
101. Wood, C.C. Information Security Policies Made Easy, 1996
102. Woodall, J., Rebuck, D.K., and Voehl, F. *Total Quality in Information Systems and Technology,* January 1997
103. Yuan, R. and Strayer, T.W. Virtual Private Networks: Technologies and Solutions, 2001

The Institute of Internal Auditors (IIA)

Publications can be ordered from the IIA, 249 Maitland Avenue, Altamonte Springs, FL 32701-4201. They can also be ordered through the Web at URL address http://www.theiia.org/.

1. Austin, G.R. Systems Auditing Capability Framework, 1998
2. Berstein, P.L. Against the Gods: The Remarkable Story of Risk, 1998
3. Bragg, S. Advanced Accounting Systems, 1997
4. Coopers & Lybrand LLP. SAP R/3: Its Use, Control, and Audit, 1997
5. UNIX Security and Control, 1996
6. David, J.S. and Steinbart, P.J. Data Warehousing and Data Mining: Opportunities for Internal Auditors, 2000
7. Deloitte & Touche LLP. The Current Impact of Information Technology on Internal Auditing Departments, 1996
8. Firgo, M.L. The Impact of Business Process Reengineering on Internal Auditing, 1995

9. Friedlob, G.T., Plewa, F.J., Schleifer, L., and Schou, C.D. *An Auditor's Guide to Encryption*, 1997
10. Client/Server in an Open Systems Environment, 1997
11. Electronic Commerce: Control Issues for Securing Virtual Enterprises, 1998
12. Johnson, S. *Who Moved My Cheese?* 1998
13. Kaplan, J.M. *An Auditor's Guide to Internet Resources,* 2nd Edition, 1997
14. Kelly, S. Data Warehousing in Action, 1997
15. Integrating PCs into the Internal Audit Process, 2000
16. www.STOPTHIEF.net: Protecting Your Identity on the Web, 1999
17. McNamee, D.W. Business Risk Assessment, 1998
18. MIccolis, J.A., Hively, K., and Merkley, B. *Enterprise Risk Management: Trends and Emerging Practices*, 2001
19. Parker, X.L. *An E-Risk Primer*, 2001
20. Ramamoorti, S. Using Neural Networks for Risk Assessment in Internal Auditing: A Feasibility Study, 1998
21. Rockefeller, B.W. Using SAP R/3 FI: Beyond Business Process Reengineering, 1998
22. Walker, P.L., Shenkir, W.G., and Barton, T.L. *Enterprise Risk Management: Pulling It All Together*, 2002

International Federation for Information Processing

Publications can be ordered from Kluwer Academic Publishers, 101 Philip Drive, Assinippi Park, Norwell, MA 02061. They can also be ordered through the International Federation for Information Processing Web site at URL address http://www.ifip.or.at/public.htm.

1. Atluri, V., Jajodia, S., and George, B. *Multilevel Secure Transaction Processing,* 1999
2. Atluri, V. and Samarati, P. *Security of Data Transaction Processing*, 2000
3. Carlsen, J. and Yngstroem, L. Information Security in Research & Business, 1997
4. Eloff, J.H.P. and von Solms, S.H. *Information Security the Next Decade*, 1995
5. Eloff, J.H.P., Labuschagne, L., von Solms, R., and Verschuren, J. *Information Security Management and Small Systems Security*, 1999
6. Falkenberg, E.D., Lyytinen, K., and Verrijn-Stuart, A.A. *Information Systems Concepts: An Integrated Discipline Emerging*, 2000
7. Falkenberg, E.D., Hesse, W., and Olive, A. *Information System Concepts: Towards a Consolidation of Views*, 1995
8. Gritzalis, D. Reliability, Quality, and Safety of Software-Intensive Systems, 1997
9. Jajodia, S. Database Security XII Status and Prospects, 1999
10. Jajodia, S., List, W., McGregor, G., and Strous, L. *Integrity and Internal Control in Information Systems*, 1998

11. Katsikas, S. Communications & Multimedia Security, Vol. 3, 1996
12. Katsikas, S. and Gritzalis, D. Information Systems Security Facing the Information Society of the 21st Century, 1997
13. Kautz, K. and Pries-Heje, J. Diffusion and Adoption of Information Technology, 1996
14. Samarati, P. and Sandhu, R. *Database X Status and Prospects*, 1997
15. Spooner, D.L., Demurjian, S.A., and Dobson, J.E. *Database Security IX Status and Prospects,* 1996
16. Terashima, N. and Altman, E. *Advanced IT Tools,* 1996

International Federation of Accountants (IFAC)

Publications can be ordered from the IFAC, 535 Fifth Avenue, 26th Floor, New York, NY 10017. They can also be ordered through the Web at URL address http://www.ifac.org/.

1. A Framework for Reporting on the Credibility of Information, February 1998
2. Codifying Power and Control: Ethical Codes in Action, 2000
3. Enhancing Shareholder Wealth by Better Managing Business Risk, 2000
4. Executive Checklist 1, 1999
5. Implementation of Information Technology Solutions, 2000
6. Information Technology in the Accounting Curriculum, 1998
7. Into the Twenty-First Century with Information Management, 2000
8. IT Service Delivery and Support, 2000
9. Managing Information Technology Planning for Business Impact, August 1998
10. Managing Security of Information, January 1998
11. The Measurement and Management of Intellectual Capital: An Introduction, 2000
12. IFAC Handbook of International Information Technology Guidelines, 2000
12. Information Security Governance: Guidance for Boards of Directors and Executive Management, 2001
14. Board Briefing on IT Governance, 2001

Quality Assurance Institute

Publications can be ordered from the Quality Assurance Institute, 7575 Dr. Phillips Boulevard, Suite 350, Orlando, FL 32819. They can also be ordered through the Web at URL address http://www.qaiusa.com/products/index.html.

1. Perry, W.E. *Effective Methods for Software Testing,* 1995
2. *Hatching the Information Services Measurement Activity*, Book 3, 1995
3. *Hatching the Information Services Quality Function*, Book 1, 1995

4. *Hatching the Information Services Quality Function*, Book 2, 1995
5. Perry, W.E. and Rice, R.W. *Surviving the Top Ten Challenges of Software Testing*, 1995
6. *Establishing a Software Defect Management Process*, 1995
7. *Service-Level Agreements*, 1998

Other Publications

This section provides selected references from various publishers categorized according to current topics of interest to IT auditors. Some publications can be ordered directly from the publishers. Most can also be ordered through the internet at URL address http://www.amazon.com.

Best Practices in Information Technology

1. Blakemore, J. Quality Habits of Best Business Practice, 1996
2. Devaraj, S. IT Payoff: Measuring the Business Value of Information Technology Investments, *1/e* 2002
3. Goldblatt, J.J. Special Events: Best Practices in Modern Event Management, 1997
4. Pickup, P. Intranets: Best Practice in Planning, Implementation, and Use, 1998
5. Regester, M. and Larkin, J. Risk Issues and Crisis Management: A Casebook of Best Practice, 1998
6. Roth, J. Control Model Implementation: Best Practices, 1997
7. Sadler, P. Management Consultancy: A Handbook of Best Practice, 1998
8. Toney, F. Best Practices of Project Management Groups in Large Functional Organizations, 1997
9. U.S. Congress House Committee on Government Reform and Oversight; Subcommittee on Government Management, Information, and Technology. *Using the Best Practices of Information Technology in Government*, 1997
10. Wheeler, D.A. et al. Software Inspection: An Industry Best Practice, 1996
11. Zari, M. Benchmarking for Best Practice: Continuous Learning through Sustainable Innovation, 1998
12. Zari, M. Best Practice: Process Innovation Management, 1999

Computer Hardware and Software

1. Colberg, T.P. The Pricewaterhouse EDI Handbook, 1995
2. Downes, L., Mui, C., and Negroponte, N. *Unleashing the Killer App: Digital Strategies for Market Dominance,* 1998
3. Glass, R.L. *Software Runaways: Monumental Software Disasters, 1/e* 1998
4. McKie, S. Client/Server Accounting: Reengineering Your Account Systems, January 1997

5. The Technology Guide to Accounting Software: A Handbook for Evaluating Vendor Applications, April 1997
6. Mitrakas, A. Open EDI and Law in Europe: A Regulatory Framework, 1997
7. O'Leary, D.E. and Watkins, P.R. Expert Systems and Artificial Intelligence in Internal Auditing, August 1995
8. Visual Explanations: Images and Quantities, Evidence and Narrative, March 1997
9. Verity, B. *Guide to Network Cabling Fundamentals*, 2003

Computer, Network, and Information Security

1. Berkowitz, B.D. and Goodman, A.E. *Best Truth: Intelligence in the Information Age*, March 2000
2. Butler, J.G. and Badura, P. Contingency Planning and Disaster Recovery: Protecting Your Organization's Resources, June 1997
3. Cretaro, P. Lab Manual for Security + Guide to Network Security Fundamentals, 2003
4. Holden, G. *Guide to Network Defense and Countermeasures*, 2003
5. Holden, G. *Guide to Firewalls and Network Security*, 2004
6. Hutt, A.E., Bosworth, S., and Hoyt, D.B. *Computer Security Handbook*, September 1995
7. Konicek, J. and Little, K. Security, ID Systems, and Locks: The Book on Electronic Access Control, August 1997
8. Panko, R.R. *Corporate Computer and Network Security*, 2004
9. Penfold, R.R.C. Computer Security: Business at Risk, June 1999
10. Pipkin, D.L. *Information Security*, May 2000
11. Pfleeger, C.P. *Security in Computing*, September 1996
12. Shaw, P.D. Managing Legal and Security Risks in Computing and Communications, May 1998
13. Stallings, W. Network Security Essentials: Applications and Standards, 2000
14. Stallings, W. *Cryptography and Network Security*, 2003
15. Summers, R.C. Secure Computing: Threats and Safeguards, January 1997
16. Wayner, P. Digital Copyright Protection, May 1997

Enterprise Resource Planning (ERP) Systems

1. Anderegg, T. ERP: A-Z Implementer's Guide for Success, December 2000
2. Anderegg, T. Scorecard System for World Class Enterprise Resource Management: ERP Systems, April 2000
3. Carroll, B. Lean Performance ERP Project Management: Implementing the Virtual Supply Chain, February 2002

4. Clott, J. and Raff, S. *PeopleSoft Application Development Tools,* September 1999

5. George, J. *SAP Workbench Organizer,* October 1999

6. Hamilton, S. Maximizing Your ERP System: A Practical Guide for Managers, October 2002

7. Jacobs, F.R. and Whybark, D.C. *Why ERP? A Primer on SAP Implementation,* January 2000

8. Lientz, B.P. and Rea, K.P. *Project Management for the 21st Century,* 2nd Edition, March 1998

9. Lozinsky, S. Enterprise-Wide Software Solutions: Integration Strategies and Practices, April 1998

10. Maciariello, J.A. and Kirby, C.J. *Management Control Systems: Using Adaptive Systems to Attain Control,* 2nd Edition, 1994

11. McHugh, P., Merli, G., and Wheeler, W.A., III. Beyond Business Processing Reengineering: Towards the Holonic Enterprise, 1995

12. Norris, G. et al. E-Business and ERP: Transforming the Enterprise, May 2000

13. Norris, G. E-Business and ERP: Transforming the Enterprise, July 2000

14. O-Leary, D. Enterprise Resource Planning Systems: Systems, Life Cycle, Electronic Commerce, and Risk, January 2000

15. Ptak, C.A. ERP Tools, Techniques, and Applications for Integrating the Supply Chain, September 1999

16. Shields, M. E-Business and ERP: Rapid Implementation and Project Planning, April 2001

17. Shtub, A. Enterprise Resource Planning: The Dynamics of Operations Management, March 1999

18. Snevely, R. *Enterprise Data Center Design and Methodology, 1/e* 2002

19. Wallace, T. and Kremzar, M. ERP: Making it Happen: The Implementer's Guide to Success with Enterprise Resource Planning, July 2001

20. Welti, N. Successful SAP R3 Implementation: Practical Management of ERP Projects, March 1999

21. Yourdon, E. Death March: The Complete Software Developer's Guide to Surviving "Mission Impossible" Projects, 1997

Information Technology and Accounting Systems

1. Bodnar, G.H. and Hopwood, W. *Accounting Information Systems,* January 1998

2. Boockholdt, J.L. Accounting Information Systems: Transaction Processing and Controls, October 1995

3. Hollander, A., Denna, E., and Cherrington, J.O. *Accounting Information Technology and Business Solutions*, June 1998

4. Gelinas, U., Sutton, S., and Orma, A. *Accounting Information Systems*, May 2001
5. Govindarajan, V. and Anthony, R. *Management Control Systems*, August 2000
6. Moscove, S.A., Simkin, M.G., and Bagranoff, N.A. *Core Concepts of Accounting Information Systems*, February 1996
7. Potter, D.A. Automated Accounting Systems and Procedures Handbook, June 1991
8. Romney, M. and Steinbart, P. *Accounting Information Systems*, June 2002
9. Sutton, S.G. Advances in Accounting Information Systems 1996, Vol. 4, December 1996
10. Vasarhelyi, M.A. Artifical Intelligence in Accounting and Auditing: Using Expert Systems, February 1995
11. Vasarhelyi, M.A. and Kogan, A. Artifical Intelligence in Accounting and Auditing: Towards New Paradigms, Vol. 4, January 1998
12. Vaassen, E.H. Accounting Information Systems: A Managerial Approach, April 2002
13. Wilkinson, J.W. and Cerullo, M.J. Accounting Information Systems: Essential Concepts and Applications, December 1996

The Internet, E-Commerce, and Web Security

1. Allamaraju, S. *Professional Java E-Commerce*, February 2001
2. Bekkers, V., Koops, B.-J., and Nouwt, S. Emerging Electronic Highways: New Challenges for Politics and Law, 1996
3. Cameron, D. Security Issues for the Internet and the World Wide Web, 1996
4. Chissick, M. and Kelman, A. *E-Commerce: Law and Practice*, March 2000
5. Cohen, E.E. Accountant's Guide to the Internet, February 1997
6. Cranor, L. *Web Privacy with P3P*, September 2002
7. Dustin, E., Rashka, J., McDiarmid, D., and Mielson, J. *Quality Web Systems: Performance, Security, and Usability*, August 2001
8. Faulkner Information Services. Alternatives for Secure Online Transactions, May 2001
9. Ferrera, G.R. et al. *CyberLaw: Texts and Cases, 2/e* 2004
10. Ford, W. and Baum, M.S. *Secure Electronic Commerce, 2/e* 2001
11. Garfinkel, S. and Spafford, G. *Web Security and Commerce*, June 1997
12. Greenstein, M. and Vasarhelyi, M. Electronic Commerce: Security, Risk Management, and Control with PowerWeb Passcode Card (E-Commerce), July 2001
13. Graff, J. Cryptography and E-Commerce: A Wiley Tech Brief, December 2000
14. Harrison, R. *ASP/MTS/ADSI Web Security*, March 1999

15. Held, J. and Bowers, J. Securing E-Business Applications and Communications, June 2001
16. Jennings, C. et al. The Hundredth Window: Protecting Your Privacy and Security in the Age of the Internet, May 2000
17. Killelea, P. *Web Performance Tuning,* 2nd Edition, March 2002
18. Kyas, O. Internet Security: Risk Analysis, Strategies, and Firewalls, December 1997
19. Macgregor, R.S. www.security: How to Build a Secure World Wide Web Connection, 1996
20. McClure, S., Shah, S., and Shah, S. *Web Hacking: Attacks and Defense*, August 2002
21. Meyer, C. and Davis, S. Blur: The Speed of Change in the Connected Economy, March 1998
22. Oppliger, R. Security Technologies for the World Wide Web, November 1999
23. O'Neill, M. *Web Services Security*, January 2003
24. Phaltankar, K.M. Practical Guide for Implementing Secure Intranets and Extranets, December 1999
25. Peikari, C. and Fogie, S. *Windows.Net Server Security Handbook*, April 2002
26. Rescorla, E. SSL and TLS: *Designing and Building Secure Systems*, October 2000
27. Rubin, A., Geer, D., and Ranum, M. *Web Security Sourcebook*, June 1997
28. Scambray, J. and Shema, M. *Hacking Exposed™ Web Applications*, June 2002
29. Schetina, E., Green, K., and Carlson, J. *Internet Site Security*, March 2002
30. Smith, G. E-Commerce: A Control and Security Guide, December 2001
31. Splaine, S. Testing Web Security: Assessing the Security of Web Sites and Applications, October 2002
32. Stein, L.D. Web Security: A Step-by-Step Reference Guide, 1998
33. Sybex Inc. and Lierly, M. *Security Complete*, August 2001
34. Trevedi, R., Whitney, D., Galbraith, B., Prasad, D.V., Janakiramin, M., Hiotis, A., and Hnakison, W. *Professional Web Services Security*, December 2002

IT Auditing and Control Systems

1. Arter, D. Quality Audits for Improved Performance, December 2002
2. Barnard, S. Clinical Audit in Physiotherapy: From Theory into Practice, September 1998
3. Cangemi, M. and Singleton, T. *Managing the Audit Function: A Corporate Audit Department Procedures Guide,* April 2003
4. Chan, S. EDI Control, Management, and Audit Issues, 1995

5. Dayton, D. *Information Technology Audit Handbook,* April 1997
6. Dustin, E. et al. Automated Software Testing: Introduction, Management, and Performance, July 1999
7. Gallegos, F. et al. *Information Technology Control and Audit,* July 1999
8. Hall, J.A. *Information Systems Auditing and Assurance,* June 1999
9. Kimbell, L. *Audit,* May 2003
10. Kuong, J.F. and MASP Consulting Staff. Client/Server Control, Security, and Audit (MAP-34), 1996
11. MASP Consulting Staff. Data Communication Networks Audit Work Plan (AP-3), 1997
12. MASP Consulting Staff. Local Area Network Audit Work Plan (AP-4), 1996
13. MASP Consulting Staff. Reengineering and Business Process Redesign — Management Control and Audit Implications (MAP-37), 1997
14. Piattini, M. *Auditing Information Systems*, December 1999
15. Marcella, A.J. *EDI Security, Control, and Audit*, March 2003
16. Russell, J.P. *The Quality Audit Handbook*, December 1999
17. Russell, J.P. After the Quality Audit: Closing the Loop on the Audit Process, May 2000
18. Weber, R. *Information Systems Control and Audit,* 1999.

Privacy of Information

1. Agre, P.E. and Rotenberg, M. *Technology and Privacy: The New Landscape*, October 1997
2. Bloustein, E.J. and Pallone, N.J. *Individual and Group Privacy*, December 2002
3. Cady, G.H., McGregor, P., and Beverley, J. Protect Your Digital Privacy! Survival Skills for the Information Age, December 2001
4. Caloyannides, M.A. *Computer Forensics and Privacy*, December 2001
5. Cate, F.H. Privacy in the Information Age, November 1997
6. Chesbro, M. Freeware Encryption and Security Programs: Protecting Your Computer and Your Privacy, September 2001
7. Cobb, S. Privacy for Business: Web Sites and E-mail, October 2002
8. Decew, J.W. In Pursuit of Privacy: Law, Ethics, and the Rise of Technology, June 1997
9. Erbschloe, M. The Executives Guide to Privacy Management, 2001
10. Erbschloe, M. and Vaca, J. Net Privacy: A Guide to Developing & Implementing an Ironclad E-business Privacy Plan, 2001
11. Fischer-Hubner, S. and Fisher-Hubner, G. *IT-Security and Privacy*, September 2001
12. Garfinkel, S. *Web Security, Privacy, and Commerce,* 2nd Edition, January 2002
13. Garfinkel, S. Database Nation: The Death of Privacy in the 21st Century, January 2001

14. Henderson, H. *Privacy in the Information Age*, November 1999
15. Hunter, R. World without Secrets: Business, Crime, and Privacy in the Age of Ubiquitous Computing, April 2002
16. Hyatt, M.S. and Hyatt, M. *Invasion of Privacy: How to Protect Yourself in the Digital Age,* April 2001
17. Jennings, C., Fena, L., and Dyson, E. The Hundredth Window: Protecting Your Privacy and Security in the Age of the Internet, June 2000
18. Kahin, B. and Nesson, C. Borders in Cyberspace: Information Policy and the Global Information Infrastructure, March 1997
19. Klosek, J. *Data Privacy in the Information Age,* August 2000
20. Marcella, A.J. *Privacy Handbook: Guidelines, Exposures, Policy Implementation, and International Issues,* April 2003
21. Melanson, P.H. and Summers, A. Secrecy Wars: National Security, Privacy, and the Public's Right to Know, January 2002
22. Miller, M. *Absolute PC Security and Privacy,* August 2002
23. Peters, T.A. Computerized Monitoring and Online Privacy, October 1999
24. Pfleeger, C. *Security in Computing,* 3rd Edition, December 2002
25. Santiago, J. and Love, P. *Internet Privacy Protection Guide*, November 1999
26. Scambray, J. et al. *Hacking Exposed*, 2001
27. Schneier, B. and Banisar, D. The Electronic Privacy Papers: Documents on the Battle for Privacy in the Age of Surveillance, August 1997
28. Whitaker, R. The End of Privacy: How Total Surveillance Is Becoming a Reality, February 1999

Quality Assurance

1. American Institute of Certified Public Accountants. Guide for Establishing and Maintaining a System of Quality Control for a CPA Firm's Accounting and Auditing Practice, 1996
2. Bernowski, K. and Stratton, B. 101 Good Ideas: How to Improve Just About Any Process, February 1999
3. Bradley, V.J. Quality Assurance in a Rapidly Changing World: Challenges and Opportunities in a Changing World, March 2003
4. Burrill, C.W. et al. Achieving Quality through Continual Improvement, July 1998
5. Evans, J.R. *The Management and Control of Quality*, September 1998
6. George, S. Uncommon Sense: Creating Business Excellence in Your Organization, December 1996
7. Ginac, F.P. Customer Oriented Software Quality Assurance, December 1997

8. Horch, J.W. *Practical Guide to Software Quality Management,* August 1996
9. Hughes, T. and Williams, T. *Quality Assurance: A Framework to Build On*, October 1995
10. Lewis, W.E. Software Testing and Continuous Quality Improvement, April 2000
11. Peach, R.W. *The ISO 9000 Handbook*, November 1996
12. Ratliff, T.A. The Laboratory Quality Assurance System: A Manual of Quality Procedures and Forms, March 2003
13. Regal, T. and Russell, J.P. After the Quality Audit: Closing the Loop on the Audit Process, May 2000
14. Schulmeyer, G. *The Handbook of Software Quality Assurance,* January 1999
15. Silverman, L.L. and Propst, A.L. *Critical SHIFT: The Future of Quality in Organizational Performance,* June 1999
16. Zuckerman, A. International Standards Desk Reference: Your Passport to World Markets: ISO 9000, Ce Mark, Qs-9000, Ssm, ISO 14000, Q 9000, American, European, and Global Standards Systems, December 1996

Risk Management

1. Barton, T.L., Shenkir, W.G., and Walker, P.L. Making Enterprise Risk Management Pay Off: How Leading Companies Implement Risk Management, February 2002
2. Braun, E. Technology in Context: Technology Assessment for Managers, May 1998
3. Crouhy, M., Mark, R., and Galai, D. *Risk Management*, April 2001
4. Ennals, R. Executive Guide to Preventing Information Technology Disasters, January 1996
5. Erbschloe, M. *Guide to Disaster Recovery,* 2003
6. Hall, E.M. Managing Risk: Methods for Software Systems Development, February 1998
7. Hoffman, D.G. Managing Operational Risk: 20 Firmwide Best Practice Strategies, January 2002
8. Janczewski, L. Internet and Intranet Security Management: Risks and Solutions, July 2000
9. Karolak, D.W. and Karolak, N. *Software Engineering Risk Management*, January 1998
10. Lochhead, D. *Shifting Realities: Information Technology and the Church,* January 2000
11. Moynihan, T. Coping with IS/IT Risk Management: The Recipes of Experienced Project Managers, April 2002
12. Myerson, M. Risk Management Processes for Software Engineering Models, January 1997

13. Ould, M.A. *Managing Software Quality and Business Risk,* October 1999
14. Pritchard, C. *Risk Management: Concepts and Guidance,* 2nd Edition, November 2001
15. Peltier, T.R. Information Security Risk Analysis, January 2001
16. Remenyi, D. *Stop IT Project Failures Through Risk Management,* August 1999
17. Schreider, T. Encyclopedia of Disaster Recovery, Security, & Risk Management, 1998
18. Shaw, P.D. Managing Legal and Security Risks in Computing and Communications, May 1998
19. Taylor, I. *Procurement of Information Systems: Getting Value from Suppliers in High Risk, Hi Tech, and Highly Competitive Markets,* March 2001

Appendix III
Professional Standards that Apply to Information Technology (Audit, Security, and Privacy Issues)

The purpose of this appendix is to identify, review, and categorize both standards and guidelines related to information technology (IT) established by professional organizations in the fields of accounting, audit, and technology. The organizations are listed in Exhibit 1. Upon review, the standards and guidelines relating to IT have been categorized into three areas: audit, security, and privacy issues.

In addition to categorizing these professional organizations, other information was also collected for those readers interested in contacting the professional organizations for additional information and updates. This information includes contact address, contact telephone, contact facsimile, contact Internet home page, and contact e-mail address.

The information sources used to collect information relevant for this research project have been noted in each of the corresponding professional organizations following the contact information.

With the exception of the *CICA Handbook*, dated 1991 (revised), the majority of the information collected for this research project was taken from the professional organization's main Internet home page (Web site).

American Institute of Certified Public Accountants (AICPA)

The American Institute of Certified Public Accountants and its predecessors have a history dating back to 1887, when the American Association of Public Accountants was formed. In 1916, the American Association was succeeded by the Institute of Public Accountants at which time there were 1150 members. The name was changed to the American Institute of

Exhibit 1. Standards and Guidelines Organizations Listed in This Appendix

- American Institute of Certified Public Accountants (AICPA)
- The Institute of Internal Auditors (IIA)
- Information Systems Audit Control Association (ISACA)
- Canadian Institute of Chartered Accountants (CICA)
- International Federation of Accountants (IFAC)
- Information System Security Association (ISSA)
- Society for Information Management (SIM)
- Association of Information Technology Professionals (AITP)
- International Federation for Information Processing (IFIP)
- Association for Computing Machinery (ACM)
- The Institute of Chartered Accountants in Australia (ICAA)
- National Institute of Standards and Technology (NIST)
- General Accounting Office (GAO)
- The International Organization of Supreme Audit Institutions (INTOSAI)

Accountants in 1917 and remained so until 1957, when the name was again changed to the American Institute of Certified Public Accountants. The American Society of Certified Public Accountants was formed in 1921 and acted as a federation of state societies. The Society was merged into the Institute in 1936 and, at that time, the Institute agreed to restrict its future members to CPAs.

```
American Institute of Certified Public Accountants
1211 Avenue of the Americas
New York, NY 10036-8775
Telephone:  (212) 596-6200
Facsimile:  (212) 596-6213
Web site:   http://www.aicpa.org
e-mail:     https://util.aicpa.org/feedback/general.htm
```

Information Source

http://www.aicpa.org

1. Halper, S., *Handbook of EDP Auditing*, Warren, Gorham & Lamont, Inc., Boston, MA, 1985.
2. Carmichael, D.R., The auditor's new guide to errors, irregularities, and illegal acts, *J. Acc.,* September 1988.
3. Hernandez, P., Practical IT Auditing, *IS Audit Control J.,* Vol. 3, 1998

Authoritative Guide

Statements on Audit Standards (SASs) (see Exhibit 2) are issued by the Auditing Standards Board (ASB) of the AICPA and are recognized as interpretations of the ten generally accepted auditing standards. SASs usually apply only in situations where auditing services are being performed.

Exhibit 2. American Institute of Certified Public Accountants (AICPA) Statement on Audit Standards (SAS)

Authoritative Guide	Summary	Category
SAS 1 1972	**SAS 1, Codification of Auditing Standards and Procedures** SAS 1 represents a broad codification of auditing standards and procedures. It contains the following statements in AU Sections 320.33, .34, .37, .57, .58, .65, .66, and .68 "Methods of Data Processing," regarding the auditor's basic responsibility of the EDP systems.	Audit
SAS 3 1974	**SAS 3, The Effects of EDP on the Auditor's Study and Evaluation of Internal Controls (Replaced by SAS 48)** The first SAS to mention "EDP" was SAS 3, which was published in 1974. An excerpt from the SAS states that: "because the method of data processing used may influence the organization and procedures employed by an entity to accomplish the objectives of accounting control, it may also influence the procedures employed by an auditor in his study and evaluation of accounting control to determine the nature, timing, and extent of audit procedures to be applied in his examination of financial statements." This SAS was the first to introduce that auditors now have the responsibility to assess the risk associated to the financial statements within the EDP environment.	Audit
SAS 9 1975	**SAS 9, The Effect of an Internal Audit Function on the Scope of the Independent Auditor's Examination** If the external auditors decide that the internal auditors' work may have bearing their her own procedures, the standard set forth in SAS 9 (AU Section 322) requires that external auditors also review the competence and objectivity of the internal auditors and evaluate their work. To review the competence, external auditors are required by the standard to inquire about the qualification of the internal audit staff, including, for example, consideration of the practices for hiring, training, and supervising the internal audit staff, especially in relation to their technical EDP capabilities.	Audit
SAS 16 1976	**SAS 16, The Independent Auditor's Responsibility for Detection of Errors or Irregularities (Replaced by SAS 53)** The auditor is required to plan the audit to search for material errors and irregularies. EDP environments are not exempt.	Audit

Exhibit 2. American Institute of Certified Public Accountants (AICPA) Statement on Audit Standards (SAS) (Continued)

Authoritative Guide	Summary	Category
SAS 17 1976	**SAS 17, Illegal Acts by Clients (Replaced by SAS 54)** The auditor should be aware of the possibility that illegal acts with an indirect effect on financial statements may have occurred.	Audit
SAS 20 1977	**SAS 20, Required Communication of Material Weaknesses in Internal Accounting Control** SAS 20 (AU Section 323) requires that the external auditor communicates material weaknesses in the internal accounting control to senior management and the board of directors or its audit committee. SAS 20 notes that the auditor may become aware of the existence of material weaknesses in the internal accounting control through an initial review of the system, tests of compliance, and/or substantive tests. The nature, extent, and timing of the audit tests are affected by the existence of a material weakness in internal accounting control.	Audit
SAS 22 1978	**SAS 22, Planning and Supervision** SAS 22 (AU Section 311.03), with SAS 48 integrated, has the required planning consideration expanded. Paragraphs AU Section .09 and .10 summarize those aspects of computer processing that may have an effect on planning and examination of financial statements. They also describe how the auditor might consider the need for specialized skills to determine the effects of computer processing on the examination.	Audit
SAS 23 1978	**SAS 23, Analytical Review Procedures** SAS 23 (AU Section 318.07), as amended by SAS 48, is expanded to include features that the auditor should consider when planning and performing analytical review procedures. 07e notes: "The increased availability of data prepared for management's uses when computer processing is used." Computer systems have created an ability (which may not be practical in manual systems) to store, retrieve, and analyze data for use in achieving broader management objectives. These data and analyses, although not a necessary part of the basic accounting records, may be valuable sources of information for the auditor to use in applying analytical review procedures, other substantive tests, or compliance testing.	Audit

Exhibit 2. American Institute of Certified Public Accountants (AICPA) Statement on Audit Standards (SAS) (Continued)

Authoritative Guide	Summary	Category
SAS 31 1980	**SAS 31, Evidential Matter** SAS 31 (AU Section 326.12), as amended by SAS 48, makes it clear that audit evidence is not affected by the use of computer processing. Only the method by which the auditor gathers that evidence can be affected.	Audit
SAS 47 1982	**SAS 47, Audit Risk and Materiality in Conducting an Audit** Control risk is defined as the possibility of a misstatement occurring in an account balance or a class of transactions that (1) could be material when aggregated with misstatements in other balances or classes and (2) will not be prevented or detected on a timely basis by the system of internal control. Control risk, like inherent risk, cannot be changed by the auditor. The client's design of internal control that produces the current financial statements must be treated as a given factor. Of course, the auditor can make recommendations for improving the system, which may affect the audit engagement of the next period. In general, the stronger the internal control, the more likely that material misstatements will be prevented or detected by the system (AU 312.20).	Audit
SAS 48 1984	**SAS 48, The Effects of Computer Processing on the Examination of Financial Statements** The AICPA issued SAS 48 in 1984, which superseded SAS 3. This SAS is more direct in indicating that auditors should (i.e., must) consider computer controls during the planning phase of an audit. The SAS dictates that auditors should consider the extent to which the computer is used, complexity of the computing system, structure of the computer processing activities, and the availability of data from the computer system. This SAS also suggests that CAATs might increase the efficiency of performing audit procedures in a computerized environment. By utilizing CAATs, an entire population can be reviewed, instead of a sample (N=n).	Audit

Exhibit 2. American Institute of Certified Public Accountants (AICPA) Statement on Audit Standards (SAS) (Continued)

Authoritative Guide	Summary	Category
SAS 53 1989	**SAS 53, The Auditor's Responsibility to Detect and Report Errors and Irregularities (Revises SAS 16)** SAS 53 throws that comfortable preconceived notion of the auditor on the heap of discarded audit folklore. Auditors cannot assume management is honest or dishonest. They should take a hard, cold look at the possibility of management misrepresentation at the start of the audit and reexamine the likelihood of management misrepresentations as the audit progresses. The EDP environment is not exempt for this SAS.	Audit
SAS 54 1989	**SAS 54, Illegal Acts by Clients (Revises SAS 17)** Evaluation of audit tests results may cause auditors to question whether there is a possible illegal act. For example, illegal acts may be indicated by unauthorized transactions, improperly recorded transactions, and large payments for unspecified services to consultants or other affiliated parties. SAS 54 indicates that when auditors believe there is a possible illegal act, they should obtain sufficient information to evaluate the effect on the financial statements.	Audit
SAS 55 1989	**SAS 55, Consideration of the Internal Control Structure in a Financial Statement Audit** SAS 55 points out that auditors should perform "independent checks on performance and proper valuation of recorded amounts such as ... computer-programmed controls ... " Because most companies use computers to process transactions, it is only logical that many internal controls would be placed in the computer programs. The SAS also mentions an extremely important point: "The auditor also considers his assessment of inherent risk, his judgments about materiality, and the complexity and sophistication of the entity's operations and systems, including whether the method of controlling data processing is based on manual procedures independent of the computer or is *highly dependent on computerized controls*" [emphasis added]. As an entity's operations and systems become more complex and sophisticated, it may be necessary to devote more attention to internal control structure elements to obtain the understanding of them that is necessary to design effective substantive tests.	Audit

Exhibit 2. American Institute of Certified Public Accountants (AICPA) Statement on Audit Standards (SAS) (Continued)

Authoritative Guide	Summary	Category
SAS 56 1989	**SAS 56, Analytical Procedures** According to SAS 56, analytical procedures are a required part of the overall review of the audit. At this stage, the objective of the procedure is to assess whether the financial statements appear to warrant the anticipated audit opinion. An approach to the overall review is noted in AU 329.22. (Evaluate the adequacy of the data collected in response to unusual or unexpected balances identified as part of the preliminary analysis. Identify any other unusual or unexpected balances not previously identified.)	Audit
SAS 60 1989	**SAS 60, Communication of Internal Control Structure Related Matters Noted in an Audit** The standards established by SAS 60 apply to all engagements, regardless of whether the client has an audit committee. Reportable conditions related to the client's internal control structure must be communicated to someone (e.g., owner/manager). These reportable conditions noted in AU 325.21 include evidence that a system fails to provide complete and accurate output consistent with the entity's control objective because of misapplication of control procedures.	Audit
SAS 61 1990	**SAS 61, Communication with Audit Committees** SAS 61 concludes that certain matters related to the audit should be communicated to those who have responsibility for oversight of the financial reporting process. The recipient of the communication will be the audit committee (or "individuals with a level of authority and responsibility equivalent to an audit committee in organizations that do not have one, such as the board of directors, board of trustees, an owner in an owner-managed enterprise, or others who may have engaged the auditor"). Although the audit committee is to receive the communication, the audit may also provide the information to the entity's management or other within the entity that may benefit from communication (AU 380.01).	Audit

**Exhibit 2. American Institute of Certified Public Accountants (AICPA)
Statement on Audit Standards (SAS) (Continued)**

Authoritative Guide	Summary	Category
SAS 65 1990	**SAS 65, The Auditor's Consideration of the Internal Audit Function in an Audit of Financial Statements** SAS 65 requires that, in all engagements, the auditor develop some understanding of the internal audit function (EDP audit, if available) and determine whether that function is relevant to the assessment of control risk. Thus, if there is an internal audit function, it must be evaluated. The evaluation is not optional (AU 322.05).	Audit
SAS 70 1992	**SAS 70, Reports on the Processing of Transactions by Service Organizations** The standards established by SAS 70 are also applicable to service organizations that develop, provide, and maintain software used by user organizations. On the other hand, the standards are not applicable to the audit of a client's transactions that arise from financial interests in partnerships, corporations, and joint ventures, when the entity's proprietary interest is accounted for and reported. In addition, SAS 70 would not apply then the service organization executes transactions based on specific authorizations granted by the user organization. For example, the user auditor would not consider the control procedures of a broker that simply executes security transactions for the user organization (AU 324.03).	Audit

Exhibit 2. American Institute of Certified Public Accountants (AICPA) Statement on Audit Standards (SAS) (Continued)

Authoritative Guide	Summary	Category
SAS 80 1996	**SAS 80, Amendment to Statement on Auditing Standards No. 31, Evidential Matter** SAS 80 is directly aimed at improving auditing in the surroundings of EDP. This SAS was published in 1996 and has made a profound impact on the auditing profession. An excerpt from SAS 80 states: "In entities where significant information is transmitted, processed, maintained, or accessed electronically, the auditor may determine that it is not practical or possible to reduce detection risk to an acceptable level by performing only substantive tests for one or more financial statement assertions. For example, the potential for improper initiation or alteration of information to occur and not be detected may be greater if information is produced, maintained, or accessed only in electronic form. In such circumstances, the auditor should perform tests of controls to gather evidential matter to use in assessing control risk, or consider the effect on his or her report."	Audit
SAS 87 1998	**SAS 87, Restricting the Use of an Auditor's Report** SAS 87 provides guidance to help auditors determine whether an engagement requires a restricted-use report and, if so, what elements to include in that report. Existing auditing standards for engagements require that each restricted-use report contain guidance related to the applicable engagement. This statement unifies that guidance. A restricted-use report is one that is intended only for specified parties. The need for restriction on the use of a report may result from the purpose of the report, the nature of the procedures applied in its preparation, the basis of or assumptions used in its preparation, the extent to which the procedures performed generally are known or understood, and the potential for the report to be misunderstood when taken out of the context in which it was intended to be used.	Audit

Exhibit 2. American Institute of Certified Public Accountants (AICPA) Statement on Audit Standards (SAS) (Continued)

Authoritative Guide	Summary	Category
SAS 88 1999	**SAS 88, Service Organizations and Reporting on Consistency** *Part 1 — Service Organizations* Part 1 of this SAS clarifies the applicability of SAS 70, "Reports on the Processing of Transactions by Service Organizations," by replacing existing language with the language and concepts in SAS 55, "Consideration of Internal Control in a Financial Statement Audit," as amended by SAS 78, to state that the SAS is applicable if an entity obtains services from another organization, which are part of the entity's information system. It provides guidance to help auditors determine whether services are part of an entity's information system and also revises and clarifies the factors a user auditor should consider in determining the significance of a service organization's controls to a user organization's controls. In addition, it clarifies the guidance on determining whether information about a service organization's controls is necessary to plan the audit and that information about a service organization's controls may be obtained from a variety of sources. Finally, it changes the title of SAS 70 from "Reports on the Processing of Transactions by Service Organizations" to "Service Organizations." *Part 2 — Reporting on Consistency* Part 2 of this SAS amends AU sec. 420, "Consistency of Application of Generally Accepted Accounting Principles" to conform the list of changes that constitute a change in the reporting entity (AU sec. 420.07) to the guidance in paragraph 12 of Accounting Principles Board Opinion No. 20, *Accounting Changes.* Clarify that an auditor need not add a consistency explanatory paragraph to the auditor's report when a change in the reporting entity results from a transaction or event. Eliminate the requirement for a consistency explanatory paragraph in the auditor's report if a pooling of interests is not accounted for retroactively in comparative financial statements. Eliminate the requirement to qualify the auditor's report and consider adding a consistency explanatory paragraph to the report if single-year financial statements that report a pooling of interests do not disclose combined information for the prior year.	Audit

Exhibit 2. American Institute of Certified Public Accountants (AICPA) Statement on Audit Standards (SAS) (Continued)

Authoritative Guide	Summary	Category
SAS 89 1999	**SAS 89, Audit Adjustments** This SAS amends 3 SASs to establish audit requirements designed to encourage management to record adjustments aggregated by the auditor. It also clarifies management's responsibility for the disposition of financial statement misstatements brought to its attention. The amendments are: • Add an item to the list of matters in SAS 83, "Establishing an Understanding With the Client," "Appointment of the Independent Auditor" (AU sec 310.06), that generally is addressed in the engagement letter. This item indicates that management is responsible for adjusting the financial statements to correct material misstatements and for affirming to the auditor in the representation letter that the effects of any uncorrected misstatements aggregated by the auditor during the current engagement and pertaining to the latest period presented are immaterial, both individually and in the aggregate, to the financial statements taken as a whole • Add an item to the list in SAS 85, "Management Representations" (AU sec. 333.06), of matters that should be addressed in a representation letter. This item is management's acknowledgment that it believes that the effects of any uncorrected financial statement misstatements aggregated by the auditor during the current engagement and pertaining to the latest period presented are immaterial, both individually and in the aggregate, to the financial statements taken as a whole. It also would require that a summary of the uncorrected misstatements be included in or attached to the letter. • Require the auditor to inform the audit committee, as defined in SAS 61, "Communication With Audit Committees" (AU sec. 380), about uncorrected misstatements aggregated by the auditor during the current engagement and pertaining to the latest period presented that were determined by management to be immaterial, both individually and in the aggregate, to the financial statements taken as a whole.	Audit

Exhibit 2. American Institute of Certified Public Accountants (AICPA) Statement on Audit Standards (SAS) (Continued)

Authoritative Guide	Summary	Category
SAS 90 1999	**SAS 90, Amendment to SAS 61** This is effective for audits of financial statements for periods ending on or after December 15, 2000. Earlier application is permitted. Amendment to SAS 71 — Effective for reviews of interim financial information for interim periods ending on or after March 15, 2000. Earlier application is permitted. *The Amendment to SAS 61:* • Requires an auditor to discuss certain information relating to the auditor's judgments about the quality, not just the acceptability, of the company's accounting principles with the audit committees of SEC clients • Encourages a three-way discussion among the auditor, management, and the audit committee *The Amendment to SAS 71:* • Clarifies that the accountant should communicate to the audit committee or be satisfied, through discussions with the audit committee, that matters described in SAS 61 have been communicated to the audit committee by management when they have been identified in the conduct of interim financial reporting • Requires the accountant of an SEC client to attempt to discuss with the audit committee the matters described in SAS 61 prior to the filing of the form 10-Q	Audit

**Exhibit 2. American Institute of Certified Public Accountants (AICPA)
Statement on Audit Standards (SAS) (Continued)**

Authoritative Guide	Summary	Category
SAS 91 2000	**SAS 91, Statement on Auditing Standards Federal GAAP Hierarchy** On October 19, 1999, the AICPA Council adopted a resolution recognizing the Federal Accounting Standards Advisory Board (FASAB) as the body designated to establish generally accepted accounting principles (GAAP) for federal governmental entities under Rule 203, "Accounting Principles," of the AICPA's *Code of Professional Conduct.* The AICPA members may now express an opinion that the financial statements of a federal governmental entity are in conformity with GAAP if they are prepared in conformity with the accounting principles promulgated by the FASAB. Pursuant to the resolution, Statements of Federal Financial Accounting Standards (SFFAS) issued by the FASAB since March 1993 are recognized as GAAP for the applicable federal governmental entities. In response to the Council resolution, the AICPA Auditing Standards Board issued Statement on Auditing Standards (SAS) No. 91, *Federal GAAP Hierarchy.* The SAS amends SAS 69, "The Meaning of Present Fairly in Conformity with Generally Accepted Accounting Principles in the Independent Auditor's Report" (AICPA, *Professional Standards*, vol. 1, AU sec. 411) to reflect FASAB pronouncements in the GAAP hierarchy as sources of established accounting principles.	Audit
SAS 92 2000	**SAS 92, Auditing Derivative Instruments, Hedging Activities, and Investments in Securities** SAS 92, "Auditing Derivative Instruments, Hedging Activities, and Investments in Securities," was issued to help auditors plan and perform auditing procedures for financial statement assertions about derivative instruments, hedging activities, and investments in securities. The new standard supersedes SAS 81, "Auditing Investments."	Audit

Exhibit 2. American Institute of Certified Public Accountants (AICPA) Statement on Audit Standards (SAS) (Continued)

Authoritative Guide	Summary	Category
SAS 93 2000	**SAS 93, Omnibus Statement on Auditing Standards — 2000** • Withdraws SAS 75, "Engagements to Apply Agreed-Upon Procedures to Specified Elements, Accounts, or Items of a Financial Statement" in order to consolidate the guidance applicable to agreed-upon procedures engagements in professional standards. The guidance currently in SAS 75 will be incorporated in Statements on Standards for Attestation Engagements (SSAE) No. 10, "Attestation Standards: Revision and Recodification." The withdrawal of SAS 75 is concurrent with the effective date of SSAE No. 10. SSAE No. 10 is effective for agreed-upon procedures engagements for which the subject matter or assertion is as of or for a period ending on or after June 1, 2001, with earlier application permitted. • Amends SAS 58, "Reports on Audited Financial Statements," to include a reference in the auditor's report to the United States as the country of origin of the accounting principles used to prepare the financial statements and the auditing standards that the auditor follows in performing the audit. The amendment to SAS 58 also: • Withdraws Auditing Interpretation No. 13, "Reference to Country of Origin in the Auditor's Standard Report" (AICPA, *Professional Standards*, vol. 1, AU sec. 9508.53-.55), of SAS 58 • Revises references to or examples of auditors' reports in other SASs to include an identification of the country of origin of the accounting principles used to prepare the financial statements and of the auditing standards the auditor followed in performing the audit • Amends SAS 69, "The Meaning of Present Fairly in Conformity with Generally Accepted Accounting Principles in the Independent Auditor's Report" (AICPA, *Professional Standards*, vol. 1, AU sec. 411.01), to reflect the new requirement to include in the auditor's report an identification of the United States as the country of origin of GAAP. The title of SAS 69 also is amended and is now, "The Meaning of Present Fairly in Conformity with Generally Accepted Accounting Principles"	Audit

Exhibit 2. American Institute of Certified Public Accountants (AICPA) Statement on Audit Standards (SAS) (Continued)

Authoritative Guide	Summary	Category
SAS 93 (Continued)	The amendment to SAS 58 is effective for reports issued or reissued on or after June 30, 2001, with earlier application permitted. Amends SAS 84, "Communications between Predecessor and Successor Auditors" (AICPA, Professional Standards, vol. 1, AU sec. 315.02), to clarify the definition of predecessor auditor. This amendment is effective for audits of financial statements for periods ending on or after June 30, 2001, with earlier application permitted.	Audit
SAS 94 2001	**SAS 94, The Effect of Information Technology on the Auditor's Consideration of Internal Control in a Financial Statement Audit** SAS 94, "The Effect of Information Technology on the Auditor's Consideration of Internal Control in a Financial Statement Audit," provides guidance to auditors about the effect of information technology (IT) on internal control and on the auditor's understanding of internal control and assessment of control risk. SAS 94 amends SAS 55, "Consideration of Internal Control in a Financial Statement Audit."	Audit
SAS 95 2001	**SAS 95, Generally Accepted Auditing Standards** An independent auditor plans, conducts, and reports the results of an audit conducted in accordance with generally accepted auditing standards (GAAS). Auditing standards provide a measure of audit quality and the objectives to be achieved in an audit. Auditing procedures differ from auditing standards. Auditing procedures are acts that the auditor performs during the course of an audit to comply with auditing standards.	Audit

Exhibit 2. American Institute of Certified Public Accountants (AICPA) Statement on Audit Standards (SAS) (Continued)

Authoritative Guide	Summary	Category
SAS 96 2001	**SAS 96, Audit Documentation** SAS 96, "Audit Documentation," provides general guidance on the content and extent of audit documentation. It also adds specific documentation guidance to certain other SASs. The new standard supersedes SAS 41, "Working Papers." SAS 96 reaffirms the objectives in SAS 41 that audit documentation serves mainly to provide the "principal support for the auditor's report," and to help the auditor conduct and supervise the audit. Although SAS 96 retains much of the guidance in SAS 41, it provides more specific guidance and requirements than SAS 41.	Audit
SAS 97 2002	**SAS 97** This amendment revises SAS 50, "Reports on the Application of Accounting Principles" (AICPA, *Professional Standards* AU sec. 625), to prohibit an accountant from providing a written report on the application of accounting principles not involving facts and circumstances of a specific entity. This SAS covers performance standards as well as reporting standards. The standard is effective for written reports issued or oral advice provided on or after June 30, 2002.	Audit

Exhibit 2. American Institute of Certified Public Accountants (AICPA) Statement on Audit Standards (SAS) (Continued)

Authoritative Guide	Summary	Category
SAS 98 2002	**SAS 98** SAS 98 amends the following: • SAS 95, "Generally Accepted Auditing Standards," AICPA, *Professional Standards*, vol. 1, AU sec. 150.05 • SAS 25, "The Relationship of Generally Accepted Auditing Standards to Quality Control Standards," AICPA, *Professional Standards*, vol. 1, AU sec. 161.02 and .03 • SAS 47, "Audit Risk and Materiality in Conducting an Audit," AICPA, *Professional Standards*, vol. 1, AU sec. 312.34–.41 • SAS 70, "Service Organizations," AICPA, *Professional Standards*, vol. 1, AU sec. 324, and rescinds Interpretation No. 6, "Responsibilities of Service Organizations and Service Auditors with Respect to Subsequent Events in a Service Auditor's Engagement," of SAS 70 • SAS 58, "Reports on Audited Financial Statements," AICPA, *Professional Standards*, vol. 1, AU sec. 508.65 • SAS 8, "Other Information in Documents Containing Audited Financial Statements," AICPA, *Professional Standards*, vol. 1, AU sec. 550.07 • SAS 52, "Required Supplementary Information," AICPA, *Professional Standards*, vol. 1, AU sec. 558.08 and .10 • SAS 52, Required Supplementary Information, AICPA, *Professional Standards*, vol. 1, AU sec. 558.02 • SAS 29, "Reporting on Information Accompanying the Basic Financial Statements in Auditor-Submitted Documents," AICPA, *Professional Standards*, vol. 1, AU sec. 551.12 and .15 • SAS 1, "Codification of Auditing Standards and Procedures," AICPA, *Professional Standards*, vol. 1, AU sec. 561.03, "Subsequent Discovery of Facts Existing at the Date of the Auditor's Report" • SAS 1, Codification of Auditing Standards and Procedures, AICPA, *Professional Standards*, vol. 1, AU sec. 560.01, "Subsequent Events"; and amendment to SAS 1, "Codification of Auditing Standards and Procedures," AICPA, *Professional Standards*, vol. 1, AU sec. 530.03–.05, "Dating of the Independent Auditor's Report"	Auditing

Exhibit 2. American Institute of Certified Public Accountants (AICPA) Statement on Audit Standards (SAS) (Continued)

Authoritative Guide	Summary	Category
SAS 99 Dec 2002	**SAS 99** SAS 99 supersedes SAS 82, "Consideration of Fraud in a Financial Statement Audit," AICPA, *Professional Standards*, vol. 1, AU sec. 316, and amends SAS 1, "Codification of Auditing Standards and Procedures," AICPA, *Professional Standards*, vol. 1, AU sec. 230, "Due Professional Care in the Performance of Work," and SAS 85, "Management Representations," AICPA, *Professional Standards*, vol. 1, AU sec. 333. SAS 90 establishes standards and provides guidance to auditors in fulfilling their responsibility, as it relates to fraud, in an audit of financial statements conducted in accordance with GAAS. Contents of this statement include: • Description and characteristics of fraud • The importance of exercising professional skepticism • Discussion among engagement personnel regarding the risks of material misstatement due to fraud • Obtaining information needed to identify risks of material misstatement due to fraud • Identification of risks that may result in a material misstatement due to fraud • Assessment of the identified risks after taking into account an evaluation of the entity's programs and controls • Response to the results of the assessment • Evaluation of audit evidence • Communication about fraud to management, the audit committee, and others • Documentation of the auditor's consideration of fraud	Audit

Exhibit 2. American Institute of Certified Public Accountants (AICPA) Statement on Audit Standards (SAS) (Continued)

Authoritative Guide	Summary	Category
SAS 100 March 2003	**SAS 100** SAS 100 supersedes SAS 71, Interim Financial Information, AICPA, *Professional Standards*, vol. 1, AU sec. 722. This statement establishes standards and provides guidance on the nature, timing, and extent of the procedures to be performed by an independent accountant when conducting a review of interim financial information — defined as: financial information or statements covering a period less than a full year or for a 12-month period ending on a date other than the entity's fiscal year end. This Statement provides guidance on the application of the fieldwork and reporting standards to a review of interim financial information, to the extent those standards are relevant	Audit

The Institute of Internal Auditors (IIA)

Established in 1941, the IIA serves more than 60,000 members in internal auditing, governance and internal control, IT audit, education, and security from more than 100 countries. The world's leader in certification, education, research, and technological guidance for the profession, the institute serves as the profession's watchdog and resource on significant auditing issues around the globe. Presenting important conferences and seminars for professional development, producing leading-edge educational products, certifying qualified auditing professionals, providing quality assurance reviews and benchmarking, and conducting valuable research projects through the IIA Research Foundation are just a few of the institute's many activities. The IIA also provides internal auditing practitioners, executive management, boards of directors, and audit committees with standards, guidance, and information on internal auditing best practices. The institute is a dynamic international organization that meets the needs of a worldwide body of internal auditors. The history of internal auditing has been synonymous with that of the IIA and its motto, "Progress through Sharing."

The Institute of Internal Auditors (IIA)
247 Maitland Avenue
Altamonte Springs, FL 32701-4201
Telephone: (407) 937-1100
Facsimile: (407) 937-1101

Web site: http://www.theiia.org/
e-mail: iia@theiia.org

Information Source

http://www.theiia.org/

Authoritative Guide

The International Standards for the Professional Practice of Internal Auditing (see Exhibit 3) are issued by the Professional Standards and Responsibilities Committee, the senior technical committee designated by The Institute of Internal Auditors, Inc., to issue pronouncements on auditing standards. These statements are authoritative interpretations of the Standards for the Professional Practice of Internal Auditing. Organizations, internal auditing departments, directors of internal auditing, and internal auditors should strive to comply with the Standards. The implementation of the Standards and related statements will be governed by the environment in which the internal auditing department carries out its assigned responsibilities. The adoption and implementation of the Standards and related statements will assist internal auditing professionals in accomplishing their responsibilities. The Standards are divided into two areas: performance and attribute. They were revised in 2000.

Exhibit 3. The Institute of Internal Auditors (IIA) Performance and Attribute Standards

Authoritative Guide	Summary	Category
Performance Standard 2000	**Performance Standard 2000, Managing the Internal Audit Activity** This performance standard states: "The chief audit executive should effectively manage the internal audit activity to ensure it adds value to the organization."	Audit
Performance Standard 2010	**Performance Standard 2010, Planning** The purpose of this statement is to describe the elements of audit planning. This performance standard states: "The chief audit executive should establish risk-based plans to determine the priorities of the internal audit activity, consistent with the organization's goals." Note that this Standard has implementation standard 2010.A1, which addresses Assurance Engagements, and implementation standard 2010.C1, which addresses Consulting Engagements.	Audit

Exhibit 3. The Institute of Internal Auditors (IIA) Performance and Attribute Standards (Continued)

Authoritative Guide	Summary	Category
Performance Standard 2020	**Performance Standard 2020, Communication and Approval** The purpose of this statement is to describe the elements of communication and approval. This performance standard states: "The chief audit executive should communicate the internal audit activity plans and resource requirements, including significant interim changes to senior management and to the board for review and approval. The chief audit executive should also communicate the impact of resource limitations."	Audit
Performance Standard 2030	**Performance Standard 2030, Resource Management** The purpose of this statement is to describe the elements of resource management. This performance standard states: "The chief audit executive should ensure that internal audit resources are appropriate, sufficient, and effectively deployed to achieve the approved plan."	Audit
Performance Standard 2040	**Performance Standard 2040, Policies and Procedures** The purpose of this statement is to describe the elements of policies and procedures. This performance standard states: "The chief audit executive should establish policies and procedures to guide the internal audit activity."	Audit
Performance Standard 2050	**Performance Standard 2050, Coordination** The purpose of this statement is to describe the elements of coordination. This performance standard states: "The chief audit executive should share information and coordinate activities with other internal and external providers of relevant assurance and consulting services to ensure proper coverage and minimize duplication of efforts."	Audit

Exhibit 3. The Institute of Internal Auditors (IIA) Performance and Attribute Standards (Continued)

Authoritative Guide	Summary	Category
Performance Standard 2060	**Performance Standard 2060, Reporting to the Board and Senior Management** The purpose of this statement is to describe the elements of reporting to the board and senior management. This performance standard states: "The chief audit executive should report periodically to the Board and Senior Management on the internal audit activity's purpose, authority, responsibility, and performance relative to its plan. Reporting should include significant risk exposures and control issues, corporate governance issues, and other matters needed or requested by the board and senior management."	Audit
Performance Standard 2100	**Performance Standard 2100, Nature of Work** The purpose of this statement is to describe the elements of nature of work. This performance standard states: "The internal audit activity evaluates and contributes to the improved risk management, control, and governance systems."	Audit
Performance Standard 2110	**Performance Standard 2110, Risk Management** The purpose of this statement is to describe the elements of risk management. This performance standard states: "The internal audit activity should assist the organization by identifying and evaluating significant exposures to risk and contributing to the improvement of risk management and control systems." Note that this standard is supported by supplemental directives governing Assurance Engagements and Consulting Engagements.	Audit, security, and privacy
Performance Standard 2120	**Performance Standard 2120, Control** The purpose of this statement is to describe the elements of control. This performance standard states: "The internal audit activity should assist the organization in maintaining effective controls by evaluating their effectiveness and efficency and by promoting continuous improvement." This standard is supported by supplemental directives governing Assurance Engagements and Consulting Engagements.	Audit, security, and privacy

Exhibit 3. The Institute of Internal Auditors (IIA) Performance and Attribute Standards (Continued)

Authoritative Guide	Summary	Category
Performance Standard 2130	**Performance Standard 2130, Governance** The purpose of this statement is to describe the elements of governance. This performance standard states: "The internal audit activity should contribute to the organization's governance process by evaluating and improving the process through which (1) values and goals are established and communicated, (2) the accomplishment of goals is monitored, (3) accountability is ensured and (4) values are preserved." This standard is supported by supplemental directives governing Assurance Engagements and Consulting Engagements, Performance Standard 2030, Resource Management.	Audit, security, and privacy
Other IIA Performance Standards	The remaining performance and attribute standards can be found at the IIA Web site at www.theiia.org The remaining performance standards areas are identified as Engagement Planning, Planning Considerations, Engagement Objectives, Engagement Scope, Engagement Resource Allocation, Engagement Work Program, Performing the Engagement, Identifying Information, Analysis and Evaluation, Recording Information, Engagement Supervision, Communicating Results, Criteria for Communicating, Quality of Communications, Errors and Omissions Engagement Disclosure of Noncompliance with the Standards, Disseminating Results, Monitoring Progress and Management's Acceptance of Risk. The IIA's Attribute Standards cover: (1) Purpose, Authority and Responsibility, (2) Organizational Independence, (3) Individual Objectivity, (4) Impairments to Independence or Objectivity, (5) Proficiency, (6) Due Professional Care (7) Continuing Professional Development, (8) Quality Assurance and Improvement Program (Quality Program Assessments, Internal Assessments, External Assessments, Reporting on the Quality Program, Use of "Conduct in Accordance with the Standards," Disclosure of Noncompliance).	Audit

Note that these Standards were substantially revised and issued in December 2000.

Information Systems Audit and Control Association (ISACA)

A worldwide not-for-profit member association of more than 17,000 information systems (IS) professionals, it is dedicated to IS audit, control, and security practitioners through a commitment to education, certification, and standards and an associated not-for-profit foundation committed to expanding the knowledge base of the profession through a commitment to research.

Information Systems Audit and Control Association (ISACA)
3701 Algonquin Road, Suite 1010
Rolling Meadows, IL 60008
Telephone: (847) 253-1545
Facsimile: (847) 253-1443
Web site: http://www.isaca.org
e-mail: membership@isaca.org, education@isaca.org, publication@ isaca.org, certification@isaca.org, conference@iscaa.org, bookstore@isaca.org, research@isaca.org

Authoritative Guide

A Statement on Information System Auditing Standards (SISAS) (see Exhibit 4) is issued by the Standards Board of the ISACA and is recognized as the system auditing standards.

Exhibit 4. Information Systems Audit and Control Association (ISACA) Statement on Information System Audit Guidelines

Authoritative Guide	Summary	Category
IS Audit Guideline May 1, 1999	**Audit Charter** The purpose of this guideline is to assist the IS auditor to prepare an audit charter to define the responsibility, authority, and accountability of the IS audit function. This guideline is aimed primarily at the internal IS audit function, however, aspects could be considered for other circumstances. This guideline provides guidance in applying IS auditing standards. The IS auditor should consider it in determining how to achieve implementation of the above standard, use professional judgment in its application, and be prepared to justify any departure.	Audit

Exhibit 4. Information Systems Audit and Control Association (ISACA) Statement on Information System Audit Guidelines (Continued)

Authoritative Guide	Summary	Category
IS Audit Guideline May 1, 1999	**Outsourcing of IS Activities to Other Organizations** An organization (the service user) may partially or fully delegate some or all of its IS activities to an external provider of such services (the service provider). IS activities that could be outsourced include IS functions such as, data center operations, security, and application system development and maintenance. The responsibility for confirming compliance with contracts, agreements, and regulations remains with the service user. The rights to audit are often unclear. The responsibility for auditing compliance is also often not clear. The purpose of this guideline is to set out how the IS auditor should comply with Standards 010.010, 050.010, and 060.020 in this situation. This guideline provides guidance in applying IS auditing standards. The IS auditor should consider it in determining how to achieve implementation of the above standards, use professional judgment in its application, and be prepared to justify any departure.	Audit

Exhibit 4. Information Systems Audit and Control Association (ISACA) Statement on Information System Audit Guidelines (Continued)

Authoritative Guide	Summary	Category
IS Audit Guideline April 1, 2002	**Effect of Nonaudit Role on the IS Auditor's Independence** In many organizations, the expectation of management, IS staff, and internal audit is that IS auditors may be involved in nonaudit roles such as: • Defining IS strategies relating to areas such as technology, applications, and resources • Evaluating, selecting, and implementing technologies • Evaluating, selecting, customizing, and implementing third-party IS applications and solutions • Designing, developing, and implementing custom-built IS applications and solutions • Establishing best practices, policies, and procedures relating to various IS functions • Designing, developing, and implementing security and control The nonaudit role, in general, involves participation in the IS initiatives and IS project teams, and in working in advisory/consultative capacities on a full-time or part-time basis. Examples include: • Assigning or loaning temporarily full-time IS audit staff to the IS project team • Assigning part-time IS audit staff as a member of the various project structures such as project steering group, project working group, evaluation team, negotiation and contracting team, implementation team, quality assurance team, and trouble shooting team • Acting as an independent advisor or reviewer on an ad hoc basis Such nonaudit roles are an important part of the IS auditor's contribution to the education and training of other members of the organization. They enable IS auditors to use their expertise and their knowledge of the organization to provide a unique and valuable contribution to the efficiency and effectiveness of the organization's IS investments. They also provide opportunities to raise the profile of the IS audit function and to give IS audit staff valuable practical experience.	Audit

Exhibit 4. Information Systems Audit and Control Association (ISACA) Statement on Information System Audit Guidelines (Continued)

Authoritative Guide	Summary	Category
	When the IS auditor has been involved in a nonaudit role in an IS initiative, and an audit is subsequently/concurrently performed of that initiative or the related IS function, recommendations and conclusions arising from that audit may be perceived by the recipients as not objective. In this situation, the perception may be that both the independence and the objectivity of the IS auditor have been impaired by the nonaudit involvement	
	The purpose of this guideline is to provide a framework to enable the IS auditor to:	
	• Establish when the required independence may be, or may appear to be, impaired • Consider potential alternative approaches to the audit process when the required independence is, or may appear to be, impaired • Determine the disclosure requirements	
IS Audit Guideline September 1, 2000	**Organizational Relationship and Independence** The purpose of this guideline is to expand on the meaning of "independence" as used in Standards 020.010 and 020.020 of the Information Systems Auditing Standards and to address the IS auditor's attitude and independence in IS auditing. This guideline provides guidance in applying IS auditing standards. The IS auditor should consider it in determining how to achieve implementation of the above standards, use professional judgment in its application, and be prepared to justify any departure.	Audit
IS Audit Guideline April 1, 2002	**Irregularities and Illegal Acts** The purpose of this guideline is to provide guidance to the IS auditor on the definition of irregularities and illegal acts and the IS auditor's consideration when performing work.	Audit

Exhibit 4. Information Systems Audit and Control Association (ISACA) Statement on Information System Audit Guidelines (Continued)

Authoritative Guide	Summary	Category
IS Audit Guideline November 1, 1999	**Audit Considerations for Irregularities** Some irregularities may be considered fraudulent activities. The determination of fraudulent activities depends on the legal definition of fraud in the jurisdiction pertaining to the audit. Irregularities include, but are not limited to, deliberate circumvention of controls with the intent to conceal the perpetuation of fraud, unauthorized use of assets or services, etc., and abetting or helping to conceal these types of activities Nonfraudulent irregularities may include: • Intentional violations of established management policy • Intentional violations of regulatory requirements • Deliberate misstatements or omissions of information concerning the area under audit or the organization as a whole • Gross negligence • Unintentional illegal acts This guideline provides guidance in applying IS auditing standards. The IS auditor should consider it in determining how to achieve implementation of the above standards, use professional judgment in its application, and be prepared to justify any departure.	Audit
IS Audit Guideline May 1, 1999	**Due Professional Care** The purpose of this guideline is to clarify the term "due professional care" as it applies to the performance of an audit in compliance with Standards 030.010 and 030.020 of the IS Auditing Standards. The guideline provides guidance in applying IS auditing standards. The IS auditor should consider it in determining how to achieve implementation of the above standards, use professional judgment in its application, and be prepared to justify any departure.	Audit

Exhibit 4. Information Systems Audit and Control Association (ISACA) Statement on Information System Audit Guidelines (Continued)

Authoritative Guide	Summary	Category
IS Audit Guideline May 1, 1999	**Materiality Concepts for Auditing Information** The IS auditing guideline on planning the IS audit states, "In the planning process the IS auditor should normally establish levels of materiality such that the audit work will be sufficient to meet the audit objectives and will use audit resources efficiently." Financial auditors ordinarily measure materiality in monetary terms because what they are auditing is also measured and reported in monetary terms. IS auditors may audit nonfinancial items, e.g., physical access controls, logical access controls, and program change controls, and systems for personnel management, manufacturing control, design, quality control, password generation, credit card production, and patient care. IS auditors may therefore need guidance on how materiality should be assessed in order to plan their audits effectively, focus their efforts on high-risk areas, and assess the severity of any errors or weaknesses found. This guideline provides guidance in applying IS auditing standards. The IS auditor should consider it in determining how to achieve implementation of the above standard, use professional judgment in its application, and be prepared to justify any departure.	Audit
IS Audit Guideline November 1, 2001	**Planning** The purpose of this guideline is to define the components of the planning process as stated in Standard 050.010 of the Standards for IS auditing. This guideline also provides for planning in the audit process to meet the objectives set by CoBiT®.	Audit

Exhibit 4. Information Systems Audit and Control Association (ISACA) Statement on Information System Audit Guidelines (Continued)

Authoritative Guide	Summary	Category
IS Audit Guideline September 1, 2000	**Use of Risk Assessment in Audit Planning** The level of audit work required to meet a specific audit objective is a subjective decision made by the IS auditor. The risk of reaching an incorrect conclusion based on the audit findings (audit risk) is one aspect of this decision. The other is the risk of errors occurring in the area being audited (error risk). Recommended practices for risk assessment in carrying out financial audits are well documented in auditing standards for financial auditors, but guidance is required on how to apply such techniques to IS audits. Management also bases its decisions on how much control is appropriate upon assessment of the level of risk exposure that they are prepared to accept. For example, the inability to process computer applications for a period of time is an exposure that could result from unexpected and undesirable events (e.g., data center fire). Exposures can be reduced by the implementation of appropriately designed controls. These controls are ordinarily based upon probabilistic estimation of the occurrence of adverse events and are intended to decrease such probability. For example, a fire alarm does not prevent fires, but is intended to reduce the extent of fire damage. This guideline provides guidance in applying IS auditing standards. The IS auditor should consider it in determining how to achieve implementation of the above standards, use professional judgment in its application, and be prepared to justify any departure.	Audit
IS Audit Guideline November 1, 2001	**Effect of Third Parties on an Organization's IT Controls** This guideline sets out how the IS auditor should comply with the ISACA standards and CobiT when assessing the effects a third party has on an organization's information system controls and related control objectives. This guideline is not intended to provide guidance on how IS auditors report on third-party provider controls in accordance with other standard-setting entities.	Audit

Exhibit 4. Information Systems Audit and Control Association (ISACA) Statement on Information System Audit Guidelines (Continued)

Authoritative Guide	Summary	Category
IS Audit Guideline May 1, 1999	**Audit Documentation** The purpose of this guideline is to describe the documentation that the IS auditor should prepare and retain to support the audit. This guideline provides guidance in applying IS auditing standards. The IS auditor should consider it in determining how to achieve implementation of the above standards, use professional judgment in its application, and be prepared to justify any departure.	Audit
IS Audit Guideline August 1, 2001	**Application Systems Review** The purpose of this guideline is to describe the recommended practices in performing an application systems review. The purpose of an application systems review is to identify, document, test, and evaluate the controls over an application that are implemented by an organization to achieve relevant control objectives. These control objectives can be categorized into control objectives over the system and the related data.	Audit
IS Audit Guideline June 19, 1998	**Audit Evidence Requirement** The purpose of this guideline is to define the word "evidence" as used in Standard 060.020 of the Standards for Information Systems Auditing and to address the type and sufficiency of audit evidence used in IS auditing. This guideline provides guidance in applying IS auditing standards. The IS auditor should consider it in determining how to achieve implementation of the above standard, use professional judgment in its application, and be prepared to justify any departure.	Audit

Exhibit 4. Information Systems Audit and Control Association (ISACA) Statement on Information System Audit Guidelines (Continued)

Authoritative Guide	Summary	Category
IS Audit Guideline November 1, 1999	**Audit Sampling** The purpose of this guideline is to provide guidance to the IS auditor to design and select an audit sample and evaluate sample results. Appropriate sampling and evaluation will meet the requirements of "sufficient, reliable, relevant, and useful evidence" and "supported by appropriate analysis." The IS auditor should consider selection techniques that result in a statistically based representative sample for performing compliance or substantive testing. Examples of compliance testing of controls where sampling could be considered include user access rights, program change control procedures, procedures documentation, program documentation, follow-up of exceptions, review of logs, software licenses audits, etc. Examples of substantive tests where sampling could be considered include reperformance of a complex calculation (e.g., interest) on a sample of accounts, sample of transactions to vouch for supporting documentation, etc. This guideline provides guidance in applying IS auditing standards. The IS auditor should consider it in determining how to achieve implementation of the above standard, use professional judgment in its application, and be prepared to justify any departure. Other useful references on audit sampling include the International Standard on Auditing #530, Audit Sampling and other Selective Testing Procedures, issued by the International Federation of Accountants (IFAC).	Audit

Exhibit 4. Information Systems Audit and Control Association (ISACA) Statement on Information System Audit Guidelines (Continued)

Authoritative Guide	Summary	Category
IS Audit Guideline April 1, 2002	**IT Governance** The COBIT® *Executive Summary* states: "Organizations must satisfy the quality, fiduciary and security requirements for their information, as for all assets. Management must also optimize the use of available resources including data, application systems, technology, facilities, and people. To discharge these responsibilities, as well as to achieve its objectives, management must establish an adequate system of internal control." Use of technology in all aspects of economic and social endeavors has created a critical dependency on IT to initiate, record, move, and manage all aspects of economic transactions, information, and knowledge, creating a critical place for IT governance within enterprise governance. High profile problems (for example: system failures resulting from virus attacks, loss of trust, or systems availability due to Web site hacking) experienced by a variety of public and private sector organizations have focused attention on enterprise governance issues. The formal means by which management discharges its responsibility to establish an effective system of internal control over an organization's operational and financial activities can be subject to public scrutiny and often forms part of the audit scope for both internal and external IS auditors. The purpose of this guideline is to provide information on how an IS auditor should approach an audit of the IT governance — covering the appropriate organizational position of the IS auditor concerned, covering issues to consider when planning the audit, and evidence to review when performing the audit. This guideline also provides guidance on reporting lines and content and the follow-up work to be considered.	Audit

Exhibit 4. Information Systems Audit and Control Association (ISACA) Statement on Information System Audit Guidelines (Continued)

Authoritative Guide	Summary	Category
IS Audit Guideline November 1, 1999	**Effect of Pervasive IS Controls** The management and monitoring of any organization, department, or function has an effect on the way in which that organization, department, or function behaves, including the way in which it applies controls. This principle applies as much to the use of IS as it does to a manufacturing organization, an accounts payable department, or a treasury function. The effectiveness of the detailed IS controls operated within an organization is limited by the effectiveness of the management and monitoring of the use of information systems in the organization as a whole. This is often recognized in guidelines for financial audits, where the effect of "general" controls in the IS environment upon "application" controls in the financial systems is acknowledged. For example, the U.K. Auditing Guideline 3.2.407 (Auditing in a Computer Environment) states: "Strong general controls contribute to the assurance which may be obtained by an auditor in relation to application controls. Unsatisfactory general controls may undermine strong application controls or exacerbate unsatisfactory application controls." The Information Systems Audit and Control Foundation's "Control Objectives for Information and related Technology" (CobiT) provides a framework that can assist the IS auditor in differentiating between: the detailed IS controls, which are directly relevant to the IS audit scope, and the features of IS management and monitoring, which contribute to the assurance that may be obtained by an IS auditor in relation to those detailed IS controls The general/application control split was specifically designed to apply to audits whose objective is to form an opinion on whether or not the financial information is free of material misstatement (financial audits).	Audit

Exhibit 4. Information Systems Audit and Control Association (ISACA) Statement on Information System Audit Guidelines (Continued)

Authoritative Guide	Summary	Category
IS Audit Guideline November 1, 1999 (Continued)	When internal auditors and independent consultants perform IS audits, the audit objective and scope are ordinarily different from those for financial audits. The systems in use are a combination of manual and computer processes, and the control objectives must be for the entire process, which may be either wider or narrower than accounting records. Therefore, the controls framework used for financial audits may not be appropriate for some IS audits.	Audit
	In order to form an opinion on the effectiveness of the detailed controls being audited, the IS auditor should consider the need to assess the effectiveness of management and monitoring of information systems, even where such matters are outside the agreed scope for the audit. The outcome of such consideration may range from an extension of the agreed scope to an appropriately qualified report.	
	The total population of management and monitoring controls is broad, and some of these controls may not be relevant to the specific audit objective. In order to assess the audit risk and determine the appropriate audit approach, the IS auditor needs a structured method of determining:	
	• Those management and monitoring controls that are relevant to the audit scope and objectives • Those management and monitoring controls that should be tested • The effect of the relevant management and monitoring controls on the audit opinion	
	This may be achieved using a framework of controls specific to the use of IS and related technology, which helps the IS auditor to focus on the key controls that affect the IS and operations being audited.	
	This guideline provides guidance in applying IS auditing standards. The IS auditor should consider it in determining how to achieve implementation of the above standard, use professional judgment in its application, and be prepared to justify any departure.	

Exhibit 4. Information Systems Audit and Control Association (ISACA) Statement on Information System Audit Guidelines (Continued)

Authoritative Guide	Summary	Category
IS Audit Guideline June 19, 1998	**Use of Computer Assisted Audit Techniques (CAATs)** Computer Assisted Audit Techniques (CAATs) are important tools for the IS auditor in performing audits. CAATs include many types of tools and techniques, such as generalized audit software, utility software, test data, application software tracing and mapping, and audit expert systems. CAATs may be used in performing various audit procedures including: • Tests of details of transactions and balances • Analytical review procedures • Compliance tests of IS general controls • Compliance tests of IS application controls • Penetration testing	Audit
IS Audit Guideline February 1, 1998	**Using the Work of Other Auditors and Experts** The interdependency of customers' and suppliers' processing and the outsourcing of noncore activities mean that an IS auditor (internal or external) will often find that parts of the environment being audited are controlled and audited by other independent functions or organizations. This guideline sets out how the IS auditor should comply with the above standard in these circumstances. Compliance with this guideline is not mandatory, but the IS auditor should be prepared to justify deviation from the standard.	Audit
IS Audit Guideline June 19, 1998	**Report Content and Form** The purpose of this guideline is to describe the recommended practices for preparing and issuing an IS audit report ("report"). This guideline provides guidance in applying IS auditing standards. The IS auditor should consider it in determining how to achieve implementation of the above standard, use professional judgment in its application, and be prepared to justify any departure.	Audit

Exhibit 4. Information Systems Audit and Control Association (ISACA) Statement on Information System Audit Guidelines (Continued)

Authoritative Guide	Summary	Category
Documents Withdrawn Title		Withdrawal date
SISAS 3 (Evidence Requirement)		June 19, 1998
SISAS 7 (Audit Reports)		June 19, 1998
SISAS 9 (Use of Audit Software Tools)		June 19, 1998
SISAS 4 (Due Professional Care)		October 1, 1999
SISAS 6 (Audit Documentation)		October 1, 1999
SISAS 2 (Involvement in the System Development Process)		March 1, 2000
SISAS 8 (Audit Considerations for Irregularities)		March 1, 2000
SISAS 1 (Attitude & Appearance — Organizational Relationship)		September 1, 2000
SISAS 5 (The Use of Risk Assessment in Audit Planning)		September 1, 2000

The **Guidelines** provide examples of different types of IS audit work and set requirements for the work and its reporting. They are standards to the extent that an IS auditor should be prepared to justify departures from them but is not required to follow them.

The **Standards** define mandatory requirements for IS auditing and reporting.

The Canadian Institute of Chartered Accountants (CICA)

The Canadian Institute of Charted Accountants, like the profession it serves, reflects the national character of Canada; its members work in virtually all streams of Canadian life. The CICA serves not only the accounting profession at the national and international level, but it provides significant input to the public and private sectors through Canada regarding business practices and government legislation. In its organization, the profession reflects the federalism of Canada. Through a system of interlocking membership, chartered accountants automatically become members of CICA upon admission to a provincial institute. The institute was established in 1972 and is governed by the 23-member board of governors.

The Canadian Institute of Chartered Accountants (CICA)
277 Wellington Street West
Toronto ON M5V 3H2 Canada
Telephone: (416)977-3222
Facsimile: (416)977-8585
Web site: http://www.cica.ca
E-mail: customer.service@cica.ca

Information Source

http://www.cica.ca

1. "Auditing in an Electronic Data Processing Environment," *CICA Handbook*, The Canadian Institute of Chartered Accountants, August 1981.
2. Section 1000-9200, *CICA Handbook*, The Canadian Institute of Chartered Accountants, August 1991.
3. Accounting Guideline AcG-10, "The Year 2000 Issue," The Canadian Institute of Chartered Accountants, June 1998.
4. Assurance and Related Services Guideline AuG-22, "The Year 2000 Issue — Considerations for Audit Planning and Communications of Matters," The Canadian Institute of Chartered Accountants, February 1998.
5. Assurance and Related Services Guideline AuG-23, "The Year 2000 Issue — The Auditor's Consideration of Financial Statement Disclosures, the Going Concern Assumption, and Other Matters," The Canadian Institute of Chartered Accountants, June 1998.
6. Assurance and Related Services Guideline AuG-24, "The Year 2000 Issue — Service Auditor Responsibilities and Audit Evidence Considerations When an Entity Uses a Service Organization," The Canadian Institute of Chartered Accountants, June 1998.

Authoritative Guide

The Accounting Research and Auditing Standards Committees were established in 1973 when the board of governors decided to split its predecessor, the Accounting and Auditing Research Committee, into two separate committees (see Exhibit 5). By far the most important responsibility of both committees is the issuance of accounting recommendations and auditing recommendations for the *CICA Handbook*. Only these committees have been given the authority to issue pronouncements without reference to the board of governors. Information about the *CICA Handbook* can be obtained by the members at: http://handbook.cica.ca/

International Federation of Accountants (IFAC)

IFAC is an organization of national professional accountancy organizations that represent accountants employed in public practice, business and industry, the public sector, and education, as well as some specialized groups that interface frequently with the profession. Currently, it has 140-member bodies in 101 countries, representing 2 million accountants. Full membership in IFAC automatically includes membership in the International Accounting Standards Committee (IASC).

International Federation of Accountants
535 Fifth Avenue, 26th Floor
New York, NY 10017

Exhibit 5. The Canadian Institute of Chartered Accountants (CICA) Accounting Recommendations and Auditing Recommendations

Authoritative Guide	Summary	Category
CICA Handbook Section 1508	**CICA Handbook Section 1508, *Measurement Uncertainty*** Financial statements may be affected by the Year 2000 issue — disclosures in accordance with *Measurement Uncertainty*, Section 1508, such as those necessary when it is reasonably possible that the recognized amount of accounts receivable or loans receivable could change by a material amount in the near term because they are due from entities not ready for the year 2000.	Audit
CICA Handbook Section 3025	**CICA Handbook Section 3025, *Impaired Loans*** Financial statements may be affected by the Year 2000 issue — reduction in the carrying amount of impaired loans in accordance with *Impaired Loans,* Section 3025.	Audit
CICA Handbook Section 3060	**CICA Handbook Section 3060, *Capital Assets*** Financial statements may be affected by the Year 2000 issue — write downs and amortization policies in accordance with *Capital Assets*, Section 3060, such as those related to computer hardware planned to be abandoned because it cannot process transactions with Year 2000 data, or capital assets or inventories containing software that cannot deal with Year 2000 data.	Audit
CICA Handbook Section 3280	**CICA Handbook Section 3280, *Contractual Obligations*** Financial statements may be affected by the Year 2000 issue — disclosure in accordance with *Contractual Obligations*, Section 3280, such as disclosure of costs contracted to complete year 2000 conversions.	Audit
CICA Handbook Section 3290	**CICA Handbook Section 3290, *Contingencies*** Financial statements may be affected by the Year 2000 issue: • Recognition and disclosure in accordance with *Contingencies,* Section 3290, when, for example, the recent sales of a software vendor and installer may not have been Year 2000 ready, although they were represented as such on installation	Audit

Exhibit 5. The Canadian Institute of Chartered Accountants (CICA) Accounting Recommendations and Auditing Recommendations (Continued)

Authoritative Guide	Summary	Category
CICA Handbook Section 5100	**CICA Handbook Section 5100, *Generally Accepted Auditing Standards*** The general standard (Generally Accepted Auditing Standards, Section 5100) states in part: "The examination should be performed...by a person having adequate technical training and proficiency in auditing..." In an EDP environment, to enable compliance with the standards contained in Section 5100, proficiency would require a knowledge of how the characteristics of EDP affects the accounting function, internal control, and auditing techniques.	Audit
CICA Handbook Section 5140	**CICA Handbook Section 5140, *Knowledge of the Client's Business*** The auditor, in obtaining a knowledge of the client's business and determining his tentative audit strategy, should consider aspects of the EDP environment.	Audit
CICA Handbook Section 5150	**CICA Handbook Section 5150, *Planning and Supervision*** In some situations, the auditor may find it necessary to use assistants with extensive EDP knowledge. Even if the assistants are not directly employed by the auditor and are not trained in accounting and auditing, their work forms are an integral part of the audit examination; therefore, the auditor should possess sufficient knowledge to discharge his or her supervisory responsibilities as outlined in *Planning and Supervision*, Section 5150.	Audit

Exhibit 5. The Canadian Institute of Chartered Accountants (CICA) Accounting Recommendations and Auditing Recommendations (Continued)

Authoritative Guide	Summary	Category
CICA Handbook Section 5200 to 5220	**CICA Handbook Section 5200-5220, *Internal Controls*** *Internal Control,* paragraph 5220.06 states: "The auditor should review those internal control systems on which he intends to rely." Although there are many types of internal controls in an EDP environment (for example, organizational, operating, and processing controls), only some of these may be relevant to the auditor in a particular system. The auditors' review is likely to be conducted with greater efficiency if they first determine which controls are of audit significance and select those that achieve their audit objective in the most efficient way. The objectives of performing compliance and substantive procedures are not altered by the existence of an EDP environment. As indicated in *Internal Controls,* paragraph 5215.16, some audit procedures may fulfill both compliance and substantive objectives.	Audit
CICA Handbook Section 5360	**CICA Handbook Section 5360, *Using the Work of a Specialist*** When the evaluation of the additional financial statement disclosure requires knowledge of computerized systems beyond the auditor's expertise, the auditor would need to use the work of a specialist; for example, when an entity with diverse operations and complex, technology-reliant systems describes the results of its assessment of the effects of the Year 2000 issue and its plans to remediate and replace systems. In these circumstances, the auditor would refer to the guidance set out in *Using the Work of a Specialist,* Section 5360.	Audit
CICA Handbook Section 5510	**CICA Handbook Section 5510, *Reservations in the Auditor's Report*** If additional financial statement disclosure about the Year 2000 issue includes statements that are not factual, or that cannot be verified, or that are inconsistent with the required inherent uncertainty disclosure, the auditor would ask management to correct or remove them. If such statements are not corrected or removed, the auditor would refer to *Reservations in the Auditor's Report,* Section 5510.	Audit

Telephone: (212) 286-9344
Facsimile: (212) 286-9570
Web site: http://www.ifac.org
E-mail: mariahermann@ifac.org (Maria Hermann)

Information Source

http://www.ifac.org

Authoritative Guides

Auditing and related services: **International Standards on Auditing — Codified Introductory Matters (ISA)** is issued by the IFAC and gives recognized standards and/or guidelines.

Education: **International Education Guidelines (IEG)** are issued by the IFAC and are recognized as standards and/or guidelines.

Financial and management accounting: **International Management Accounting Practice Statements** and **International Management Accounting Studies Statements** are issued by the IFAC and are recognized as standards and/or guidelines.

Information Technology: **International Information Technology Guidelines** are issued by the IFAC and are recognized as standards and/or guidelines. The Information Technology Committee is in the process of developing a series of international guidelines to assist management in both understanding and ultimately managing the risks associated with information technology.

Public Sector: **International Public Sector Guidelines** are issued by the IFAC and are recognized as standards and/or guidelines.

* Detailed information relating to authoritative guides was not available for review. See Exhibit 6.

Exhibit 6. International Federation of Accountants (IFAC) Guidelines

Authoritative Guide	Summary	Category
ISA-100*	ISA-100, Assurance Engagements	Audit
ISA-120*	ISA-120, Framework of ISAs	Audit
ISA-200*	ISA-200, Objective and General Principles Governing an Audit of Financial Statements	Audit
ISA-210*	ISA-210, Terms of Audit Engagements	Audit

Exhibit 6. International Federation of Accountants (IFAC) Guidelines (Continued)

Authoritative Guide	Summary	Category
ISA-220*	ISA-220, Quality Control for Audit Work	Audit
ISA-230*	ISA-230, Documentation	Audit
ISA-240*	ISA-240, The Auditor's Responsibility to Consider Fraud and Error in an Audit of Financial Statements	Audit
ISA-240A*	ISA-240A, Fraud and Error	Audit
ISA-250*	ISA-250, Consideration of Laws and Regulations in an Audit of Financial Statements	Audit
ISA-260*	ISA-260, Communications of Audit Matters with Those Charged with Governance	Audit
ISA-300*	ISA-300, Planning	Audit
ISA-500*	ISA-500, Audit Evidence	Audit
ISA-501*	ISA-501, Audit Evidence — Additional Considerations for Specific Items	Audit
ISA-505*	ISA-505, External Confirmations	Audit
ISA-510*	ISA-510, Initial Engagements — Opening Balances	Audit
ISA-520*	ISA-520, Analytical Procedures	Audit
ISA-540*	ISA-540, Audit of Accounting Estimates	Audit
ISA-550*	ISA-550, Related Parties	Audit
ISA-560*	ISA-560, Subsequent Events	Audit
ISA-570*	ISA-570, Going Concerns	Audit
ISA-580*	ISA-580, Management Representations	Audit
ISA-600*	ISA-600, Using the Work of Another Auditor	Audit
ISA-610*	ISA-610, Considering the Work of Internal Auditing	Audit
ISA-620*	ISA-620, Using the Work of an Expert	Audit
ISA-700*	ISA-700, The Auditor's Report on Financial Statements	Audit
ISA-710*	ISA-710, Comparatives	Audit
ISA-720*	ISA-720, Other information in documents containing audited financial statements	Audit
ISA-800*	ISA-800, The Auditor's Report on Special Purpose Audit Engagement	Audit
ISA-810*	ISA-810, The Examination of Prospective Financial Information	Audit
ISA-910*	ISA-910, Engagements to Review Financial Statements	Audit

Exhibit 6. International Federation of Accountants (IFAC) Guidelines (Continued)

Authoritative Guide	Summary	Category
ISA-920*	ISA-920, Engagements to Perform Agreed-Upon Procedures Regarding Financial Informational	Audit
ISA-930*	ISA-930, Engagements to Compile Financial Information	Audit
ISA-1004*	ISA-1004, The Relationship between Banking Supervisors and Banks' External Auditors	Audit
ISA-1005*	ISA-1005, The Special Consideration in the Audit of Small Entities	Audit
ISA-1006*	ISA-1006, Audits of the Financial Statements of Banks	Audit
ISA-1007*	ISA-1007, Communications with Management (deleted)	Audit
ISA-1010*	ISA-1010, The Consideration of Environmental Matters in the Audit of Financial Statements	Audit
ISA-1011*	ISA-1011, Implications for Management and Auditors of the Year 2000 Issue (deleted)	Audit
ISA-1012*	ISA-1012, Auditing Derivative Financial Instruments	Audit
ISA-1013*	ISA-1013, Electronic Commerce: Effect on the Audit of Financial Statements	Audit
Study 1*	Study 1, The Determination and Communication of Levels of Assurance Other than High	Security
International Information Technology Guideline No. 1	International Information Technology Guideline No. 1 Managing Security of Information This guideline is the first of the series and covers security. In addition to generating better awareness of the importance of security to organizations today, it provides a framework for designing, implementing, and managing effective security over information.	Security

Information System Security Association (ISSA)

The Information Systems Security Association (ISSA) is an international organization of information security professionals and practitioners. It provides education forums, publications, and peer interaction opportunities that enhance the knowledge, skill, and professional growth of its members.

Information System Security Association (ISSA)
7044 S. 13th Street
Oak Creek, WI 53154
Telephone: (414) 768-8000
Facsimile: (414) 768-8001

710

Exhibit 7. Information System Security Association (ISSA) Guideline for Information Valuation (GIV) Publication

Authoritative Guide	Summary	Category
GIV *	**Guideline for Information Valuation (GIV) publication** Created by a knowledgeable task force of ISSA members. These guidelines, created exclusively by ISSA, provide the tools necessary for assigning value to an organization's information assets.	Security, privacy

Web site: http://www.uh.edu/~bmw/issa/frame.html
E-mail: MbrMktg@NaSPA.Net (Meg)

Information Source

http://www.uh.edu/~bmw/issa/frame.html

Authoritative Guide

Guideline for Information Valuation (GIV) publication — It has been created exclusively by a knowledgeable task force of ISSA members, and these guidelines provide the tools necessary for assigning value to an organization's information assets.

* Detailed information relating to authoritative guides was not available for review. See Exhibit 7.

Society for Information Management (SIM)

The Society for Information Management comprises 2700 senior executives who are corporate and divisional heads of information technology (IT) organizations and their management staff, leading academicians, consultants, and other leaders who shape and influence the management and use of IT.

Society for Information Management (SIM)
401 North Michigan Avenue
Chicago, IL 60611-4267
Telephone: (312) 527-6734
Facsimile: (800) 387-9746
Web site: http://www.simnet.org
E-mail: SIM_Central@simnet.org

Information Source

http://www.simnet.org

Exhibit 8. Society for Information Management (SIM)

Authoritative Guide	Summary	Category
N/A	N/A	N/A

Authoritative Guide

The Society for Information Management has not issued authoritative guides to date. However, SIM has issued several press releases on technology-related topics and may be found at the following Web site http://www.simnet.org/public/aboutsim/pressrls/. See Exhibit 8.

Association of Information Technology Professionals (AITP)

AITP is the professional association comprising of career-minded individuals who look to expand their talents — employers, employees, managers, and programmers who share an enthusiasm for knowledge. The organization aims to provide avenues for all members to become teachers, as well as students, and to open doors to exchange ideas with other professionals in an effort to become more marketable.

Association of Information Technology Professionals (AITP)
401 North Michigan Avenue, Suite 2200
Chicago, IL 60622-4267
Telephone: (800) 224-9371/(312) 245-1070
Facsimile: (847) 527-6636
Web site: http://www.aitp.org/
E-mail: aitp_hq@aitp.org

Information Source

http://www.aitp.org/

Authoritative Guide

The Association of Information Technology Professionals has not issued authoritative guides to date. However, AITP has two publications.

Information Executive

Each monthly issue of the *Information Executive* focuses on current industry topics from technical and managerial viewpoints to help information systems and data processing individuals understand and meet the most important challenges of the IS industry. Contributions from industry experts, practitioners, and educators are regular features of *Information Executive* topics, which cover a full range of industry issues, including client/server management, project management, online services, down-

Exhibit 9. Association of Information Technology Professionals (AITP)

Authoritative Guide	Summary	Category
N/A	N/A	N/A

sizing, rightsizing, LANs, microcomputers, workstations, security, disaster recover, systems integration, and total quality management.

The Nanosecond

This newsletter is published for the AITP student members and faculty advisors. Published six times a year, each issue contains articles that are contributed by AITP student members, student advisors, and professionals within the industry. In addition to student chapter information, there are also articles featured that address the key topics of interest to students. See Exhibit 9.

International Federation for Information Processing (IFIP)

IFIP is a nongovernmental, nonprofit umbrella organization for national societies working in the field of information processing. It was established in 1960 under the auspices of UNESCO as an aftermath of the first World Computer Congress held in Paris in 1959. Today, IFIP has several types of members and maintains friendly connections with specialized agencies of the UN system and nongovernmental organizations. Technical work, which is the heart of IFIP's activity, is managed by a series of technical committees.

IFIP Secretariat
Hofstraße 3,
A-2361 Laxenburg, Austria
Telephone: + 43 2236 73616
Facsimile: + 43 2236 736169
Web site: http://www.ifip.or.at/homeintro.html
E-mail: ifip@ifip.or.at

Information Source

http://www.ifip.or.at/homeintro.html

Authoritative Guide

IFIP Technical Committee (TC) and Working Group (WG) — Aims and Scopes. There are aims shared by all or most committees that are not subject specific. They are as follows:

- To establish and maintain liaison with national and international organizations with allied interests and to foster cooperative action, collaborative research, and information exchange
- To identify subjects and priorities for research, to stimulate theoretical work on fundamental issues, and to foster fundamental research that will underpin future development
- To provide a forum for professionals with a view to promote the study, collection, exchange, and dissemination of ideas, information, and research findings, and thereby promote the state of the art
- To seek and use the most effective ways of disseminating information about our work including the organization of conferences, workshops, and symposia, and the timely production of relevant publications
- To have special regard for the needs of developing countries and to seek practical ways of working with them
- To encourage communication and to promote interaction between users, practitioners, and researchers
- To foster interdisciplinary work and, in particular, to collaborate with other technical committees (TC) and working groups (WG)

* Detailed information relating to authoritative guides was not available for review. See Exhibit 10.

Association for Computing Machinery (ACM)

ACM, the Association for Computing Machinery, is an international scientific and educational organization dedicated to advancing the arts, sciences, and applications of IT. ACM functions as a locus for computing professionals and students working in the various fields of IT. ACM is the world's oldest and largest educational and scientific computing society. Since 1947, ACM has provided a vital forum for the exchange of information, ideas, and discoveries. Today, ACM serves a membership of more than 80,000 computing professionals in more than 100 countries in all areas of industry, academia, and government.

Association for Computing Machinery (ACM)
One Astor Plaza
1515 Broadway
New York, NY 10036
Telephone: (212) 626-0500/(US-Canada) 800-342-6626
Facsimile: (212) 944-1318
Web site: http://www.acm.org
E-mail: webmaster@acm.org

Information Source

http://www.acm.org

Exhibit 10. International Federation for Information Processing (IFIP), IFIP Technical Committee (TC), and Working Group (WG) — Aims and Scopes

Authoritative Guide	Summary	Category
WG 8.6 est. 1994	**WG8.6, Transfer and Diffusion of Information Technology** Aims • To foster understanding and improve research in practice, methods, and techniques in the transfer and diffusion of IT within systems that are developed and in the development process Scope • Diffusion, transfer, and implementation of both mature and immature information technologies and systems in organizations and among organizations, sectors, and countries • Transfer of technology to be incorporated in systems for customers and clients • Transfer of both system and development technologies to technologists, developers, managers, and sponsors of systems • Development of frameworks, models, and terminology for IT transfer and diffusion • Identification of risk factors and barriers to success in technology transfer and strategies for addressing them • Determination of conditions or scenarios under which specific transfer and diffusion techniques are applicable • Methods to evaluate the efficiency, effectiveness, and value of technology transfer programs and approaches, including time and effort estimators and metrics • Organization design and process issues related to technology transfer and diffusion • Case studies of technology transfer and diffusion to provide instances to guide research, development, and practice • Standards and intellectual property issues that inhibit or facilitate IT transfer	Privacy
WG 8.8 *	**WG 8.8, Smart Cards** (tentative)	Security, privacy

Exhibit 10. International Federation for Information Processing (IFIP), IFIP Technical Committee (TC), and Working Group (WG) — Aims and Scopes (Continued)

Authoritative Guide	Summary	Category

WG 9.6
est. 1990,
revised 1992
	WG 9.6, Information Technology Misuse and the Law
	Aims
	• To develop an understanding, in IFIP committees and national bodies, of:
	  – threats to IT system security
	  – risks to people and organizations arising from these threats
	• To propose and evaluate general legal prescriptions to counteract these threats and to deal with these risks
	• To initiate information exchange on threats, their origin, and likely implications (such as viruses, acts of sabotage, worms etc.) and their likely impacts
	• To propose and evaluate appropriate courses of action
	Scope
	• Analysis of existing and emerging threats to IT systems security and concomitant risks to people, organizations, and society as a whole
	• Analysis of confidentiality, integrity, availability, and reliability (safety)
	• Analysis of existing legal prescriptions and their ability to limit such threats
	• Analysis of ethical standards to influence the extent to which such threats can be countered
	• Analysis of ethical standards and other social factors applicable to professional behavior and responsibilities in the context of IT systems
	• New legal, social, and organizational consequences of the development and use of IT systems
	• Possible solutions
		Security, privacy

TC 11 est. 1984	**TC 11, Security and Protection in Information Processing Systems** Aims • To increase the reliability and general confidence in information processing, as well as to act as a forum for security managers and others professionally active in the field of information processing security Scope • The establishment of a frame of reference for security common to organizations, professionals, and the public • The promotion of security and protection as essential parts of information processing systems	Security

Exhibit 10. International Federation for Information Processing (IFIP), IFIP Technical Committee (TC), and Working Group (WG) — Aims and Scopes (Continued)

Authoritative Guide	Summary	Category
WG 11.1 est. 1985, revised 1992	**WG11.1, Information Security Management**	Security

WG11.1, Information Security Management

Aims

• As management, at any level, may be increasingly held answerable for the reliable and secure operation of the information systems and services in their respective organizations in the same manner as they are for financial aspects of the enterprise, the Working Group (WG) will promote all aspects related to the management of information security.

• These aspects cover a wide range, from purely managerial aspects concerning information security, (like upper management awareness and responsibility for establishing and maintaining the necessary policy documents), to more technical aspects (like risk analysis, disaster recovery, and other technical tools) to support the information security management process

Scope

• To study and promote methods to make senior business management aware of the value of information as a corporate asset, and to get their commitment to implementing and maintaining the necessary objectives and policies to protect these assets

• To study and promote methods and ways to measure and assess the security level in a company and to convey these measures and assessments to management in an understandable way

• To research and develop new ways to identify information security threats and vulnerabilities that every organization must face

• To research and identify the effect of new and changed facilities and functions in new hardware and software on the management of information security

• To study and develop means and ways to help information security managers to assess their effectiveness and degree of control

• To address the problem of standards for information security

**Exhibit 10. International Federation for Information Processing (IFIP),
IFIP Technical Committee (TC), and Working Group (WG) — Aims and
Scopes (Continued)**

Authoritative Guide	Summary	Category
WG 11.2 est. 1985, revised 1992, 1995	**WG11.2, Small System Security** Aims • To investigate methods and issues in the area of information security, particularly those related to small systems Scope • To promote awareness and understanding of small systems security • To provide a forum for the discussion and understanding of small system security matters • To advance technologies and methodologies that support small systems security • To contribute, as feasible and appropriate, to international standards for small system security	Security
WG 11.3 est. 1987	**WG11.3, Database Security** Aims • To promote wider understanding of the risks to society of operating database systems that lack adequate measures for security or privacy • To encourage the application of existing technology for enhancing the security of database systems Scope To advance technologies that support: • the statement of security requirements for database systems • the design, implementation, and operation of database systems that include security functions • the assurance that the implemented database systems meet their security requirements	Security

Exhibit 10. International Federation for Information Processing (IFIP), IFIP Technical Committee (TC), and Working Group (WG) — Aims and Scopes (Continued)

Authoritative Guide	Summary	Category
WG 11.4 est. 1985, revised 1992, 1997	**WG11.4, Network Security** Aim • To study and promote internationally accepted processes that will enable management and technicians to fully understand their responsibility in respect to the reliable and secure operation of the information networks that support their organizations, their customers, or the general public. To study and promote education and training in the application of security principles, methods, and technologies to networking Scope • To promote the awareness and understanding of the network aspect of information systems security • To provide a forum for the discussion, understanding, and illumination of network security matters • To study and identify the managerial, procedural, and technical aspects of network security and hence to define the network security issues • To study and describe the risks that arise from embedding an information system in a network environment • To advance technologies and practices that support network security controls, make possible the statement of requirements for network security, and in general, advance the foundation for effective network security • To contribute, as feasible and appropriate, to international standards for network security	Security

Exhibit 10. International Federation for Information Processing (IFIP), IFIP Technical Committee (TC), and Working Group (WG) — Aims and Scopes (Continued)

Authoritative Guide	Summary	Category
WG 11.5 est. 1987, revised 1989 and 1991	**WG11.5, Systems Integrity and Control** Aims • To promote awareness of the need to ensure proper standards of integrity and control in information systems in order to ensure that data is complete and in accordance with its owners' expectations Scope • To study and promote the use of appropriate control measures to ensure that data integrity requirements are satisfied within information systems • To study and promote the use of advanced auditing tools and techniques as a means to identify integrity and control weaknesses • To promote EDP auditing function as a tool for senior management to obtain an independent and objective appraisal of the effectiveness and continuing appropriateness of integrity and control measures within information systems • To promote the mutual understanding of EDP audit, security, and development functions between personnel engaged in those functions	Audit, security

Exhibit 10. International Federation for Information Processing (IFIP), IFIP Technical Committee (TC), and Working Group (WG) — Aims and Scopes (Continued)

Authoritative Guide	Summary	Category
WG 11.8 est. 1991	**WG11.8, Information Security Education** Aims • To promote information security education and training at the university level and in government and industry Scope • To establish an international resource center for the exchange of information about education and training in information security • To develop model courses in information security at the university level • To encourage colleges and universities to include a suitable model course in information security at the graduate or undergraduate level in the disciplines of computer science, information systems, and public service • To develop information security modules that can be integrated into a business educational training program or introductory computer courses at the college or university level • To promote an appropriate module about information security to colleges and universities, industry, and government • To collect, exchange, and disseminate information relating to information security courses conducted by private organizations for industry • To collect and periodically disseminate an annotated bibliography of information security books, feature articles, reports, and other educational media	Security

Authoritative Guide

Editor-in-Chief: Carl Cargill, SunSoft (A division of Sun Microsystems). As the push for standardization becomes international in scope, understanding the development and use of standards is critical. Producers and users of standards in business, government research, and academia will benefit from StandardView's practical and theoretical information on all aspects of standardization with an emphasis on how standards affect the daily work of all IT professionals. See Exhibit 11.

APPENDICES

Exhibit 11. Association for Computing Machinery (ACM) StandardView

Authoritative Guide	Summary	Category
StandardView Volume 2, No. 2 June 1994	**Standardizing information technology security** Warwick Ford (Pages 64–71)	Security
StandardView Volume 2, No. 2 June 1994	**Using standards as a security policy tool** J. M. Ferris (Pages 72–77)	Security
StandardView Volume 2, No. 2 June 1994	**Internet security standards: past, present, and future** Stephen Kent (Pages 78–85)	Security
StandardView Volume 2, No. 2 June 1994	**The government information locator service: a user-based approach to standards** William E. Moen and Charles R. McClure (Pages 86–95)	Privacy
StandardView Volume 2, No. 3 September 1994	**Open geodata access through standards** Clem Henriksen, J. P. Lauzon, and Scott Morehouse (Pages 169–174)	Security
StandardView Volume 2, No. 3 September 1994	**SQL and beyond** Mark Ashworth (Pages 175–178)	Security
StandardView Volume 2, No. 4 December 1994	**Modeling NII services: future needs for standards and interoperability** Christopher Dabrowski, William Majurski, Wayne McCoy, and Shukri Wakid (Pages 203–217)	Privacy
StandardView Volume 2, No. 4 December 1994	**Federal networking standards: policy issues** David C. Wood (Pages 218–223)	Security, Privacy
StandardView Volume 3, No. 1 March 1995	**EDIFACT for business computers: has it succeeded?** Airi Salminen (Pages 33–42)	Privacy
StandardView Volume 3, No. 2 June 1995	**Arguments for weaker intellectual property protection in network industries** Joseph Farrell (Pages 46–49)	Privacy

Exhibit 11. Association for Computing Machinery (ACM) StandardView (Continued)

Authoritative Guide	Summary	Category
StandardView Volume 3, No. 2 June 1995	**Telecommunications standardization and intellectual property rights: a fundamental dilemma?** Mark Shurmer and Gary Lea (Pages 50–59)	Privacy
StandardView Volume 3, No. 2 June 1995	**Tension and synergism between standards and intellectual property** Oliver R. Smoot (Pages 60–67)	Privacy
StandardView Volume 3, No. 2 June 1995	**Economics of intellectual property protection for software: the proper role for copyright** Frederick R. Warren-Boulton, Kenneth C. Baseman, and Glenn A. Woroch (Pages 68–78)	Privacy
StandardView Volume 3, No. 3 September 1995	**Standardizing agent technology** Sankar Virdhagriswaran, Damian Osisek, and Pat O'Connor (Pages 96–101)	Privacy
StandardView Volume 4, No. 1 March 1996	**Recommendations for the global information highway: a matter of standards** Ken Krechmer (Pages 24–28)	Security, privacy
StandardView Volume 4, No. 3 September 1996	**The Internet Society of New Zealand: roles, goals, and ambitions** Roger Hicks (Pages 155–160)	Security
StandardView Volume 4, No. 4 December 1996	**Users and standardization — worlds apart? The example of electronic mail** Kai Jakobs, Rob Procter, and Robin Williams (Pages 183–191)	Privacy
StandardView Volume 5, No. 1 March 1997	**World Wide Web distributed authoring and versioning (WebDAV): an introduction** E. James, Jr. Whitehead (Pages 3–8)	Privacy
StandardView Volume 5, No. 1 March 1997	**Requirements for distributed authoring and versioning on the World Wide Web** J.A. Slein, F. Vitali, E.J. Whitehead, Jr. and D.G. Durand (Pages 17–24)	Privacy
StandardView Volume 5, No. 1 March 1997	**Justifying the need for distributed authoring: a compelling reason** Carl F. Cargill (Pages 25–29)	Privacy

Exhibit 11. Association for Computing Machinery (ACM) StandardView (Continued)

Authoritative Guide	Summary	Category
StandardView Volume 5, No. 1 March 1997	**The quest for information technology standards for the global information infrastructure** Michael D. Hogan and Shirley M. Radack (Pages 30–35)	Security, privacy
StandardView Volume 5, No. 3 September 1997	**Trust and traceability in electronic commerce** Dennis D. Steinauer, Shukri A. Wakid, and Stanley Rasberry (Pages 118–124)	Security, privacy
StandardView Volume 6, No. 2 June 1998	**Representing compatibility and standards: a case study of Web browsers** Giancarlo Succi, Paolo Predonzeni, Andrea Valerio, and Tullio Vernazza (Pages 69–75)	Privacy
StandardView Volume 6, No. 2 June 1998	**The business benefit of standards** Graham B. Bird (Pages 76–80)	Privacy
StandardView Volume 6, No. 2 June 1998	**Standards and innovation in technological dynamics** Dominique Foray (Pages 81–84)	Privacy
StandardView Volume 6, No. 2 June 1998	**User participation in standards setting — the panacea?** Kai Jakobs, Rob Procter, and Robin Williams (Pages 85–89)	Security, privacy
StandardView Volume 6, No. 2 June 1998	**Standards and standardization on the eve of a new century** Enrico Zaninotto (Pages 90–93)	Privacy
StandardView Volume 6, No. 3 June 1998	**Keeping an electronic commerce shop** Katy Dickinson (Pages 106–109)	Security
StandardView Volume 6, No. 3 June 1998	**Creating usable E-Commerce sites** Janice Anne Rohn (Pages 110–115)	Security
StandardView Volume 6, No. 3 June 1998	**E-Commerce and security** Whitfield Diffie (Pages 116–117)	Security

The Institute of Chartered Accountants in Australia (ICAA)

The Institute was established by Royal Charter in 1928 following antecedent bodies dating from 1885. It currently operates under a Supplemental (amending) Charter granted by the Governor-General on March 17, 1988. The Institute sets the technical and ethical standards for members and provides leadership for the profession. The ethical rulings issued by the Institute, along with current accounting and auditing standards, are binding on members. A major part of the Institute's activities involves representing members at the highest levels with governments, business and professional organizations, academic institutions, and the news media.

The Institute of Chartered Accountants in Australia (ICAA)
Level 14
37 York Street
Sydney NSW 2000 Australia
Telephone: 61-2-9290 1344
Facsimile: 61-2-9262 1512
Web site: http://www.icaa.org.au
E-mail: rebekah@icaa.org.au

Information Source

http://www.icaa.org.au or http://www.icaa.org.au/index.cfm

Authoritative Guide

The purpose of this auditing standard (AUS) is to establish standards and provide guidance on obtaining an understanding of the internal control structure and on audit risk and its components: inherent risk, control risk, and detection risk.

Auditing Guidance Statements (AGS) are issued by the Auditing Standards Board when the Board wishes to provide guidance on procedural matters, guidance on entity or industry specific issues, or believes an underlying principle in an auditing standard requires clarification, explanation, or elaboration. Auditing guidance statements do not establish new auditing standards, do not amend existing auditing standards, and are not mandatory. See Exhibit 12.

National Institute of Standards and Technology (NIST)

The major focus of NIST activities in IT is developing tests, measurements, proofs of concept, reference data, and other technical tools to support the development of pivotal, forward-looking technology. Under Section 512 of the Information Technology Reform Act of 1996 and the Computer Security Act of 1987, Public Law 104-106, NIST develops standards, guidelines, and associated methods and techniques for federal computer systems.

Exhibit 12. The Institute of Chartered Accountants in Australia (ICAA) Auditing Standard (AUS) and Auditing Guidance Statements (AGS)

Authoritative Guide	Summary	Category
AUS 214 August 1995	**AUS 214, Auditing in a CIS Environment** The purpose of this auditing standard (AUS) is to establish standards and provide guidance regarding auditing in a computer information systems (CIS) environment. For the purposes of AUSs, a CIS environment exists when a computer of any type or size is involved in the processing by an entity of financial information of significance to the audit, whether that computer is operated by the entity or a third party.	Audit
AUS 402 August 1995	**AUS 402, Risk Assessments and Internal Controls** The Information System .20 The auditor should obtain an understanding of the information system sufficient to identify and understand: (a) Major classes of transactions in the entity's operations (b) How such transactions are initiated (c) Significant accounting records and supporting documents and accounts in the financial report (d) The accounting and financial reporting process from the initiation of significant transactions and other events to their inclusion in the financial report .21 Obtaining an understanding of the information system would require the auditor to obtain an understanding of how the information database is held, updated, and secured, including supporting documentation.	Audit

Exhibit 12. The Institute of Chartered Accountants in Australia (ICAA) Auditing Standard (AUS) and Auditing Guidance Statements (AGS) (Continued)

Authoritative Guide	Summary	Category
AUS 404 August 1995	**AUS 404, Audit Implications Relating to Entities Using a Service Entity** .03 "Service entity" means an entity that provides services to the user to record, process, execute transactions, maintain related accountability for these transactions, or any combination thereof. Examples of such service entities include: (a) A computer service bureau that provides data processing functions for other entities .07 A user may employ a service entity to record various transactions and process-related data. For example, a user entity may engage a computer service bureau to process payrolls, orders, billings, collections, or specialized accounting functions such as credit card transactions or to maintain a general ledger system. When, for example, a service entity executes transactions at the specific authorization of the user (such as processing of check account transactions by a bank), or acts as simple custodian of assets (such as safe custody of share scrip), confirmation and/or inspection procedures performed by the user auditor (which corroborate the records maintained by the user entity) ordinarily constitute sufficient appropriate audit evidence concerning the existence of those transactions and assets.	Audit
AUS 512 August 1995	**AUS 512, Analytical Procedures** .19 The complex techniques are more advanced models of the simple quantitative procedures and are appropriate where financial relationships involve two or more variables. Their use may be facilitated by the use of computer programs. As with all quantitative techniques, the auditor uses the information provided by these models within the context of the knowledge of the entity's business that has been obtained and would exercise professional judgment in its evaluation.	Audit

Exhibit 12. The Institute of Chartered Accountants in Australia (ICAA) Auditing Standard (AUS) and Auditing Guidance Statements (AGS) (Continued)

Authoritative Guide	Summary	Category
AUS 514 April 1998	**AUS 514, Audit Sampling and Other Selective Testing Procedures** .16 Audit sampling for tests of control is generally appropriate when application of the control leaves evidence of performance (for example, initials of the credit manager on a sales invoice indicating credit approval or evidence of authorization of data input to a microcomputer-based data processing system).	Audit
AUS 604 August 1995	**AUS 604, Considering the Work of Internal Auditing** .12 When obtaining an understanding and performing a preliminary assessment of internal auditing, an important criterion is: (c) Technical competence: Whether internal auditing is performed by persons having adequate technical training and proficiency as internal auditors. The external auditor may, for example, review the policies for hiring and training the internal auditing staff and their experience and professional qualifications.	Audit
AUS 606 August 1995	**AUS 606, Using the Work of an Expert** .06 Although the auditor may use the work of an expert as audit evidence, the auditor retains full responsibility for the audit opinion on the financial report. .07 During the audit the auditor may need to obtain, in conjunction with the entity or independently, audit evidence in the form of reports, opinions, valuations, and statements of an expert.	Audit

Exhibit 12. The Institute of Chartered Accountants in Australia (ICAA) Auditing Standard (AUS) and Auditing Guidance Statements (AGS) (Continued)

Authoritative Guide	Summary	Category
AUS 804 April 1998	**AUS 804, The Audit of Prospective Financial Information** .16 The auditor should obtain a sufficient level of knowledge of the business to be able to evaluate whether all significant assumptions required for the preparation of the prospective financial information have been identified. The auditor would also need to become familiar with the entity's process for preparing prospective financial information, for example, by considering: (a) The internal controls over the system used to prepare prospective financial information and the expertise and experience of those persons preparing the prospective financial information (b) The nature of the documentation prepared by the entity supporting management's assumptions (c) The extent to which statistical, mathematical, and computer-assisted techniques are used and the reliability	Audit
AGS 1018 August 1995	**AGS 1018, CIS Environment — Stand-Alone Microcomputers** The purpose of this statement is to help the auditor implement AUS 214, "Auditing in a CIS Environment," by describing microcomputer systems used as stand-alone workstations. The statement describes the effects of the microcomputer on the internal control structure and on audit procedures.	Audit
AGS 1020 October 2001	**AGS 1020, CIS Environment — Online Computer Systems** The purpose of this statement is to help the auditor implement AUS 214, "Auditing in a CIS Environment," by describing online computer systems. The statement describes the effects of an online computer system on the internal control structure and on audit procedures. Computer systems that enable users to access data and programs directly through terminal devices are referred to as online computer systems. Such systems may be based on mainframe computers, minicomputers, or microcomputers structured in a network environment.	Audit

Exhibit 12. The Institute of Chartered Accountants in Australia (ICAA) Auditing Standard (AUS) and Auditing Guidance Statements (AGS) (Continued)

Authoritative Guide	Summary	Category
AGS 1022 October 2001	**AGS 1022, CIS Environment — Database Systems** The purpose of this statement is to help the auditor implement AUS 214, "Auditing in a CIS Environment," by describing online computer systems. The statement describes the effects of an online computer system on the internal control structure and on audit procedures. Database systems are comprised principally of two essential components — the database and the database management system (DBMS). Database systems interact with other hardware and software aspects of the overall computer system.	Audit
AGS 1034 April 1998	**AGS 1034, Implications for Management and Auditors of the Year 2000 System Issue** The Year 2000 issue has had much publicity, but although all entities should be aware of it, responses are varied, with some entities still doing little. The issue is simple to explain; it has risen because where computerized systems identify the year using two digits only, the digits 00 may be misinterpreted, for example, as 1900 or a special code or an error condition, potentially causing errors or operational failure of computerized systems. In addition, some computerized systems do not properly perform calculations with dates beginning in 1999 because these systems use the digits 99 in date fields to represent something other than the year 1999. The impact of these issues is not simple to predict because, even though the basic Year 2000 issue is well publicized, there are new issues emerging and, as a result, appropriate further guidance may need to be developed. The Year 2000 issue may manifest itself before, on, or after January 2000, and its effects on financial reporting and operations may range from inconsequential errors to entity failure.	Audit

National Institute of Standards and Technology
Conformance Testing Group
Building 820, Room 562
Gaithersburg, MD 20899-0001
Telephone: (301) 975-3283
Facsimile: (301) 948-6213
Web site: http://www.itl.nist.gov
e-mail: itlab@nist.gov

Information Source

http://www.itl.nist.gov

Authoritative Guide

Under the Information Technology Management Reform Act (Public Law 104-106), the Secretary of Commerce approves standards and guidelines that are developed by the NIST for federal computer systems. These standards and guidelines are issued by NIST as Federal Information Processing Standards (FIPS) for use government-wide. NIST develops FIPS when there are compelling federal government requirements such as security and interoperability, and there are no acceptable industry standards or solutions. See Exhibit 13.

Exhibit 13. National Institute of Standards and Technology (NIST) Federal Information Processing Standards (FIPS)

Authoritative Guide	Summary	Category
FIPS 31 June 1974	**FIPS 31, Guidelines for Automatic Data Processing Physical Security and Risk Management** Provides guidance to federal organizations in developing physical security and risk management programs for their ADP facilities. Can be used as a checklist for planning and evaluating security of computer systems.	Security

**Exhibit 13. National Institute of Standards and Technology (NIST) Federal
Information Processing Standards (FIPS) (Continued)**

Authoritative Guide	Summary	Category
FIPS 46-3 October 25, 1999	**Data Encryption Standard (DES)** The selective application of technological and related procedural safeguards is an important responsibility of every federal organization in providing adequate security to its electronic data systems. This publication specifies two cryptographic algorithms, the Data Encryption Standard (DES) and the Triple Data Encryption Algorithm (TDEA), which may be used by federal organizations to protect sensitive data. Protection of data during transmission or while in storage may be necessary to maintain the confidentiality and integrity of the information represented by the data. The algorithms uniquely define the mathematical steps required to transform data into a cryptographic cipher and also to transform the cipher back to the original form. The DES is being made available for use by federal agencies within the context of a total security program consisting of physical security procedures, good information management practices, and computer system/network access controls. This revision supersedes FIPS 46-2 in its entirety.	Security
FIPS 48 April 1, 1977	**FIPS 48, Guidelines on Evaluation of Techniques for Automated Personal Identification** Discusses the performance of personal identification devices, how to evaluate them, and considerations for their use within the context of computer system security.	Security, privacy
FIPS 73 June 30, 1980	**FIPS 73, Guidelines for Security of Computer Applications** Describes the different security objectives for a computer application, explains the control measures that can be used, and identifies the decisions that should be made at each stage in the life-cycle of a sensitive computer application. For use in planning, developing, and operating computer systems which require protection.	Security
FIPS 74 April 1, 1981	**FIPS 74, Guidelines for Implementing and Using the NBS Data Encryption Standard** Provides guidance for the use of cryptographic techniques when such techniques are required to protect sensitive or valuable computer data. For use in conjunction with FIPS PUB 81.	Security, privacy

Exhibit 13. National Institute of Standards and Technology (NIST) Federal Information Processing Standards (FIPS) (Continued)

Authoritative Guide	Summary	Category
FIPS 81 December 2, 1980	**FIPS 81, DES Modes of Operation** Defines four modes of operation for the DES that may be used in a wide variety of applications. The modes specify how data will be encrypted (cryptographically protected) and decrypted (returned to original form). This standard has been adopted as a voluntary industry standard, ANSI X3.106-1983.	Security, privacy
FIPS 83 September 29, 1980	**FIPS 83, Guideline on User Authentication Techniques for Computer Network Access Control** Provides guidance in the selection and implementation of techniques for authenticating the users of remote terminals in order to safeguard against unauthorized access to computers and computer networks.	Security
FIPS 102 September 27, 1983	**FIPS 102, Guideline for Computer Security Certification and Accreditation** Describes how to establish and how to carry out a certification and accreditation program for computer security. Certification consists of a technical evaluation of a sensitive system to see how well it meets its security requirements. Accreditation is the official management authorization for the operation of the system and is based on the certification process.	Security
FIPS 112 May 30, 1985	**FIPS 112, Password Usage** Defines 10 factors to be considered in the design, implementation, and use of access control systems that are based on passwords. It specifies minimum security criteria for such systems and provides guidance for selecting additional security criteria for password systems that must meet higher security requirements.	Security
FIPS 113 May 30, 1985	**FIPS 113, Computer Data Authentication** Specifies a Data Authentication Algorithm (DAA) that, when applied to computer data, automatically and accurately detects unauthorized modifications, both intentional and accidental. Based on FIPS PUB 46, this standard is compatible with requirements adopted by the Department of Treasury and the banking community to protect electronic fund transfer transactions.	Security

Exhibit 13. National Institute of Standards and Technology (NIST) Federal Information Processing Standards (FIPS) (Continued)

Authoritative Guide	Summary	Category
FIPS 140-2 May 25, 2001	**Security Requirements for Cryptographic Modules — (Supersedes FIPS PUB 140-1, 1994 January 11)** FIPS 140-2 was recently approved by the Secretary of Commerce. It specifies the security requirements that will be satisfied by a cryptographic module, providing four increasing, qualitative levels intended to cover a wide range of potential applications and environments. The areas covered, relating to the secure design and implementation of a cryptographic module, include specification; ports and interfaces; roles, services, and authentication; finite state model; physical security; operational environment; cryptographic key management; electromagnetic interference/electromagnetic compatibility (EMI/EMC); self-tests; design assurance; and mitigation of other attacks.	Security, privacy
FIPS 161-2 May 22, 1996	**FIPS 161-2, Electronic Data Interchange (EDI)** FIPS 161-2 adopts, with specific conditions, the families of EDI standards known as X12, UN/EDIFACT, and HL7 developed by national and international standards developing organizations. FIPS 161-2 does not mandate the implementation of EDI systems within the federal government, but requires the use of the identified families of standards when federal agencies and organizations implement EDI systems.	Privacy
FIPS 180-1 April 17, 1995	**FIPS 180-1, Secure Hash Standard (SHS)** Specifies a Secure Hash Algorithm to be used by both the transmitter and intended receiver of a message in computing and verifying a digital signature.	Privacy
FIPS 181 October 5, 1993	**FIPS 181, Automated Password Generator (APG)** Specifies a standard to be used by federal organizations that require computer generated pronounceable passwords to authenticate the personal identity of an automated data processing (ADP) system user and to authorize access to system resources. The standard describes an automated password generation algorithm that randomly creates simple pronounceable syllables as passwords. The password generator accepts input from a random number generator based on the Data Encryption Standard (DES) cryptographic algorithm defined in Federal Information Processing Standard 46-2.	Security

Exhibit 13. National Institute of Standards and Technology (NIST) Federal Information Processing Standards (FIPS) (Continued)

Authoritative Guide	Summary	Category
FIPS 185 February 9, 1994	**FIPS 185, Escrowed Encryption Standard (EES)** This nonmandatory standard provides an encryption/decryption algorithm and a Law Enforcement Access Field (LEAF) creation method that may be implemented in electronic devices and may be used at the option of government agencies to protect government telecommunications. The algorithm and the LEAF creation method are classified and are referenced, but not specified, in the standard. Electronic devices implementing this standard may be designed into cryptographic modules that are integrated into data security products and systems for use in data security applications. The LEAF is used in a key escrow system that provides for decryption of telecommunications when access to the telecommunications is lawfully authorized.	Security
FIPS 186-2 January 27, 2000	**FIPS 186-2 Digital Signature Standard (DSS)** This standard specifies algorithms appropriate for applications requiring a digital, rather than written, signature. A digital signature is represented in a computer as a string of binary digits. A digital signature is computed using a set of rules and a set of parameters such that the identity of the signatory and integrity of the data can be verified. An algorithm provides the capability to generate and verify signatures. Signature generation makes use of a private key to generate a digital signature. Signature verification makes use of a public key that corresponds to, but is not the same as, the private key. Each user possesses a private and public key pair. Private keys are kept secret; public keys may be shared. Anyone can verify the signature of a user by employing that user's public key. Signature generation can be performed only by the possessor of the user's private key. This revision supersedes FIPS 186-1 in its entirety.	Security
FIPS 188 September 6, 1994	**FIPS 188, Standard Security Label for Information Transfer** Defines a security label syntax for information exchanged over data networks and provides label encodings for use at the application and network layers. ANSI/TIA/EIA-606-1993	Security

**Exhibit 13. National Institute of Standards and Technology (NIST) Federal
Information Processing Standards (FIPS) (Continued)**

Authoritative Guide	Summary	Category
FIPS 190 September 28, 1994	**FIPS 190, Guideline for the Use of Advanced Authentication Technology Alternatives** Describes the primary alternative methods for verifying the identities of computer system users, and provides recommendations to federal agencies and departments for the acquisition and use of technology that supports these methods.	Security
FIPS 191 November 9, 1994	**FIPS 191, Guideline for the Analysis of Local Area Network Security** Discusses threats and vulnerabilities and considers technical security services and security mechanisms	Security
FIPS 196 February 18, 1997	**FIPS 196, Entity Authentication Using Public Key Cryptography** Specifies two challenge–response protocols by which entities in a computer system may authenticate their identities to one another. These protocols may be used during session initiation and at any other time that entity authentication is necessary. Depending on which protocol is implemented, either one or both entities involved may be authenticated. The defined protocols are derived from an international standard for entity authentication based on public key cryptography, which uses digital signatures and random number challenges.	Security, privacy
FIPS 197 November 26, 2001	**FIPS 197, Advanced Encryption Standard (AES)** The Advanced Encryption Standard (AES) specifies an FIPS-approved cryptographic algorithm that can be used to protect electronic data. The AES algorithm is a symmetric block cipher that can encrypt (encipher) and decrypt (decipher) information. Encryption converts data to an unintelligible form called ciphertext; decrypting the ciphertext converts the data back into its original form, called plaintext.	Security, privacy

Exhibit 13. National Institute of Standards and Technology (NIST) Federal Information Processing Standards (FIPS) (Continued)

Authoritative Guide	Summary	Category
FIPS 198 March 2002	**The Keyed-Hash Message Authentication Code (HMAC)** This standard describes a keyed-hash message authentication code (HMAC), a mechanism for message authentication, using cryptographic hash functions. HMAC can be used with any iterative approved cryptographic hash function, in combination with a shared secret key. The cryptographic strength of HMAC depends on the properties of the underlying hash function. The HMAC specification in this standard is a generalization of Internet RFC 2104, HMAC, Keyed-Hashing for Message Authentication, and ANSI X9.71, Keyed Hash Message Authentication Code.	Security, privacy

General Accounting Office (GAO)

The U.S. General Accounting Office (GAO) is a nonpartisan agency within the legislative branch of the government. GAO conducts audits, surveys, investigations, and evaluations of federal programs. This work is done at the request of congressional committees or members, or to fulfill GAO's specifically mandated or basic legislative requirements. GAO's findings and recommendations are published as reports to Congressional members or delivered as testimony to Congressional committees.

U.S. General Accounting Office
P.O. Box 37050
Washington, D.C. 20013
Telephone: (202) 512-6000
Facsimile: (202) 512-6061
Web site: http://www.gao.gov
e-mail: documents@gao.gov

Information Source

http://www.gao.gov

1. Government Financial Management TOPICS, Association of Government Accountants, May/June 1998, Vol. 37, No. 5.

Authoritative Guide

Government Accounting Standards (The Yellow Book) contains standards for audits of government organizations, programs, activities, and functions, and of government assistance received by contractors, non-profit organizations, and other nongovernment organizations. These standards, often referred to as generally accepted government auditing standards (GAGAS), are to be followed by auditors and audit organizations when required by law, regulation, agreement, contract, or policy. They pertain to auditors' professional qualifications, the quality of audit effort, and the characteristics of professional and meaningful audit reports. Other guides provide assistance, including IMTEC (Information Technology), OP (Office of Policy), and AIMD (Accounting and Information Management Division).

Exhibit 14. General Accounting Office (GAO) Government Accounting Standards (The Yellow Book)

Authoritative Guide	Summary	Category
GAGAS 2.5 June 1994	**Financial Audits 2.5** Financial related audits may, for example, include audits of the following items: c. Internal controls over financial reporting and/or safeguarding assets, including controls using computer-based systems	Audit
GAGAS 3.8 June 1994	**Continuing Education Requirement 3.8** The continuing education and training may include such topics as current developments in audit methodology, accounting, assessment of internal controls, principles of management or supervision, financial management, statistical sampling, evaluation design, and data analysis. It may also include subjects related to the auditor's field of work, such as public administration, public policy and structure, industrial engineering, economics, social sciences, or computer science.	Audit

Exhibit 14. General Accounting Office (GAO) Government Accounting Standards (The Yellow Book) (Continued)

Authoritative Guide	Summary	Category
GAGAS 4.29 June 1994	**Safeguarding Controls 4.29** Understanding these safeguarding controls can help auditors assess the risk that financial statements could be materially misstated. For example, an understanding of an auditee's safeguarding controls can help auditors recognize risk factors such as: c. Lack of controls over computer processing, such as lack of controls over access to applications that initiate or control the movement of assets d. Failure to develop or communicate adequate policies and procedures for security of data or assets, such as allowing unauthorized personnel to have ready access to data or assets	Audit, Security
GAGAS 6.56 June 1994	**Test of Evidence 6.56** The auditors' approach to determining the sufficiency, competence, and relevance of evidence depends on the source of the information that constitutes the evidence. Information sources include original data gathered by auditors and existing data gathered by either the auditee or a third party. Data from any of these sources may be obtained from computer-based systems.	Audit
GAGAS 6.62 June 1994	**Test of Evidence 6.62** **Validity and Reliability of Data from Computer-Based Systems** Auditors should obtain sufficient, competent, and relevant evidence that computer-processed data are valid and reliable when those data are significant to the auditors' findings. This work is necessary regardless of whether the data are provided to auditors or auditors independently extract them. Auditors should determine if other auditors have worked to establish the validity and reliability of the data or the effectiveness of the controls over the system that produced the data. If they have, auditors may be able to use that work. If not, auditors may determine the validity and reliability of computer-processed data by direct tests of the data. Auditors can reduce the direct tests of the data if they test the effectiveness of general and application controls over computer-processed data, and these tests support the conclusion that the controls are effective.	Audit

Exhibit 14. General Accounting Office (GAO) Government Accounting Standards (The Yellow Book) (Continued)

Authoritative Guide	Summary	Category
IMTEC 8.1.4 December 1992	**IMTEC 8.1.4 — Information Technology: An Audit Guide for Assessing Acquisition Risk** This guide is intended for use in planning and conducting risk assessments of computer hardware and software, telecommunications, and system development acquisitions. A risk assessment is the process of identifying potential risks in a system under development and then determining the significance of each risk in terms of its likelihood and impact on the acquisition's cost, schedule, and ability to meet the agency's needs. Such assessments may have their greatest impact if carried out early, when an agency can more easily alter its acquisition plans and strategy to manage and control the identified risks.	Audit
IMTEC 11.1.2 August 1992	**IMTEC 11.1.2 — Planning, Preparing, Documenting, and Referencing SAS Products** The SAS system is a software system for data analysis. It is primarily used for information storage and retrieval, data modification and programming, report writing, statistical analysis, graphics, and file handling. It is used extensively within the General Accounting Office (GAO) to retrieve, analyze, and present data. Evaluators, programmers, and analysts use SAS because it is comprehensive and flexible. Because properly planning, preparing, documenting, and referencing SAS products can be intricate and demanding, this guide was developed to enable GAO's SAS users to develop products that conform to GAO quality control and workpaper documentation standards. The guide recommends SAS features that are consistent with GAO standards and warns against using those that are not. Although SAS has nonaudit applications, such as management information systems, this guide is intended for audit and program evaluation applications. While this guide is specific to SAS, the principles discussed here apply to other analytical packages.	Audit

Exhibit 14. General Accounting Office (GAO) Government Accounting Standards (The Yellow Book) (Continued)

Authoritative Guide	Summary	Category
GAO-03-273G External Version 1 October 2002	**GAO-03-273G — Assessing the Reliability of Computer-Processed Data** The purpose of this guide is to help GAO staff meet the Yellow Book standard for ensuring that computer-based data are reliable — complete and accurate. The guide also provides a helpful conceptual framework to expedite job performance and help staff address standards for assessing internal controls and compliance with applicable laws and regulations.	Audit
GAO–01-121G February 2001	**Electronic Law Enforcement: Introduction to Investigations in an Electronic Environment GAO-01-121G** Guidance from GAO on how to proceed with investigations in a computer-based environment	Audit
AIMD 98-68 May 1998	**Executive Guide: Information Security Management: Learning From Leading Organizations GAO/AIMD-98-68** Increased computer interconnectivity and the popularity of the Internet are offering organizations of all types unprecedented opportunities to improve operations by reducing paper processing, cutting costs, and sharing information. However, the success of many of these efforts depends, in part, on an organization's ability to protect the integrity, confidentiality, and availability of the data and systems it relies on. This guide is one of a series of GAO publications that is intended to define actions federal officials can take to better manage their information resources.	Audit
GAO-01-376G February 2001	**Executive Guide: Maximizing the Success of Chief Information Officers: Learning from Leading Organizations GAO-01-376G** Briefing by CIOs from leading organizations and best practices achieved	Audit
AIMD-12.19.6 June 2001	**Federal Information System Controls Audit Manual: Volume I Financial Statement Audits. AIMD-12.19.6** Download appendices 1–4 and 10 that allow users to enter data to support the gathering and analysis of audit evidence	Audit

Exhibit 14. General Accounting Office (GAO) Government Accounting Standards (The Yellow Book) (Continued)

Authoritative Guide	Summary	Category
AIMD 98-89 March 1998	**AIMD 98-89 Measuring Performance and Demonstrating Results of Information Technology Investments** The Government Performance and Results Act of 1993 requires government executives to focus on defining missions, setting goals, measuring performance, and reporting accomplishments. In addition, with the passage of the Federal Acquisition Streamlining Act of 1994 (FASA) and the Clinger–Cohen Act of 1996, performance-based and results-oriented decision making is now required for all major investments in IT. Clearly, this intense focus on results is one of the most important management issues now confronting federal agencies. To assist federal agencies in understanding and devising effective IT measurement implementation approaches, GAO examined certain public and private organizations well known for their IT performance, leadership, and management expertise. Similar to our past efforts examining comprehensive information management practices of other leading organizations, the GAO has taken the lessons learned from these organizations and developed a suggested framework for agencies to consider when designing and implementing its IT performance management approaches. GAO has briefed numerous CIOs, agency executives, and agency IT managers on its work as part of its effort to advance a pragmatic understanding of what is required to effectively measure the contribution of IT to mission performance and program outcomes. By using comprehensive performance information, more informed decisions can be made about IT investments at a time when resources are limited and public demands for better government service are high. Ultimately, the success of results-oriented reform legislation will demand concerted management effort and long-term commitment. The key practices and steps outlined in this guide can help agencies achieve success.	Audit

Exhibit 14. General Accounting Office (GAO) Government Accounting Standards (The Yellow Book) (Continued)

Authoritative Guide	Summary	Category
AIMD 00 21.3.1 November 1999	**AIMD 00 21.3.1 Standards for Internal Control in the Federal Government** These standards define the minimum level of quality acceptable for internal control in government and provide the basis against which internal control is to be evaluated. These standards apply to all aspects of an agency's operations: programmatic, financial, and compliance. However, they are not intended to limit or interfere with duly granted authority related to developing legislation, rule-making, or other discretionary policy-making in an agency. These standards provide a general framework. In implementing these standards, management is responsible for developing the detailed policies, procedures, and practices to fit their agency's operations and to ensure that they are built into and an integral part of operations.	Audit
GAO-02-121 January 2002	**Human Services Integration: Results of a GAO Cosponsored Conference on Modernizing Information Systems, GAO-02-121** Issues involving the modernization of information today — complexities, changing technology, cost of change, management issues and problems	
GAO/ AIMD-10.1.13 February 1997	**Information Technology Investment Evaluation Guide. Assessing Risks and Returns: A Guide for Evaluating Federal Agencies' IT Investment Decision Making, GAO/AIMD-10.1.13** Guide on how to assess and evaluate IT investment decisions	
GAO/ AIMD-00-33 November 1999	**Information Security Risk Assessment: Practices of Leading Organizations, GAO/AIMD-00-33** Practices of some of the leading organization in performing information security risk assessments	

International Organization of Supreme Audit Institutions (INTOSAI)

The International Organization of Supreme Audit Institutions (INTOSAI) is the professional organization of Supreme Audit Institutions (SAIs) in countries that belong to the United Nations or its specialized agencies. SAIs play a major role in auditing government accounts and operations and in promoting sound financial management and accountability in their governments. INTOSAI supports its members in this task by providing opportunities to share information and experiences about the auditing and evaluation challenges facing them in today's changing and increasingly interdependent world. INTOSAI was founded in 1953 and has grown from the original 34 countries to a membership of 175 SAIs.

INTOSAI — Austrian Court of Audit
Rechnungshof, Fach 240
A-1033 VIENNA
AUSTRIA
Telephone: + 43 (1) 711 71 8456
Facsimile: + 43 (1) 718 94 25
Web site: http://www.intosai.org

Information Source

http://www.intosai.org

Authoritative Guide

INTOSAI offers two guidelines.

Auditing Standards

Auditing Standards Committee, Chair: Riksrevisionsverket (The Swedish National Audit Office), Sweden

Issued by the Auditing Standards Committee at the XIVth Congress of INTOSAI in 1992 in Washington, D.C., as amended by the XVth Congress of INTOSAI 1995 in Cairo, Egypt.

Guidelines for Internal Control Standards

Internal Control Standards Committee, Chair: Állami Számvevöszék (State Audit Office), Hungary

Issued by Internal Control Standards Committee, International Organization of Supreme Audit Institutions, June 1992. See Exhibit 15.

Exhibit 15. International Organization of Supreme Audit Institutions (INTOSAI) Auditing Standards and Guidelines for Internal Control Standards

Authoritative Guide	Summary	Category
AS No. 2	2. The INTOSAI auditing standards consist of four parts: (a) Basic postulates (b) General standards (c) Field standards (d) Reporting standards INTOSAI has developed these standards to provide a framework for the establishment of procedures and practices to be followed in the conduct of an audit, including audits of computer-based systems. They should be viewed in the particular constitutional, legal, and other circumstances of the Supreme Audit Institution (SAI).	Audit
AS No. 12	12. SAIs often carry out activities that by strict definition do not qualify as audits, but which contribute to better government. Examples of nonaudit work may include: (a) Gathering data without conducting substantial analysis (b) Legal work (c) An information mission of the elected assembly as regards the examination of draft budgets (d) An assistance mission for members of the elected assemblies as regards investigations and consultations of SAIs' files (e) Administrative activities (f) Computer-processing functions. These nonaudit activities provide valuable information to decision makers and should be of consistently high quality.	Audit
AS No. 144	144. Where accounting or other information systems are computerized, the auditor should determine whether internal controls are functioning properly to ensure the integrity, reliability, and completeness of the data.	Audit

745

Exhibit 15. International Organization of Supreme Audit Institutions (INTOSAI) Auditing Standards and Guidelines for Internal Control Standards (Continued)

Authoritative Guide	Summary	Category
AS No. 153	153. The audit findings, conclusions, and recommendations must be based on evidence. Since auditors seldom have the opportunity of considering all information about the audited entity, it is crucial that the data collection and sampling techniques are carefully chosen. When computer-based system data are an important part of the audit and the data reliability is crucial to accomplishing the audit objective, auditors need to satisfy themselves that the data are reliable and relevant.	Audit
ICS No. 68	68. It may be appropriate for various central organizations to become involved to some extent in setting internal controls to be followed by all agencies. In some instances, the controls may be quite specific (for example, in matters relating to revenue collections, contract award, specifications for computerized information systems, and human resource management). In other areas, especially those dealing with managerial controls, the controls may have to be more general. In either situation, the internal controls must permit the exercise of managerial judgment and initiative aimed at improving economy, efficiency, and effectiveness.	Audit

Appendix IV
Glossary

abend   The abnormal termination of a computer application or job because of a nonsystematic condition or a failure that causes a program to halt.

acceptance confidence level   The degree of certainty in a statement of probabilities that a conclusion is correct. In sampling, a specified confidence level is expressed as a percentage of certainty.

acceptance testing   The formal testing conducted to determine whether a software system satisfies its acceptance criteria. It enables the customer to determine whether to accept the system or not.

access   The ability and the means necessary to approach, store, or retrieve data or to communicate with or make use of any resources of a computer information system.

access category   An authorization that defines the resources in a computer-based system to which a user, program, or process is granted access.

access control   The process of allowing only authorized users, programs, or other computer systems (i.e., networks) to access the resources of a computer system.

access control mechanisms   Hardware, software, or firmware features, and operating and management procedures in various combinations designed to detect and prevent unauthorized access and to permit authorized access to a computer system.

access list   A catalog of users, programs, or processes and the specifications of the access categories to which each is assigned.

access period   A segment of time, generally expressed on a daily or weekly basis, during which access rights prevail.

access type   The nature of access granted to a particular device, program, or file (e.g., read, write, execute, append, modify, delete, or create).

accountability   The quality or state that enables attempted and committed violations of computer systems security to be traced to individuals who may then be held responsible.

accumulator   An area of storage in memory used to develop totals of units or items being computed.

active wire-tapping   The attachment of an unauthorized device (e.g., a computer terminal) to a communications circuit to gain access to data by generating false messages or control signals or by altering the communications of legitimate users.

Ada   A programming language that allows use of structured techniques for program design; a concise but powerful language designed to fill government requirements for real-time applications.

adaptive filter Prompts user to rate products or situations and also monitors your actions over time to find out what you like and dislike.

adaptivity The ability of intelligent agents to discover, learn, and take action independently.

add-on security The retrofitting of protection mechanisms, implemented by hardware, firmware, or software, on a computer system that has become operational.

administrative security The management constraints, operational procedures, accountability procedures, and supplemental controls established to provide an acceptable level of protection for sensitive data.

adware Software to generate ads that installs itself on your computer when you download some other (usually free) program from the Web.

affiliate programs Arrangements made between E-commerce sites that direct users from one site to the other and by which, if a sale is made as a result, the originating site receives a commission.

agent In the Client/Server Model, the part of the system that performs information preparation and exchange on behalf of a client or server application.

aging The identification, by date, of unprocessed or retained items in a file. This is usually done by date of transaction and classifying items according to ranges of data.

alphabetic test The check on whether an element of data contains only alphabetic or blank characters.

alphanumeric A character set that includes numeric digits, alphabetic characters, and other special symbols.

American National Standards Institute (ANSI) The agency that recommends standards for computer hardware, software, and firmware design and use.

American Standard Code for Information Interchange (ASCII) A byte-oriented coding system based on an 8-bit code and used primarily to format information for transfer in a data communications environment.

analysis and design phase The phase of the systems development life cycle in which an existing system is studied in detail and its functional specifications are generated.

anonymous Web browsing (AWB) Services hide your identity from the Web sites you visit.

anti-virus software Detects and removes or quarantines computer viruses.

application Computer software used to perform a distinct function. Also used to describe the function itself.

application architects IT professionals who can design creative technology-based business solutions.

application generation subsystem Contains facilities to help you develop transaction-intensive applications.

application layer The top-most layer in the Open Systems Interconnection (OSI) Reference Model providing such data communication service is invoked through a software package.

application program Interface (API)   A set of calling conventions defining how a service is invoked through a software package.

application service provider (ASP)   Provides an outsourcing service for business software applications.

application software   Software that enables you to solve specific problems or perform specific tasks.

arithmetic operator   In programming activities, a symbol representing an arithmetic calculation or process.

annual loss expectancy (ALE)   In risk assessment, the average monetary value of losses per year.

arithmetic logic unit (ALU)   A component of the computer's processing unit, in which arithmetic and matching operations are performed.

array   Consecutive storage areas in memory that are identified by the same name. The elements (or groups) within these storage areas are accessed through subscripts.

artificial intelligence (AI)   A field of study involving techniques and methods under which computers can simulate human intellectual activities such as learning.

artificial neural network (ANN)   Also called a neural network; an artificial intelligence system that is capable of finding and differentiating patterns.

ASCII   See American Standard Code for Information Interchange.

assembler language   A computer programming language in which alphanumeric symbols represent computer operations and memory addresses. Each assembler instruction translates into a single machine-language instruction.

assembler program   A program language translator that converts assembler programs into machine code.

assertion   A logical expression specifying a program state that must exist or a set of conditions that program variables must satisfy at a particular point during program execution.

association control service element (ACSE)   Part of the application layer of the OSI Model. ASCE provides the means to exchange authentication information coming from the Specific Application Service Element (SASE) of the OSI Model.

asynchronous transfer mode (ATM)   A transfer mode in which data is transmitted in the form of 53-byte units called "cells." Each cell consists of a 5-byte header and a 48-byte payload. The term "asynchronous" in this context refers to the fact that cells from any one particular source need not be periodically spaced within the overall cell stream. In other words, users are not assigned a set position in a recurring frame as is common in circuit switching.

audio output   Voice synthesizers that create audible signals resembling a human voice out of computer-generated output.

audio response system   The method of delivering output by using audible signals and transmitters that simulate a spoken language.

audit   An independent review and examination of system records and activities that test for the adequacy of system controls, ensure compliance with established policy and operational procedures, and recommend any indicated changes in controls, policies, and procedures.

audit risk   The probable unfavorable monetary effect related to the occurrence of an undesirable event or condition.

audit trail   A chronological record of system activities that is sufficient to enable the reconstruction, review, and examination of each event in a transaction from inception to output of final results.

authentication   The act of identifying or verifying the eligibility of a station, originator, or individual to access specific categories of information. Typically, a measure designed to protect against fraudulent transmissions by establishing the validity of a transmission, message, station, or originator.

authorization   The granting of right of access to a user, program, or process.

autofilter function   Filters a list and allows you to hide all the rows in a list except those that match criteria you specify.

automated security monitoring   The use of automated procedures to ensure that the security controls implemented within a computer system or network are not circumvented or violated.

automatic speech recognition (ASR)   A system that not only captures spoken words but also distinguishes word groupings to form sentences.

autonomy   The ability of an intelligent agent to act without your telling it every step to take.

B2B marketplace   An internet-based service that brings together many buyers and sellers.

backbone   The primary connectivity mechanism of a hierarchical distributed system. All systems that have connectivity to an intermediate system on the backbone are assured of connectivity to each other. This does not prevent systems from setting up private arrangements with each other to bypass the backbone for reasons of cost, performance, or security.

backbone network   A network that interconnects various computer networks and mainframe computers in an enterprise. The backbone provides the structure through which computers communicate.

back-propagation neural network   A neural network trained by someone.

backup operation   A method of operation used to complete essential tasks (as identified by risk analysis) subsequent to the disruption of the information processing facility and continuing to do so until the facility is sufficiently restored.

backup procedures   Provisions made for the recovery of data files and program libraries and for the restart or replacement of computer equipment after the occurrence of a system failure or disaster.

backward chaining   A process related to an expert system inference engine that starts with a hypothesis and attempts to confirm that the hypothesis is consistent with information in the knowledge base.

bandwidth   The range of frequencies assigned to a channel or circuit. The difference expressed in hertz (cycles per second) between the highest and lowest frequencies of the transmission band.

banner ad   A small ad on one Web site that advertises the products and services of another business.

bar code   A series of solid bars of different widths used to encode data. Special optical character recognition (OCR) devices can read this data.

bar code reader   Captures information that exists in the form of vertical bars whose width and distance from each other determine a number.

baseband   Characteristic of any network technology that uses a single carrier frequency and requires all stations attached to the network to participate in every transmission. See broadband.

BASIC   See Beginner's All-Purpose Symbolic Instruction Code.

basic text formatting tag   HTML tags that allow you to specify formatting for text.

batch control   A computer information processing technique in which numeric fields are totaled and records are tabulated to provide a comparison check for subsequent processing results.

baud   Signal or state change during data transmission. Each state change can be equal to multiple bits, so the actual bit rate during data transmission may exceed the baud rate.

Beginner's All-Purpose Symbolic Instruction Code (BASIC)   A programming language designed in the 1960s to teach students how to program and to facilitate learning. The powerful language syntax was designed especially for time-sharing systems.

benchmark test   A simulation evaluation conducted before purchasing or leasing equipment to determine how well hardware, software, and firmware perform.

between-the-lines entry   Access obtained through the use of active wiretapping by an unauthorized user to a momentarily inactive terminal of a legitimate user assigned to a communications channel.

binary digit   A state of function represented by the digit 0 or 1.

biometrics   The use of one's physical characteristics such as fingerprints, blood vessels in the retina of the eye, and the sound of one's voice to provide identification.

bit   A binary value represented by an electronic component that has a value of 0 or 1.

bits per second (bps)   The speed at which bits are sent during data transmission.

black-hat hackers   Cyber vandals.

blocking factor   The number of records appearing between interblock gaps on magnetic storage media.

block structure   In programming, a segment of code that can be treated as an independent module.

bluetooth   Technology that provides entirely wireless connections for all kinds of communication devices.

bounds checking   The testing of computer program results for access to storage outside its authorized limits.

bounds register   A hardware or firmware register that holds an address specifying a storage boundary.

branch   An alteration of the normal sequential execution of program statements.

brevity lists   A coding system that reduces the time required to transmit information by representing long, stereotyped sentences with only a few characters.

bridge   A device that connects two or more physical networks and forwards packets between them. Bridges can usually be made to filter packets, that is, to forward only certain traffic.

broadband   Characteristic of any network that multiplexes multiple, independent network carriers onto a single cable.

broadcast   A packet delivery system where a copy of a given packet is given to all hosts attached to the network. Example: Ethernet.

browser-safe colors   A range of 216 colors that can be represented using 8 bits and are visible in all browsers.

browsing   The searching of computer storage to locate or acquire information without necessarily knowing whether it exists or in what format.

buffer   A storage location used to compensate for differences in the rate of speed of data being transferred between devices.

bug   A coded program statement containing a logical or syntactical error.

burst   The separation of multiple-copy printout forms into individual sheets.

bus   A data path that connects the CPU, input, output, and storage devices.

business intelligence   Knowledge about customers, competitors, partners, and own internal operations. Business intelligence from information.

business process   A standardized set of activities that accomplishes a specific task such as processing a customer's order.

business process reengineering (BPR)   The reinventing of a process within a business.

business requirement   A detailed knowledge worker request that the system must meet to be successful.

business to business (B2B)   Companies whose customers are primarily other businesses.

business to consumer (B2C)   Companies whose customers are primarily individuals.

buyer agent or shopping bot   An intelligent agent or application on a Web site that helps customers find the products and services they want.

byte   The basic unit of storage for many computers; typically, one configuration consists of eight bits used to represent data plus a parity bit for checking the accuracy of representation.

byte–digit portion   Usually, the four rightmost bits in a byte.

C   A third-generation computer language used for programming on microcomputers. Most microcomputer software products such as spreadsheets and DBMS programs are written in C.

cable modem   A device that uses a TV cable to deliver an internet connection.

callback   A procedure that identifies a terminal dialing into a computer system or network by disconnecting the calling terminal, verifying the authorized terminal against the automated control table, and then, if authorized, reestablishing the connection by having the computer system dial the telephone number of the calling terminal.

capacity planning   Determining the future IT infrastructure requirements for new equipment and additional network capacity.

cathode-ray tube (CRT)   The display device for computer terminals, typically a television-like electronic vacuum tube.

cave (cave automatic virtual environment)   A special 3-D virtual reality room that can display images of other people and objects located in other cave's all over the world.

CCITT   See Telecommunications Standardization Sector of the International Telecommunications Union (TSSUITU).

CD-R (compact disc-recordable)   An optical or laser disc that offers one-time writing capability with about 700 MB or greater of storage.

CD-ROM   A compact disk, similar to an audio compact disk, which is used to store computer information (e.g., programs, data, or graphics).

CD-RW (compact disc-rewritable)   A CD that offers unlimited writing and updating capabilities.

central processing unit (CPU)   The part of the computer system containing the control and arithmetic-logic units.

certification   The acceptance of software by an authorized agent, usually after the software has been validated by the agent or its validity has been demonstrated to the agent.

channel   A magnetic track running along a length of tape that can be magnetized in bit patterns to represent data.

character   A single numeric digit, special symbol, or letter.

check digit   A numeric digit that is used to verify the accuracy of a copied or transcribed number. The numeric digit is typically appended to the end of a number.

chief information officer (CIO)   The title for the highest-ranking MIS officer in the organization.

chip   A wafer containing miniature electronic imprinted circuits and components.

choice   The third step in the decision-making process where you decide on a plan to address the problem or opportunity.

class   Contains information and procedures and acts as a template to create objects.

clickstream   A stored record of a Web surfing session containing information such as Web sites visited, how long the user was there, what ads were looked at, and the items purchased.

click-throughs   A count of the number of people who visit one site and click on an ad, and are taken to the site of the advertiser.

client   A workstation in a network that is set up to use the resources of a server.

client/serve   A network in which several PC-type systems (clients) are connected to one or more powerful, central computers (servers). In databases, this term refers to a model in which a client system runs a database application (front end) that accesses information in a database management systems situated on a server (back end).

Client/Server Architecture   A local area network (LAN) in which microcomputers called servers provide specialized service on behalf of the user's computers which are called clients.

Client/Server Model   A common way to describe network services and the model user processes (programs) of those services. Examples include the name-serve/name-resolver paradigm of the DNS and file-server/file-client relationships such as NFS and diskless hosts.

cipher system   A system in which cryptography is applied to plaintext elements of equal length.

ciphertext   Encoded text or signals produced through the use of cipher systems.

coaxial cable   A medium used for telecommunications. It is similar to the type of cable used for carrying television signals.

COBOL   See Common Business-Oriented Language.

Conference on Data Systems Languages (CODASYL)   A Department of Defense-sponsored group that studies the requirements and design specifications for a common business programming language.

code generator   A precompiler program that translates fourth-generation language-like code into the statements of a third-generation language code.

code system   Any system of communication in which groups of symbols represent plaintext elements of varying length.

coder   The individual who translates program design into executable computer code.

coding   The activity of translating a set of computer processing specifications into a formal language for execution by a computer.

cold site   A separate facility that does not have any computer equipment but is a place where the knowledge workers can move after the disaster.

collaboration system   A system that is designed specifically to improve the performance of teams by supporting the sharing and flow of information.

collaborative filtering   A method of placing you in an affinity group of people with the same characteristics.

collaborative planning, forecasting, and replenishment (CPFR)   A concept that encourages and facilitates collaborative processes between members of a supply chain.

collaborative processing enterprise information portal   Provides knowledge workers with access to workgroup information such as e-mails, reports, meeting minutes, and memos.

co-location   A vendor that rents space and telecommunications equipment to other companies.

754

Common Business-Oriented Language (COBOL)   A high-level programming language for business computer applications.

COM (computer output microfilm)   The production of computer output on photographic film.

common carrier   An organization or company that provides data or other electronic communication services for a fee.

communications medium   The path or physical channel in a network over which information travels.

Communications Protocol (protocol)   A set of rules that every computer follows to transfer information.

communications satellite   A microwave repeater in space.

communications security   The level of protection that ensures the authenticity of telecommunications. The application of measures taken to deny unauthorized persons access to valuable information that might be acquired from the network.

communications service provider   A third party who furnishes the conduit for information.

communications software   Helps you communicate with other people.

complementor   Provides services that complement the offerings of the enterprise and thereby extend its value-adding capabilities to its customers.

compare   A computer-applied function that examines two elements of data to determine their relationship to one another.

compartmentalization   The isolation of the operating system, user programs, and data files from one another in main storage to protect them against unauthorized or concurrent access by other users or programs. This also includes the division of sensitive data into small, isolated blocks to reduce risk to the data.

competitive advantage   Providing a product or service in a way that customers value more than what the competition is able to do.

compiler   A program that translates high-level computer language instruction into machine code.

completeness   The property that all necessary parts of an entity are included. Completeness of a product often means that the product has met all requirements.

composite primary key   The primary key fields from two intersecting relations.

compromise   Unauthorized disclosure or loss of sensitive information.

compromising emanations   Electromagnetic emanations that convey data and, if intercepted and analyzed, could compromise sensitive information being processed by a computer system.

computer-aided design (CAD)   A term used to describe the use of computer technology as applied to the design of problems and opportunities.

computer-aided instruction (CAI)   The interactive use of a computer for instructional purposes. Software provides educational content to students and adjusts its presentation to the responses of the individual.

computer-aided manufacturing (CAM)   The use of computer technology as applied to the manufacturing of computer technology as applied to the manufacturing of goods and services.

computer-aided software engineering (CASE)   Tools that automate the design, development, operation, and maintenance of software.

computer crime   The act of using IT to commit an illegal act.

computer ethics   The issues and standards that support the proper use of IT which are not criminal or threatening to another person or organization.

Computer Fraud and Abuse Act (P.L. 99-474)   Computer Fraud and Abuse Act of 1986. Strengthens and expands the 1984 Federal Computer Crime Legislation. Law extended to computer crimes in private enterprise and anyone who willfully disseminates information for the purpose of committing a computer crime (i.e., distribute phone numbers to hackers from a Bulletin Board System [BBS]).

Computer Matching Act (P.L. 100-503)   The Computer Matching and Privacy Act of 1988 ensures privacy, integrity, and verification of data disclosed for computer matching and establishes data integrity boards within federal agencies.

computer network   Two or more computers connected so that they can communicate with each other and share information, software, peripheral devices, and processing power.

computer output microfilm (COM)   The production of computer output on photographic film.

computer program   A series of operations that perform a task when executed in logical sequence.

computer security   The practice of protecting a computer system against internal failures, human error, attacks, and natural catastrophes, which might cause improper disclosure, modification, destruction, or denial-of-service.

Computer Security Act (P.L. 100-235)   The Computer Security Act of 1987 directs the National Bureau of Standards, now known as the National Institute of Standards and Technology (NIST), to establish a computer security standards program for federal computer systems.

computer system   An interacting assembly of elements, including at least computer hardware and usually software, data procedures, and people.

computer system security   All of the technological safeguards and managerial procedures established and applied to computers and their networks (including related hardware, firmware, software, and data) to protect organizational assets and individual privacy.

computer virus   Software that is written with malicious intent to cause annoyance or damage.

concealment systems   A method of keeping sensitive information confidential by embedding it in irrelevant data.

concentrator   A computer that consolidates the signals from any slower speed transmission lines into a single faster line or performs the reverse function.

concurrent processing   The capability of a computer to share memory with several programs and simultaneously execute the instructions provided by each.

conditional branch   The alteration of the normal sequence of program execution following the text of the contents of a memory area.

conditional formatting   Highlights the information in a cell that meets some specified criteria.

condition test   A comparison of two data items in a program to determine whether one value is equal to, less than, or greater than the second value.

confidentiality   A concept that applies to data that must be held in confidence and describes that status or degree of protection that must be provided for such data about individuals as well as organizations.

configuration management   The use of procedures appropriate for controlling changes to a system's hardware, software, or firmware structure to ensure that such changes will not lead to a weakness or fault in the system.

connectivity software   Enables a computer to "dial up" or connect to another computer.

consistency   Logical coherency among all integrated parts; also, adherence to a given set of instructions or rules.

console operator   Someone who works at a computer console to monitor operations and initiate instructions for efficient use of computer resources.

constant   A value in a computer program that does not change during program execution.

contingency plans   Plans for emergency response, backup operations, and post-disaster recovery maintained by a computer information processing facility as a part of its security program.

control   Any protective action, device, procedure, technique, or other measure that reduces exposures.

control break   A point during program processing at which some special processing event takes place. A change in the value of a control field within a data record is characteristic of a control break.

control field   A field of data within a record used to identify and classify a record.

controllable isolation   Controlled sharing in which the scope or domain of authorization can be reduced to an arbitrarily small set or sphere of activity.

controlled sharing   The condition that exists when access control is applied to all users and components of a resource-sharing computer system.

control logic   The specific order in which processing functions are carried out by a computer.

control signals   Computer-generated signals for the automatic control of machines and processes.

control statement   A command in a computer program that establishes the logical sequence of processing operations.

control structure   A program that contains a logical construct of sequences, repetitions, and selections.

control totals   Accumulations of numeric data fields that are used to check the accuracy of the input, processing, or output data.

control unit A component of the CPU that evaluates and carries out program processing and execution.

control zone The space surrounding equipment that is used to process sensitive information and that is under sufficient physical and technical control to preclude an unauthorized entry or compromise.

conversational program A program that permits interaction between a computer and a user.

conversion The process of replacing a computer system with a new one.

conversion rate The percentage of customers who visit a Web site and actually buy something.

cookie A small record deposited on the hard disk by a Web site containing information about users and their Web activities.

copyright The legal protection afforded to the expression of an idea, such as a song or a game and some types of proprietary documents.

correctness The extent to which software is free from design and coding defects (i.e., fault free). Also, the extent to which software meets its specified requirements and user objectives.

cost/benefit analysis Determination of the economic feasibility of developing a system on the basis of a comparison of the projected costs of the proposed system and the expected benefits from its operation.

cost-risk analysis The assessment of the cost of potential risk of loss or compromise of data in a computer system without data protection versus the cost of providing data protection.

counterfeit software Software that is manufactured to look like the real thing and sold as such.

courseware Computer programs used to deliver educational materials within computer-assisted instruction systems.

cracker A hacker for hire; a person who engages in electronic corporate espionage.

crash-proof software Utility software that helps save information if the system crashes and the user is forced to turn it off and then back on.

critical success factor (CSF) A factor simply critical to the organization's success.

crossover The process within a genetic algorithm where portions of the good outcome are combined in the hope of creating an even better outcome.

crosstalk An unwanted transfer of energy from one communications channel to another.

CRT A monitor that looks like a television set.

CRUD (create, read, update, delete) The four primary procedures or ways a system can manipulate information.

culture The collective personality of a nation, society, or organization, encompassing language, traditions, currency, religion, history, music, and acceptable behavior, among other things.

custom auto filter function   Allows one to hide all the rows in a list except those that match criteria specified.

customer-integrated system   An extension of a TPS that places technology in the hands of an organization's customers and allows them to process their own transactions.

customer relationship management (CRM) system   Uses information about customers to gain insights into their needs, wants, and behaviors in order to serve them better.

cryptanalysis   The deciphering of encrypted messages into plaintext without initial knowledge of the key employed in the encryption algorithm.

cryptographic system   The documents, devices, equipment, and associated techniques that are used as a unit to provide a single means of encryption.

cryptography   The art or science that applies the principles, means, and methods for producing encrypted text and converting encrypted messages into plaintext.

cryptology   The field of study that encompasses both cryptography and cryptanalysis.

cyberterrorist   One who seeks to cause harm to people or destroy critical systems or information.

data   Raw facts and figures that are meaningless by themselves. Data can be expressed in characters, digits, and symbols, which can represent people, things, and events.

data administration   The function in an organization that plans for, oversees the development of, and monitors the information resource.

data administration subsystem   Helps manage the overall database environment by providing facilities for backup and recovery, security management, query optimization, concurrency control, and change management.

database   An integrated aggregation of data usually organized to reflect logical or functional relationships among data elements.

database administrator   A person who is in charge of defining and managing the contents of the database.

database management system (DBMS)   The software that directs and controls data resources.

database-based workflow system   Stores the document in a central location and automatically asks the knowledge workers to access the document when it is their turn to edit the document.

data communications   The transmission of data between two or more Web sites through the use of public and private communications channels or lines.

data contamination   A deliberate or accidental process or act that compromises the integrity of the original data.

data definition language (DDL)   A set of instructions or commands used to define data for the data dictionary.

data dictionary   A document or listing defining all items or processes represented in a data flow diagram or used in a system.

data diddling   A type of computer crime where information and data flowing in or out of a computer is being altered.

data element   The smallest unit of data accessible to a database management system or a field of data within a file processing system.

Data Encryption Standard (DES)   A cipher standardized by the U.S. National Bureau of Standards (NBS). DES is a symmetric block cipher with a block length of 64 bits and effective key length of 56 bits.

data flow analysis   A graphic analysis technique to trace the behavior of program variables as they are initialized, modified, or referenced during program execution.

data flow diagram   A descriptive modeling tool providing a graphic and logical description of a system.

data integrity   The state that exists when automated information or data is the same as that in the source documents and has not been exposed to accidental or malicious modification, alteration, or destruction.

data link layer   The OSI layer that is responsible for data transfer across a single physical connection or series of bridged connections between two network entities.

data management system   System software that supervises the handling of data required by programs during execution.

data mart   Subset of a data warehouse in which only a focused portion of the data warehouse is stored.

data mining   A methodology used by organizations to better understand their customers, products, markets, or any other phase of the business.

data-mining agent   An intelligent agent or application that operates in a data warehouse discovering information.

data-mining tool   Software tool used to query information in a data warehouse.

data protection engineering   The methodology and tools used to design and implement data protection mechanisms.

data representation   The manner in which data is characterized in a computer system and its peripheral devices.

data security   The protection of data from accidental or malicious modification, destruction, or disclosure.

data segment   A collection of data elements accessible to a database management system; a record in a file processing system.

data-dependent protection   The protection of data at a level that is commensurate with the sensitivity of the entire file.

data warehouse   A logical collection of information, gathered from many different operational databases, used to create business intelligence that supports business analysis activities and decision-making tasks.

deadlock   A condition that occurs when two users invoke conflicting locks in trying to gain access to a specific record or records.

debugging The process of correcting static and logical errors detected during coding. With the primary goal of obtaining an executable piece of code, debugging shares certain techniques and strategies with testing but differs in its usual ad hoc application and scope.

decentralized computing An environment in which an organization splits computing power and locates it in functional business areas as well as on the desktops of knowledge workers.

decipher The ability to convert, by use of the appropriate key, enciphered text into its equivalent plaintext.

decision processing enterprise information portal Provides knowledge workers with corporate information for making key business decisions.

decision support system (DSS) A computer information system that helps executives and managers formulate policies and plans. This support system enables the users to access information and assess the likely consequences of their decisions through scenario projections.

decrypt Synonymous with decipher.

dedicated mode The operation of a computer system such that the central computer facility, connected peripheral devices, communications facilities, and all remote terminals are used and controlled exclusively by the users or groups of users for the processing of particular types and categories of information.

dedicated server A microcomputer used exclusively to perform a specific service, such as to process the network operating system.

degauss To erase or demagnetize magnetic recording media (usually tapes) by applying a variable, alternating current (AC) field.

demand aggregation Combines purchase requests from multiple buyers into a single large order, which justifies a discount from the business.

denial-of-service (DoS) attack The attacker floods a Web site with many electronic message requests for service that it slows down or crashes the network or computer targeted.

design Considering possible ways of solving the problem, filling the need, or taking advantage of the opportunity.

design and implementation A phase of the systems development life cycle in which a set of functional specifications produced during systems analysis is transformed into an operational system for hardware, software, and firmware.

desktop computer The most popular choice for personal computing needs.

desktop publishing The use of computer technology equipped with special hardware, firmware, and software features to produce documents that look equivalent to those printed by a professional print company.

digit A single numeral representing an arithmetic value.

digital cash An electronic representation of cash. Also called e-cash.

digital divide The fact that different peoples, cultures, and areas of the world or within a nation do not have the same access to information and telecommunications technologies.

digital economy   Marked by the electronic movement of all types of information, not limited to numbers, words, graphs, and photos but also including physiological information such as voice recognition and synthesization, biometrics (a person's retina scan and breath, for example), and 3-D holograms.

digital subscriber line (DSL)   A high-speed Internet connection using phone lines that allows the use of phone for voice communications at the same time.

directory engine search   Organizes listings of Web sites into hierarchical lists.

direct access   The method of reading and writing specific records without having to process all preceding records in a file.

direct organization   A method of file organization under which records are located on the basis of their keys and associated addresses on the storage media.

disaster recovery cost curve   Charts (1) the cost to the organization due to the unavailability of information and technology, and (2) the cost to the organization of recovering from a disaster over time.

disaster recovery plan   A detailed process for recovering information or an IT system in the event of a catastrophic disaster such as a fire or flood.

disintermediation   The use of the Internet as a delivery vehicle whereby intermediate players in a distribution channel can be bypassed.

disk address   The positioned location of a data record on magnetic disk storage.

diskette   A flexible disk storage medium most often used with microcomputers; also called a floppy disk.

disk optimization software   Utility software that organizes information on the hard disk in the most efficient way.

distributed computing environment (DCE)   An architecture of standard programming interfaces, conventions, and server functionalities (e.g., naming, distributed file system, remote procedure call) for distributing applications transparently across networks of heterogeneous computers. Promoted and controlled by the Open Software Foundation (OSP), a consortium led by Hewlett-Packard, Digital Equipment Corp, and IBM.

distributed denial-of-service (DDoS) attack   Multiple computers flooding a Web site with so many requests for service that it slows down or crashes.

documentation   The written narrative of the development, workings, and operation of a program or system.

domain   A part of the naming hierarchy in the Internet. Syntactically, an Internet domain name consists of a sequence of names (labels) separated by periods (dots), e.g., tundra.mpk.ca.us. In OSI, domain is generally used as an administrative partition of a complex distributed system, as in MHS Private Management Domain (PRMD) and Directory Management Domain (DMD).

domain name system (DNS)   The distributed name and address mechanism used in the Internet.

downtime   A period of time in which the computer is not available for operation.

DSS shell   A set of programs that can be used for constructing a decision support system.

dump The contents of a file or memory that are output as listings. These listing may be formatted.

dynamic analysis The execution of program code to detect errors by analyzing the code's response to input.

dynamic processing The technique of swapping jobs in and out of computer memory. This technique can be controlled by the assignment priority and the number of time slices allocated to each job.

eavesdropping The unauthorized interception of information-bearing emanations through methods other than wiretapping.

ebXML A set of technical specifications for business documents built around XML designed to permit enterprises of any size and in any geographical location to conduct business over the Internet.

echo The display of characters on a terminal output device as they are entered into the system.

edit The process of inspecting a data field or element to verify the correctness of its content.

EDP auditor A professional whose responsibility is to certify the validity, reliability, and integrity of all aspects of the computer information system environment of an organization, a.k.a. IS auditor, CIS auditor, or IT auditor.

E-government The application of E-commerce technologies in government agencies.

electronic bill resentation and payment (EBPP) A system that sends people their bills over the Internet and gives them an easy way to pay.

electronic business XML See ebXML

electronic catalog Designed to present products to customers via the Internet.

electromagnetic emanations Signals transmitted as radiation through the air or conductors.

electronic bulletin board An application program that lets users contribute messages via e-mail that can be routed or shared with users.

Electronic Communications Privacy Act (P.L. 99-508) Electronic Communication Privacy Act of 1986 extends the Privacy Act of 1974 to all forms of electronic communication, including e-mail.

electronic data interchange (EDI) A process whereby such specially formatted documents as an invoice can be transmitted from one organization to another.

electronic document file A magnetic storage area that contains electronic images of papers and other communications documents.

electronic job market Consists of employers using the Internet to advertise for and screen potential employees.

electronic portfolio Collection of Web documents used to support a stated purpose such as writing skills.

electronic journal A computerized log file summarizing, in chronological sequence, the processing activities and events performed by a system. The log file is usually maintained on magnetic storage media.

electronic mail (e-mail)   Formal or informal communications electronically transmitted or delivered.

electronic office   An office that relies on word processing, computer systems, and communications technologies to support its operations.

e-mail software (electronic mail software)   Enables people to electronically communicate with other people by sending and receiving e-mail.

emanation security   The protection that results from all measures designed to deny unauthorized persons access to valuable information that might be derived from interception and analysis of compromising emanations.

encipher   The process of converting plaintext into unintelligible form by means of a cipher system.

encapsulation   The technique used by layered protocols in which a layer adds header information to the protocol data unit (PDI) from the layer above.

encryption   The use of algorithms to encode data in order to render a message or a file readable only for the intended recipient.

encryption algorithm   A set of mathematically expressed rules for encoding information, which renders it unintelligible to those who do not have the algorithm decoding key.

end-to-end encryption   The encryption of information at the point of origin within the communications network and postponing of decryption to the final destination point.

enterprise application integration (EAI)   The process of developing an IT infrastructure that enables employees to implement new or changing business processes.

enterprise application integration middleware (EAI middleware)   Allows organizations to develop different levels of integration from the information level to the business process level.

enterprise information portal (EIP)   Allows knowledge workers to access company information via a Web interface.

enterprise resource planning (ERP)   The method of getting and keeping an overview of every part of the business, so that production and selling of goods and services will be coordinated to contribute to the company's goals.

enterprise software   A suite of software that includes (1) a set of common business applications; (2) tools for modeling how the organization works; and (3) development tools for building applications unique to the organization.

entity class   A concept — typically people, places, or things — about which information can be stored and then identified with a unique key called the primary key.

entity-relationship (ER) diagram   A graphic method of representing entity classes and their relationships.

entity barrier   A product or service feature that customers have come to expect from companies.

entrapment   The deliberate planting of apparent flaws in a system to detect attempted penetrations or confuse intruders about which flaws to exploit.

erasable programmable read-only memory (EPEOM)   A memory chip that can have its circuit logic erased and reprogrammed.

E-tailor   An Internet retail site.

Ethernet card   The most common type of network interface card.

ethical (white-hat) hacker   A computer security professional who is hired by a company to break into its computer system.

ethics   The principles and standards that guide people's behavior towards others.

evolution checking   Testing to ensure the completeness and consistency of a software product at different levels of specification when that product is a refinement or elaboration of another.

exception report   A manager report that highlights abnormal business conditions. Usually, such reports prompt management action or inquiry.

executive information system (EIS)   A very interactive IT system that allows the user to first view highly summarized information and then choose how to see greater detail, which may be an alert to potential problems or opportunities.

expandability   Refers to how easy it is to add features or functions to a system.

expansion bus   Moves information from the CPU and RAM to all other hardware devices such as a microphone or printer.

expansion card   A circuit board that is inserted into an expansion slot.

expansion slot   A long skinny pocket on the motherboard into which an expansion card can be inserted.

expert system   The application of computer-based artificial intelligence in areas of specialized knowledge.

explanation module   The part of an expert system where the "why" information, supplied by the domain expert, is stored to be accessed by knowledge workers who want to know why the expert systems asked a question or reached a conclusion.

exposure   A form of possible loss or harm (e.g., erroneous record keeping, unmaintainable applications, or business interruptions) that affects the profitability of the going concern.

extended binary-coded decimal interchange code (EBCDIC)   A data representation and code system based on the use of an 8-bit byte.

external information   Describes the environment surrounding the organization.

extraction engine   Smart software with a vocabulary of job-related skills that allows it to recognize and catalog terms in a scannable resume.

extranet   An intranet that is restricted to an organization and certain outsiders, such as customers and suppliers.

facsimile (fax)   A technology used to send document images over telecommunications lines.

fail safe   The automatic termination and protection of programs or other processing operations when a hardware, software, or firmware failure is detected in a computer system.

fail soft   The selective termination of nonessential processing affected by a hardware, software, or firmware failure in a computer system.

failure access   Unauthorized and usually inadvertent access to data resulting from a hardware, software, or firmware failure in the computer system.

failure control   The methodology used to detect and provide fail-safe or fail-soft recovery from hardware, software, or firmware failure in a computer system.

Fair Credit Reporting Act (P.L. 91-508)   A federal law that gives individuals the right of access to credit information pertaining to them and the right to challenge such information.

Fair Use Doctrine   Allows the use of copyrighted material in certain situations.

fault   A weakness of the system that allows circumventing protective controls.

feasibility study   An investigation of the legal, political, social, operational, technical, economic, and psychological effects of developing and implementing a system.

feature analysis   The step of ASR in which the system captures the users' words as spoken into a microphone, eliminates any background noise, and converts the digital signals of speech into phonemes (syllables).

feature creep   Occurs when developers add extra features that were not part of the initial requirements.

Federal Computer Fraud Act   The Counterfeit Access Device and Computer Fraud and Abuse Act of 1986 outlaws unauthorized access to the federal government's computers and financial databases as protected under the Right to Financial Privacy Act of 1978 and the Fair Credit Reporting Act of 1971. This Act is an amendation of the 1984 Federal Computer Fraud Act.

fetch protection   A system-provided restriction to prevent a program from accessing data in another user's segment of storage.

fiber distributed data interface (FDDI)   A standard for a 100 Mbps token-passing ring network operating over fiber optics.

fiche   A sheet of photographic film containing multiple microimages; a form of computer output microfilm.

field   A basic unit of data, usually part of a record that is located on an input, storage, or output microfilm.

file   A basic unit of data records organized on a storage medium for convenient location, access, and updating.

file creation   The building of master or transaction files.

file inquiry   The selection of records from files and immediate display of their contents on a terminal output device.

file maintenance   The changing of master file by changing the contents of existing records, adding new records, or deleting old records.

file protection   The aggregate of all processes and procedures established in a computer system and designed to inhibit unauthorized access, contamination, or elimination of a file.

File Transfer Protocol (FTP)   The Internet protocol (and program) used to transfer files between hosts.

file updating   The posting of transaction data to master files or maintenance of master files through record additions, changes, or deletions.

firmware Software or computer instructions that have been permanently encoded into the circuits of semiconductor chips.

financial cybermediaries Internet-based companies that make it easy for one person to pay another over the Internet.

financial EDI (FEDI) The use of EDI for payments.

firewall Hardware and/or software that protects a computer or network from intruders.

flame To express strong opinion or criticism of something, usually as a frank inflammatory statement in an electronic message.

flat-panel display Thin lightweight monitor that takes up much less space than a CRT.

floppy disk A flexible removable disk used for magnetic storage of data, programs, or information.

Foreign Corrupt Practices Act The Act covers an organization's system of internal accounting control and requires public companies to make and keep books, records, and accounts that, in reasonable detail, accurately and fairly reflect the transactions and disposition of company assets and to devise and maintain a system of sufficient internal accounting controls. This Act was amended in 1988.

foreign key A primary key of one file (relation) that appears in another file (relation).

forensic image copy An exact copy or snapshot of the contents of an electronic medium.

formal analysis The use of rigorous mathematical techniques to analyze a solution. The algorithms may be analyzed for numerical properties, efficiency, and correctness.

format The physical arrangement of data characters, fields, records, and files.

Formula Translation (Fortran) A high-level programming language developed primarily to translate mathematical formulas into computer code.

formulary A technique for permitting the decision to grant or deny access to be determined dynamically at access time rather than at the time the access list is created.

front office space The primary interface to customers and sales channels.

Fortran See Formula Translation.

fourth-generation language (4GL) A computer language that is easy to learn and use and often associated with rapid applications development.

front-end computer A computer that off-loads input and output activities from the central computer so it can operate primarily in a processing mode; sometimes called a front-end processor.

FTP (File Transfer Protocol) server Maintains a collection of files that can be downloaded.

function In computer programming, a processing activity that performs a single, identifiable task.

functional specification   The main product of systems analysis, which presents a detailed logical description of the new system. It contains sets of input, processing, storage, and output requirements specifying what the new system can do.

functional testing   The application of test data derived from the specified functional requirements without regard to the final program structure.

gateway   A product that enables two dissimilar networks to communicate or interface with each other.

genetic algorithm   An artificial intelligence system that mimics the evolutionary, survival-of-the-fittest process to generate increasingly better solutions to a problem.

general-purpose computer   A computer that can be programmed to perform a wide variety of processing tests.

geographic information system (GIS)   A decision support system designed specifically to work with spatial information.

gigabyte (G byte)   The equivalent of one billion bytes.

gigahertz   The number of billions of CPU cycles per second.

global digital divide   The term used specifically to describe differences in IT access and capabilities between different countries or regions of the world.

global economy   One in which customers, businesses, suppliers, distributors, and manufacturers operate without regard to physical and geographical boundaries.

global positioning system   A collection of 24 earth-orbiting satellites that continuously transmit radio signals to determine an object or target's current longitude, latitude, speed, and direction of movement.

global reach   The ability to extend a company's reach to customers anywhere through an Internet connection and at a lower cost.

glove   An input device that captures and records the shape, movement, and strength of the users' hands and fingers.

Government OSI Profile (GOSIP)   A U.S. government procurement specification for OSI protocols.

government to business (G2B)   The E-commerce activities performed between a government and its business partners for purposes such as purchasing materials or soliciting and accepting bids for work.

government to consumer (G2C)   The E-commerce activities performed between a government and its citizens or consumers, including paying taxes and providing information and services.

government to government (G2G)   The E-commerce activities limited to a single nation's government focusing on vertical integration (local, city, state, and federal) and horizontal integration (within the various branches and agencies).

graphics output   Computer-generated output in the form of pictures, charts, and line drawings.

graphics software   Helps the user create and edit photos and art.

graphics terminal   An output device that displays pictures, charts, and line drawings, typically a high-resolution CRT.

graphical user interface (GUI)   An interface (e.g., in Macintosh, Microsoft Windows, or Motif) in which the user can manipulate icons, windows, pop-down menus, or other related constructs.

grid computing   Harnesses computers together by way of the Internet or a virtual network to share CPU power, databases, and storage.

group document databases   A powerful storage facility for organizing and managing all documents relayed to specific teams.

groupware   Software designed to function over a network to allow several people to work together on documents and files.

GUI (graphical user interface) screen design   The ability to model the information system screens for an entire system.

hacking   A computer crime in which a person breaks into an information system simply for the challenge of doing so.

hacktivist   A politically motivated hacker who uses the Internet to send a political message of some kind.

handshaking procedure   Dialogue between a user and a computer, two computers, or two programs to identify the user and authenticate the identity. This is done through a sequence of questions and answers that are based on information either previously stored in the computer or supplied to the computer by the initiator of the dialogue.

Handspring   A type of PDA that runs on the Palm Operating System (Palm OS).

hard disk   A fixed or removable disk mass storage system permitting rapid direct access to data, programs, or information.

hardware   The physical equipment or devices included in computer systems.

hardware key logger   A hardware device that captures keystrokes on their way from the keyboard to the motherboard.

heading tag   HTML tag that puts certain information, such as the title, at the top of the page.

headset   It combines input and output devices that (1) capture and record the movements of the user's head, and (2) contains a screen that covers the user's field of vision and displays various views of an environment based on the head's movements.

help desk   Responds to knowledge workers' questions.

hertz   One cycle per second.

high capacity floppy disk   Storage device that holds between 100MB and 250MB of information. Superdisks and Zip disks are examples.

high-level language   The class of procedure-oriented language.

HIPAA Act of 1996 The Administrative Simplification provisions of the Health Insurance Portability and Accountability Act of 1996 (HIPAA, Title II) require the Department of Health and Human Services to establish national standards for electronic healthcare transactions and national identifiers for providers, health insurers, and employers. It also addresses the security and privacy of health data. Adopting these standards will improve the efficiency and effectiveness of the nation's healthcare system by encouraging the widespread use of electronic data interchange in healthcare.

holographic device A device that creates, captures, and displays images in true three-dimensional form.

home PNA (home phoneline networking alliance) Allows one to network home computer using telephone wiring.

Homeland Security Act of 2002 The Act restructures and strengthens the executive branch of the federal government to better meet the threat to the United States posed by terrorism. In establishing a new department of Homeland Security, the Act for the first time creates a Federal department whose primary mission will be to help prevent, protect against, and respond to acts of terrorism on the U.S. soil.

horizontal market software Application software that is general enough to be suitable for use in a variety of industries.

hot site A separate and fully equipped facility where the company can move after a disaster and resume business.

HTML document A file made from the HTML language.

HTML tag Specifies the formatting and presentation of information in an HTML document.

Hypertext Markup Language A language created by programmers at the CERN in Switzerland to create Web pages.

Hypertext Transfer Protocol (HTTP) The communications protocol that supports the movement of information over the Web, essentially from a Web server to the user.

humanware Computer programs that interface or communicate with users by means of voice-integrated technology, interpret user-specified command, and execute or translate commands into machine-executable code.

hypermedia An extension to hypertext in which frames contain graphics, illustrations, images, audio, animation, text, and other forms of information or knowledge.

hypertext Text that is held in frames; authors develop or define the linkage between frames.

icon A pictorial symbol used to represent data, information, or a program on a GUI screen.

identification The process, generally employing unique machine-readable names, that enables recognition of users or resources as identical to those previously described to the computer system.

impact printer A hard-copy device on which a print mechanism strikes against a ribbon to create imprints on paper. Some impact printers operate one character at a time; others strike an entire line at a time.

impersonation An attempt to gain access to a system by posing as an authorized user.

implant chip A technology-enabled microchip implanted into the human body.

implementation The specific activities within the systems development life cycle through which the software portion of the system is developed, coded, debugged, tested, and integrated with existing or new penetration.

implementation phase Distributes the system to the knowledge workers who begin using the system in their everyday jobs.

incomplete parameter checking A system fault that exists when all parameters have not been fully checked for correctness and consistency by the operating system, leaving the system vulnerable to penetration.

indexed sequential filing A file organization method in which records are maintained in logical sequence and indices (or tables) are used to reference their storage addresses. The method allows direct and serial access to records.

indirect material Material that is necessary for running a modern corporation but does not relate to the company's primary business activities. Commonly called MRO materials.

inference engine A system of computer programs in an expert systems application that uses expert experience as a basis for conclusions.

information Meaningful data; the result of processing data by computer or other means.

information age A time when knowledge is power.

information decomposition Breaking down the information for ease of use and understandability.

information float The amount of time it takes to get information from its source into the hands of the decision makers.

information granularity The extent of detail within the information.

information-literate knowledge workers Can define what information they need, know how to obtain that information, understand the information once they receive it, and act appropriately to help the organization achieve the greatest advantage.

information partnership Two or more companies that cooperate by integrating their IT systems, thereby providing customers with the best of what each has to offer.

information resource management A concept or practice in which information is recognized as a key asset to be appropriately managed as a vital resource.

information technology (IT) Any computer-based tool that people use to work with the information processing needs of an organization.

information view Includes all of the information stored within a system.

infrared A wireless communications medium that uses light waves to transmit signals or information.

inheritance The ability to define superclass and subclass relationships among classes.

inkjet printer Makes images by forcing ink droplets through nozzles.

input controls Techniques and methods for verifying, validating, and editing data to ensure that only correct data enters a system.

input device A tool used to capture information and commands by the user.

inquiry processing The process of selecting a record from a file and immediately displaying its contents.

insourcing It means that IT specialists within the organization will develop the system.

instance An occurrence of an entity class that can be uniquely described.

inspection A manual analysis technique that examines the program requirements, design, or code in a formal and disciplined manner to discover errors.

instrumental input The capture of data and its placement directly into a computer by machines.

integrated circuit A miniature microchip incorporating circuitry and semi-conductor components. The circuit elements and components are created as a part of the same manufacturing process.

Integrated Services Digital Network (ISDN) An emerging technology that is being offered by the telephone carriers of the world. ISDN combines voice and digital network services in a single medium making it possible to offer customers digital data services as well as voice connections through a single wire. The standards that define ISDN are specified by ITU-TSS.

integration Allows separate systems to communicate directly with each other by automatically exporting data files from one system and importing them into another.

integration testing The orderly progression of testing in which software, hardware, or both are combined and tested until all intermodule communication links have been integrated.

integrity checking The testing of programs to verify the soundness of a software product at each phase of development.

intellectual property Intangible creative work that is embodied in physical form.

intelligence The first step in the decision making process where a problem, need, or opportunity is found or recognized. Also called the diagnostic phase of decision making.

intelligent agent Software that assists the user in performing repetitive computer-related tasks.

interactive chat Lets the user engage in real-time exchange of information with one or more individuals over the Internet.

interactive video A system in which video segments are integrated via a menu-based processing application.

interblock gap (IBG) A blank space appearing between records or groups of records on magnetic storage media.

interdiction Impeding or denying someone the use of system resources.

interface analysis   The checking and verification process that ensures intermodule communications links are performed correctly.

interleaving   The alternating execution of programs residing in the memory of a multiprogramming environment.

intermediary   A specialist company that provides services better than its client companies.

internal information   Information that describes specific operational aspects of the organization.

internal accounting control   The process of safeguarding the accounting functions and processes of a business. This process includes validating that the accounting system complies with the appropriate, generally accepted accounting principles and that audit trails exist for verification of all processes.

internal control   The method of safeguarding business assets, including verifying the accuracy and reliability of accounting data, promoting operational efficiency, and encouraging adherence to prescribed organizational policies and procedures.

international government-to-government (IG2G)   The E-commerce activities performed between two or more governments, including foreign aid.

international virtual private network (IVPN)   Virtual private networks that depend on services offered by phone companies of various nationalities.

International Standards Organization (ISO)   Best known for the 7-layer OSI Reference Model and ISO 17799 and ISO 9000. See OSI.

Internet   The Internet consists of large national backbone networks (such as MILNET, NSFNET, and CREN) and a myriad of regional and local campus networks all over the world. The Internet uses the Internet protocol suite. To be on the Internet the user must have IP connectivity, i.e., be able to Telnet to or ping other systems. Networks with only e-mail connectivity are not actually classified as being on the Internet.

Internet address   A 32-bit address assigned to hosts using TCP/IP.

Internet backbone   The major set of connections for computers on the Internet.

Internet protocol (IP)   The network layer protocol for the Internet protocol suite.

Internet server computer   Computer that provides information and services on the Internet.

Internet service provider (ISP)   A company that provides individuals, organizations, and businesses access to the Internet.

Internet telephony   A combination of hardware and software that uses the Internet as the medium for transmission of telephone calls in place of traditional telephone networks.

Interorganizational System (IOS)   Automates the flow of information between organizations to support the planning, design, development, production, and delivery of products and services.

intersection relation   A relation the user creates to eliminate a many-to-many relationship. Also called a composite relation.

intranet   An internal organizational Internet that is guarded against outside access by a special security feature called a firewall.

intrusion-detection software   Looks for unauthorized users on the Internet.

Ida (infrared date association) port   A port for wireless devices that works in essentially the same way as the remote control on TV.

IRC (Internet Relay Chat) server   Supports the use of discussion groups or chat rooms.

IT infrastructure   The hardware, software, and telecommunications equipment that when combined provides the underlying foundation to support the organization's goal.

investigation   The phase of the systems development life cycle in which the problem or need is identified and a decision made on whether to proceed with a full-scale study.

ISO 9000   A certification program that demonstrates an organization adheres to steps that ensure quality of goods and services.

isolation   The separation of users and processes in a computer system from one another as well as from the protection controls of the operating system.

Java   An object-oriented programming language that was developed by Sun Microsystems and is used in developing applications on the Web and other environments.

job   A complete set of programs to be executed in sequence on a computer.

job accounting system   A set of systems software that can track the services and resources used by computer system account holders.

job queue   A set of programs held in temporary storage and awaiting execution.

joint application development (JAD)   Occurs when knowledge workers and IT specialists meet, sometimes for several days, to define or review the business requirements for the system.

Just in Time (JIT)   An approach that produces or delivers a product or service just at the time the customer wants it.

Kermit   A popular file transfer and terminal emulation program.

key   A control field in a record that uniquely identifies the record or classifies it as a member of a segment of records within a file. In cryptography, a sequence of symbols that controls encryption and decryption.

Keyboard   Today's most popular input technology.

key generation   The origination of a key or set of distinct keys.

key logger (or key trapper) software   A program that, when installed on a computer, records every keystroke and mouse click.

key-to-disk device   A keyboard unit that records data as patterns of magnetic spots onto magnetic disks.

key-to-tape device   A keyboard unit that records data as patterns of magnetic spots onto magnetic tape.

kilobyte (K byte)   The equivalent of 1,204 bytes.

knowledge acquisition   The component of the expert system that the knowledge engineer uses to enter the rules.

774

knowledge base   The part of an expert system that contains specific information and facts about the expert area. Rules that the expert system uses to make decisions are derived from this source.

knowledge-based system   An artificial intelligence system that applies reasoning capabilities to reach a conclusion. Also known as an expert system.

knowledge engineer   The person who formulates the domain expertise of an expert system.

knowledge worker   Works with and produces information as a product.

language processing   The step of ASR in which the system attempts to analyze and make sense of the user's verbal instructions by comparing the word phonemes generated in step 2 with a language model database.

language translator   Systems software that converts programs written in assembler or a higher-level language into machine code.

laser printer   An output unit that uses intensified light beams to form an image on an electrically charged drum and then transfers the image to paper.

last mile bottleneck problem   Occurs when information is traveling on the Internet over a very fast line for a certain distance and then comes near the user where it must travel over a slower line.

legacy system   A previously built system using older technologies such as mainframe computers and programming languages such as COBOL.

limit check   An input control text that assesses the value of a data field to determine whether values fall within set limits.

line printer   An output unit that prints alphanumeric characters one line at a time.

linkage   The purposeful combination of data or information from one information system with that from another system in the hope of deriving additional information.

link encryption   The application of online crypto-operations to a link of a communications system so that all information passing over the link is encrypted in its entirety.

Linux   An open source operating system that provides a rich operating environment for high-end workstations and network servers.

list   A collection of information arranged in columns and rows in which each column displays one particular type of information.

list definition table   A description of a list by column.

local area network (LAN)   The physical connection of microcomputers with communication media (e.g., cable and fiber optics) that allows the sharing of information and peripherals among those microcomputers.

lock/key protection system   A protection system that involves matching a key or a password with a specified access requirement.

logical error   A programming error that causes the wrong processing to take place in a syntactically valid program.

logical file organization   The sequencing of data records in a file according to their key.

Logical Link Control (LLC)   The portion of the link level protocol in the 802 standards that is in direct contact with higher-level layers.

logical operation   A comparison of data values within the arithmetic logic unit. These comparisons show when one value is greater than, equal to, or less than a second value.

logical operator   A symbol used in programming that initiates a comparison operation of two or more data values.

logical organization   Data elements organized in a manner that meets human and organizational processing needs.

loophole   An error of omission or oversight in software, hardware, or firmware that permits circumventing the access control process.

machine language   Computer instructions or code representing computer operations and memory addresses in a numeric form that is executable by the computer without translation.

Mac OS   The operating system for today's apple computers.

macro viru   A computer virus that spreads by binding itself to software such as Word or Excel.

magnetic ink character recognition (MICR)   An input method under which data is encoded in special ink containing iron particles. These particles can be magnetized and sensed by special machines and converted into computer input.

magnetic disk   A storage device consisting of metallic platters coated with an oxide substance that allows data to be recorded as patterns of magnetic spots.

magnetic tape   A storage medium consisting of a continuous strip of coated plastic film wound onto a reel and on which data can be recorded as defined patterns of magnetic spots.

mail gateway   A machine that connects two or more e-mail systems (especially dissimilar mail systems on two different networks) and transfers messages between them. Sometimes the mapping and translation can be quite complex, and generally it requires a store-and-forward scheme whereby the message is received from one system completely before it is transmitted to the next system after suitable translations.

mailing list   Discussion groups organized by area of interest.

mail server   Provides e-mail services and accounts.

mainframe computer   A computer designed to meet the computing needs of hundreds of people in a large business environment.

maintenance phase   Monitors and supports the new system to ensure it continues to meet the business goals.

maintenance programmer   An applications programmer responsible for making authorized changes to one or more computer programs and ensuring that the changes are tested, documented, and verified.

management information systems (MIS)   Deals with the planning, development, management, and use of information technology tools to help people perform tasks related to information processing and management.

marketing mix   The set of marketing tools that a firm uses to pursue its marketing objectives in the target market.

mass customization   When a business gives its customers the opportunity to tailor its product or service to the customer's specifications.

master file   An automated file that contains semipermanent or permanent information and is maintained over a time period required by organizational policy.

matrix display   The alphanumeric representation of characters as patterns of tiny dots in specific positions on a display terminal.

matrix printer   A hard-copy printing device that forms alphanumeric characters with small pins arranged in a matrix of rows and columns.

mature system   A fully operational system that performs all the functions it was designed to accomplish.

M-commerce   The term used to describe E-commerce conducted over a wireless device such as a cell phone or personal digital assistant.

md5 hash value   A mathematically generated string of 32 letters and digits that is unique for an individual storage medium at a specific point in time.

media   The various physical forms (e.g., disk, tape, and diskette) on which data is recorded in machine-readable formats.

megabyte (M byte)   The equivalent of 1,048,576 bytes.

megahertz (MHz)   The number of millions of CPU cycles per second.

memory   The area in a computer that serves as temporary storage for programs and data during program execution.

memory bounds   The limits in the range of storage addresses for a protected region in memory.

memory chips   A small integrated circuit chip with a semiconductor matrix used as computer memory.

menu   A section of the computer program — usually the top-level module — that controls the order of execution of other program modules. Also, online options displayed to a user prompting the user for specific input.

message handling system (MHS)   The system of message user agents, message transfer agents, message stores, and access units that together provide OSI e-mail. MHS is specified in the ITU-TSS X.400 series of recommendations.

message transfer agent (MTA)   An OSI application process used to store and forward messages in the X.400 message handling system. Equivalent to Internet mail agent.

messaging-based workflow system   Sends work assignments through an e-mail system.

metatag   A part of a Web site text not displayed to users but accessible to browsers and search engines for finding and categorizing Web sites.

microcomputer   A small microprocessor-based computer built to handle input, output, processing, and storage functions.

microfilm   A film for recording alphanumeric and graphics output that has been greatly reduced in size.

micro-payment A technique to facilitate the exchange of small amounts of money for an Internet transaction.

microphone For capturing live sounds, such as human voice.

microprocessor A single small chip containing circuitry and components for arithmetic, logical, and control operations.

Microsoft Windows 2000 Millennium (Windows 2000Me) An operating system for a home computer featuring utilities for setting up a home network and performing video, photo, and music editing and cataloging.

Microsoft Windows 2000 Professional (Windows 2000 Pro) An operating system for people who have a personal computer connected to a network of other computers at work or at school.

Microsoft Windows XP Home Microsoft's latest upgrade to Windows 2000Me, with enhanced features for allowing multiple users to use the same computer.

Microsoft Windows XP Professional (Windows XP Pro) Microsoft's latest upgrade to Windows 2000 Pro.

microwave A type of radio transmission used to transmit information.

millions of instructions per second (MIPS) Used as a measure for assessing the speed of mainframe computers.

minicomputer Typically a word-oriented computer whose memory size and processing speed falls between that of a microcomputer and a medium-sized computer. Sometimes called mid-range computer.

MIPS See millions of instructions per second.

modeling The activity of drawing a graphical representation of a design.

model management Component of a DSS that consists of the DSS models and the DSS model management system.

modem (modulator/demodulator) A device that converts the digital language of the PC to a series of high- and low-pitched tones for transmission over analog telephone lines.

monitoring and surveillance agents (or predictive agents) Intelligent agents that observe and report on equipment.

mouse A hardware device used for moving a display screen cursor.

multiaccess rights terminal A terminal that may be used by more than one class of users, for example, users with different access rights to data or files.

multidimensional analysis (MDA) tools Slice and dice techniques that allow viewing multidimensional information from different perspectives.

multifunction printer Scans, copies, and faxes as well as prints.

multiprocessing A computer operating method under which two or more processors are linked and execute multiple programs simultaneously.

multiprogramming A computer operating environment in which several programs can be placed in memory and executed concurrently.

multitasking Allows the user to work with more than one piece of software at a time.

municipal area network (MAN) A network that covers a metropolitan area.

mutation   The process within a genetic algorithm of randomly trying combinations and evaluating the success or failure of the outcome.

mutually suspicious   Pertaining to a state that exists between interactive processes (systems or programs), each of which contains sensitive data and is assumed to be designed to extract data from the other and to protect its own data.

NAK attack   A penetration technique that capitalizes on an operating system's inability to handle asynchronous interrupts properly.

National Science Foundation (NSF)   Sponsors of the NSFNET.

National Science Foundation Network (NSFNET)   A collection of local, regional, and mid-level networks in the U.S. tied together by a high-speed backbone. NSFNET provides scientists access to a number of supercomputers across the country.

natural language   A language that is used in communication with computers and that closely resembles English syntax.

network   An integrated, communicating aggregation of computers and peripherals linked through communications facilities.

network access point (NAP)   A point on the Internet where several connections converge.

Network Basic Input Output System (NetBIOS)   The standard interface to networks on IBM PC and compatible system.

Network File Systems (NFS)   A distributed file system developed by Sun Microsystems which allows a set of computers to cooperatively access each other's files in a transparent manner.

network hub   A device that connects multiple computers into a network.

Network Information Center (NIC)   Originally there was only one, located at SRI International and tasked to serve the ARPANET (and later DDN) community. Today, there are many NICs, operated by local, regional, and national networks all over the world. Such centers provided user assistance, document service, training, and much more.

Network Service Provider (NSP)   Owns and maintains routing computers at NAPs and even the lines that connect the NAPs to each other. For example, MCI and AT&T.

networking   A method of linking distributed data processing activities through communications facilities.

network layer   The OSI layer that is responsible for routing, switching, and subnetwork access across the entire OSI environment.

neural network (NN)   A type of system developed by artificial intelligence researchers used for processing logic.

nonprocedural language   A programming language with fixed logic, which allows the programmer to specify processing operations without concern for processing logic.

nonrecurring (ad hoc) decision   One that is made infrequently and may have different criteria for determining the best solution each time.

nonstructured decision   A decision for which there may be several right answers and there is no precise way to get a right answer.

normalization   A process of assuring that a relational database structure can be implemented as a series of two-dimensional relations.

notebook computer   A highly portable, battery powered microcomputer with a display screen, carried easily in a briefcase, and used away from a user's work-place.

numeric test   An input control method to verify that a field of data contains only numeric digits.

object   An instance of a class.

object program   A program that has been translated from a higher-level source code into machine language.

objective information   Quantifiably describes something that is known.

object-oriented approach   Combines information and procedures into a single view.

object-oriented database   Works with traditional database information and also complex data types such as diagrams, schematic drawings, videos, and sound and text documents.

object-oriented programming language   A programming language used to develop object-oriented systems. The language groups together data and instructions into manipulative objects.

office automation   The application of computer and related technologies to office procedure.

online analytical processing (OLAP)   The manipulation of information to support decision-making.

online processing   Often called interactive processing. An operation in which the user works at a terminal or other device that is directly attached or linked to the computer.

online training   Runs over the Internet or off a CD-ROM.

online transaction processing (OLTP)   The gathering of input information, processing that information, and updating.

open network computing (ONC)   A distributed applications architecture promoted and controlled by a consortium led by Sun Microsystems.

Open Systems Interconnection (OSI)   An international standardization program to facilitate communications among computers from different manufactures. See ISO.

operand   The portion of a computer instruction that references the memory address of an item to be processed.

operating system (OS)   The various sets of computer programs and other software that monitor and operate the computer hardware and the firmware to facilitate use of the hardware.

operating system software   System software that controls the application software and manages how the hardware devices work together.

operational database   A database that supports online transaction processing (OLTP).

operational management   Manages and directs the day-to-day operations and implementations of the goals and strategies.

operation code   The portion of the computer instruction that identifies the specific processing operation to be performed.

optical character recognition (OCR)   An input method in which handwritten, typewritten, or printed text can be read by photosensitive devices for input to a computer.

optical disk   A disk that is written to or read from by optical means.

optical fiber   A form of transmission medium that uses light to encode signals and has the highest transmission rate of any medium.

optical mark recognition (OMR)   Detects the presence of or absence of a mark in a predetermined place (popular for multiple choice exams).

output controls   Techniques and methods for verifying that the results of processing conform to expectations and are communicated only to authorized users.

output device   A tool used to see, hear, or otherwise accept the results of information-processing requests.

outsourcing   The delegation of specific work to a third party for a specified length of time, cost, and level of service.

overlapped processing   The simultaneous execution of input, processing, and output functions by a computer system.

overwriting   The obliteration of recorded data by recording different data on the same surface.

Packet Internet Groper (PING)   A program used to test reachability of destinations by sending them an ICMP (Internet Control Messaging Protocol) echo request and waiting for a reply. The term is used as a verb: "Ping host X to see if it is up."

packet switching   A switching procedure that breaks up messages into fixed length units (called packets) at the message source. These units may travel along different routes before reaching their intended destination.

paging   A method of dividing a program into parts called pages and introducing a given page into memory as the processing on the page is required for program execution.

Palm   A type of PDA that runs on the Palm Operating System (Palm OS).

Palm Operating System   The operating system for Palm and Handspring PDAs.

parallel connector   Has 25 pins that fit into the corresponding holes in the port. Most printers use parallel connectors.

parallel conversion   The concurrent use of new system by its users.

parity bit   A bit attached to a byte that is used to check the accuracy of data storage.

partition   A memory area assigned to a computer program during its execution.

Pascal   A computer programming language designed especially for writing structured programs. This language is based on the use of a minimum set of logical control structures.

passive wiretapping   The monitoring or recording of data while it is being transmitted over a communications link.

password   A protected word or string of characters that identifies or authenticates a user, a specific resource, or an access type.

pattern classification   The step of ASR in which the system matches the user's spoken phonemes to a phoneme sequence stored in an acoustic model database.

peer-to-peer network   A network in which a small number of computers share hardware (such as a printer), software, and information.

penetration   A successful unauthorized access to a computer system.

penetration profile   A delineation of the activities required to effect penetration.

penetration signature   The description of a situation or set of conditions in which a penetration might occur.

penetration testing   The use of special programmer or analyst teams to attempt to penetrate a system to identify security weaknesses.

performance   Measures how quickly an IT system performs a certain process.

performance monitor   A set of systems software that tracks service levels provided by a computer system.

permission marketing   When a person has given a merchant permission to send special offers.

personal agent (or user agent)   An intelligent agent that takes action on the user's behalf.

personal computer   A commonly used term that refers to a microcomputer. Often called a PC.

personal digital assistant (PDA)   A small hand-held computer that helps surf the Web and perform simple tasks such as note taking, calendaring, appointment scheduling, and maintaining an address book.

personal finance software   Helps the user maintain a checkbook, prepare a budget, track investments, monitor credit card balances, and pay bills electronically.

personal information management (PIM) software   Helps create and maintain (1) lists, (2) appointments and calendars, and (3) points of contact.

personalization   When a Web site can know enough about the user's likes and dislikes that it can fashion offers that are more likely to appeal to the user.

personal productivity software   Helps the user perform personal tasks — writing a memo, creating a graph, and creating a slide presentation — that can usually be done even if the user does not own a computer.

phased conversion   The system installation procedure that involves a step-by-step approach for the incremental installation of one portion of a new system at a time.

physical layer   The OSI layer that provides the means to activate and use physical connections for bit transmission. In plain terms, the physical layer provides the procedures for transferring a single bit across a physical media.

physical organization   The packaging of data into fields, records, files, and other structures to make them accessible to a computer system.

piggyback entry   Unauthorized access to a computer system that is gained through another user's legitimate connection.

pirated software   The unauthorized use, duplication, distribution, or sale of copyrighted software.

pivot table   Enables to group and summarize information.

plaintext   Intelligible text or signals that have meaning and can be read or acted on without being decrypted.

planning phase   Involves determining a solid plan for developing information system.

plotter   A graphics output device in which the computer drives a pen that draws on paper.

PNA adapter card   An expansion card that is put into the user's computer to act as a doorway for information flowing in and out.

Pocket PC   A type of PDA that runs on Pocket PC OS that used to be called Windows CE.

Pocket PC OS (or Windows CE)   The operating system for the Pocket PC PDA.

pointing stick   Small rubber-like pointing device that causes the pointer to move on the screen as the user applies directional pressure. Popular on notebooks.

point-of-sale (POS)   Applications in which purchase transactions are captured in machine-readable form at the point of purchase.

Point-to-Point Protocol (PPP)   The successor to SLIP, PPP provides router-to-router and host-to-network connections over both synchronous and asynchronous circuits.

polymorphism   Having many forms.

polling   A procedure by which a computer controller unit asks terminals and other peripheral devices in a serial fashion if they have any messages to send.

port   An outlet, usually on the exterior of a computer system, that enables peripheral devices to be connected and interfaced with the computer.

Portable Document Format (PDF)   The standard electronic distribution file format for heavily formatted documents such as a presentation resume because it retains the original document formatting.

postscript   A language used to describe the printing of images and text and typically used with laser printing capability. Word processor or desktop publishing applications generate postscript code for higher quality laser products.

preprocessors   Software tools that perform preliminary work on a draft computer program before it is completely tested on the computer.

presentation layer   The OSI layer that determines how application information is represented (i.e., encoded) while in transit between two end systems.

presentation resume   A format-sensitive document created in a word processor to outline job qualifications in one to two printed pages.

presentation software   Helps create and edit information that will appear in electronic slides.

primary key   A field (or group of fields) that uniquely describes each record.

principle of least privilege   A security procedure under which users are granted only the minimum access authorization they need to perform required tasks.

print suppress   The elimination of the printing of characters to preserve their secrecy — for example, the characters of a password as they are keyed by a user at a terminal or station on the network.

privacy   The right of people to be left alone when they want to be, to have control over their own personal possessions, and not to be observed without their consent.

Privacy Act of 1974   The federal law that allows individuals to know what information about them is on file and how it is used by all government agencies and their contractors. The Electronic Communication Act of 1986 is an extension of the Privacy Act.

privacy protection   The establishment of appropriate administrative, technical, and physical safeguards to protect the security and confidentiality of data records against anticipated threats or hazards that could result in substantial harm, embarrassment, inconvenience, or unfairness to any individual about whom such information is maintained.

private branch exchange (PBX)   A central telecommunications switching station that an organization uses for its own purposes.

privileged instructions   A set of instructions generally executable only when the computer system is operating in the executive state (e.g., while handling interrupts). These special instructions are typically designed to control such protection features as the storage protection features.

procedure   Manipulates or changes information.

procedural language   A computer programming language in which the programmer must determine the logical sequence of program execution as well as the processing required.

procedure division   A section of a COBOL program that contains statements that direct computer processing operations.

procedure view   Contains all of the procedures within a system.

profile filtering   Requires that the user choose terms or enter keywords to provide a more personal picture of preferences.

process description   A narrative that describes in sequence the processing activities that take place in a computer system and the procedures for completing each activity.

processing controls   Techniques and methods used to ensure that processing produces correct results.

processor   The hardware unit containing the functions of memory and the central processing unit.

program analyzers   Software tools that modify or monitor the operation of an application program to allow information about its operating characteristics to be collected automatically.

program development process   The activities involved in developing computer programs, including problem analysis, program design, process design, program coding, debugging, and testing.

program maintenance   The process of altering program code or instructions to meet new or changing requirements.

programmable read-only memory (PROM)   Computer memory chips that can be programmed permanently to carry out a defined process.

programmer   The individual who designs and develops computer programs.

programmer/analyst   The individual who analyzes processing requirements and then designs and develops computer programs to direct processing.

programming language   A language with special syntax and style conventions for coding computer programs.

Programming Language/1 (PL/1)   A general-purpose, high-level language that combines business and scientific processing features. The language contains advanced features for experienced programmers yet can be easily learned by novice programmers.

programming specifications   The complete description of input, processing, output, and storage requirements necessary to code a computer program.

project manager   An individual who is an expert in project planning and management, defines and develops the project plan, and tracks the plan to ensure all key project milestones are completed on time.

project milestone   Key date by which a certain group of activities needs to be performed.

project plan   Defines the what, when, and who questions of system development including all activities to be performed, the individuals or resources who will perform the activities, and the time required to complete each activity.

project scope   Clearly defines the high-level system requirements.

project scope document   A written definition of the project scope and usually no longer than a paragraph.

project team   A team designed to accomplish specific one-time goals, which is disbanded once the project is complete.

Prolog   A language widely used in the field of artificial intelligence.

proof-of-concept prototype   A prototype used to prove the technical feasibility of a proposed system.

proof of correctness   The use of mathematical logic to infer that a relation between program variables assumed true at the program entry implies that another relation between program variables holds at program exit.

protection ring   A hierarchy of access modes through which a computer system enforces the access rights granted to each user, program, and process, ensuring that each operates only within the authorized access mode.

protocol   A set of instructions required to initiate and maintain communication between sender and receiver devices.

protocol data unit (PDU)   This is OSI terminology for "packet." A PDU is a data object exchanged by protocol machines (entities) within a given layer. PDUs consist of both protocol control information (PCI) and user data.

prototype   A usable system or subcomponent that is built inexpensively or quickly with the intention of modifying or replacing it.

pseudoflow   An apparent loophole deliberately implanted in an operating system program as a trap for intruders.

pseudocode   Program processing specifications that can be prepared as structured English-like statements which can then be easily converted into source code.

psychographic filtering   Anticipates the user's preferences based on the answers given to a questionnaire.

public key encryption (PKE)   An encryption system that uses two keys: a public key that everyone can have and a private key for only the recipient.

public network   A network on which the organization competes for time with others.

purging   The orderly review of storage and removal of inactive or obsolete data files.

push technology   An environment in which businesses and organizations come to the user with information, services, and product offerings based on the user profile.

query and reporting tools   Similar to QBE tools, SQL, and report generators in the typical database environment.

query-by-example tools (QBE)   Helps the user graphically design the answer to a question.

queue   A waiting line in which a set of computer programs is in secondary storage awaiting processing.

random access   A method that allows records to be read from and written to disk media without regard to the order of their record key.

random-access memory (RAM)   Computer memory chips used to store programs and data temporarily during processing, a technology that is used heavily in microcomputers.

read-only memory (ROM)   Computer memory chips with preprogrammed circuits for storing such software as word processors and spreadsheets.

real-time processing   Computer processing that generates output fast enough to support multiple activities being performed concurrently.

real-time reaction   A response to a penetration attempt that can prevent actual penetration because the attempt is detected and diagnosed in time.

record block   A group or collection of records appearing between interblock gaps on magnetic storage media. This group of records is handled as a single entity in computer processing.

record blocking   A technique of writing several records to magnetic storage media in between interblock gaps or spaces.

recovery   The restoration of the information processing facility or other related assets following physical destruction or damage.

recovery procedures   The action necessary to restore a system's computational capability and data files after system failure or penetration.

recurring decision   A decision that you have to make repeatedly and often periodically, whether weekly, monthly, quarterly, or yearly.

reduced instruction set computing (RISC)   A method of processing by which the set of instructions available to the computer is a subset of that found on conventional computers.

regression testing   The rerunning of test cases that a program has previously executed correctly to detect errors create during software correction or modification.

relation   Describes each two-dimensional table or file in the relation model (hence its name relational database model).

relational database   Uses a series of logically related two-dimensional tables or files to store information in the form of a database.

remanence   The residual magnetism that remains on magnetic storage media after degaussing.

Remote File System (RFS)   A distributed file system, similar to NFS, developed by AT&T and distributed with their UNIX System V operating system. See Network File System.

remote procedure call (RPC)   An easy and popular paradigm for implementing the client/server model of distributed computing. A request is sent to a remote system to execute a designated procedure using arguments supplied and the result returned to the caller.

repeater   A device that propagates electrical signals from one cable to another without making routing decisions or providing packet filtering. In OSI terminology, a repeater is a physical layer intermediate system. See bridge and router.

report   Printed or displayed output that communicates the content of files and other activities. The output is typically organized and easily read.

Report Program Generator (RPG)   A nonprocedural programming language used for many business applications.

report writing   The process of accessing data from files and generating it as information in the form of output.

request for comments (RFC)   The document series begun in 1969, which describes the Internet suite of protocols and related experiments. Not all (in fact very few) RFCs describe Internet standards, but all Internet standards are written up as RFCs.

request for proposal (RFP)   A formal document that describes in detail logical requirements for a proposed system and invites outsourcing organizations (vendors) to submit bids for its development.

requirement definition document   Defines all of the business requirements, prioritizes them in order of business importance, and places them in a formal comprehensive document.

residue   Data left in storage after processing operations and before degaussing or rewriting has occurred.

resolution of a printer The number of dots per inch (dpi) a printer produces, which is the same principle as the resolution in a monitor.

resolution of a screen The number of pixels a screen has. Pixels (picture elements) are the dots that make up an image on the screen.

resource In a computer system, any function, device, or data collection that can be allocated to users or programs.

resource sharing In a computer system, the concurrent use of a resource by more than one user, job, or program.

risk analysis An analysis that examines an organization's information resources, its existing controls, and its remaining organization and computer system vulnerabilities. It combines the loss potential for each resource or combination of resources with an estimated rate of occurrence to establish a potential level of damage in dollars or other assets.

risk assessment Synonymous with risk analysis.

risk management Consists of the identification of risks or threats, the implementation of security measures, and the monitoring of those measures for effectiveness.

rlogin A service offered by Berkeley UNIX that allows users of one machine to log into other UNIX systems (for which they are authorized) and interact as if their terminals were connected directly. Similar to Telnet.

robot A mechanical device equipped with simulated human senses and the capability of taking action on its own.

robotics The use of automated equipment for production work and other mechanical tasks.

rule based expert The type of expert system that expresses the problem-solving process as rules.

router A system responsible for making decisions about which of several paths will be followed by network (or Internet) traffic. To do this, it uses a routing protocol to gain information about the network, and algorithms to choose the best route based on several criteria known as "routing metrics." In OSI terminology, a router is a network layer intermediate system. See gateway, bridge, and repeater.

safeguard Synonymous with control.

Safe Harbor Principles The set of rules to which U.S. businesses that want to trade with the European Union (EU) must adhere.

sales force automation (SFA) system Automatically tracks all of the steps in the sales process.

sanitizing The degaussing or overwriting of sensitive information in magnetic or other storage media.

Sarbanes–Oxley Act of 2002 The most dramatic change to federal securities laws since the 1930s, the Act radically redesigns federal regulation of public company corporate governance and reporting obligations. It also significantly tightens accountability standards for directors and officers, auditors, securities analysts, and legal counsel.

satellite modem A modem that allows Internet access from a satellite dish.

scalability Refers to how well a system can adapt to increased demands.

scannable resume (ASCII resume, plain-text resume) Designed to be evaluated by skills-extraction software and typically contains all resume content without any formatting.

scanner Captures images, photos, and artwork that already exist on paper.

scavenging The searching of residue for the purpose of unauthorized data acquisition.

scheduling program A systems program that schedules and monitors the processing of production jobs in the computer system.

scope creep Occurs when the scope of the project increases.

script bunny (or script kiddie) Someone who would like to be a hacker but does not have much technical expertise.

search engine A facility on the Web that helps the user find sites with the information the user wants.

secure operating system An operating system that effectively controls hardware, software, and firmware functions to provide the level of protection appropriate to the value of the data resources managed by the operating system.

security audit An examination of data security procedures and measures to evaluate their adequacy and compliance with established policy.

security controls Techniques and methods to ensure that only authorized users can access the computer information system and its resources.

security filter A set of software or firmware routines and techniques employed in a computer system to prevent automatic forwarding of specified data over unprotected links or to unauthorized persons.

security kernel The central part of a computer system (hardware, software, or firmware) that implements the fundamental security procedures for controlling access to system resources.

security program A systems program that controls access to data in files and permits only authorized use of terminals and other related equipment. Control is usually exercised through various levels of safeguards assigned on the basis of the user's need to know.

seepage The accidental flow of data or information to unauthorized individuals that is presumed to be protected by computer security safeguards.

selection A program control structure created in response to a condition test in which one of two or more processing paths can be taken.

self-organizing neural network A network that finds patterns and relationships in vast amounts of data by itself.

self sourcing (or knowledge worker/end-user development) The development and support of IT systems by knowledge workers with little or no help from IT specialists.

selling prototype A prototype used to convince people of the worth of a proposed system.

semiconductor Material used in electronic components that possesses electrical conducting qualities of conductors and resistors.

sensitive information   Any information that requires protection and that should not be made generally available.

sequential organization   The physical arrangement of records in a sequence that corresponds with their logical key.

serial connector   Usually has 9 holes but may have 25 that fit into the corresponding number of pins in the port. Serial connectors are often used for monitors and certain types of modems.

Serial Line IP (SLIP)   An IP used to run over serial lines such as telephone circuits or RS-232 cables interconnecting two systems. SLIP is now being replaced by Point-to-Point Protocol. See Point-to-Point Protocol.

serial organization   The physical arrangement of records in a sequence.

serial processing   The processing of records in the physical order in which they appear in a file or on an input device.

server farm   A location that stores a group of servers in a single place.

service level agreement (SLA)   Defines the specific responsibilities of the service provider and sets the customer expectations.

service program   An operating system program that provides a variety of common processing services to users (e.g., utility programs, librarian programs, and other software).

session layer   The OSI layer that provides means for dialogue control between end systems.

shared information   An organization's information is in one central location allowing anyone to access and use it as they need it.

sign-off   The knowledge workers' actual signatures indicating they approve all of the business requirements.

simulation   The use of an executable model to represent the behavior of an object. During testing, the computational hardware, the external environment, and even the coding segments may be simulated.

Simple Mail Transfer Protocol (SMTP)   The Internet e-mail protocol.

Simple Network Management Protocol (SNMP)   The network management protocol of choice for TCP/IP-based Internets.

simultaneous processing   The execution of two or more computer program instructions at the same time in a multiprocessing environment.

skill words   Nouns and adjectives used by organizations to describe job skills that should be woven into the text of applicants' resumes.

slack space   The space left over from the end of the file to the end of the cluster.

slave computer   A front-end processor that handles input and output functions for a host computer.

smart cards   Plastic cards the size of a credit card that contain an embedded chip on which digital information can be stored.

sociability   The ability of intelligent agents to confer with each other.

social engineering   A person conning his way into acquiring information that the person has no right to.

software   Computer programs, procedures, rules, and possibly documentation and data pertaining to the operation of the computer system.

software life cycle   The period of time beginning when a software product is conceived and ending when the product is no longer available for use. The software life cycle is typically broken into phases (e.g., requirements, design, programming, testing, conversion, operations, and maintenance).

software suite   Bundled software that comes from the same publisher and costs less than buying all the software pieces individually.

sort   The arrangement of data in ascending or descending, alphabetic or numeric order.

source document   The form that is used for the initial recording of data prior to system input.

source program   The computer program that is coded in an assembler or higher-level programming language.

spam   Unsolicited e-mail.

spoofing   The deliberate inducement of a user or resource to take incorrect action, such as forging the return address on an e-mail message so the message appears to come from someone other than the actual sender.

spooling   A technique that maximizes processing speed through the temporary use of high-speed storage devices. Input files are transferred from slower, permanent storage and queued in the high-speed devices to await processing, or output files are queued in high-speed devices to await transfer to slower storage devices.

spreadsheet software   Computer software that divides a display screen into a large grid. This grid allows the user to enter labels and values that can be manipulated or analyzed.

SQL   See Structured Query Language.

spyware (or sneakware or stealthware)   Software that comes hidden in free downloadable software and tracks the user's online movements.

stacked-job processing   A computer processing technique in which programs and data awaiting processing are placed into a queue and executed sequentially.

standards audit   The check to ensure that applicable standards are properly used.

statement testing   A test method of satisfying the criterion that each statement in a program be executed at least once during the program testing.

static analysis   The direct analysis of the form and structure of a product that does not require its execution. It can be applied to the requirements, design, or code.

steganography   The hiding of information inside other information.

storage media   Physical hardware on which programs and data are maintained in machine-readable format.

strategic management   Provides an organization with overall direction and guidance.

structured design   A methodology for designing systems and programs through a top-down, hierarchical segmentation.

structured programming   The process of writing computer programs using logical, hierarchical control structures to carry out processing.

Structured Query Language (SQL)   The international standard language for defining and accessing relational database.

subjective information   Attempts to describe something that is unknown.

subroutine   A segment of code that can be called up by a program and executed at any time from any point.

subscript   A value used in programming to reference an item of data stored in a table.

supercomputer   The fastest, most powerful, and expensive type of computer.

supply chain   The paths reaching out to all of a company's suppliers of parts and services.

supply-chain management (SCM) system   Tracks inventory and information among business processes and across companies.

swapping   A method of computer processing in which programs not actively being processed are held on special storage devices and alternated in and out of memory with other programs according to priority.

switch   A device that connects multiple computers into a network in which multiple communications links can be in operation simultaneously.

switching costs   Costs that can make customers reluctant to switch to another product or service.

symbolic evaluation   The process of analyzing the path of program execution through the use of symbolic expressions.

symbolic execution   The analytical technique of dissecting each program path.

syntax   The statement formats and rules for the use of a programming language.

system bus   The electronic pathways that move information between basic components on the motherboard, including the pathway between the CPU and RAM.

system integrity   The state that exists when there is complete assurance that under all conditions a computer system is based on the logical correctness and reliability of the operating system and the logical completeness of the hardware, software, and firmware that implement the protection mechanisms and data integrity.

system integrity procedures   Procedures established to ensure that hardware, software, firmware, and data in a computer system maintain their state of original integrity and are not tampered with by unauthorized personnel.

systems analysis   The process of studying information requirements and preparing a set of functional specifications that identify what a new or replacement system should accomplish.

systems design   The development of a plan for implementing a set of functional requirements as an operational system.

systems development life cycle (SDLC)   The systematic systems building process consisting of specific phases — for example, preliminary investigation, requirements determination, systems analysis, systems design, systems development, systems implementation, and systems operation and maintenance.

Systems Network Architecture (SNA)   IBM's proprietary network architecture.

systems software   The programs and other processing routines that control and activate the computer hardware facilitating its use.

system test   The process of testing an integrated hardware/software system to verify that the system meets its specified requirements.

table   An area of computer memory containing multiple storage locations that can be referenced by the same name.

table driven   An indexed file in which tables containing record keys (i.e., disk addresses) are used to retrieve records.

tactical management   Develops the goals and strategies outlined by strategic management.

tape management system   Systems software that assesses the given information on jobs to be run and produces information for operators and librarians regarding which data resources (e.g., tapes and disks) are needed for job execution.

task management system   It allocates the processor unit resources according to priority scheme or other assignment methods.

TCP/IP (Transport Control Protocol)   See Internet Protocol.

technical architecture   Defines the hardware, software, and telecommunications equipment required to run the system.

technological attack   An attack that can be perpetrated by circumventing or nullifying hardware, software, and firmware access control mechanisms rather than by subverting system personnel or other users.

technology-literate knowledge worker   A person who knows how and when to apply technology.

telecommunications   Any transmission, emission, or reception of signs, signals, writing, images, sounds, or other information by wire, radio visual, satellite, or electromagnetic systems.

Telecommunications Standardization Sector of the International Telecommunications Union (ITU-TSS)   A unit of the International Telecommunications Union (ITU) of the United Nations. An organization with representatives from the post office, telegraph, and telecommunications agencies (PTTs) of the world. ITU-TSS produces technical standards, known as recommendations, for all internationally controlled aspects of analog and digital communications.

telecommunications device   A tool used to send information to and receive it from another person or location.

telecommuting   The use of communications technologies (such as the Internet) to work in a place other than a central location.

teleprocessing   Information processing and transmission performed by an integrated system of telecommunications, computers, and person-to-machine interface equipment.

teleprocessing security   The protection that results from all measures designed to prevent deliberate, inadvertent, or unauthorized disclosure or acquisition of information stored in or transmitted by a teleprocessing system.

Telnet The virtual terminal protocol in the Internet suite of protocols. Allows users of one host to log into a remote host and interact as normal terminal users of that host.

temporary advantage An advantage that, sooner or later, the competition duplicates or leap frogs with a better system.

terabyte (TB) Roughly 1 trillion bytes.

terminal identification The means used to establish the unique identification of a terminal by a computer system or network.

test condition A detailed step the system must perform along with the expected result of the step.

test data Data that simulates actual data to form and content and is used to evaluate a system or program before it is put into operation.

test data generators Computer software tools that help generate files of data that can be used to test the execution and logic of application programs.

testing The examination of the behavior of a program through its execution on sample data sets.

thin client A workstation with a small amount of processing power and costing less than a full-powered workstation.

threat monitoring The analysis, assessment, and review of audit trails and other data collected to search out system events that may constitute violations or precipitate incidents involving data privacy.

three-dimensional (3D) technology Presentations of information that give the user the illusion that the object viewed is actually in the room with the user.

three generic strategies Cost leadership, differentiation, and a focused strategy.

thrill-seeker hacker A hacker who breaks into computer systems for fun.

throughput The process of measuring the amount of work that a computer system can execute within a specified period of time.

time-dependent password A password that is valid only for a certain period of time of the day or during a specified time interval.

top-level domain Three-letter extension of a Web site address that identifies its type.

touchpad Popular on notebook computers, a stationary mouse that is touched with the finger.

touch screen Special screen the user touches to perform a particular function.

trackball An upside-down, stationary mouse in which the ball is moved instead of the device. Used mainly for notebooks.

traditional technology approach Has two primary views of any system — information and procedures — and it keeps these two views separate and distinct at all times.

traffic flow security The protection that results from those features in some cryptography equipment that conceal the presence of valid messages on a communications circuit, usually by causing the circuit to appear busy at all times or by encrypting the source and destination addresses of valid messages.

transactional processing system (TPS)   The processing of transactions as they occur rather than in batches.

transaction file   A collection of records containing data generated from the current business activity.

Transmission Control Protocol (TCP)   The major transport protocol in the Internet suite of protocols providing reliable, connect-oriented, full duplex streams.

transceiver   The physical device that connects a host interface to a local area network, such as Ethernet. Ethernet transceivers contain electronics that apply signals to the cable and sense collisions.

transnational firm   A firm that produces and sells products and services all over the world.

transport layer   The OSI layer that is responsible for reliable end-to-end data transfer between end systems.

trapdoor   A breach created intentionally in a computer system to collect, alter, or destroy data.

Trojan horse   A computer program that is apparently or actually useful and contains a trap door.

Trojan horse software   Software the user does not want that is hidden inside software the user wants.

Trojan horse virus   Hides inside other software. Usually an attachment or download.

true search engine   Uses software agent technologies to search the Internet for key words and then places them into indices.

Trusted Computer Security Evaluation Criteria (TCSEC)   A security development standard for system manufacturers and a basis for comparing and evaluating different computer systems. Also known as the Orange Book.

turnkey system   A complete, ready-to-operate system that is purchased from a vendor as opposed to a system developed in-house.

twisted-pair wire   A communication medium that consists of pairs of wires that are twisted together and bound into cable.

unallocated space   The set of clusters that has been marked as available to store information but has not yet received a file, or still contains some or all of a file marked as deleted.

uninstaller software   Utility software that can be used to remove software that the user no longer wants from the hard disk.

URL (uniform resource locator)   An address for a specific Web page or document within a Web site.

USB (Universal Serial Bus)   It is becoming the most popular means of connecting devices to a computer. Most standard desktops today have at least 2 USB ports, and most standard notebooks have at least one.

user acceptance testing (UAT)   Determines if the system satisfies the business requirements and enables the knowledge workers to perform their jobs correctly.

user agent   An intelligent agent that takes action on the user's behalf.

user documentation   Highlights how to use the system.

user interface management   The component of the expert system that is used to run a consultation.

unit testing   The testing of a module for typographic, syntactic, and logical errors and for correct implementation of its design and satisfaction of its requirements.

universal product code (UPC)   An array of varied width lines that can be read by special machines (e.g., OCR devices) and converted into alphanumeric data. This method is used to mark merchandise for direct input of sales transactions.

UNIX   An operating system initially developed by Bell Labs. Used primarily on engineering workstations and computers, and networked systems. UNIX is difficult for nontechnical people to use but is becoming increasingly popular in the business environment in supporting GUI applications.

update   The file processing activity in which master records are altered to reflect the current business activity reflected in transaction files.

utility software   Software that provides additional functionality to the operating system.

validation   The determination of correctness with respect to the user's needs and requirements of the final program or software produced from a development effort.

validation, verification, and testing   Used as an entity to define a procedure of review, analysis, and testing to discover errors throughout the software life cycle. Determines that functions operate as specified and ensures the production of quality software.

value-added network (VAN)   A semipublic network that provides services beyond the movement of information from one place to another.

value chain   A tool that views the organization as a chain or series of processes, each of which adds value to the product or service for the customer.

value network   All the resources behind the click on a Web page that the customer does not see, but that together create the customer relationship-service, order fulfillment, shipping, financing, information brokering, and access to other products.

verification   A demonstration of the consistency, completeness, and correctness of the software at and between each stage of the development life cycle.

verify   The process of ensuring that transcribed data has been accurately keyboarded.

vertical market software   Application software that is unique to a particular industry.

video disk   An optical disk that can store images.

videotext   Generic text that refers to a computer information system that uses television, telecommunication, and computer technologies to access and manipulate large, graphics-oriented databases.

virtual marketing   Encourages users of a product or service supplied by a B2C (buyer to customer) company to ask friends to join.

virtual memory   A method of extending computer memory by using secondary storage devices to store program pages that are not being executed at the time.

virtual private network (VPN) Uses software to establish a secure channel on the Internet for transmitting data.

virtual reality A three-dimensional computer simulation in which the user actively and physically participates.

virtual workplace A technology-enabled workplace — no walls, no boundaries, work anytime, anyplace. Linked to other people and information the user needs.

virus Software that is written with malicious intent to cause annoyance or damage.

voice mail An e-mail system that allows a regular voice message to be digitally stored at the receiving location and converted back to voice form when it is accessed.

voice synthesizer An input and output device that can either interpret and convert human speech into digital signals for computer processing or convert digital signals into audible signals that resemble human speech.

walker An input device that captures and records the movement of the feet as the user walks or turns in different directions.

walk-through A manual analysis technique in which the module author or developer describes the module's structure and logic to colleagues.

wearable computer A fully equipped computer that is worn just like a piece of clothing or attached to a piece of clothing similar to the way the cell phone is carried on the belt.

Web authoring software Helps design and develop Web sites and pages that are published on the Web.

Web browser software Enables the user to surf the Web.

Web farm Either a Web site that has multiple servers or an ISP that provides Web site outsourcing services using multiple servers.

Web log Consists of one line of information for every visitor to a Web site and is usually stored on a Web server.

Web page A specific portion of a Web site that deals with a certain topic.

Web portal A site that provides a wide range of services including search engines, free e-mail, chat rooms, discussion boards, and links to hundreds of different sites.

Web server Provides information and services to Web surfers.

Web services Software applications that talk to other software applications over the Internet using XML as a key enabling technology.

Web site A specific location on the Web where the user can visit, gather information, and order products.

Web site address A unique name that identifies a specific site on the Web.

Web space A storage area where the user's Web site can be kept.

whitehat (or ethical) hacker A computer security professional who is hired by a company to break into its computer system.

wide area networks (WAN) A communications network that covers a broad geographic area.

WiFi (wireless fidelity) A way of transmitting information in a wave form that is reasonably fast and is often used for notebooks. Also known as IEEE 802.11b.

wired communications Media that transmit information over a closed connected path.

wireless communications Media that transmit information through the air.

wireless Internet service provider (wireless ISP) A company that provides the same services as a standard Internet service provider except that the user does not need a wired connection for access.

wireless local area network (WLAN) A local area network using wireless communication protocol.

wireless network access point A device that allows computers to access a network using radio waves.

word In computer memory, a contiguous set of bits used as a basic unit of storage. Words are usually 8,16, 32, or 64 bits long.

word processing The use of computers or other technology for storage, editing, correction, revision, and production of textual files in the form of letters, reports, and documents.

workflow Defines all of the steps or business rules, from beginning to end, required for a process to run correctly.

workgroup A group of people who can work together to achieve a common set of goals, linked together via technological tools and hardware.

workshop training Held in a classroom environment and led by an instructor.

World Wide Web or Web A multimedia-based collection of information, services, and Web sites supported by the Internet.

worm A type of virus that spreads itself not just from file to file but from computer to computer via e-mail and other Internet traffic.

X.500 A ITU-TSS international standard that binds a public key to a directory name.

X.400 A ITU-TSS international standard for reformatting and sending Internet work via e-mail.

XML (eXtensible Markup Language) A coding language for the Web that lets computers interpret the meaning of information in Web documents.

X-Open A group of computer manufacturers who promote the development of portable applications based on UNIX. They publish a document called the X-Open Portability Guide.

X/recommendations The ITU-TSS documents that describe data communication network standards. Well-known ones include: X.25 Packet Switching Standard, X.400 Message Handling System, and X.500 Directory Services.

Zip drive A high capacity, removeable diskette drive that typically uses 100MB Zip disks or cartridges.

Appendix V
Sample Audit Programs

Audit Program for Systems Maintenance

I. Systems Maintenance

Objective: Determine that all maintenance activity is performed and documented according to installation standards and procedures by reviewing documentation related to systems maintenance.

Audit steps

1. Determine whether standards have been established for the documentation of systems maintenance.

2. Evaluate existing standards to determine whether they are comprehensive enough and cover such issues as compliance with ISO 17799.

3. Review a sample of existing documentation to determine whether it complies with installation standards.

4. Ascertain whether systems maintenance documentation is maintained in a secure environment and protected against tampering.

II. Change Procedures

Objective: Determine whether all changes to the system are completely documented and tested to ensure the desired results by reviewing documentation related to system changes (maintenance) and evaluating its adequacy.

Audit steps

1. Interview appropriate personnel to determine:
   - Documentation standards that relate to system changes
   - Testing standards that relate to system changes

2. Select a sample of completed system changes and determine whether:
   - Documentation is in accordance with installation standards.
   - Documentation provides a clear explanation of the change made and the reason for the change.
   - Documentation has been appropriately reviewed and approved.

- Test plans for the change are in compliance with installation standards.
- The test plan thoroughly tested the implemented change.
- The test plan and the results of the test were reviewed and approved.

3. Evaluate the review process related to system changes and determine whether:
   - A peer review of system changes is done before they are submitted for approval.
   - Operations management reviews and approves system changes before implementation.
   - Errors were identified, corrected, retested, documented, and reviewed for approval before release for use.

4. Assess whether the controls over documentation and test results are adequate to prevent tampering.

III. Implementation of System Changes

Objective: The implementation of system changes should be performed by a group other than the group responsible for the system (for example, systems software changes should be implemented by someone other than a systems programmer). All procedures related to the implementation of system changes should be reviewed.

Audit steps

1. Identify the personnel responsible for implementing system changes and determine whether an adequate separation of duties exists.

2. Determine whether adequate communication links exist between the change implementation group and the other data processing and user groups involved in the change process.

3. Determine the adequacy of documentation supplied to the change implementation group to support the change.

4. Determine whether the change documentation includes the date and time at which changes will be installed.

5. Determine that documentation similar to that given to the change implementation group has been released to system users to inform them of the impending changes.

6. Determine whether system changes have been installed in an orderly manner (i.e., in compliance with standards and procedures).

7. Determine whether system changes are evaluated and accepted after installation.

8. Determine whether computer operators cannot reverse system changes without assistance from the change implementation group.

IV. System Change Log

Objective: Determine whether a chronological record of all system changes is maintained by reviewing records of all system changes.

Audit steps

1. Determine whether a log exists to record all changes made to the system.
2. Review the log for completeness and for evidence of management approval.

ISO 9001 Review: Conclusion and Documents

In this section a New York company's ISO 9001 review is examined in terms of lessons learned that can be applied to similar audits. The initial NSAI audit was conducted over a three-day period. The net result was a total of 52 Corrective Action Requests (CARs) written of which one was deleted, two were issued to the corporate phase review process, and eight were issued to software. The site was certified pending a resolution of issues within 90 days.

Notes on audits for use by guides:

- First and most important in this NSAI review was beginning each new piece of an audit with a manager. Allowing upper management to answer the broad questions and paint an overview of their projects, processes, and interdependencies made it easier for the auditor to isolate and identify the appropriate project and the next layer of management to approach. (The auditor's questions are best answered by management; at the lowest technical level the answers are generally too focused and detailed and served only to confuse the audit.)
- The more the guide knows about all the processes used as well as the history of the processes, the better. There were many times in this audit when it appeared that a process not known to the guide was being followed or that the process had actually been changed during the course of the project. If a project passes through many different people during its cycle, this is not always obvious to the person being audited (who is usually the last to touch the project). In some instances in this audit the guide could help point the person being audited to the process or procedure that the auditor was looking for or to the person who really knew where specific information was kept.
- The more the guide knows about the projects and their history, the better. For example, avoid, if possible, projects that may be associated with CARs or other nonstandard processes or projects that have been through numerous changes in personnel, management,

or processes. Such projects can pose a challenge as an auditor tries to trace their development against the company's current processes. They may also pose a challenge in finding someone who remembers what happened during an early phase. (Of course, this is less of a problem if record keeping has been maintained in good shape throughout the life of the project.) Care must be taken, however, to ensure the auditor has a choice of projects so as to avoid creating the belief that he was directed to the "perfect" project.

- At least in this audit the guide was not only welcomed but also asked by the auditor to feel free to interject comments or questions that would help the audit. It is one role of the guide to help translate the auditor's questions into local terminology. The guide was not prevented from making suggestions to the person being audited such as, "Why don't you show item X?" or "Why don't you pull out procedure X and we'll follow that?"
- The NSAI auditor in this review was very disturbed by the company's untidy offices. The feeling was "How can you produce a controlled product out of an uncontrolled environment." Even so, because the staff did produce the items needed for the audit, there was nothing in this area that could be cited. This pointed out a need for the company to examine its quality records procedures and the audit guide anticipated producing future recommendations in this area.

A breakdown of the 52 CARs cited in the audit is as follows:

- *Document Control (4):* Documents that were current and in use but lacked information such as page numbers, approval, etc.
- *Quality System (2):* Portions of the company's quality procedures were not completely documented.
- *Design Verification (1):* The company was requested to add and document a step in one of the product initiation processes.
- *Process Control (1):* No evidence was found of a documented and controlled process for a significant step in the product cycle.

Lessons Learned — 9001 Review

The staff associated with the New York City review and the ISO certification effort was asked for their reaction to the process. Following are excerpted quotes summarizing their comments:

- Expect to be challenged. You will not get complete buy-in because people are being asked to go beyond the scope of what they believe they were hired to do. It is important that employees have a forum to vent their frustrations. Such comments can be a good indicator of the attitude and commitment employees are making and how well they understand why the company has chosen specific approaches to meeting its business needs.

- It was very poor planning to let another group within our facility have its own ISO certification in the same plant with the rest of us. It increases COTS and duplicates services.
- It is much harder to achieve and maintain certification for a site which does not have a single site manager ... If we could change the world we would have all orgs in New York City report up to one manager who is located here.
- We did too much work when we first started. We had people with backgrounds in product quality assurance running the program and they make it a major effort. Perhaps if we had known, we would not have had these same people calling the shots. We might have more quickly gone to the streamlined internal auditing system.
- ... A site-wide document control system and team .... Common numbering and formats would have helped. More document templates would have helped. Developing our own on-line document control system has been a tragedy of errors. Don't do it.

Conclusion

In terms of the description, experience, and examples given above regarding ISO certification, the IS auditor can contribute to the training and development of internal staff in performing the audit process. There are a number of questions the organization must ask itself in performing this function. It is an intensive effort and process that must be followed and performed to the letter. There must be a commitment to training, learning, and education if it is to succeed. Management and corporate must support the process.

APPENDICES

Document 1. Audit Analysis

Analysis Date: _____   Analyzed by: _____

Audit Date: _____   Audit Number: _____

ISO 9001 Clause Number	OUTCOME P = Passed N = Not Covered # = No. of CARs	ISO 9001 CLAUSE Name
4.1	_____	Management responsibility
4.2	_____	Quality system
4.3	_____	Contract review
4.4	_____	Design control
4.5	_____	Document control
4.6	_____	Purchasing
4.7	_____	Purchaser supplied product
4.8	_____	Product identification and traceability
4.9	_____	Process control
4.10	_____	Inspection and testing
4.11	_____	Inspection, measuring, and test equipment
4.12	_____	Inspection and test status
4.13	_____	Control of nonconforming product
4.14	_____	Corrective action
4.15	_____	Handling, storage, packaging, and delivery
4.16	_____	Quality records
4.17	_____	Internal quality audits
4.18	_____	Training
4.19	_____	Servicing
4.20	_____	Statistical techniques

Document 2. ISO 9000 Reference Card

Orange County Software Engineering
ISO 9001 Reference Card
Orange County Quality Policy

Unisys Quality Policy

We are committed to quality and excellence in all endeavors. We have set our goals to achieve customer satisfaction — to deliver error-free, competitive products and customer solutions on time with service second to none.

Seven Quality Beliefs

1. Quality is the responsibility of every employee.
2. Quality improvement results from management leadership.
3. Quality attributes should be viewed from the customer's view.
4. Focus for improvement must be on each job at each step of the process.
5. No level of defect is acceptable.
6. Commitment to continuous improvement.
7. Quality improvement reduces costs.

Orange County Quality System

QC Quality System Manual [QSM]

→ Global Policies, Processes, and Procedures
[Phase Review SMM], Process Guides

→ Local Policies, Processes, and Procedures
[Work Instructions, Handbooks, and Guides]

→ Checklists and Forms

OC Software Engineering ISO 9001 Reference Card

APPENDICES

Document 3. ISO 9001 Principle Themes

Documentation:	Record what you do.
Practices:	Do what you have documented.
Records:	Keep evidence of what you have done.
Audits:	Check what you do.
Corrective Action:	Correct discrepancies that are found.

Phase Review Phases

Phase 1: Study [Feasibility]
Phase 2: Design [Design Review]
Phase 3: Develop [Coding, Inspection, Unit Test, Integration Test]
Phase 4: Quality [System & Field Test]
Phase 5: Evaluate [Continuation]
Phase 6: Withdraw [Terminate Support]

Software Engineering Organization
ISO 9001 News

Check A-Mail Newsgroup WC.QIT for latest news on ISO 9001 status and issues. The Software Engineering ISO 9001 Review Board is also available to address questions on ISO 9001.

What do I say to an auditor?

1. Listen to the questions.
2. Give answers that are brief and to the point.
3. Be truthful.
4. Focus on facts not opinions.
5. If you don't know the answer, say so (it's ok!).
6. You may refer the auditor to someone who will know the answer.
7. Remember — the auditor is looking at your group's processes, not you.

What questions might an auditor ask?

1. What is your job?
2. What processes and procedures do you follow to do your job?
3. How do these processes and procedures relate to the Phase Review or other processes?
4. What are your qualifications to do this job?
5. How do you know that the specification you are working to is still current?
6. Are you familiar with the Orange County Quality Policy?
7. How were you trained to do your job?
8. Can you show me the process document you use for process "x?"

Document 4. Sample CAR Forms

Software House   **New York City**

CORRECTIVE ACTION REQUEST
QUALITY SYSTEM AUDIT

CAR Number:

Area Audited: Audit Date:

Area Manager:

Responsible Manager: Audit Number:
                                                      Reference No:

NONCOMPLIANCE has been identified as defined below. Please respond to this noncompliance by indicating the nature of corrective action you are planning and the date it will become effective. Per the referenced DI, your response is required within five working days.

Process Being Audited:

Local Reference: QSM Ref:

Procedure Name:

Finding:

Recommendation:

Audited By: Car Date:

Observed By:

Approved By: Approval Date:

Reference: DI 34700047   Side 1 of 2 Sides   Form: F-3470S020 1/01

APPENDICES

CORRECTIVE ACTION REQUEST

Closing Meeting Date: CAR Number:

Planned Corrective Action: To be completed by CAR Addressee

Committed Completion Date:

Closure Criteria: To be completed by Auditor

Commitment:

Responsible Manager Signature: Date Signed:

Status Update:
Item Changed: To be completed by Auditor
                          Date: By:

Corrective Action Verified: To be completed by Auditor

Signature: Date:

Distribution: To be completed by Auditor
Controlled Copy:
                          Auditor until closure, then
                          Quality System Coordinator
                                              Copies:
    Manager of the area audited
    Responsible Manager
    Quality System Coordinator until closure, then Auditor

Note: Redistribute copies each time information content is updated

Reference: DI 34700047   Side 2 of 2 Sides   Form: F-34705020 1/01

Document 5.

**Software House INTERNAL ISO 9001/9002 QUALITY AUDIT   IAF-03
CORRECTIVE ACTION REQUEST FORMREV B**

PAGE 1 OF _____

Issued to: Issued by: Date Issued:

Audit#:   CAR#:

Nonconformity with Description:

Nonconformity with Paragraph:

Auditee Concurrence with Nonconformity Descripton and Corrective Action
Commitment:

Date for Completion of CAR:

Signed: Position: Date:

Follow-Up/Close-Out Action:

Correction Action Verified   Signed:
Date CAR Closed: Position:
                                    Date:

Detroit Facility Procedure #43578921-00

Audit Program for Operating System Security Evaluation

Location:_____   Date:_____

Initial Checklist

Before Beginning the Audit, the Auditor Should Locate the Following Documents for
Easy Access:

1. A list of all hardware configurations showing all devices,
   communication lines, and operating systems   _____
2. A list of operating systems being used or planned, with version and
   release levels, brief descriptions, target dates for implementation,
   and management approvals   _____
3. A list of application systems in production with a brief description
   of each   _____
4. A list of utilities for each operating system, detailing utility name,
   purpose, approvals required to use the utility, names or classes of
   individuals authorized to use each utility, levels of access control
   over each utility, and monitoring policies and procedures   _____
5. An organizational chart of the IT department showing names and
   position titles   _____

1.	SYSTEMS DOCUMENTATION REVIEW **Objective:** To ensure that current documentation is available, adequate, and safeguarded for each operating system version. Recommendations resulting from the systems documentation review should cite appropriate control objectives, reference numbers, and applicable workpapers.	
Audit Test No.	**Action**	**Source of Information or Documentation**
1.1	**Vendor-Supplied Systems Documentation**	
1.1.1	Identify the vendor-supplied documentation for each operating system.	
1.1.2	Determine whether vendor-supplied documentation is complete and current for each operating system in use.	
1.2	**System Documentation for Internal Modifications**	
1.2.1	Identify the documentation for operating system modifications.	

1.2.2	Confirm that the following documentation is available for each operating system modification: • Detailed description of the operating system • Security features • Detailed description of system utilities • Control or command language requirements • User error messages • Error detection and correction features • A list of all files and modules used by the operating system	
1.2.3	Verify that documentation is complete and current for each operating system modification.	
1.2.4	Review the procedures that restrict operating system documentation to authorized personnel.	
1.2.5	Confirm that backup copies of operating system and utility documentation are available.	
2.	**UTILITIES REVIEW** **Objective:** To ensure that all utilities are adequately restricted to authorized users. Recommendations resulting from the utilities review should cite appropriate control objectives, reference numbers, and applicable workpapers.	

Audit Test No.	Action	Source of Information or Documentation
2.1	Determine whether all users are restricted from copying or renaming utility programs.	
2.2	Confirm that all programming, debugging, and file-altering utilities are restricted from unauthorized personnel.	
2.3	Determine whether necessary approvals are obtained before utilities are used.	
2.4	Determine whether any utilities can bypass controls in the operating system or security software.	
2.5	Determine whether any utilities can be used when the operating system or security software is not running.	

2.6	When the operating system is not running, determine whether operating system modules are protected from access.	
2.7	Confirm that utility use is monitored by management.	
3.	**SYSTEM SECURITY REVIEW** **Objective:** To determine whether controls adequately prevent the unauthorized modification or use of the operating system. Recommendations resulting from the system security review should cite appropriate control objectives, reference numbers, and applicable workpapers.	
Audit Test No.	**Action**	**Source of Information or Documentation**
3.1	**Privileges and Quotas**	
3.1.1	Identify which user and system privileges should not be restricted.	
3.1.2	Identify which user and system privileges should be restricted.	
3.1.3	Determine whether management periodically reviews the user authorization file for accounts with unnecessary privileges or quotas or unusual attributes and determine whether this review is documented.	
3.1.4	Obtain a listing of the user authorization file for all on-site computer systems. This listing should show all privileges and quotas assigned to each user.	
3.1.5	Identify all users with privileges that should be restricted and determine whether they require all the assigned privileges to perform their job functions.	
3.1.6	Identify all users with quotas in excess of those necessary to perform their functions.	
3.2	**File Protection**	
3.2.1	Describe the universal file-protection schemes for operating system files for all systems.	
3.2.2	Evaluate the file-protection schemes for adequacy and appropriateness.	
3.2.3	Determine whether user groupings are appropriate.	

3.2.4	Obtain directory listings indicating owner, protection, size, backup date, and creation date for all system and user files.	
3.2.5	Identify all system directories.	
3.2.6	Confirm that all files in system directories are authorized.	
3.2.7	Determine whether the online system files are adequately protected.	
3.2.8	Confirm that application users are assigning appropriate file protections.	
3.2.9	Verify that application command files do not contain embedded passwords or sensitive materials.	
3.2.10	Compare file sizes from the directory listings with file records to determine whether any unauthorized modifications have been made to the system or security software. Hash totals, byte counts, and so on may be used.	
3.2.11	If operating system source code is present at this location, determine whether it is licensed.	
3.2.12	Determine whether operating system source code is adequately safeguarded (i.e., offline, backed up, and restricted to authorized personnel).	
3.3	**Sysgen**	
3.3.1	Identify all command files used in system start-up.	
3.3.2	Determine that start-up command files do not undermine privileges or file-protection controls by granting terminals, users, or processes added abilities.	
3.3.3	Identify all processes created at system start-up.	
3.3.4	Verify that all processes created at system start-up (i.e., control programs) are approved by management and perform only authorized functions.	

4.	**SYSTEM ENVIRONMENT CONTROL REVIEW** **Objective:** To determine whether the operating system holds all users and processes in a controlled environment. Recommendations resulting from the system environment control review should cite appropriate control objectives, reference numbers, and applicable workpapers.	
Audit Test No.	**Action**	**Source of Information or Documentation**
4.1	**Access Procedures**	
4.1.1	Identify the methods that the operating system uses to control access to the computer system and its resources.	
4.1.2	Determine whether all users are uniquely identified to the system by at least one of the following: • User identification and password • Key or badge • Physical characteristics	
4.1.3	Confirm that automatic log-ons are not enabled on the system. (Note: the Digital Equipment Corporation VMS specifies automatic terminal log-ons in the file sysalf.dat.)	
4.1.4	Verify that a user cannot circumvent the defined and authorized access procedures.	
4.1.5	Confirm that log-ons are disabled when the operating system is not functioning or partially functioning.	
4.1.6	Determine whether passwords are changed regularly.	
4.1.7	Confirm that the ability to change passwords is restricted to authorized personnel.	
4.1.8	Verify that passwords are arbitrary and difficult to compromise.	
4.1.9	Determine whether all terminals connected to the system are positively identified, preferably by unique hardwired terminal IDs.	
4.1.10	Verify that the operating system or security software notifies operations of all unauthorized access attempts.	

4.1.11	Discover whether a line or terminal is disabled after a predetermined number of unauthorized access attempts.	
4.1.12	Confirm that procedures are documented for, and followed by, operations for the identification of individuals responsible for unauthorized access attempts.	
4.1.13	Determine whether users are restricted to specific days and hours of computer resource use.	
4.1.14	Identify which log-on flags are available under the operating system and security software at this site.	
4.1.15	Verify that appropriate log-on flags are set for each user.	
4.1.16	Determine whether users are restricted to specific computer resources (e.g., specific terminals and printers).	
4.1.17	If operating system source code is available, review the modules controlling access to computer resources for any control weaknesses.	
4.2	**Users**	
4.2.1	Confirm that a formal procedure has been established for authorizing the use of computer resources and creating user accounts.	
4.2.2	Review the process by which management approves user accounts, user identification codes, privileges, and quotas.	
4.2.3	Determine whether the name, address, telephone number, and reason for using a computer account is documented for all users.	
4.2.4	Verify that every user account is used solely by the individual it is assigned to.	
4.2.5	Confirm that it is not possible for any user to emulate the operating system of other users.	
4.2.6	Determine whether the operating system restricts users to their own work area.	
4.2.7	Verify that applications users are limited to applications-controlled environments.	

4.2.8	Review the procedures for ensuring that the system does not provide information on the bypassing of operating system or security software controls (e.g., online help procedures that show how to log on and bypass log-on or application command files).	
4.2.9	Confirm that users are automatically logged off when activity ceases for a predetermined length of time.	
4.2.10	Determine whether all dormant user accounts are removed from the user authorization file.	
4.2.11	Verify that log-ons are disabled for all field service and system default accounts when they are not in use.	
4.2.12	Review the formal procedures for authorization, authentication, and monitoring of field service personnel.	
4.3	**Operations**	
4.3.1	Determine whether operators are required to use hard-copy terminals or whether their terminal sessions are logged.	
4.3.2	Verify that access as a system console is restricted to authorized operations personnel.	
4.3.3	Confirm that unauthorized personnel cannot take logical control of the system console or become as powerful as the system console without the knowledge of operations personnel.	
4.3.4	Determine whether the uses of all operator and special functions are logged.	
4.3.5	Verify that the operating system or security software prevents operators from modifying application data or programs while online.	
4.3.6	Review the operating system controls to prevent computer operators from modifying applications data or processes in main storage.	
4.3.7	Determine whether the computer system's clock is protected from unauthorized access or modification.	

5.	REMOTE ACCESS AND COMMUNICATIONS REVIEW	
	Objective: To determine whether dial-up and network users are properly controlled. Recommendations resulting from the remote access and communications review should cite appropriate control objectives, reference numbers, and applicable workpapers.	
Audit Test No.	**Action**	**Source of Information or Documentation**
5.1	Determine whether all lines of communication are disabled when not in use.	
5.2	Review how dial-up users are identified to the system.	
5.3	Confirm that the operating system or security software access controls cannot be bypassed by dial-up or network users.	
5.4	Verify that all dial-up and network sessions are prearranged with computer operations and preauthorized.	
5.5	Review the call-in/dial-back procedure used and confirm that all dial-out accesses use prearranged telephone numbers and terminals.	
6.	REVIEW OF INTERFACES WITH OTHER OPERATING SYSTEMS	
	Objective: To ensure that when more than one operating system is used concurrently, the appropriate operating system retains control over system resources and that the operating systems do not undermine the controls of each other. Recommendations resulting from the review of interfaces with other operating systems should cite appropriate control objectives, reference numbers, and applicable workpapers.	
Audit Test No.	**Action**	**Source of Information or Documentation**
6.1	Determine whether two or more operating systems can run concurrently on the computer system.	
6.2	Identify the relationship between the operating systems.	
6.3	Identify which operating system controls which system resources.	

Audit Test No.	Action	Source of Information or Documentation
6.4	Confirm that neither operating system undermines controls of the other.	
7.	**SOFTWARE MODIFICATIONS REVIEW** **Objective:** To determine whether operating system modifications are tested, documented, and performed according to established procedures. Recommendations resulting from the software modifications review should cite appropriate control objectives, reference numbers, and applicable workpapers.	
7.1	**Testing**	
7.1.1	Review the adequacy of procedures used for testing operating system modifications for program bugs.	
7.1.2	Review the adequacy of procedures used for testing utility modifications for program bugs.	
7.1.3	Determine whether the systems supervisor or systems staff, other than the original system programmer, reviews all system and utility testing before cataloging for production.	
7.1.4	Review the procedures by which environmental testing is authorized before being performed.	
7.1.5	Review system test documentation for adequacy of the tests that were performed.	
7.2	**Production Update**	
7.2.1	Identify the formal procedures established for initiation and implementation of operating system and utility changes.	
7.2.2	Confirm that there is an authorization procedure for all operating systems and utility changes, and that the procedure requires the approval of system management before cataloging.	
7.2.3	Verify that computer operations require formal approval before implementing any new or changed operating system software or utilities.	

		Source of Information or Documentation
7.2.4	Determine whether full consideration is given to security requirements before the implementation of new system software, module updates, or utilities in accordance with organizational policies.	
7.2.5	Review the system modification history log that records changes to the operating system and utilities.	
7.2.6	Determine whether all modifications to system software are logged in the system modification history log.	
7.3	**Maintenance**	
7.3.1	Record the number of systems programmers assigned to system maintenance; all required maintenance of the existing operating systems and utilities should be able to be performed promptly.	
7.3.2	Review the controls over emergency changes and patches made by system programmers.	
7.3.3	Confirm that formal system maintenance requests must fully explain the change to be made, the reason for the change, and the cost justification.	
8.	**AUTOMATED LOGS REVIEW** **Objective:** To determine whether automated logs are produced, reviewed, and stored as appropriate to record significant system events. Recommendations resulting from the automated logs review should cite appropriate control objectives, reference numbers, and applicable workpapers.	
Audit Test No.	**Action**	**Source of Information or Documentation**
8.1	Determine whether automated logs are produced for: • Operating system accesses • Utilities accesses • Network accesses • System halts and restarts • Software modifications • Accesses to the system clock	
8.2	Confirm that automated logs cannot be turned off by unauthorized users.	
8.3	Verify that automated logs are reviewed for any unusual activity.	

Audit Test No.	Action	Source of Information or Documentation
8.4	Determine whether a retention schedule is available for automated logs.	
8.5	Review the procedures by which the operations division follows the retention schedule.	
9.	**ERROR HANDLING REVIEW** **Objective:** To ensure that the operating system maintains control of users and processes during error handling and provides information on error resolution. Recommendations resulting from the error handling review should cite appropriate control objectives, reference numbers, and applicable workpapers.	
Audit Test No.	**Action**	**Source of Information or Documentation**
9.1	Determine whether system error traps are sufficient to control all users upon error detection.	
9.2	Verify that the operating system produces error messages for all system errors.	
9.3	Review operating system and utility error messages to ensure that they accurately describe the cause of the error and suggest any corrective actions required.	
10.	**SYSTEM BACKUP REVIEW** **Objective:** To ensure that all necessary versions of the operating systems and utilities in use are properly backed up. Recommendations resulting from the system backup review should cite appropriate control objectives, reference numbers, and applicable workpapers.	
Audit Test No.	**Action**	**Source of Information or Documentation**
10.1	Review the procedures by which operators periodically back up the operating system.	
10.2	Determine whether the backup procedures are adequate.	
10.3	Confirm that previous versions of the operating system are retained intact until new versions or modifications are completely tested and accepted by all affected users.	

11.	**ADMINISTRATIVE CONTROLS REVIEW**	
	Objective: To ensure that separation of duties is adequate and that personnel policies are properly adhered to. Recommendations resulting from the administrative controls review should cite appropriate control objectives, reference numbers, and applicable workpapers.	
Audit Test No.	**Action**	**Source of Information or Documentation**
11.1	Verify that only systems programmers write operating system software.	
11.2	Verify that systems programmers do not write application programs.	
11.3	Ensure that applications programmers and operations staff are not allowed to make direct program calls to operating system modules but must instead use the command language provided by the operating system.	
12.	**SECURITY SOFTWARE REVIEW**	
	Objective: To determine whether the security software used provides an adequate level of control over system resources. Recommendations resulting from the security software review should cite appropriate control objectives, reference numbers, and applicable workpapers.	
Audit Test No.	**Action**	**Source of Information or Documentation**
12.1	Determine whether security software is used to control applications, functions, and other bank resources.	
12.2	Identify the specific resources that the security software protects or monitors.	
12.3	Determine whether security software is transparent to all users.	
12.4	Review the procedures for preventing and detecting hostage situations involving users without the knowledge of the perpetrators (e.g., special log-on ID or password).	
12.5	Verify that the security software features cannot be bypassed or overridden.	

12.6	Determine whether output from the security software is reviewed periodically by supervisory personnel.	
12.7	Confirm that security breaches are followed up by appropriate security personnel.	

Index

Index

Index